The Palgrave Handbook of Sustainable Peace and Security in Africa

Dan Kuwali
Editor

The Palgrave Handbook of Sustainable Peace and Security in Africa

palgrave
macmillan

Editor
Dan Kuwali
University of Pretoria
Pretoria, South Africa

ISBN 978-3-030-82019-0   ISBN 978-3-030-82020-6 (eBook)
https://doi.org/10.1007/978-3-030-82020-6

© The Editor(s) (if applicable) and The Author(s), under exclusive license to Springer Nature Switzerland AG 2022
This work is subject to copyright. All rights are solely and exclusively licensed by the Publisher, whether the whole or part of the material is concerned, specifically the rights of translation, reprinting, reuse of illustrations, recitation, broadcasting, reproduction on microfilms or in any other physical way, and transmission or information storage and retrieval, electronic adaptation, computer software, or by similar or dissimilar methodology now known or hereafter developed. The use of general descriptive names, registered names, trademarks, service marks, etc. in this publication does not imply, even in the absence of a specific statement, that such names are exempt from the relevant protective laws and regulations and therefore free for general use.
The publisher, the authors and the editors are safe to assume that the advice and information in this book are believed to be true and accurate at the date of publication. Neither the publisher nor the authors or the editors give a warranty, expressed or implied, with respect to the material contained herein or for any errors or omissions that may have been made. The publisher remains neutral with regard to jurisdictional claims in published maps and institutional affiliations.

Cover credit: FrankRamspott

This Palgrave Macmillan imprint is published by the registered company Springer Nature Switzerland AG
The registered company address is: Gewerbestrasse 11, 6330 Cham, Switzerland

To Uhuru—that he, too, shall be an extraordinary luminary...

Foreword

The Palgrave Handbook of Sustainable Peace and Security in Africa is a comprehensive compendium of intellectually illuminating discussion on how to overcome contemporary peace and security challenges in Africa. This 34-chapters volume is predominantly authored by up-and-coming African luminaries, scholars and practitioners, supported by an equally eminent and experienced expert from beyond the continent. The Handbook comes at a time when there is an emerging consensus that Africa's peace and security is pivotal to the international community's continued stability and prosperity. Indeed, gone past are the days when the destabilization of the continent served other States' interests. In an increasingly interwoven World, it is unimaginable that Africa can sneeze alone without the rest of the world catching a cold.

The Handbook presents theoretical underpinnings as well as in-depth discussions on current and future human security challenges; and forward-looking solutions which are drawn from various interlocking fields such as International Law, International Relations, peace and security studies, development economics, political philosophy, among others. From a critical theorization of African concept of sustainable peace and security, to a detailed evaluation of peace and security on the continent including emerging global pandemics such as corona virus (Covid-19), the Handbook provides solid understanding of contemporary issues with an aim of informing present and future practice. This conversation is not only pertinent but also timely, at a juncture when regional institutions consistently contributing to democratization and peacebuilding in their neighbourhoods, especially in the face of the African Union (AU) Agenda 2063.

While tackling perennial problems to peace and security on the continent, the Handbook also interrogates emerging threats such as terrorism, violent extremism, xenophobia, cybercrimes and irresponsible use of Artificial Intelligence (AI) on the battlefield. In an age where the role of women in peace and security cannot be overemphasized, the Handbook eloquently investigates the invaluable contribution of women in multidimensional peace support operations. The role of international partners has also been addressed in a manner that redefines the way the continent relates to the rest of the world. More importantly, the issue of financing the continent's peace, an elephant in the room, is interrogated in the face of increasing and competing priorities for African states.

Consequently, the Handbook is akin to the proverbial chameleon in that it observes behind, remains aware of the present while looking forward. The intellectually rigorous and research-based strategies provided in the Handbook, while not claiming to be panacea to the myriad challenges facing the continent, uniquely reflect and involve all relevant stakeholders. Moving forward, this Handbook will assist scholars, practitioners and policymakers alike, to reflect on their theoretical approaches in countering threats to peace and security on the continent. Beyond finding African solutions to African problems, the volume will also act as a compass to political leaders in the implementation of the AU Master Roadmap of Practical Steps to Silence the Guns in Africa (Lusaka Master Roadmap 2016). Thus, immensely contributing to the search for lasting solutions to the continent's peace, security and development.

Johannesburg, South Africa   Gilbert M. Khadiagala

Gilbert M. Khadiagala Jan Smuts Professor of International Relations and Director of the African Centre for the Study of the United States (ACSUS) at the University of the Witwatersrand, Johannesburg, South Africa.

ACKNOWLEDGEMENTS

An immense debt of gratitude to all the contributors to this publication for sparing their time to write insightful chapters despite tight schedules and deadlines. Colleagues at Palgrave Macmillan and the anonymous reviewers provided immeasurable support towards the fruition of this publication. The Commander of the Malawi Defence Force, General Vincent Thom Nundwe and his Deputy, Lieutenant General (Dr.) Paul Valentino Phiri were very supportive to afford me time to work on this volume. Justice Professor Redson Kapindu, Justice Dingiswayo Madise, Professor Address Malata, Professor Jonathan Makuwira, Mr. Bernard Ndau, the late Bishop Dr. C. J. Tsukuluza and the former Attorney-General of the Republic of Malawi, Dr. Chikosa Mozesi Silungwe provided invaluable inspiration.

In one way or the other, Messrs Justin and Maina Mkandawire, Richard and Pamela Kuwali, Thokozire Kuwali, Ben Wandawanda, Likhwa Mussa, Shadreck Mhango and Major Emmanuel Mlelemba rendered a very helpful hand in the course of this publication. Lt. Col Gilbert Mittawa, Captain Prince Bright Majiga, Captain Tadziwana Kapeni, Ms. Chimwemwe Fabiano and Ms. Gloria David Phiri played a monumental role to put the manuscript together including Brigadier General (Dr.) Godard Busingye. As always, my wife, Chimwemwe together with my mum, Florence, and Mafunase Kuwali offered the much-needed moral support along the way. My son, Uhuru Joseph, has been a pillar of strength.

Any opinion expressed in this volume is solely that of the individual authors and not of the institutions they represent.

Lilongwe, Malawi
March 2021

Dan Kuwali
Centre for Human Rights
University of Pretoria
Pretoria, South Africa

Centre for Strategic Studies
Malawi University of Science and
Technology
Thyolo, Malawi

CONTENTS

Part I Conceptualising Sustainable Peace and Security in Africa

1   **Introduction**   3
Dan Kuwali

2   **The Concept of Peace: An African Perspective**   15
Desire Hakorimana and Godard Busingye

3   **Sustaining Peace in Africa**   35
Youssef Mahmoud and Chimwemwe A. Fabiano

4   **The African Union Agenda for Sustainable Peace
and Security**   47
Dan Kuwali

Part II A Regional Focus to Peace and Security in Africa

5   **Securing Peace and Security in North Africa**   81
Dan Kuwali and Prince Bright Majiga

6   **Building Peace in East Africa**   95
Godard Busingye

7   **Securing Lasting Peace in West Africa**   109
Bright Nkrumah

8   **Peace and Security in Central Africa**   125
Peter J. Mugume

9   **Sustaining Peace and Security in Southern Africa**   143
Mphatso Jones Boti Phiri

xi

xii CONTENTS

Part III   Emerging Threats to Peace and Security in Africa

10   Cybersecurity Threats in Africa   159
Tabitha Mwangi, Tracy Asava, and Iretioluwa Akerele

**11   The Proliferation of Popular Protests and Coups d'Etas
in Africa**   181
Prince Bright Majiga

12   Countering Violent Extremism in Africa   197
Dan Kuwali

13   The Future of Violence in Africa   217
Dan Kuwali

14   Social Media, Peace and Security in Africa   241
Peter Makossah and Gilbert Mittawa

15   Emerging Epidemics and Pandemics in Africa   253
Chikondi M. Mandala and John C. Phuka

Part IV   Perennial Problems to Peace and Security in Africa

16   Protection of Human and People's Rights in Africa   275
Gloria David Phiri and Chikondi M. Mandala

17   The Governance Conundrum in Africa   291
Tadziwana Kapeni

18   Organized Crime in Africa   303
Mlowoka Noel Kayira

19   Resource Conflicts in Africa   323
Godard Busingye

20   Combating Piracy in African Waters   343
Prince Bright Majiga

21   Post-Electoral Violence in Africa   365
Archiles A. Bwete, Leonard Hatungimana,
and Wilson N. Parsauti

22   Illicit Small Arms and Light Weapons in Africa   383
Gilbert Mittawa

23   Weapons of Mass Destruction in Africa   397
Godard Busingye, Sarah Mukashaba, and Christable Tusiime

CONTENTS xiii

Part V Strategies for Sustaining Peace and Security in Africa

24 Securing a Path to Security and Peace: Building a People's Trust in the Military 417
Mark D. Maxwell

25 Addressing Youth Unemployment in Africa 433
Mphatso Jones Boti Phiri

26 Increasing the Role of Women in Peace and Security in Africa 445
Thomasin Tumpale Gondwe and Laika Nakanga

27 Respecting the Law of Armed Conflict in Africa 461
Dan Kuwali

28 Promoting Peace and Reconciliation in Africa 489
Ibrahim Mohammed Machina and Lawan Cheri

29 Enhancing Conflict Resolution in Africa 505
Elias O. Opongo

30 Preventing Illicit Resources Outflows from Africa 525
George Chikondi Chipembere Lwanda

31 Curbing the Migrant Crisis in the Mediterranean Sea 545
Godard Busingye and Daniel Mayombo

32 Financing the African Peace and Security Agenda 561
Cephas Lumina

33 Commend and Condemn: Combating Corruption in Africa 581
Dan Kuwali

Part VI Securing Sustainable Peace and Security in Africa

34 Conclusion 599
Dan Kuwali

Index 611

NOTES ON CONTRIBUTORS

Iretioluwa Akerele is an information security professional who has acquired technical knowledge and practical experience in leading practices. She is currently an information security lead consultant that has worked to align several organizations in Nigeria and across Africa to information security best practice standards. She is passionate about contributing to information security research and recently published "SWOT analysis of Information Security Management System" ISO 27001 in International Journal Services Operations and Informatics. She also started a Cyber Security mentoring and training programme to help people acquire the required knowledge to succeed in their cybersecurity education or job role.

Ms. Tracy Asava is a graduate who acquired a B.Sc. in Applied Computer Science from United States International University—Africa. She concentrated in Forensic IT and Cybercrime, which majors on the use of IT to investigate crimes committed in the cyberspace. She is passionate about web design and development, systems analysis and design, object-oriented programming and database development and maintenance.

Mr. Archiles Angelo Bwete is a Ugandan Lawyer and Writer serving in the Uganda Peoples' Defence Forces. He holds a Bachelor of Laws Degree from Makerere University and a Post Graduate Diploma in Legal Practice from the Law Development Centre, Kampala Uganda. He is an advocate of Courts of Judicature in Uganda, a member of Uganda Law Society and East African Law Society.

Dr. Mphatso Jones Boti Phiri, MP is a Senior Lecturer at the School of Public Administration, University of Malawi. He earned his Ph.D. at Coventry University, specializing in regionalism and leadership of peace and security in Africa. He has special interest in human security. He is a retired military officer after 12 years in Malawi Defence Force.

Godard Busingye Associate Professor Godard Busingye (Brig Gen) holds a Doctor of Laws Degree (LL.D.) of Makerere University, Uganda, a Master of Laws (LL.M.) Degree of Makerere University, Uganda, a Bachelor of Laws Degree (LL.B.) (Hons.) of Makerere University, Uganda, a Postgraduate Diploma in Legal Practice of the Law Development Centre, Uganda, a Diploma in Law of the Law Development Centre, Uganda, and a Diploma in Secondary Education, National Teachers College, of the Institute of Teacher Education, Kyambogo, Uganda. He is an Advocate of Courts of Judicature of Uganda and an *Emeritus* Member of the Committee on Continuing Legal Education of the Uganda Law Society. He is the Chief of Legal Services in the Uganda Peoples' Defence Forces/Ministry of Defence and Veteran Affairs, Uganda. He is a Friend of, and Visiting Lecturer, at the International Institute of Humanitarian Law (IIHL), Sanremo, Italy. He is the Vice President (EAC), African Military Forum (AMLF), and has obtained several short certificate courses and awards in the field of international humanitarian law, human rights, gender and the law, and environmental law and policy.

Lawan Cheri is a political scientist with specialization in Public Administration and strong interest in Conflict Management. He is a Lecturer with Public Administration Department in Federal Polytechnic Damaturu, Nigeria and a visiting Senior Lecturer with the Department of Public Administration, Yobe State University, Damaturu, Nigeria.

Chimwemwe A. Fabiano holds a Bachelor of Arts degree in Social and Political Philosophy from the University of Malawi and is pursuing a Master of Arts in International Cooperation and Humanitarian Aid with Kalu Institute, Spain. Chimwemwe has considerable experience working in Malawi, Mozambique, Zambia within the development and humanitarian sector focusing on gender justice. Chimwemwe's research interests lie at the intersection of various development agendas vis-à-vis feminist theory. This includes gender; the youth, leadership, peace and security and the politics of knowledge production.

Thomasin Tumpale Gondwe is a Bachelor of Laws (Honours) graduate from the University of Malawi, Chancellor College. She has been an advocate of the Supreme Court, High Court and Subordinate Courts of Malawi since 2015. She joined the Malawi Defence Force in 2017 as a Legal Officer and currently holds the rank of Major. From September 2019 to January 2021, she deployed on a peacekeeping mission in the Democratic Republic of the Congo under MONUSCO as a legal advisor to the Malawi Battalion. She was a key leader of the Female Engagement Team during her tour of duty. Her research interest is gender and the law.

Lt. Col Desire HAKORIMANA is a military officer in the Burundi National Defense Force. He is a Lawyer and holds a master's degree in Human Rights and Peaceful Resolution of conflicts from UNESCO Chair and a Diploma in Crime Scene Investigation from Benin in 2009. He is a visiting lecturer of Law at several military and civilian universities located in Burundi including the University of NGOZI, Burundi Military Academy (ISCAM), Senior Command and Staff College (ESCEM), and Burundi Military Intelligence School. He has served as the Burundian Contingent Legal Officer and in 2015–2016 as Senior Provost Marshal to the African Union Mission in Somalia (AMISOM). He is a founding President of the African Military Law Forum (AMLF) where he now sits as the Vice President of its Advisory Council. He is the Secretary of the Military Committee of the African Bar Association.

Major Leonard Hatungimana is a Burundian Lawyer and Writer serving in the Burundi National Defence Forces. He holds two Bachelor's Degrees in Law and Public Administration. He has served twice in the African Union Mission in Somalia under the Burundi Contingent. He has served in various capacities in the Burundian National Army. He has done various military and civilian courses.

Tadziwana Kapeni is a Commissioned Officer in the Malawi Defence Force. Currently, he is a training officer at the Malawi Armed Forces College (MAFCO). Capt Kapeni holds a Bachelor's of Arts Degree in Education Summa Cum Laude from the University of Eastern Africa-Baraton, Kenya He has also held various military appointments such as Platoon Commander, Mechanical Transport Officer, Adjutant and Staff Officer in the Public Information Office at the Malawi Defence Force Headquarters.

Mr. Mlowoka Noel Kayira is a Deputy Commissioner in the Malawi Police Service (MPS) responsible for the Central Eastern Region of Malawi. He has served in the Malawi Police Service for 20 years. He holds a Bachelor of Laws (with Honours) from the University of Malawi, a master's degree in Public Policy and Management with Distinction from Monash University, Australia. He also has a Bachelor of Arts (Humanities) degree from the University of Malawi. Currently, he is pursuing a Doctoral of Philosophy (Ph.D.) degree in Public Administration and Management with the University of Malawi. He has served the Malawi Police Service in various capacities including Deputy Director for Community Policing in Malawi, Commandant for the Malawi Police College in Zomba, Head of Professional Standards Unit and Director of Training and Human Resource Development for the Malawi Police Service. He is an adjunct lecturer at the University of Malawi in Law Enforcement, Management, and Leadership. His areas of interest include Criminal Law, Constitutional and Administrative Law, Leadership, Public Management, and Police Procedures.

Dan Kuwali serves in the Malawi Defence Force as Chief of Legal Services and Judge Advocate with the rank of Brigadier General. He is the Senior Partner in a law firm, KD Freeman & Associates; Extraordinary Professor of International Law at the Centre for Human Rights, Faculty of Law, University of Pretoria; Visiting Professor, Raoul Wallenberg Institute of Human Rights and Humanitarian Law, Lund University, Adjunct Professor, Malawi University of Science and Technology; Professor of Law, University of Lilongwe; Fellow, Carr Centre for Human Rights Policy, Harvard Kennedy School of Government; President of the Governing Council of the African Military Law Forum; Member of the Governing Council of the African Bar Association and Editor, *African Yearbook of International Humanitarian Law*. He served as a Division Legal Advisor, the then United Nations (UN) Mission in the Democratic Republic of the Congo (MONUC). He recently published the Oxford Bibliography on "Forceful Intervention to Protect Human Rights." His publications include: *Responsibility to Protect: Implementation of Article 4(h) Intervention* (Martnus Nijhoff, 2011); *Africa and the Responsibility to Protect* (Routledge, 2014), *By All Means Necessary: Protecting Civilians and Preventing Mass Atrocities in Africa* (Pretoria University Law Press, 2017), among scores of other peer reviewed publications.

Professor Cephas Lumina is a Visiting Professor of Law at the University of Lusaka, an Advocate of the High Court of Zambia, a Member of the United Nations Committee on the Rights of the Child and, formerly, a full Research Professor of Constitutional and Human Rights Law at the University of Fort Hare (2014–2019) and Extra-Ordinary Professor of Human Rights Law at the University of Pretoria (2010–2018) in South Africa. From March 2008 to May 2014, he served as the UN Independent Expert on the effects of foreign debt and other related international financial obligations of States on the full enjoyment of all human rights, particularly economic, social and cultural rights. In that capacity, he wrote the UN Guiding Principles on Foreign Debt and Human Rights, which were endorsed by the UN Human Rights Council in July 2012, and contributed to the development of other international human rights standards, including the guiding principles on extreme poverty and human rights and the draft declaration on the right to international solidarity. Professor Lumina holds a Ph.D. in International Human Rights Law (Griffith University, Australia), an LL.M. in International Human Rights Law (University of Essex, United Kingdom) and an LL.B. (with Merit) (University of Zambia), among other qualifications. He has more than 30 years legal practice, research and university lecturing experience in several countries. He has published several articles, book chapters and official reports and presented papers at numerous international conferences. His latest book, *Sovereign Debt and Human Rights* (co-edited with Professor Ilias Bantekas), was published by Oxford University Press in November 2018. Professor Lumina is a member of the editorial boards of the *International Human Rights Law Review*, *African Yearbook of International Humanitarian Law* and *Southern African Public Law*.

Mr. George Chikondi Chipembere Lwanda a strategist, is a 2018 Asia Global Fellow at Hong Kong University's Asia Global Institute, an alumnus of the Mo Ibrahim-SOAS University of London Governance for Development in Africa Initiative and an alumnus of the TRALAC trade law programme. He is currently a senior development coordination officer with the United Nations Development Coordination Office.

Mr. Ibrahim Mohammed Machina is a Lecturer at the Department of Political Science, Federal University Gashua, Nigeria. He was a Fellow on the African Leadership Centre's (ALC) 2019/2020 Peace and Development Fellowship for Young African Scholars. Holds a master's in International Relations and Diplomacy from Nile University of Nigeria, Abuja and is pursuing another master's in Security, Leadership, and Society at King's College London and another M.Sc. in International Relations and Diplomacy from Nile University of Nigeria, Abuja. His research interests include peace, security and development in Africa, community resilience to violent extremism, and the role of young people in countering violent extremism.

Ambassador Dr. Youssef Mahmoud is Senior Adviser at the International Peace Institute (IPI) supporting the sustainable development and peace operations programmes and serving as focal point on mediation and prevention policies and practices. He is a former United Nations (UN) Under-Secretary-General and has headed peace operations in Burundi, the Central African Republic and Chad. Prior to these assignments, he held other senior UN positions, notably as UN Resident Coordinator in Guyana, Director in the UN Department of Political Affairs, and Head of the Office of the Under-Secretary-General for Political Affairs. In 2015, he served as member of the UN Secretary-General High-Level Panel on Peace Operations (HIPPO) and simultaneously a member of the High-Level Advisory Group for the Global Study on Security Council Resolution 1325 on Women, Peace and Security. In 2019, he led an independent strategic review of the UN peace operation in the Democratic Republic of the Congo (MONUSCO), pursuant to UN Security Council Resolution 2463. He periodically writes on the theory and practice of the evolving concept of sustaining peace and on political transitions in Africa, with particular focus on Tunisia. He is currently a Visiting Professor at the African Leadership Centre, King's College, London, and serves on the Boards of several non-profit organizations in the United States and Tunisia. Dr. Mahmoud has a Ph.D. in Linguistics from Georgetown University, Washington, D.C.

Captain Prince Bright Majiga is a commissioned officer in the Malawi Defence force Force. He holds a Bachelor of Arts (Education) degree from Mzuzu University. He has attended several courses including the International Officer Tactical Intelligence course at the United States Army Intelligence Center for Excellence, State Border Security in Egypt, and IHL at the IIHL, San Remo, Italy, among others. He has previously worked as a Platoon Commander, Battalion Intelligence Officer, Protocol and Foreign Relations Officer and All Source Analyst. He also deployed as a Military Information Officer for the Malawi Battalion in the DRC. Captain Majiga has also published several articles in Malawian diaries. Before joining the MDF, he

xx NOTES ON CONTRIBUTORS

also taught at the Catholic University of Malawi and the Natural Resources College. His research interests include: conflict prevention, management resolution in local communities, intelligence analysis and conduct in resource poor situations and the Blue economy.

Ms. Chikondi M. Mandala is a PhD candidate at the University of Kent where she is a Next Generation Scholar. Ms. Mandala has been involved with legal research and maintaining MalawiLII at the Gender and Justice Unit; has conducted research on trade, entrepreneurship and development with the New Markets Lab; has done work on women's access to justice with the Women Judges Association of Malawi; and has conducted research on the advancement of rights of incarcerated persons with the Centre for Human Rights, Education, Advice, and Assistance.

She has been a judicial officer for eight years at the Malawi Judiciary. She holds a Master of Laws (LLM) from Harvard University where she was a Fulbright Scholar, and a Bachelor of Laws (LLB) (Honours) from the University of Malawi.

Mark "Max" Maxwell is a retired U.S. Army Judge Advocate with a rank of Colonel. He is currently the Deputy Legal Counsel, U.S. Africa Command. The opinions in this article are the author's and do not reflect the opinions of the U.S. Government or U.S. Africa Command. The author would like to thank both Mr. Mike Leonard and Ms. Gisela Westwater for their review of this article. They improved it greatly but all the mistakes remain the author's.

Lt Daniel Mayombo holds a Master of Laws Degree (LL.M.) from the University of Amsterdam, The Netherlands, a Bachelor of Laws Degree (LL.B.) from Makerere University, Uganda, a Post Graduate Diploma in Legal Practice of the Law Development Centre, Kampala, Uganda. He is a Legal Officer in the Chieftaincy of Legal Services, Uganda Peoples' Defence Forces. He has attended several short courses in international humanitarian law at the Legal Training Centre (LTC), Uganda.

Lt Col Gilbert Mittawa is a Deputy Chief of Legal Services in the Malawi Defence Force (MDF) with the rank of Lieutenant Colonel and alumnus of the Defence Institute of International Legal Studies, Rhode Island, United States. He is a graduate of the University of Rwanda and the Rwanda Defence Force Command and Staff College. He is also a Legal Consultant at KD Freeman & Associates (Law Offices), Lilongwe, Malawi. He teaches and publishes mostly on Public International Law, focusing on International Law, Security and Human Rights.

Mr. Peter Makossah is a lawyer, independent filmmaker, multi-platform journalist, communications specialist, and security intelligence expert based in the United Kingdom (UK). He holds a master's degree in law (LL.M.) and a bachelor's degree in Law (LL.B.) from Nottingham Law School at the Nottingham Trent University in the UK. He possesses a Bachelor of Science degree (BSc) in Digital Video and Broadcast Production from the University of De Montfort in Leicester, UK, a Higher National Diploma in Media Production in Digital Video and Audio Production for Film and TV from Confetti Institute of Creative Technologies in Nottingham, UK, and a diploma in Journalism and Media Studies from University of Malawi. He worked for the Malawi's two daily newspapers, *The Times Group* and *The Nation* as an investigative journalist. He also served in the Malawi Police Service in the Criminal Investigations Department and served as the Police Deputy National Spokesperson. He is an ardent Social Justice advocate.

Dr. Peter J. Mugume is Lecturer, Researcher and Coordinator of postgraduate programmes at the Center for Conflict Management (CMM) of the University of Rwanda (UR) where he is also a Lecturer of peace, and development and also coordinates the Social and Military Sciences programme at the School of Governance in the College of Arts and Social Sciences (CASS) of the UR) and at Stockholm University in Sweden. He has a Ph.D. in Peace and Development Research from the University of Gothenburg, Sweden, a master's degree in International Development and Social Change from Clark University, Massachusetts, United States and a Bachelor of Arts degree in Political and Administrative Sciences from the National University of Rwanda. He is the Team leader of the Peace, Conflict and Security subprogramme of the UR and Sweden's Cooperation for Research, Higher Education and Institutional Advancement. He is the Principal investigator of the 5S-Foundation Research Project of the University of Rwanda, University of Addis Ababa (Ethiopia) and University of Khartoum (Sudan) and the University of Sussex (UK). He has been involved in different research activities, among others, on Rwanda governance Barometer commissioned by the Rwanda Governance Advisory Council; *Itorero* in Post-Genocide Rwanda: Ambition, Expectation, Perception and Effects; and a baseline study on the innovations and the role of higher education institutions in Rwanda particularly the UR. He published a paper, with others, on National ownership and donor involvement: an aid paradox illustrated by the case of Rwanda. He is also involved in another book project on *Listening, Community Engagement, and Peacebuilding: International Perspectives*.

Ms. Sarah Mukashaba holds a Bachelor of Laws Degree (LL.B.) of Makerere University, Uganda, a Postgraduate Diploma in Legal Practice of Law Development Centre, Uganda. She is an Advocate of Courts of Judicature of Uganda. She is a Legal Officer in the Chieftaincy of Legal Services, Uganda Peoples' Defence Forces. She has attended a number of short certificate Courses at the International Institute of Humanitarian Law (IIHL), Sanremo, Italy; the Defence Institute of International Legal Studies (DIILS); Centre for United Nations Peacekeeping, New Delhi, India, International Peace Support Centre Kenya. She previously served as a Legal Officer for the African Union Mission in Somalia, and more recently as a Ceasefire Transitional Security Arrangement Monitoring Mechanism/IGAD Officer, in South Sudan.

Ms. Tabitha Mwangi holds a master's degree in Counter-Terrorism and Homeland Security Studies with a cluster in Cyber Terrorism from the Interdisciplinary Center (IDC), Herzliya (Israel), and an undergraduate degree in International Relations: Foreign Policy and Diplomacy with a minor in Japanese Language and Culture from United States International University—Africa (Kenya). She is a researcher and consultant on Counter-Terrorism and Security issues and heads the Security Program at the Center for International and Security Affairs (CISA) directing the organization's Security and Counter-Terrorism programmes through research, policy formulation, forums and training. Tabitha has been involved in Countering Violent Extremism (CVE) efforts through engagement with Government Agencies and NGOs. She has appeared on different media interviews, and provided analysis on terrorism and security issues to various newspapers in Kenya. Her research interests are on national and international security, counter-terrorism, violent extremist groups, cyber security and cyber terrorism.

Ms. Tabitha Mwangi is an International Security Researcher who focuses on counter-terrorism, violent extremism and cyber security issues. Tabitha holds a B.A. in International Relations from United States International University—Africa. She studied M.A. Government- Counter-Terrorism and Homeland Security with a cluster in Cyber Terrorism at the Interdisciplinary Center, Herzliya (Israel). She is an Early Career Fellow at the African Leadership Centre, King's College London. Currently, she is pursuing the Master of Advanced Studies (MAS) in International and European Security at the University of Geneva.

Major Laika Nakanga is a Legal Officer in the Malawi Defence Force with a demonstrated interest in peace and conflict resolution. She has served as a Military Legal Advisor in the United Nations Stabilization Mission in the Democratic Republic of the Congo (MONUSCO) and is currently serving as a Justice Advisor for the United Nations Mission in South Sudan (UNMISS), assisting the South Sudan Peoples Defense Force.

Mr. Wilson Parsauti Ngelech is a Kenyan lawyer and realtor. He holds a Bachelor of Laws from Moi University. He is a candidate for Master of Laws (LL.M.) at the School of Law of Makerere University.

Dr. Bright Nkrumah is a scholar-activist at the Center for Human Rights, University of the Free State. He received his DPhil from the Center for Human Rights, University of Pretoria and has published extensively on insurgency, climate change, democratization, food security, minority rights, political contestation, and youth activism.

Dr. Elias Opongo is a senior lecturer and conflict analyst at Hekima Institute of Peace Studies and International Relations, Hekima University College, and the director of the Centre for Research, Training, and Publications at the same university. He is a Jesuit priest and holds a Ph.D. in Peace Studies from the

University of Bradford, United Kingdom, and a Master of Arts degree in International Peace Studies from the University of Notre Dame, United States. He is a conflict analyst and peace practitioner. His research focus and publications have been in the areas of transitional justice, peacebuilding and conflict resolution, democracy, and state-building. One of his recent publications is *Election, Violence and Transitional Justice in Africa* by Routledge, 2022.

Ms. Gloria David Phiri earned a bachelor's degree in Criminal Justice and Security Management from the Africa Nazarene University, Kenya in 2020 where she also served as the international student President (ANUISA) from October 2019 to August 2020. She has worked as an Intern at the High Court of Malawi while pursuing her research interests, which include: environmental protection in resource poor areas, access to social justice, human rights, victimology, and sexuality rights. She's currently working for Tumaini Letu, where she deals with the protection of human rights for refugees for the organization.

Dr. John C. Phuka is an Associate Professor from the Department of Public Health at Kamuzu University of Health Sciences formerly College of Medicine, University of Malawi. He is a former Dean of Public Health and served as the Co-Chairperson of the Presidential Taskforce on COVID-19. During public health emergencies, Dr Phuka supports the Government to ensure the resilience of the health system and advocates for the utilization of health services among the public.

Lt. Christable Tusiime holds a Bachelor of Laws Degree (LL.B.) (Hons.) of Uganda Christian University, Mukono, Uganda, a Postgraduate Diploma in Legal Practice of the Law Development Centre, Uganda, a Diploma in Law of the Law Development Centre, Uganda. She is an Advocate of Courts of Judicature of Uganda. She is in the Chieftaincy of Legal Services, Uganda Peoples' Defence Forces/Ministry of Defence and Veteran Affairs, Uganda. She has attended a number of short certificate courses, including at the Defense Institute of International Legal Studies, DIILS, Rhode Islands, United States and the International Institute of Humanitarian Law (IIHL), Sanremo, Italy.

ABBREVIATIONS AND ACRONYMS

AAFC	Allied Armed Forces of the Community
ACtJHR	African Court of Justice and Human Rights
ADF	Allied Democratic Forces
AfCFTA	African Continental Free Trade Agreement
AFISMA	African-Led International Support Mission in Mali
Africa CDC	The African Centre for Disease Control and Prevention
AIMS 2050	Africa's Integrated Maritime Strategy 2050
AMIS	Africa Union Mission in Sudan
AMISOM	African Union Mission in Somalia
AMV	Africa Mining Vision
ANC	African National Congression
API	First additional Protocal
APSA	African Peace and Security Architecture
AQIM	Al Queda in the Islamic Maghreb
ASF	African Standby Force
ATM	Auto Teller Machine
ATT	Arms Trade Treaty
AU	African Union
AUC	African Union Commission
AUCPCC	Convention on Preventing and Combating Corruption
AU-Led RCI-LRA	African Union-Led Regional Cooperation Initiative for the Elimination of the Lords Resistance Army
AU-RECsMOU	African Union Constitutive Act and a Memorudum of Understanding Between African Union and Regional Economic Community
CADSP	Common African Defence and Security Policy
CAR	Central African Republic
CB	Chemical and Biological
CBRN	Chemical, Biological, Radiological and Nuclear
CEDAW	Convention on the Elimination of All Forms of Discrimination Against Women
CEN–SAD	Community of Sahel–Saharan States

xxvi   ABBREVIATIONS AND ACRONYMS

CEWS	Continental Early Warning Systems
CFA	Cooperative Framework Agreement
CIA	Central Intelligence Agency
CIMIC	Civil-Military Coordination
COMESA	Common Market for Eastern and Southern Africa
Covid-19	Corona Virus Disease of 2019
CPC	Coalition of Patriots for Change
CPI	Corruption Perception Index
CSO	Civil Society Organisations
CSSDCA	Conference on Security, Stability, Development and Cooperation in Africa
CTSAMVM	Transnational Security Arrangements Monitoring and Verification Mechanism
CVE	Countering Violent Extremism
DDR	Disarmament, Demobilization and Reintegration
DNA	Deoxyribonucleic Acid
DPKO	Department of Peacekeeping Operations
DRC	Democratic Republic of the Congo
EAC	East African Community
EASF	East African Standby Force
ECCAS	Economic Community of Central African States
ECOMOG	Economic Community of West African States Monitoring Group
ECOWAS	Economic Community of West African States
EDF	European Development Fund
EEZ	Exclusive Economic Zone
EloGE	Europe's European Label of Governance Excellence
ERM	Early Response Mechanism
EU	European Union
EVD	Ebola Virus Disease
FDLR	Forces Démocratiques de Libération du Rwanda
FET	Female Engagement Teams
FIB	Force Intervention Brigade
FRELIMO	Frente de Libertação de Moçambique (lit. Liberation Front of Mozambique)
GA	General Assembly
GDP	Gross Domestic Product
HIV/AIDS	Human Immunodeficiency Virus, Acquired Immunodeficiency Syndrome
HRBA	Human Rights Based Approach
HRDC	Human Rights Defenders Coalition
HRW	Human Rights Watch
iARMS	Illegal Arms Records and Tracing Management Systems
ICC	International Criminal Court
ICCPR	International Convention on Civil and Political Rights
ICGLR	International Conference for Great Lakes Region
ICJ	International Court of Justice
ICRC	International Red Cross Committee
ICT	Internet Communication Technology
IED	Improvised Explosive Device

IFF	Illicit Financial Flows
IGAD	Inter-Governmental Authority on Development
IGAD SSP	Security Sector Programme
IGO	Inter-Governmental Organisation
IHL	International Humanitarian Law
IHRL	International Human Rights Law
ILO	International Labour Organisation
IMO	International Maritime Organisation
INTERPOL	International Criminal Police
IS	Islamic State
ISIS	Islamic State of Iraq and al-Sham
IUU	Illegal, Unreported and Unregulated
KANU	Kenya African National Union
LGBTQ/I	Lesbians, Gays, Bisexuals, Transgenders and Queers/Intersexuals
LoAC	Law on Armed Conflict
LRA	Lords Resistance Army
M&E	Monitoring and Evaluation
M23	March 23 Movement
M5-RFP	June 5 Protest Movement
MAPROBU	African Prevention Mission (Specific to Burundi)
MFN	Most Favoured Nation Principle
MI	Military Intelligence
MICOPAX	Mission for the Consolidation of Peace in the Central African Republic
MINUSCA	United Nations Multidimensional Integrated Stabilization Mission in the Central African Republic
MINUSMA	Multidimensional Integrated Stabilization Mission in Mali
MISCA	African-Led International Support Mission in the Central African Republic
MNJTF	Multi-National Joint Task Force
MOJWA	Movement for the Oneness and Jihad in West Africa
MONUSCO	United Nations Stabilization mission in the Democratic Republic of the Congo
MOU	Memorudum of Understanding
MOWCA	Maritime Organisation of West and Central African States
MSM	Muhutu Social Movement
MUJAO	Movement Pour l'Unification et le Jihad en Afrique de l'Quest
NASG	Non-State Armed Group
NATO	North Atlantic Treaty Organisation
NCAC	National Constitutional Amendment Committee
NEPAD	New Partnership for Africa's Development
NetPeace	Network of African Journalists for Peace
NEWC	National Early Warning Centre
NGO	Non-Governmental Organization
NIA	National Intelligence Agency
NIS	National Integrity System
NRM	National Resistance Movement
NSA	National Security Agency

xxviii ABBREVIATIONS AND ACRONYMS

NSAW	Non State Armed Groups
NVAA	National Vulnerability Assessment and Analysis
NVAC	National Vulnerability Assessment Committee
OAU	Organization of African Unity
OCG	Organised Crime Groups
ODM	Orange Democratic Movement
PDSC	Protocol on Defence and Security Cooperation
PNU	Party of National Unity
POC	Protection of Civilians
POW	Panel of the Wise
PSC	Peace and Security Council
PSOD	Peace Support Operations Divisions
RCI-LRA	Regional Cooperation Initiative for the Elimination of the Lords Resistance Army
REC	Regional Economic Communities
reCAPP	Regional Cooperation Agreement on Combating Piracy and Armed Robbery Against Ships in Asia
RECs/RMs	Regional Economic Communities/Regional Mechanisms
RENAMO	Mozambican National Resistance
REWC	Regional Early Warning Centre
RGI	Resource Governance Index
RVAA	Regional Vulnerability Assessment and Analysis
RVAC	Regional Vulnerability Assessment Committee
SADC	Southern Africa Development Community
SALW	Small Arms and Light Weapons
SANAB	South African Narcotics and Alcohol Bureau
SAPS	South African Police Service
SAR	Search and Rescue
SARPCCOO	Southern Africa Regional Police Chiefs Cooperation Organization
SAS	Small Arms Survey
SASS	South African Secret Service
SDGs	Sustainable Development Goals
SGBV	Sex and Gender Based Violence
SIPO	Strategic Indication Plan for the Organisation
SIPRI	Stockholm International Peace Research Institute
SOE	State Owned Entreprises
SSP	Security Security Program
SUA	Convention for the Suppression of Unlawful Acts against the Safety of Maritime Navigation
TCC	Troops Contributing Countries
TJRC	Truth Justice and Reconciliation Committee
TOC	Transnational Organised Crime
TRC	Truth and Reconciliation Commission
UCDP	Uppsala Conflict Data Programme
UMA	Arab Maghreb Union
UN	United Nations
UNCLOS	United Nations Convention on the Law of the Sea
UNDP	United Nations Development Programme

UNFCCC	United Nations Framework Conventional Climate Change
UNGA	United Nations General Assembly
UNHCR	United Nations High Commission for Refugees
UNMISS	United Nations Missions in South Sudan
UNODA	United Nations Office for Disarmament Affairs
UNODC	United Nations Office of Drugs and Crime
UNSC	United Nations Security Council
UNSCR	United Nations Security Council Resolution
UNTOC	United Nations Convention Against Transnational Organised Crime
UPR	Universal Period Review
US	United States
VAA	Vulnerability Assessment and Analysis
WANEP	West African Network for Peacebuilding
WCO	World Customs Organisation
WMD	Weapons of Mass Destruction
WPS	Women, Peace and Security
WTO	World Trade Organisation

LIST OF FIGURES

Fig. 30.1	Countries covered	527
Fig. 30.2	Number of armed conflicts globally (1946–2019)	528
Fig. 30.3	IFF and security interaction (*Source* Tax Justice Network, 2014)	531
Fig. 30.4	Correlation between corruption and GDP growth (*Source* Kaufmann et al. 2010)	533
Fig. 30.5	What is the Resource Governance Index	536

LIST OF TABLES

Table 10.1	Non-state actors in cyberspace operations	165
Table 30.1	African conflicts fueled by minerals	529
Table 30.2	Overview of thematic areas assessed	534
Table 30.3	General summary of the likelihood of IFF activity	537
Table 30.4	General summary of the likelihood of IFF activity	538
Table 30.5	Areas of significant progress fighting IFF activity	539
Table 30.6	Summary of proposed priority focus areas	540

PART I

Conceptualising Sustainable Peace and Security in Africa

CHAPTER 1

Introduction

Dan Kuwali

BACKGROUND

Africa has been referred to as the 'troubled continent' because of perpetual wars and perennial problems of peace and security that have ravaged the continent over the years.[1] The challenges facing Africa today remain complex and massive, while its institutions are relatively weak and lack resources.[2] This is supported by the fact that The 2020 Global Peace Index shows that six of the reported 11 least peaceful countries in the world are from Africa, in ascending order as follows: Afghanistan, Syria, Iraq, South Sudan, Yemen, Somalia, Libya, the Democratic Republic of the Congo (DRC), Central African Republic (CAR), Russia and Sudan.[3] Further, the first 10 of the 13 situations under investigations of the International Criminal Court (ICC)

---

[1] Lansana Gberie, 'Africa: The Troubled Continent', 104(415) *African Affairs* (2005), pp. 337–342.

[2] Dan Kuwali, Squaring the Circle: The Role of the African Peace and Security Architecture, Tony Karbo and Kudrat Virk (eds.), *The Palgrave Handbook of Peacebuilding in Africa*, Palgrave-Macmillan, 2018, pp. 45–63, p. 46.

[3] Global Peace Index, Statistics Times, as of 11 June 2020, available at: https://statisticstimes.com/ranking/globa-peace-index.php (accessed 23 February 2021).

D. Kuwali (✉)
University of Pretoria, Pretoria, South Africa

© The Author(s), under exclusive license to Springer Nature Switzerland AG 2022
D. Kuwali (ed.), *The Palgrave Handbook of Sustainable Peace and Security in Africa*, https://doi.org/10.1007/978-3-030-82020-6_1

3

concern eight African countries[4] while seven of the 14 existing United Nations (UN) peace support operations are deployed on the content also point to the prevalence of conflicts in Africa.[5]

This is underscored by the fact that over 60 per cent of deliberations of the UN Security Council focus on Africa, particularly on issues bordering on international peace and security.[6] The fact that all the six countries currently considered on the UN Peacebuilding Commission agenda also lends credence to Gberie's claim of Africa as a 'troubled' continent.[7] The desire to end the protracted conflicts and internecine wars in Africa explain why the African Union (AU) resolved to develop a strategy to achieve peace and security on the continent.

In June 2015, the AU adopted Agenda 2063 as a blueprint for continent-wide socioeconomic transformation over a period of 50 years. The AU Agenda is a strategic framework synthesised from, and intended to, accelerate the implementation of both erstwhile and existing continental, sub-regional and national initiatives for growth and sustainable development; that have been distilled into seven (7) aspirations, 20 goals and 39 priorities with concomitant targets and indicators.[8] At the heart of the AU Agenda 2063 is the aspiration for a peaceful and secure Africa emanating from the continental organization's 50th Anniversary Solemn Declaration (2013) vision of ending all wars in Africa by 2020 and 'silencing the guns' (also known as Vision 2020).[9]

---

[4] International Criminal Court, 'Situations Under Investigation', available at: https://www.icc-cpi.int/pages/situation.aspx (accessed 24 August 2020).

[5] John Campbell, 'Global Peacekeeping Operations Overwhelmingly African and in Africa', Council on Foreign Relations, 10 July 2018, available at: https://www.cfr.org/blog/global-peacekeeping-operations-overwhelmingly-african-and-africa#:~:text=Afr ican%20peacekeeping%20missions%20accounted%20for,the%20majority%20of%20those% 20troops.&text=The%20African%20bloc%20is%20the,will%20replace%20Ethiopia%20in% 202019 (accessed 24 August 2020) .See also Stale Ulriksen and Giovanna Bono, 'Conclusion: Economic and Diplomatic Tools vs. Military Might', 11(3) *International Peacekeeping* (2004), pp. 561–571, p. 561.

[6] Centre for Conflict Resolution, 'Towards a New Pax Africana: Making, Keeping, and Building Peace in Africa', Concept Paper, Research Seminar, 28–20 August, Stellenbosch, South Africa, p. 6.

[7] Namely, Burundi, Sierra Leone, Guinea, Guinea-Bissau, Liberia, and Central African Republic. See United Nations Association in Canada, 'UN Peacekeeping: From Peacekeeping to Peacebuilding', available at: http://www.unac.org/peacekeeping/en/un-pea cekeeping/fact-sheets/from-peacekeeping-to-peacebuilding/ (accessed 24 August 2020). See also Gberie, footnote 1 above.

[8] African Union (AU), 'Agenda 2063', available at: https://au.int/en/agenda2063 (accessed 22 May 2018); and United Nations (UN), 'Transforming Our World: The 2030 Agenda for Sustainable Development', available at: https://sustainabledevelopment. un.org/?menu=1300 (accessed 22 May 2018). See also United Nations, General Assembly Resolution A/RES/70/1, UN Doc A/RES/70/1 (25 September 2015).

[9] The AU Assembly of Heads of State and Government adopted the 50th Anniversary Solemn Declaration on 25 May 2013 during the ccommemoration of the OAU/AU's Golden Jubilee.

To this end, the framework specifically targeted the year 2020 as the deadline by which all guns were supposed to be silent in Africa. Vision 2020 also envisaged that there would be functional mechanisms for peaceful resolution of conflicts at all levels to nurture a culture of peace and tolerance among the peoples of Africa. Realizing the likelihood of not achieving the Vision 2020, in June 2020, the AU Commissioner for Peace and Security, Ambassador Smail Chergui, blamed the Corona virus disease of 2019 (COVID-19) for considerably slowing down the momentum of the silencing the guns agenda and end conflicts and crises in Africa.[10] However, Ambassador Chergui conceded that terrorists and armed groups have failed to heed the calls for a ceasefire.[11] In an attempt to provide a solution to blurred future of the Vision 2020, Ambassador Cessouma Minata Semate, the AU Commissioner for Political Affairs advised that 'a sustainable strategy to silence the guns must directly address the structural root causes of violent conflict in Africa, including governance deficits, as well as promote equitable management of natural resources for the overall benefit of the citizenry'.[12]

By February 2021, Africa was far from achieving its Vision 2020. Notwithstanding this ambitious determination, there has been escalating instability and insecurity in several regions and countries on the continent. Some regions in Africa have seen the most rapid growth in violent extremist activity worldwide since the adoption of Vision 2020. The continent has also become a nexus of criminal networks and illicit drug and human trafficking. Some regions have experienced a rise in farmer-herder violence. The continent also has one of the fastest population growth rates globally, despite being among the poorest and facing some of the most fragile environmental conditions. Apart from African migrants constituting a significant share of those trying to cross the Mediterranean Ocean into Europe, the continent also hosts a huge population of refugees and internally displaced persons.

The AU Master Roadmap of Practical Steps to Silence the Guns in Africa by Year 2020 ('Lusaka Master Roadmap 2016') aptly notes that '[m]ost crises and violent conflicts in Africa are being driven by poverty, economic hardships, violation or manipulation of constitutions, violation of human rights, exclusion, inequalities, marginalization and mismanagement of Africa's rich ethnic diversity, as well as relapses into the cycle of violence in some post-conflict settings and external interference in African affairs'.[13] The unfathomable ramifications of proliferation of small arms and light weapons (SALW) into Africa;

---

[10] African Union, Press Release: African Union calls for redoubling of efforts to silence the guns in Africa, Addis Ababa, 8 June 2020, Relief Web, available at: https://relief.int/reporrt/world/press-release-african-union-calls-redoubling-efforts-sil ence-guns-afrca (accessed 20 February 2021).

[11] As above.

[12] As above.

[13] The AU Master Roadmap of Practical Steps to Silence the Guns in Africa by Year 2020 ("Lusaka Master Roadmap 2016"), available at: https://int/sites/default/files/docume nts/37996-doc-au-roadmap-silencing-guns-2020.pdf.en.pdf (accessed 24 February 2021).

endemic corruption, illicit financial inflows and governance deficits are among the factors contributing to the threats to peace and security on the continent.[14] It has also been reported that some states outside Africa are fighting proxy wars and fuelling ongoing conflicts on the continent.[15]

More effort is needed to end the conflict and achieve peace in the Democratic Republic of the Congo (DRC), Horn of Africa; the Sahel and the Lake Chad basin; in Western Sahara, where efforts are ongoing to implement the Nouakchott decision; Libya, where political dialogue seems to be a more viable solution than military might; Somalia where the African Union Mission in Somalia (AMISOM) is facing incessant hurdles; in the Central African Republic (CAR) where efforts have intensified to ensure the rigorous application of peace and reconciliation agreements; and in Cameroun, where dialogue is continuing and attention is required.[16]

It is against this background that this edited volume engages in a discursive exploration of the evolving threats to peace and security on the continent in order and to provide recommendations on how to encounter such challenges to achieve peace on the continent. The contributors to this discussion are highly respected multidisciplinary academics, policymakers and practitioners with recognized contribution to peace and security on the continent. The main objective is to provide readily available research-based policy recommendation on steps that are needed to effectively silence the guns on the continent in order to achieve sustainable peace and security in Africa.

METHODOLOGY

The multitude of literature on peace and security in Africa is scattered. This Handbook addresses this concern as a multidisciplinary and comprehensive volume with contributions from practitioners, academicians, researchers and policymakers who are predominantly from the continent. Contributors have written extensive essays on various topics, paying particular attention on how to overcome the challenges to, in order to achieve, peace and security in Africa. The discussion involves multidisciplinary and transdisciplinary research on peace and security in Africa in a more contemporary, structured and easily accessible form. The golden thread running through all the 34 essays is the quest to find African solutions to African problems, particularly focusing on innovative ways and best practices to overcome the threats to peace and security on the continent.

[14] African Union, footnote 10 above.

[15] See statement of the Incoming Chairperson of the Commission. His Excellency Cyril Ramaphosa, African Union, 33rd Ordinary Session of the Assembly: Meeting of the Assembly of the African Union Begins, Press Release No: /2020 Date: 09/02/2020, Addis Ababa, Ethiopia, available at: https://au.int/en/newsevents/20200209/3rd-ord inary-session-assembly (accessed 20 February 2021).

[16] As above.

The central thesis of the Handbook is that if the drivers of conflict and violence in Africa include socioeconomic challenges such as poverty, high unemployment, marginalization, proliferation of arms and bad governance and corruption, then respect for human rights and humanitarian law, good governance, rule of law and regulation of weaponry are key to achieving peace and security on the continent. This view calls for promotion of liberal democracy, which includes respect for the rule of law and democratic governance coupled with inclusive economic development, which provide better prospects for peace and stability on the continent.[17] Further, considering that the predominant protagonists in these conflicts are the youth who do not have stable economic opportunities, it is imperative to address the factors that lead the youth to be disgruntled in order to reduce escalation of violence in Africa.

The contributors to the volume have provided in-depth and critical analysis of the contemporary threats to peace and security in Africa, especially challenges, opportunities and strategies to achieve a peaceful and secure Africa. With regard to methodology or approach, this volume provides a thematic and analytical discussion on the threats to peace and security in Africa, from an African epistemological perspective. The authors do this by identifying issues and providing recommendations through discourse analysis. The golden thread running through all the chapters is that while the AU has adopted an ambitious African Peace and Security Architecture (APSA), it lacks formidable preventive mechanisms for the myriad and evolving challenges on the continent. All the contributors agree that peace, security, good governance and socioeconomic development should be pursued simultaneously.[18]

Outline of Chapters

Including this prefatory chapter, this volume has 34 chapters, which are grouped into six parts as outlined below.

Conceptualizing Peace and Security in Africa

The first part of the Handbook seeks to theorize the elusive concept of sustainable peace and security in Africa. After Dan Kuwali outlines the raison d'être of the Handbook and the background of the discussion in this chapter, in Chapter 2, Desire Hakorimana and Godard Busingye engage in an exploratory discussion of the concept of peace and security from an African Point of view. The concept of peace in Africa is not merely the absence of violence, but also the ability of a society to respond to the needs of its citizens, reduce the

---

[17] See also Anton de Plesis and Anja Kaspersen, '7 Trends Shaping the Future of Peace and Security in Africa', World Economic Forum 21 June 2016, available at: https://weforum.org/agenda/2016/06/7-trends-shaping-the-african-security-landscape/ (accessed 24 February 2021).

[18] See also The Lusaka Master Roadmap 2016, footnote 13 above.

number of conflicts, and resolve existing disputes.[19] While security relates to the protection from harm in every imaginable way.[20] In this way, Africans view peace as a precious good for all humanity and contend that the main constraint to peace on the continent is due to the exogenic forces of imperial colonialism.

In Chapter 3, Youssef Mahmoud and Chimwemwe Fabiano, while agreeing with Hakorimana and Busingye, wonder why Africa continues to be subservient to the externally driven, liberal peacebuilding project focused on rebuilding the neo-colonial state, politics and economy. Then in Chapter 4, Kuwali, in his assessment of the capacity of the APSA, note that it is a 'two-legged tripod' in that it has early warning mechanisms and corresponding early response mechanisms but lacks formidable preventive mechanisms.

A Regional Focus to Peace and Security in Africa

The second part looks at the various challenges in African Regional Economic Communities (RECs) and Regional Mechanisms (RMs). In doing so, Kuwali and Prince Bright Majiga in Chapter 5, navigate the multifaced transnational threats in North Africa, a region with the continent's largest economies and three key funders of the AU, which include terrorism, illicit proliferation of arms and proxy wars and explore why international cooperation in light of the region's unique geopolitics can contribute to securing peace and security in North Africa.[21] The ricochet of the Arab Spring of 2011 still resonates in some countries in the region with a likelihood of civil unrest coupled with identity politics and sectarianism being a key characteristic of the political landscape.[22]

In Chapter 6, Busingye, challenges the East African Community (EAC) States to adhere to their obligations under the EAC Treaty in order to ensuring peace, safety and security in the region. In Chapter 7, Bright Nkrumah contends that the interlocking nature of the various crises including insurgent groups and the proliferation of SALW across porous borders have contributed to the spilling over of crises in the region hence he advocates for a robust regional approach for timely decisive action to prevent crises in the region.

With a focus on Central Africa in Chapter 8, Peter Mugume is of the view that peace and security in that part of Africa can be achieved through conflict resolution approaches that manifest objectivity and takes into account the geopolitical complexities in the region. In Chapter 9, Mphatso Jones Boti Phiri notes that there is little or no threat of state-to-state conflict in

---

[19] Olusola Adeyoose, 'Achieving Sustainable Peace and Security in Africa', *The Guardian*, 22 October 2017, available at: https://guardian.ng/opinion/achieving-sustainable-peace-and-security-in-Africa/ (accessed 23 February 2021).

[20] As above.

[21] The three key funders of the AU in North Africa include Algeria, Egypt and Tunisia.

[22] African Development Bank Group, Jobs for Youths in Africa: Catalyzing Youth Opportunity across Africa, available at: https://afdb-org/kr/wp-content/uploads/2018/02/Bottom-3-English.pdf (accessed 2 March 2021).

Southern Africa. However, he observes that the Southern African Development Community (SADC) is ill prepared to manage threats such as the emergency of terrorist groups and crisis of governance, natural disasters hence the need for international corporation in capacity building of national early warning systems and crisis management. The Sub-Saharan Africa continues to be the epicentre of HIV/AIDS, with the highest rate of infection and malaria in the world.[23]

Emerging Threats to Peace and Security in Africa

The third part of the Handbook takes stock of the contemporary and emerging challenges to peace and security in Africa. In Chapter 10, Tabitha Mwangi, Tracy Asava and Iretioluwa Akerele interrogate the increased Internet penetration on the continent, which inadvertently exposes a considerable population to cyber threats. To mitigate such risks, she advises governments to adopt proactive cybersecurity policy and legislative frameworks through multidisciplinary approaches between public and private sector players. In Chapter 11, Prince Bright Majiga notes that mediocre leadership, poor governance, corruption, shabbily run elections are some of the grievances that have triggered a proliferation of popular protests and coups d'états on Africa. Majiga argues that these can be avoided if African States improve their governance systems and provide socioeconomic development to their citizens in order to reduce areas of discontent.

In agreement with Majiga, in Chapter 12, Kuwali candidly presents his Ten C's strategy for countering violent extremism in Africa. Kuwali goes further to look at the crystal ball to discern trends for the future of violence on the continent in Chapter 13. Kuwali is concerned that future hostilities will continue to be asymmetric against an amorphous enemy on an undefined battlefield with innocent civilians forming the bulk of victims. The hostilities will be based more on exclusivist identities as opposed to political or ideological agenda. He counsels that the APSA should also actively engage States to adopt mediation to resolve disputes and eradicate marginalization.

In Chapter 14, Peter Makossah and Gilbert Mittawa debate whether social media is a necessary evil that has become an integral part of political uprisings and revolutions all over the world. In Chapter 15, Chikondi Mandala and John Phuka provide a prognosis of the emerging epidemics and pandemics in Africa, with a focus on Covid-19. Mandala and Phuka also explore the parameters of the use of law in disasters when social systems are disrupted and suggest the need for law's flexibility, and innovations towards resilience mechanisms for peace and security.

---

[23] UNAIS, 'Seizing the Moment: Tackling Entrenched Inequalities to End Epidemics', Global AIDS Update, 2020, pp. 8–11.

Perennial Problems to Peace and Security in Africa

Part four contains a gloomy picture of some of the factors that have contributed to the breakdown of peace and insecurity on the continent. For example, in Chapter 16 Gloria David Phiri and Mandala note that violation of human rights obligations is a contributing factor to conflicts in Africa and reiterate the clarion call on the urgent need for the protection of human rights in Africa. In Chapter 17 Kapeni hypothesizes that poor governance and leadership pose a threat to peace and security of many African countries, therefore, with good leadership and good governance skills, a country can develop politically, socially and economically. In Chapter 18, Noel Kayira unpacks a catalogue of organized crimes in Africa, which are exacerbated by corruption among law enforcement officials, globalization, advancement in technology, porous borders as well as weak governments and civil wars in some parts of Africa. In order to arrest the problem of organized crimes, Kayira advocates for a holistic approach that will enable the AU and its member states to join efforts to prevent, monitor, investigate and prosecute perpetrators of these crimes.

In Chapter 19, Busingye laments that lack of democratic management of natural resources coupled with the insatiable interest of external actors in Africa's natural resources, continue to fuel armed conflicts on the continent and proposes adoption of all-inclusive governance framework for natural resources that guard against abuse by former colonial interference. In Chapter 20, Majiga observes a worrying surge in acts of piracy and attacks against shipping vessels on African coastal lines and the lack the technical and logistical capability as well as financial resources to counter the threat effectively, which call for international corporation to curb the vice.

In Chapter 21, Archiles Bwete, Leonard Hatungimana and Wilson Parsauti attribute ethnicity and economic factors as the common causes of post-electoral violence in Africa and advocate for promotion of democracy and rule of law and, education and sensitization of the African people to end electoral violence. In Chapter 22, Gilbert Mittawa asserts that the proliferation of illicit SALW in Africa undermines Africa's socioeconomic development under AU Agenda 2063 and goes further to underscore the need for adoption of coherent and coordinated international and regional strategies to regulate the SALW on the continent. In Chapter 23, Christable Tusiime, Sarah Mukashaba and Busingye also recommend adoption of a coordinated continental approach to prohibition of weapons of mass destruction (WMD), which have remained elusive in the global and regional peace and security architectures.

Strategies for Achieving Peace and Security in Africa

Part five of the Handbook is dedicated to devising strategies to counter the evolving threats to peace and security in Africa. In Chapter 24, Mark Maxwell posits that the immense promise of the APSA is undermined by pockets where security and peace are elusive and advises that the building blocks to a nation's security must include professionalization of military and through commitment to the rule of law. Maxwell aptly posits that with trust comes security and with security comes peace. In Chapter 25, Boti Phiri tracks the repercussion of unemployment and the youth bulge in Africa, and is of the view that addressing youth unemployment is key to curbing conflicts on the continent, including post-election violence and insurgency.

In Chapter 26, Thomasin Gondwe and Laika Nakanga examine the challenges encountered in the implementation of UN Security Council resolutions on participation of women in peace processes and highlight the impact of the inclusion of women at strategic, operational and tactical levels, especially towards increasing operational effectiveness in peacekeeping operations. In Chapter 27, Kuwali recommends that considering the changing and dynamic nature of armed conflicts in Africa, it is crucial to develop mechanisms to ensure that all actors involved are taking their respective responsibilities seriously and that proper oversight is exercised in order to silence the guns on the continent. In Chapter 28, Ibrahim Machina Mohammed and Lawan Cheri examine the key factors that drive conflicts on the continent and outlines practical steps and strategies for promoting peace and reconciliation in order to end armed conflicts and build peace in Africa.

In Chapter 29, Elias Opongo asserts that the African continent faces four categories of conflicts that are closely interconnected, namely: armed conflicts between the state and armed groups; sectarian violence (ethnic or religious) led by insurgents; political violence advanced by the state against the population; and low-key communal conflicts. Opongo argues that these conflicts can be resolved through effective and efficient conflict resolution mechanisms as well as all-inclusive economic and political strategies aimed at improving socioeconomic conditions of the majority of the population. In Chapter 30, George Chipembere-Lwanda reveals why preventing illicit resource outflows from Africa is key to ending conflicts and promoting socioeconomic development on the continent.

In Chapter 31, Busingye and Daniel Mayombo lucidly demonstrate how the migrant crisis in the Mediterranean Sea partly stems from displacements of persons due to armed conflicts, political persecution, poverty, gender discrimination and unfavourable climatic conditions on the continent, among others. Africans have suffered unimaginable loss and suffering resulting from the unseaworthy boats operated by gangs of human traffickers. As such, Busingye and Mayombo recommend a re-thinking of the human rights and political governance regimes in Africa to dissuade migrants from leaving the continent and risking their lives on such precarious expeditions.

In Chapter 32, Cephas Lumina grapples with the challenges as well as the initiatives undertaken by the AU to secure sustainable and predictable financing for the effective implementation of the AU's 'Silencing the Guns by 2020' initiative. He argues that although the 2017 Kigali Financing Decision is an important step in the AU's quest for financial self-reliance, it is not certain whether it will yield the required resources.

On his part, in Chapter 33 Kuwali poignantly points out that there has been a progressive rise of corruption in Africa, which fuels greed and grievances that eventually triggers conflict. If unchallenged, corruption is likely to continue to exacerbate inequality on the continent thereby escalating violence. In order to effectively prevent corruption in Africa, Kuwali advances a commend and condemn strategy, including adoption of adequate legislation with firm punishment for corruption to arrest the greed and insatiable appetite for public resources for personal gain by unscrupulous individuals.

Securing Sustainable Peace and Security in Africa

Finally, in Chapter 34, Kuwali sums up the discussion and recommendation. There continues to be a deterioration in peace in Africa, particularly in countries such as South Sudan, Somalia, Libya, the Democratic Republic of the Congo (DRC), Central African Republic (CAR) and Sudan.[24] Asymmetric warfare, terrorism, and violent extremism, ethnic tensions, violent electoral crises, transnational crimes, resource conflicts, global pandemics, among others, are some of the challenges that have hampered the development of the continent.[25] The drivers of conflict and violence on the continent relate to socioeconomic challenges such as high youth unemployment rate, lack of equal opportunities, urbanization, poverty, inequality, proliferation of SALW, competition over natural resources; bad governance and corruption.[26] In this case, the concept of peace in Africa is not merely the absence of violence, but also the ability of a society to respond to the needs of its citizens, reduce the number of conflicts, and resolve existing disputes.[27] While security relates to the protection from harm in every imaginable way.[28]

As such, securing peace and security in Africa is dependent on good governance, which requires responsible leadership, participatory citizenship and fair political representation. It follows that to secure sustainable peace and security in Africa; governments should respect human rights obligations that require equitable distribution of resources, bridging the poverty gap and ensuring minority voices are heard. It is also imperative to strengthen democratic institutions, promote representative governance and abhor all forms of discrimination in order to achieve sustainable peace and security.[29] Engaging

[24] Global Peace Index, Statistics Times, as of 11 June 2020, available at: https://statisticstimes.com/ranking/globa-peace-index.php (accessed 23 February 2021).

[25] Adeyoose, footnote 20 above.

[26] De Plesis and Kaspersen, footnote 17 above.

[27] Adeyoose, footnote 17 above.

[28] As above.

[29] As above.

unemployed youths will prevent them from being willing tools in the hands of extremist groups and non-state armed groups.[30] The emergence of Covid-19 has brought health to the front and centre on issues of peace and security. Making health care affordable via creation and strengthening of insurance schemes will enable even the least privileged of our population to access care when the need arises thereby bringing about peace and security.[31] With a peaceful and secured Africa, we will be able to develop human capital and attain sustainable development.[32]

It is reassuring that the AU recognizes that national and regional governance institutions need to be strengthened to counter contemporary challenges to peace and security. The AU's African Governance Architecture (AGA) should be fully engaged and integrated in responses to Africa's peace and security and development challenges.[33] There should also be coordination between the APSA and the New Partnership for Africa's Development (NEPAD), which explicitly recognizes that: '[p]eace, security, democracy, good governance, human rights, and sound economic management are conditions for sustainable development.'[34] Given the nature of the peace and security on the continent, the APSA cannot work in isolation, it has to consistently and coherently coordinate with human rights institutions and organs meant to promote socioeconomic well-being of individuals on the continent. Therefore, coordination of AGA, APSA, NEPAD and the AU Human and People's Rights legal and judicial frameworks is critical in the implementation of the AU Master Roadmap of Practical Steps to Silence the Guns in Africa by Year 2020 (Lusaka Master Roadmap 2016).[35]

As a component of NEPAD, the African Peer Review Mechanism (APRM) is designed to promote structural conflict prevention through good governance. Importantly, the Conference on Security Stability, Defence and Cooperation in Africa (CSSDCA) propounds that stability calls for the rule of law and 'good governance' and the full protection of human rights, which are key

---

[30] As above.

[31] Adeyoose, footnote 17 above.

[32] As above.

[33] Shamil Idriss and Mike Jobbins, 'Achieving Peace in the Great Lakes Region', *Africa in Focus*, Brookings, 6 February 2015, available at: www.brookings.edu/blog/africa-in-focus/2015/02/06/achieving-peace-in-the-great-lakes-region/ (accessed 23 February 2021).

[34] See also United Nations, Declaration on the New Partnership for Africa's Development, UN Doc.GA/57/L.2/Rev.1 (16 September 2002).

[35] African Union, the AU Master Roadmap of Practical Steps to Silence the Guns in Africa by Year 2020 (Lusaka Master Roadmap 2016), available at: https://au.int/sitesdefault/files/documents/37996-doc-au-roadmap-silencing-guns-2020.pdf.en-pdf (accessed 24 February 2021).

14   D. KUWALI

to the prevention of human rights violations, and the root causes of conflicts.[36] Considering that development, security and human rights are intertwined in a symbiotic relationship, the AU should focus more on improving human security and promoting rule of law, good governance and economic development in AU States, which are crucial to the prevention of conflicts.[37] Therefore, in light of the AU's current context of chronic underfunding and excessive dependency on external funding, the best way to cut costs for the APSA is to avoid conflicts, promote good governance and respect for human rights and the rule of law.

Against this background, it is hoped that the Handbook will be of value and interest to varied audience at global, regional and national level, including, development partners, policymakers, practitioners, academics, security analysts and politicians as well as students, researchers involved in peace, security and development studies.

---

[36] *See* Department of Foreign Affairs, *The Report on the Implementation of the Conference on Security Stability, Defence and Cooperation in Africa*, Republic of South Africa ['CSSDCA'], p. 2.

[37] J. Busumtwi-Sam, 'Architects of Peace: The African Union and NEPAD', 7 *Georgetown Journal of International Affairs* (2006), pp. 71–81, pp. 76–77.

CHAPTER 2

The Concept of Peace: An African Perspective

Desire Hakorimana and Godard Busingye

INTRODUCTION

The concept of peace in Africa has been shaped by the continent's colonial history. The first post-colonial African leaders such as Kwame Nkrumah saw Africa transcending into the new horizons of peace. Nkrumah envisioned peace in Africa developing from the concerns of the individual to address issues of the sub-systemic which was the state and finally settled on the systemic which, is the African continent as a whole and thereafter the World.[1] Kwame Nkrumah's mission in the world was to dismantle colonialism in Africa. His vision was the restoration of the dignity that was lost because of slavery and colonialism to enable the Africans to function freely in the forthcoming unified world society as an equal player and partner.[2] Potekhin has observed that imperialists are disturbed by Africans' determination to independently define their future without consulting them, hence they are now increasingly

[1] Dodoo, Vincent, Kwame Nkrumah's Mission and Vision for Africa and the World, *The Journal of Pan African Studies*, Vol. 4, No. 10 (January 2012).

[2] As above.

D. Hakorimana
Burundi National Defence Force, Gitega, Burundi

G. Busingye (✉)
Kampala International University, Kampala, Uganda

© The Author(s), under exclusive license to Springer Nature
Switzerland AG 2022
D. Kuwali (ed.), *The Palgrave Handbook of Sustainable Peace
and Security in Africa*, https://doi.org/10.1007/978-3-030-82020-6_2

15

supplementing economic fetters with ideological persuasion, retaining more ideological servitors and dumping propaganda material into Africa.[3]

The thesis and antithesis of peace in the African perspective is a function of the continent's colonial history. Colonial history disoriented the African mind and eroded the traditional concept of peace. Africans' exposure to the 'western civilization' enabled the latter to erode the peaceful environment that prevailed on the continent before the advent of colonialism. Conscious of that horrendous background, Africans have now resolutely assumed responsibility to maintain their peace in the neo-colonial period.[4]

COLONIALISM AND THE EROSION OF PEACE IN AFRICA

Today, Africans are filled with euphoria as they attempt to go back to the drawing board to craft a new concept of peace that adequately answers their philosophical aspirations. Attempts to overcome the colonial political history hysteria by the first crop of African leaders at the time of independence came up with two views about Africanized peace concept, *Pax Africana*[5] and *Negritude*.[6] Each of these paradigms espouses the desire and anger the post-colonial leaders had, which inspired them to rid the continent of the worst memories associated with the imperial colonial rule. which now resurfaces in the globalized era of the United Nations (UN).

The current Internet revolution, where face-to-face meetings are now held online, via Zoom or any other virtual platforms, brings the global community together, without individuals travelling distances for meetings.[7] Virtual meetings are, however, a threat to the African culture of communal meetings. As expounded by Tabitha Mwangi and Tracy Asava in Chapter 10 and also Dan Kuwali in Chapter 13, this problem is compounded by the use of cyber technology in warfare, which enables the developed world to use such

---

[3] Potekhin, Ivan, Pan-Africanism and the Struggle of the Two Ideologies, accessed at: https://www.sahistory.org.za/sites/default/files/archive-files/Acn1964.0001.9976.000.019.Oct1964.7.pdf, on 27 October 2020.

[4] Dersso, S. A., The Quest for Pax Africana: The Case of the African Union's Peace and Security Regime, *African Journal on Conflict Resolution*, Vol. 12, No. 2 (2012).

[5] Ndlovu-Gatsheni, S. J., 'My Life Is One Long Debate': Ali A Mazrui on the Invention of Africa and Postcolonial Predicaments, Archie Mafeje Research Institute University of South Africa, Public Lecture delivered at the University of the Free State (UFS) on 'Ali A. Mazrui Memorial Event' hosted by the Vice Chancellor and Rector & the Centre for African Studies, Albert Wessels Auditorium, Bloemfontein Campus, 30 October 2014.

[6] Lundahl, M., Negritude—An Anti-Racist Racism? (Or Who Is the Racist?), published in Negritude: Legacy and Present Relevance, red Isabelle Constant, Cambridge Scholars Publishing, 2009.

[7] Li, C., and Lalani, F., The COVID-19 Pandemic Has Changed Education Forever, The World Economic Forum COVID Action Platform, 29 April 2020, accessed at: https://www.weforum.org/agenda/2020/04/coronavirus-education-global-covid19-online-digital-learning/, on 12 December 2020.

technologies to fight wars from faraway places.[8] Indirect rule policies are now tools to foreign domineering powers, and the purpose for them is expressly to destabilize the African continent so that they remain in control when they are looked to for solutions to African problems.[9]

Evoking the traditional values of togetherness, unity and harmony, however, Africans have been able to restate their position with clarity on what kind of peace they want and what that means to them.[10] Africans now act as if they were no longer chained down by their former tormentors and colonizers, much as that remains a fallacy.[11] On the face of it, African leaders do not have to refer to their former colonizers or other imperialistic Western Powers before making decisions concerning their destiny. The caveat, however, is that inroads of imperialistic powers cannot wholly be wished away, these shall still come on board through grants, aid and donations, which in most of the cases are conditional.[12] The peaceful environment on the African continent, must therefore, be analysed within a context of multifaceted players, the Africans themselves, and their grant, aid donor-linked partners from the Western World. Unable to fully wriggle out of the shackles of colonial history, Africans remind themselves of the horrific socioeconomic and political exposure they suffered at the hands of their former western imperialistic colonial powers, largely through their racist policies.[13]

Immediately after their first encounter with Western colonial powers, Africans started experiencing untold suffering as they gradually lost grasp of their traditional values and cultural practices.[14] They were victims of slave trade, participated in the notorious World Wars, on behalf of their colonizers, and thereafter suffered as victims of the Cold War between the United States of America (US) and its Allies and the former Union of Soviet Socialist Republics

---

[8] Oakes, F. C., and Govern, K. H., Introduction: Cyber and the Changing Face of War, Penn Law: Legal Scholarship Repository, University of Pennsylvania, Carey Law School, 2015, accessed at: https://scholarship.law.upenn.edu/cgi/viewcontent.cgi?article=2567&context=faculty_scholarship, on 10 December 2020.

[9] Kaoma, K. J., African Religion and Colonial Rebellion, *Journal for the Study of Religion*, Vol. 29, No. 1 (2016), pp. 57–84 (28 pages), available at: https://www.jstor.org/stable/24805707.

[10] Dersso, footnote 4 above.

[11] African Union Agenda 2063 A Shared Strategic Framework for Inclusive Growth and Sustainable Development, Background Note August 2013.

[12] Heldring, L., and Robinson, J., Colonialism and Development in Africa, VOX EU.CEPR, 2013, accessed at: https://voxeu.org/article/colonialism-and-development-africa, on 7 December 2020.

[13] Rusagara, F. K., Resilience of a Nation: A History of the Military in Rwanda, Fountain Publishers, Kigali, Rwanda, 2009, pp. 89–106.

[14] Rodney, W., How Europe Underdeveloped Africa, Chapter II: How Africa Developed Before the Coming of the Europeans—Up to the Fifteenth Century, East African Educational Publishers, Kampala, 1981, pp. 33–71.

(USSR).[15] Azikiwe sums up this history that slavery contributed to depopulating Africa; capitalism denuded the continent's wealth; colonialism deprived Africa of its birthright, and imperialism emasculated its livelihood and peaceful enjoyment of the bounties of the good earth.[16]

Colonialism profoundly transformed and mangled the political landscape of the African continent through the imposition of the modern state. Each pre-colonial state had several characteristics: one ethnic community inhabited a 'common territory; its members shared a tradition, real or fictitious, of common descent; and they were held together by a common language and a common culture. Few African nations were also states in the modern of European sense, although they were certainly political societies. In contrast, the states created by European imperialists, comprising the overwhelming majority of the continent, ordinarily contained more than one nation.[17]

The particular historical political era where Africa is today is neo-colonialism. Mazrui considers that 'neo-colonialism' is an indirect political and economic manipulation, paradigm, designed to perpetuate external control in Africa in more subtle ways—the actual activity of manipulation which an external power might carry out or attempt to carry out.[18] Neo-colonialism can conveniently be understood to mean administering a former colony through its own executive government.[19] Neo-colonialism has a direct bearing on African peace today. While Africans would like to have peace within their organic philosophy of Pan-Africanism, they may never do so, because the neo-colonialism agenda is so oppressive to them and dictates, indirectly, what policies must be implemented in the former colonies.[20] Broadly speaking, peace in the African perspective encapsulates elements of socioeconomic and

[15] United Nations, Remember Slavery, available at: https://www.un.org/en/events/slaveryremembranceday/, where it is stated that every year 25 March, is the International Day of Remembrance of the Victims of Slavery and the Transatlantic Slave Trade. The Day offers the opportunity to honour and remember those who suffered and died at the hands of the brutal slavery system.

[16] Azikiwe, Nnamdi, "The Future of Pan Africanism", Blackpast, African American History, available at: https://www.blackpast.org/wp-content/uploads/prodimages/files/blackpast_images/Nnamdi_Azikiwe.jpg.

[17] Mutua, M., The Banjul Charter and the African Cultural Fingerprint: An Evaluation of the Language of Duties, *Virginia Journal of International Law*, Vol. 35 (1995), p. 339, in Heyns, C., and Stefiszyn, K., (eds.), Human Rights, Peace and Justice in Africa: A Reader, Centre for Human Rights, Pretoria University Law Press, 2006, p. 54.

[18] Mazrui, A. A., Neo-dependency and Africa's Fragmentation, in Coetzee, P. H., and Roux, A. P. J. (eds.), The African Philosophy Reader, Second Edition, A Text with Readings, Routledge, London, 2003, p. 619.

[19] As above, p. 620.

[20] Ebatamehi, S., Pan-Africanism: The Only Solution To Neo-Colonialism, The African Exponent, online Magazine, 2020, accessed at: https://www.africanexponent.com/post/9142-african-unity-is-our-only-resistance-to-neo-colonialism, on 7 December 2020.

peace, which, when unpacked imply unity, solidarity and the elimination of tribalism, religious divisiveness or any form of sectarian divide.[21]

THEORETICAL AND CONCEPTUAL ASPECTS OF PEACE FROM AN AFRICAN PERSPECTIVE

Before colonialism, Africans lived harmoniously with one another because they enjoyed the available resources communally and believed in *Ubuntu* (togetherness).[22] In case of any conflict, Africans had organized ways of restoring peace. They did that through mediation by the leaders in the community.[23] Colonialists divided the continent into small States or amalgamated small African States into larger political entities to suit their interests. In addition, colonialists introduced ideologies such as capitalism that distorted African peace.[24] Today, Africans tolerate and live together, but in a changed environment, created by colonialists.[25] With respect to the neo-colonial African continent, each constituent country has a unique history and geographical conditions. It is also impacted differently by the global geopolitics. Moreover, African countries are at different stages of economic development and have varied internal democracies and public policies. African countries equally have different patterns of internal and international interactions.[26] The African continent can be summed up as a mosaic of economic, geo-political, and economic outlay, incapable, at least in the foreseeable future, to attain continental peace as envisaged under the Pan-African and African Renaissance paradigms.

Majority of African countries were colonies of the western powers, which shaped their histories and also distorted their plans for future political, social,

[21] Marie-Aude Fouere, Julius Nyerere, Ujamaa, and Political Morality in Contemporary Tanzania, African Studies Review April 2014, available at: http://journals.cambridge.org/ASR.

[22] Asike, J. C., The Philosophical Concept of "Ubuntu" as Dialogic Ethic and the Transformation of Political Community in Africa, *Ogirisi: A New Journal of African Studies*, Vol. 12s (2016), available at: http://dx.doi.org/10.4314/og.v12is1.1.

[23] Ajayi, A. T., Methods of Conflict Resolution in African Traditional Society, African Research Review, *An International Multidisciplinary Journal, Ethiopia*, Vol. 8, No. 2, Serial No. 33 (April 2014), pp. 138–157, ISSN 1994-9057 (Print) ISSN 2070-0083 (Online) http://dx.doi.org/10.4314/afrrev.v8i2.9.

[24] Michalopoulos, S., and Papaioannou, E., Pre-colonial Ethnic Institutions and Contemporary African Development, *Econometrica*, Vol. 81, No. 1 (January 2013), pp. 113–152, https://doi.org/10.3982/ECTA9613.

[25] Nkrumah, B., and Busingye, G., No Peace, No War: Protection of Civilians in The Great Lakes Region of Africa in Kuwali & Viljoen (eds.), By All Means Necessary: Protecting Civilians and Preventing Mass Atrocities in Africa, Pretoria University Law Press (PULP), 2017, pp. 342–355.

[26] Annan, K., The Causes of Conflict and the Promotion of Durable Peace and Sustainable Development in Africa, 1998, in Heyns, C., and Stefiszyn, K. (eds.), Human Rights, Peace and Justice in Africa: A Reader, Centre for Human Rights, Pretoria University Law Press, 2006, p. 240.

cultural and economic development. Colonialism, first and foremost, aimed at exploiting its victims and this exploitation was justified through a racial prejudice: the inferior intellectual capacity of the exploited.[27] One of the African philosophies associated with the concept of peace in the African perspective is *Negritude*. This philosophy began a discourse on racism, Eurocentric ideas, colonialism and contributed to theories and critical thinking that ultimately formed the basis for much of the post-colonial debate.[28] According to Kasanda, the concern for African identity rests on two premises: the rehabilitation of African identities and the threat to cultural homogenization due to globalization.[29] This view is largely championed by the proponents of the *Negritude* paradigm, spearheaded by Leopold Senghor.

According to this paradigm, it is essential to assume being black, to cultivate one's pride and self-appreciation. This is summed up in the famous aphorism, 'the emotion is as *negro* as the reason is *Hellenic*'.[30] To the proponents of *Negritude*, there can be no peace on the African continent without Africans having self-esteem in themselves, as blacks, with a cultural background unadulterated by imperialism. The philosophy of *Negritude* asserts that, contrary to Western people for whom reason constitutes the fundamental characteristic, black people are characterized by the ascendancy of emotion. Emotion defines their epistemology and configures their world view.[31] The paradigm of *Negritude* is, however, critiqued as antiracist racism, simply because it dichotomizes between the Africans and the Hellenics.[32]

Conceptually, 'peace' has diverse dimensions. Some conceptualize peace as living in an environment free of armed conflict or war. *Pax Africana*, a peace 'that is protected and maintained by Africa herself', is one of the several dimensions of the theoretical conceptualization of African peace.[33] To Mazrui, *Pax Africana* is not about the imposition of peace on others but rather about Africans taking custodianship of African peace and security, and addressing

---

[27] Address delivered by Leopold Sedar Senghor, President of the Republic of Senegal (1979), reprinted in Heyns, C. (ed.), Human Rights Law in Africa Leiden: Martinus Nijhoff, in Heyns, C., and Stefiszyn, K. (eds.), Human Rights, Peace and Justice in Africa: A Reader, Centre for Human Rights, Pretoria University Law Press, 2006, p. 50.

[28] Triglone, T., Negritude's Legacy in African Political Ideology, 2011, accessed at: https://www.academia.edu/5736107/Negritudes_legacy_in_modern_African_political_ide ology, on 8 November, 2020.

[29] Kasanda, A., Reviewing the African Identity Discourses, Ethinophilosophy and Negritude, Book Chapter In Contemporary African Social and Political Philosophy, (1st Ed), 2018, Routledge, eBook ISBN9781351209922.

[30] Kasanda, A., Analyzing African Social and Political Philosophy: Trends and Challenges, *Journal of East–West Thought*, Summer, Vol. 5, No. 2 (June 2015), p. 38.

[31] As above.

[32] Lundahl, footnote 6 above.

[33] Dersso, footnote 10 above.

the structural causes of conflict on their own continent.[34] Peace per se, is, however, relative, and not a constant phenomenon; it keeps changing with events and times. Mohammed opines that "for peace to be irreversible in Africa, more work needs to be done to address, in a coherent and more coordinated manner, the structures, attitudes, and processes that perpetuate conflict and instability".[35]

With time, Africans have realized that to attain sustainable peace, there is need to shift from the current top-down approach to a more people-centred paradigm with a specific focus on peace dividends especially for women and children.[36] The proposed people-centred approach is indeed necessary to include each and every stakeholder in discussions aimed at ensuring lasting peace, even in war-torn countries like the Democratic Republic of the Congo (DRC), the Central African Republic (CAR) and Libya. This approach is relevant much as a greater proportion of Africans live free of war today than ever in the post-independence period.[37] Those living in such an environment, however, cannot boast of living in a world of peace because their fellow Africans on the continent are living in war and war-like environments. As pointed out by Kuwali in Chapter 27, armed conflicts, low human development, poverty and environmental degradation are the most severe problems human beings are confronted with, and which continue to deny them the right to peace.[38] These problems are cross-cutting, and adversely affect the resource envelope of the continent.

The African Peace and Security Architecture (APSA), which is an African home-grown outfit to deal with all peace and security related issues on the continent, depends on the resource contributions from member States of the African Union (AU).[39] The over-dependence on external funding by the AU has been aptly discussed by Cephas Lumina in Chapter 32. One condition for peace is probably an equitable relation, but there may also be violence in a non-exploitative system if something goes wrong within one single actor.[40]

[34] Mazrui, A. A., Towards a Concept of "Pax Africana" in Karbo, T., and Virk, K. (eds.), The Palgrave Handbook of Peacebuilding in Africa, 2018. Palgrave Macmillan, Cham. https://doi.org/10.1007/978-3-319-62202-6_2.

[35] Mohammed, F. K., Pax Africana: Peacebuilding in Africa, March 14, 2018, International Peace Institute, 50 Years, accessed at: https://www.ipinst.org/2018/03/pax-africana-peacebuilding-in-africa#8, on 7 December 2020.

[36] As above.

[37] Burbach, David T., The Coming Peace: Africa's Declining Conflicts, 2016, accessed at: https://www.oxfordresearchgroup.org.uk/Blog/the-coming-peace-africas-declining-conflicts, on 29 October 2020.

[38] Ramirez, Claudia A., Peace, Security, and Sustainable Development in Africa, Area Studies—Africa (Regional Sustainable Development Review)—Vol. II—Peace, Security, and Sustainable Development in Africa.

[39] African Union Commission, African Peace and Security Architecture (APSA), 2010 Assessment Study Report.

[40] Galtung, Johan, Peace by Peaceful Means, Peace and Conflict, Development and Civilization, International Peace Research Institute, Oslo, 1996.

Using the trending language used for patients with Coronavirus disease of 2019 (Covid-19), peace or lack of it, like patients, can manifest itself with clear symptoms, and hence provide clear signals to the health workers to treat; or may be asymptomatic, and pose a challenge to the health workers to identify the patients, without testing, and either treat or isolate the patient. Clear symptoms of lack of peace on the African continent manifest in cases of violent armed conflict,[41] while asymptomatically disenfranchisement of the citizens of a particular country remains a brewing pot for lack of peace.[42] Using the analogy of the diagnosis-prognosis-therapy triangle, Galtung theorizes that peace, or lack of it, has a direct correlation to the medical identification of the problem, isolating it and treating it.[43] Galtung's theory, just like that of symptomatic and asymptomatic conditions of a Covid-19 case, is a useful tool when theorizing peace from the African perspective.

A discussion of the concept of peace in the African perspective insinuates political peace and not peace in general terms. Political peace in Africa has changed through times, right from the pre-colonial, colonial, neo-colonial to date.[44] Political peace, which must be the concern for the African continent, however, may not be maintained without the consonance of exogenic factors, previously colonialism, and presently, globalism. Political peace must be enjoyed by each and every citizen in a given country.[45] Short of that, those oppressed by actions of other political actors, shall not be at peace, and will only be at peace when they violently remove their oppressors from the political seats.[46] From a theoretical perspective, peace is intangible, elusive, and always ruptured by wars and other forms of violent conflict.[47] Peace is a background condition for the perception of everything else, a physical phenomenon affecting all sentient beings, something whose presence or absence is best measured on a continuum or spectrum.[48] Rationally, therefore, it is not possible to talk of peace from an African perspective, in isolation of

---

[41] Nkrumah and Busingye, footnote 25 above, pp. 342–355.

[42] Weinstein, J. M., and Francisco, L., The Civil War in Mozambique: The Balance Between Internal and External Influences, in Collier, P., and Sambanis, N. (eds.), Understanding Civil War: Evidence and Analysis, Volume 1: Africa, The International Bank for Reconstruction and Development/The World Bank, 2005.

[43] Galtung, footnote 41 above.

[44] Rusagara, footnote 13 above, pp. 71–81.

[45] The Constitutive Act of the African Union, Adopted by The Thirty-Sixth Ordinary Session of the Assembly of Heads of State and Government 11 July 2000—Lome, Togo; Preamble, recites inter alia that: peace, security and stability as a prerequisite for the implementation of our development and integration agenda.

[46] Museveni, Y. K., What Is Africa's Problem? Speeches and Writings on Africa by Yoweri Kaguta Museveni, NRM Publications, Kampala, Uganda, 1992, p. 39.

[47] Webel C., Introduction: Toward a Philosophy and Metapsychology of Peace, in Webel, C., and Galtung, J. (eds.), Handbook of Peace and Conflict Studies, Routledge, London, 2007.

[48] As above, 2007, p. 11.

peace, or lack of it in other parts of the world. For example, there was no peace on the African continent during World War I (WWI) and World War II (WWII), and even during the Cold War. Wig notes that "each of these political episodes had its unique peace paradigm".[49]

In Africa, where customary institutions are plentiful and many states have low capacity, strong pre-colonial institutions can serve as tools for peaceful bargaining and thus conflict reduction.[50] Wig further argues that when groups have centralized customary institutions, they can make their promises to respect agreements more credible by enshrining them in centralized political authorities.[51] When agreements are guaranteed by a customary institution, such as a king or a traditional legislature, this raises the cost of violating the agreement, since reneging will have reputation costs for the customary institutions.[52] Pre-colonial Africa was at peace with itself—Africans versus Africans.

Webel considers that peace is a primary requirement of the human condition itself as it is needed for survival of mankind. Perhaps 'peace' is like 'happiness', 'justice', 'health' and other human ideals, something every person and culture claims to desire and venerate, but which few if any, achieve, at least on an enduring basis.[53] Webel elaborates further that peace in its progressive or dialectical mode denotes active individual and collective self-determination and emancipatory empowerment.[54] On his part, Dersso opines that the change in the nature of conflicts, which led to the recognition that Africa, needs to develop its own means for overcoming the challenges of peace and security facing it.[55] That, however, does not mean that the African continent would henceforth be peaceful. Violent armed conflicts have ravaged the continent almost instantaneously with the time when African countries started to rid themselves of the colonial powers.[56]

The foregoing analysis does not succinctly delineate what conceptually, 'peace' is, rather it alludes to the fact that 'peace' is and remains a theoretical paradigm. Lack of conceptual clarity on what peace is, necessitates individuals, states and regional blocs to have their own conceptualization of peace. Such conceptualization, however, must be based on their individual experiences, past and present, of peace. The argument advanced in this paper is that much as there is no succinct definition of peace in the available literature, Africans

---

[49] Wig, T., Pre-colonial Institutions and Peace in Africa, Oxford Research Group, Breaking the cycle of violence, 25 November 2016, accessed at: https://www.oxfordresearchgroup.org.uk/Blog/pre-colonial-institutions-and-peace-in-africa, on 9 November 2020.

[50] As above.

[51] As above.

[52] As above.

[53] Webel, footnote 48 above.

[54] As above.

[55] Dersso, footnote 34 above.

[56] Rusagara, footnote 45 above.

know the exact meaning of peace, how they enjoyed it before the advent of colonial imperialism, the current status of peace on the continent, and what they want for the future.

It is also argued that it is fallacious to talk about an African perspective of peace for a continent of diversity in almost every aspect—the peoples. Moreover, there is disconnect between the pre-colonial, colonial and post-colonial African continent, each having its unique political and cultural features. The colonial effects were not homogeneous across the continent. Some countries were colonized by Italians, others by the British, the French, the Portuguese and the Dutch. Each of those colonizers had different policies in the countries they colonized. The Dutch colonizers in South Africa had the intention of assimilating themselves into the country and practised an *Apartheid* policy. The British largely relied on the indirect rule policy in the colonies they occupied, while the French directly ruled their colonies.

COLONIAL LEGACY AND PEACE IN AFRICA

Colonial institutions in Africa weakened African peace by forcefully replacing African traditional institutions with foreign constructed democraticgovernance ideologies. Africa has surmounted the challenges of slavery, colonization, exploitation, neo-colonialism and imperialism.[57] Africa has, since the departure of colonial powers, and the dismantling of *Apartheid*, made profound strides to establish systems of democratic governance that have broadened competitive politics, induced leadership turnovers, invigorated civic action and resuscitated economies for growth and development.[58] Some parts of the continent, however, remain saddled by violent conflicts and instability that are linked to competition over power, resources and the mismanagement of diversity.[59]

The ethnic, sectarian and religious fissures, largely introduced and entrenched by the colonial powers, exacerbate divisionism amongst the hitherto coherent traditional communities.[60] It also foments conflict amongst those communities and hence becomes a platform for the escalation of social, economic and political tensions and instability on the continent. Silencing the guns in Africa by 2020 is the collective responsibility of African States that should ultimately culminate in States that can enhance dignity, prosperity,

---

[57] Economic Commission for Africa (ECA), Common African Position on the Post-2015 Development Agenda, UNECA, 2014, accessed at: https://sustainabledevelopment. un.org/index.php?page=view&type=400&nr=1329&menu=35#:~:text=Published%20in% 20March%202014%2C%20the,urbanization%2C%20climate%20change%20and%20inequal ities.&text=The%20African%20Position%20is%20an%20African%20Union%20(UN)%2Ds ponsored%20document, on 20 November 2020.

[58] As above.

[59] As above.

[60] Rodney, footnote 14 above.

and security in national, regional, and continental domains.[61] The peaceful resolution of wars, when achieved on the continent, will contribute significantly to the goals of the Common African Position (CAP) on the Post-2015 Development Agenda and the Africa Agenda 2063.[62]

The CAP on the post-2015 Development Agenda is the embodiment of unity. The Position recognizes rising trends such as population growth and the youth bulge, urbanization, climate change and inequalities, which have also been ably discussed in this Handbook. It reiterates the importance of prioritizing structural transformation for inclusive and people-centred development in Africa.[63] Within the ambit of this Agenda, the post-2015 Development Agenda was intended to be Member State-driven, and in this regard, Africa is expected to stand together in solidarity in negotiating an outcome that can result in the collective ownership of the new agenda.[64]

The continuum of the agenda of the former Africa's imperialistic powers on the continent, and the latter's failure to ensure peace for Africans as a condition precedent to the continent-wide development, created the inertia for the 'African solutions to African problems' paradigm on the continent.[65] The story told by Africans, undoubtedly, points to the reality that Africans, in their diversity, know what peace means to them and why they need it.[66] It is ironical, however, to note that African Governments are unable, and probably unwilling to fund the Peace Fund, one of the pillars of APSA, yet the responsibility for peace building squarely lies on them.[67] APSA is Africa's vehicle for attainment of peace on the continent. As discussed by Lumina in Chapter 32, the AU has not provided adequate financial support for this important undertaking. As a result, these critical activities are heavily dependent on the financial support of external partners, with more than 95 per cent of such activities

---

[61] It is important to note that the set date of 2020 for silencing the guns on the African continent did not anticipate that that milestone would be achieved. Rather, it was intended to inspire African States to work towards creating a peaceful environment, without shooting guns. The failure to achieve this milestone, should not, therefore, be seen as a setback towards the concept of silencing guns on the African continent. It remains inspiring for each and every State to do so.

[62] Economic Commission for Africa, footnote 58 above.

[63] As above.

[64] As above.

[65] Kasaija, P. A., The African Union's Notion of 'African Solutions to African Problems' and the Crises in Côte d'Ivoire (2010–2011) and Libya (2011), *African Journal on Conflict Resolution*, Vol. 12 No. 2 (2012).

[66] See for example, Article 124 (1) of the Treaty for the Establishment of the African Union, 1999, which recites as follows: The Partner States agree that peace and security are pre-requisites to social and economic development within the Community and vital to the achievement of the objectives of the Community.

[67] UNSCR Resolution 2282 (2016), adopted by the UNSC on 27 April 2016, at its 7680th Meeting.

funded by external partners, including conflict prevention, mediation, special envoys and special political missions.[68]

The gaps in raising funds for the African home-grown peace, notwithstanding, Africans relentlessly work towards attaining this virtue. The African continent with its diverse customs and cultures is bound together not by the geographical accident, but, by what the former President of the Republic of South Africa Nelson Mandela put clearly that Africans "human compassion binds us the one to the other-not in pity or patronizingly, but as human beings who have learnt how to turn our common suffering into hope for the future".[69] Mandela's words resonate well with Africans past experience and sum up why Africans yearn for peace, and are prepared to do all it takes to have it, to themselves, by themselves and protect it.

THE AFRICAN UNION FRAMEWORK FOR PEACE

Africans have from time immemorial remained seized of need to enjoy their inalienable right to control their own destiny.[70] They, however, do not have the requisite capacity, financial, human and in some cases, will, to ensure peace for all Africans. As discussed in detail in the subsequent chapters, countries like Libya, CAR, South Sudan, Somalia, and Ethiopia are now in state of misery due to lack of peace for their citizenry, yet the AU has structures which can be relied upon to ensure that peace is maintained all over the continent. For example, when fully operational, the APSA, with its elaborate mechanisms is capable of ensuring peace throughout the continent.[71] The APSA, however, remains weak in regard to fulfillment of its mandate due to a number of constraints, major of which is lack of adequate funding. In Chapter 32, Lumina correctly notes that AU Members are unable to fully fund the operations of APSA; they rely heavily on Development Partners for much of the funding for the operations of APSA.[72]

In regard to mandate for APSA to ensure peace on the African continent, Article 3 (f) of the AU Constitutive Act enjoins member states to promote peace, security and stability on the continent; while Article 4(i) requires member States to peacefully co-existence live in peace and security with each other. Principle 4(j) of the African Union Constitutive Act upholds the right

[68] AU Peace Fund, Silencing the Guns, Securing Predictable and Sustainable Financing for Peace in Africa, August 2016.

[69] Simon and Schuster, Nelson Mandela, Notes to the Future: Words of Wisdom, ATRIA Books, New York, 2012.

[70] The Organization of African Unity Charter, Addis Ababa, Ethiopia, 25 May 1963; the Preamble.

[71] Established by the Protocol on the Establishment of the Peace and Security Council in July 2002.

[72] The East African, AMISOM programmes stall due to lack of funds, Tuesday March 21, 2017, accessed at: https://www.theeastafrican.co.ke/tea/news/east-africa/amisom-programmes-stall-due-to-lack-of-funds--1363438, on 12 December 2020.

of Member States to request intervention from the Union in order to restore peace and security. Article 9 (g) of the African Union Constitutive Act, gives mandate to the Executive Council on the restoration of peace on the continent. The reality is, whether or not such assistance is sought, the African Union does not have the capacity to respond to the request. This is clearly illustrated by the call to restore peace in countries like the DRC, Libya and Somalia, but which call may only be responded to after the African Union has secured funding from Development Partners, and belatedly.

The AU Peace and Security Council is established under Article 5(2) of the AU Constitutive Act, as a standing decision-making organ for the prevention, management and resolution of conflicts on the continent.[73] The Peace and Security Council is a collective security and early-warning arrangement to facilitate timely and efficient response to conflict and crisis situations in Africa. The Peace and Security Council is supported by the Commission, a Panel of the Wise, a Continental Early Warning System, an African Standby Force and a Special Fund.[74] Notwithstanding existence of such an elaborate system, the concept of peace on the African continent remains constrained by three things: technological underdevelopment, organizational incompetence and military impotence.[75]

APSA works with Regional Economic Communities (RECS) in a collaborative manner. The RECS, which include the Economic Community of West African States (ECOWAS), the East African Community (EAC) and the Southern African Development Cooperation (SADC), are equally not able to sustain peace within their jurisdictions, yet the AU seeks to collaborate with them to ensure continental peace. With its perennial cries for funding, the APSA has never been fully operational nor has it ever acted in a timely manner to conflicts and crises on the continent as envisaged in the instruments of its establishment. The on-going political crisis in Cameroon, which has resulted in fragrant violation of human rights and hence destabilization of continental peace has not been given the attention it deserves. The political divide between Morocco and the breakaway Western Sahara Republic worsens day by day because of APSA's weaknesses *vis-à-vis* the strong vested foreign interests in the politics of the Northern part of the continent.[76] It is possible that one of the constraints to the AU mechanisms for response to such scenarios shall

---

[73] Protocol relating to the Establishment of the Peace and Security Council of the African Union, 2002, Article 2 (1).

[74] Protocol relating to the Establishment of the Peace and Security Council of the African Union, 2002, Article 2 (2).

[75] Ali Mazrui, Reith Lectures 1979: The African Condition: Lecture 6: In Search of Pax Africana Transmission: 12 December 1979—Radio 4, accessed at: http://downloads.bbc.co.uk/rmhttp/radio4/transcripts/1979_reith6.pdf, on 20 October 2020.

[76] Powell, A., US Proclamation Giving Morocco Sovereignty Over Disputed Region Draws Backlash in Africa, VOA News (online), December 11, 2020, accessed at: https://www.voanews.com/usa/us-proclamation-giving-morocco-sovereignty-over-disputed-region-draws-backlash-africa, on 12 December 2020.

for a long time remain lack of adequate funding from Development Partners, some of who have vested interests in the crisis.[77]

RE-INCARNATION OF THE AFRICAN PEACE PARADIGM

The forceful physical departure of colonial powers from the African continent, notwithstanding, their tenterhooks, and policies have not been fully dismantled. The numbers of wars and other forms of conflict on the continent today have direct links with the former colonial masters for the particular countries where the conflicts take place. The French, for example, have direct interests in what takes place in the CAR, Mali and even Rwanda. The British remain deeply concerned with what takes place in all their former colonies on the African continent. Mutua, citing Hansen, states:

> African leaders have adopted and continued to use political forms and precedents that grew from, and were organically related to, the European experience. Formal declarations of independence from direct European rule do not mean actual independence from European conceptual dominance. African leaders and peoples have gone through tremendous political changes in the past hundred years. These profound changes have included the transformation of African societies and polities. They are still composed of indigenous African units, such as lineage, village, tribe and chieftainship, but they have been transformed around European units, such as the colony, district, political party and state.[78]

Recent attempts to return to the cherished African philosophy of peace are succinctly encapsulated in the Africa Agenda 2063.[79] Africa Agenda 2063 is a shared framework for inclusive growth and sustainable development for Africa to be realized in the next fifty years. It is a continuation of the Pan-African struggles started a number of decades ago. The current African stature for peace is to strive for unity, self-determination, freedom, progress and collective prosperity pursued under *Pan-Africanism* and *African Renaissance*.[80] Successive African leaders worked hard to ensure they come up with an acceptable concept of peace, for the African people.

---

[77] The Conversation, African Union needs a more robust response to conflict in Cameroon, an African online Magazine, March 2, 2020, accessed at: https://theconversat ion.com/african-union-needs-a-more-robust-response-to-conflict-in-cameroon-132449, on 12 December 2020.

[78] Mutua, footnote 14 above.

[79] African Union Agenda 2063, A Shared Strategic Framework for Inclusive Growth and Sustainable Development, Background Note August 2013.

[80] African Union Commission, Agenda 2063, The Africa We Want, Addis Ababa, Ethiopia, 2015; see also Young, K. B., Towards a Holistic Review of Pan-Africanism: Linking the Idea and the Movement, *Nationalism and Ethnic Politics*, Vol. 16, No. 2 (2010), see also Kah, H. K., Kwame Nkrumah and The Panafrican Vision: Between Acceptance And Rebuttal, *Austral: Brazilian Journal of Strategy & International Relations*, Vol. 5, No. 9 (January/June 2016), pp. 141–164 e-ISSN 2238–6912 | ISSN 2238–6262.

On his part, Mwalimu Julius Kambarage Nyerere, the First President of the United Republic of Tanzania, worked hard to ensure that people from different cultures and backgrounds live and work together productively and in peace.[81] For example, he was the architect of an exemplary mode of uniting two sovereign states in Africa in which, despite the existence of all the ingredients of disunity, has endured for over five decades now.[82] For the well-being of individuals and the nation in general, Nyerere was committed to peace and unity initiatives in Tanzania, especially in the area of religious tolerance, specific actions were taken to engender tolerance in matters of faith and manage potential cracks to Tanzania. Nyerere created a socialist society which was based on three principles: equality and respect for human dignity; sharing of the resources which are produced by Tanzanian's efforts; work by everyone and exploitation by none.[83]

To Nyerere, there would be no peace in Africa if there would be no tolerance, despite the diverse cultural backgrounds of the various African people. Shivji describes Nyerere as an ardent and militant African nationalist and an equally convinced and persuasive Pan-Africanist, who arrived at continental Pan-Africanism through his country's nationalism.[84] Africa's future hope is peace, and nothing short of that. Broadly, Pan-Africanism has since its inception become the cornerstone of the struggle for many African post-colonial leaders in their agitation for an independent Africa. It advocated for the political unity of the continent.[85] It also advocated for the resolution of African problems by Africans.[86] The possibility of having a lasting African solution to African problems, and hence sustainable peace on the African continent, however, remains elusive. Due to historical reasons, it is not possible for

[81] Eckert A., Julius Nyerere, Tanzanian Elites, and the Project of African Socialism, in Dülffer, J., and Frey, M. (eds.), Elites and Decolonization in the Twentieth Century, Cambridge Imperial and Post-Colonial Studies Series, 2011, Palgrave Macmillan, London. https://doi.org/10.1057/9780230306486_12.

[82] Simeon Mesaki and Mrisho Malipula, Julius Nyerere's Influence and Legacy: From a Proponent of Familyhood to a Candidate for Sainthood, *International Journal of Sociology and Anthropology*, Vol. 3, No. 3 (March 2011), pp. 093–100. Available online http://www.academicjournals.org/ijsa ISSN 2006- 988x ©2011 Academic Journals.

[83] As above.

[84] Issa G. Shivji, Nationalism and Pan-Africanism: Decisive Moments in Nyerere's Intellectual and Political Thought, *Review of African Political Economy*, Vol. 39, No. 131 (March 2012), pp. 103–116.

[85] Kah, H. K., Kwame Nkrumah and The Panafrican Vision: Between Acceptance and Rebuttal, *Austral: Brazilian Journal of Strategy & International Relations*, Vol. 5, No. 9 (January/June 2016), pp. 141–164, e-ISSN 2238-6912 | ISSN 2238-6262; see also the Organization of African Unity Charter, Addis Ababa, Ethiopia, 25 May 1963, whose main theme was African Unity.

[86] Ani, N. C., African Solutions to African Problems: Assessing the African Union's Application of Endogenous Conflict Resolution Approaches, PhD Thesis, University of KwaZulu-Natal, 2016.

Africans to garner adequate home-grown resources to resolve their problems without foreign interventions.

Another view being advanced is to adopt a middle ground paradigm of 'appropriate solutions to the continental problems.[87] The latter paradigm seems realistic because it accommodates the problematic reality that Africans still live in. It also takes care of the fact that Africans still need the hand of their former tormentors to create a peaceful environment—one that does not wholly alienate the western powers. This view is based on an understanding that, due to historical reality, any notion of peace in an African perspective must be squeezed into a European perspective.[88]

Moreover, western world powers must remain on board, this time under the auspices of the globalized outfit of the United Nations.[89] Within the ambit of the United Nations Charter, peace is an international peace good, and should not be disintegrated.[90] The main argument advanced in this paper, therefore, is that many Africans wish for a reversal of the political landscape from the colonial hegemonic background to the hands of Africans, which is impracticable in the prevailing global order. Attempts to reverse the *status quo*, however, remain only ideal, but difficult to achieve. A middle ground is required if Africans are to enjoy sustainable peace, which encompasses activities aimed at preventing the outbreak, escalation, continuation and recurrence of conflict.[91]

While adopting Agenda 2063, the Heads of State and Government of the AU Member States did not define, in discrete terms, what the term 'peace' means in their perspective. Their conscience was nonetheless informed by the dire need for Africans to be at peace with themselves. Principle 4 (i) of the AU Constitutive Act envisages a peaceful co-existence of Member States and their right to live in peace and security. The call for peaceful co-existence of AU Member States, must, however, be made well aware of continent's political history, characterized by colonialism as the major force that distorted peace for Africans. Moreover, the end of colonialism was not smooth and peaceful, and that left a political and socioeconomic gap to be filled by the first post-colonial African political elites. In addition to having been dragged by the colonial powers to fight wars on their behalf, the African continent has, since

---

[87] ISS, 18 September 2008: African Solutions to African Problems, ISS Today, accessed at: https://issafrica.org/iss-today/african-solutions-to-african-problems, on 19 November 2020.

[88] Brown, W., Africa and International Relations: A Continent on an IR Theory, Anarchy and Statehood, *Review of International Studies*, Vol. 32, No. 1 (January 2006), pp. 119–143 (25 pages).

[89] Saul, R. R., The Collapse of Globalism and the Reinvention of the World, Atlantic Books, London, 2005.

[90] United Nations Charter, 1945, Preamble.

[91] UNGA & UNSC, A/RES/70/262 and S/RES/2282 (2016).

the departure of colonialists experienced violent armed conflicts in many parts, and some are still on-going.[92]

In order for the African continent to be at peace with itself, the Heads of State and Government, resolutely believe, it has to: 'accelerate the African Renaissance through integrating principles of Pan-Africanism in all policies anchored in our belief in common destiny and shared values'.[93] Principles of Pan-Africanism, however, can be steered forward if Africans are able to continue the struggle against neo-colonialism and support the right to self-determination of people still under the strong influence of neo-colonial rule, direct and indirect. The ever-increasing appetite for secession of constituent parts of African States, which has never been peaceful, equally erodes African peace. The Eritrea Secession War,[94] the Sudan-South Sudan Secession War,[95] the current Ethiopia-Tigray Crisis[96] and the Libyan experience after the Arab Spring revolution confirm lack of peace within Africa's independent States. Such events are also pointers to the fact that it is not possible to have a uniform concept of peace from the African perspective. These events clearly demonstrate the role played by external influence in distorting peace on the African continent. External influence on the African continent remains a vibrant political factor much as the colonial powers were forcefully ejected from the continent.

A tool towards empowerment of Africans to sustainable peace requires them to, amongst others; eradicate recurrent conflicts through addressing the root causes of these conflicts.[97] The latter can, however, only be achieved if African leaders adopt good governance and democratic principles within their countries.[98] One of the most challenging, and probably the most prominent brewery for violent armed conflicts on the African continent has been lack of transparency by political leaders, when it comes to holding political elections.

[92] See for example, Nkrumah and Busingye, footnote 56 above, pp. 342–355.

[93] African Union, Agenda 2063.

[94] Plaut, M., and Gilkes, P., Conflict in the Horn: Why Eritrea and Ethiopia are at War, Reliefweb, Briefing Paper, New Series No. 1 March 1999, accessed at: https://reliefweb. int/report/eritrea/conflict-horn-why-eritrea-and-ethiopia-are-war, on 12 December 2020.

[95] Yousif, A., and Rothbart, D., Sudan and South Sudan: Post-Separation Challenges, Beyond Intractability, 2012, accessed at: https://www.beyondintractability.org/casestudy/ yousif-rothbart-sudan-south-sudan, on 12 December 2020.

[96] Schweers, P., Thaker, P., Wade, S., and Raleigh, C., The Escalation of the Tigray Crisis: Ethiopia Edges Towards the Abyss? ISS, Monday 30 November 2020, accessed at: https://www.iiss.org/events/2020/11/ethiopia-tigray-crisis, on 12 December 2020.

[97] Nkrumah and Busingye, footnote 92, above, pp. 342–355.

[98] African Charter on Democracy, Elections and Governance, adopted on January 30, 2007, entered into force on February 15, 2012.

Countries such as the CAR,[99] Equatorial Guinea,[100] Rwanda[101] and South Sudan[102] have at different times been plunged into violent armed conflicts due to issues relating to lack of transparency and undemocratic rule in those countries.

Internal political strife and unconstitutional changes of governments still persist on the African continent in spite of the strong wording in Article 4 (q) of the AU Constitutive Act regarding unconstitutional changes of governments. Under the African Charter on Democracy, Elections and Governance, Article 17 State Parties re-affirm their commitment to regularly holding transparent, free and fair elections in accordance with the AU's Declaration on the Principles Governing Democratic Elections in Africa. That, however, has not always been the case for some countries. In countries where regular elections are held, the results have been disputed, which in some cases result in internal civil strife.

It is worth noting that the post-colonial era of Africa is largely influenced by the new forms of domination, espoused within the globalization paradigm. A pertinent question to be asked is 'can Africa have its own theoretical concept of peace, in isolation, without being conditioned by what happens in other parts of the world?' In this regard, Oloya for example observes that after the 9/11 terrorist attack in the US, the then President George W. Bush spelt out what the new global order looked like after the attack of pursuing countries that aided or provided safe haven to terrorists.[103]

In addition to the former colonial powers, the globalization concept, disguisedly clothed as the United Nations (UN) framework, has brought onto the African continent other powerful vampires, who front economic development as a vehicle for entrenching themselves in the natural resources richly endowed African continent. Countries like the US, the Russian Republic and China are some of the superpowers that have entrenched their indirect economic and political rule in many African countries. Within the new outfit of globalism, the gained African independence is waning away rapidly

[99] After François Bozizé seized power in 2003, the Central African Republic Bush War (2004–2007) began with the rebellion by the Union of Democratic Forces for Unity (UFDR) in North-Eastern CAR, led by Michel Djotodia.

[100] The Guinea-Bissau Civil War was fought from 7 June 1998 to 10 May 1999 and was triggered by an attempted coup d'état against the government of President João Bernardo Vieira led by Brigadier-General Ansumane Mané.

[101] The Event That Sparked the Genocide at 8:30 p.m. on April 6, 1994, President Juvénal Habyarimana of Rwanda was returning from a Summit in Tanzania when a surface-to-air missile shot his plane out of the sky over Rwanda's capital city of Kigali. President Juvénal Habyarimana died in that crash, and thereafter, genocide, which had earlier been taking place at a low scale, was blown out of proportions.

[102] Civil war along ethnic lines broke out in December 2013, in South Sudan, following President Salva Kiir's accusations that former Vice President Riek Machar was plotting a coup d'état.

[103] Oloya, Opiyo, Black Hawks Rising: The Story of AMISOM's Successful War Against Somali Insurgents, 2007–2014, Helion & Company, England, 2016, p. 35.

as African governments get entangled in debt repayment traps set for them by the seemingly friendly economic allies.[104]

Africa as a whole has begun to make significant economic and political progress in recent years, but in many parts of the continent progress remains threatened or impeded by conflict.[105] Now that the African countries have attained sovereignty, they naturally wish to implement independent policies that differ from that of their former rulers and indeed very often this cut right across the latter's interests. According to Potekhin, upon realization that the Marxist-Leninism ideology provided a better alternative to the western imperialist capitalist ideology, many African countries vowed to take non-capitalist measures to development.[106] Potekhin further avers that:

> 'Because the imperialists are seriously disturbed by the Africans' determination to choose their own way forward without consulting them on the matter they are now more than ever supplementing economic fetters with ideological persuasion. Never before have they retained such a large staff of ideological servitors as in the independent African countries today. Never before have they dumped such a tremendous amount of propaganda material onto Africa'.[107]

The aggressive western influence on the African continent is then reinforced by the rush onto the continent by the hitherto non-colonizers of the African countries like the US and China who are now on board with their entrenched foreign policies for the African continent.[108] On the face of it, their foreign policies for Africa appear pro-Africa, but hidden in them is the reality of self-aggrandizement by the policy framers in those countries. The increasing debt burden on some African countries, interference in the sovereign interests of African countries sometimes under the guise of superintending over the human rights regimes on the African continent, are pointers to the very problem of elusive peace on the African continent.[109]

---

[104] Globalism and Crisis, in J. Fürst, S. Pons, and M. Selden (eds.), The Cambridge History of Communism (The Cambridge History of Communism, pp. 21–278), Cambridge: Cambridge University Press, 2017.

[105] Annan, Kofi, footnote 26 above, p. 239.

[106] As above, footnote 3.

[107] As above.

[108] Gyimah-Boadi, E., Signé, L., and Sanny, A. J., US Foreign Policy Toward Africa: An African Citizen Perspective, Africa in Focus, Brookings, 23 October 2020, accessed at: https://www.brookings.edu/blog/africa-in-focus/2020/10/23/us-foreign-policy-toward-africa-an-african-citizen-perspective/, on 12 December 2020; see also Sun, Y., Africa in China's Foreign Policy, Brookings, April 2014, accessed at: https://www.brookings.edu/wp-content/uploads/2016/06/africa-in-china-web_cmg7.pdf, on 12 December 2020.

[109] Goldsmith, C., Is a New Debt Crisis Mounting in Africa? World Finance: The Voice of the Markets, August 2019, accessed at: https://www.worldfinance.com/special-reports/is-a-new-debt-crisis-mounting-in-africa, on 12 December 2020.

Conclusion

Africans through their traditional institutions maintained peace amongst themselves. They had adequate means of resolving conflicts amongst themselves, if such cropped up. The advent of colonialism, however, forcefully disorganized and disrupted the tempo at which African traditional institutions were operating in maintaining peace on the continent. Colonial force was so destructive that it is no longer possible for Africans to go back and utilize the traditional methods of maintaining and restoring peace in the face of neo-colonial Western policies and in the globalized environment. The AU with its structures and mechanisms, however, has the capacity to resolve continental problems, but lacks the resources, largely financial, to put in place robust systems to ensure sustainable continental peace.

Africans understand that peace is a precious good for all humanity. Africans, know what peace means, want have peace, but they do not have and enjoy it in its totality. The main constraint to peace on the African continent is in the realm of intervening exogenic forces of imperial colonialism. These forces existed in the colonial period, in the immediate post-colonial period, and are now present under the guise of globalization. Global interests are much broader than imperial colonial powers. The role played by the popularity of Africa's developmental dictatorships or developmental patrimonialism for regenerating conflict-prone States has to be clearly understood as one of the factors contributing to degeneration of peace on the African continent. In political terms, and as a move to deconstructing the potency of such paradigms, Pan-Africanists must emphasize the dire need for regular, fair and free elections to test the peace claims of such leaders.

Africans, however, are not lying down waiting for divine intervention or peace to fall unto them from heaven. They have through the medium of Pan-Africanism been able to put a strong and concerted resistance to foreign domination, but with little success. In order for Africans to enjoy sustainable peace, therefore, Africans must understand the dynamics prevailing at the time and, using a historical analysis, know how to maintain their peace within a globalized environment. It is clear that whatever happens, Africans cannot restore peace to themselves in a manner that it will be the same as that prior to colonialism. Mechanisms that were used to disseminate information about peace to Africans in the pre-colonial era, such as family or clan talks whenever it was possible for them to come together, are no longer applicable in the current globalized environment. The Internet revolution has also fundamentally changed the arenas of meetings, reducing the chances of face-to-face meetings, which were a virtue of Africans. In order for the African continent to enjoy a befitting peace environment, Africans must be able to set aside adequate funds that can enable the APSA to operate independently of the Western powers.

CHAPTER 3

Sustaining Peace in Africa

Youssef Mahmoud and Chimwemwe A. Fabiano

INTRODUCTION

Africa has been the most important regional setting for international peace-making, peacebuilding and peacekeeping and has had a critical impact in defining their possibilities and limitations. In many instances, the continent has been the graveyard of short-term interventions driven by a myopic international peacebuilding agenda. Whether it is the United Nations (UN) or the African Union (AU), efforts to build peace have largely focused on rebuilding the neo-colonial state, politics and economy with its underlying, top-down logic of violence rather than transforming society as a whole.

For centuries, philosophers, scholars and practitioners have written about or expounded on how peace is attained, cultivated, restored and sustained. They range from Kant's Perpetual Peace 1795[1] to Galtung's negative and positive peace, to Richmond's conceptualization of Peace in International Relations

[1] Immanuel Kant, To perpetual peace: A philosophical sketch.

[2] Oliver P. Richmond "Peace in International Relations Theory", in Oliver P. Richmond, S. Pogodda, & J. Ramović (eds.), *The Palgrave Handbook of Disciplinary and Regional Approaches to Peace.*

[3] David J. Francis (ed.), *Peace and Conflict in Africa.*

Y. Mahmoud (✉)
International Peace Institute (IPI), New York, NY, USA

C. A. Fabiano
Kalu Institute, Madrid, Spain

© The Author(s), under exclusive license to Springer Nature Switzerland AG 2022
D. Kuwali (ed.), *The Palgrave Handbook of Sustainable Peace and Security in Africa*, https://doi.org/10.1007/978-3-030-82020-6_3

35

Theory,[2] to David J. Francis's Peace and Conflict in Africa.[3] In the last decade there have been steady attempts, notably by the Institute of Economics and Peace to measure peace world-wide both in its positive[4] and negative[5] incarnations. The 2020 Global Peace Index for example, found that world peacefulness has deteriorated over four of the previous five years.

Another notable advance is the adoption in 2016 of landmark resolutions by the UN ushering the concept of sustaining peace as an overarching framework for building peace in societies under stress or emerging from conflict.[6] In 2014, two years prior to the adoption of the resolutions on sustaining peace, a group of scientists from different disciplines at Columbia University launched the Sustaining Peace Project aimed at providing an evidence-based understanding of the basic conditions and processes that increase the likelihood of sustaining peace in societies that chose peace over war.[7] The project is meant to fill a gap left by peace practice which tends to focus on negative peace-reducing war, rather than on peace as a positive state.[8] To ground their findings about the factors that drive peace, the scientists chose Mauritius, among other countries, to understand how this African island nation-state, considered as one of the most peaceful countries in the world, sustains peace.[9]

Following the UN's adoption of the resolutions on sustaining peace, in 2017 the International Peace Institute (IPI) launched a series of high-level conversations. The aim of these conversations was to develop a shared understanding of the practical implications of sustaining peace on the ground, using empirical contributions from the Sustaining Peace Project and the Institute for Economics and Peace. The policy briefs for these conversations and the subsequent outcomes were published in 2018 under the title "Sustaining Peace in Practice: Building on What Works."[10]

In a parallel process, as discussed by Desire Hakorimana and Godard Busingye in the preceding chapter, a number of African scholars have delved into the rich repertoire of African indigenous and endogenous peacebuilding

---

[4] Institute for Economics & Peace. Positive Peace Report 2019: Analysing the Factors That Sustain Peace (2016).

[5] 2020 Global Peace Index https://www.visionofhumanity.org/maps/.

[6] SC/12340 Security Council Unanimously Adopts Resolution 2282 (2016) on Review of United Nations Peacebuilding Architecture, 27 April 2016.

[7] Peter T. Coleman, Joshua Fisher, Douglas P. Fry, Larry S. Liebovitch, A. Chen-Carrel, & G. Souillac, "How to Live in Peace? Mapping the Science of Sustaining Peace: A Progress Report", *American Psychologist* (2020); Peter T. Coleman, Douglas P. Fry, Larry S. Liebovitch, Jaclyn Donahue, Joshua Fisher, Beth Fisher-Yoshida, & Philippe Vandenbroeck, *The Science of Sustaining Peace Ten Preliminary Lessons from the Human Peace Project* (2017).

[8] Peter T. Coleman "Half the Peace: The Fear Challenge and the Case for Promoting Peace" (2018).

[9] Allegra Chen-Carrel, "Researchers Study How Mauritius Achieves and Sustains Peace" (2020).

[10] Youssef Mahmoud, Lesley Connolly, & Delphine Mechoulan (eds.), "Sustaining Peace in Practice: Building on What Works" (2018).

approaches and interrogated their relevance for laying the foundations for self-sustaining peace. In this endeavor, they did not shy away from highlighting the limitations inherent in some of these approaches while making the case that integrating them in the AU's peacebuilding agenda could help the shift toward a "decolonial peace" on the continent.

This chapter, therefore, takes a critical look at these normative and empirical advances and examines how they could inform the development of an African agenda for sustaining peace that leverages existing formal and informal African capacities for peace.[11] The chapter further proposes a number of policy and programmatic components that can serve as the founding pillars for such a strategy.

THE SUSTAINING PEACE AGENDA: NORMATIVE AND EMPIRICAL ADVANCES

The UN Sustaining Peace Framework

In 2016, the UN Security Council and General Assembly adopted identical landmark resolutions 2282 and 70/262, respectively, offering sustaining peace as the overarching framework for revitalizing the peacebuilding work of the organization. The resolutions were the intergovernmental response to recommendations contained in a 2015 review of the UN Peacebuilding Architecture (PBC).[12] The review found that the predominant peacebuilding approach gave power and agency to external actors who tended to define the problems and prescribe remedies.[13] The PBC review contended that such an approach sidelined existing national, local, endogenous efforts and aptitude for building and sustaining peace.

The resolutions, picking up on some of the language contained in the review, defined sustaining as "a goal and a process to build a common vision of a society, ensuring that the needs of all segments of the population are taken into account."[14] It emphasized that sustaining peace is a shared task and responsibility that needs to be fulfilled by the Government and all other national stakeholders, and should flow through all three pillars of the United Nations engagement at all stages of conflict.

---

[11] Tim Murithi, "African Approaches to Building Peace and Social Solidarity", *African Journal on Conflict Resolution* (2006).

[12] United Nations, The challenge of sustaining peace: Report of the advisory group of experts for the 2015 review of the United Nations peacebuilding architecture.

[13] Cedric de Coning, "Peace: Can a New Approach Change the UN?".

[14] A/72/707–S/2018/43 Peacebuilding and sustaining peace: Report of the Secretary-General (2018).

The African Union and Sustaining Peace

In January 2015 the AU adopted *Agenda 2063: The Africa We Want*.[15] Under Aspiration 4, the Agenda calls for a peaceful and secure Africa grounded in grass-rooted social cohesion, management of diversity and equitable socioeconomic transformation. It envisions that mechanisms for peaceful prevention and resolution of conflicts will be functional at all levels, and that a culture of peace and tolerance shall be nurtured in Africa's children and youth through peace education. It emphasizes the need to recognize existing capacities for peace particularly among under-represented and marginalized groups of people such as women and the youth.

Through Agenda 2063, the AU recognizes the need to strengthen human rights, social economic well-being, governance and peace culture simultaneously. In many respects, the AU Agenda resonates with the UN 2030 agenda also adopted in 2015 where peace is treated both as a governance and development function as well as an enabler and outcome of sustainable development. In its pursuit for sustainable peace in Africa, Agenda 2063 also recognizes the need to nurture conscious and transformative leadership that will drive the agenda and defend Africa's interests.[16] A leadership that is not only grounded in local context but pursues the decolonization of the African state and society in order to give rise to what has been termed as decolonial peace.[17]

Freeing Sustaining Peace from Liberal Peacebuilding

Despite the undeniable normative shift ushered by the UN sustaining peace resolutions, their policy and programmatic interpretations remain beholden to the liberal, top-down peacebuilding agenda largely focused on rebuilding the neo-colonial state, politics and economy. It is feared that rebranding various existing peacebuilding activities under the new nomenclature of sustaining peace risks contributing to a conceptual muddle, possibly confusion both for member states and practitioners. In practice, not unlike peacebuilding, sustaining peace continues to be perceived as a package of interventions relevant solely to contexts where conflict is manifest, proximate or threatens to return. It is still wedded to the predominant belief that if you analyze and address the root causes of conflict, peace will ensue. Thus, the factors associated with peace are understood to be the inverse of those leading to war and conflict, despite evidence to the contrary.[18]

---

[15] African Union, "Agenda 2063: The Africa We Want", Available at: https://au/en/agenda2063/overview (accessed 18 March 2021).

[16] African Union, Agenda 2063: The Africa We Want (2015).

[17] Siphamandla Zondi, "African Union Approaches to Peacebuilding: Efforts at Shifting the Continent Towards Decolonial Peace", *African Journal for Conflict Resolution* (2017).

[18] Paul F. Diehl, "Exploring Peace: Looking Beyond War and Negative Peace", *International Studies Quarterly* (2016).

In agreement with Hakorimana and Busingye in Chapter 2, it would seem that the "silencing the guns" vision as articulated under Aspiration 4 of the AU Agenda 2063 has also fallen prey to the same assumption, namely that if guns were removed by 2020, there would be peace on the continent. While violent conflict remains one of the biggest challenges standing in the way of a peaceful and prosperous Africa, conflicts do not start simply because arms are available.[19] In this connection, some analysts have maintained that as long as Africa's aspirations for peace continue to be depicted negatively, that is as the absence of conflict, sustaining peace will remain an elusive goal.[20] Additionally, the goal is even more unattainable if state-building is equated with peacebuilding, particularly in contexts where the state has been captured by predatory elites concerned more with power than governance.[21] In fact various scholars have pointed out that before its liberal co-optation, peacebuilding was at the core a grassroots, bottom-up activity rooted in societies' cultures and identities.[22]

The Science of Sustaining Peace

Until recently, normative peace scholarship and practice have mainly focused on the prevention of conflict, de-escalation or mitigation of aggression, peacekeeping, peacemaking and peacebuilding in the context of war. This assumes that doing so will lay the foundations for self-sustainable peace, yet all that is essentially achieved through these efforts is negative peace or absence of violence.[23] To address this deficit, a multidisciplinary team of researchers housed at the Earth Institute, Columbia University sets out to study the dynamics of sustainably peaceful societies using models and methods from complex science (applied mathematics). Their findings validate existing peace theory and practice by various critical scholars. For example, their research established that sustainable peace is rooted in communities. That "in situations of insecurity, violence, and conflict, it is people within the everyday

---

[19] Youssef Mahmoud, "What Kind of Leadership Does Sustaining Peace Require?", *Global Observatory* (2019), International Peace Institute.

[20] Youssef Mahmoud, "Freeing Prevention from Conflict: Investing in Sustaining Peace", Global Observatory.

[21] Oliver Richmond, "Becoming Liberal, Unbecoming Liberalism: Liberal-Local Hybridity via the Everyday as a Response to the Paradoxes of Liberal Peacebuilding", *Journal of Intervention and Statebuilding* (2009).

[22] Roger Mac Ginty, "Indigenous Peace-Making Versus the Liberal Peace", *Cooperation and Conflict* (2008).

[23] Peter T. Coleman, Douglas P. Fry, Larry S. Liebovitch, Jaclyn Donahue, Joshua Fisher, Beth Fisher-Yoshida, & Philippe Vandenbroeck, *The Science of Sustaining Peace Ten Preliminary Lessons from the Human Peace Project* (2017)—unpublished conference paper; Youssef Mahmoud & Anupah Makoond, "Can Peacebuilding Work for Sustaining Peace?", *Global Observatory* (2018), International Peace Institute.

spaces who mobilize and act to minimize risk, foster relationships and build structures and practices of peace."[24]

Furthermore, their research corroborated the argument that "top-down one-size-fits-all approaches to policymaking in peace and development are often ineffectual and unsustainable."[25] They learned that community-initiated programs are usually more effective. As discussed by Mphatso Jones Boti-Phiri in Chapter 25 as well as Thomasin Gondwe and Laika Nakanga in Chapter 26, community-initiated programs allow for more genuine inclusion of women, the youth and other marginalized groups who typically have a more grounded and informed insight of the local challenges and sustainable solutions. Nonetheless, this does not mean local initiatives do not have challenges. Interestingly, in a related study political scientist Valerie Hudson found that the state of physical security of women and level of violence against women in society is a better predictor of state peacefulness than levels of democracy, wealth or religion.[26]

The research also found that countries with a well-articulated and shared vision for. peace tends to be peaceful. A shared vision for peace entails strong mutuality and commitment to see through peace processes. According to the sustaining peace scientists, such a vision includes an ethic for interethnic and intergroup unity, care and nurturance of others that is at least as strong as the value of peace as something that needs to be secured and defended.[27] Additionally, the peace scientists were able to determine that war and peace are not two ends of one continuum, that the drivers and inhibitors of peaceful relations are often categorically different from those of violence and war.[28]

The anthropological strand of this research also identified a number of core peace features that characterize peaceful intergroup relations. The first factor identified was an overarching social identity that unites groups across their differences by "expanding the 'us to include the "them," akin to the humanistic concept of *Ubuntu* of Southern Africa which says—*I am because we are.*[29] The second factor that characterizes peaceful intergroup relations are interconnections and constructive interactions among subgroups through trade, intermarriage, sports or education, among other things. The third factor is cooperative forms of interdependence and shared goals due to mutual ecological, economic and common security interests. Fourth is socialization that includes non-violent and warring ethos that are buttressed by symbols and

[24] Helen Berents & Siobhan McEvoy-Levy "Theorising Youth and Everyday Peace(building)", *Peacebuilding*.

[25] Coleman et al., footnote 23 above.

[26] As above.

[27] As above.

[28] As above.

[29] See also Dan Kuwali, "Decoding Afrocentrism: Decolonizing Legal Theory", in Oche Onazi (ed.), *African Legal Theory and Contemporary Problems*, Edward Elgar Publishing Ltd, 2013, pp. 71–92.

ceremonies that celebrate and reinforce peacefulness. The fifth factor is functional superordinate institutions that promote intergroup integration. Sixth is fair and constructive conflict management mechanisms that help manage disputes between members of different groups when they arise; and the seventh and final factor is visionary leadership and inclusion.

Toward an African Agenda for Sustaining Peace

Notwithstanding the above findings, post-conflict contexts continue to be subjected to external, short-term interventions driven by the liberal and top-down Eurocentric perspective[30] that are largely heedless of the important contributions local community can make toward building lasting peace. This has prompted some African scholars to call for a shift toward a decolonial peace that puts the citizens and indigenous peace structures and processes at the center of building lasting peace.[31] This chapter proposes several key pillars which if properly conceived and developed could serve as a foundation for an African agenda for consolidating and sustaining peace.

The agenda is informed by the global and regional understanding of peace,[32] and by the findings of the sustaining peace research. More importantly, it is anchored in the rich repertoire of the indigenous and endogenous peace capacities of African societies in their complex plurality.[33] To this end, the following seven policy and programmatic components are offered as founding pillars where sustaining peace rather than just ending conflict constitutes the entry point and end goal.[34]

A Peace to Be Sustained Rather Than Built

For the purpose of the proposed agenda, peace is essentially defined as the deliberate preservation of harmonious and trusting relations in a society and the deployment of norms, values and structures that facilitate collective actions to repair those relations when they are ruptured and nurture them when restored. The relational lens adopted here in defining peace treats peace as the norm in human interactions rather than the exception, the exception being breaches and challenges caused by unresolved conflict. It specifically steers

---

[30] Youssef Mahmoud, "(High-Level Independent Panel on Peace Operations) on UN Peacekeeping Operations—Security Council 8033rd Meeting" (29 August 2017).

[31] Siphamandla Zondi, "Decolonial Peace". See also David J. Francis (ed.), *Peace and Conflict in Africa*, London/New York: Zed Books, 2008.

[32] Isaac Olawale Albert, "Understanding Peace in Africa", in David J. Francis (ed.), *Peace and Conflict in Africa* (2008).

[33] Tim Murithi, "African Approaches to Building Peace and Social Solidarity", *African Journal on Conflict Resolution* (2006).

[34] Youssef Mahmoud, Lesley Connolly, & Delphine Mechoulan (eds.), "Sustaining Peace in Practice: Building on What Works" (2018).

clear of what is termed the peace continuum,[35] ushered by the discourse around the 2016 UN resolutions on sustaining peace where states, under the guise of national ownership, are still considered, despite rhetoric to the contrary, to be primary actors in starting and ending wars and consolidating peace, leaving only a marginal role for "we, the people."

More importantly, the above definition takes into account the findings from the emerging sustaining peace science research. The definition has also been informed by other considerations which include the following three. First, that all societies possess attributes that contribute to sustaining peace, whether their institutions, their culture, their policies or the less tangible, quotidian and tacit norms of interaction between individuals and groups.[36] Second, that peace, like a tree, grows from the bottom up. Unlike the rule of law and security, it cannot be enforced from the top. It must be woven into society from within and from below by fostering systemic partnerships and incentives to maintain it. Third, that while there is still no clear understanding of how to link bottom-up and top-down efforts effectively for the purposes of sustained peace,[37] what is known is that only a combination of local, provincial, national, regional and international efforts can lead to sustainable peace.[38] This has led certain international peacebuilding partners to call for an approach that builds peace from the inside-out,[39] rather than from top-down or bottom-up where the emphasis is more on the process than the outcome. It is up to local communities in partnership with intermediate and national governance structures to shape the outcome, as exemplified by the innovative, ground-up *Fambul Tok* process in Sierra Leone.[40]

African Repertoire of Formal and Informal Infrastructures of Peace

As mentioned above, African scholars and practitioners have documented the rich repertoire of African formal and informal practices, approaches and processes for building and sustaining peace. One of the most noteworthy contributions is by Murithi, who has documented and conceptualized indigenous and endogenous approaches to peacebuilding, conflict management in

---

[35] Christian Davenport, Erik Melander, & Patrick M. Regan, *The Peace Continuum: What It Is and How to Study It*.

[36] Douglas Fry, *The Human Potential for Peace: An Anthropological Challenge to Assumptions About War and Violence*.

[37] Séverine Autesserre, "Going Micro: Emerging and Future Peacekeeping Research", *International Peacekeeping*.

[38] Severine Autesserre, "The Trouble with the Congo: Local Violence and the Failure of International Peacebuilding".

[39] Libby Hoffman, "Building Peace from the Inside Out: A Transformational Approach to Partnership" (2019).

[40] Fambul Tok, https://fambultok.org/programs/wan-fambul-framework.

post-colonial Africa.[41] Among the examples he cites are community-based peacemaking processes as practiced by the *Tiv* community in Nigeria, the *Guurti* system in Somaliland, the *Mato Oput* in Northern Uganda and the *Ubuntu* tradition in southern Africa. Murithi believes that these indigenous processes have a value added in terms of sustaining peace, given that they are inclusive and draw upon local cultural assumptions, norms and values as well as grassroot notions of justice. He makes a case for integrating some of these endogenous approaches within national constitutions as alternative forms of restorative justice.

Other scholars have offered the traditional *Gacaca* system in post-genocide Rwanda that combines both punitive and restorative justice as a means to fast-track transitional justice and reconciliation processes.[42] Despite the limitations inherent in some of these processes including a predisposition to patriarchy and gender-based violence, these practices if strategically leveraged can go a long way toward tempering the top-down, liberal peacebuilding prescriptions and help build lasting peace. Given that peace is both an enabler and outcome of AU Agenda 2063 and the UN 2030 Agenda for sustainable development, a deliberate integration of traditional peacebuilding approaches would make the progress achieved thus far less reversible, particularly in the face of new and debilitating crises such as the Covid-19 pandemic.

Analysis of the Drivers of Conflict and the Causes of Peace

For decades and as alluded earlier, peace and conflict research has primarily focused on addressing and preventing the problems associated with conflict and violence and not on the solutions associated with peace. A basic assumption inherent in this approach is that if a society can gain a sophisticated enough understanding of the root causes of conflict, violence, oppression and war, it will be better able to resolve them and thus foster and sustain, peace. This amounts to saying that a person is healthy because s/he is free of diseases. The study of disease has certainly led to breakthroughs in our understanding of how to treat and cure illness. But as Steve Killelea points out, it was only when medical science started to look deeper into healthy human beings—the study of wellness rather than illness—that we gained a better understanding of what we need to do to stay healthy and avoid sickness.[43] This could only be learnt by studying, among other things, the regenerative capacities, that enable people to remain healthy even in challenging circumstances.

By the same token, while analyzing the root causes of conflict is an important aspect of peacebuilding, the causes of sustainable peace would be better served if the challenges facing countries under stress are framed in terms of the

[41] Tim Murithi, "African Indigenous and Endogenous Approaches to Peace and Conflict Resolution", in David J. Francis (ed.), *Peace and Conflict in Africa*.

[42] David J. Francis (ed.), *Peace and Conflict in Africa*.

[43] Steve Killelea, *Peace in the Age of Chaos: The Best Solution for a Sustainable Future*.

inadequate self-organizing capacity of the society to anticipate, manage, mitigate and resolve conflicts.[44] Seen through this lens, the search for underlying causes becomes the search for why this capacity is inadequate, and how it can be reinforced—rather than merely looking for the causes of today's conflicts. As Phil Vernon points out, this analytical shift helps identify opportunities for strengthening what is already working even amidst devastation.[45] Focusing on what is still going strong and not only what is wrong,[46] takes people away from the obsessive examination of their conflicts, and provides a welcome opportunity to embrace a different challenge. In long-lasting conflicts, attempting to understand the causes of the problem often involves looking backward and apportioning blame, which is hardly a recipe for repairing broken relations, let alone rebuilding trust and laying the foundations for lasting peace.

Considering the above, a peace and conflict analysis in the context of an African agenda for sustaining peace would need to follow two simultaneous steps. The first is to indeed analyze the drivers of conflict with a view to addressing its immediate deleterious consequences. The second is to map the resilient capacities of peace that are still working and propose ways for strengthening them. Among these capacities are the indigenous and endogenous infrastructures of peace outlined above. Sustainable peace has greater chance to take root, if peacebuilders build on what people have and what they know.[47]

In this case, the search for existing capacities for peace and how they can be reinforced is employed along with the mapping of the underlying causes of conflict. As Phil Vernon points out, this analytical shift helps identify opportunities for strengthening what is already working even amidst devastation.[48] Focusing on what is still going strong and not only what is wrong[49] fundamentally shifts from the obsessive examination of conflicts and provides an opportunity to map out evidence and practices of peace rather than violence as a point of entry.

[44] Cedric de Coning, "Peace: Can a New Approach Change the UN?".

[45] Phil Vernon, "The Root Causes of What? How Root Causes Analysis Can Get in the Way of Peacebuilding", *Peacebuilding, International Development & Poetry* (2018).

[46] Cormac Russell, "Sustainable Community Development: From What's Wrong to What's Strong", *Tedx Exeter*.

[47] Youssef Mahmoud et al., "Sustaining Peace in Practice: Building on What Works" (2018).

[48] Phil Vernon, "The Root Causes of What? How Root Causes Analysis Can Get in the Way of Peacebuilding", *Peacebuilding, International Development & Poetry* (2018).

[49] Cormac Russell, "Sustainable Community Development: From What's Wrong to What's Strong", *Tedx Exeter*.

Incubating Leadership for Sustaining Peace

A key determinant for the viability of the proposed African strategy for sustaining peace is leadership. Leadership for sustaining peace[50] may be defined as the processes that create and nurture an empowering environment that unleashes the positive energy and potential of people at all levels of society so they can resolve conflict non-violently and participate in co-charting a path toward every day, positive peace.[51] A fundamental tenet of leadership for sustaining peace is that it is not entirely vested in an individual leader.[52] Rather it entails facilitating exchange of ideas, influence and establishing mutuality among various groups of people toward a consolidated vision of peace. Leadership for sustaining peace entails, as sketched above, rethinking the ways we analyze peace and conflict contexts.

To be a viable component of the proposed African strategy for sustaining peace, such leadership should be incubated in future generation of young leaders. This would be consistent with the call in AU's Agenda 2063 which calls for a transformative leadership in order to secure peace. It is also consistent with the findings of the sustaining peace research project relating to the importance of visionary leadership to secure/build and sustain peace. One could envisage the integration of such leadership component in the entrepreneurial leadership courses offered by the African Leadership University at its Mauritius campus.

Invest in Peace Education and Culture

Another key component to sustaining peace is peace education. Worldviews like that of *Ubuntu* among other humanistic African traditions offer rich foundational principles and practices for a robust peace education program. Such programs would be equally consistent with the spirit and the letter of Agenda 2063.

A Tool for Measuring Peacefulness

The positive peace index and its pillars of peace developed by the Institute for Economics and Peace have greatly contributed to our understanding of the key attitudes, structures and institutions that underpin peaceful societies, many of which are in Africa. It would advance the credibility of the African sustaining peace agenda if an African peace index based on data provided by the continent were to be developed. Such an index would complement ongoing efforts to develop an African Human Security Index.

---

[50] Youssef Mahmoud, "What Kind of Leadership Does Sustaining Peace Require?", *Global Observatory* (2019).

[51] Roger Mac Ginty, "Everyday Peace: Bottom-up and Local Agency in Conflict-Affected Societies", *Security Dialogue* (2014).

[52] Fumni Olonisakin, "Towards Re-conceptualising Leadership for Sustainable Peace".

Predictable and Flexible Financing

Without a dedicated financial facility, the proposed African agenda for sustaining peace would be unattainable. For so long, peace interventions have been funded by western nations, some of whom have agendas which do not necessarily allow for sustainable peace to take root on the continent. In order for it to be African owned-led and owned, the majority of the funds should come from Africans themselves, particularly if we want to sustain the ongoing efforts to decolonize the powerful, Eurocentric epistemology that has for decades informed the peacebuilding enterprise on the continent, without much to show for it. Borrowed water, the African saying goes, does not quench thirst.

CONCLUSION

The primary purpose of this chapter is to drive home the argument that the African continent has a rich and varied repertoire of formal and informal capacities, knowledge and experiences to decolonize the study of peace and develop an integrated agenda for sustaining peace. To lay the foundations for such an agenda and its main constituent components, this discussion provides a critical review of the genesis of the international and regional sustaining peace enterprise as well as its practical implications for durable peace in Africa. It also highlights some of the key findings emerging from recent scientific efforts to study and measure peace directly and not only through conflict. It proposed several policy and programmatic components that could serve as a foundation for the agenda, offering, where needed a rationale for each.

The discussion further points out that in order for the African sustainable peace agenda to be viable, it must address some of the limitations inherent in some of the endogenous peace approaches. It advocates the need for sustainable and predictable financing the majority of which should be provided by Africans. One of the proposed components of the Agenda that can benefit from a meaningful financial support is the development of a positive peace index to measure peacefulness on the continent with an aim of making a judicious assessment of the multiple factors that account for the prevailing oases of peace which tend to be sacrificed on the altar of our infatuation with what is wrong with Africa.

CHAPTER 4

The African Union Agenda for Sustainable Peace and Security

Dan Kuwali

INTRODUCTION

Africa has seen and continues to experience escalating levels of conflicts in the region. As narrated by Desire Hakorimana and Godard Busingye in Chapter 2 as well as Youssef Mahmoud and Chimwemwe Fabiano in Chapter 3, Vision 2020 adopted by the African States to make a commitment to silence the guns in 2020 was adopted on the premise that Africa must take responsibility of its destiny. Why haven't the guns been silenced in some countries so far? What has been done so far since the adoption of the theme? People are still fighting in Somalia, the Democratic Republic of the Congo (DRC), on the coasts of Mozambique, in the Central African Republic, Mali, Nigeria, South Sudan among other intra state and interstate conflicts. Despite constructing a forward-looking African Peace and Security Architecture (APSA), the question remains, why Africa is still experiencing insecurity, instability, disruption of political congruence, attrition of social cohesion and thwarted efforts on spearheading the theme of silencing the guns in Africa.

It has been noted that the continuing 'insecurity, instability, disruption of political harmony, erosion of social cohesion, destruction of the economic fabric and public despondency in various parts of Africa call on the Peace and Security Council (PSC) to play a locomotive role in spearheading strategic

D. Kuwali (✉)
University of Pretoria, Pretoria, South Africa

© The Author(s), under exclusive license to Springer Nature Switzerland AG 2022
D. Kuwali (ed.), *The Palgrave Handbook of Sustainable Peace and Security in Africa*, https://doi.org/10.1007/978-3-030-82020-6_4

47

interventions to put this sad situation to an end'.[1] Poverty, human rights violations, lack of inclusion in governance, inequalities are some of the vices that are fueling conflicts in Africa.[2] It is more than obligatory to have cognizance that the quest to silence the guns in Africa requires concerted efforts of all leaders in Africa and beyond. Thus, in accord with Mark Maxwell in Chapter 24, partnerships must be forged to realise peace and stability in Africa. It must be put on record that skirmishes happening in a number of countries in Africa affect the efforts of silencing the guns.

As such on peace and security partnerships, UN Security Council Resolution 2320 of November 2016 calls on both the AU and the UN to further enhance their strategic partnership to end violent conflicts in Africa.[3] As discussed by Tadziwana Kapeni in Chapter 17, good leadership and good governance play a vivacious role in making sure that the demands of the electorates are met more especially removing them from the quagmire of poverty and economic hardships. Leaders must prioritise economic, technological, social and political developments of their countries. However, the pursuit of peace, security and socioeconomic development must be done simultaneously.[4] Therefore, this discussion explores ways and means on how the APSA can counter contemporary peace and security challenges on the continent.

CONTEMPORARY PEACE AND SECURITY CHALLENGES IN AFRICA

Terrorism and/extremism is a global phenomenon. The rise in terrorism and extremism in Africa is further compromising the efforts to make Africa secure. The vices aforementioned have led to a number of deaths, most of whom are civilians with a larger percentage being women and children. Terrorism and/extremism have also led to destruction of property and has led to severe instability prevalent in the north, east, west and Horn of Africa. Since 2006, terrorism has increased by 1000% margin with 22 African states being targeted.[5] Thousands of people have died and displaced at the hands of Boko Haram in Nigeria. Somalia is failing to get on its feet because of the actions of Al-Shabaab which has in the recent past destabilised and thwarted the efforts towards achieving social and economic development. Mozambique

---

[1] Practical Steps to Silence the Guns in Africa by the Year 2020—A Speech by Mr. Osman Keh Kamara to African Union Peace and Security Council, 6 December 2016 available at https://apctimes.com/practical-steps-to-silence-the-guns-in-africa-by-the-year-2020/ (accessed on 20 August 2020).

[2] As above.

[3] S/RES/2320 (2016), Resolution 2320, adopted by the Security Council at its 7816th meeting on 18 November 2016.

[4] Kamara 2016.

[5] THE AFRICAN UNION AND COUNTER-TERRORISM article available at https://nesa-center.org/the-african-union-and-counter-terrorism/ (accessed on 23 November 2020).

has lately seen terrorists affiliated to Islamic State committing atrocities with civilians largely being victims in gas-rich Northern Province of Cabo Delgado. Terrorism and extremism have often been driven, according to the terrorists and extremists, by unemployment, rigged elections, corruption and violence.[6]

Most conflicts in Africa emanate from electoral processes. As stated by Archiles Bwete and his colleagues in Chapter 21, electoral processes are methods that individual countries adopt for choosing their national leaders. Throughout the world are distinct processes and there is substantial argument regarding which one is the best. Countries choose a particular process considering their political and economic conditions. Democratic governance is determined by the electoral process. Flawed electoral processes have a huge impact on elections and democratic governance. Lately, the African continent has suffered flawed electoral processes which in turn negatively affected elections and democratic governance. As a result of flawed elections and undemocratic governance, management of national affairs has been marred by corruption, lack of inclusiveness and participation and lack of accountability and responsibility. These have resulted in conflicts and instability in Africa.

Drug trafficking and human trafficking in Africa is not a novel phenomenon. Almost each and every country in the African continent has experienced and continues to experience the depravities. Most people trafficked and/or involved in drug trafficking are from countries experiencing conflicts and economic hardships. Currently, there are 12 countries in Africa experiencing armed conflict. Statistically, 99 per cent of the people are trafficked within their own country in West Africa; 83 per cent of people are trafficked in North Africa; 90 per cent are trafficked in East Africa and 62 per cent are trafficked in Southern Africa.[7] From the statistics, it can be seen that no part of Africa has been spared. Armed and extremist groups have flourished in conflict prone regions due to human trafficking. Human trafficking has enabled the groups to raise revenue and expand their power and military capabilities.[8] Extremist groups such as the self-proclaimed Islamic State in Iraq and Syria and Boko Haram in Nigeria have had women and girls being enslaved and revenue generated from sex trafficking.[9] The instability in Libya amid breakdown of the rule of law and the rise of militias fighting for control and power—has created a fertile ground for traffickers.

As the world is enjoying technological advancements, Africa has not been spared. The information, communication and technologies have proved to

---

[6] Andrew Harding, Mozambique President visits region beset by Islamists, 2020 BBC News, 14 August 2020.

[7] The Africa Center for Strategic Studies, Myths about Human Trafficking in Africa July 26, 2019 available at https://africacenter.org/spotlight/myths-about-human-trafficking-in-africa (accessed on 19 November 2020).

[8] Jamille Bigio and Rachel Vogelstein, The Security Implications of Human Trafficking, Discussion paper, Council on Foreign Relations (2019).

[9] Ibid.

be indispensable tools for governments, civil society, businesses and individuals across the continent. It is an open secret that these technologies have had tremendous positive effects on social and economic development. On the other hand, these developments have presented the world with new challenges notably cybercrime. In the twenty-first century, increasing cybercrime poses a threat to national, regional and international peace and security.[10] As such, citizens, governments and businesses must be protected from cybercrime and enhance cybersecurity. It is imperative therefore, that states must develop and enact effective legislative mechanisms to combat cybercrime. We hear of Russia meddling with United States elections using the internet, collapse of critical infrastructures and communication networks of nations by cybercriminals. Africa must adopt measures to prevent these challenges so as to ensure peace and security of its citizens and governments as adopted at the AU Convention on Cybersecurity and personal data protection as guided by the Constitutive Act of the AU adopted in 2000.[11]

Climate change in itself does not pose a security threat but its effects thereof exacerbate efforts towards achieving peace and security. Effects of climate change are being felt across the globe with recent reports of severe drought in some parts of Africa, flooding, heatwaves and wildfires. These changes of the climate have a huge impact on the African population. Many African states hinge their economic development on agriculture. Flooding causes deaths, dispersion, diseases as well as famine if the crops are washed away and so does drought. Consequently, poverty creeps in and this make people vulnerable. Climate changes have the capacity to make states vulnerable to violence, instability and conflict for example in North Kordonfan in Sudan and Lake Chad region.[12] These areas have seen weakening local conflict resolution and governance mechanism and recruitment of non-state armed opposition groups respectively due to famine and fragile economies.[13]

How Can the APSA Counter Contemporary Peace and Security Challenges?

On the premise of preventing and managing conflicts, the AU fashioned the APSA as an instrument to be used to counter and respond to conflicts in Africa in line with the provisions of the Constitutive Act of the AU and PSC

---

[10] Jeffrey Kurebwa and Jaquiline Tanhara, Cybercrime as a Threat to Zimbabwe's Peace and Security, 2020. 10.4018/978-1-7998-2466-4.ch066 available at www.researchgate.net/publications (accessed on 15 September 2020).

[11] AU Convention on Cybersecurity and personal data protection by the 23rd ordinary session of the Assembly, held in Malabo, Equatorial Guinea on 27 June 2014. This convention has of late become to be known as the Malabo Convention.

[12] United Nations, Climate Security Mechanism, Briefing Note, New York, 2020.

[13] As above.

protocol.[14] The AU took a bold step to come up with this mechanism so as to experience gradual decrease and elimination of conflicts from the region. It must be noted however, that States are main actors in this pursuit without which the APSA will just be another barking dog without substantial action to show for it.[15] Africa has experienced blunt effects of conflicts across the region which have had adverse economic and social consequences.

More Action, Less Politics: The Role of the AU Assembly of Heads of State and Government

Article 4(h) is clear that it is the AU Assembly of Heads and Government that will make a decision for intervention. A decision to intervene is by consensus or, failing which, only requires an endorsement of two-thirds of the Member States. Flowing from Article 11 of the AU Act, no single Member of the AU has the power to veto as opposed to the UN Security Council. The AU Assembly, which is composed of Heads of State and Government or their duly accredited representatives, is the supreme organ of the AU. Article 7 of the AU Act as well as Rule 18 of the Rules of Procedure of the AU Assembly specify that the Assembly shall take decisions by consensus or, failing which, by a two-thirds majority of the AU Member States. Two-thirds of the total membership of the AU shall form a quorum.

According to Article 4(1) of the Rules of Procedure of the AU Assembly, the Assembly shall decide on intervention in a Member State. It shall also determine the sanctions to be imposed on any Member State for non-payment of assessed contributions, violation of the principles enshrined in the AU Act and the rules of the AU as well as noncompliance with the decisions of the AU and unconstitutional changes of government. The AU Commission shall also collaborate with the United Nations (UN), its agencies, other relevant international organisations (IGOs), research centres, academic institutions and non-international organisations (NGOs), to facilitate the effective functioning of the Continental Early Warning System (CEWS). It is conceivable that there may be instances when it is generally agreed that some form of action is necessary as was the case on Libya in 2012, but there is no agreement on its form or objective, its mandate and duration.[16]

Pursuant to Rules 33 and 34 of the Rules of Procedure of the AU Assembly, if a decision is made as a Regulation or Directive then it is automatically

---

[14] Yayew Genet Chekol, 'Major Successes and Challenges of African Peace and Security Architecture,' 5(2) *International Journal of Political Science* (2019), pp. 1–8 available at www.arcjournals.org (accessed on 18 February 2021).

[15] As above.

[16] *See also* Kioko, *supra* footnote 9, pp. 822–824.

binding on the Member States and shall be enforceable 30 days after the publication in the AU Official Journal or as specified by the decision.[17] However, if a decision is taken as a Recommendation, Declaration, Resolution or Opinion then it is not binding. Non-implementation of Regulations and Directives attracts appropriate sanctions under Article 23 of the AU Act. The forms that sanctions may take include the denial of transport and communications links with other Member States, and other measures of a political and economic nature to be determined by the AU Assembly. Thus, any decision to take a decisive action to counter threats to peace and security on the continent largely depends on the decision of the AU Assembly. This is strengthened by the fact that the AU Assembly also has the responsibility to monitor the implementation of policies and decisions of the AU as well as ensure compliance by all Member States through appropriate mechanisms in accordance with Rule 4(1)(b) of the Rules of Procedure of the AU Assembly.

Heartbeat of APSA: The Need for a Proactive Role of the Peace and Security Council (PSC)

The AU's PSC has effectively replaced the historic OAU's Central Organ for the Mechanism for Conflict Prevention, Management and Resolution.[18] In order to move from the confinement of purely reacting to events, the PSC was established recognising that the AU required more effective policy channels through which it could tackle conflicts more proactively. According to Article 2 of the PSC Protocol, the PSC is 'a collective security and early-warning arrangement to facilitate timely and efficient response to conflict and crisis situations in Africa'.[19] The PSC has considerable powers serving as the standing decision-making vehicle for the prevention, management and resolution of conflicts.

Pursuant to, and as buttressed by, the need to promote peace, security and stability in Africa, the main objectives of the PSCare, inter alia, to: anticipate conflicts and undertake preventive diplomacy; make peace through use of

---

[17] The AU Assembly gives directives to the Executive Council (of Ministers of Foreign Affairs), the PSCor the Commission on the management of conflicts, wars, acts of terrorism, emergency situations and the restoration of peace, but it may delegate to any other AU organ. Cf. The Constitutive Act of the African Union, 2000 ['AU Act']; Arts. 7 of the Act and Art. 9(g); and Rules 4(1) (d) and 4(2) 6 and 18 of the Rules of Procedure of the AU Assembly; see also Kioko, supra footnote 9, p. 816.

[18] The fourth recital of the Preamble of the PSC Protocol states that pursuant to a decision of the 37th Ordinary Session of the OAU Assembly of Heads of State and Government in Lusaka, Zambia in July 2001, the Assembly 'decided to incorporate the Central Organ of the AOU Mechanism for Conflict, Prevention, Management, and Resolution as one of the organs of the Union'.

[19] The PSC Protocol was endorsed on 9 July 2002 at the First Ordinary Session of the Assembly of the AU in Durban, South Africa. It was adopted pursuant to Art. 5(2) of the AU Act, which empowers the AU to establish other 'organs that the Assembly may decide to establish'.

good offices, mediation, conciliation and enquiry; undertake peace support operations and interventions; engage in peace-building and post-conflict reconstruction; undertake humanitarian action and disaster management as stipulated in Article 7 of the PSC Protocol. The PSCwill also form vital part of the African regional human and peoples' rights system.[20]

Article 7 of the PSC Protocol is a clear manifestation by the architects of the African peace and security framework to construct a proactive human security structure on the continent insofar as the tasks shift the focus from the traditional state-centric approach to human security. The PSC meets regularly and recommends action to the AU Assembly, which stands as the supreme organ of the AU. However, the AU Assembly can delegate authority to the PSC to make decisions on its behalf. The PSC is supported by the chairperson of the AU Commission who, importantly, also has official oversight of a number of key peace and security structures meant to contribute to operational conflict prevention, mediation and management. The peace and security activities of the AU are supported by a 'Peace Fund' used to provide the necessary financial resources for peace missions and other operational activities germane to peace and security.

There are a number of means by which an item may be placed on the agenda of the PSC. According to Article 8(10)(c) of the PSC Protocol, these include submission by a Member State, by the Chairperson of the AU Commission, by the Panel of the Wise, by a Regional Mechanism or by the Pan-African Parliament. Civil Society Organisations may also make representations to the PSC. This important provision is designed to address the problem of political will and sovereignty of Member States, and to ensure that the initiation of action is not left to Member States alone.[21] The PSCseems to be 'more democratic than its UN counterpart as it does not provide for permanent membership or for any veto power' and that all decisions are by consensus, that no Member State can deadlock the activities of the PSC.[22]

Despite the broad powers accorded to the PSC, the PSC lacks the mandate to make the final decision to take action against peace and security on the continent as the final decision lies with the AU Assembly. Although such a requirement is necessary to avoid possible abuse, it does not only make the decision-making procedure convoluted, but also in situations where urgent action is needed the AU Assembly may decide not to take action because of the inherent political nature of the AU Assembly. The problem here is that the AU Assembly meets only once a year and takes decisions on the basis of consensus or failing that, a two-thirds majority. The process of taking action such as the right of intervention under Article 4(h) of the AU Act would

[20] Levitt, *supra* footnote 5, p. 110.

[21] G. Puley, The Responsibility to Protect: East, West, and Southern African Perspectives on Preventing and Responding to Humanitarian Crises, Working Paper, Project Ploughshares 05–5, 2005.

[22] Levitt, *supra* footnote 5, p. 116.

54   D. KUWALI

therefore be time-consuming. In crisis situations like those that have occurred in Liberia, Rwanda, Sierra Leone and Sudan, a few weeks delay in action could come at the expense of thousands of lives.

By way of illustration, by ratifying the PSC Protocol, all AU Member States are expected to implement the decisions of the PSC. In case of noncompliance, the PSC Protocol provides no instrument and institutions for the enforcement of the decisions of the PSC. The AU Act, in general terms, provides that the AU Assembly will ensure compliance with the decisions of the AU pursuant to Article 23(2) of the AU Act. Although this may apply to the decisions of the PSC as well, it is not only unclear as to what measures the AU Assembly may take, but also the process will be lengthy and ineffective.[23] The PSC launching statement proclaims its mission that the PSC 'shall not shrink from decisive actions to overcome the challenges confronting the continent' and that '[h]enceforth, there will be no conflict on [the African] continent that will be considered out of bounds for the [the AU]'.[24]

Although the PSCcan recommend a course of action to the AU Assembly, there is a significant danger in the PSCbeing essentially a political body and not legal or judicial body, to make a finding for example, whether war crimes, genocide and crimes against humanity are occurring in a given situation.[25] This explains why there should be more coordination between the African Commission of Human and Peoples' Rights and the PSCin terms of Article 19 of the PSC Protocol. Further, in order for the PSCto be effective AU States 'need to make realistic commitments about the amount of human and tangible resources needed to "endow it".'[26]

The Need for Actionable Intelligence: The Continental Early Warning System (CEWS)

Article 12 of the PSC Protocol establishes the CEWS in order to facilitate the anticipation and prevention of conflicts in Africa. According to the PSC Protocol, the CEWS shall develop an early warning module to be used to analyse developments within the continent and to recommend the best course of action. The information gathered through the CEWS shall be used to timely inform the PSC on potential conflicts and threats to peace and security in Africa and recommend the best course of action. In collaboration with the AU Commission, the UN, its agencies, research centres, academic institutions and nongovernmental organisations (NGOs), the CEWS shall develop an early

[23] G. Alemu, available at: www.ossrea.net/publications/newsletter/oct05/article8.htm (10 May 2008).

[24] Quoted by C. Van der Westhuizen, 'The AU's Peace and Security Council: On a Tightrope Between Sovereignty and Human Rights?' 42 *Global Insight* (2005), p. 6.

[25] *Cf.* A. Abass, 'The Darfur Crisis: The Role of the African Union in Darfur,' 24(65) *Utrecht Journal of International and European Law* (2007), pp. 47–57, p. 49.

[26] Levitt, *supra* footnote 5, p. 116.

warning module based on clearly defined and accepted political, economic, social, military and humanitarian indicators. Cilliers and Sturman have noted that in theory this requirement sets the stage for an 'objective' process to which the CEWS tracks the situation in its Member States, and alerts the PSCwhen there are indicators of an impending crisis. However, '[b]eyond the implied investment in software and data processing, the module would somehow have to quantify what "standard deviation" from the norm would trigger reports to the PSC'.[27]

Given that early warning mechanisms have been weak, the CEWS is designed to anticipate and prevent conflicts. The CEWS is charged with the task of collecting and analysing data. The heart of the CEWS is an observation headquarters called the 'Situation Room' in the Conflict Management Directorate under the Peace and Security Department. In theory, the Situation Room is connected to the observation and monitoring units of the sub-regional mechanisms in each of Africa's five regions to share information on impending conflicts with the PSC. The information collected and analysed through the CEWS is meant to be used timely by the chairperson of the AU Commission to provide the PSCwith advice on appropriate responses to potential or actual conflict. The CEWS seems to be well positioned to give early warning of conflicts that could brew into mass atrocity crimes if the international community does not act.

Respect for human rights is a viable and less costly method of conflict prevention than reaction after violence erupts. As such, human rights monitoring constitutes an effective means for early warning and preventive action. The CEWS is a key institution for better prevention strategies. The challenge is to translate the ambitious network of the CEWS into practice and to develop a mechanism whereby access is systematically granted to the grassroots. In addition, there should be strategic partnerships and collaboration among sub-regional early warning capacities, human rights monitoring bodies with the CEWS and the Situation Room. The idea is to establish a credible continental early warning system that is capable of preventing potential flashpoints from erupting into grave circumstances. It would be reasonable to suggest that AU States should set up national frameworks for conflict prevention from the grass root level where it would be possible to monitor the problems evolving in a community that may threaten peace and security.[28] Importantly, having created an early warning network there is need to create early action mechanisms, and more crucially, preventive mechanisms.

[27] *For more details see* J. Cilliers & K. Sturman, 'The Right of Intervention: Enforcement Challenges for the African Union,' 11(3) *African Security Review* (2002), pp. 101–102.

[28] *See* B.A. Kiplagat, 'Regional Co-operation in Africa,' in *Conflict Prevention and Peacebuilding in Africa*, Report from the Maputo Conference, 28–29 June 2001, Danish Ministry of Foreign Affairs, Danida, 2001, p. 20.

The Right of Initiative of the Panel of the Wise

In terms of Article 11 of the PSC Protocol, the Panel of the Wise has the responsibility to advise the PSC and the Chairperson of the AU Commission on all issues pertaining to conflict prevention and the promotion and maintenance of peace, security and stability in Africa. The Panel of the Wise can thus serve as an impartial mechanism for advising on a decision to take a decisive action against a threat to peace and security on the continent. The 'Panel of the Wise' consists of five highly respected African personalities from various segments of society who have made outstanding contribution(s) to the cause of peace, security and development on the continent. The Panel meets regularly and assists the PSC and the Chairperson of the AU Commission with the promotion and maintenance of peace, security and stability on the continent. It is also mandated to take appropriate action to support the efforts of the PSC and those of the Chairperson of the AU Commission for the prevention of conflicts, and to pronounce itself on issues relating to the promotion and maintenance of peace, security and stability in Africa.[29]

The Panel of the Wise will constitute people with expertise and extensive experience on issues affecting the continent and who will, principally engage in conflict prevention and diplomacy. This underscores the importance of the 'right of initiative' of the Panel of the Wise to serve as an alternative avenue for conflict resolution and mobilise support for action when action is needed.[30] The Panel of the Wise should use its 'right of initiative' to examine existing initiatives, domestic, national and regional, with the aim of improving civilian protection on the continent. For example, in the event of an impending crisis, such as the case of Zimbabwe around 2008, the Panel of the Wise should play its advisory role to ensure compliance of international obligations and protection of fundamental human rights by States.

It is, thus, important to adopt a coherent and integrated approach to the prevention of threats to peace and security on the continent by strengthening the relationship between and among the key organs of the AU human security architecture to ensure better coordination on topical issues that require coordinated action by the AU. To this end, with its utility role, the Panel of the Wise can coordinate the myriad activities of AU organs and human rights institutions and promote a culture of prevention among AU Member States, in accordance with their respective mandates. Since violations usually occur in conflict situations, there is also need that the Panel of the Wise should be supported by dedicated mediation mechanism to effectively prevent and resolve conflicts in order to prevent mass atrocity crimes on the continent.[31]

---

[29] The Panel builds on a longstanding African tradition of mediation by African 'elder statesmen' to help bring an end to armed conflicts and is seemingly a derivative of the 'Council of Elders' of the ECOWAS peace and security structure.

[30] *See also* Samkange, *supra* footnote 30, p. 83.

[31] *See* 'The World Summit Outcome,' *supra* footnote 8, paras. 149–151.

The Role of the African Standby Force (ASF) in Protection of Civilians

In order to enable the PSC to perform its responsibilities with respect to the deployment of peace support missions and interventions, Article 13(1) of the PSC Protocol establishes an African Standby Force (ASF). Significantly, the ASF is established in order to enable the PSC to perform its responsibilities with respect to the deployment of peace support missions and intervention pursuant to Article 4(h) and (j) of the AU Act. The ASF constitutes standby multidisciplinary contingents, with civilian and military components in their countries of origin which are ready for rapid deployment at appropriate notice.[32] It is clear that the AU has adopted a proactive and interventionist stance to security challenges on the continent.

Inspired by the theme of building robust African regional capacities for peace operations, the ASFis intended for rapid deployment for a multiplicity of peace support operations that may include, inter alia, preventive deployment, peacekeeping, peace-building, post-conflict disarmament, demobilisation, re-integration and humanitarian assistance. The ASFis intended to address the perennial problems relating to the safety and security of civilian populations in armed conflicts in Africa.[33] The ASFoperates at three possible levels: as an African Force under the AU; as a Regional Standby Forces at the level of a Regional Mechanisms for conflict prevention, management and resolution or at the level of a lead nation intervening on behalf of the AU. These regional standby forces can be deployed under AU mandates and placed under AU or UN operational control, as applicable. The chain of command for the ASF is through the Chairperson of the AU Commission, the AU's Commission's appointment of a Special Representative and a Force Commander.[34]

Given that most of the staff, logistics and equipment is drawn from regionally based resources, the use of the epiphany term 'African' may be misleading.[35] Similarly, the term 'Force' seems to subdue its civilian components. Be that as it may, it is more urgent now than ever to expedite the establishment of the sub-regional standby forces within the policy framework of the ASF. AU Member States are expected to provide well equipped contingents rapidly, and to provide 'all forms of assistance and support' to their troops once deployed.[36] However, most countries need to improve on the

---

[32] *For details on this point see* J. Cilliers, 'The African Standby Force: An Update on Progress,' ISS Paper 160, Pretoria: Institute of Security Studies, March 2008, p. 4.

[33] The ASF will consist of a system of five regionally managed multidisciplinary contingents comprising 3000–4000 troops, between 300 and 500 military observers, police units and civilian specialists on standby in their countries of origin. *See also* Powell, *supra* footnote 3.

[34] PSC Protocol 13, African Standby Force.

[35] Puley, *supra* footnote 25, pp. 3–4.

[36] PSC Protocol, Article 15.

maintenance of complex equipment, strategic mobility, advanced command, control, and intelligence, airpower and naval power.[37]

The ASF is supported by the Military Staff Committee (MSC) comprising of senior military officers of the Members of the PSC and is mandated to advise and assist in all questions relating to military and security requirements for the promotion and maintenance of peace and security in Africa. In any event, it is imperative that the AU must be capable of deploying African missions not only for peacekeeping but also for peace enforcement and post-conflict activities.[38] Accordingly, the ASF is meant to undertake observation and monitoring, preventive deployment, peacekeeping and multidimensional peacekeeping, intervention to prevent or halt mass atrocity crimes like genocide, and engagement in peace-building tasks, including post-conflict disarmament and demobilisation. The ASF is also mandated to undertake tasks that fit within a civilian protection mandate. Ideally, the ASF should be deployed under a mandate from the UN, but the AU can also authorise the deployment of peacekeepers as a regional organisation in terms of Chapter VIII of the UN Charter; although the legality of such enforcement action without the UN Security Council authorisation will be questionable.

Tellingly, the role of intervention forces pursuant to Article 4(h) is akin to law enforcement. As such, there is also need for the creation of a standing police capacity that includes forces who straddle the military-police divide, such as *gendarmerie* in France or *carabinieri* in Italy.[39] All in all, there is need to forge predictable partnerships and arrangements between the AU, and the UN[40] as well as relevant organisations such as NATO and the EU. In the final analysis, it is possible to argue that the idea of having a ready and capable ASFwould reinforce a culture of taking action, and erode the sense of resignation that tolerates mass atrocity crimes.[41] Egregious atrocities are

[37] D.C. Peifer (ed.), *Stopping Mass Killings in Africa; Genocide, Airpower and Intervention*, Alabama: Air University Press, 2008, pp. 6, 44.

[38] *See* Report of the 4th Meeting of African Chiefs of Defence Staff and Experts on the Establishment of the African Standby Force and the Common African Defence and Security Policy, EXP/Def&SecRpt (IV), January 2004.

[39] *See* ICISS Report, *supra* footnote 6, *see also* G. Däniker, *The Nature and the Use of Armed Forces*, Geneva: United Nations Institute for Disarmament Research, 1999.

[40] *For more details see* Mepham & Ramsbotham, *supra* footnote 10, p. xiii, *see also* Dr. Mohamed Bin Chambas, Executive Secretary, ECOWAS, 25 May 2005, 'Forward I' in Aboagye and Bah (eds.), *supra* footnote 13, p. xviii, pp. xv–xix; *see* The Brahimi Report, *supra* footnote 51, p. xi; *cf.* Bah, *supra* footnote 13, pp. 45–46; *see* F.B. Aboagye & A.M.S. Bah, 'Synergies of Regional and UN Interventions The Contribution of the UN Mission in Liberia to Civilian Protection,' in F.B. Aboagye & A.M.S. Bah (eds), *A Tortuous Road to Peace: The Dynamics of Regional, UN and International Humanitarian Intervention in Liberia*, Pretoria: ISS, 2005, pp. 99–126, p. 123; *see also* Powell, *supra* footnote 3, pp. 23–24.

[41] L. Feinstein, 'Darfur and Beyond: What Is Needed to Prevent Mass Atrocities'. 22 *Council Special Report*, New York: Council on Foreign Relations, 2007, p. 20; *see also* 'The Responsibility to Protect: Moving the Agenda Forward,' Ottawa: United Nations Association in Canada, 2007, p. 29.

committed against civilians mainly because the belligerents do not comply with the principles of IHL. Therefore, by ensuring compliance with human rights and IHL, the ASFwould, to a large extent, guarantee the protection of the rights of the civilian population and prevention of mass atrocity crimes.

The Oversight Role of the African Commission of Human and Peoples' Rights

The African Commission of Human and Peoples' Rights (the African Commission) is a quasi-judicial body, modelled on the UN Human Rights Committee, with no binding powers. In particular, the African Commission's functions are limited to examining state reports, considering communications alleging violations, and interpreting the African Charter on People's and Human Rights (the Banjul Charter) at the request of a State Party, the AU or any Organisation recognised by the AU. As ably discussed by Gloria Phiri and Chikondi Mandala, the scantiness of the enforcement and compliance control mechanism contained in the Banjul Charter, however, is hardly surprising given the paucity of democracy and the prominence of autocracy on the continent at the time the Banjul Charter was adopted.[42] Notably, all AU States are members of the African Commission which is mandated to monitor the implementation of the Banjul Charter.

A noteworthy provision is Article 19 of the PSC Protocol, which specifically provides that the PSC will 'seek close cooperation' with the African Commission 'in all matters relevant to its objects and mandate' and that the PSC should also inform the PSC of relevant issues. However, it is unclear how and in what form the African Commission will 'bring to the attention' of the PSC relevant information.[43] Given that the African Commission is mandated to receive complaints from States, individuals and NGOs, its close cooperation with the PSC has potential to detect threats to peace and security on the continent and inform the PSC to take preventive action. The recognition of the African Commission in Article 19 of the PSC Protocol is an important development because it recognises and codifies the link between conflict, human rights violations and the right to intervene.[44]

In the past, state practice under the OAU showed that, due to the interpretation given to the non-interference principle, the OAU was not considered to

---

[42] At that time very few African States (i.e., Gambia, Senegal, and Botswana), could vaunt of a democratic regime respectful of at least the fundamental human rights. *See* Project on International Courts and Tribunals, African Court of Human and Peoples' Rights, available at: www.pict-pcti.org/courts/ACHPR.html (12 December 2007).

[43] Levitt, as above footnote 5, p. 124.

[44] As above.

be competent even to discuss 'internal events' of a Member State or pass resolutions on them without the permission of the concerned State.[45] However, caution must be taken to avoid the ineffectiveness of the link between the African Commission and the erstwhile OAU Assembly of Heads of State and Government. It should be noted that under Article 58 of the Banjul Charter, the African Commission is mandated to draw the attention of the AU Assembly to cases of 'the existence of a series of serious or massive violation' of the Banjul Charter.

Yet, while the African Commission referred a number of cases to the then OAU Assembly, it made no response to them due to procedural hiccups that the African Commission sent them as Annual Activity Reports.[46] Nonetheless, given that the African Commission occupies a central role in the AU having a close cooperation with the PSC and mandated to report to the AU Assembly on serious violations of the Banjul Charter, it has an important role to spearhead the coordination and enhance interaction of these organs with the African Court in order to strengthen the protection of human rights and preventions of conflicts on the continent.[47] The immediate role the African Commission can play is to provide an authoritative report to the PSC on human rights deprivations, which can serve as the basis for deciding on the relevant action to be taken.[48]

The Enforcement Role of the African Court of Justice and Human Rights

The African regional human rights system operates under the umbrella of the AU. Before the adoption of the Protocol on the establishment of an African Court of Human and Peoples' Rights (ACtHPR Protocol), the protection of the rights listed in the African Charter rested solely with the African Commission. The long awaited African Court of Human and Peoples' Rights was established as a complement to, not as a panacea for, the protective activities of the under-resourced and ineffectual African Commission.[49] The establishment of the ACtHPR dealing with violations of human rights abuses and rendering binding judgements was long overdue given the backdrop of the region's dismal human rights record. Some say that 'that the Court is intended to make up for the many shortcomings of the Commission, which has had little

---

[45] K. van Walraven, *Dreams of Power: The Role of the Organisation of African Unity in the Politics of Africa (1963–1993)*, Ridderkerk: Ridderprint, 1996, p. 295.

[46] R. Murray, *Human Rights in Africa–From the OAU to the African Union*, Cambridge: Cambridge University Press, 2004, pp. 59–60.

[47] *Cf.* Assembly/AU/Dec.6 (II), Draft Decision on 60th Annual Activity Report on the African Commission on Human and Peoples' Rights-Doc. Assembly/AU/7(II).

[48] Murphy, *supra* footnote 36, p. 351.

[49] It took six years to be ratified by just 15 Member States. Although the African Court on Human and Peoples' Rights is operational, the Court of Justice is yet to be ratified; *cf.* Assembly/AU/Dec.45, (III).

4 THE AFRICAN UNION AGENDA FOR SUSTAINABLE PEACE AND SECURITY 61

impact since its establishment in 1987'.[50] Central to these is the fact that the African Commission does not make recommendations on the communications it hears but rather 'it submits reports to the Assembly of Heads of State, who act– or more often, do not act – on these findings'.[51]

While Article 18 of the AU Act provides for the establishment of a Court of Justice, the AU Assembly decided to merge the Court of Justice with the barely established African Court on Human and Peoples' Rights to ensure adequate resources to fund a single effective continental court.[52] In July 2008 the AU Summit adopted the 'Protocol on the Statute of the African Court of Justice and Human Rights' (the Single Protocol), which resulted from the merger of the African Court on Human and Peoples' Rights and the Court of Justice of the African Union. The single Protocol shall enter into force 30 days after the deposit of the instruments of ratification by 15 Member States in terms of Article 9(1) of the 'Single Protocol'.

According to Article 28 of the Statute of the African Court of Justice and Human Rights (ACtJHR Statute), the African Court shall have jurisdiction over all cases and all legal disputes submitted to it in accordance with the present Statute which relate to: (a) the interpretation and application of the AU Act; (b) the interpretation, application or validity of other AU Treaties and all subsidiary legal instruments adopted within the framework of the AU; (c) the interpretation and the application of the Banjul Charter, the Charter on the Rights and Welfare of the Child, the Protocol to the African Charter on Human and Peoples' Rights on the Rights of Women in Africa, or any other legal instrument relating to human rights, ratified by the States Parties concerned; (d) any question of international law; (e) all acts, decisions, regulations and directives of the organs of the AU; (f) all matters specifically provided for in any other agreements that States Parties may conclude among themselves, or with the AU and which confer jurisdiction on the African Court; (g) the existence of any fact which, if established, would constitute a breach of an obligation owed to a State Party or to the AU; (h) the nature or extent of the reparation to be made for the breach of an international obligation.

---

[50] *See* Cilliers & Sturman, *supra* footnote 37, p. 105; *but see* the Protocol on the Statute of the African Court of Justice and Human Rights [the 'Single Protocol'], available at: www.africa-union.org/root/au/Documents/Treaties/treaties.htm (12 December 2008), Art. 2 of the Single Protocol.

[51] Cilliers & Sturman, *supra* footnote 37, p. 104; *see also* D. Geldenhuys, 'Brothers as Keepers: Africa's New Sovereignty Regime,' in 28(2) *Strategic Review for Southern Africa* (2006), p. 19.

[52] The decision was made in June 2004. According to Art. 7 of the 'Single Protocol,' the old ACtHPR Protocol shall remain in force for a transitional period of one year to enable the African Court on the Human and Peoples' Rights to implement measures necessary. The single Protocol replaces the Protocol to the African Charter on Human and Peoples' Rights on the Establishment of an African Court on Human and Peoples' Rights adopted in 1998 (the ACtHPR Protocol), and the Protocol for the transfer of its prerogatives, assets, rights, and obligations to the ACtJHR. *See* the Single Protocol, *supra* footnote 73.

In terms of Article 29 of the ACtJHR Statute, State Parties to the ACtJHR Protocol, the AU Assembly, the PAP and other organs of the AU authorised by the AU Assembly, is entitled to submit cases to the ACtJHR on any issue or dispute provided for in Article 28 of the ACtJHR Statute.[53] Article 30 of the ACtJHR Statute provides for standing on human rights and the following entities shall also be entitled to submit cases to the African Court on any violation of a right guaranteed by the Banjul Charter, by the Charter on the Rights and Welfare of the Child, the Protocol to the African Charter on Human and Peoples' Rights on the Rights of Women in Africa or any other legal instrument relevant to human rights ratified by the States Parties concerned: (a) State Parties to the present Protocol; (b) the African Commission on Human and Peoples' Rights; (c) the African Committee of Experts on the Rights and Welfare of the Child; (d) African Intergovernmental Organisations accredited to the AU or its organs; (e) African National Human Rights Institutions.

However, according to Article 30(f) of the ACtJHR Statute, individuals and NGOs accredited to the AU or to its organs can only submit cases against States if the State concerned has made a declaration accepting the competence of the African Court to do so under Article 8 of the 'Single Protocol'. Unless States make such a declaration, this limitation renders access to justice illusory for human rights victims. This development is in stark contrast with the practice of African regional and sub-regional human rights mechanisms which have long recognised individual petitions for human rights abuses. The procedures of the African Commission and sub-regional courts such as the Court of Justice of the ECOWAS, the East African Court of Justice (EACJ) and the SADC Tribunal clearly demonstrate that victims require direct access to human rights institutions in order to ensure effective protection of human rights in the region.[54]

Unlike the African Commission, the African Court has the power, if it considers that there was a violation of a human or peoples' right, to order any appropriate measures in order to remedy the situation, including granting fair compensation pursuant to Article 45 of the ACtJHR Statute. Article 46 of ACtJHR Statute dictates that States Parties to the 'Single Protocol' are required to comply with, and guarantee the execution of, any judgements of the African Court. This is a significant development in the African human

---

[53] A staff member of the AU on appeal, in a dispute and within the limits and under the terms and conditions laid down in the Staff Rules and Regulations of the AU; obviously, the Court shall not be open to States, which are not members of the AU. The Court shall also have no jurisdiction to deal with a dispute involving a Member State that has not ratified the Protocol. *see* the Statute of the African Court of Justice and Human Rights [the 'ACtJHR Statute'] attached to the Single Protocol, available at: www.africa-union.org/root/au/Documents/Treaties/treaties.htm (12 December 2008), Art. 29(1)(c) and 29(2) of the ACtJHR Statute.

[54] The International Centre for the Legal Protection of Human Rights, available at: www.interights.org/AfricanSingleProtocolAdopted/index.htm (29 July 2008).

rights system because it ensures that African States should be more accountable for human rights violations. The Decisions of the African Court are final and binding on State Parties to the 'Single Protocol' and they can be referred to the AU Assembly for enforcement. Where a party has failed to comply with a judgement, the African Court shall refer the matter to the AU Assembly, which shall decide upon measures to be taken to give effect to that judgement. Article 23(2) of the AU Act gives the AU Assembly the power to impose sanctions on States that refuse to comply with decisions made by any AU organ, including the African Court. However, the AU has not been decisive in acting against errant governments. Thus, if the African Court is not empowered to punish States that do not comply with its judgements, it will have less impact on civilian protection and the prevention of mass atrocity crimes.[55]

An important catalyst for recourse to the African Court is, inter alia, Article 28(d) of the ACtHPR Statute which provides that actions may be brought before the Court on the basis of any question of international law. An obvious example would be the interpretation of the often politico-legal penumbra issue of whether or not genocide has been committed in a given situation, as in the Darfur scenario. Further, according to Article 53(1) of the ACtJHR Statute, the African Court may give an advisory opinion on any legal question at the request of the AU Assembly, the Pan-African Parliament, the Executive Council, the PSC, the Economic, Social and Cultural Council (ECOSOCC), the Financial Institutions or any other organ of the AU as may be authorised by the AU Assembly. The generous jurisdiction of the African Court provides wide latitude to engage the African Court to deal, in some way, with cases of mass atrocity crimes to change behaviour of repressive States and individual perpetrators.

If the proposal to have the African Court determine the existence of war crimes, genocide or crimes against humanity in Article 4(h) is accepted, it may be worthwhile to have the African Court decide by way of summary procedure. Given that the determination of the African Court may not per se authorise nor justify recourse to armed force, the immediate reaction open to the AU would be to intervene to protect the population at risk, secure access to victims or prevent the continuation of mass atrocity crimes.[56] The African Court can also provide legal clarity, for instance, on the dilemma in cases of trade-off between peace and justice in post-conflict settings and the often one-sided victor's justice for war crimes. The African Court might also be asked to offer an opinion in order to clarify the scope of the AU's right to intervene embodied in Article 4(h) of the AU Act.[57]

---

[55] Mepham & Ramsbotham, *supra* footnote 10, p. 33.

[56] *Cf.* A. de Hoogh, *Obligations Erga Omnes and International Crimes: A Theoretical Inquiry into the Implementation and Enforcement of the International Responsibility of States*, The Hague: Kluwer Law International, 1996, p. 404.

[57] Puley, *supra* footnote 25, pp. 22–23.

64   D. KUWALI

Furthermore, according to Article 31 of the ACtJHR Statute, the African Court can apply as sources of law any relevant human rights instrument ratified by the State in question, including the general principles of law recognised universally or by African States. In other words, the African Court could become the judicial arm of panoply of human rights agreements to which AU States are parties such as the UN Bill of Rights, the Genocide Convention, the 1949 Geneva Conventions and the ICC Statute.[58] All these instruments are crucial to prevent mass atrocity crimes in Article 4(h). Thus, Article 28 of the ACtJHR Statute is an important provision for dispute settlement and implementation control system, particularly where international treaties do not contain judicial mechanisms of ensuring their implementation.

Lessons learnt from history are that crimes enumerated in Article 4(h) are committed under the hand of the State or those who wield state-like power. This fact begs the difficult question of who will try the perpetrators of war crimes, genocide or crimes against humanity. In the words of Schabas, 'if a country's rulers are behind the crime, can its courts seriously be expected to hand out justice? Where those responsible for genocide have been vanquished – Germany in 1945 or Rwanda in 1994 – there may be modest hope of progress with prosecution. Where they have prevailed, impunity would seem to be the order of the day'.[59] The African Court may, however, be one of the possible fora for bringing such cases. Although the African Court cannot actually prosecute perpetrators of human rights violations, its involvement in cases relating to them can serve far-reaching goals.

Given the inter-State complaint procedure and the limited NGO access to the African Court, its judgement can put pressure on governments to comply with extraterritorial obligations such as the *aut dedere aut judicare* principle and duty to cooperate with efforts to bring perpetrators of atrocities to justice. The African Court can also establish an authoritative factual record and adjudicate state responsibility for human rights violations, which may provide psychological support to victims. Its decisions can also serve the cause of development of jurisprudence by interpreting unsettled legal issues such as determining the occurrence of genocide in a given situation. The African Court will also have a potential for parties to initiate cases relatively quickly and inexpensively since its work will not require apprehension of offenders.

To this end, the African Court may serve the most useful purpose as an adjunct to other mechanisms of individual accountability. Such legal suits may clarify international obligations concerning arrest, prosecution, extradition or judicial assistance and encourage recalcitrant States to comply with them. For example, if a State has custody of an 'indictee' and refuses requests for extradition to a competent national or international tribunal, a case may be brought

[58] Project on International Courts and Tribunals, *supra* footnote 65.

[59] W.A. Schabas, 'Genocide Convention at Fifty,' *Special Report*, Washington, DC: United States Institute of Peace, 1999, p. 4.

to induce that State to extradite the indictee.[60] By the same token, if a State refuses to investigate abuses or grants an amnesty to perpetrators in violation of its international law obligations to prosecute them, a suit might be brought against that State to restrain it from doing so.[61]

While the adoption of the 'Single Protocol' and the concomitant ACtJHR Statute is a progressive development, yet, an obvious weakness which threatens the effectiveness of the African Court to direct civilian protection is the lack of provision of standing to individuals and NGOs. As it stands, the Protocol establishing the African Court allows only African States and IGOs, such as SADC or ECOWAS, as well as the African Commission to bring cases before the African Court. Article 8 of the 'Single Protocol' as read with Article 30(f) of the ACtJHR Statute provides for an additional declaration to be signed by a State Party upon ratification of the 'Single Protocol', accepting the competence of the African Court to hear cases from NGOs and individuals.[62] It is unlikely whether States will be bold enough to make such a declaration. This pessimism provokes the question as to whether ordinary people, who are invariably the victims, will ever be able to bring cases before the African Court. These 'questions of access will determine whether the Court will become the principal protector of human rights on the continent or another toy telephone institution'.[63]

Drawing from the experience of the African Commission where almost all the cases were brought by individuals and NGOs, it will be defeating the *effet utile* of the African Court to deny individuals and NGOs standing before the African Court. It should be recalled that human rights violations are committed against individuals and not States.[64] In the same vein, non-state actors equally commit violations as evidenced by the stripping of the human rights of the acholi people by the Lord's Resistance Army (LRA) in northern Uganda; the Janjaweed against civilians in Darfur or the warlords who recruit school children in eastern DRC. In any event, the Kampala Document, which recommended the establishment of the African Court, intended the African Court to adjudicate between States and people's rights.[65] In addition, impeding NGOs' access to the African Court runs against the spirit of the AU Act and the PSC Protocol which have provided significant space for

---

[60] S.R. Ratner & J.S. Abrams, *Accountability for Human Righhts Atrocities in International Law: Beyond the Nuremberg Legacy*, 2nd edn, Oxford: Oxford University Press, 2001, pp. 225–227.

[61] Ibid.

[62] The original draft by experts in 1995 gave access to individual victims and enabled NGOs to represent them. This was watered down in the final version adopted by the OAU Heads of State in 1998; *cf.* Art. 5 of the Single Protocol, *supra* footnote 73.

[63] Cilliers & Sturman, *supra* footnote 37, p. 104.

[64] Out of the 280 cases brought before the African Commission over the years, 279 were made by individuals and NGOs, and only one by a State Party against another State Party. Ibid., pp. 103–104.

[65] *See* The Kampala Document, *supra* footnote 57.

66   D. KUWALI

civil society engagement within the realm of peace and security of the country of which protection of human rights is an important component.[66]

Given that the 'Single Protocol', which established the African Court, allows African governments and IGOs as well as the African Commission to bring cases before the African Court, these institutions should closely coordinate in pursuing delinquent States beyond borders and bring them to justice through the African Court. It is thus important that African judicial institutions need to be strengthened, and an emphasis placed on the creation of credible enforcement mechanisms that will back up the judgments of the African Court.[67] Therefore, the stakeholder community, AU States, civil society, the AU should all seek to intensify efforts to urge States to ratify the 'Single Protocol', and AU States should make the declaration allowing for individual petitions.[68]

The Role of the Pan-African Parliament on Continental Governance

The Pan-African Parliament (PAP) is another utility pillar of the AU's continental governance. Each Member State is represented in the PAP by five members. Equally important are the objectives of PAP that include, inter alia, the promotion of peace and security, human rights, democracy in Africa and the encouragement of good governance, transparency and accountability in Member States. Meanwhile in its nascent stage, PAP is limited to exercising advisory and consultative powers but is intended to be the legislative body of the AU, after five years of existence.[69] Pursuant to Article 18(1) of the PSC Protocol, PAP submits reports to the PSC including a separate report on the 'state of peace and security on the continent'.[70]

The articulated vision for PAP is that of providing a common platform for African peoples and grassroots organisations to be involved in discussions and decision-making regarding issues facing the continent.[71] In this case, PAP may examine, discuss, express an opinion and make recommendation on such matters relating to human rights, the consolidation of democratic institutions and the culture of democracy, and the promotion of good governance and the rule of law. According to van Dijk, PAP is an 'international institution which

[66] *Cf.* the PSC Protocol, Arts 8, 11, 12(3), 13(3) and 20, *supra* footnote 21; *see also* Resolution on the Co-operation between the African Commission on Human and Peoples' Rights and NGOs Having Observer Status with the Commission 1998.

[67] Mepham & Ramsbotham, *supra* footnote 10, p. 33.

[68] *See* Article 8 of the 'Single Protocol,' *supra* footnote 73; *see also* Artilce 30 (f) of the 'ACtJHR Statute,' *supra* footnote 76; *see also* the International Centre for the Legal Protection of Human Rights, *supra* footnote 77.

[69] Art. 11, Protocol to the Treaty Establishing the African Economic Community Relating to the Pan-African Parliament, CM/2198(LXXII), Annex I.

[70] Levitt, *supra* footnote 5, p. 124.

[71] G. Hugo, 'The Pan-African Parliament: Is the Glass Half-Full or Half-Empty?' *ISS Paper 168*, Pretoria: Institute of Security Studies, 2008, 1.

is able to distinguish between the individual interests of the States and the common interest of mankind'.[72]

PAP is entitled to intrude into the domestic domain of Members States and to call them to account.[73] On this note, some of PAP's notable achievements are dispatches of observer missions to Darfur in 2004, to Mauritania after the *coup d'état* in 2005, to the DRC to monitor the elections in 2006, later to the Central African Republic and to Zimbabwe in 2008. On this footing, PAP can be another far-reaching tool upholding the principle of 'sovereignty as a responsibility' in the transformation from a culture of sovereign impunity to that of accountability.

However, critics have indicated that PAP's resolutions and recommendations 'go largely un-noticed, and are often ignored or not taken seriously by the AU'.[74] This mutation is viewed as 'indicative of lack of clarity on power relations' between PAP and other AU organs, given that PAP's decisions are not binding on other AU organs.[75] As a way forward, PAP should utilise the space created by the various provisions such as Articles 5 and 17 of the AU Constitutive Act and Article 18 of the PSC Protocol to fully engage with other AU organs within the sphere of its responsibility to promote peace and security, human rights, democracy, good governance and accountability on the continent.[76]

The Role of the Civil Society in Peace, Security and Governance

There is a new paradigm of civil society involvement and engagement in influencing and shaping the process and ends of peace-building, including constitutional, socio-political and judicial and security reforms. This is evident from the objectives of the AU Act which, inter alia, aim at building a partnership between governments and all segments of the civil society, promotion of democratic principles and institutions, popular participation and good governance and participation of the African peoples in the activities of the AU. How to translate these principles into genuine working partnerships between the AU and African civil society organisations has been taken up by an AU-Civil Society Provisional Working Group. This group has focused its attention on ECOSOCC as the primary vehicle for formal representation of civil society within the AU.

The AU Act envisages ECOSOCC as an advisory organ composed of different social and professional groups of the Member States of the AU. According to Article 4 of the ECOSOCC Statutes, ECOSOCC comprises

---

[72] P. van Dijk, 'The Law of Human Rights in Europe—Instruments and Procedures for a Uniform Implementation,' 6(2) *AEL* (1997), pp. 22–50.

[73] *See also* Geldenhuys, *supra* footnote 74, pp. 18–19.

[74] Hugo, *supra* footnote 94, p. 5.

[75] Ibid.

[76] Ibid., pp. 5–9.

68   D. KUWALI

of 150 civil society organisations representing social groups such as women, youth, the elderly and disabled persons; professional groups such as doctors, lawyers, media and business organisations; NGOs and community-based organisations; trade unions and employers; and traditional leaders, academia, religious and cultural associations. ECOSSOC aims at promoting the participation of African civil society in the implementation of the AU's policies and programmes. To ensure the independence of ECOSOCC, Article 10 of the Statutes of ECOSOCC provides for a Selection Committee, made up of civil society organisations, to invite candidatures for membership to ECOSOCC and to process applications for membership.[77]

In the spirit of popular participation, the AU should develop strong links with civil society organisation at the national, sub regional and continental levels. The development and strengthening of such links will ensure that issues such as human rights, good governance and conflict prevention should receive relevant inputs from the citizenry at the grass root level. It is imperative that the AU establishes mechanisms that would facilitate an interface between the African civil society and itself, as well as to provide inputs and explore modalities for effective engagement of civil society organisations within the framework of the CSSDCA and ECOSOCC. For their part, civil society organisations should make themselves familiar with policies germane to human security at the national, sub-regional and continental levels, so as to allow them to make meaningful contribution. This underscores the importance of implementing the 'Livingstone Formula' that has been developed to define and map areas for constructive engagement and collaborations between the AU Peace and Security Council and the civil society organisations.[78] ECOSOCC is a vital channel for enforcement of human rights in so far as it has unquestionable *locus standi* before the African Court.

The African Peer Review Mechanism as a Tool for Prevention of Conflicts in Africa

One of the systems for monitoring adherence to the rule of law is the African Peer Review Mechanism (APRM), which requires that States, after 18 months, should submit to base review. Afterwards, there is a review at three and five years with a possibility of ad hoc review and that an impending crisis may justify a review. The APRM operates on the basis of voluntary accession and is designed as a mechanism for 'self-monitoring' by the participating Members States. States choose peer review by signing an additional Memorandum of

---

[77] Cilliers & Sturman, *supra* footnote 37, p. 103.

[78] *See* Institute of Security Studies, *Operationalising the African Peace and Security Architecture: Challenges and Opportunities*, Report of the ISS Seminar 20 March 2009, p. 4 [ISS Report on APSA].

see also Bah, *supra* footnote 13, pp. 45–46.

Understanding.[79] The fact that membership is not mandatory makes the APRM porous if a target State has not subscribed to its membership. States that are patently in breach of AU standards of governance are unlikely to submit themselves to peer evaluation. Rather than risk being 'named and shamed' by their counterparts, deviant States will prefer to steer clear of the APRM. This is true considering the current list of 38 signatories out of the 55 Members States of the AU.[80] Still, non-APRM participants will be held accountable through other general mechanisms of the AU. Non-APRM Members, however, stand to lose from foreign assistance since donor partnership of the New Partnership for Africa's Development (NEPAD) is conditional on all NEPAD elements of which good governance and peer review is a crucial component.[81]

The apparent challenge for the AU and NEPAD in developing the institutional capacity for peace, therefore, is to develop a political-normative framework, based on existing principles of international law that provides a foundation for stable political relations and for managing socioeconomic change within and across the African continent. The goal is explicitly political, i.e., the creation and maintenance of responsive, representative and responsible domestic governance.[82] The NEPAD Heads of States Implementation Committee should thus incorporate protection criteria into the indicators of the APRM. The integration of NEPAD into the AU structure could

---

[79] *See generally* J. Cilliers, 'Regional African Peacekeeping Capacity—Mythical Construct or Essential Tool?' in *From Peacekeeping to Complex Emergencies: Peace Support Missions in Africa*, Johannesburg: South African Institute for International Affairs and ISS, 1999, *supra* footnote 377.

[80] As of 19 March 2021, the Members are: Algeria, Angola, Benin, Burkina Faso, Cameroon, Chad, Côte d'Ivoire, Djibouti, Egypt, Equatorial Guinea, Ethiopia, Gambia, Gabon, Ghana, Kenya, Lesotho, Liberia, Malawi, Mali, Mauritania, Mauritius, Mozambique, Republic of Niger, Namibia, Nigeria, Republic of Congo, Rwanda, *São Tomé and Príncipe*, Senegal, Sierra Leone, South Africa, Sudan, Tanzania, Togo, Tunisia, Uganda and Zambia. See African Union, African Peer Review Mechanism (APRM), available at: https://au.nt/en/organs/aprm (accessed 18 March 2021). See Geldenhuys, *supra* footnote 74, pp. 21–22.

[81] Although the NEPAD is focused on economic development, it explicitly recognises that 'peace, security, democracy, good governance, human rights and sound economic management are conditions for sustainable development'. NEPAD proposes systems for monitoring adherence to the rule of law that can promote respect for human rights, in addition to serving as a check to prevent conditions in a given country from deteriorating to the point of insurgency or conflict. NEPAD sets out a series of peace and security priorities to respond to different stages of conflict that correspond with the report's prevention-reaction-rebuilding framework. In parenthesis, NEPAD has been given global legitimacy with the UN General Assembly's unanimous adoption of the 'Declaration on the New Partnership for Africa's Development' in September 2002. *See also* United Nations, Declaration on the New Partnership for Africa's Development, UN Doc.GA/57/L.2/Rev.1 (16 September 2002).

[82] J. Busumtwi-Sam, 'Architects of Peace—The African Union and NEPAD,' 7 *Georgetown Journal of International Affairs* (2006), pp. 71–81, pp. 76–77.

70   D. KUWALI

encourage more AU States to sign on to the APRM, thereby strengthening governance-related standards.[83]

The implementation of APRM may enhance sustained peace and security in Africa by articulating a strong stance on domestic governance issues that are at the root of instability and insecurity on the continent.[84] There is a need for civil society groups to come together to put pressure on governments to protect civilians.[85] The monitoring Mechanism of the CSSDCA offers the AU a comprehensive peer review process that is premised on the combination of a bottoms-up and top-down approach. Importantly, the Framework of Implementation and monitoring performance contained in the Memorandum of Understanding on CSSDCA involves governments through inter-Ministerial Committees, RECs, civil society organisations and independent research agencies. Thus, it involves a process of interaction at various levels that allows for, and encourages, cross-verification and cross-substantiation, as well as mediation at the same levels to promote changes.[86]

In spite of being voluntary, the APRM is highly intrusive insofar as it probes both structures and functioning of a participating State's political system, lock, stock and barrel. Under the APRM, a group of African 'eminent persons' is to conduct periodic reviews of Members' 'policies and practices' to ascertain progress being made towards achieving mutually agreed goals. The actual reviews are undertaken by Peer Review Teams. Upon completion of the review of a country, the Review Team submits the report to the APRM participating Heads of State and Government. If inadequacies are reported and the State concerned shows 'demonstrable will' to rectify the shortcomings, participating States are obliged to assist their peer and urge the international community to do likewise.

In the absence of political will to mend its ways, peers should first engage the errant government in 'constructive dialogue' before giving notice of their collective intention to take 'appropriate measures'. While the 'measures have not been spelt out, it is doubtful whether the drafters of the APRM document had military intervention in mind. The APRM document, however,

---

[83] However, in the worst case, it could result in weakening of those standards by those AU States with little interest in subscribing to a process of peer review. Ibid., p. 78.

[84] Ibid.

[85] *See* Background Research: International Commission on Interventional and State Sovereignty, the Responsibility to Protect, available at: www.iciss.ca/01_Section_A-en.asp (2 May 2008); *see also* Report on the Implementation of the CSSDCA, *supra* footnote 57.

[86] For example, Human Rights Committee concluding observations: Argentina, CCPR/CO/70/ARG, para. 9 (2000), in which the HRC recommended that Argentina take measures 'to ensure that persons involved in gross human rights violations are removed from military or public service' after noting its concern 'that many persons whose actions were covered by [amnesty] laws continue to serve in the military or in public office, with some having enjoyed promotions in the ensuing years' and 'at the atmosphere of impunity for those responsible for gross human rights violations under military rule'.

states that punitive measures should always be utilised as a last resort.[87] Thus, the peer review process is a useful initiative in raising awareness about relevant governance and political issues of a particular country, all of which might represent conflict vulnerabilities and thus need to be addressed with appropriate measures.[88]

This lack of decisive action informs the need for the APRM to collaborate with the African Commission to assess and take effective action where country examinations or individual communications reveal patterns of grave and systematic violations. States might refrain from engaging in it or might not accept the results presented by the review. However, after a breach of the AU Act, even if dialogue is privileged, political pressure, economic sanctions and any other appropriate enforcement action can be taken. The further coordination and involvement of AU institutions such as the PAPand the proposed African Court will help boost the legitimacy of the APRM. For instance, the APRM may provide political backing for the monitoring bodies by placing political pressure on governments that ignore or challenge the findings of human and peoples' rights bodies in Africa and decisions of the AU.[89] In essence, the APRM is designed to promote structural conflict prevention through good governance. As such, the APRM is another manifestation of the regional transition from a culture of sovereign impunity to a culture of accountability.

If it is effectively supported, the APRM can lay the foundations for a paradigm shift on the continent in efforts to consolidate Africa's fragile democracies and improve democratic governance and prevent conflicts. Experts have, however, noted that if all 53 Member States of the AU joined the APRM, it would take about ten years, at the current pace of activities, to conduct a continent-wide review. It is, therefore, important to increase the institutional capacity of the Eminent Panel of the APRM and its support staff.[90] The APRM or the African Commission and the African Court would thus provide political backing for the monitoring bodies by placing political pressure on governments that ignore or challenge the findings of relevant human rights institutions including UN treaty bodies or special procedures. This further

---

[87] Geldenhuys, *supra* footnote 74, pp. 15–17.

[88] A. Abass, 'Consent Precluding State Responsibility: A Critical Analysis,' 53 *International & Comparative Law Quarterly* (2004), pp. 211–225, p. 51.

[89] *See* R. Gossen *&* S. Sharma, 'Advancing NEPAD through The Responsibility to Protect,' Policy Brief, The Liu Institute for Global Issues, July 2003; *see also* Powell, *supra* footnote 3, pp. 14–15.

[90] *See* Centre For Conflict Resolution, Building An African Union For The 21st Century: Relations With Regional Economic Communities (RECs), NEPAD and Civil Society, Policy Seminar Report The Vineyard Hotel, Cape Town, 20–22 August 2005, Cape Town, 2005, p. 11.

72   D. KUWALI

expose the need for an instrument to outline practical measures for cooperation and coordination between the AU and the Human Rights Council, UN treaty bodies or mechanisms in the field of human rights as well as Law of Armed Conflict (LoAC).

THE ROLE OF SRMs AND RECs
IN OVERCOMING PEACE AND SECURITY THREATS

The OAU divided Africa into five regions, aligning with a number of existing RECs.[91] While these RECs were initially established for regional economic development, they subsequently also evolved into regional security arrangements.[92] This was due to the endemic insecurity and instability which was a major impediment to integration and development on the continent.[93] With the exception of the Arab Maghreb Union (AMU), ECOWAS,[94] SADC and the Economic Community of Central African States (ECCAS), have developed security mechanisms to operate within the context of a broader regional integration agenda. In Eastern Africa (the horn of Africa), the reinvigorated Inter-Governmental Authority on Development (IGAD) has developed a peace and security mandate and established a conflict prevention, management and resolution mechanism.[95]

---

[91] *See* OAU, Resolution CM/Res464 (XXVI), Twenty-Sixth Ordinary Session of the Council of Ministers, Addis Ababa, 23 February–1 March 1976.

[92] The Common Market for Eastern and Southern Africa (COMESA) too has not adopted a formal protocol on peace and security although it has formally endorsed a number of State-centric guiding principles, including non-aggression between Member States and the peaceful resolution of disputes between Member States. The Eastern African Community (EAC) has developed a Memorandum of Cooperation in Defence and has held joint meetings on small arms and light weapons, joint exercises for peace operations training, counter-terrorism and disaster management. *Cf.* Powell, *supra* footnote 3.

[93] *See* M. Mwanasali, 'From the Organization of African Unity to the African Union,' in M. Baregu & C. Landsberg (eds.), *From Cape to Congo: Southern Africa's Evolving Security Challenges*, London: Boulder Lynne Rienner Publishers, 2003.

[94] *For views on* ECOWAS *see* Ambassador Jacques Paul Klein, Special Representative of the Secretary General, United Nations Mission in Liberia (UNMIL) and Coordinator of the UN Operations in Liberia, 25 May 2005, 'Forward II,' in Aboagye & Bah (eds.), *supra* footnote 13, p. xxii, pp. xxi–xxiv, pp. 1–2; *see also* Aboagye & Bah, *supra* footnote 63, pp. 73–98, p. 122; Bah, *supra* footnote 13, p. 30; *see also* G.J. Yoroms, 'Mechanism for Conflict Management in ECOWAS,' Accord Occasional Paper, No. 8. 1999, pp. 3–4; *cf.* Proposed concept of ECOWAS Standby Brigade, May 2004; *see also* ECOMIL *After-Action Review, Final Report*, Abuja, August 2004.

[95] In contrast to ECOWAS and SADC, IGAD does not possess the operational infrastructure to respond militarily to conflict. Instead, it has focused its efforts on 'conflict prevention' through the on-going formation of a continental early warning system, and 'conflict resolution' by mediating the peace processes in Sudan and offering critical support to the Somalia–Djibouti-led peace process. In March 2005 member states of IGAD revised its Charter in order to authorise the deployment of a peacekeeping mission to support the Somalia peace process; *cf.* Centre for Conflict Resolution, *A More Secure Continent:*

The 1991 Abuja Treaty, which sought to rationalise the pan-African and regional agendas, stressed that the RECs would form the constitutive elements of a pan-African integration agenda. The AU and its Common African Defence and Security Policy (CADSP) have retained and reiterated this organisational structure. To be sure, Article 16 of the PSC Protocol outlines that regional mechanisms will form the 'building blocks' of the AU's peace and security architecture, including the ASF and CEWS. The PSC Protocol in Article 7(j) reinforces this relationship by emphasising the importance of harmonisation, coordination and cooperation between the AU and the regional mechanisms, and ensuring effective partnerships between the regional mechanisms and the PSC. The prominent role the AU has assigned to the RECs will allow the AU to build on their comparative advantage, experience and established frameworks and mechanisms for conflict prevention, management and resolution.

Regional organisations' proximity to the conflict provides them with a better understanding of its dynamics, key players and context-specific management and resolution options. At least in theory, this proximity also allows regional organisations to initiate rapid and less expensive responses to conflict than the UN. Further, regional leaders and organisations may also be considered more accountable and legitimate than pan-African and international organisations. It is conceivable to suggest that the AU's emerging peace and security regime may have a greater stake in finding a peaceful solution to conflict than more distant powers.[96] Sub-regional organisations also play an important role within the African peace and security agenda as they serve as the main interlocutors between each individual African State and the continental body. Yet, on the one hand, regional organisations have manifold shortcomings with adverse impact on the construction of a continental peace and security architecture. Apart from the usual resource and capacity constraints, regional organisations' proximity to conflict can also compromise the neutrality and impartiality of this response. Ibok succinctly notes that 'proximity generates tension and undermines the spirit of impartiality between neighbours, sometimes to the extent that neighbours become part of the problems'.[97]

The other is the existence of regional hegemonic actors which may influence the shape of regional peace and security agendas to suit the domestic problems and national interests of these powerful States. Reliance on regional powers also raises questions about how to fashion regional responses to mass atrocity

---

African Perspectives on the UN High-Level Panel Report, A More Secure World: Our Shared Responsibility, Seminar Report, Somerset West, Cape Town, 23–24 April 2005, p. 25.

[96] *See* M. Juma & A. Mengistu, 'The Infrastructure of Peace in Africa: Assessing the Peace-building Capacity of African Institutions,' New York: International Peace Academy, September 2002.

[97] Ibok (2004), *supra* footnote 4, pp. 7–9.

74   D. KUWALI

crimes in which the hegemonic State is a party to the conflict.[98] In this category, regional organisations lack capacity to organise coherent interventions owing to the uneven political and economic development of Member States, differing political and security agendas and visions and competition between States. This undermines the consensus required to pursue a collective security mandate and execute effective responses to mass atrocity crimes.

On the other hand, there are myriad challenges confronting the interoperability and harmonisation of the AU and regional organisations as well as between regional organisations themselves. For instance, the broad differences in the peace and security mandates of regional organisations, including ECOWAS' tradition of intervention versus the strong non-intervention norms in East Africa, will complicate a coherent pan-African approach to conflict.[99] Further, the construction of a continental security architecture built on regional capacities may be undermined by the fact that the AU and RECs have not been able to formalise a clear division of labour and responsibilities for conflict prevention, management and resolution on the continent. Some regional organisations such as ECOWAS consider the UN, and not the AU, as the central political authority on matters pertaining to peace and security.[100]

This underscores the need for RECs to consolidate in order to feed into the AU. If the AU is to construct a formidable human security architecture against mass atrocity crimes using regional arrangements as building blocks, then significant effort must be made towards harmonising the respective agendas of RECs. 'Otherwise', analysts have cautioned, 'the PSCwill risk becoming another "security council of five," and be left to decide the destiny of the remaining members, with the outside chance of rendering itself completely ineffective'.[101] In fact, regional and sub-regional action

[98] International Peace Academy, Refashioning the Dialogue: Regional Perspectives on the Brahimi Report on UN Operations, New York, 2001.

[99] See Powell, *supra* footnote 3, p. 69.

[100] See EXP/AU-Recs/ASF/Comm (I) At an Experts' Meeting in Addis Ababa in March 2005, the AU and the RECs (ECOWAS, ECCAS, IGAD, COMESA, EAC and SADC) agreed to consider a draft Memorandum of Understanding on conflict prevention, resolution and management but were not able to come to a final agreement on modalities. This is due to a resistance on the part of Member States to confer greater decision-making authority to the AU in some cases, in part because regional organisations provide an alternative forum to exercise influence and leverage greater institutional support for specific political agendas than might be possible in organisations with a larger and more diverse membership. Moreover, ECOWAS and SADC actually have more experience in executing military responses to conflict than the AU, which—with the exception of AMIB and AMIS—has only undertaken observer missions; *see* Powell, *supra* footnote 3, p. 69.

[101] More so, while the AU has the right to intervene under Article 4(h) and 4(j) of the Act and Article 7(e) of the Protocol of the PSC compels the AU to intervene whereas Article 11 of the SADC Organ on Politics, Defence and Security Cooperation Protocol (PPDSC) does not firmly provide for such intervention. In addition, SADC will only respond to a heavy, forceful and well-informed sub-regional bottom-up approach. In relation to internal and external threats the CADSP deals with both simultaneously while in the SADC provisions, these matters are dealt with separately both in the PPDSC and the

and co-operation is critical to the capacity of African countries to defend their collective interests or advance Africa's priorities among the broader international community. Continent-wide, regional and sub-regional capacity building in conflict prevention and management needs to be given the highest priority, for when action is needed the stark reality is that it is most likely to take the form of sub-regional action.

A common thread running through the agendas of the RECs is clearly the foursome of security, stability, development and cooperation. This suggests that common ground for harmonising agendas of the RECs can be found in the CSSDCA, which posits that peace, security and stability are the pillars for development and cooperation in Africa.[102] The CSSDCA emphasises that the security, stability and development of African States are inseparably interlinked and that the security of each African country is similarly linked to that of other African countries and the African continent as a whole. The thrust of the CSSDCA is that exercise of responsible sovereignty is the key to security, failing which cooperation among neighbours is required to deal with internal problems and conflicts.[103]

Importantly, the CSSDCA embraces both state security and human security. It propounds that stability calls for the rule of law, accountable governments and democratic procedures, the free participation of the citizenry in governance and the full protection of human rights.[104] All these principles contribute to the prevention of human rights violations, and the root causes of

Mutual Defence Pact (MDP). Furthermore, decision-making processes between the two also differ. Whereas AU decisions are by consensus and voting in the event of a deadlock, decision-making in SADC is based invariably on consensus. Ibid.

[102] The CSSDCA, which is loosely modelled on the Organization for Security and Cooperation in Europe (OSCE), also has a peer review implementation similar to the APRM. The CSSDCA process has also developed a framework of activity that would serve the monitoring and evaluation goals of the AU Assembly as prescribed in Art. 9(e) of the AU Act. The obligations and frameworks of behaviour set for values, commitments and actions to be taken, and key performance indicators enunciated in the Memorandum of Understanding on the Security, Stability, Development and Cooperation Calabashes under the CSSDCA meet the highest comparable regional and international standards. It is also remarkable that the Member States in consensus agreed and committed themselves in clear and unequivocal terms on standards to stand by them and to respect and implement all this undertakings in the conformity with Arts 9(e) and 23(2) of the AU Act; *see* the Report on the implementation of the CSSDCA, *supra* footnote 57.

[103] The CSSDCA is one of the two special programmes of the AU, the other being NEPAD. Initially, the CSSDCA was a framework for the adoption of common values for the AU as well as benchmarks against which successes could be measured, while NEPAD was an action programme for achieving the objectives of the AU and the continent as a whole. One of the main characteristics of the CSSDCA initiative was its provision of a mechanism for monitoring and facilitating the implementation of OAU/AU decisions. Although there is convergence and complementarity between the objectives of the CSSDCA and NEPAD in the context of the AU, there are areas of overlap and possible duplication that need to be addressed; *cf.* Report on the implementation of the CSSDCA, *supra* footnote 57.

[104] *See also* Bah, *supra* footnote 13, pp. 35–36.

conflicts on the continent. It follows from this reasoning that RECs can build a common front in the investigation, extradition and prosecution of perpetrators of gross human rights violations on the continent. Unlike membership of NEPAD which is voluntary, all AU Members States are Members to the CSSDCA. Thus, the CSSDCA serves as a major vehicle through which the AU can collectively translate into concrete, achievable and measurable results, the vision and agenda of the AU in the realm of peace, security, development and integration.

CONCLUSION

The contemporary security challenges faced by Africa exhibits the social and economic complexities that the continent is facing. The APSA, which is considered as a promising African security ingenuity, has somewhat ascertained lacking in some aspects because of its stance of putting out the fire when it has burst forth than preventing it from flaring up at the outset. Although African states have taken ambitious steps into adopting numerous instruments on governance, human rights and humanitarian law augmented by the construction of the APSA, numerous conflicts and violations of human rights and international humanitarian norms still take place on the continent. African leaders must formulate and take deliberate effective measures and apparatuses to prevent and manage conflicts in their infancy.

Despite the adoption of numerous conventions on international human rights and humanitarian law, there are still numerous occurrences of violations of human rights and international humanitarian standards resulting into mass atrocity crimes. This points to the need for creating a 'climate of compliance'. International instruments are essential tools for the legal protection of civilians and prevention of mass atrocity crimes. In order to promote compliance, the AU PSC should encourage AU States to ratify the core human rights and humanitarian treaties, to withdraw reservations, take all measures to ensure their implementation in practice and to disseminate these fundamental international norms within national armed forces and police and among all sectors of society.[105] The PSC should also ensure that AU States ratify and implement the provisions of the Rome Statute as a concrete measure aimed at enforcing respect for international human rights law and IHL.[106]

Although the AU has set up human security architecture with an early warning system, still to be constructed is an effective early response and, crucially, mechanism for timely preventive action. This suggests the need to cultivate a culture of prevention. Timely and adequate response to early warning will enhance chances of preventing mass atrocity crimes. As such, apart from the information from CEWS, the PSC should utilise the human

[105] *See also* United Nations, Report of the Secretary-General to the Security Council on the Protection of Civilians in Armed Conflict, S/1999/957, 8 September 1999, para. 36.

[106] Ibid., para. 38(4).

rights information and analysis emanating from the AU human rights institutions such as the African Commission and independent experts as well as the UN human rights mechanisms including the UN Human Rights Council, treaty bodies and other reliable sources, as indicators for potential preventive action.[107]

As rightly asserted by Dan Kuwali in Chapter 34, the AU, APSA and RECs must embrace inclusion if Africa is to experience peace and security, without which, the continent will continue bearing excruciating effects of conflicts. Human rights and governance mechanisms must be given considerable attention to counter specific regional security threats. Although human security has been given prominence, the contemporary security threats such as environmental degradation, human trafficking, drug abuse, cybercrime and diseases must also be looked into with the eagle's eye. Subsequently, the PSC must broaden its mandate and activities to include these threats. Peace and security are key to the full realisation of the AU agenda 2063 and its aspirations.

[107] Ibid., para. 45.

PART II

A Regional Focus to Peace and Security in Africa

CHAPTER 5

Securing Peace and Security in North Africa

Dan Kuwali and Prince Bright Majiga

INTRODUCTION

North Africa is often loosely defined, but for the purposes of this chapter, it encompasses the States of the Arab Maghreb Union (Algeria, Libya, Mauritania, Morocco and Tunisia) together with Egypt.[1] With the exception of Mauritania, this group of States lies on the northern littoral of the African continent, between the Mediterranean Sea to the North and the Sahara to the South. Although North African countries were among the founding members of the erstwhile Organization for African Unity (OAU) in 1963, Egypt later gravitated towards the Arab World, drawn in by the Arab–Israeli conflict since the 1970s, while Morocco withdrew its membership from the OAU in 1987 in response to the former continental organisation's recognition of Western Sahara. Meanwhile, Libya and Algeria, continued to play instrumental roles in the affairs of the OAU and its successor, the African Union (AU).

North Africa is home to some of the most economically and militarily powerful States in Africa, with Algeria, Egypt and Libya being three of the five countries that contributed 65 per cent of the Member State portion of the African Union (AU) operational budget in 2014. However, security in this region has since taken a serious turn for the worse. Not only has the region seen the outbreak of civil war in Libya since 2011, a revolution and emerging insurgency in Egypt in 2011 and 2019, but the problem of terrorism has also worsened to unprecedented heights with the regional expansion of the Islamic

---

D. Kuwali · P. B. Majiga (✉)
Malawi Defence Force, Lilongwe, Malawi

© The Author(s), under exclusive license to Springer Nature
Switzerland AG 2022
D. Kuwali (ed.), *The Palgrave Handbook of Sustainable Peace and Security in Africa*, https://doi.org/10.1007/978-3-030-82020-6_5

81

State. In addition, declining oil prices have had an impact and are likely to continue to affect the major producers in the region, namely Algeria, Egypt and Libya.

Despite the North Africa–Sub Saharan divide and the limited role of countries like Egypt and Tunisia in the affairs of the AU, as a region, North Africa has always held a concentration of the continental body's biggest financial contributors. Before the fall of President Colonel Muammar Gaddafi in 2011, Libya, Algeria, Egypt, Nigeria and South Africa contributed 15 per cent each to the AU's budget.[1] With Morocco joining the AU in 2017, Egypt, Algeria and Morocco now each contribute 9.6 per cent of the total AU budget, as do Nigeria and South Africa.[2]

The peace and security implications of the Arab Spring are of great significance, not only to North Africa, but also to the African continent as a whole. Up until the Arab Spring in 2011, North Africa was a relatively stable region on the continent. Human development, that is to say, levels of poverty, education and health, had progressively improved in the region, although governments in Egypt and Tunisia struggled to maintain a large public sector amidst a growing population, while continuing to subsidize basic goods that had been key to the social contract between people and the government.[3] State presence and penetration in Tunisia, Egypt and Libya was quite palpable, and ensured "security" in these countries. But that came at the cost of civil liberties and brutal suppression of opposition.

By 2013, the North African region had seen profound changes. The popular protests termed "Arab Spring" that started in Tunisia in 2010, had taken root in Egypt and Libya. The Egyptian President Hosni Mubarak was ousted after 30 years in power, giving way to democratic elections in 2012 that saw the ascendancy of the Muslim Brotherhood to power, only to be taken out by the military in 2013. The then Tunisian President, Ben Ali, fled to Saudi Arabia, giving way for a bumpy but promising transition to electoral democracy in the country. In Libya, popular protests that started in 2010 turned into a bloody civil war and saw a proliferation of armed groups, which has spilled over to destabilize North Africa and the Sahel region. To this day, the legality, proportionality and necessity of the intervention of the North Atlantic Treaty Organization (NATO) in March 2011 to enforce a "no fly zone", is questioned. NATO (particularly France and the United States) and the AU—which at that time was negotiating a dignified exit for President Gaddafi—could not

[1] Allinson T. 2019. Can Abdel-Fattah el-Sissi Make Egypt Great Again? *Deutsche Welle.* https://www.dw.com/en/can-abdel-fattah-el-sissi-make-egypt-great-again/a-48474675; and Allison, S. 2011. Who Will Fund the AU? *The Daily Maverick.*

[2] African Union. 2018a. *African Union Handbook 2019.* https://au.int/sites/default/files/pages/31829-fileau_handbook_2019_english.pdf.

[3] Se Devarajan, S. 2015. What is the Social Contract and Why Does the Arab World Need a New One? *Arab Voices.* World Bank Blogs. https://blogs.worldbank.org/arabvoices/what-social-contract-and-why-doesarab-world-need-new-one; and Winckler, O. 2013. *The 'Arab Spring': Socioeconomic Aspects.* Washington: Middle East Policy Council.

see eye to eye on the matter. North Africa's current destabilization is largely attributed to the Libyan crisis and increasingly tied to the rise of armed groups and jihadist in the Sahel region.[4]

For the AU, stabilizing North Africa through the provisions of the African Peace and Security Architecture (APSA) poses a particular challenge as there is no functional regional organization it can work with.[5] The Arab Maghreb Union, of which Algeria, Morocco, Libya and Mauritania are members, can barely carry out its basic functions, let alone overcome the political and economic dynamics among its members to facilitate regional stability.[6] It is particularly strangled by the tensions between Morocco and Algeria, which, in an attempt to maintain regional hegemony, undermine each other's initiatives. In the absence of one unified sub-regional organization, however, countries like Algeria, Morocco and Egypt initiate new or boost existing bi- or multilateral economic and security cooperation mechanisms between and among each other as well as with other countries in the Sahel and West Africa, rendering the AU a distant observer.

Unprecedented levels of conflict and violence in North Africa pose new challenges to practitioners and policymakers. In light of armed conflict and perceived instability in the region, the systems and institutions that promised order are fragile, fragmented and stressed, especially state structures, economic networks and the social fabrics. State authorities struggle to provide even the minimum level of security to engender the trust and stability to end conflict or build sustainable peace. Where violence and displacement continue, people fearing anarchy and distress have sought security and basic services in informal networks with ever-shifting dynamics. New elite configurations in the form of war lords who are often armed with strong and tangled vested interests in the conflict-driven informality, compete for power and resources nationally and locally. Competition among international and regional states only adds to the pressure. Urban areas have come under particular stress as targets of violence in a highly urbanized region leaving millions of people displaced.

---

[4] Lounnas, D. and Messari, N. 2018. Algeria–Morocco Relations And Their Impact On The Maghrebi Regional System. MENARA Working Papers 20; and Larémont, R.R. 2015. After the Fall of Qaddafi: Political, Economic, and Security Consequences for Libya, Mali, Niger, and Algeria. *Stability: International Journal of Security and Development* 2(2): 1–8. http://doi.org/10.5334/sta.bq.

[5] Kuwali D. 2018. 'Squaring the Circle: The Role of the African Peace and Security Architecture' In: Karbo T., Virk K. *The Palgrave Handbook of Peacebuilding in Africa.* Cham: Palgrave Macmillan, 45–63. Available at https://doi.org/10.1007/9783-319-622 02-6_3.

[6] Abderrahmane, A. 2012. *Hope for Reviving the Arab Maghreb Union (UMA).* Tshwane/Pretoria: Institute for Security Studies; and Boukhars, A. 2018. *Maghreb: Dream of Unity, Reality of Divisions.* Doha: Aljazeera Centre for Studies.

There are two key regional organizations in North Africa, namely the Arab Mahgreb Union (AMU) founded in 1989[7] and the Community of Sahel-Saharan States (CEN-SAD) founded in 1998.[8] AMU and CEN-SAD are formally recognized by the AU as Regional Mechanisms (RMs)/Regional Economic Communities (RECs), and thus part of the APSA. However, the AMU has never formalized its relationship with the AU by signing the Protocol on Relations between the RECs and the AU. In addition, there is the North African Regional Capability (NARC), founded in 2007,[3] which is the RM in charge of managing the North African standby force contribution to the African Standby Force (ASF). In order to understand the regional realities and peculiarities of the region, the ensuing discussion looks into obstacles to securing peace and security in North Africa.

Main Challenges to Peace and Security in North Africa

North Africa faces a myriad of challenges, with each country in the region experiencing peculiar problems. However, some of the problems in the region are widespread, complicating governance and security issues. These include but are not limited to: youth unemployment and discontent, terrorism and violent extremism, armed conflict, governance deficits, irregular migration, human trafficking, among others.[9]

Youth Unemployment and Discontent

Economic and social challenges are key underlying causes of instability in North Africa. Unemployment rates, particularly among the youth, are high in all countries in the region. In Tunisia, 36 per cent of those aged 15–24 were out of work in 2018. This figure stood at 34 per cent in Egypt and 42 per cent in Libya.[10] In comparison, the average youth unemployment rate in middle-income countries was 14 per cent that year.[11]

---

[7] Member states include Algeria, Libya, Mauritania, Morocco and Tunisia.

[8] Member states include (North African in bold): Benin, Burkina Faso, Central African Republic, Chad, Côte d'Ivoire, Djibouti, Egypt, Eritrea, Gambia, Ghana, Guinea Bissau, Kenya, Liberia, Libya, Mali, Morocco, Niger, Nigeria, Senegal, Sierra Leone, Somalia, Sudan, Togo and Tunisia. 3 Member states include Algeria, Libya, Mauritania, Tunisia, Egypt and Western Sahara.

[9] Adriana Lins de Albuquerque Challenges to Peace and Security in North Africa: Accounting for the Lack of Regional Institutional Response Studies in African Security September 2015. www.foi.se/africa.

[10] ILO. "Unemployment, Youth Total (% of Total Labor Force Ages 15–24)". International Labour Organization, ILOSTAT Database. 2019. https://data.worldbank.org/indicator/SL.UEM.1524.ZS?locations=EG-TN-MA-DZ-XP.

[11] Ibid.

The uprisings that occurred across the North Africa region in 2011 were rooted in socioeconomic discontent.[12] This discontent has not been adequately addressed by the region's post-revolutionary governments, as evidenced by the high incidence of economically rooted protest in North Africa over the past few years. In Morocco's Rift Valley, frustration about corruption and stalled economic development led to unrest in late 2016 and early 2017. In Egypt, protests also erupted in late 2016 in response to subsidy cuts and other painful austerity measures associated with a US$ 12 billion International Monetary Fund (IMF) loan. There have been sporadic displays of public outrage since then as the prices of fuel, public transportation, electricity and other goods and services have been increased. Given that economic hardship fuels instability, the failure of governments across the region to meaningfully tackle their populations' grievances in this respect represents a latent security issue.

Insecurity

The anarchy in Libya that emerged following the NATO bombing and fall of President Muammar Ghaddafi in 2011 has evolved into a full-scale civil war, with two main factions, both referring to themselves as the government, fighting for control of the country. The faction based in Misurata and with a provisional government in Tripoli comprises Islamists and local militias, whereas the faction based in the East and led by General Khalifa Hiftir comprises anti-Islamists.

A third party has now emerged in the Libyan civil war, namely the Islamic State (IS), affiliates of which have expanded their territory in the country, targeting security forces and civilians. Islamic State appears to be establishing branches across North Africa, with local groups throughout the region, but especially in Egypt and Libya, pledging fealty. Nearly a decade later, Libyans continue to struggle to end their violent conflict and build state institutions. External actors have exacerbated Libya's problems by funneling money and weapons to proxies that have put various interests above those of the Libyan people. The efforts by the United Nations (UN) to negotiate a sustainable peace have yet to reach fruition and been overshadowed by competing peace gatherings sponsored by various foreign governments.

Meanwhile, Libya's borders remain porous, particularly in the southern Fezzan, facilitating an increase in trafficking and smuggling of illicit materials, including weapons. At the subnational level, many local conflicts reflect long-standing feuds between various factions, tribes and ethnic groups. In the shadow of the ongoing conflict around Tripoli, the prospects for a political solution are dimmed by the country's deep political and tribal divides. The Libyan conflict affects relations between other States in North Africa and

[12] Julio Miranda Calha, Security and stability in Africa—Opportunities for NATO. 12 October 2019.

increasingly draws in outside actors on both side of the conflict. This is similar to the impact of the impasse over the Western Sahara, in that it has exacerbated long-standing tensions between Algeria and Morocco.

Terrorism and Violent Extremism

The threat posed by extremist militant groups in the Middle East and North Africa (MENA) region appears to have slightly decreased in recent years. This decrease is linked to Daesh's recent retreat from Iraq and Syria, as well as to the reduced impact of its local affiliate in Egypt. However, the collapse of Daesh has created a potential new terrorist threat in the form of returning North African Daesh fighters. Although many are presumed to have been killed in combat, the danger that returnees could pose should not be underestimated: they have gained military experience, ideological training and connections with fellow jihadists from around the world. This could pose a real threat to Libya where continued chaos, insecurity and the lack of governance provide an opportunity for the continuation of jihadist activities.

An even bigger concern for Egypt is dealing with a variety of home-grown terrorist organizations and jihadist extremists, which have been increasing their visibility in Sinai and staging attacks elsewhere in Egypt since 2013.[13] The Daesh in the Sinai Province (formerly known as Ansar Bait al-Maqdis) continues to be the most active terrorist group in Egypt, operating in the northern Sinai Peninsula. Islamic State is also present in the Sinai province of Egypt and has carried out attacks in Cairo, Alexandria and Minya.[14] Although it initially targeted the Egyptian army, this Daesh affiliate has increasingly focused its operations on Coptic Christians, Sufi Muslims and foreign tourists. There is also a growing militant threat in the Western Desert in the form of Ansar al-Islam, a new group composed mostly of former Egyptian army officers and soldiers that has pledged allegiance to Al-Qaeda in the Islamic Maghreb (AQIM). In addition, smaller extremist cells stage attacks on security forces in urban areas. In February 2018, the Egyptian government launched a major campaign aimed at eliminating Daesh and other militant groups in the Sinai. On a national scale, the government has reacted to these terrorist activities with a harsh military crackdown and repressive legal measures, including repeated extensions of the nationwide state of emergency since April 2017.

---

[13] Ragab, E. 2016. *Counter Terrorism in Egypt: Effectiveness and Challenges.* Euro-Mediterranean Study Commission. https://css.ethz.ch/content/dam/ethz/special-interest/gess/cis/center-for-securitiesstudies/resources/docs/IEMed-euromesco30.pdf.

[14] Egypt Today. 2019c. *Global Condemnation of Sheikh Zowayed's Terror Attack Killing.* www.egypttoday.com/Article/1/68169/Global-condemnation-of-Sheikh-Zowayed%E2%80%99s-terrorattack-killing-7. Accessed 31 March 2021; Dawoud K. 2018. *Downplaying Terror Attacks in Egypt.* Washington: Carnegie Endowment for International Peace. https://carnegieendowment.org/sada/77687; and Maguid, M. 2017. *Egypt's Role in Libya: Attempts and Risks of Solving the Crisis.* Giza: Egypt Today. www.egypttoday.com/Article/2/4687/Egypt%E2%80%99s-role-in-Libya-Attempts-and-risks-of-solving-the-crisis. Accessed 30 March 2021.

However, this approach also fuels further radicalisation, with Ansar al-Islam, for example, declaring a "Holy War" against the Egyptian state. The growing threat of terrorism in the Middle East, North Africa and the Sahel, and the increasing mobility and ideological alignment of terrorist groups across these regions, have had serious implications for Egypt.

Democracy Deficits

Tunisia is the only country that has successfully managed to transition from autocracy following the Arab Spring, making it the region's only democracy. In contrast, Egypt's Mohamed Morsi of the Muslim Brotherhood, the president elected in the country's first free parliamentary election since the ousting of President Hosni Mubarak, was himself ousted in a military coup d'état backed by popular protests in 2013. The coup leader, General Abdel Fattah Al-Sisi, was subsequently elected president following an election widely considered by international observers as flawed. The new government's heavy-handed repression of political dissident suggests the country has returned to its autocratic ways.

IRREGULAR MIGRATION, HUMAN TRAFFICKING AND BORDER SECURITY

North Africa continues to be an "area of origin, transit and final destination" for migrants and refugees from sub-Saharan Africa and the Middle East.[15] Despite some efforts to mitigate the challenge, most agreements have not addressed the factors that spur emigration and have, therefore, exacerbated insecurity in North Africa in some ways. There continues to be a lucrative people smuggling business in Libya's southern deserts and there is "increased evidence of connections between organized criminal networks and terrorist groups".[16]

The illicit flow of militants and migrants as well as of weapons, fuel and drugs across Libya's borders is related to the fragmentation and low professionalism of the country's security forces, its outdated border-security infrastructure and the disintegration of its justice system.[17] Despite troop deployment and enforcement of other measures, including security walls, this creates new security challenges, with border communities facing potential abuse of power by border-security services. This is particularly true as

[15] European Commission. "North of Africa". European Commission. 2019. https://ec. europa.eu/trustfundforafrica/region/north-africa_en.

[16] European Commission. "Dismantling the Criminal Networks Operating in North Africa andIinvolved in Migrant Smuggling and Human Trafficking". European Commission. December 4 2017. https://ec.europa.eu/europeaid/dismantling-criminal-networks-operating-north-africa-andinvolved-migrant-smuggling-and-human_en.

[17] US Department of State. "Country Reports on Terrorism 2017—Libya". *Refworld*. September 9, 2018. https://www.refworld.org/docid/5bcf1f9713.html.

these public officers come under increased economic stress as they are cut off from smuggling revenues, and therefore, becoming increasingly susceptible to radicalisation.

Accounting for the Lack of a Regional Institutional Response in North Africa

Neither AMU nor CEN-SAD has done much to manage the various challenges to peace and security that have emerged in the region since 2011. The following section seeks to explain what accounts for this institutional handicap. The conflict between Algeria and Morocco over the status of Western Sahara has more or less deadlocked the AMU, which has been largely dormant for close to two decades. Although there has been no fighting for the last 24 years between Morocco and the opposing Polisario Front, which is the Western Sahara independence movement, the conflict remains unresolved.[18] It is AMU's stalemate that inspired Libya's Ghaddafi to create CEN-SAD.

Since Morocco, but not Algeria, is a member of CEN-SAD, the organization does not face the same problems over Western Sahara as AMU. Another strength of CEN-SAD is that, in contrast to AMU, it includes the military powerhouse Egypt. Nevertheless, the fall of Ghaddafi has left CEN-SAD in disarray, resulting in institutional inertia as regards dealing with issues of regional security. Lately, however, there have been signs of attempts to revive both organizations, with Tunisia seeking to take the reins of the AMU and Morocco those of CEN-SAD. Yet, meetings by these organizations have produced little to date in terms of actual management of security in the region.

Finally, there is NARC, whose standby force is meant to be used for managing regional security. The main reason why NARC remains a moot cause is because its standby force has not yet reached the initial operational capacity, making it the regional standby force whose development is furthest beyond schedule. NARC's development has been lagging since its creation, and up to 2011 primarily due to disagreements among States in the region on how to proceed. Following 2011, NARC has largely fallen by the way-side, largely due to the security situation in Libya, where the RM is based. The AU is currently looking into relocating NARC to another more suitable North African country.

Given the institutional stalemate in the region, the request by the recognized government of Libya in August 2015 that the League of Arab States (LAS) intervene militarily to fight IS is perhaps not surprising. Whereas LAS Member States quickly agreed that IS in Libya needs to be countered, the organization has decided to delay indefinitely the decision of whether to form

---

[18] Morocco left the AU in direct reaction to Western Sahara having been admitted as a member by its precursor organization, the Organization of African Unity (OAU).

a regional force and engage militarily. Hence, an institutional response to the turmoil in Libya by an organization with regional member states appears distant, at best.

CONFLICT TRAPS—COMPLEXITY OF SECURING PEACE IN NORTH AFRICA

Violence in North Africa has erupted as a result of an accumulation of many unaddressed grievances. As the transitions to either peace or violence are gradual processes—rather than one-time breaking points—the persistence of underlying grievances such as exclusion of some segments of the population injustice, or inequality and people's strategies for coping with instability pushes a country to move into and out of violence. These cycles of violence sustain "conflict traps" that cannot be escaped until these underlying dynamics are addressed.[19] In MENA, the most recent violence expresses the explosion of unaddressed grievances that have been accumulating for decades, leading to the protracted and often localized conflicts in the aftermath of the Arab Spring.

To understand the complexities, there is need to look at the situation from a human security perspective. First, there is a strong relationship between poverty and peace and security.[20] Second, disruptive political transitions as evident in times of change, including transitions from autocracy to democracy are often unstable and prone to violence. Third, lack of respect for human rights has potential to generate conflict and violence. Fourth, unmet needs of youth or imbalances in economic benefits, and social and economic exclusion could also undermine peace and security. Fifth, violence can generate more violence in response when a country that has experienced large-scale violence is susceptible to more of the same.

For example, in the case of Libya, the near decade of civil war in Libya highlights the paramount starting point of establishing a lasting peace that provides security for the country's people. The situation in Libya also illustrates some of the transversal aspects, including migrants who cross the Sahel seeking access to Europe as well as internal displaced persons (IDPs). At the same time, neighbouring Mauritania and Sudan are faced with complex and deeply rooted development issues linked to the failures of the political leadership to manage their economies as well as deep seated corruption. Mauritania can also illustrate the transboundary issues as highlighted in the connections with the

---

[19] Study on the interlinkages between the development, peace and security, human rights and humanitarian pillars in North Africa Stephen Commins, Inception Report Final draft. November 11, 2020.

[20] United Nations Trust Fund for Human Security. 2016. Human Security Handbook—An Integrated Approach for the Realization of Sustainable Development Goals and the Priority Areas of the International Community and the United Nations System. https://www.un.org/humansecurity/wp-content/uploads/2017/10/h2.pdf.

Sahel initiative.[21] For Tunisia, Morocco, Algeria and Egypt, the continuing ricochet from the Arab Spring shows how the tensions over human rights is having an impact across the region, linked with specific economic development dilemmas, the youth bulge and pressures for employment opportunities.

Transboundary issues include the ongoing unresolved tensions over the status of the Western Sahara territory which leads to tensions between Mauritania, Algeria and Morocco, as well as the unresolved status of the displaced populations currently residing in camps. Egypt and Sudan are currently engaged in major diplomatic negotiations with Ethiopia over Issues in Transboundary Water Use in the River Nile Basin associated in recent years with the new Nile Dam, which is perceived as a serious threat to their economies.

North Africa is a region where demands for political and economic change (notably ignited by the Arab Spring movements in 2011 and following in countries such as Tunisia and Egypt), along with various forms of pressures for fundamental reforms, a number of which have led to large protest movements and, in the case of Libya the collapse of the political system into civil war. Several countries in the region are undergoing social and political upheavals amidst contested elections, violence between entities claiming authority over geographic space and low-level challenges to state authority by a variety of social and political groups. These immediate political conflicts overlay and in some ways are embedded in the political economy of the region. These range from rapid growth in demand for employment by youth, rural to urban migration and structural changes in their economies, driven both by exogenous factors and by the decisions of the government.

Political tensions and polarization were key factors surrounding electoral politics in countries such as Tunisia and Algeria in 2019, and they are likely to remain significant for both countries.[22] While both countries, as well as Morocco and Egypt, continue to face economic problems, there are difficulties in seeking to implement economic reforms, as well-connected and powerful interests attempt to protect their control that was exercised under earlier regimes. Public anger at the political class is increasing due to failure to address underlying economic crises including inflation, and persistent youth unemployment.

Unequal distribution of wealth across North Africa and concentration of the levers of production in the hands of a few groups in each country, particularly those who have been in power for a long time, continues to contribute to political and social unrest. Coupled with a lack of mechanisms for redistribution of wealth, persistent corruption and nepotism based on strongly

---

[21] ICG, Crisis Watch, Libya, September 2020; Wolfram Lacher Libya's Fragmentation: Structure and Process in Violent Conflict., I.B. Tauris, 2020 Libya Cash Working Group, Libya: Rapid Market Assessment. April 2020.

[22] Adel Abdel Ghafar and Anna Jacobs, Could Morocco's Political Shakeup Empower More Radical Elements, Brookings. April 17, 2017; and Annabelle Houdret and Astrid Harnisch, Decentralisation in Morocco. The Current Reform and Its Possible Contribution to Political Liberalisation. December 2016.

patrimonial systems, enables the persistence of inequality, in spite of progress made in some countries. This leads to an enduring sense of exclusion across large sections of society, including sections of the youth. It is precisely the lack of change to this status quo position that provided a central impetus for the continuation of protests in the decade following the Arab Spring.

In summary, all four countries in the region face domestic political pressures born of distinct individual factors yet share a regional set of pressures. These range from the complex "democratic transition" amid secular-religious fault lines in Tunisia, to the street protests against the old regime in Algeria, the tradeoffs involved in political reform and stability in Morocco and the closing of political space in Egypt.[23]

The human development indicators for Sudan and Mauritania are distinct from those of Egypt, Libya, Morocco, Tunisia and Algeria. In the latter five, there remain serious difficulties with access to development opportunities and inclusive benefits of development. Thus, the nature of development as a process of inclusive economic growth remains a problem. Despite the level of development in the five countries compared to the first two, development is still a problem due to the lack of inclusiveness and uneven opportunities and benefits, which were notable drivers for the "Arab Spring".

Sudan's economic decay helped drive the December Revolution, a movement which began on 19 December, 2018, when the price of bread rose due to a government decree.[24] The government was seen as following a top down fiscal policy with the poor and vulnerable groups bearing a heavy burden. The protests grew in size and the demands expanded with the specific call for the overthrow of the President. The various economic interests, including labour organizations and farmers associations were vocal from the beginning that it was not just about the political leadership, but the economic plight of citizens. Mauritania also faced political tensions after the change of government in 2019.[25] Much of the popular anger was based on the hard evidence of the corruption of the old regime coupled with the poor economic prospects for most citizens. Across the region, young people have become more engaged in the political process, sometimes linked with political parties, sometimes with fluid social movements, and increasingly energized by the frustration that is widespread over economic inequality and what many perceive as an unresponsive political system.[26]

---

[23] Sarah Yerkes and Zeineb Ben Yahmed, Tunisia's Political System from Stagnation to Competition, 2019, Carnegie Endowment.

[24] ICG, Crisis Watch, Sudan. September 2020.

[25] Haim Malka, Turbulence Ahead: The North Africa Maghreb in 2019, CSIS.

[26] AU-EU/Decl.1(V). 2017. Investing in Youth for Accelerated Inclusive Growth and Sustainable Development, 7–10. https://au.int/sites/default/files/documents/37754-doc-5th_au-eu_abidjan_declaration.pdf.

AGAINST ALL ODDS: OVERCOMING SECURITY HURDLES IN NORTH AFRICA

As in many conflict-ridden regions in Africa, the temptation has been to use the military to deal with issues. However, tapping into the wisdom of Ero, the AU should focus on developing an overall "sustainable security" strategy that links hard security to broader peace, development and human security concerns.[27] Ero is right that the "military may win battles but it cannot sustain wider security on its own".[28] Therefore, military solutions should be principally applied where there is a high security issue. Breaking the cycle of violence can be achieved only if policymakers avoid rebuilding the institutions, networks and dynamics responsible for and benefiting from the conflict, and instead focus on the key drivers and enablers of sustainable peace.

The traditional reconstruction approach—applied after the clear ending of a conflict and focused primarily on a clear and stable central government as the key counterpart for implementing a top-down approach to reconstruction—cannot ensure sustainable peace in today's conflict situations. Complementing top-down approaches with local and community-based bottom-up approaches will enhance the likelihood of achieving peace in the long term. While it may lead to a temporary stabilization, it does not address fully or effectively the conflict's dynamics, causes and consequences, which is crucial in building sustainable peace.

North Africa's recent gravitation towards sub-Saharan Africa could pay positive dividends to the African integration agenda (economically and security-wise). It is particularly pertinent as the continent strides towards the goals laid out in the AU Agenda 2063.[29] More specifically, the success of the African Continental Free Trade Area, and the AU reform process, requires the full attention and participation of all AU Member States if it is to bear fruit.

In the domain of security management, the intricacies and complexities of conflict dynamics in different regions of the continent—not least in North Africa and the Sahel—need concerted action by the AU and other regional bodies. But in the absence of a functioning regional organization to act as a lead, and with a concentration of influential countries like Egypt, Algeria and Morocco with big economies making significant contributions to the AU budget, the role of the AU in stabilizing the region will continue to be marginal. Moreover, if tensions between Algeria and Morocco are not progressively resolved, there is a risk that the AU will become another platform where Algeria, Morocco and Egypt play out regional competitions and promote their narrow national security interests vis-à-vis key issues—over security in the Sahel

[27] Comfort Ero, Crisis Group Africa Program Director, to the 975th session of the African Union Peace and Security Council. Speech: Peace, Security and Development: Taking Security Challenges into Account in Development Financing. 27 January 2021.

[28] Ibid.

[29] Agenda 2063. The Africa We Want. Available at https://au.int/sites/default/files/documents/36204-docagenda2063_popular_version_en.pdf.

region and the Saharawi cause, and for Egypt over Libya and the Horn of Africa. It also remains to be seen how Algeria manages its internal political transition, and whether things at home will affect its role in the AU or in North Africa.

There is need to implement robust national action plans to mainstream youth in peace and security processes at the local, subnational and national levels. Further, States need to take concrete measures, including substantial investment in education and employment opportunities to reduce youth vulnerability and susceptibility to activities that threaten peace and security; and use youth-friendly and Information, Communication and Technology (ICT)-based methods to communicate with and disseminate information that promotes the culture of peace and tolerance. As elaborated by Dan Kuwali in Chapter 12, this would also run counter to terrorists methods of recruiting and radicalizing youths which is now being more internet based.[30]

[30] African Development Bank Group, Jobs for Youths in Africa: Catalyzing Youth Opportunity across Africa. Available at https://afdb.org/kr/wp-content/uploads/2018/02/Bottom-3-English.pdf. Accessed 2 March 2021.

CHAPTER 6

Building Peace in East Africa

Godard Busingye

INTRODUCTION

Peace, safety and security are a composite good which cannot be enjoyed if one element is missing. In the case of East Africa, this good is provided for in the Treaty for the Establishment of the Community. Providing for this good in the treaty, however, does not guarantee that it shall be so enjoyed. Certain enablers must be put in place for the peoples of the Community to realise their aspirations. Unfortunately, even with key enablers such as the Protocols and Mechanisms required to operationalise the treaty provisions having been put in place, their operationalization still remains farfetched.

It is noteworthy that the East African Community is a treaty based international organisation established in 1999. Being a product of international law makes it not specifically enforced in the EAC Partner States which follow a dualist approach in the ratification of treaties. This weakness of international law, coupled with the Partner States insistence on strict observance of their sovereign rights, thwarts the whole essence of the treaty regarding ensuring peace, safety and security.

[1] African Union, Main successes of the AU in Peace and Security, challenges and mitigation measures in place, 27 Jan 2017, accessed at: https://reliefweb.int/rep ort/world/main-successes-au-peace-and-security-challenges-and-mitigation-measures-place, on 1 March, 2021.

G. Busingye (✉)
Kampala International University, Kampala, Uganda

© The Author(s), under exclusive license to Springer Nature Switzerland AG 2022
D. Kuwali (ed.), *The Palgrave Handbook of Sustainable Peace and Security in Africa*, https://doi.org/10.1007/978-3-030-82020-6_6

95

The EAC is one of the Regional Economic Communities (RECs) of the African Union (AU). Broadly, the AU works towards attaining peace, safety and security for all the peoples of the continent.[1] The strategic vision of the AU expressed in its Agenda 2963 on silencing guns on the continent acts as a cornerstone for the working systems of all the continental RECs.[2] Building on the momentum set by the AU under Agenda 2063, the EAC Partner States undertook to ensure peace, safety and security within the Community and in its neighbourhood.[3] EAC consists of six Partner States, namely; the Republic of Burundi, Republic of Kenya, Republic of South Sudan, the Republic of Rwanda, the Republic of Uganda and the United Republic of Tanzania. Originally, under the 1967, the EAC consisted of three Partner States, namely the Republic of Kenya, the Republic of Uganda and the United Republic of Tanzania.[4]

The 1967 EAC outfit, however, collapsed in 1977 due to a number of reasons, including, ideological differences between the Partner States.[5] The collapse of the 1967 EAC was a drawback to a foundation for peace, safety and security established by the pre-colonial, and immediate postcolonial African State structures. By way of illustration, in the 1970s, there was no peace, security or safety of persons in Uganda, which was experiencing serious human rights abuses from the dictatorial regime of Idi Amin. The spill over of the dire situation in Uganda adversely affected enjoyment of peace, safety and security of citizens in other EAC Partner States.

The United Republic of Tanzania and the Republic of Kenya, in a sisterly and brotherly manner received many Ugandans who fled their country and hosted some of them for years, until their forceful return home in 1979. In 1978, the United Republic of Tanzania, provided bases and military support to Ugandans in exile, who fought their way back home, and overthrew the

---

[2] Ernest Toochi Aniche, Is African Peace and Security Architecture the Solution? Analysing the Implications of Escalating Conflicts and Security Challenges for African Integration and Development, A Paper Delivered at the 30th Annual Conference of the Nigerian Political Science Association Southeast Chapter on the theme: Elections, Security Challenges and African Development at University of PortHarcourt, Rivers State on June 26–28, 2016.

[3] Treaty for the Establishment of the East African Community, 1999, Article 5 (3) (f).

[4] Walter Rodney, How Europe Underdeveloped Africa, Bogle-L'Ouverture Publications, London and Tanzanian Publishing House, Dar-Es-Salaam, 1973, Transcript from 6th reprint, 1983, http://abahlali.org/files/3295358-walter-rodney.pdf, accessed on 21 November 2019.

[5] Dickson Kanakulya, Governance and Development of the East African Community: The Ethical Sustainability Framework, Linköping University, Department of Culture and Communication, 2015, p. 6, http://liu.diva-portal.org/smash/get/diva2:878457/FUL LTEXT02.pdf, accessed on 18 November 2019.

Idi Amin regime in April, 1979.[6] For the period of the war, Tanzanians lost property, some Tanzanians died at the battlefield and the country's economy was adversely affected.[7]

It can rightly be stated that Uganda exported its political instability to the United Republic of Tanzania, thereby creating an insecure atmosphere in that country. Relative peace returned to Uganda in 1979, but that was short lived. Fighting erupted on 6 February, 1981 between the Government of President Milton Obote who was elected on 10 December, 1980 and Yoweri Museveni, who was part of the Ugandans that overthrew Idi Amin in 1979.[8] The East African region was again plunged into chaos with many Ugandans fleeing to the traditional hosts, Kenya and Tanzania. The situation in Uganda returned to normalcy in 1986 after the Museveni led National Resistance Army/Movement captured political power and established a pro-people centred form of governance. The eventual eruption of armed political dissent in Uganda hardly a year of the National resistance Army/Movement taking over political seat in Uganda, however, destabilised the peace, safety and security not only in Uganda, but also in the whole of the EAC. In a bid to enhance cooperation among EAC Partner States, Uganda, Tanzania and Kenya revived the EAC in the 1999.

The 1999 Treaty created room for expansion of the Community, if the joining members were ready to meet the criteria set for them. There was hope, that in the interest of peace, safety and security within the Community, more countries neighbouring the current EAC Partner States would be admitted to the Community. The expansion of the EAC after the coming into force of the 1999 Treaty, however, created additional problems to the region. Instability in the new Partner States, namely Rwanda, Burundi and South Sudan, has been felt in the other Partner States as if it was generated from within their countries. For example, it cannot be said that Rwanda has fully recovered from the aftermaths of the early 1990s genocide, whose effects were felt in the other Partner States. The Republic of Burundi is still struggling to recover from the long period of political upheavals in the country, while the Republic of South Sudan is still grappling with its internal political issues. Apart from a few pockets of insecurity in some of the EAC Partner States, the region is relatively peaceful.

---

[6] Samuel Sejjaaka, A Political and Economic History of Uganda, 1962–2002, 2004, https://doi.org/10.1057/9780230522503_6, accessed at: https://www.researchgate.net/publication/304737518_A_Political_and_Economic_History_of_Uganda_1962-2002, on 1 March, 2021.

[7] Peter F. B. Nayenga, Review: The Overthrowing of Idi Amin: An Analysis of the War Reviewed Work: War in Uganda: The Legacy of Idi Amin by Tony Avirgan, Martha Honey, Africa Today, Vol. 31, No. 3, Libya: Unpublicized Realities (3rd Qtr., 1984), pp. 69–71 (3 pages), available at: https://www.jstor.org/stable/4186254, accessed on 1 March, 2021.

[8] Museveni, Y. K., Sowing the Mustard Seed: The Struggle for Freedom and Democracy in Uganda (2nd Edition), Moran (E.A) Publishers Limited, 2016, p. 161.

Antecedents to the Peace, Safety and Security Challenges in the EAC

Before the advent of colonial rule, and formation of the formal State structures, people in the EAC Partner States were connected to each other through their social relations, albeit among several nationalities. Traditional African social values, which were familial, and communal in character, cemented values of peace, safety and security for the East Africans. The formation of States during the colonial period, and the latter adoption of the regional outfit for the formed States, however, changed the *status quo*. Currently EAC Partner States operate within the broader spectre of regionalism to promote their aspiration reading peace, safety and security.

This scenario has some noticeable advantages over a situation where States attempt to handle their political, social, economic and even environmental issues individually. There are disadvantages as well. The status of the EAC as a REC of the AU enables it to operate within the framework of the African Peace and Security Architecture (APSA). APSA aims at ensuring peace, safety and security of the African continent. Operationally, however, the primary responsibility to ensure peace, safety and security in the EAC lies with the citizens of the Community and their political leadership. Each Partner State of the Community has its internal legal mechanisms to regulate aspects of peace, safety and security, which are capped in their national Constitutions. Internal legal mechanisms, must, however, conform to the broader concept of the composite peace, safety and security under international law.[9]

Within the ambit of the EAC Treaty, Partner States undertook to plan and direct their policies and resources with a view to creating conditions favourable for the development and achievement of the objectives of the Community.[10] At the same time, EAC Partner States are expected to coordinate, through the institutions of the Community, their economic and other policies to the extent necessary to achieve the objectives of the Community.[11] The EAC members further have a responsibility to abstain from taking any measures likely to jeopardise the achievement of those objectives or the implementation of the provisions of this Treaty.[12] The relationship between the Partner States, however, remains delicate and precarious because any suspicions by one Partner State that any others are working against its downfall can bring the Community to a total collapse.[13]

---

[9] See for example, The Constitutive Act of the African Union, 2000, Article 3 (f); The Charter of the United Nations, 1945, Article 1, and Article 39.

[10] The Treaty for the Establishment of the East African Community, 1999, Article 8 (a).

[11] The Treaty for the Establishment of the East African Community, 1999, Article 8 (b).

[12] The Treaty for the Establishment of the East African Community, 1999, Article 8 (c).

[13] Paul Nantulya, Escalating Tensions between Uganda and Rwanda Raise Fear of War, Africa Centre for Strategic Studies, July 3, 2019, accessed at: https://africacenter.org/spotlight/escalating-tensions-between-uganda-and-rwanda-raise-fear-of-war/, on 25 February, 2021.

Admitting new members to the Community, namely the Republic of Burundi, the Republic of Rwanda and South Sudan should not be wholly praised as a measure to consolidate peace, safety and security in the Community. Each of those countries joined the EAC but remained constrained by the desire to fulfil her overarching national interests, which may not wholly be in line with those of the broader EAC outfit. Worse still, the mechanisms through which EAC Partner States sought to attain a peaceful safe and secure environment have not been fully operationalized. These include, an East African Customs Union and a Common Market and integral parts thereof, and subsequently a Monetary Union and ultimately a Political Federation.[14]

As a measure for the assured peace, safety and security in the EAC, Partner States envisaged that there would be free movement of labour, goods, services, capital and the right of establishment.[15] This aspiration, however, has not been fully realised. Suspicions and intrigue between some EAC Partner States exist and this is a precursor to the eventual failure of the EAC to achieve its set objectives under the 1999 Treaty.

THE YEARNED FOR END STATE

Hope for a peaceful, safe and secure East Africa remains high on the agenda of the peoples and leaders of the East African region. Attainment of this end state, however, remains constrained by a number of factors, which broadly include political and state fragility, resource scarcities and environmental degradation.[16] Specific constraints emanate from colonial history, porous borders, proliferation of criminality into the region, intra-community conflicts, conflicts from the neighbouring environs and globalisation. Each of these factors is discussed in a fair detail below. Colonial border demarcation did not take into account the historical and traditional ties that united the people of the East African region. Ethnicities and their social, economic and political values were divided by the political State boundaries.[17] Economic activities such as cattle rearing, which shared similar resources namely, water and pastures were forcefully separated into different countries. Political ties were severed by the same factor of colonial border marking. For example, the tribes on the Western border of Kenya are the same as those on the Eastern border of Uganda with Kenya. They share similar dialects, and other cultural values, but are unable

[14] The Treaty for the Establishment of the East African Community, 1999, Preamble, paragraph 14 and Article 2 (2).

[15] The Treaty for the Establishment of the East African Community, 1999, Article 76 (1).

[16] Gilbert M. Khadiagala, Eastern Africa: Security and the Legacy of Fragility, Africa Program Working Paper Series, 2008, p. 1.

[17] Sadia Hassanen, Return, Resettlement or Reintegration in the Aftermath of Conflict, in Clara Fischer and Ruth Vollmer (eds.), brief 39 Migration and Displacement in Sub-Saharan Africa The Security-Migration Nexus II, Bonn International Center for Conversion, 2009, p. 48.

to freely socialise due to the politics created for them by the former colonial masters. Similar patterns appear at other borders of the other Partner States. Problems created by colonial history are exacerbated by strict adherence to the traditional concept of state sovereignty.

Due to constraints reminiscent in the concept of state sovereignty, EAC Partner States still hold on to their sovereign rights and including boundaries. Crossing such boundaries by citizens of other EAC Partner States is not always welcome. In some cases, such as that between Rwanda and Uganda, a diplomatic feud stopped most cross-border movements between the two countries. That situation has had a huge effect on daily life for families in both countries.[18] Such a scenario is undesirable, it instils fear and a growing sense of insecurity between the citizens of the two neighbouring countries, belonging to the EAC. Moreover, such a scenario is detrimental to the economic welfare of EAC and the continental vision of economic integration.[19]

There is also a stalemate in the East African Community created by some Partner States rejecting agricultural produce from sister Partner States. This move is criticised as being contrary to the letter and spirit of the EAC Treaty and Protocols made under it, which aim at widening and deepening cooperation among Partner States.[20] It creates a sense of economic insecurity among citizens of the EAC, who have historically traded together, but who must now see themselves as enemies of each other. This scenario demonstrates how difficult it is for the leaders of the EAC to commit themselves to ensure peace, safety and security within the Community. The discussed challenges, however, do not stand alone. There is another problem which thwarts enjoyment of peace, safety and security in the EAC, the issue of porous borders.

The EAC Partner States are unable to ensure maximum security all round their political boundaries, both within the Community region and with the neighbouring countries. The expanse of porous borders both within the EAC and its regional neighbours facilitate criminal elements to infiltrate and

---

[18] Catherine Byaruhanga, How the Rwanda-Uganda border crossing came to a halt, BBC Africa, Cyanika border post, Uganda, Published 9 March 2019, accessed at: https://www.bbc.com/news/world-africa-47495476, on 7 March, 2021.

[19] Samson S. Wasara, Conflict and State Security in the Horn of Africa: Militarization of Civilian Groups, The African Journal of Political Science and International Relations (2002), Vol. 7 No. 2, p. 40; see also Sekou Toure Otondi, The Uganda and Rwanda Conflict Is Shameful and Shows the East African Community Must Be Reformed, The African Exponent, March 20th, 2019, accessed at: https://www.africanexponent.com/bpost/5134-uganda-and-rwanda-conflict-its-high-time-to-reform-the-eac, on 2 March, 2021; Dick Mugahe, The Root Cause of the Tension and Conflict Between Uganda and Rwanda: A Deeper Analysis, The New Times, 20 May, 2019, accessed at: https://www.newtimes.co.rw/news/root-cause-tension-and-conflict-between-uganda-and-rwanda-deeper-analysis, on 2 March, 2021.

[20] Treaty for the Establishment of the East African Community, 1999, Article 5 (1); see also Mulengera News reporters, Lawyer Fred Muwema Makes the Necessary Noise: Who Will Eat Maize Kenyans Have Rejected? Accessed at: https://mulengeranews.com/lawyer-fred-muwema-makes-the-necessary-noise-who-will-eat-maize-kenyans-have-rejected/, on 10 March, 2021.

proliferate arms into Partner States. In regard to porous borders, which are associated with vast ungoverned turbulent neighbourhoods, Khadiagala observes that 'Africa contains vast territorial regions in which the reach and authority of States has not been adequately secured. In these regions, governments compete for resources, legitimacy, and loyalty with groups and movements that have diverse grievances and contest violently among one another'.[21] While within the Partner States, criminal elements, including terrorists, cause mayhem and generally destabilise the peace of the EAC citizens. Widespread criminality, sometime with a political mind-set is not always easy to detect and deal with decisively by State security agencies of the EAC. For example, until 2015, the Allied Democratic Alliance (ADF) rebel leader, Jamil Mukuru had been able to move in and out of Uganda to recruit, abduct and commit atrocities against innocent Ugandans without being arrested.

It could be said that there were gaps in the security circles in Uganda and other EAC Partner States, and that is why he could not be arrested. He was, however, later arrested in a neighbouring country.[22] Earlier on in 1998, ADF rebels had crossed into Uganda from the Democratic Republic of Congo (DRC) through the country's porous western border and killed, abducted students and torched school property at Kicwamba Technical Institute.[23] In July, 2010, Al Shabaab terrorists infiltrated Uganda and carried out two deadly bomb attacks in Kampala City.[24] The same terrorist group has on several occasions infiltrated Kenya and committed crimes therein.[25] The threat posed by terrorists groups in the EAC, and the actual manifestations of their acts, after crossing into the region through porous borders, makes it difficult

---

[21] Gilbert M. Khadiagala, Silencing the Guns: Strengthening Governance to Prevent, Manage, and Resolve Conflicts in Africa, New York: International Peace Institute, May 2015, p. 18; see also Sewanyana, L., The Use of Traditional Communications in Conflict Management: The Case of Uganda, Michigan State University Library, available at: http://digital.lib.msu.edu/projects/africanjournals/, accessed on 20 December, 2019.

[22] Zurah Nakabugo, ADF leader Jamil Mukulu 'Arrested', The Observer Newspaper, April 24, 2015, accessed at: https://observer.ug/news-headlines/37497-adf-leader-jamil-mukulu-arrested, on 7 March, 2021.

[23] Human Rights Watch (HRW), HRW Condemns Deadly Attack by Ugandan Rebels on School Children, 1998, accessed at: https://www.hrw.org/news/1998/06/10/hrw-condemns-deadly-attack-ugandan-rebels-school-children, on 1 March, 2021.

[24] Chris Harnisch, Al Shabaab's First International Strike: Analysis of the July 11 Uganda Bombings, Critical Threats, July 14, 2010, accessed at: https://www.criticalthreats.org/analysis/al-shabaabs-first-international-strike-analysis-of-the-july-11-uganda-bombings, on 2 March, 2021.

[25] Thomas Mukoya (Reuters Reporter), Al-Shabab Claims Lethal Attack on Hotel Complex in Nairobi, Kenya, The World, January 15, 2019 · 11:30 AM EST, accessed at: https://www.pri.org/stories/2019-01-15/al-shabab-claims-lethal-attack-hotel-complex-nairobi-kenya, on 2 March, 2021, see also Loulla-Mae Eleftheriou-Smith, Kenya Garissa University Attack: Al-Shabaab Gunman Abdirahim Abdullahi Identified as Son of Kenyan Government Official, The Independent Newspaper online, Wednesday 23 September 2015, accessed at: https://www.independent.co.uk/news/world/africa/kenya-garissa-university-attack-al-shabab-gunman-abdirahim-abdullahi-identified-son-kenyan-government-official-10156726.html, on 7 March, 2021.

102   G. BUSINGYE

for East Africans to enjoy the yearned for peace, security and safety in their homes.

The long-standing problem of proliferation of arms into the region from neighbouring countries increases fear and lack of enjoyment of peace, security and generally makes East Africans unsafe in their home countries. Some of the neighbouring countries to the EAC region have had long term insecurity problems which require arms and ammunitions to sustain. As revealed by Gilbert Mittawa in Chapter 22, some of the insurgents' trade in arms with criminal elements in the EAC Partner States. The demand for arms and ammunitions by individuals in the EAC is catapulted by the failure of governments to provide adequate security to the vulnerable pastoral communities such as the Karimojongs in the North Eastern Uganda, the Dinka in South Sudan and the Turkana in North Western Kenya. These pastoral communities have historically engaged in conflicts associated with cattle raids.[26] These are pastoral communities, whose livelihoods have historically been threatened by animal thieves, who in many cases are armed. In the case of the Karimojongs, limited amounts of small arms continue to be smuggled into the sub region through the various porous borders with South Sudan and Kenya causing insecurity in the sub region.[27]

These pastoral communities purportedly require arms to guard their livestock from thieves. They, however, in a number of cases use them to commit crimes. Acquisition of these arms is costly both in terms of money required to purchase them and human beings, who are maimed or killed when these communities engage in fighting either with government forces or other pastoral communities. Wairagu observes that 'the acquisition of arms and ammunition for self-preservation impoverishes the affected communities. That reverses any advances made towards attainment of peace security and safety'.[28] On their part, Ndawana et al. consider the problem of proliferation of SALW a global problem.[29] SALW in the hands of illegal non-states actors, especially within the EAC subverts most of the initiatives put in place to ensure peace, safety and security in the bloc.

Impoverishment of the affected communities is multifaceted, it costs money to purchase arms and ammunitions for individuals' self-preservation, yet that responsibility lies on the East African governments, and weapons purchased are

---

[26] Gilbert M. Khadiagala, Eastern Africa: Security and the Legacy of Fragility, Africa Program Working Paper Series, 2008, pp. 8–9.

[27] Government of the Republic of Uganda, Office of The Prime Minister, Ministry for Karamoja Affairs, Karamoja Integrated Development Plan 2 (KIDP 2) p. 4.

[28] Francis K. Wairagu, Small Arms and Conflicts in the Great Lakes Region, in Nyambura Githaiga, Regional dimensions of Conflict in the Great Lakes, ISS Workshop Report, Nairobi, 12–13 September 2011, pp. 5–7.

[29] Ndawana, W. M., HOVE Sylvester D. GHULIKU, Tanzania: Small Arms Proliferation in East Africa and National Security, Conflict Studies Quarterly Issue 23, April 2018, pp. 48–77, at p. 49, available online at: https://doi.org/10.24193/csq.23.3, accessed on 17 November, 2019.

used in criminal activities to terrorise innocent citizens. That further erodes the hope for a peaceful environment in the region. The total outcome of all this is a reality that the affected communities continue sinking into abject poverty. Living in abject poverty is by itself not peaceful, nor is it secure or safe for anyone. Unfortunately, the EAC Partner States lack resources to create a safe environment and to monitor all peace, safety and security related activities such as proliferation of SALW and infiltration of rebel and terrorist groups along their borders.[30] Unabated proliferation of SALW in the EAC region raises doubts as to whether or not East Africans are about to enjoy lasting peace, safety and security in their countries.

Apart from the conflicts between pastoral communities, there are other pockets of instability in the EAC Partner States caused by inter-tribal rivalries over land and control of other resources. For example, the Bakonzo have frequently been attacking their neighbours, the Basongora and other tribes in the South Western town of Kasese, in Uganda. In a recent incident, the clashes started when a group of Bakonzo armed with spears and *pangas* attacked the Basongora pastoralists who were grazing cattle, blowing up a conflict that has been brewing for years. Nine people died in the attack and seven cows were looted.[31] This and other similar examples in the EAC, including the post-election violence in Kenya, in 2007–8,[32] what is currently happening in South Sudan[33] and the Republic of Burundi[34] paint a negative picture in terms of peace, safety and security in the EAC.

Peace, safety and security in the East African Partner States are also directly and indirectly affect by armed conflicts in neighbouring countries. Some East African States, namely Uganda and Rwanda, had to effectively deploy their armed forces in the DRC in a bid to arrest the situation out of home. Uganda and Rwanda, however, ended up being peace, security and safety disruption

---

[30] Dulo Nyaoro,Society for International Development (SID), EAC Integration and Cross Border Migration: Key Issues for the Regional Agenda, accessed at: https://www.sid int.net/content/ea-integration-and-cross-border-migration-key-issues-regional-agenda, on 2 December, 2019.

[31] Basaija Idd, Nine Injured in Fresh Bakonzo, Basongora Clashes in Kasese, Uganda Radio Network online, 10 Aug 2020 04:59, accessed at: https://ugandaradionetwork. net/story/five-injured-in-fresh-bakonzo-basongora-clashes-in-kasese-, on 2 March, 2021.

[32] Dickson Nkonge Kagema, The Aftermath of the 2007/08 Post-Election Violence in Kenya and the Role of Religion, January 2019, https://doi.org/10.15640/ijpt.v7n1a9, accessed at: https://www.researchgate.net/publication/339598592_The_Aftermath_of_ the_200708_Post-Election_Violence_in_Kenya_and_the_Role_of_Religion, on 6 March, 2021.

[33] PaanLuel Wël, The Importance of Peace and Political Stability in South Sudan (Part 8), accessed at: https://paanluelwel.com/2018/03/22/the-importance-of-peace-and-pol itical-stability-in-south-sudan-part-8/, on 6 March, 2021.

[34] Foreign & Commonwealth Office (UK), Burundi continues to constitute a threat to international peace and security, Statement by David Clay, UK Political Coordinator at the UN, at the Security Council briefing on the situation in Burundi, 31 October 2019, accessed at: https://www.gov.uk/government/speeches/burundi-continues-to-constitute-a-threat-to-international-peace-and-security, on 8 March, 2021.

104   G. BUSINGYE

agents in the DRC, when some of their elements engaged in criminal acts. The Government of the DRC, which had invited them, then attempted to forcefully send them away.[35] In the case of Somali, the Republic of Burundi, the Republic of Kenya and the Republic of Uganda deployed their forces in Mogadishu to fight Al Shabab, much as their home countries still face dire challenges regarding peace, safety and security. In the case of Uganda and Kenya, their participation in the fight against the Al Shabab forces in Mogadishu has not only taken a toll on their deployed forces, some of who die at the frontline, but has also been viewed as increasing chances of being targeted by the Al Shabab in their home countries.[36]

The mass movements of irregular migrants, refugees, internally displaced persons (IDPs) within and into the EAC Partner States might be seen as extending a gesture of hope for such categories of persons under international law. Irregular migrants, however, cause political, social and economic stress in the host communities. In some cases, they become a source of actual insecurity in the host communities.[37] The outfit of the East African Community envisages a seamless and borderless Community where citizens belong to the EAC, not Partner States.[38] The recent introduction of an East African Passport aims at achieving this objective. Displaced persons within the Community are, therefore, expected to move freely within the Community, much as there are still hurdles to this programme.

This, however, does not happen and citizens of particular EAC Partner States can only be IDPs in their own countries. Once they cross the colonial boundaries, they are treated as if they are not citizens of the EAC, a fact that further erodes confidence built between their Governments over time. That is the case, because, Partner States have not yet fully embraced

[35] UN Report on The Illegal Exploitation of the DRC, October 2002; see also, the Case of Democratic Republic of the Congo V. Uganda, The International Court of Justice, No. 116 (2005), paras 29–30.

[36] Thomas Mukoya (Reuters Reporter), Al-Shabab claims lethal Attack on Hotel Complex in Nairobi, Kenya, The World, January 15, 2019 · 11:30 AM EST, accessed at: https://www.pri.org/stories/2019-01-15/al-shabab-claims-lethal-attack-hotel-complex-nairobi-kenya, on 2 March, 2021; see also Loulla-Mae Eleftheriou-Smith, Kenya Garissa University Attack: Al-Shabaab Gunman Abdirahim Abdullahi Identified as Son of Kenyan Government Official, The Independent Newspaper online, Wednesday 23 September 2015, accessed at: https://www.independent.co.uk/news/world/africa/kenya-garissa-uni versity-attack-al-shabab-gunman-abdirahim-abdullahi-identified-son-kenyan-government-official-10156726.html, on 7 March, 2021.

[37] Siân Herbert & Iffat Idris, Refugees in Uganda: (in)stability, Conflict, and Resilience, Rapid Literature Review, Birmingham, UK: GSDRC, University of Birmingham, April 2018; see also Khoti Kamanga, Forced Displacement and Conflict in the Great Lakes Region, in Nyambura Githaiga, Regional Dimensions of Conflict in the Great Lakes, ISS Workshop Report, Nairobi, 12–13 September 2011, pp. 20–27, and Kelly Abale, Armed S.Sudanese Arrested in Uganda, Eye Radio, accessed at: https://eyeradio.org/armed-s-sud anese-arrested-in-uganda/, on 7 March, 2012.

[38] The Protocol on the Establishment of the East African Community Common Market, 2009, Articles 6 and 7.

the ideals of a political federation and as such remain royal to their sovereign rights at the expense of the EAC political federation. Other irregular migrants from near and far, have historically been accommodated in the EAC. These, too, add to the stress on the existing peace, safety and security in the EAC. They can, however, not be sent back to countries where they ran from under international law.[39]

It is important to note that in a globalised world, ensuring peace, safety and security is no longer a preserve of a single country or a group of a few of them, such as the EAC. A global world is a single entity, and lack of peace, safety or security in any other part of the world has a direct impact on countries far away from the epicentre of the instability. Political, economic or social instability in the EAC may owe much of its cause to internal factors, however the interplay between internal and external factors in a geo-political world must be appreciated regarding what happens in the EAC. Indeed, geo-political and economic interests of the international community play a significant role in societal development in the EAC.[40]

For example, the rapid spread of the novel coronavirus SARS-CoV2 (COVID-19), from Wuhan, China in late 2019, where it was first reported to the rest of the world, shows how vulnerable countries in the EAC are to the global effects of such a disease. Indeed, East Africans must have had their unique challenges, but effects of COVID-19, further deteriorated the already uncomfortable situation on terms of peace, safety and security in the EAC Partner States. The rapid spread of this disease was facilitated by the quick means of air transport that connects the world in a few hours. On the other part, when there are instabilities in far way parts of the world, which generate the irregular movement of persons from those areas, a refugees' crisis may be experienced in any part of the world. The East African region is indeed a home of refugees from such distant areas.[41]

Much as the foregoing discussion seems to paint a gloomy picture to globalisation, there are peace dividends that can only be realised in a globalised world, especially where States belong to a multitude of international organisations at the same time.[42] Rwengabo observes that security cooperation in the EAC portrays interlocked institutional features. Some features apply only

[39] The Refugee Convention, 1951, Article 33.

[40] Antony Otieno Ong'ayo, Political instability in Africa: Where the problem lies and alternative perspectives, the African Diaspora Policy Centre, Amsterdam, Presented at the Symposium 2008: "Afrika: een continent op drift" Organised by Stichting Nationaal Erfgoed Hotel De Wereld Wageningen, 19th of September, 2008, accessed at: https://www.diaspora-centre.org/DOCS/Political_Instabil.pdf, on 8 March, 2021.

[41] Esther Chelule, Journal of International Academic Research For Multidisciplinary: Impact Factor 1.393, ISSN: 2320–5083, Vol. 2, No. 3 (April 2014).

[42] Irit Back, IGAD1 and South Sudan: Success and Failure in Mediation, Telaviv Notes, Telavivi University, Vol. 8, No. 23 (December 25, 2014); and James Karuhanga, EALA South Sudan Members Want EAC role in IGAD-led Talks, The New Times Newspaper, Rwanda's Leading Daily, April 24, 2018, accessed at: https://www.newtimes.co.rw/news/eala-south-sudan-members-want-eac-role-igad-led-talks, on 10 March, 2021.

to the EAC; others encompass non-East African Community (EAC) States under the Eastern Africa Standby Force (EASF), the International Conference for the Great Lakes Region (ICGLR), with Inter-Governmental Authority on Development (IGAD) and the Southern African Development Cooperation (SADC).[43]

The outcome of the combined effort by these international organisations has been increased safety and security, reduction of conflict and risk factors of conflict and increased capacity of positive peace for the EAC.[44] For example, peace negotiations that have brought relative peace, safety and security in South Sudan were brokered under the auspices of two international organisations, the Intergovernmental Authority on Development (IGAD) and the EAC. South Sudan is a member of the EAC as well as IGAD. It remains a possibility that if such were handled by one international organisation, South Sudan would not have accepted the terms set for it due to one reason or the other.

Conclusion

The logical conclusion drawn from the foregoing discussion is that there can be no peace within the East African Community if there is no peace in any part of the world. It also follows that ensuring peace, safety and security in the EAC must be done in line within a broader framework under the auspices of the Afrin Union, and its other RECs and the United Nations. EAC's colonial and post-colonial history, and its current politically turbulent neighbourhood decrease the chances of citizens of the EAC to enjoy durable peace, safety and security. Proliferation of SALW into the EAC weakens the efforts undertaken to ensure peace, safety and security within the EAC.

The most outstanding factors include, the polarised geo-politics within the ambit of globalisation, taking sovereign interests by Partner States to be superior to those of the Community, instability within particular EAC Partner States, instability within the immediate neighbourhood of the EAC, coupled with the fact of porous borders, which are difficult to closely monitor and supervise and prevent infiltration and proliferation of insecurity into the Community. It is also a problem for the EAC Partner States to ensure peace, safety and security in the region due to internal governance issues within particular EAC Partner States. Attention by EAC Partner States to the spill overs of terrorist activities from their hubs in the EAC neighbouring disrupt the established mechanisms for peace, safety and security in the Community.

---

[43] Rwengabo, S., Institutional Design and the Implementation of the African Peace Security Architecture in Eastern Africa, Africa Development / *Afrique et Développement*. Vol. 41, No. 4 (2016), pp. 107–138, CODESRIA, available at: https://www.jstor.org/stable/90013891.

[44] Solomon Dersso, East Africa and the Intergovernmental Authority on Development: Mapping Multilateralism In Transition No. 4, International peace Institute, October 2014.

It is, therefore, recommended that Partner States should enhance their cooperation in the peace and security sector with a view to attaining political federation in the near future. EAC Partner States should equally enhance collaboration with international organisations charged with the responsibility of maintaining international peace, safety and security. They should also adhere to and remain committed to observe their obligations to ensure peace, safety and security in accordance with principles of international law.

CHAPTER 7

Securing Lasting Peace in West Africa

Bright Nkrumah

INTRODUCTION

Since the unwilling departure of colonial masters from the shores of Africa, the continent has witnessed a proliferation of Regional Economic Communities (RECs). The emergence of most bodies may be tied to one or more of the following reasons: (i) capturing dormant political space created since the departure of colonial powers; (ii) battle insurgent movements in post-Cold War (iii) managing inflow of refugees due to electoral and ethnic conflicts; (iv) provide support for fragile states against invasion by external powers; and (v) establish hegemony as the primary power for safeguarding civilians in the sub-region (Tavares and Tang 2011; Nkrumah and Busingye 2017). One REC whose orientation meets these benchmarks is the Economic Community of West African States (ECOWAS).[1] Since its launch in 1975, the organisation has asserted its position as an important interventionist body by managing inter-and-intra-state conflicts in the region.

[1] The organisation has 15 member states: Benin, Burkina Faso, Cape Verde, Côte d'Ivoire, The Gambia, Ghana, Guinea, Guinea-Bissau, Liberia, Mali, Niger, Nigeria, Senegal, Sierra Leone, and Togo.

B. Nkrumah (✉)
University of the Free State, Bloemfontein, South Africa

© The Author(s), under exclusive license to Springer Nature Switzerland AG 2022
D. Kuwali (ed.), *The Palgrave Handbook of Sustainable Peace and Security in Africa*, https://doi.org/10.1007/978-3-030-82020-6_7

109

West Africa, historically, has been a land of bloody civil wars and insurgencies.[2] From the late 1950s when the first country in the sub-region, Ghana gained independence, West Africa has been immersed in the protracted military overthrow of governments with dire ramifications for civilians.[3] These acts of aggression climaxed in the 1990s and 2000s when Liberia, Sierra Leone, Guinea-Bissau and Mali were engulfed in a series of coup d'état and resultant instabilities.[4] In each of these cases, ECOWAS successfully intervened, using military repression to contain the hostilities. The golden thread which runs through all these interventions was the collective support from member states in terms of logistics and troops contributions.

Yet, in contemporary times, the sub-region faces a new form of security threat, the rise of extremist groups and the proliferation of small arms. The most notorious of these groups has been Boko Haram. The rub, however, is that in contrast to popular opinion, Boko Haram is not the only extremist group undermining peace and security in the sub-region. The uprising of militant groups such as *Al-Qaeda in the Islamic Maghreb* (AQIM), Islamic State (ISIS), and *Ansar al-Shari*a and *Al-Murabitum* seeking to operationalise Sharia law in Niger, Mali, Chad and Cameroon provides some indication of ECOWAS's ineffective security machinery in safeguarding populations from radical organisations.[5] The battle for control of these insurgents makes humanitarian crises one of the biggest challenges confronting the sub-region.

Thus, despite ECOWAS's early successes in containing hostilities in the sub-region, the REC has rarely channelled this collective commitment towards addressing ongoing insurgencies against civilians. In seeking to understand this irony, the chapter will be divided into four parts, excluding the present introduction. The next section traces the evolution of ECOWAS security architecture, what factors necessitated its shift from mainly economic community to a somewhat security organisation. The third section considers the current state of extremism, the potential impact of their operations, and what measures individual member states (IMS) have taken to contain insurgents. The fourth section interrogates *why* ECOWAS has not demonstrated sufficient commitment towards tackling extremism around the Lake Chad Basin (LCB). The fifth section provides recommendations on how to mobilise political will from unaffected IMS, the African Union and the international community in managing violent attacks in the sub-region. This section is an attempt to

---

[2] The nouns, extremist (groups) and insurgents will be used interchangeably as they seek to achieve a common objective: the use of force to destabilise the country and instil fear in civilians.

[3] Ghana gained independence in 1957.

[4] B Nkrumah & L Viljoen (2014) 'Lessons from ECOWAS for the Implementation of Article 4(h).' In Kuwali, D & Viljoen, F (eds.), *Africa and the Responsibility to Protect: Article 4(h)*, pp. 251–264, Routledge: United Kingdom.

[5] MN Mutasa & C Muchemwa (2021) 'Ansar Al-Sunna Mozambique: Is It the Boko Haram of Southern Africa?' *Journal of Applied Security Research*, https://doi.org/10.1080/19361610.2021.1882281.

critically assess the possible role and prospects of ECOWAS security architecture in forestalling humanitarian crises, and making the sub-region a better place for civilians, particularly women and children. The last section serves as a conclusion.

Historical Evolution of ECOWAS Security Architecture

The Economic Community of West African States (ECOWAS) was established on 28 May 1975 as a regional economic community (REC) to foster economic development and trade among member states.[6] Nonetheless, following the end of the cold war, the sub-region witnessed an upsurge of ethnic violence, coup d'états, and bloody civil wars which threatened human and state security in the sub-region (Nkrumah and Viljoen 2014). The new development somewhat altered the focus of the organisation, by incorporating security roles into its primary obligation.

Like elsewhere, since the state's sovereignty is jealously guarded in the region, the REC adopted two overarching security instruments: the 1978 Non-Aggression Treaty, and 1981 *Protocol Relating to Mutual Assistance of Defence.*[7] The cardinal objective of these instruments was to pave the way for sub-regional intervention in a situation where an internal crisis might have a spill-over effect and destabilise the sub-region. In specific reference to humanitarian interventions, article 4 of the 1981 Protocol obliges the REC to intervene in any internal hostilities within ECOWAS states, when such violence tends to spread to other jurisdictions in the sub-region.

After amending its founding Treaty in 1993, ECOWAS evolved into a full-scale security organisation. This assertion hinges on the adoption of other normative frameworks which aim to address different facets of security issues in the sub-region. As their names reflect, the instruments include the 1998 *Declaration of a Moratorium on Light Weapons in West Africa*; 1999 *Protocol Relating to the Mechanism for Conflict Prevention, Management, Resolution, Peacekeeping and Security* (1999 *Mechanism*); and the 2001 *Protocol on Democracy and Good Governance.*[8] These instruments have guided the region's peace support operations (PSOs) from the early 2000s onwards.

In re-echoing the mandate of ECOWAS under the 1981 Protocol, the 1999 Mechanism authorises REC to conduct humanitarian interventions to save the lives of civilians. The content of the instrument seems to underscore the common principle that instability in one country, is instability in the entire

[6] Nkrumah and Viljoen, footnote 4 above.

[7] ECOWAS (1981) 'Protocol Relating to Mutual Assistance on Defence' Document A/SP3/5/81.

[8] M Juma (2006) 'Compendium of Key Documents Relating to Peace and Security in Africa' Pretoria University Law Press: Pretoria.

sub-region.[9] This notion holds as countries with common borders tend to be affected by the political crisis in neighbouring countries, particularly in terms of refugee inflows. This projection seems to have informed article 40 of the Mechanism which imposed an obligation on ECOWAS to 'intervene to alleviate the suffering of the populations and restore life to normalcy in the event of crises, conflict, and disaster'. To ensure the operationalisation of this provision, REC established the Mediation and Security Council (MSC) to oversee negotiations and security engagement.[10]

The litmus test of the 1999 Mechanism occurred in post-election crisis Côte d'Ivoire. In September 2002, dissidents comprising ex-military personnel, calling themselves Patriotic Movement of Côte d'Ivoire (MPCI) instructed President Laurent Gbagbo to resign.[11] This insurrection gained much publicity in the region and beyond, as Gbagbo accused two ECOWAS states, Liberia and Burkina Faso of covertly supporting the rebel group.[12] Following immediate, yet unsuccessful intervention by France in the same month, then Chairman ECOWAS, Senegalese President Abdoulaye Wade deployed a mediation mission to attempt a peace accord between the two factions.

To prove the neutrality of the mission, diplomats from Liberia and Burkina Faso were excluded. Yet, the mission failed to achieve its intended aspiration when the president failed to enter into a truce with the rivals. In his capacity as head of the mediation mission, Togolese President, Gnassingbe Eyademan recommended the deployment of troops to contain the mutiny. With further authorisation by the African Union (AU) and United Nations (UN), the ECOWAS MSC deployed multinational troops to Côte d'Ivoire in April 2003.[13] The composition of troops from Benin, Ghana, Gambia, Guinea-Bissau, Mali, Niger, Nigeria and Togo, was an illustration of the collective willingness of ECOWAS states to commit resources to contain hostilities within their region.

Ultimately, the brigade assisted in the disarmament and demobilisation of the forces, leading to the establishment of a new government of national reconciliation under the Linas-Marcoussis Agreement.[14] The collective deployment of troops may have been informed by two reasons: (i) in the spirit of neighbourliness and safeguarding the other from degrading into a

[9] EK Aning (2004) 'Investing in Peace and Security in Africa: The Case of ECOWAS' *Conflict, Security & Development*, 4(3), 533–542.

[10] E de Wet (2014) 'The Evolving Role of ECOWAS and the SADC in Peace Operations: A Challenge to the Primacy of the United Nations Security Council in Matters of Peace and Security' *Leiden Journal of International Law*, 27(2), 353–370.

[11] Nkrumah & Viljoen (footnote 5 above).

[12] B Charbonneau (2012) 'War and Peace in Côte d'Ivoire: Violence, Agency, and the Local/International Line' *International Peacekeeping*, 19(4), 508–524.

[13] AJ Bellamy & PD Williams (2011) 'The New Politics of Protection? Côte d'Ivoire, Libya and the Responsibility to Protect' *International Affairs*, 87(4), 825–850.

[14] P Richards (2011) 'A Systematic Approach to Cultural Explanations of War: Tracing Causal Processes in Two West African Insurgencies' *World Development*, 39(2), 212–220.

fragile state; and (ii) shared consciousness that non-assistance will result in an influx of refugees, causing competition over scarce resources. Despite these noble intentions, a detractor could counter that the display of unity was a quest for equality in regional affairs, irrespective of the human and logistical burden they each had to borne. In other words, the shared ownership was an attempt to limit the hegemony of one state, Nigeria, in the sub-regional polity.

Such an assertion may be underpinned by Nigeria's earlier unilateral interventions in Liberia and Sierra Leone which was largely criticised by individual ECOWAS states as arbitrary (Berger 2001). Regardless of these contentions, the REC in 2005 converged with its development partners in Ghana to deliberate on the establishment of an ECOWAS Standby Force (ESF) to timeously respond to atrocities in the sub-region.[15] The draft report of the workshop, convened by the Kofi Annan International Peacekeeping Training Centre (*KAIPTC*), observed that an ESF could complement the efforts of local military and police forces in containing insurgencies.[16] The document eventually resulted in the establishment of an ESF in 2009.[17]

The ESF draws its mandate from article 21 of the 1999 Mechanism which obliged the REC to compose a multi-purpose standby force for immediate deployment in times of crises. This provision implicitly speaks to article 1 of the UN Charter which mandates states to take 'effective collective measures for the prevention and removal of threats to the peace'. Thus, as its name reflects, the standby force is a backup or special troop made up of civilians, police and military officers for immediate deployment for PSOs. Composed of more than 2000 military personnel with different ranks, the troops are partitioned into two infantry battalions, with Nigeria leading the Eastern Battalion and Senegal commanding the Western Battalion.[18]

To a great extent, the launch of the ESF was a landmark as it gave an impetus to the REC's security outlook on two fronts: (i) re-assert its hegemony in regional peacekeeping; (ii) rapidly deploy troops for PSOs. Yet, sporadic deployment of the ESF is not cast in stone as the REC first needs to seek authorisation from the target state, and then the backing of the Authority of Heads of State and Government (the ECOWAS Authority). In this regard, collaboration with the target state is very important as the opposite could

---

[15] The P3 partners are composed of ECOWAS Mission Planning Management Cell; Standby High Readiness Brigade for UN Operations; and partners from the African Union, Netherlands, Germany, France, Denmark, Canada, UK, USA, and the European Union.

[16] M Malan (2006) 'Developing the ECOWAS Civilian Peace Support Operations Structure: Report of an Expert's Workshop' Retrieved from https://reliefweb.int/sites/reliefweb.int/files/resources/01A573BF5E777E34C12572D0004502F5-kapitc-peacekeeping-feb06.pdf.. (Accessed 28 February 2021).

[17] BT Afolabi (2009) 'Peacemaking in the Ecowas Region: Challenges and Prospects' *Conflict Trends, 2009*(2), 24–30.

[18] CI Obi (2009) 'Economic Community of West African States on the Ground: Comparing Peacekeeping in Liberia, Sierra Leone, Guinea Bissau, and Côte D'Ivoire' *African Security*, 2(2–3), 119–135.

be construed as an intrusion or a breach of the sanctity of sovereignty, an act which the 1981 Protocol (see Preamble) strongly condemns. Having said that, ECOWAS in line with the notion of responsibilities to protect may deploy the ESF into a member state, if it is convinced that such a state is unable or unwilling to protect its.[19]

Needless to say that ECOWAS remains a subsidiary of its mother body, the AU. In 2015, the continental body adopted its Agenda 2063, as a shared strategic framework for sustainable development. Yet, since socio-economic transformation cannot be attained in an unstable environment, the framework admonishes African states and REC to promote a culture of tolerance and end all violence. Yet, like other RECs, this aspiration has remained a pipedream for millions of West Africans as insurgency continues to destabilise the sub-region. An insurgency may be depicted as a state of armed conflict incited by a select group of people, either to cause fear among non-combatants or coerce the state to succumb to specific demands.[20] This definition slightly differs from dissent or protest action, which is a form of collective action waged by civilians to nudge their government to improve their standards of living, without the use of force.

It is important to indicate that while individual states have developed a knack for ensuring that protest actions such as EndSARS do not exacerbate into national turmoil, the same may not be said of insurgents. At present, five out of the fifteen ECOWAS member states in the Lake Chad Basin (LCB) have become the theatre for the operations of a Jihadist terrorist organisation, Boko Haram.[21] The activities of the group around the Lake have made the location one of the darkest zones in the region, with Nigeria becoming the third most impacted country by terrorism globally.[22] While some attempts have been made by the REC to contain the insurrection, this attempt seems to be ineffective as the terrorist group continues to cause a humanitarian crisis in Chad, Cameroon, Mali, Niger and Nigeria.[23]

---

[19] D Kuwali (2013) 'Humanitarian Rights': Bridging the Doctrinal Gap between the Protection of Civilians and the Responsibility to Protect' *Journal of International Humanitarian Legal Studies*, *4*(1), 5–46.

[20] JD Fearon & DD Laitin (2003) 'Ethnicity, Insurgency, and Civil War' *American Political Science Review*, *97*(1), 75–90.

[21] The affected countries are Cameroon, Chad, Niger, and Nigeria. See OO Oluwaniyi (2021) 'Why are women victims or perpetrators in Nigeria's Boko Haram? Recruitment, roles, and implications' *Journal of Contemporary African Studies*. 10.1080/02589001.2020.1849580.

[22] IEP (Institute for Economics & Peace) (2020) Global Terrorism Index 2020: Ten Countries Most Impacted by Terrorism. Retrieved from https://visionofhumanity.org/wp-content/uploads/2020/11/GTI-2020-web-1.pdf (Accessed 28 February 2021), 18.

[23] SK Okunade & O Ogunnubi (2020) 'Insurgency in the Border Communities of North-Eastern Nigeria: Security Responses and Sustainable Solutions' *The Round Table*, *109*(6), 684–700.

The State of Insurgency in West Africa

On a canvas of broad strokes, (West) Africans are naturally non-violent. The continent's belief system and practices teach its young generation that taking a human life is an abomination or a taboo. Nhlapo (2017) captures it well when he mooted that even in pre-colonial African societies, it was a heinous infringement of moral duty for a man to execute another, as the act establishes a spiritual barrier between the wrongdoer and the ancestral realm. What, then, explains the sudden ideological shift, from non-violence to mass atrocities against fellow Africans. It is essential to reiterate that contemporary insurgencies in the West African sub-region did not emerge out of a vacuum. One might argue that the underlying pull of many extremist groups has been influenced by religious or socio-economic factors.

In other words, the upsurge in extremism is a spill-over of the plethora of localised vulnerabilities triggered by poor governance and economic deprivation.[24] Moreover, the intensity and passion with which these extremists conduct their operations, and the grievous harms inflicted on civilians, might perhaps suggest that recent insurrections might have underlining factors that ought to be examined.[25] In the case of Boko Haram, disempowerment and social injustice from political leaders seem to have fuelled their aggression. To expand on this hypothesis, perhaps a brief history of the evolution of Boko Haram will suffice.

In 2002, Boko Haram began in north-eastern Nigeria as a local Salafist sect. As an ultraconservative ideology, Salafism is grounded in Sunni Islam and admonishes adherents to strictly adhere to the teachings of the Quran.[26] Like other founders of militant Islamist organisations, Boko Haram's founder, Mohammed Yusuf, lived a normal life. Besides being a smallholder, he was known for arranging marriages and giving alms to the needy (Onuoha 2010). For Yusuf, the economic situation in Nigeria transcended mere survival. It altered his perspective and shaped his political thoughts. Since the attainment of independence, and the country's exportation of crude oil in 1960, the non-oil producing north-eastern parts have been systematically marginalised from economic resources, thereby exacerbating their service delivery and underdevelopment.[27]

The disempowerment and marginalisation of natives in the north-eastern region are illustrative of the lack of employment opportunities, poor health care systems and road infrastructures, as well as, long distances children have

---

[24] JT Omenma, IM Abada & Z Omenma (2020) 'Boko Haram Insurgency: A Decade of Dynamic Evolution and Struggle for a Caliphate' *Security Journal*, *33*, 376–400.

[25] M Bøås & F Strazzari (2020) 'Governance, Fragility, and Insurgency in the Sahel: A Hybrid Political Order in the Making' *The International Spectator*, *55*(4), 1–17.

[26] M Nwankpa (2020) 'Understanding the Local–Global Dichotomy and Drivers of the Boko Haram Insurgency' *African Conflict and Peacebuilding Review*, *10*(2), 43–64.

[27] WO Iyekekpolo (2020) 'Political Elites and the Rise of the Boko Haram Insurgency in Nigeria' *Terrorism and Political Violence*, *32*(4), 749–767.

to cover to access education. Given this condition, while 98% of children in southern states including Imo are literate, only 34 and 46% of girls and boys respectively are literate in a northern state like Borno.[28] Thus, as a form of self-empowerment, natives have mobilised themselves into community networks along ethnic and religious lines to provide support for individual members. One of such groups was/is Boko Haram.

In 2002, Boko Haram emerged as a grassroots movement providing safety nets for vulnerable groups such as children, the unemployed and widows.[29] Due to this social network and support, it gained considerable popularity among residents in north-eastern Nigeria and Borno in particular where impoverished populations continue to approach it for financial assistance. It is noted that the group provides capital incentives, in the form of loans to aspiring entrepreneurs and dowry for young men who find it difficult to marry, particularly in light of hikes in Nigeria's marriage market.

It could be argued that Yusuf did not envision his small group of followers to mobilise into a large-scale dissident. Yet, from 2009, the group started launching a violent jihad against other Muslim sects and Salafists which opposed its radical interpretation of the Quran and Sunna. Following a joint task force operation by the Nigerian army which resulted in the execution of Yusuf in 2009, the group was placed under a new and extremely violent leader, Abubakar Shekau.[30] Since he assumed power in 2009, Shekau has violently expanded the group's operations to neighbouring states, while leaving behind a trail of humanitarian crisis across the north-eastern region.

One could, therefore, argue that the magnet for recruitment of youth into the group may be tied to two elements: (i) opposition to conservative Muslims; and (ii) safety net or source of sustenance. In simple terms, growing unemployment among the youth in the region, coupled with rising inflation have repositioned extremist groups as an attractive occupation for the young generation. This is more so as they somewhat find a livelihood from the loot and spoils. It will, nonetheless, be farfetched to suggest that all the members of the group voluntarily enlisted. It is fair to argue that a disproportionate percentage were abducted and indoctrinated to embrace its radical interpretation of the Quranic.[31] These teachings may nudge abductees to inflict harm on infidels, as well as other sects which are opposed to their abductors' doctrines.

---

[28] H Matfess (2016) 'Here's why so many people join Boko Haram, despite its notorious violence' *The WashingtonPost*. Retrieved from https://www.washingtonpost.com/news/monkey-cage/wp/2016/04/26/heres-why-so-many-people-join-Boko-haram-despite-its-notorious-violence/ . (Accessed 28 February 2021), para. 6.

[29] F Onuoha (2012) 'The Audacity of the Boko Haram: Background, Analysis and Emerging Trend' *Security Journal*, 25, 134–151.

[30] S MacEachern (2020) 'Boko Haram, Bandits and Slave-Raiders: Identities and Violence in a Central African Borderland' *Canadian Journal of African Studies*, 54(2), 247–263.

[31] S Oyewole (2015) 'Boko Haram: Insurgency and the War against Terrorism in the Lake Chad Region' *Strategic Analysis*, 39(4), 428–432.

Since the atrocities of Boko Haram and other insurgents have stretched to neighbouring Cameroon and Chad, these countries along with Nigeria formed Multinational Joint Task Force (TJF) against Boko Haram in April 2012.[32] Nonetheless, ineffective coordination between member states as well as lack of institutional capacity hindered the effectiveness of the task force to successfully repel the extremist. Undoubtedly, weariness about the prospect of the TJF to manage violent attacks tempted Nigeria to revisit an ancient practice of hiring mercenaries for PSOs. In December 2014, Nigeria enlisted the services of South African mercenaries to counter Boko Haram activities in its north-eastern region.[33] But what good does it serve a nation to enlist mercenaries or civilian contractors to undertake essential security tasks in combat? A response to this discursive question rests in the long trajectory of empires contracting skilled civilians to perform security functions in battles.

Mercenarism could be classified as the second-oldest enterprise globally.[34] Traces of foreign soldiers hired for battle could be located in the later Middle Ages, when mediaeval Europe's military resources of coping with external aggression and growing resistance from below were obsolescent. Consequently, Alexander solicited the services of 5000 mercenaries in his 334 B.C. Asian invasion, while his Persian rivals at Issos composed of 10,000 Greek recruitments.[35] Besides war, contracted forces were used to address the evolving complex demands of a modernising society, including tax collection, safeguarding merchants' trade routes and law enforcement. These soldiers of fortune have subsequently been active in the American Revolution and participated in some of the 1960s African liberation guerrilla warfare.[36]

In contemporary times, mercenaries, rebranded as private security companies remain a dominant force in the UK's war effort. Moreover, these private soldiers have been known to constitute the second-largest contingent in the 2003 US-led coalition force in Iraq.[37] In West Africa, the hiring of mercenaries is not a new phenomenon. Two states are known to have solicited the services of foreign-trained soldiers to manage domestic threats. It is observed that in 2009, Cameroonian President Paul Biya conscripted Israeli mercenaries, Avi Sivan, Eran Moas and Erez Zuckerman in the formation of an

---

[32] IO Albert (2017) 'Rethinking the Functionality of the Multinational Joint Task Force in Managing the Boko Haram Crisis in the Lake Chad Basin' *Africa Development*, XLII (3), 119–135.

[33] T Tayo (2021) 'Soldiers for Rent in the Boko Haram Crisis' Retrieved from https://issafrica.org/iss-today/soldiers-for-rent-in-the-boko-haram-crisis (Accessed 28 February 2021).

[34] SE Finer (1976) 'The Second Oldest Trade' *New Society*, 129–31.

[35] VG Kiernan (1957) 'Foreign Mercenaries and Absolute Monarchy' *Past & Present*, 11, 66.

[36] P Gleijeses (1994). 'Flee! The White Giants Are Coming!': The United States, the Mercenaries, and the Congo, 1964–65' *Diplomatic History 18*(2), 207–237.

[37] SV Percy (2007) 'Mercenaries: Strong Norm, Weak Law' *International Organization*, 61(2), 367–397.

elite unit, Rapid Intervention Battalion (RIB), to contain the insurgents.[38] Though it is an ancient profession, it is important to underscore that the practice of hiring mercenaries is an affront to two international instruments. Both the UN (1989) and AU (1977) Mercenary Conventions proscribes Cameroon and Nigeria from hiring soldiers of fortune. It was, therefore, no surprise that upon his election in 2015, Nigeria's ex-military general, president Muhammed Buhari slammed his predecessor's use of mercenaries, whom he claimed failed to safeguard local communities.[39]

As a result, in 2015, the TJF was restructured and upgraded with the inclusion of troops from Benin. Yet, with countless unsuccessful attempts at annihilating extremist groups, the TJF was rebranded into the G5 Sahel Joint Task Force in 2017 (Dieng 2019). The label G5 is reflective of the five-member states drawn from three RECs: ECOWAS (Burkina Faso, Mali, and Niger), Economic Community of Central African States (ECCAS, Chad), and Arab Maghreb Union (Mauritania). Devastatingly, like its predecessor, the G5 has been unsuccessful in countering illegal migration, criminal groups and insurgents. For this reason, the continued operation of the force has been subject to scrutiny, as it has neither wooed the support of the local populace nor stabilised prime border areas including the Liptako-Gourma region.[40] It is important to underscore that the failure of G5 in tackling violence in the affected countries may be tied to three major setbacks: (i) logistical constraints; (ii) insufficient technological equipment; and (iii) a limited number of troops.

In recognition of these tipple constraints, ECOWAS established the Accra Initiative (AI) in September 2017 to complement the efforts of the transnational troops operating in the sub-region.[41] With brigades drawn from Benin, Burkina Faso, Côte d'Ivoire, Ghana and Togo, the ad-hoc sub-regional security arrangement was charged with the mandate of combating violent extremism, transnational organised crimes and forestalling spill-over of terrorism.[42] Still, nearly half-decade since its launch, the AI has been unable

---

[38] E Freudenthal & Y van der Weide (2020) 'Making a Killing: Israeli Mercenaries in Cameroon' *African Arguments*. Retrieved from https://africanarguments.org/2020/06/making-a-killing-israeli-mercenaries-in-cameroon/ (Accessed 28 February 2021).

[39] L Binniyat (2015) 'Buhari Slams the Military for Hiring Mercenaries to fight Boko Haram' *NewsRescue* Retrieved from Accessed https://newsrescue.com/buhari-slams-military-for-hiring-mercenaries-to-fight-Boko-haram/ (Accessed 28 February 2021).

[40] A Boutellis & Y Mahmoud (2017) 'Investing in Peace to Prevent Violent Extremism in the Sahel-Sahara Region' *Journal of Peacebuilding and Development*, *12*(2), 80–84; KM Osland & HU Erstad (2020) 'The Fragility Dilemma and Divergent Security Complexes in the Sahel' *The International Spectator*, *55*(4), 18–36.

[41] ECRF (European Council on Foreign Relations) (2017) Accra Initiative. Retrieved from https://ecfr.eu/special/african-cooperation/accra-initiative/ (Accessed 28 February 2021).

[42] S Kwarkye, EJ Abatan, & M Matongbada, M. (2019) 'Can the Accra Initiative prevent terrorism in West African Coastal States?' *ISS AFRICA* Retrieved from https://issafrica.org/iss-today/can-the-accra-initiative-prevent-terrorism-in-west-african-coastal-states (Accessed 28 February 2021).

to jointly thwart the operations of extremists and illicit arms trade in the region. The direct impact of the rising extremism in the sub-region is manifested in the proliferation of illicit trade in ammunitions, explosives, and small arms, which could lead to the formation of similar extremist groups in other ECOWAS states. This sorry state of affairs triggers a discursive question; what factors underpin ECOWAS's ineffectiveness in addressing insurgency in the sub-region? In responding to the question, the next question traces the institutional and logistical constraints which hinder ECOWAS security operations in the sub-region.

CHALLENGES

Several factors may be listed as the major reasons which make PSOs uniquely challenging for the REC, particularly in hostile hotspots such as the LCB. The first conundrum may be tied to the multiplicity of tasks often assigned to peacekeepers, like the TJF and G5. Given their limited budget, they are often charged to restore peace, enforce embargos, sanctions, disarm and reintegrate extremists within a short period. Although all the functions seem to be synonymous with the duties of soldiers, the latter seems to be a good fit for social workers rather than soldiers. Yet, since they are obliged to perform this role, the troops are sometimes confronted with the difficult task of integrating self-demobilised ex-combatants into local communities.

The challenge, however, exacerbates in localities where victims seek retribution over reconciliation, and thus, agitate for prosecution (Ike, et al. 2021). This contention may sometimes pose a considerable challenge to force commanders on the ground, as a significant percentage may be experienced with riffles, rather than as conciliators. To this end, in deploying troops to conflict zones such as the LCB, ECOWAS ought to enlist the assistance of diplomats to liaise with local civilians on the need to embrace and treat with kindness ex-combatants who have returned to their fold. Thus, with the promise of successful (re)integration, coupled with the possibility of employment, some members of extremist groups might be willing to down their weapons, rather than fostering feud with the REC.

The second broaches on poor communication and coordination.[43] Infantry brigades ought to complement each other and adopt uniform strategies, especially if the war against insurgency is to be won. Yet, since troops are drawn from 15 different nationalities, with different languages and training, it becomes cumbersome to train them to operate as a single unit. This barrier may trickle down to strategic or tactical setbacks, as troops might have a

---

[43] S Agbo, L Gbaguidi, C Biliyar, Seydou Sylla, Mukeh Fahnbulleh, John Dogba, Sakoba Keita, S Kamara, A Jambai, A Harris, T Nyenswah, M Seni, S Bhoye, S Duale & A Kitua (2019) 'Establishing National Multisectoral Coordination and Collaboration Mechanisms to Prevent, Detect, and Respond to Public Health Threats in Guinea, Liberia, and Sierra Leone 2016–2018' *One Health Outlook, 1*(4), 1–13.

different understanding of their core mandates, particularly as some key terminologies could be misunderstood in the process of translating documents into common languages for individual forces. As opposed to insurgents who are more likely drawn from the same location with a common language, ECOWAS being Anglophone, Francophone and Lusophone speaking sub-region, the language barrier could greatly hinder effective communication among its troops. Thus, poor communication will ultimately impact coordination and timely deployment of troops, as illustrated by the lack of the REC's presence in hostile hotspots, such as the LCB.

The third challenge may be traced to the ancient quandary of lack of political will by IMS for immediate deployment of troops. In conforming to conventional standards of military intervention, the deployment of troops for PSOs ought to be sanctioned by the ECOWAS Authority, the AU and with the backing of the UN. This implies that although there might be extremists destabilising and/or terrorising civilians in a particular jurisdiction, commanders of brigades cannot deploy their troops without prior authorisation by the coalitions of ECOWAS and AU states. Since political support for such missions is often tied to resource commitments, it could prove cumbersome in garnering consensus from the 15 IMS at the sub-regional level, thereby hampering the rapid response to atrocities. The delay could be aggravated by (dis)agreement among ECOWAS and the AU members, particularly over the approach or modalities which such intervention ought to assume.

The contestation could trickle down to differences between Anglophone and Francophone blocs over strategies, which insurgent groups ought to negotiate with or forcefully repelled. As an illustration, while Anglophone countries hailed Nigeria's PSOs in Liberia, the Francophone camp condemned it as overly aggressive. Thus, while some in the ECOWAS caucus and 53+ in the AU chamber may prefer troops' deployment, others might advocate for negotiation with extremists. Drawing from the ongoing hostilities in Libya, although dialogue may not be a preferred remedy under hostile conditions, the use of force does not always guarantee a successful peacekeeping operation either. As evidenced in the peacebuilding efforts in Mali and Chad, the dialogue could be a key entry point to ending hostilities. Even where such consensus is built, there is an enigma of insufficient pre-deployment briefing and training to ensure brigades fully understand, and comply with Rules of Engagement (RoE). This predicament could be further complicated by the different languages, training and disciplines which could influence their understanding of what is expected of them, and how to operationalise such tasks.

Another tactical challenge is in terms of the type of training and ammunitions which troops are acquainted with.[44] Drawn from different regiments in different countries, some troops are more likely to be disciplined and well

---

[44] K Aning & F Edu-Afful (2017) 'Peacekeeping in a Francophone Space: Experiences of Ghanaian Peacekeepers in Côte d'Ivoire' *The Round Table*, 106(4), 375–391.

trained than others. These distinctive features could stir discontent and frustration among elite groups as they might have doubts regarding the capabilities of the next soldier to brave gunfire during an ambush. In similar terms, whereas some from developing countries such as Ghana, Nigeria and Senegal are likely to be exposed to sophisticated ammunitions and technologies, others from less developed countries such as Liberia and Niger are unlikely to be exposed to contemporary weaponry as these poor countries might be unable to afford. This incoherence to a great extent might impact the speed or duration within which troops could be trained to achieve uniformity in the use of weapons during humanitarian interventions.

The fifth setback ties to the question of financial and technical capacity.[45] ECOWAS's insufficient and unsustainable financial stream greatly inhibits its effort to successfully deploy peacekeepers, such as the ESF, to hostile zones. As it stands now, whereas IMS with smaller economies might be unable to deploy large contingents and resources for security operations, those with large budgets are inclined to safeguard their national security. Against this backdrop, the latter is more inclined to channel a larger proportion of its budget into domestic security upgrades, rather than transnational PSOs.

Finally, in terms of personnel, given that a significant number of ECOWAS states lack sufficient military and police force, they find it difficult to deploy their best security forces.[46] The unwillingness may sometimes be informed by fears that perhaps the absence of their skilled security personnel could inspire a coup against the government or similar insurrection locally. Also, the intensity of hostilities further serves as a deterrent to non-affected countries as some might perceive it as a suicidal mission to deploy their countrymen to harsh terrain with little prospect for their safe return. Consequently, the few troops which are deployed by the JTF and G5 were thinly spread across the vast terrestrial region of LCB, thereby unable to cover the entire conflict zone. This trend is more troubling as ISIS continues to consolidate its Islamic State in West Africa Province (ISWAP) offshoots as part of an effort to increase its presence across the sub-region.[47] In light of these constraints, the next section carefully considers possible avenues which could improve the REC's counter-insurgent response.

[45] OO Akanji (2019) 'Sub-Regional Security Challenge: ECOWAS and the War on Terrorism in West Africa' *Insight on Africa*, 11(1) 94–112.

[46] AJ Ateku (2020) 'Regional Intervention in the Promotion of Democracy in West Africa: An Analysis of the Political Crisis in the Gambia and ECOWAS' Coercive Diplomacy' *Conflict, Security & Development*, 20(6), 677–696.

[47] E Beevor & F Berger (2020) 'ISIS Militants Pose a Growing Threat Across Africa' Retrieved from https://www.iiss.org/blogs/analysis/2020/06/csdp-isis-militants-africa (Accessed 28 February 2021).

Recommendation

Presently, the increasing intensity of extremism in the sub-region provides an entry point for IMS to foster cooperation for an effective PSOs. ECOWAS could reclaim its rightful place as effective security machinery if the necessary support is provided by member states, in terms of logistics and personnel for insurgencies and illicit trade in small weapons. In the area of logistical support for troops, ECOWAS could source external funding by enhancing existing ties and building new partnerships with donors. To attract sufficient financial support, the REC ought to outline specific incentives for contributors, such as acknowledgement or allocation of special status for donors, as well as states which make considerable donations to PSOs. Such a commitment by the REC could enable the ESF, TJF and G5 to enhance their operational capability and effectively disarm Boko Haram and other insurgents in the sub-region. The provision of logistics could be directed towards the recruitment, accessing modern ammunitions and capacity development of troops to bring them up to a speed of techniques in contemporary guerrilla warfare.

The second recommendation is building a strong alliance with continental bodies such as the AU. From the onset, ECOWAS security architecture was inspired by the African Union's security mechanism. While these two bodies share similar structures, it remains ambiguous the extent to which these institutions collaborate and/or complement the work of the other. Whereas the AU (2008) attempted to forge some form of alliance with RECs, and in particular with Eastern and Northern Africa standby brigades, specific partnership with ECOWAS security structure remains ambiguous. Yet, in light of the benefit of fostering alliance, the ECOWAS must revisit its relationship with the AU in mapping clearer guidelines on shared expertise, logistics and responsibilities. A consideration of this partnership is timely particularly in light of the sinews of extremist groups and their transnational operations.

As illustrated by the operations of Boko Haram, the scope of operations of some extremists transcends the boundaries of one country, and even the sub-region into other terrains where ECOWAS forces may not have the mandate to follow suit. Thus, through a partnership with the AU, ECOWAS troops could cross political boundaries under the banner of the AU and quell extremism even beyond the borders of the sub-region. This collaboration is timely given the sophistication and tact with which contemporary extremists conduct their operations. Consequently, ECOWAS-AU forces could combine forces in the realm of solid intelligence gathering and air power to match the skills of insurgents.

Ultimately, the ECOWAS troops contingent could draw inspiration from the extensive experience of the AU peacekeepers in safeguarding civilians from atrocities and displacement. Indeed, this aspiration calls into question the resource capacity of the REC, which could be thinly stretched if its brigades seek to annihilate insurgents in the sub-region. ECOWAS could offset this challenge in three spheres: (i) mobilising logistical support among member states, particularly those with the means to contribute more; (ii) enhancing the partnership with the AU; and (iii) seek donor funding.

Tied to the above recommendation is the duplication of effort between the ECOWAS and the AU.[48] Interestingly, both organisations share similar structures: from Early Warning Systems (EWS), Council of the Wise/Elders, to Standby Forces. Nonetheless, although AU as a supranational organisation could play an oversight role in sub-regional conflicts, it has been known to directly deploy its security machinery to intervene in these hostilities. The role of the AU, under this circumstance (though commendable), could also be construed as duplication of efforts, and therefore wasting essential resources, which could otherwise be channelled to the operations of the REC.

This was evident in the conflicting and sometimes overlapping strategies of ECOWAS and AU forces which prolonged the resolution of the Mali crisis in 2012 (Darkwa 2017). For this reason, since the ECOWAS has an advanced EWS, the continental body could rely on the diagnostic reports of the former, rather than conducting its internal assessment. Thus, as the REC is directly in touch with the situation in the sub-region, the AU could channel some assistance to the ECOWAS's EWS to ensure that accurate and timely reports are dispatched to the ECOWAS Authority for proactive intervention.

Finally, the urgency for employment opportunities cannot be underestimated. The poor economic state of West Africa, exacerbated by Covid-19 job losses could potentially incite more civilians to join the camps of extremist groups. This projection is likely as the frequent looting and ransoms obtained by insurgents could be an attractive venture for (overly)ambitious youth. It is therefore imperative for regional leaders to provide urgent stimulus to contain the economic shocks of the Covid-19 crisis, to provide skills and employment for millions of the region's unemployed youth. To this end, combating security threats in the region requires a paradigm shift, in terms of shifting to a smart counter-insurgency response (SCR). This approach may be construed as the ability of ECOWAS to effectively combat military incursions by combining elements of soft power and hard power.

Whereas hard power involves the deployment of troops to quell insurrections, a soft response encompasses non-military initiatives such as the creation of employment opportunities, integration of ex-insurgents in national troops and promotion of religious tolerance in local communities. Aside from improving the living conditions of many young graduates, boosting economic opportunities in the public and private sectors could play a key role in the recruitment and disarmament of insurgents. It will be difficult, if not nearly impossible for extremists to surrender their weapons if there are no prospects of successful reintegration into community life, particularly in terms of earning

---

[48] HE Henke (2020) 'A Tale of Three French Interventions: Intervention Entrepreneurs and Institutional Intervention Choices' *Journal of Strategic Studies*, 43(4), 583–606.

a minimum wage that could sustain themselves and their immediate dependents. In the case of Boko Haram, Nigeria and affected countries ought to adopt radical economic policies to transform north-eastern parts.

These transformations could be directed towards improving access to social amenities, financial support for young entrepreneurs and social security to vulnerable groups. Perhaps these reforms will limit the rising discontent among some residents in these parts of the country, as well as discredit the propaganda of the insurgent group. This recommendation extends to other states in the sub-region, as rising unemployment has the potential of breeding further extremisms and violent attacks against civilians. Thus, in the REC's effort towards peacebuilding, individual states need to create favourable economic conditions, including provisions of loans for aspiring entrepreneurs, accessible and quality healthcare and educational systems for the socio-economic development of local civilians.

CONCLUSION

ECOWAS was once a force to reckon with in containing insurrections. Since its establishment in 1975, it has continued to be instrumental in preventing hostilities and perpetuation of violent attacks against local civilians in the sub-region. Its contribution to PSOs has evolved in two-phases: (i) norm-creation and (ii) institutional-building. On one hand, the adoption of the 1999 Mechanism provides expansive powers for the formation of a comprehensive REC security cluster to forestall instabilities. On the other hand, the creation of the ESF greatly enhanced its PSOs and averted humanitarian crises. Despite these gains, its impact in containing ongoing insurgencies in the LCB has been insignificant, making individual states in the region more fragile and volatile than others in the continent.

The chapter realised that lack of political will, poor coordination and insufficient logistical support are a few of the major challenges which the region's security cluster is confronted with. The chapter, thus, observed that in forestalling increasing the ranks of extremists, ECOWAS leaders must blend military deployment with an economic incentive. The chapter observes that REC brigades need regular training in advanced technology to match the complex nature of contemporary guerrilla warfare. Also, there is a need for frequent recruitment of troops, as an enormous depletion in their number could lead to their outnumbering and eventual annihilation by their opponents.

The chapter argues that, although the use of force could repel insurgents from committing further acts of violence, there is also need to improve the socio-economic conditions of impoverished communities, as deprivation could be an important driver for the insurgency. In sum, the account of this chapter yields lessons and insights for other RECs, such as the Arab Maghreb, ECCAS and Southern African Development Community as they revamp their security frameworks to contain instabilities in Libya, Somalia, South Sudan, the Central African Republic and the Democratic Republic of Congo.

CHAPTER 8

Peace and Security in Central Africa

Peter J. Mugume

REASONS FOR THE CONFLICT IN THE REGION

The Central African region is comprised of countries including CAR, Burundi, Rwanda, Angola, Cameroon, Democratic Republic of Congo, Chad, Republic of Congo, Equatorial Guinea, Gabon and Sao Tome and Principle.[1] Most of the countries in Central African region have experienced violent conflicts and the 1994 genocide against Tutsi in Rwanda. As indicated by Debos among 11 ECCAS member countries only a few have escaped serious crisis and violent conflict during the last few decades.[2] According to Gabriella and Magadalena, Central Africa is one of the most volatile regions on the African continent where poor governance, armed conflicts and transnational crimes contribute to the persistent insecurity of states and peoples.[3] Debos also indicates that the porosity of national borders and between the different zones of conflict

---

[1]ADB (2019), Central Africa Regional Integration Strategy Paper 2019–2025, June 2019. (Available at www.adb.org. Accessed on March 11, 2021).

[2]Marielle Debos (2008), Fluid loyalties in a Regional Crisis: Chadian "Ex-Liberators" in the Central African Republic. African Affairs, 427.

[3]Gabriella and Magadalena (2015), Challenges to Peace and Security in Central Africa: The Role of ECASS, Studies in African Security, Swedish Defence Research Agency, Stockholm.

P. J. Mugume (✉)
University of Rwanda, Kigali, Rwanda

© The Author(s), under exclusive license to Springer Nature
Switzerland AG 2022
D. Kuwali (ed.), *The Palgrave Handbook of Sustainable Peace and Security in Africa*, https://doi.org/10.1007/978-3-030-82020-6_8

and the proliferation of illegal arms and weapons increases the risk of spill over from conflicts in neighbouring states.[4]

As narrated by Gilbert Mittawa in Chapter 22, small arms proliferation is considered to have the capacity for stimulating the backlashes including undermining development, weakening government ability to function, hampering peace and provoking humanitarian disaster, and can lead to detrimental long-term societal changes.[5] This issue does not only affect the Central African region but also other regions including the Horn of Africa and West African regional countries including Ethiopia and Nigeria, respectively. Adesoji Adeniyi in the Oxfam report on the Human Cost of Uncontrolled Arms in Africa points out that the question of uncontrolled arms, their acquisition and their transfer is a recurring security dilemma in Africa.[6] This report also asserts that concentration of most of Africa's 100 million uncontrolled small arms and light weapons in crisis zones and other security challenge environments often exacerbates and elongates conflicts.

In line with what Barman, Adesoji Adeniyi also argues that illicit arms and light weapons bring devastating costs to individuals, families and communities who experience displacement, erosion of social cohesion and trust, gender-based violence (GBV), injuries and fatalities.[7] The literature about this issue indicates that most conflicts in Africa do involve non state actors such as militias, warlords and terror groups that benefit through using uncontrolled arms. This is common with the Central African region's countries such as CAR, Democratic Republic of the Congo (DRC) and their neighbouring countries such as Burundi. The African Development Bank also points out that Central African region is characterised by political instability and volatile security environment due to activities of terrorist groups from the Lake Chad Basin which stems from northern Cameroon, western Chad, south eastern Niger, north-eastern Nigeria and outbreak of multifaceted conflicts including conflicts over control of natural resources.[8]

In agreement with Tadziwana Kapeni and Dan Kuwali in Chapters 17 and 34, respectively, apart from proliferation of uncontrolled arms in this region, another reason for the conflicts in the Central African region is related to governance issues. Weak political legitimacy leading to fragile social cohesion threatens the stability of political structures and challenges the capacities

---

[4] Marielle Debos Fluid Loyalties in a regional Crisis: Chadian "Ex-Liberators" in the Central African Republic. African Affairs, 427.

[5] Eric Barman (2004), "Trends and Dynamics of illicit Arms Proliferation in Nigeria: A Small Arms Survey Perspective", presented at the National Consultative Forum on Proliferation of SALWs in Nigeria, Abuja, 2–4 June.

[6] Adesoji Adeniyi (2017, p. 3), Adesoji Adeniyi (2017), The Human Cost of Uncontrolled Arms in Africa: Cross National Research on Seven African Countries, Oxfam Research Reports.

[7] Barman footnote 5 above.

[8] African Development Bank (2019, p. 17), Central Africa Regional Integration Strategy Paper 2019–2025, June 2019 (Available at www.adb.org. Accessed on March 11, 2021).

of Central African States institutions.[9] These factors indicated by different authors above have also been mentioned by Baregu who grouped them into five challenges and argues that they have shaped the form and nature of intervention in the region, in the search for peace, stability and development.[10] Those challenges include: presence of a number of "negative forces"/illegal armed; persistence of climate of tension and mistrust among political leaders; proliferation of small arms and light weapons; illegal exploitation of natural resources; contested boundaries; and population displacements. Although Baregu's points were made in reference to the International Conference of the Great Lakes Region (ICGLR), they can be relevant for the Central African region whose member countries are also members of the ICGLR. These challenges are sometimes related and have worked hand in hand to accelerate conflict in this region based on the interests of individual actors.

MAIN ACTORS IN THE PEACE AND SECURITY IN THE REGION

Conflicts in this region involve different actors both internal and external ones, and one of the vexing features of the conflict in the region is the issue of a multiplicity of actors and complexity of interests.[11] As further indicated by Baregu apart from the visible internal parties to the conflict who are relatively easy to identify, there are a number of actors lurking in the background but actively working in the background. Such actors may be seen to adopt strategies that help them to play roles intended to promote either the resolution of conflicts or their intensification. Across the Central African region, there have been some allegations that some Non-Governmental Organizations (NGOs) acting in such a way in the DRC.

Internal actors include individual governments and armed groups such as Mai Mai from the Democratic Republic of the Congo, Anti-Baraka, Seleka and the Coalition of Patriots for Change (CPC) from CAR. External actors are here categorised into two parts. The first part includes terror groups such as Boko Haram, FDLR, and ADF among other groups. It should be reminded that some armed groups operate across states' borders whereby some of them originate from neighbouring countries. For the purpose of this chapter, the actors that originate from neighbouring countries are referred to as Negative Forces (NF), whereas those originating from within countries where they are playing some role(s) in the conflict are referred to as armed groups (AG).

---

[9] Angela Meyer, 2011 as cited by Olumide Adetekunbo Fafore (2016, p. 56), Preventing Conflict in Central Africa: ECCAS caught Between Ambitious, Challenges and Reality. Institute for Security Studies, Issue 3/August 2015, Olumide Adetokunbo Fafore (2016), The African Union and Peace and Security in Central Africa, Journal of African Union Studies (JoAUS), Vol. 5, No. 2, (2016), pp. 51–66.

[10] Mwesiga Baregu (2011, pp. xiv–xv), Understanding Obstacles to Peace: Actors, Interests, and Strategies in Africa's Great Lakes Region, Fountain Publishers, Kampala.

[11] Mwesiga Baregu, Understanding Obstacles to Peace: Actors, Interests, and Strategies in Africa's Great Lakes Region, Fountain Publishers, Kampala (2011, p. 14).

The second part includes individual countries such as France and Russia in addition to international and regional organisations such as United Nations (UN) through MONUSCO and United Nations Multidimensional Integrated Stabilization Force in CAR (MINUSCA), African Union (AU) and Economic Community of Central African States (ECCAS). It should be noted that other regional bodies such as the Economic Community of West African States (ECOWAS) and Southern African Development and Economic Community (SADC) have also been involved in the conflict in Central African region.

Ethnic ideologies whereby, for example, as mentioned by Abdurrahim Sıradağ elites from CAR have used ethnic groups and religion as a political means to stay in power, and strengthen political positions, developing and shaping their politics according to their own ethnic identities and so increasing political tension and sparing violence.[12] Sıradag's main point here is that the struggle in CAR is driven by competition for power among elite groups. The examples provided here to illustrate this argument is the former CAR's presidents such as Andre Kolingba who strengthened his own ethnic group Yakoma, through provision of opportunities to the government positions and facilitations against other groups in the country, Ange Felix Patasse also favoured his group the Sara Kaba who fought against the Yakoma, Francois Bozize also strengthened his group the Bbaya by gifting them with high positions in the government.

The above assertion by Sıradag is not unique for CAR alone, but also can be relevant for other countries in the region including Cameroon, Chad, Burundi and DRC. Some authors such as Baregu consider such elite groups in power to be common with in situation of weak states that suffer from diminished capacity to exercise legitimate control and authority of government, maintenance of law and order, provision of social services, and defence of state sovereignty and it becomes worse in cases of collapsed or failed states.[13] This issue has partly contributed to the conflict in CAR for some time. This failure provides opportunity for mistrust among the elites. As indicated in some case the CAR's leaders have not trusted the National Army-Central African Armed Forces (FACA) and this mistrust partly contributes to establishment of militia groups to protect the leaders.[14]

Trinidad also points out that the failure of institutions in CAR particularly between FACA and Presidential Guard have led to human rights abuses

---

[12] Abdurrahim Sıradağ (2016), Abdurrahim Sıradağ (2016), Eplaining the Conflict in Central African Republic: Causes and Dynamics, King Fahd University of Petroleum and Minerals, Saudi Arabia, The journal of Transdisciplinary Studies, Vol. 9 No. 3 (2016).

[13] Buregu, footnote 11 above, p. 1.

[14] Annette Weber and Markus Kaim (2014, pp. 1–2), Central African Republic in Crisis: African Union Mission Needs United Nations Support. (SWP Comment, 15/2014). Berlin: Stiftung Wissenschaft und Politik—SWP—Deutsches Institut für Internationale Politik und Sicherheit. https://nbn-resolving.org/urn:nbn:de:0168-ssoar-388025.

in the country.[15] This creates a situation of insecurity that has facilitated the emergence of armed groups not only in CAR but also in some other Central African region's member countries such as DRC. Currently the situation in CAR is unpredictable considering the security developments in post-election period where the country is threatened by six armed groups that came together under the Coalition of Patriots for Change that is fighting the government of the CAR's President Faustin Archange Touadera.

The creation of the Coalition of Patriots for Change in CAR to fight the current government makes the AUs' desire to silence guns particularly in this country far from achievable. The coalition of the Patriots for Change is blamed for the attempted coup on January 13, 2021 which was done in violation of the commitments that were made by signatories to the APPR-CAR. The post-electoral violence situation in CAR is worrisome considering its consequences such as the influx of refugees fleeing this violence to the neighbouring countries especially DRC. Post-electoral violence in CAR has worsened the humanitarian situation in the country and its neighbours that receive the refugees. The Coalition of Patriots for Change has not only fought the Central African government military, but it has also fought the MINUSCA force, sometimes killing its service members. Although these rebels have been defeated in some places that they had captured earlier by the government forces with the help of its allies notably Russian paramilitaries and Rwanda force, they have already caused damage in terms of infrastructure and deterioration of education and health services.

The identity politics issue in this region has affected Rwanda and Burundi for some time. The Hutu Tutsi issue has seriously affected the politics in both Rwanda and Burundi and is blamed for the 1994 Genocide against Tutsi and its effects in the Central African and Great Lakes region of Africa. The effects of genocide have been felt by the DRC that welcomed the former genocidal force since 1994. Those effects have not only affected the DRC in terms of its peace, security and political developments, it also affects the political developments in the region and countries relationships. The 1994 genocide against Tutsi contributed to the mushrooming of Negative forces in the Eastern DRC that have seriously affected peace and security in the country and worsened humanitarian situation in the Central African region.

The 2018 UN report of Experts on the DRC, indicates that armed groups continue to pose security threat to peace and security in the DRC and its neighbours.[16] This report also points out that some of these groups have been working hand in hand with the government forces *FARDC* which is also mentioned as working with fighters such as Nduma Defense du Congo-Rénové (NDC-R). DRC still hosts a number of Negative Forces operating on

---

[15] Trinidad (2014, p. 8), Deiros, Trinidad (2014), Central African Republic: e Invention of a Religious Con ict. No. 67, the Spanish Institute for Strategic Studies (IEEE).

[16] United Nations Security Council (2018), Final Report of the Group of Experts on the Democratic Republic of the Congo, June 2018. New York.

its territory, some of which originate from its neighbouring countries such as Rwanda, Uganda and Burundi.

These forces have flourished in its Eastern parts in particular probably due to its vegetated terrain that has favoured their operations from this country and their countries of origin where they cause insecurity by attacking security forces and civilian population in most cases. The NFs appear to have a strategic objective of securing political power from their countries of origin. They include *Forces démocratiques de libération du Rwanda* (FDLR) from Rwanda, Allied Democratic Forces (ADF) and Lord's Resistance Army (LRA) from Uganda, *Forces Nationales De Liberation* (FNL), Red-Tabara, *Forces républicaines du Burundi* (FOREBU) and *Forces populaires du Burundi* (FPB) from Burundi.

All these NFs, except LRA whose operations traverse DRC through CAR, Uganda and South Sudan, operate from the Eastern DRC. Apart from these NFs, DRC also has Armed Groups (AGs) originating from within its own territory. Although NFs and AGs sometimes pursue different objectives, they also tend to work together in pursuing their interests and thus cause instability in this region particularly in areas they control. In addition to the loss of lives, NFs and AGs also contribute to the displacement and refugees.

As mentioned above, apart from the DRC where most NFs fighting Rwanda, Burundi and Uganda are based, they also cause trouble in their countries of origin including Rwanda where such forces are opposed to the socio-political establishment through the launching of attacks. The negative forces originating from Rwanda are in one way or the other related with the 1994 Genocide against Tutsi after which the Ex-Forces Armee Rwandaise (FAR), Interahamwe militias and their government fled Rwanda and established camps in the former Zaire and the Federal Republic of Tanzania. In the immediate post-genocide period, the NF formed *Rassemblement pour la Democratie et le Retour au Rwanda* (RDR) which was seen as a threat to Rwanda's national security.

RDR was later transformed into *Parti pour la Libération du Rwanda* (PALIR) which formed an armed wing known as *Armée de Libération du Rwanda* (ALIR). It was this armed group that in mid-May 1998 launched incursions into Rwanda particularly in its northern parts. The attacks by both negative forces mentioned above prompted Rwanda to launch pre-emptive attacks in 1996 and 1998 to then Zaire to pursue the NFs hideouts in eastern parts of that country. ALIR was later divided into two parts notably ALIR 1 and ALIR 2. These two forces were later merged and transformed into what became the *Forces Démocratiques de Libération du Rwanda* (FDLR). This change of ALIR to form a political wing-FDLR also had its military wing called *Forces combattantes Abacunguzi* (FOCA), the *Conseil National pour le Renouveau et la Démocratie* (CNRD)-*Ubwiyunge, Ralliement pour l'unité et la Démocratie* (RUD)-*Urunana*. The number of NFs mushroomed either from splitting of the existing ones or new ones and they keep destabilising DRC and Rwanda to date.

These NFs throughout their process of change have sought alliances both within the DRC and beyond. They have also been fighting among themselves with the help of their allies. All these have affected peace and security within DRC particularly its Eastern part and neigbours of Burundi and Rwanda. The activities of these forces have also affected the relationship of countries beyond the ECCAS region. For example, the current security situation between Uganda and Rwanda can be partly attributed to this issue.

Apart from both North and South Kivu provinces, Ituri province is also seriously affected by the conflict and security situation across the region according to the UNHCR remains fragile.[17] ADF, FDLR and the Mai-Mai armed groups have been fighting with FARDC in North Kivu province. South Kivu is still experiencing conflict particularly in the regions of Minembwe where the fighting is seriously affecting the Banyamulenge community. The insecurity situation in this region has accelerated the violence in areas of Fizi, Itombwe, Bijomba and Uvira. The fighting in these regions has caused the displacement of millions of people both internally where they are forced to be.

Recently there have been military attacks from the Western and Southern Rwanda by the negative forces from both DRC and Burundi according to the media and security reports. Although Uganda is not a member of ECCAS it is worth mentioning its Negative Force-ADF apparently destabilises DRC more than it apparently does to its country of origin. It blamed civil society organisations among others for committing atrocities in the Ituri region. However, Uganda is still concerned that the ADF may launch some attacks on its territory.

As indicated earlier above, there also are NFs that originate from Burundi. It is because of this issue that Burundi is also concerned that those forces can attack it any time. The situation in Burundi is worsened by the mistrust it has for Rwanda which it accuses of supporting the Negative Forces against the Burundi government. However, Rwanda denies the allegation that it supports any NF from Burundi, and it also accuses Burundi of supporting NFs fighting its government including Paul Rusesabagina's Rwanda Movement for Democratic Change-National Liberation Front (RMDC-FLN) which is blamed for recent killings and lootings in the Western province of Rwanda.

As is the case of some other ECCAS member countries such as CAR and DRC, Cameroon is also affected by persistent insecurity that stems from for example its colonial and post-colonial history such as contested state structures. The situation in this country is also fueled by the political and social economic imbalance among the regions and population in addition to the negative and terrorism forces such as Boko Haram which contributes to havoc in Cameroon. Although Boko Haram is sometimes traced from Nigeria its spillover effects have seriously affected Cameroon in terms of loss of lives and properties. The other key issue for Cameroon is the separatist groups in the

---

[17] UNHCR (2020), Bi-Weekly Emergency Update, Ituri, North Kivu and South Kivu Provinces Democratic Republic of the Congo, 25 May–8 June 2020.

North West and South West who are fighting for the independence of the two Anglophone regions-North West and South West to form the Ambazonia state.

Cameroon, Chad and CAR have had suspicion over insecurity and alliance of (for example) Chad with the Seleka rebel movement which is a key actor in the conflict in CAR, and Cameroon accepting to host the disposed CAR' leader Francois Bozize.[18] As indicated elsewhere, like Cameroon, Angola has also had a key role in influencing geopolitical situation of Central Africa inter alia through its decisive interventions during conflicts in the DRC and CAR and it continues to increase its economic position through oil exploitation.[19]

Politics in CAR particularly over resources derails its peace and security initiatives including those involving external actors. The suspicion has kept the security situation in this part of the region calm but capricious. The operation by external forces especially those from outside Africa have accelerated the conflict in CAR for example whereby it took sides and facilitated Anti-Balaka militias in terms of its military capacity, disarmed Seleka group.[20] Apart from France which is considered to be the most important factor for strengthening the EU's peacekeeping mission in CAR, the European Union (EU) has also been actively involved in peace and security in Central African region in pursuit of its economic interests.[21]

MECHANISMS FOR SILENCING GUNS IN THE REGION

It has been indicated in the second part of this chapter that the actors in the conflicts in the Central African region include those who accelerate conflict and those who attempt to prevent it. In this regard this part focuses on some actors' attempts to prevent the conflict. UN and AU have been key organisations that have attempted to prevent the conflict and thus promote peace and security across the region. The UN through MONUC which was later transformed into Stabilisation Mission in the Democratic Republic of Congo (MONUSCO) has been praised by mainly international NGOs on one hand for being instrumental in peacekeeping in DRC.

The credit for the MONUSCO in peace keeping in this country is based on the claim that it has contributed to the reunification of the country because

[18] Stephen W. Smith (2015; Marchal R., 2015), The Elite's Road to Riches in a Poor Country, in Eds Lombard and Carrayannis, 2015.

[19] Cristopher Stevens et al. (2008), The New EPAs: Comparative Analysis of their Content and the Challenges for 2008. ECDPM Policy Management Report no. 14, March, 2008 Maastricht.

[20] Abdurrahim Ingerstad (2014), Central African Republic-Trapped in a Cycle of Violence: Causes, Conflict Dynamics and Prospects for Peace. Stockholm: Swedish Defence Research Agency (FOI).

[21] Abdurrahim Sıradağ (2016), Explaining the Conflict in Central African Republic: Causes and dynamics, King Fahd University of Petroleum and Minerals, Saudi Arabia, The journal of Transdisciplinary Studies, Vol. 9, No. 3 (2016).

its presence has led to preventing the recurrence of a major violent conflict and facilitating the International and national actors to provide services and to stimulate the local economy and for supporting democratic politics and justice.[22] On the other hand, MONUC/MONUSCO has been criticised for its failure to end conflict in the DRC despite having the largest number in any UN peace keeping missions. The missions have been criticised for failure to protect civilians from being massacred. Yet, it was mandated to do that by the UN Security Council Resolution 1291 that called on MONUC to take "necessary action" to protect civilians under threat of eminent violence in deployment areas of its "infantry battalions" This mandate was also reiterated in the extended Mandate of 2012 UN Security Council Resolution 2053 (2012) which transformed MONUC into MONUSCO. MONUSCO like its predecessor MONUC has up to now failed to stop the killing of civilians mainly in the Eastern parts of the DRC.

Another major UN peacekeeping mission in ECCAS member countries is MINUSCA. The mission was mandated to protect civilians and support the transition processes in the CAR. The MINUSCA replaced Mission Internationale à la Central Afrique sous Conduite Africaine (MISCA) which was put in place by the AU's Peace and Security Council (PSC) to resolve the crisis and reaffirmed by the UN Security Council Resolution 2027 (2013). In addition, ECCAS has played a key role in preventing conflict in the Central African region through its efforts in mediating the conflict in CAR. Apparently, the Angolan president João Lourenço is also trying to mediate in tackling the post-electoral violence in CAR. Angolan attempts in this regard are also in line with the support of the International Conference of the Great Lakes Region's (ICGRL) which is also involved in tackling conflict in CAR. Angola is not only attempting to tackle the conflict in the CAR but it has also recently encouraged Rwandan and Ugandan leaders to have talks with an of diffusing the current security situation between their sister countries. The role of ICGRL in the enhancement of peace and security in the Central African region can also be seen through its Expanded Joint Verification Mechanisms now based in Goma, DRC.

Other external actors in line with peace and security in the region include the European Union, the United States (US) which contributed logistical and financial means to facilitate MISCA in its efforts to end the crisis. On the request from the CAR government, Rwanda and Russia have sent troops to prevent the violence during and after the election whereas France has contributed flyover missions in CAR. These countries' roles are crucial in the prevention of post-electoral violence in the CAR.

Other external actors include international civil society organisations. On this list of actors in the peace and security enhancement in the Central African

---

[22] Alexandra, Novosselof (2019), The Effectiveness of the UN Mission in the Democratic Republic of the Congo. https://theglobalobservatory.org/2019/12/effectiveness-un-mission-democratic-republic-of-the-congo/. (Accessed on February 22, 2021).

region we can also add local civil society organisations which most of the time work with the International civil society organisations. The forces do not only include regional economic communities or regional mechanisms, but also civil society organisations, private sector and human rights organisations. There is a wider way of sources that provide information where in CAR MINUSCA paved a way for the UN mission in Central Africa. Responding and preventing conflict is not only a responsibility of ECCAS but also individual states have the responsibility to prevent the conflicts. This responsibility should be exercised even after the conflict context when there is sustainable disarmament programme to ensure that combatants do not return to conflict. Silencing guns means focussing on the underlying causes of conflicts make and to make sure that prevention is sustainable such that there is no need to resort to weapons as a result.

The Central African region can make a difference through the prevention of conflicts rather than implementing the tools of conflict management when the conflicts have started. In this regard, more efforts should be directed to prevention than reacting to conflicts after they have escalated. This is in line with the African initiative to work with armed groups to negotiate and work with governments. The APSA road map builds on AU Peace and Security Council with a focus on preventive and post-conflict strategies to achieve the goal of silencing the guns through strategic priorities of prevention, crisis/conflict management, post-conflict reconstruction, strategic security issues and coordination and partnerships.

There have been mechanisms put in place by individual countries, and organisations with other partners. July 2006 AU adopted (Peace conflict reconstruction and development—PCRD) in Banjul on reconstruction based on—monitoring and to ensure that peace agreements are complemented by sustained post-conflict reconstruction and peacebuilding efforts to address root causes underlining their outbreak. For example, regional cooperation initiatives for the elimination of LRA.

In the CAR, mechanisms through agreements have been considered in this regard. The Political Agreement for Peace and Reconciliation in the CAR in February 2019 between the Government of CAR on the one hand and the armed groups, on the other hand, was signed in Khartoum, Sudan. This agreement reiterated the commitment of African and international instruments and the constitution of the CAR of 2016 and other contribution through different dialogues and resolutions concerning the situation in CAR. This agreement recognises the decisions of the regional bodies including the AU, the Economic Community of Central African States (ECCAS) and the International Conference of the Great Lakes Region (ICGLR).[23]

---

[23] See the Political Agreement for Peace and Reconciliation in the Central African Republic-15 February 2019. https://documents-dds-ny.un.org/doc/UNDOC/GEN/N19/044/63/PDF/N1904463.pdf?OpenElement. (Accessed on November 27, 2020).

This agreement also mentioned specific issues of that have to be considered for the peace and security in CAR to flourish. It mentions issues of disarmament, demobilisation, reintegration and repatriation (DDRR). The critical role of the region and international community is mentioned in the agreement and it clearly states the sanctions in relation to the AU Peace and Security Council in addition to the UN Security Council resolution whereby they can impose sanctions to the parties that fail to adhere to the agreement. Although this is an important point for the successful implementation of the agreement, it may not be a guarantor of the peace and security of the CAR. As presented in another section above the conflict in CAR has multiple actors who may not necessarily be easily managed and thus made accountable for crimes committed because of the way they transform and breed new AGs.

Regional initiatives to silence guns together have been taken including those taken by the AU to coordinate a unified regional political process to defeat the Lord Resistance Army.[24] The regional initiative against the LRA is flexible and original mechanisms to promote collective security by pooling the resources and capabilities of the countries of the sub-region to address the LRA problem.[25] Maphosa also points out that the regional cooperative initiative for elimination of LRA is a peace support model that highlights the multifarious presence of collaboration and regional cooperation which necessitates a shared planning and unambiguous mandates of operation, with clear coordination of military and non-military utilities. He also recommends the mechanism to be applied to eliminate Boko Haram insurgency and other AGs from parts of Africa.

Challenges in Silencing Guns in Central African Region

As presented in the above section, the peace and security situation in Central African region is still problematic and silencing guns is still a challenge. Different factors contribute to this situation. Overarching challenge behind this is governance issues. It needs to be highlighted that these two countries are the most affected by the insecurity. And they have more AGs and NF than any other ECASS member country.

Poor political and military institutions are common such that most countries in this region have had political instability for quite many years. The fragility of Central African political context is reflected in high scores on many rankings regarding corruption and poor governance where it has been

---

[24] AU (2010), Decisions, Declarations and Resolution Adopted. In 'Proceedings of the Fifteenth Ordinary Session of the Assembly of the Union', Kampala, Uganda, 27 July 2010.

[25] Maphosa S.B. (2013), 'Preparing for Peace: The AU Regional Cooperation Initiative for the Elimination of the LRA in Central Africa', Discussion paper, No. 85, Asia Policy Brief, March 2013.

136   P. J. MUGUME

mentioned in 2016 that three out of eleven ECCAS member states belonged to the top ten fragile states notably CAR, DRC and Chad.[26] In the same vein Congo Brazzaville, Chad, the CAR and the DRC are in top 20 of the corruption perception index, with the exception of São Tomé and Príncipe.[27]

It is important also to mention the issue of insufficient resources by regional bodies such as ECASS. The Regional Economic Communities (RECs) including ECCAS have faced different issues such as political consensus to create an effective peace keeping operation; ineffective coordination among the different peace keeping operations deployed by regional, sub-regional and international actors, and the economic and logistical challenge that hamper the effectiveness of operations.[28] The issue of logistical and financial support has not only affected ECASS member countries such CAR, Burundi but has also manifested in Somalia and South Sudan. Insufficiency of resources that hamper operational effectiveness of ECASS member countries has probably necessitated the international actors to intervene in peace and security-related activities in the AU's member countries through its RECs and/or the UN for the case of CAR in 2013.

ECCAS was established in 1983 and started its operations in 1985. The aim of ECCAS is to promote and strengthen cooperation in order to realise a balanced and self-sustained economic development of member countries. This makes ECCAS more of an economic body rather than a peace and security centred one. However, one of its objectives is to foster peaceful relations between member countries, although this appears to be a secondly objective. This may be a challenge and can hinder the organization's activities from the effective promotion of peace and security.

The availability of natural resources has partly facilitated insecurity in the region.[29] In this vein Meyer points out that Central Africa's significant wealth in minerals, oil and timber, together with governments' failure to access and effectively manage resources, represents a substantial conflict factor, and weak, limited or non-existent state control over mines and resources makes these resources a potential income source for criminal groups and rebel

---

[26] Fragile States Index (2016), Fund for Peace Available on http://www.transparency.org/news/feature/corruption_perceptions_index_2016. (Accessed on March 10, 2021).

[27] Transparency International (2016), Sub-Saharan Africa: Corruption is a Big Issue in 2016 Elections. Available on https://www.transparency.org/en/news/africa-corruption-is-a-big-issue-in-2016-african-elections. (Accessed on March 9, 2021).

[28] Annette Weber and Markus Kaim (2014, p. 5), Central African Republic in Crisis: African Union Mission Needs United Nations Support. (SWP Comment, 15/2014). Berlin: Stiftung Wissenschaft und Politik—SWP—Deutsches Institut für Internationale Politik und Sicherheit. https://nbn-resolving.org/urn:nbn:de:0168-ssoar-388025.

[29] Paul Collier et al. (2003), Breaking the Conflict Trap: Civil War and Development Policy. Oxford: Oxford University Press; see also Ian Bannon and Paul Collier (2003), Natural Resources and Violent Conflict: options and actions.

movements.[30] This point has already been mentioned elsewhere by scholars including The 2010 UN Group of Experts report on DRC which points out that the exploitation of natural resources and illicit diamond trade by armed groups is an important cause of insecurity and conflict in Eastern DRC and the region.[31] Apart from natural resources another issue that accelerates conflict in the Central African region is the illicit flow of firearms that have flowed into the region over the years from two Congolese wars, the genocide in Rwanda, the conflict in Burundi and external sources.[32] In relation to this point, Meyer argues that Central African region is one of Africa's most fragile and vulnerable regions with several military coups, crises and conflict.[33]

Multiple and sometimes overlapping membership of some ECASS member countries and ECASS is still an issue in regional discussion. Central African Region is also considered to be a complex region in which to work regionally.[34] On one hand Central African Region is considered to be more of periphery, or leftover, of other regions than a coherent region in itself. But on other hand, there is rather a hive of competing authorities across the region, born of specific historical basis for regional initiatives, organisations and for countries to engage, all are undermined by conflict and gamesmanship, internal and cross-border conflicts, alliances and anti-alliances.[35] As an illustration, countries such as Angola and DRC are SADC members, Rwanda and Burundi are members of the EAC, DRC, Burundi, Rwanda and Angola are also member of COMESA. In addition, Rwanda, Burundi and DRC are also members of the Nile basin Initiatives (NBI). Some of these organisations have similar objectives including economic and security-related ones.

As mentioned earlier, the AU pursues peace and security through Africa's RECs precisely through regional standby forces. To focus on Central African regional forces-there is the Central Africa Standby Force (CASF) of which some member countries such as Angola, DRC and Rwanda are members. This regional force that does not involve all regional member countries and thus may not serve all countries in the region. Lack of cohesion among member countries may also affect decisions concerning peace operations in the region

---

[30] Angela Meyer (2011), Peace and Security Cooperation in Central Africa: Developments, challenges and Prospects, Nordiska Afrikainstitutet 2011.

[31] United Nations 2010. UN (2010), Final Report of the United Nations Group of Experts on the DRC (United Nations publication, 29 November 2010, S/2010/596/para.d. Available at: http://www.un.org. (Accessed on November 20, 2020). See also UNODC (2011), Organized Crime and Instability in Central Africa, A Threat Assessment, Vienna.

[32] Greenpeace (2010); Fedotov (2011).

[33] Meyer (2015), Preventing Conflict in Central Africa: ECCAS Caught Between Ambitious, Challenges and Reality. Institute for Security Studies, Issue 3/August 2015.

[34] Bruce Byiers (2017, p. 3).

[35] Lombard and Carayannis (2015), as cited in Bruce Byiers (2017, p. 3): Lombard, L., Carayannis, T. (2015), Making Sense of CAR: An Introduction, in Eds Carrayannis, T., Lombard, L. (2015), Making Sense of the Central African Republic, Zed Books, London.

as a whole. This can be so due to the divergence of interests and priorities of Central African regional member countries.

External support contributes in the promotion of peace and security in the Central African Region on one part. However, it also affects it on the other. For example, external actors from France to the UN have generally viewed CAR through the lens of the promotion of regional stability at the expense of standing firm for any kind of substantive democracy or inclusiveness in CAR politics.[36] France's role has also been considered to be influential in the politics of Gabon for some time due to its economic interests in the country in particular. Another example that is worth mentioning is the role of the Central African Region's member countries such as Chad in facilitating countries including the United States of America (USA) and France in tackling the issue of Jihadists in the region.

PROPOSED SOLUTIONS TO THE CONFLICT

In *Ending wars, Building states,* Call points out that many scholars and practitioners have for centuries sought to improve our ability to end wars.[37] However, Call also points out that civil wars-historically have been more difficult to settle and keep settled and argues that failed peacebuilding represents one of the last risk factors for new wars.[38] What this author points out here is that peace agreements sometimes fail and where they appear to have been successful like the case of the Arusha Accord for Rwanda and Burundi, they have not ended well. For the case of Rwanda and Angola in 1990s, though the agreements were not considered failed, their aftermath was not good considering that innocent people lost their lives in Rwanda during the 1994 genocide against Tutsi. The related case is from Burundi whereby despite the Arusha peace agreement to bring peace in that country, violence and conflict continues in that country. War's disruption of people, economic production, and political uncertainty combine to produce what is known as reverse development or impoverishment. This situation complicates war-torn countries where the institutions of authority have been destroyed or disrupted.[39]

[36] Lombard and Carayannis (2015) as cited by Bruce (2017, p. 15), Lombard, L., Carayannis, T. (2015), Chapter 1: Making Sense of CAR: An Introduction, in Eds Carrayannis, T., Lombard, L. (2015), Making Sense of the Central African Republic, Zed Books, London; See also Understanding Economic Integration and Peace and Security in IGAD—High-level summitry and pragmatism in a region of "persistent turbulence; European Center for Development Policy Management. Available on https://ecdpm.org/wp-content/uploads/IGAD-Background-Paper-PEDRO-Political-Economy-Dynamics-Regional-Organisations-Africa-ECDPM-2017.pdf. (Accessed on March 10, 2021).

[37] Charles T. Call (2008, p. 1), Ending Wars, Building States, In Building States to Build Peace by Charles T. Call with Vanessa Wyeth (2008), Lynne Rienner Publishers, Boulder, London.

[38] As above.

[39] Call (2008, p. 2).

Although the Central African region is still challenged by conflicts, some of which are violent, there is a serious need for the AU's standby brigades to be well coordinated and accountable to the AU's Security Council. This requires the AU to have capacity to finance the force's activities in conflict affected countries. The AU and ECCAS in particular needs to have financial capacity because, it is vital for enhancing sustainable peace and security in the Central African region to solve the issue of underfunded peace operations in the region including the one in CAR. This can also help to overcome the issue of reliance on external funding issue that comes with conditions in addition to being unreliable for the receiving countries.

Successful attempts to promote peace and security in the Central African region require dialogue between regional states starting with neighbouring states. This can enable regional member countries to mobilise their resources together in order to deal with regional peace and security challenges. The dialogue between regional states can facilitate sincere cooperation and coordination of activities to end conflicts and thus vital silencing guns in Central African Region.

With cooperation and coordination, human security-related issues can also be addressed. Women and gender-related discrimination should be eliminated, and women can play key role in the management of conflicts and thus build peace and security in the Central African Region. ECCAS member countries need to address governance issues that have derailed the region's peace and security efforts. Governance issues that have been exclusionary whereby some sections of the region's population have been excluded in the governance affairs of their countries and resources. To address governance issues there is a need to look at it not as defined and/or given by the Global West but to contextualise it and build consensus-based democratic governance that suits the individual countries.

Despite weak institutions in some member countries in the Central African region, it is necessary for individual states to put in place a strong national security force that can enhance peace and security. These measures can consolidate peace and security within the African continent leave alone the ECASS region. Before going regional or global it is essential that states start from within their home. In order to promote peace and security through conflicts prevention in the Central African region there is a need to start at the local level. There is a need to consider investing more rights from the individual family level before considering other echelons such as local, state and regional levels.

Considering the serious issue of unequal distribution of resources in the region, there is a need for mechanisms to deal with the mismanagement of natural resources in order to make them beneficial to the population. Accountable natural resources management in individual states can contribute to this. But for them to be more productive there is a need for conducive policy framework that facilitates their activities.

The ECCAS member countries need to consider reducing reliance on external partners including UN, EU, the USA, and France. It is understandably important to have partnership, but the partnership that is unfair has affected the efforts of building peace and security in the region especially due to conditions which use biassed mechanisms that are not necessarily effective in bringing peace and security in the region. These partners from the global North have attempted to bring hybrid peace in the Central African region like other parts of the global South. It has been common in this region that the one who provides financial and sometimes military dictates what should be done on the ground.[40] Such situation has created a situation of mistrust between some locals and can also be partly blamed on contributing to identity issues in the regional member countries.

There is a need for professional security sector for the promotion of peace and security in the region. Such security sector should be non-partisan, professional and subject to civilian control. Professional security sector that serves the nation interest of the country can be helpful and prevent the identity issues in the military such as regional, religious and/or ethnic-based armies for example that can easily be manipulated by individual leaders to serve their interests. The Central African region is affected by different human (in)security including economic, environmental, community, political, health and food.

For this region to pursue sustainable peace and security, these issues need to be addressed through different mechanisms including policies. In this regard, there is a need to put in place a comprehensive human security centred policy by Central African Region's states to address the human security issues. For example, food security policies are necessary if the region is to have peace and security. This issue needs to be seriously taken care of by the Central African region's governments because sometimes people cross borders in search of services including food. The policies should be backed by specific strategies for implementation since having a good policy is one thing and implementing it is another thing. It can be noted also that a state may have good strategies including specific ones but lack capacity to implement them.

ECASS member countries should be strong for the regional bodies and strong on the armed groups and negative forces and put mechanisms in place to rehabilitate the former fighters after they silence their guns. This is important because some of those have been ideologically made to believe that their survival depends on the gun and thus surrendering them would mean the end of their lives. There is a need for states to invest heavily in human security to enable countries to fight against poverty and injustice, improve their health and food security. As long as leaders in the Central African region fail to provide the basic needs to their population and address human security issues, it will still be difficult for the AU to succeed in silencing guns in this particular region leave alone by 2020 but also perhaps by 2063. It can be

---

[40] Oliver P. Richmond (2007), The Transformation of Peace, Palgrave Macmillan, New York.

difficult to promote peace in situations where people are still habouring negative attitudes towards others due to their countries' history. It is important for regional member countries to promote the reconciliation process that can be helpful in addressing post-conflict issues. Forgiveness is crucial for promoting peace in post-conflict affected countries to prevent relapse of the conflict.

CONCLUSION

This chapter presented the Central African region's member countries and reasons for conflicts, the actors in the conflict and their interests, mechanisms and challenges involved in the process of silencing guns. Silencing of guns in this region as envisaged by the AU has not been achieved looking its current security and political and economic developments.

One of the most important factors for the conflict in the region is related to conflicting interest among the political elites who struggle to have access to their countries' resources mainly through identity-based politics. Identity politics within this region are based on tribal and religious issues which are common. These issues have affected many countries in this region, but mainly the CAR, DRC, Cameroon, Rwanda and Burundi. The major consequence of these issues is exclusion of countries' part of the citizens perceived to be opponents of those in power.

These issues in addition to regionalization in DRC particular have shaped the political ideologies of ECCAS member countries. Political elites have used these as tools to mobilise their communities to support, protect and prolong their stay in power sometimes through violent conflicts. On the other the hand these issues have derailed regional member countries from having consistent national agenda for enhancing peace and security. Exclusionary governance tendencies have encouraged human insecurity in most countries of the Central African region. Due to exclusion regional member countries some of their populations have resorted to violence as a way to fight for their rights. Poverty and unequal distribution of natural resources have accelerated the human insecurity in this region.

As indicated in this chapter there is also an issue of external influence which is based on external actors' interests. Post-colonial legacy/tendencies also have contributed to prolonging of conflict in the Central African region. It is important for the AU to help its member states to promote good governance through policies that empower the population. Decentralised governance can provide a space for involving different stakeholders in their governance because it can be helpful in addressing issues of marginalisation related to religion, ethnicity and/or regionalization. In this context decentralisation should not be decentralisation by centralising where it is more of theory than a practice. Mechanisms to enhance democratic governance such as elections should be promoted through capacity building specifically in management of elections within the Central African region but also in other AU member countries before, during and after elections. Election managers need to have the autonomy to process elections and they should put national interests before political parties, religion, ethnic group(s) and /or region.

CHAPTER 9

Sustaining Peace and Security in Southern Africa

Mphatso Jones Boti Phiri

THE SOUTHERN AFRICAN DEVELOPMENT COMMUNITY (SADC) REGIONAL FRAMEWORK

The SADC is intergovernmental in nature and emphasises the centrality of sovereignty and the nation state within the context of international and regional cooperation.[1] In this light, the SADC decisions do not supersede and override the sovereign authority of the members' states. The discussion in this chapter dwells on the implications of intergovernmental organisation on disaster preparedness policy implementation within member states. States are often depicted as unitary, sovereign and rational actors following certain national interests, although such approaches have been criticised as

---

[1] D. J. Francis (2006) *Uniting Africa: Building Regional Peace and Security Systems*. Aldershot: Ashgate Publishing. T. Murithi (2017) *The African Union: Pan-Africanism, Peacebuilding and Development*. Routledge. See also T. Murithi (2008) The African Union's Evolving Role in Peace Operations: The African Union Mission in Burundi, the African Union Mission in Sudan and the African Union Mission in Somalia. *African Security Studies 17* (1), 69–82. See P. D. Williams (2008) Keeping the Peace in Africa: Why "African" Solutions are Not enough. *Ethics & International Affairs 22* (3), 309–329. See also L. Nathan (2012) *Community of Insecurity: SADC's Struggle for Peace and Security in Southern Africa*: Ashgate Publishing, Ltd; and G. Olivier (2010) Regionalism in Africa: Cooperation without Integration? *Strategic Review for Southern Africa 32* (2), 17.

M. J. Boti Phiri (✉)
The Malawi Parliament, Lilongwe, Malawi

© The Author(s), under exclusive license to Springer Nature Switzerland AG 2022
D. Kuwali (ed.), *The Palgrave Handbook of Sustainable Peace and Security in Africa*, https://doi.org/10.1007/978-3-030-82020-6_9

144   M. J. BOTI PHIRI

too simplistic.[2] States make deliberate efforts to improve their conditions, solve common problems within their region, however, in intergovernmental settings; policy implementation remains the responsibility of states.[3]

The SADC as an international institution provides a common framework for cooperation that reduces uncertainty and minimises transaction costs.[4] Within the intergovernmental scholarship, the regional bodies or institutions provide a platform for interstate bargaining. Policy making is made through negotiation among member states or through carefully circumscribed delegations or authority.[5] Theoretical debates within this perspective have dealt with questions of states' influence on collective decision making.[6] Within the liberal intergovernmentalism scholarship, states define their underlying preferences and negotiate with other states to create appropriate international institutions for collective action and fulfilment of their goals within their regions.[7]

As shown by other contributors in Part II of this Handbook, regional frameworks are not just a functional response to intra-regional economic developments but 'an essentially political process informed by multidimensional economic and strategic factors.'[8] The central point here is that a common interest among states drives integration among states. The emphasis on the central role of the state in integration provides powerful lens through which one can view and explain the integration process elsewhere. Integration

---

[2] A. Moravcsik (1999) Is Something Rotten in the State of Denmark? Constructivism and European Integration. *Journal of European Public Policy* 6 (4), 669–681. See J. Wunderlich (2008) *Regionalism, Globalisation and International Order*. Abingdon, Ashgate Publishing Group.

[3] D. K. Emmerson (Ed.) (2009a) East Asian Regionalism in a New Global Context: Balancing Representation and Effectiveness. *A Keynote Speech Delivered on March 19 to a Conference on the Philippines and Japan in East Asia and the World: Interests, Identity and Roles*, Organised by the Philippines's Asian Centre. See P. M. Evans (1995) The Prospects for Multilateral Security co-operation in the Asia/Pacific Region. *The Journal of Strategic Studies* 18 (3), 201–217. See also R. Fawn (Ed.) (2009) *Globalising the Regional, Regionalising the Global: Vol. 35, Review of International Studies*: Cambridge University Press.

[4] S. Burchill, A. Linklater, R. Devetak, J. Donnelly, T. Nardin, M. Paterson, C. Reus-Smit, and J. True (2013) *Theories of International Relations*: Palgrave Macmillan. D. K. (Ed.) (2009a) East Asian Regionalism in a New Global Context: Balancing Representation and Effectiveness. *A Keynote Speech Delivered on March 19 to a Conference on the Philippines and Japan in East Asia and the World: Interests, Identity and Roles*, Organised by the Philippines's Asian Centre.

[5] P. Pierson (1996) The Path to European Integration A Historical Institutionalist Analysis. *Comparative Political Studies* 29 (2), 123–163.

[6] A. Moravcsik (1991) Negotiating the Single European Act: National Interests and Conventional Statecraft in the European Community. *International Organization* 45 (1), 19–56. See also Y. H. Ferguson (2003) Illusions of Superpower. *Asian Journal of Political Science* 11 (2), 21–36.

[7] M. Kim (2014) Integration Theory and ASEAN Integration. *Pacific Focus* 29 (3), 374–394.

[8] M. Beeson (2005) Rethinking Regionalism: Europe and East Asia in Comparative Historical Perspective. *Journal of European Public Policy* 12 (6), 969–985, p. 970.

outcomes constrain, and control collective action problems associated with rational choices to enhance the credibility and commitments to international institutions.[9] In this light, intergovernmentalism provides an analytical framework through which we can assess SADC approach to regional security and disaster preparedness and response.

Regional coordination mechanism between SADC and Members States is mainly a network rather than a hierarchy.[10] It is also observed that the SADC regional integration is still a work in progress).[11] Although little power has been ceded to SADC to enable the region to respond to the regional directives, SADC leaders seem to agree that having a regional response to security and emergencies is a common goal. What is unclear in this instance is the extent to which SADC member states cooperate under the SADC framework in disaster response and preparedness. This chapter is, therefore, undertaken to interrogate the SADC early warning capacity, preparedness, response and disaster risk management framework.

MOTIVATIONS FOR REGIONAL COOPERATION IN DISASTER RESPONSE AND CLIMATE CHANGE

The SADC region is currently experiencing and threatened by a series of climate-related disasters, which include drought and flooding. Some examples of the climate-related disasters are tropical cyclones such as IDAI and Kenneth that hit central Mozambique, southern Malawi and eastern parts of Zimbabwe destroying almost one million hectares and widespread flooding destroyed lives, crops and infrastructure. The Tropical Cyclone IDAI in 2019 affected an estimated three million people in the three SADC Member States. At the continental level, Africa is experiencing widespread flooding, wildfires and other hazardous occurrences resulting in loss of lives and destruction of property due to global warming.[12] As seen mostly in Malawi, Zambia and Zimbabwe, the past two decades Southern Africa has experienced an increase in the frequency, magnitude and impact of drought and floods. Climate

[9] Moravcsik (1991) Negotiating the Single European Act: National Interests and Conventional Statecraft in the European Community. *International Organization 45* (1), 19–56. See also M. Beeson (2005) Rethinking Regionalism: Europe and East Asia in Comparative Historical Perspective. *Journal of European Public Policy 12* (6), 969–985.

[10] M. J. Boti-Phiri (2018) *Leadership, regionalisation of peace operations and conflict mediation: African Union and Southern African Development Community in perspective.* PhD Thesis, Coventry University.

[11] L. Nathan, L. (2012) *Community of Insecurity: SADC's Struggle for Peace and Security in Southern Africa*: Ashgate Publishing, Ltd. See also G. Olivier (2010) Regionalism in Africa: Cooperation without Integration? *Strategic Review for Southern Africa 32* (2), 17.

[12] Speech by the representative of African Union Commission, Dr. Jolly Wasambo at the twenty-third meeting of Southern African Regional Climate Outlook Forum in Luanda, Angola, to develop consensus regional climate outlook for 2019–2020 rain season.

change is expected to exacerbate the flood risks, agriculture and food security.[13] These situations have demanded some critical assessment of disaster preparedness and response in the region.

SADC Early Warning Coordination Mechanisms with Member States

In responding to the ever-growing security challenges, the Southern African Development Community established a Regional Early Warning Centre (REWC) that mainly links with National Early Warning Centres (NEWCs). The REWC is security centric and its overall objective is to strengthen the SADC mechanisms for conflict prevention, management and resolution in line with the provisions of the Protocol on Politics, Defence and Security Cooperation (OPDS) and Strategic Indicative Plan for the Organ (SIPO).[14] Some of the main functions of the Regional Early Warning Centre are to compile strategic assessments and analysis of data collected at regional level; share information on major issues posing threat to the security and stability of the region; and propose ways and means for preventing, combating and managing such threats. REWC essentially provides key inputs for the SADC Regional Vulnerability Analysis and Assessment Programme.[15]

The SADC Vulnerability Assessment and Analysis (VAA) monitors member states' capacity in dealing with external hazards such as drought, economic crises and climate change. It also includes meteorological and crop projections, household economic analysis and food and nutrition security surveys. The SADC established the Regional Vulnerability Assessment Committee (RVAC) that is linked to National Vulnerability Assessment Committees (NVACs) at the Member State level to coordinate the annual vulnerability assessment and analysis. The Regional Vulnerability Assessment and Analysis (RVAA) Programme has been implemented by SADC since 2006. The Programme builds strategies and interventions in emergencies and threats to livelihoods. The SADC RVAA Programme is aimed at reducing poverty and vulnerability through climate-resilient livelihoods in the SADC Region.[16] While it is noted that NVACs are functional and contributing to the national- regional and global reporting system and processes within the United Nations Framework Convention on Climate Change (UNFCCC) in addressing the vulnerability

[13] SADC booklet on Climate Change Adaptation in SADC; Available at: https://www.sadc.int/files/2213/5293/3544/SADC_Climate_Change_Adaptation_for_the_Water_Sector_booklet.pdf.

[14] SADC provision available at: www.sadc.int (accessed 10 December 2019).

[15] SADC provision on Regional Vulnerability Analysis and Assessment Programme. Available at: www.sadc.int (accessed 10 December 2019).

[16] RVAC has established the following technical working groups: Nutrition; Information Management; Urban Assessments; Integrated Phase Classification (IPC) for food security; Centre of Excellence (of five Universities) and Capacity Building; Markets Assessments.

issues in the region there is no evidence that the NVACs are at the same level of development in all member states.[17]

This revelation indicates significant challenges in disaster preparedness and response within the region. The chapter further discusses the challenges. It is also noted that, although the SADC RVAA Programme supports national institution building of NVACs, and strengthen their technical capacity and communication outputs, there is little evidence on the development and comprehensive coordination between the two frameworks apart from the annual reports.[18] Similarly, as noted by Gilbert Mittawa in Chapter 22, national capabilities are not yet well synchronised.

AN ASSESSMENT OF THE SADC EARLY WARNING INFRASTRUCTURE

The SADC early warning system is dependent on the member states national systems, most of which are underdeveloped. It is noted that instruments and systems to support the operationalization of the SADC Regional Disaster Preparedness and Response Strategy had not yet been implemented as of November 2019.[19] These systems include science-based early warning system in highly vulnerable areas and communities. The significance of effective and efficient National Meteorological and Hydrological Services in Member States and SADC for timely and credible weather and climate services has been underscored.[20] Such services would greatly minimise losses from the impact of adverse extreme weather and climate events such as storms, tropical cyclones, floods, heatwaves and droughts. Despite the recurrent flooding disasters in the SADC member states like Malawi, the country still lacks the flood detector and alarm system that would monitor water levels in rivers and warn vulnerable communities of the impending flooding.

[17] SADC Stakeholders root for strengthening the mainstreaming climate change into vulnerability assessments and analysis; The meeting that took place from 01 to 05 July 2019. SADC Stakeholders root for strengthening the mainstreaming climate change into vulnerability assessments and analysis.

[18] Speech by the SADC Executive Secretary, Her Excellency Dr. Stergomena Lawrence Tax at the 21st SADC Ministerial Committee of the Organ on Politics Defence and Security Cooperation held in Lusaka, Zambia. The SADC Executive Secretary urged the SADC Members States and Partners to support the operationalization of the SADC Disaster Preparedness and Response Mechanism.

[19] "SADC and European Civil Protection and Humanitarian Aid Operations discuss areas for cooperation" The SADC Executive Secretary emphasised the urgency of developing instruments and systems to support the operationalization of the SADC Regional Disaster Preparedness and Response Strategy.

[20] Speech by the SADC Senior Programme Officer for Meteorology, Dr. Prithiviraj Booneeady, at the twenty-third meeting of Southern African Regional Climate Outlook Forum in Luanda, Angola, to develop consensus regional climate outlook for 2019–2020 rain season.

Contrary to the seemingly clear picture of the SADC regional coordination provided, the member states early warning structures are mainly independent structures with much more focus on state security. The combination of early warning and state security provides an additional coordination challenges due to the secrecy nature of defence and security apparatus. Additionally, the member states early warning structures are at different levels of development thereby adding another layer of coordination challenge with the regional framework and synchronisation.

AN ASSESSMENT OF THE STATE OF PREPAREDNESS WITHIN SADC

The SADC Member States were at different stages of disaster preparedness, vulnerability assessments and analysis.[21] From this backdrop, it is challenging for SADC to have timely and credible information to respond effectively to several disasters that affect the SADC region. SADC as an intergovernmental organisation, cannot enforce any standard procedures on member states that appear to be reluctant to cede authority to the regional body and enforce its principles. Although SADC has set out some strategies for an implementation plan and a system for monitoring and evaluating disaster preparedness projects to ensure that adaptation measures remain effective in member states, there is no guarantee for their infrastructure development.[22]

Most meteorological services within SADC are not modernised and the region lacks an integrated database on weather and climate.[23] The SADC and member states partnership on disaster risk reduction has not yet developed to systematically work together to better profile disaster risks facing the region, strengthen response capacities and enable rapid reaction when natural disasters occur. Although the Regional Remote Sensing Unit has been developed at SADC, in support of early warning for food security; natural resources management and disaster management, the corresponding national remote sensing, agrometeorology and geographic information system (GIS) are at different levels of development.

[21] The Regional Vulnerability Assessment and Analysis (RVAA) Programme's regional pre-assessment workshop (05–10 May 2019) Gaborone, Botswana. SADC Member States make strides to improve the quality and relevance of vulnerability assessments and analysis.

[22] SADC booklet on Climate Change Adaptation in SADC. Available at: https://www.sadc.int/files/2213/5293/3544/SADC_Climate_Change_Adaptation_for_the_Water_Sector_booklet.pdf.

[23] Meeting report from the twenty-third meeting of Southern African Regional Climate Outlook Forum (SARCOF-23) was held in Luanda, Republic of Angola, on the 28–30 August 2019.

CHALLENGES TO SADC DISASTER RESPONSE AND RISK REDUCTION

While the SADC underlaying factor is that Member states work together in resolving regional security challenges, the institution acknowledges the challenges in disaster risk management being faced in the region. For instance, it is noted that: institutional frameworks for disaster risk reduction at the regional, national and, in some cases, local/community level, are often under-funded and not coordinated; that there is a lack of comprehensive and constantly updated risk assessments and analysis; that there is weak information and knowledge management systems, specifically in high-risk areas; and there is a need to reduce underlying risk factors.[24] The SADC further acknowledges that planning in a number of cases is not informed by a comprehensive risk analysis and thus it may not address the priority needs for effective disaster risk reduction.[25]

The Cyclone IDAI and Kenneth have increased the awareness of climate variability and the need for a comprehensive and integrated regional approach towards disaster risk reduction and mitigation. The increased frequency, intensity and severity of extreme weather conditions pose a significant challenge to the region and African continent. At the same time, developing countries such as Malawi stand to be adversely affected by climate change due little or no resilient capacity and adaptability than other developed economies.[26] Therefore, there is an urgent need for policy tools for sustainable environment and disaster preparedness by putting in place strategies for mitigation, adaptation and resilience to climate change as well as the strengthening disaster preparedness, response and recovery in the National Disaster Risk Management Policy.[27]

IMPLICATIONS ON PEACE, STABILITY AND SUSTAINABLE DEVELOPMENT IN THE REGION

Climate change and disasters pose a number of risks to SADC goals for regional economic development. For instance, cyclone IDAI caused massive infrastructure and agricultural damage that has disrupted livelihoods, and loss of life in the affected three SADC member states, thereby exacerbating human insecurity. The impact of cyclone IDAI in Malawi Mozambique and Zimbabwe caused subsequent implications on forced migration and governance.

[24] See SADC disaster risk management and vulnerability report 2017.

[25] As above.

[26] Dan Kuwali, "From the West to the Rest: Climate Change as Challenge to Human Security in Africa", 17(3) *African Security Review*, Pretoria: Institute of Security Studies, 2008, pp. 19–38.

[27] Malawi Government, "National Disaster Risk Management Policy", available at: https://www.ifrc.org/docs/IDRL/43755_malawidrmpolicy2015.pdf (accessed 22 October 2019).

The Impact of Forced Migration on Peace and Security

Cyclone IDAI in Southern Africa led to large-scale displacement and caused massive uprooting of families. The forced displacement has mostly resulted in negative consequences such as human rights violations and weakened governance and accountability. Literature shows that forced migration flows create large negative political and economic externalities.[28] Displacement-related pressure on basic human needs like shelter, food and water, can provoke inter-communal conflict, societal tensions and xenophobia in host areas.[29] Forced migration has consequences, which, in turn, may trigger more violence and displacement. The countries hit by cyclone IDAI are developing countries with few job opportunities. The cyclone, therefore, exacerbated the strain on livelihood for both host communities and migrants. This caused a depressing effect on the socio-economic and socio-political environment in the SADC region. The forced migrants in the region also placed an enormous strain on public services and infrastructure leading to a decline in the investment climate, lack of jobs and increased unskilled labour (especially within SADC).

The cyclone IDAI coupled with forced displacement have had an effect on environmental degradation that has the potential for more displacement and inter-communal conflicts. Communities that are prone to increasing environmental dilapidation and disruption have little or no safety nets, which in turn reduces their resilience to threats in their environment such as economic hardship, conflicts and diseases. Additionally, individual characteristics, such as age, gender and social group have varied consequences and response plans to recovery during disasters. Displacement affects women and children differently from men, leading to differences in the way SADC instruments can respond.[30]

RECOMMENDATIONS FOR SUSTAINED PEACE AND SECURITY WITHIN SADC

This chapter has revealed significant gaps in disaster preparedness and response in Southern Africa. Most of these gaps are mainly due to the nature of cooperation, economic development and lack of regional oversight over the state of preparedness within member states. This section provides some recommendations that can enhance significant preparedness and response to the ever-increasing threats to human security and stability in the region.

---

[28] A. Knoll and Lidet Tadesse Shiferaw (2018). Tackling the Triggers of Violence-Induced Displacement: The Contribution of the African Peace and Security Architecture and African Governance Architecture, Discussion Paper No. 228, www.ecdpm.org/dp228.

[29] I. Salehyan (2014) Forced Migration as a Cause and Consequence of Civil War. In E. Newman and K. DeRouen (Eds.), *Handbook of Civil Wars*, New York: Routledge.

[30] A. Kangas, H. Haider, and E. Fraser (2014) *Gender: Topic Guide*. Revised edition with E. Browne. Birmingham: GSDRC, University of Birmingham, UK.

Interoperability in Climate Change and Disaster Preparedness Within SADC

The occurrence of cyclones and flooding within SADC indicates that the emerging threats to security within the region goes beyond state and human security but also environmental.[31] The threats caused by floods and climate change-related disasters are multifaceted and interlinked such that they cannot be tackled by one state alone. Therefore, where environmental security is the most imminent threat to the population, it follows that the country's political, economic and social structures should assist to address such challenges within the spheres of their competence.

To effectively overcome the contemporary flooding and climate change-related challenges in SADC, it is necessary to strengthen collaboration between and among different member states as per the clear and coherent guidelines for coordination outlined in RVAA. The balancing of demands of political (sovereignty), regional cooperation and disaster preparedness and response is important within SADC member states. SADC needs to incorporate enforceable disaster preparedness and environmental measures that goes beyond the existing intergovernmental framework. To achieve this, there is a need to have enforceable standardised early warning and meteorological infrastructure in order to strengthen their operational planning, readiness and preparedness.

For member states to have functional and effectively disaster preparedness, it is imperative to ensure that there is an oversight mechanism for climate change infrastructure development in the region. SADC Disaster Risk Reduction Unit responsible for coordinating regional preparedness and response programmes for trans-boundary hazards and disasters require more empowerment for binding decisions within member states with a view to putting in place a comprehensive and well-coordinated prevention and response mechanism.

Capacity Building of National Early Warning System

Considering that the primary role of security rests on national security apparatus, early warning systems in the member states must be up to date and provide timely and relevant information for planning and response. Training and empowerment of national early warning infrastructures especially in climate change and science-based early warning system is paramount. Development of robust early warning capacity with flooding sensor alarms that can monitor river water levels can contribute to the prevention of loss of lives in vulnerable communities.

In light of their frontline role, member states should also adopt new and practical strategies to overcome sovereignty challenges that hamper regional integration processes and disaster governance. The country's security organs

[31] Michael Renner, 'Transforming Security' in World Watch Institute, *State of the World*, New York: United Nations, 1997, p. 346.

should also adopt a systems approach in order to improve security sector coordination and interoperability. To reduce the securitisation and secrecy of early warning systems, there is a need to shift most non national security early warning to NVAA that will feed into the RVAA. The need for a comprehensive national vulnerability assessment policy that enhances proactivity and coordination of the stakeholders in the region is vital. Effective and efficient response to humanitarian, peace and security concerns in SADC require more integration of the member states in the region. The national vulnerability assessment policy should also be incorporated in the development agenda and modernised early warning infrastructure and training to suit emerging environmental and disaster challenges in the region.

To prevent and respond to emerging security threats, there is a need to ensure monitoring, detection, follow up and information gathering as well as proper coordination of disaster early warning. It is important to inculcate a culture of 'information' sharing within SADC in early warning systems. For this reason, there should be a deliberate policy of sharing early warning signs and to achieve this, the member states using RVAA programme must reduce the bureaucratic requirements that hinder timely assessments of NVAA. It is also important to note that the nature and magnitude of cyclones and flooding means that one-member state cannot protect its citizens without the cooperation of other countries regardless of its capabilities. This means that disaster response is interdependent and goes beyond the national sovereignty concerns. Member states should not operate in silos but rather holistically to sustain peace and human security as well as achieve inclusive growth and sustainable development in the region. Therefore, a close cooperation in capacity building and exchange of knowledge and information between countries is a necessity. It is also crucial to share information and skills with other security agents within SADC and the AU.

Challenges in Holistic Implementation of the RVAA Programme

The Regional Vulnerability Assessment and Analysis and early warning systems cannot be analysed in isolation without considering the continental framework. It is important to appreciate the holistic implementation challenges of the continental, regional and national peace and security frameworks. It is highlighted above how the national security requirements and sovereignty hinders coordination and information sharing between member states and regional bodies.

The APSA is guided by the principle of subsidiarity, complementary and comparative advantage, where subregional actors such as the SADC are first responders to conflicts and disasters within their region. APSA, in conjunction with the Peace and Security Council (PSC) Protocol, the AU Constitutive Act and a Memorandum of Understanding between the AU and Regional Economic Communities (AU-RECs MOU), defines regionalisation of peace and security and provides rules, norms and values that guide collective action in any peace and security efforts in the continent. It is from this backdrop that APSA is not a stand-alone tool but is utilised in conjunction with other protocols and principles.

Articles 16 and 17 of the PSC Protocol stress the need for close collaboration between the AU and Regional Economic Communities (RECs) in the promotion and maintenance of peace, security and stability.[32] Additionally, Article XX (1) in the AU and RECs memorandum of understanding (MOU) provides for modalities for interaction and states that:

> Without prejudice to the primary role of the Union in the promotion and maintenance of peace, security and stability in Africa, the RECs and, where appropriate the Coordinating Mechanisms shall be encouraged to anticipate and prevent conflicts within and among their Member States and, where conflicts do occur, to undertake peace-making and peace building efforts to resolve them, including through deployment of peace support operations.

The AU PSC, as the overall mandating authority in all regional security response, makes decisions that can either be implemented by member states within RECs also referred to as RMs.[33] It is noted, in these provisions, that while the AU delegates security responses to subregions, it retains continental leadership in the promotion and maintenance of peace, security and stability. The AU-RECs MOU, Article XX (4) specifically states that: '*Nothing in this Memorandum shall prevent the Union from taking measures to maintain or restore peace and security anywhere in the continent.*' From this backdrop, the AU provisions, particularly through AU-RECs MOU and the principles of subsidiarity, complementarity and comparative advantage, provide for both hierarchical and shared coordination between AU and subregional actors.

Studies have shown that there is little power that is ceded to the African Union (AU), so that the region can be in tune with what the AU decides.[34] Although Article 16 of PSC Protocol and Article XX (4) of AU-RECs MOU establishes a hierarchy between the AU and RECs,[35] research has revealed that

---

[32] The PSC Protocol Article 16 and Article IV (ii) of the MOU, outline the principles guiding the relationship between the AU and RECs, stating that; *the implementation of the MOU shall be guided by the recognition of, and respect for, the primary responsibility of the Union in the maintenance and promotion of peace, security and stability in Africa, in accordance with Article 16 of the PSC protocol.* Additionally, Article IV (iv) calls for the; *adherence to the principles of subsidiarity, complementarity and comparative advantage, in order to optimise the partnership between the Union, the RECs and the Coordinating Mechanisms in the promotion and maintenance of peace, security and stability.*

[33] Regional economic community (REC) is used interchangeably with Regional Mechanism (RM) and subregions.

[34] M. J. Boti-Phiri (2018) *Leadership, Regionalisation of Peace Operations and Conflict Mediation: African Union and Southern African Development Community in Perspective.* PhD Thesis, Coventry University.

[35] AU leadership is clearly defined in the PSC Protocol Article 16 and further reinforced in Article IV (ii) of the MOU, outlining the principles guiding the relationship between

subregions are autonomous. Research further reveals that the AU-RECS coordination challenges also take place within the SADC. Member states within SADC continue to shape the form and content of SADC leadership in security policies. The formation of continental and regional security structures demonstrates the importance of coordination; however, there are inconsistencies and difficulties in regional policy implementations due to the lack of hierarchy and leadership.

Leadership within the SADC as a subregional security governance structure inclines towards a collaborative set-up with member states than hierarchy. This indicates the shifting nature of influence when responding to disasters and security threats within the region. From this backdrop, there are inconsistencies in the holistic implementation of the African common defence and security policy; consequently, challenging the preparedness of SADC and implementation of the Regional Vulnerability Assessment and Analysis Programme. In this light, it is important for SADC member states to reconsider their stance on sovereignty when it comes to the implementation of RVAA programme and information sharing, if they are to address security challenges that come with displacement.

Conclusion

Achieving comprehensive peace and security in the SADC region requires member states to move beyond the existing SADC intergovernmental framework and have enforceable policies in environmental management, disaster preparedness and response basic standards and science-based early warning system. As rightly pointed out by Dan Kuwali in Chapter 4, while the design and implementation of APSA have significant emphasis on AU collaboration with RECs, the research shows significant inter organisational disconnect in the promotion of peace, security and stability in Africa. Similar observation is made within the SADC regional framework and the member states. The regionalised approach to peace and security in Africa remains complex and influenced by several interrelated factors.

The roles and functions between member states and SADC in the implementation of RVAA programme are subject to the willingness of member states and leadership. While RVAA programme is a building block of the SADC response and provides a framework for responding to disasters, it has its own leadership challenges in coordinating real-time early warning. Although the

---

the AU and RECs, stating that; *the implementation of the MOU shall be guided by the recognition of, and respect for, the primary responsibility of the Union in the maintenance and promotion of peace, security and stability in Africa, in accordance with Article 16 of the PSC protocol.* Additionally, Article IV (iv) calls for the; *adherence to the principles of subsidiarity, complementarity and comparative advantage, in order to optimise the partnership between the Union, the RECs and the Coordinating Mechanisms in the promotion and maintenance of peace, security and stability.*

RVAA has encouraged member states to develop their own national structures, regional and national structures are not harmonised. The absence of established links between RVAA and NVAA and national early warning structures pose challenges in preparedness and response to disaster in the region over time.

The basic principles and protocols guiding RVAA governance require well-defined boundaries of roles and authority between the regional structure and member states. State sovereignty is, therefore, a critical element in understanding how disaster interventions will be managed in a long run. This discussion reveals a considerable gap in internal compliance with regional protocols in disaster preparedness and response. With entrenched state sovereignty, SADC member states have minimal internalisation of regional norms and values that could drive a regional response. Member states have not yet genuinely aligned themselves with a common position of the AU and SADC, making it difficult for the effective implementation of the regional vulnerability policy. Regional response to disasters and displacements is the only realistic way to mitigate human suffering and conflicts in the region. However, SADC is still lacking the necessary political will from member states. Consequently, the region will continue to experience disjointed response to disasters and displacement-induced conflicts.

PART III

Emerging Threats to Peace and Security in Africa

CHAPTER 10

Cybersecurity Threats in Africa

Tabitha Mwangi, Tracy Asava, and Iretioluwa Akerele

INTRODUCTION

Cyber-attacks originating from Africa, or directed at targets on the continent are quickly increasing with many cybercriminals seeing the continent as an area where they can operate "illegally and with impunity".[1] According to the Africa Cyber Security Report by Serianu, Africa has one of the highest cybercrime rates which affects the continent's economic, strategic and social development.[2] In 2017, for example, it was reported that Africa lost close to US$4 billion to cybercrime with Nigeria losing US$649 million, Kenya losing US$210 million and South Africa US$157 million dollars.[3]

[1] Nir Kshetri, "Cybercrime and Cybersecurity in Africa", *Journal of Global Information Technology Management* (2019) 22(2), pp. 77–81.

[2] Serianu, "Africa Cyber Security Report 2016 Achieving Cyber Security Resilience: Enhancing Visibility and Increasing Awareness", *Serianu*, 2016, available at: https://www.serianu.com/downloads/AfricaCyberSecurityReport2016.pdf (accessed 30 November 2020).

[3] Nir Kshetri, "Cybercrime and Cybersecurity in Africa", p. 77.

T. Mwangi (✉)
University of Geneva, Geneva, Switzerland

T. Asava
United States International University Africa, Nairobi, Kenya

I. Akerele
University College Cork, Cork, Ireland

© The Author(s), under exclusive license to Springer Nature Switzerland AG 2022
D. Kuwali (ed.), *The Palgrave Handbook of Sustainable Peace and Security in Africa*, https://doi.org/10.1007/978-3-030-82020-6_10

159

160   T. MWANGI ET AL.

Increased use and reliance of the Internet has made the cyberspace a major arena where state and non-state actors interact, thereby increasing the number of cyber incidents globally.[4] Africa is rapidly growing in terms of its population and global influence resulting in renewed interest on the continent by traditional and emerging powers in what some scholars have called the third scramble for the continent through increased diplomatic and commercial relations.[5] With the population rising to approximately 1.2 billion people with a median age of 19.5 years, the continent is experiencing a demographic change as these young people are in search of livelihoods, engaging with their peers across the world and are eager to express themselves freely than previous generations did, making the cyberspace an important arena for the present and future.[6] In June 2019, it was estimated that 40% of all Africans used the internet that month and that the continent had 525 million internet users, ranking the continent higher than Latin America, North America and the Middle East. Kenya, Nigeria and South Africa were countries with the highest number of internet users at the time with 83, 60 and 56% of all their populations being online, respectively.[7]

As aptly noted by Dan Kuwali in Chapter 13, given that cyber incidents have major implications for peace and security, identifying the different categories of cybersecurity threat actors is vital to ensure contextual mitigation measures to effectively respond to the specific threat.[8] Moreover, with the Corona Virus (COVID-19) pandemic making more people reliant on the internet through working and learning from home. For instance, on 3 June 2020, the African Union (AU) held a virtual meeting to deliberate on the impact of COVID-19 on transitional justice processes.[9] While the increased use of the internet in Africa is poised to bring numerous opportunities for communication, international trade and innovation, the fact that the virtual

[4] Robert Dewar, "Cyberweapons: Capability, Intent and Context in Cyberdefense", *Center for Security Studies (CSS), Trend Analysis 2* (2017), pp. 4–20.

[5] The Economist, "The New Scramble for Africa", *The Economist*, 9 March 2019, https://www.economist.com/leaders/2019/03/07/the-new-scramble-for-africa (accessed 5 December 2020).

[6] Symantec, *Cyber Crime & Cyber Security Trends in Africa*, available at: https://docs.broadcom.com/doc/cyber-security-trends-report-africa-interactive-en (accessed 30 November 2020), pp. 7–96.

[7] John Campbell, "Last Month, Over Half-a-Billion Africans Accessed the Internet", *Council on Foreign Relations*, 25 July 2019, https://www.cfr.org/blog/last-month-over-half-billion-africans-accessed-internet (accessed 5 December 2020).

[8] African Union Commission and Symantec, "Cyber Crime & Cyber Security Trends in Africa", p. 8.

[9] African Union, "Virtual Consultative Meeting of the African Union Commission on COVID-19 Pandemic and Transitional Justice in Africa", *African Union*, 1 June 2020, https://au.int/en/pressreleases/20200601/virtual-consultative-meeting-african-union-commission-covid-19-pandemic-and (accessed 5 December 2020).

space has been used for malicious intent since the 1980s with rapid sophistication in the tools and tactics used means that all efforts must be undertaken to safeguard the cyberspace.[10]

Furthermore, incidents of online election interference as seen in the 2016 elections in the United States (US), and elections elsewhere in Africa by state and non-state actors greatly threaten peace and security because the perception that elections were free and fair legitimizes a government thus acting as a tool for resolving conflicts.[11] As rightly claimed by Archiles Bwete and his colleagues in Chapter 21, failure to have free and fair elections without undue irregularities has resulted in numerous conflicts in Africa and beyond.[12]

The three main areas around which Africa's cybersecurity challenges revolve are: personal data protection, violation of intellectual property and security risk. Further, Africa's cybersecurity challenges include: inadequate technical knowledge to detect and defend against cybersecurity threats; inadequate awareness on cybersecurity threats that results in lack of prioritization in budgetary allocation; lack of implementation of cybersecurity legislation; politicization of cybersecurity legislation; increased population of young people with cyber skills and no employment thus vulnerable to engagement in cybercrime and failure to harmonize cybersecurity efforts of different stakeholders.[13] Understanding specific cybersecurity threat actors is crucial for policy makers in Africa to make context-specific recommendations that will effectively tackle this challenge.

This chapter seeks to add to the body of knowledge on cybersecurity issues by mapping various threat actors, and linking how their activities threaten peace, security and development in Africa. It also covers changes to the continent's cybersecurity posture caused by the COVID-19 pandemic, and makes recommendations that target different stakeholders in Africa. Research for this chapter was carried out using qualitative and thematic analysis.

Cyber Threat Actors

Effective cybersecurity measures require mapping out cybersecurity threat actors and their motivations to ensure that interventions made are context-specific. The cyberspace attracts various actors who pose peace and security threats because of the lack of clarity on legal frameworks for use of the space,

---

[10] Robert Dewar, "Cyberweapons: Capability, Intent and Context in Cyberdefense", p. 5.

[11] Tabitha Mwangi and Chimwemwe Fabiano, "Kremlin's Renewed Interest Russia's Emerging Threat to Elections in Africa", *The Republic*, 24 July 2020, https://republic.com.ng/june-july-2020/kremlins-renewed-interest/ (accessed 30 November 2020).

[12] Sarah Birch, Ursula Daxecker and Kristine Höglund, "Electoral Violence: An Introduction", *Journal of Peace Research* (2020) 51(1), pp. 3–14.

[13] United Nations. Economic Commission for Africa (2014). Tackling the challenges of cybersecurity in Africa. Policy Brief. No. 002, p. 6 Addis Ababa: UN. ECA. http://hdl.handle.net/10855/22544.

low cost of access, great access to sensitive information that can be used for espionage or protests and the unbalanced nature of the space (asymmetric). It is no wonder that many states have added the cyberspace as the "fifth arena, besides land, sea, air and space, in which military operations can be performed" either for defensive or offensive operations that are ran as part of other military operations, or exclusively conducted online.[14] In agreement with Kuwali in Chapter 13, threats in the cyberspace can be posed by states, non-state actors such as organized cybercriminals, cyber terrorists, insiders and human error.[15]

State Actors

As previously mentioned, the cyber domain is used by many for a wide variety of uses. In Africa, state actors have used the cyberspace to: strategically communicate about their successes and influence public opinion, conduct online election interference and manipulate public opinion, carry out online surveillance of opposition members and control the access to information during politically charged incidents by switching off the internet. As Safa posited in 2019:

> Statecraft in the cyber domain is ultimately a balancing act where governments have to balance the opportunities of new technologies with the risk that these technologies will have negative impacts on domestic politics, international relations, the rights of their citizens, and more.[16]

In April 2020, intelligence officials presented findings to the US Senate that confirmed that Russia had been involved in election interference in the 2016 US presidential elections.[17] The report listed a number of tactics used to this end including a whole range of tools such as: misinformation campaigns; surveillance of election infrastructure, unlawful access to voter databases; studying voting systems and processes; surveillance of election machines and,

---

[14] Johan Sigholm, "Non-state Actors in Cyberspace Operations", *Journal of Military Studies* (2013) 4(1), pp. 1–37.

[15] Bernard Brode, "7 Cyber Threat Actors to Watch for in 2021", *Security Info Watch*, 25 January 2021, available at: https://www.securityinfowatch.com/cybersecurity/article/21207268/7-cyber-threat-actors-to-watch-for-in-2021 (accessed 12 February 2021). Nir Kshetri, "Cybercrime and Cybersecurity in Africa", *Journal of Global Information Technology Management* (2019) 22(2), pp. 77–81.

[16] Safa Shahwan, "How Governments Can Use Cyber Tools Irresponsibly to Preserve Power" Atlantic Council, 9 October 2019, available at: https://www.atlanticcouncil.org/blogs/new-atlanticist/how-governments-can-use-cyber-tools-irresponsibly-to-preserve-power/ (accessed 30 November 2020).

[17] United States Senate, Select Committee on Intelligence, Report on Russian Active Measures Campaign and Interference in the 2016 U.S Elections, *Intelligence Senate*, available at: https://www.intelligence.senate.gov/sites/default/files/documents/Report_Volume1.pdf (accessed 30 November 2020), pp. 1–67, p. 11.

election observation. There was suspicion that the intention of the Russian interference could have included "espionage" or "undermining the integrity of elections and American confidence in democracy".[18]

In October 2019 the Internet Observatory at Stanford University allegedthat some Russian online activities in Africa have been directed towards states in different parts of the continent. The four main trends of Russian activities in Africa identified were: strong likelihood that the activities were carried out on behalf of state actors who used local languages to disinform people; social media platforms were used; trust building efforts were made through a wide array of methods and the methods used in each country varied widely depending on the main interest in that country.[19] In March 2020, social media companies—Facebook and Twitter brought down troll pages operating in West Africa that were affiliated with Russia, and were intended to shape public opinion after gaining adequate online traction.[20] Online election interference presents a major challenge to Africa's "democracy and human security" given that for close to three decades now, elections in many African states have often led to cycles of violence in states where citizens felt that the leaders in office had not gotten their positions legitimately.[21]

State actors have in the past posed a cybersecurity threat through imposition of restrictions on communication especially during politically tensed moments such as general elections. Some of the tactics that states have used to deal with this problem have included slowing down internet speeds, banning access to certain websites or shutting down the internet.[22] In 2019 it was reported that "at least 10 African countries blocked the internet".[23] In January 2021, another East African country shut down the internet on the eve of the general election by initially limiting access to specific social media platforms

---

[18] United States Senate, Select Committee on Intelligence, Report on Russian Active Measures Campaign and Interference in the 2016 U.S Elections, *Intelligence Senate*, pp. 21–35.

[19] Stanford Internet Observatory, "Evidence of Russia-Linked Influence Operations in Africa", *Stanford Internet Observatory*, available at: https://cyber.fsi.stanford.edu/io/news/prigozhin-africa, 30 October 2019 (accessed 2 December 2020).

[20] Emma Woollacott, "Russian Trolls Outsource Disinformation Campaigns to Africa", *Forbes*, 13 March 2020, available at: https://www.forbes.com/sites/emmawoollacott/2020/03/13/russian-trolls-outsource-disinformation-campaigns-to-to-africa/?sh=2507b3e61a26 (accessed 2 December 2020).

[21] Olusola Isola, "Election Violence and the Future of Democracy in Africa", Africa Up Close Wilson Center, 20 May 2018, available at: https://africaupclose.wilsoncenter.org/election-violence-and-the-future-of-democracy-in-africa/ (accessed 2 December 2020).

[22] Lisa Garbe, "What We Do (Not) Know about Internet Shutdowns in Africa", Democracy in Africa, 29 September 2020, available at: http://democracyinafrica.org/internet_shutdowns_in_africa/ (accessed 5 December 2020).

[23] Abdi Latif Dahir, "The Numbing Experience of Living Through Africa's Growing Internet Shutdowns", *Quartz Africa*, 24 June 2019, available at: https://qz.com/africa/1650545/what-does-it-feel-like-to-experience-an-internet-shutdown/ (accessed 5 December 2020).

then later blocked access to all sites with Netblocks (an internet monitoring organization stating that this had resulted in reduced connectivity in the country).[24] This is a worrying trend because the figure represents more than 18% of African countries used this strategy even though it has major impact on economies, individual freedoms, human rights and repression. The denial of citizens' freedom of expression through shutting down of the internet is a fertile ground for anti-government sentiment which can lead to social unrest and eventually escalate to violent conflict.

Research conducted in India showed that internet shutdowns do not prevent conflict and that instead:

> Violent protest generally increased on each consecutive day of disconnection relative to the typical dynamics of agitations that do not feature communication blackouts. This escalation only dissipated on the fifth consecutive day, eclipsing sheer numbers the riots that occur when communication remains available.[25]

Non-state Actors

There are diverse non-state actors who pose cybersecurity threats to different groups. The motivations for these actors include: financial gain, ego, vengeance, search for adventure, political reasons such as patriotism or desire to influence political decision makers, social reasons such as showing solidarity with different groups and lack of proper cybersecurity knowledge. The targets for these attacks could be the private sector, governments, groups aligned along certain ideological lines or individuals as shown in Table 10.1.[26]

In some cases, there are blurred lines between states and non-state actors as some states deploy non-state actors to carry out cyber activities for them, while some non-state actors can act without governments' beseeching them to do so, especially in states with very high levels of nationalism. Consequently, it is important to emphasize the need for critical thinking, and raise public awareness on fact-checking and verification tactics to ensure proper use of the cyberspace.

A significant non-state cyberattack with major implications for peace and security is the June 2020 attack by a group called Cyber-Horus Group where Ethiopia was targeted by a non-state group based in Egypt over the tension between the two states due to the Grand Ethiopian Renaissance Dam (GERD) meant for hydroelectric generation that Egypt fears will affect water quantity

---

[24] Christopher Giles and Peter Mwai, "Africa Internet: Where and How Are Governments Blocking It?" *BBC*, 14 January 2021, available at: https://www.bbc.com/news/world-africa-47734843 (accessed 24 March 2021).

[25] Jan Rydzak and Rohini Lakshané, "Internet Shutdowns in India only Fuel the Fires of Violence", *Hindustan Times*, 3 May 2019, available at: https://www.hindustantimes.com/analysis/internet-shutdowns-in-india-only-fuel-the-fires-of-violence/story-7Lf7o6Sq0q6xwfbWk0WoTM.html (accessed 15 January 2021).

[26] Johan Sigholm, "Non-State Actors in Cyberspace Operations", p. 11.

10 CYBERSECURITY THREATS IN AFRICA **165**

Table 10.1 Non-state actors in cyberspace operations[27]

Actor	Motivation	Target	Method
Ordinary citizens	None of weak [cyberspace security]	Any	Indirect
Script kiddies	Curiosity, thrills, ego	Individuals, companies, governments	Previously written scripts and tools
Hacktivists	Political or social change	Decisionmakers or innocent victims	Protests via web page defacements or DDoS attacks
Black-hat hackers	Ego, personal animosity, economic Gain	Any	Malware, viruses, vulnerability exploits
White-hat hackers	Idealism, creativity, respect for the law	Any	Penetration testing, patching
Grey-hat hackers	Ambiguous	Any	Varying
Patriot hackers	Patriotism	Adversaries of own nation-state	DDoS attacks, defacements
Cyber insiders	Financial gain, revenge, grievance	Employer	Social engineering, backdoors, manipulation
Cyber terrorists	Political or social change	Innocent victims	Computer-based violence or destruction
Malware authors	Economic gain, ego, personal animosity	Any	Vulnerability exploits
Cyber scammers	Financial gain	Individuals, small companies	Social engineering
Organized cyber criminals	Financial gain	Individuals, companies	Malware for fraud, identity theft, DDoS for blackmail
Corporations	Financial gain	ICT-based systems and infrastructures (private or public)	Range of techniques for attack or influence operations
Cyber espionage agents	Financial and political gain	Individuals, companies, governments	Range of techniques to obtain information
Cyber militias	Patriotism, professional development	Adversaries of own nation-state	Based on group capabilities

thus have socioeconomic effects in Egypt.[28] This cyberattack sought to have an "economic, psychological, and political pressure on Ethiopia" over the dam

[27] Johan Sigholm, "Non-State Actors in Cyberspace Operations", p. 11.

[28] Tomslin Samme-Nlar, "The Future of Armed Conflict in Africa: What Cyber Attacks on Ethiopian Government Tells Us", African Academic Network on Internet Policy, 8 October 2020, available at: https://aanoip.org/the-future-of-armed-conflict-in-africa-what-cyber-attacks-on-ethiopian-government-tell-us/ (accessed 30 November 2020).

project.[29] Such an attack should be taken seriously given the threats by both states to go to war over the issue, and failure to have the dispute effectively resolved through dialogue by states or the international community. In future, efforts should be made to counter such occurrences as slight miscalculations by state actors could easily move from an escalation of tensions into violent conflict involving various parties.

HACKTIVISTS

Hacktivists are individuals or groups that carry out activism activities using the cyberspace, often motivated by political and social reasons by leveraging on cyber tools that allow them to do "unusual" and "illegal" acts.[30] Methods used by hacktivists are blocking access to normal cyber operations through; "virtual sit-ins and blockades"; message overload "e-mail bombing" by repeatedly sending information to policymakers with the motive of making them exhausted enough to take actions about special interest issues; "web hacks and computer break-ins" by removing original content from websites and replacing it with messages geared towards target campaigns such as raising awareness on human rights violations; and, using malicious code to spread viruses and worms that multiply messages related to campaigns. While there might be sympathy and even support for hacktivists from some members of the general population given the different causes that they work towards, often with the intention to positively impact communities, it is important that more alternative measures are taken as the activities of hacktivists could easily lead to loopholes that can be exploited by malicious groups and actors.

THRILL SEEKERS

Most thrill seekers (also sometimes called script kiddies) are driven by curiosity and ego rather than malice. Often, they are young people with a lot of knowledge on cyberspace issues who use the domain for adventure, to show off their skills and to build their profiles. Kaspersky reported that in September 2019, there was indication that script kiddies had been responsible for a major DDoS attack that was consistent with spikes in previous years of similar attacks likely carried out by school children beginning their academic year.[31] Given that

[29] Nathaniel Allen, "Africa's Evolving Cyber Threats", *Africa Center for Strategic Studies*, 19 January 2021 (accessed 15 February 2021).

[30] Dorothy Denning, "Activism, Hacktivism, and Cyberterrorism: The Internet as a Tool for Influencing Foreign Policy", in John Arquilla, David Ronfeldt (eds.), *Networks and Netwars: The Future of Terror, Crime, and Militancy* (California: RAND, 2001), pp. 239–272.

[31] John Oates, "Back-2-School Hacking: Kaspersky Blames Pesky Script Kiddies for Rash of DDoS Cyber Hooliganism", *The Register*, available at: https://www.theregister.com/2019/11/11/kids_blamed_for_ddos_spike_in_september/, 11 November 2019 (accessed 27 December 2020).

they are not driven by economic or political interests, the likelihood of their activities leading to major disruptions are somewhat low, yet, the codes they develop can be stolen or copied by malicious actors, especially as they are likely to share information of their code via social media platforms.[32] Further, the suspicion that the Dyn DDoS[33] that affected Twitter and Amazon attack in late 2016 was caused by script kiddies is a warning that their impact should not be underestimated given the business and communication implications of the attack and all efforts should be made to protect computer systems against their activities.[34]

INSIDERS

Insiders are individuals working in organizations who based on their knowledge of the organizational cybersecurity infrastructure and processes pose a threat either deliberately or unknowingly. Imperva categorizes insiders into three groups: "malicious insiders; careless insiders; and, moles".[35] Malicious insiders pose a threat based on a deliberate decision to use access to data for selfish reasons such as sell data to competitors. Careless insiders on the other hand subconsciously affect cybersecurity due to poor cybersecurity etiquette such as using a personal device for official purposes or clicking malicious links. Finally, moles are imposters who pretend to work for the organization so that they can get access to sensitive data.[36] These individuals pose a major cybersecurity threat because as employees they are trusted by the organization and have access to critical information thus difficult to suspect. Often insider threats are driven by the desire for revenge, grievances or economic gains.[37]

The Covid-19 pandemic forced organizations to allow their employees to work from home, to use their personal devices such as phones and laptops for work, cut down on the number of employees and introduce new cybersecurity policies. As a result, organizations need to prioritize cybersecurity issues such as frequent training, impromptu checks on employees' compliance to

---

[32] Cyber Vista, "Threat Actor Profiles: Script Kiddies", *Cyber Vista*, available at: https://www.cybervista.net/threat-actor-profiles-script-kiddies/, 2 May 2017 (accessed 27 December 2020).

[33] Michael Mimoso, "Dyn DDoS Could Have Topped 1 Tbps", *Threat Post*, 27 October 2016 (accessed 27 December 2020).

[34] Cyber Vista, "Threat Actor Profiles: Script Kiddies", *Cyber Vista*, 2 May 2017 (accessed 27 December 2020).

[35] Imperva, "Insider Threat", Imperva, n.d. (accessed 19 January 2021).

[36] Imperva, "Insider Threat", Imperva, n.d. (accessed 19 January 2021).

[37] Adenike Cosgrove, "Mapping the Motives of Insider Threats", *Help Net Security*, available at: https://www.helpnetsecurity.com/2020/09/08/mapping-the-motives-of-insider-threats/, 8 September 2020 (accessed 27 December 2020).

168   T. MWANGI ET AL.

cybersecurity policies and multifactor authentication.[38] In July 2020, there were reports that cybersecurity incidents had increased by more than 50% in a period of three months mostly due to insider threats. The East African Head of the Intelligent Security Department at Dimension Data, Ishmael Muli in July 2020 asserted:

> Across East Africa, we are seeing insiders take advantage of organizations that lack visibility or the ability to investigate successful cyberattacks due to limited access controls to detect unusual activity once someone breaches their network. Some of these attacks involve manipulation of transactional data, tampering of logs to limit tracing, as well as framing legitimate users – all of which make forensic investigations difficult.[39]

Insiders cause both internal and external damage to organizations. According to a Ponemon Institute report released in 2020, the cost of insider threats has increased by 31% since 2018 to $11.45 million with incidents rising by 47%.[40] Of all inside threats reported, 62% were due to carelessness, 23% had criminal motives thus deliberate and 14% arose from the theft of credentials.[41] Internal costs caused by this threat are: costs needed for "monitoring, surveillance and investigation", "containment", post incident analysis and resumption of business processes. On the other hand, external costs include: business disruption, financial loses, loss of sensitive information and the loss of IT assets.[42]

An example of the complexity of the insider threat is the Fairfax County scam which culminated in the arrest of 281 people was carried out using fraudulent emails known as "Business Email Compromise (BEC)" which targeted a US local government office procuring computers from Dell. A web of criminals from East Africa, West Africa, Asia, North America and Europe convinced the county finance employees to send payments to a different account, and the funds were withdrawn in Nairobi.[43]

---

[38] Center for Audit Quality, "Understanding Cybersecurity and the External Audit in the COVID–19 Environment", Center for Audit Quality, 24 July 2020 (accessed 30 November 2020).

[39] Molly Wesonga, "Insiders Blamed for an Upsurge of Cybersecurity Attacks", *CIO East Africa*, 8 July 2020 (accessed 15 November 2020).

[40] Ponemon Institute, "2020 Cost of Insider Threats Global Report", *Observe IT*, 2020, available at https://www.observeit.com/ponemon-report-2020-cost-of-insider-threats-global-cyberwire/ (accessed 24 March 2021).

[41] Ponemon Institute, "2020 Cost of Insider Threats Global Report", *Observe IT*, 2020, available at https://www.observeit.com/ponemon-report-2020-cost-of-insider-threats-global-cyberwire/ (accessed 24 March 2021), p. 3.

[42] Ponemon Institute, "2020 Cost of Insider Threats Global Report", *Observe IT*, 2020, available at https://www.observeit.com/ponemon-report-2020-cost-of-insider-threats-global-cyberwire/ (accessed 24 March 2021), p. 28.

[43] Vincent Achula, "How Kenyan Scammers Stole over $3 Million from US Firms", *The East African*, 22 September 2019 (accessed 20 October 2020).

To mitigate against insider threats, there is need for automated monitoring processes, raising awareness, having regular training programmes and installing detection mechanisms.[44] Moreover, having internal and external system audits is crucial to identify blind spots that insiders may have due to confirmation bias, and high stress levels due to limited information and time especially during a major cyber security crisis.[45] Across Africa, there should be a mindset change that will make it easier for employees to report suspicions of threats without fearing that they could lose their jobs as a result.[46]

CYBERCRIMINALS

Cybercriminals are criminals who use the cyberspace to gain access to important data for use in access to finances, and are often able to get away with their crimes because of the use of "proxies and anonymity networks".[47] Cybercriminals can be broadly categorized into: identity thieves, internet stalkers and phishing scammers.[48] These criminals are able to quickly adopt to new technologies thus able to con many people because of their sophistication.[49] In Africa, cybercrime has been on the increase due to poverty, adventurism, disgruntled revenge, bad socioeconomical/political policies, negative/failed religious, cultural norms and unemployment.[50]

In July 2020, the arrest of 37-year-old Ramon Olorunwa Abbas who used the aliases "Ray Hushpuppi" and "Hush", made global headlines after law enforcement officials from the United Arab Emirates and the United States used social media platforms—Instagram and Snapchat[51] to monitor his online activities which culminated in his arrest, alongside other individuals that were working with him for laundering hundreds of millions of dollars through BEC

[44] Michele Maasberg, Craig Van Slyke, Selwyn Ellis, Nicole Beebe, "The Dark Triad and Insider Threats in Cyber Security", Communications of the ACM (2020) 63(12), pp. 64–80. https://doi.org/10.1145/3408864.

[45] Christopher Crummey, "One Big Lesson from the Cyber Range to Help Solve Confirmation Bias", *Security Intelligence*, 17 June 2019 (accessed 30 November 2020).

[46] David Whitehouse, "Cybersecurity: Companies in Africa Need to Do More to Fight Off Attacks, Says Kaspersky", *The Africa Report*, 27 January 2021 (accessed 10 February 2021).

[47] Norwich University Online, "Who Are Cyber Criminals?", *Norwich University*, 13 February 2017 (accessed 30 November 2020).

[48] Norwich University, "Who Are Cyber Criminals?".

[49] Seriana, "Africa Cyber Security Report 2016", p. 12.

[50] Serianu, "Africa Cyber Security Report 2016", 2016, p. 50.

[51] Chidinma Irene, "How the FBI used Instagram and Snapchat to Track Down an Alleged Conman in Dubai", *Quartz Africa*, 10 July 2020, available at: https://qz.com/afr ica/1879261/fbi-use-instagram-to-get-dubai-nigerian-fraudster-hushpuppi/ (accessed 10 February 2021).

according to the US Department of Justice.[52] Speaking about the arrest, Jesse Baker—a Special Agent from the US Secret Service asserted that:

> This was a challenging case, one that spanned international boundaries, traditional financial systems and the digital sphere [...] Technology has essentially erased geographic boundaries leaving trans-national criminal syndicates to believe that they are beyond the reach of law enforcement. The success in this case was the direct result of our trusted partnerships between the Department of Justice and our federal law enforcement colleagues. These partnerships helped dismantle a sophisticated organized crime group who preyed upon unsuspecting businesses.[53]

CYBERTERRORISTS

Cyberterrorism is the merging of cyberspace and terrorism, and is motivated by political reasons. Terrorists' use of the cyberspace is not a new phenomenon and J. M. Berger posits that, "jihadists [and other terrorist organizations and violent extremist groups] have figured out how to use social media to make an impact, even though their numbers are minuscule in comparison to the overall user base [...]its highly organized social media campaign uses deceptive tactics and shows a sophisticated understanding of how such networks operate".[54] The 2013 Westgate Mall attack in Nairobi Kenya perpetrated by Al Shabaab is an example of how a terrorist organization used Twitter to spread fear, share its propaganda thus "controlling the narrative and retaining an audience" during the entire attack.[55] In Nigeria, Boko Haram has also used various cyberspace platforms such as YouTube and Twitter to share unpolished videos and images meant to spread fear and delegitimize the government by depicting the government and military as weak and corrupt.[56] Compared to other terrorist organizations, Boko Haram is not keen to attract new recruits

---

[52] Department of Justice, "Nigerian National Brought to U.S. to Face Charges of Conspiring to Launder Hundreds of Millions of Dollars from Cybercrime Schemes", Press Release, The United States Attorney's General Office Central District of California, 3 July 2020.

[53] United States Attorney's Office Central District of California, "Nigerian National Brought to U.S. to Face Charges of Conspiring to Launder Hundreds of Millions of Dollars from Cybercrime Schemes", United States Department of Justice, 3 July 2020 (accessed 10 February 2021).

[54] J. M. Berger, "The Evolution of Terrorist Propaganda: The Paris Attack and Social Media", Brookings, 27 January 2015, available at: https://www.brookings.edu/testim onies/the-evolution-of-terrorist-propaganda-the-paris-attack-and-social-media/ (accessed 28 December 2020).

[55] David Mair, "#Westgate: A Case Study: How al-Shabaab used Twitter during an Ongoing Attack", *Studies in Conflict & Terrorism* (2016) 40(1), pp. 24–43.

[56] Chris Ogbondah and Pita Agbese, "Terrorists and Social Media Messages: A Critical Analysis of Boko Haram's Messages and Messaging Techniques", in Bruce Mutsvairo (ed.), *The Palgrave Handbook of Media and Communication Research in Africa* (London: Palgrave Macmillan, 2018), pp. 313–345.

through social media,[57] yet its use of the cyberspace has a lot of impact in the public perception of the Nigerian government and military.

From the mapping of both state and non-state actors, it is clear that all these actors pose major cybersecurity threats that have major peace, security and development implications. Such concerted efforts are needed to effectively tackle this global challenge.

CYBERSECURITY CHALLENGES IN AFRICA

Unless there is a clear understanding of what the cybersecurity challenges are in Africa, designing effective counter measures remains a lucid dream. The lack of a universally accepted definition of cybercrime further complicates efforts geared towards mitigating this phenomenon.[58] Furthermore, given the rapidly evolving cybersecurity landscape, new challenges are rapidly arising as both state and non-state actors adopt to emerging technologies and interventions to counter their impact.

The Africa Cyber Security Report 2016: Achieving Cyber Security Resilience: Enhancing Visibility and Increasing Awareness by Serianu identified nine major challenges to cybersecurity in Africa. These are: low awareness on cybersecurity issues which results in high vulnerability of many cyberspace users to scams; malicious employees (insiders) who use their skills and privilege to access sensitive data to their selfish advantage; widespread lack of adequate budgetary allocation for cybersecurity issues; increased use of smart devices (Internet of Things—IoT) which increase vulnerability; increased automation of business process with little regard for security protocols; widespread poor patching practices; poor implementation of cybersecurity-related legislations and policies; overload of personal information on the cyberspace that can be used for harassment, cyberbullying and to carry out targeted criminal activities such as kidnapping for ransom and lack of effective access controls to sensitive data.[59] The same report noted that there is a shortage of skilled cybersecurity professionals on the continent to effectively deal with the threat while cybersecurity knowledge in the legal profession is also lacking thus the rate of successful prosecution of cybersecurity-related criminal activity is low.[60] Moreover, many individuals affected by cybersecurity issues do not report incidents to law enforcement officials either due to lack of clear information on the

---

[57] Chris Ogbondah and Pita Agbese, "Terrorists and Social Media Messages: A Critical Analysis of Boko Haram's Messages and Messaging Techniques", pp. 336–337.

[58] Ajayi E.F.G., "Challenges to Enforcement of Cyber-Crimes Laws and Policy", *Journal of Internet and Information Systems* (2016) 6(1), pp. 1–12.

[59] Serianu, "Africa Cyber Security Report 2016", pp. 46–47.

[60] Serianu, "Africa Cyber Security Report 2016", p. 13.

right channels to use or fear of repercussions of reporting.[61] Yarik Turianskyi in 2020, argued that the decentralized nature of the cyberspace and its managements complicates legal processes stating that:

> The structure of the Internet itself, which comes down to interconnected networks using standardised routing protocols and websites that may reside anywhere in the world, even on privately owned infrastructure, exacerbates the regulatory problems resulting in jurisdictional issues.[62]

Widespread unemployment and underemployment in Africa pushes many young people to engage in criminal activities in the cyberspace as a means to support themselves and their families.[63] This is mainly due to the fact that these young people are tech-savvy and thus able to identify loopholes that other people are unaware of. The evolution of cybersecurity threats to involve transnational organized criminals further complicates the situation as talented young people can be hired and incentivized by money.

CURRENT MEASURES BEING UNDERTAKEN TO ADDRESS CYBERSECURITY ISSUES IN AFRICA

Domestic Laws and the AU Convention on Cyber Security and Personal Data Protection

Only nine African countries have cybersecurity-related laws, while 22 states have signed legislature related to this.[64] Yet, some African countries have been criticized of politicizing cyber-related laws to target their opponents and limit civic freedoms.[65] Hence, African states must ensure that their cybersecurity regulations are holistic and objective enough to allow citizens to accrue benefits from the cyberspace. To do this effectively, states must ensure that their domestic laws are balanced in terms of human rights and state responsibility to protect citizens and hold those who pose cybersecurity threats to

[61] Mark Shaw, "Africa's Changing Place in the Global Criminal Economy", *Enhancing Africa's Response to Transnational Organed Crime*, 1 September 2017, available at: https://globalinitiative.net/wp-content/uploads/2017/09/2017-09-26-enact-continental-report1.pdf (accessed 30 November 2020).

[62] Yarik Turianskyi, *Africa and Europe: Cyber Governance Lessons*, South African Institute of International Affairs, 77, January 2020, pp. 3–4.

[63] Nir Kshetri, "Diffusion and Effects of Cybercrime in Developing Economies", *Third World Quarterly* (2010) 31(7), 1057–1079.

[64] Jennigay Coetzer, "Africa's Lack of Data Protection and Cybercrime Laws Has Created Deep Vulnerabilities. But Is Change on The Way?", *Law.Com International*, https://www.law.com/international-edition/2020/05/27/africas-lack-of-data-protection-and-cybercrime-laws-has-created-deep-vulnerabilities-but-is-change-on-the-way/?slreturn=20210219070808, 27 May 2020 (accessed 19 March 2021).

[65] Yarik Turianskyi, "Cyber Crime and Data Privacy: How Africa Can Up Its Game", *Africa Portal*, available at: https://www.africaportal.org/features/cyber-crime-and-data-privacy-how-africa-can-its-game/, 5 February 2020 (accessed 17 November 2020).

others online accountable. As of January 2020, only fourteen African states had signed, and seven domesticated the law through ratification, making it impossible to have the convention enter into force as a minimum of fifteen states must domesticate it before this can happen.[66]

International Conventions

The Budapest Convention on Cybercrime developed by the Council of Europe in 2001 has been ratified by several African countries—Ghana, Mauritius, Morocco and Senegal. South Africa has signed the convention but is yet to ratify it.[67] Globally, as of 2020, this treaty had been "ratified or acceded to by sixty-four states".[68] This international criminal justice convention demands that states criminalize crime committed using or against computers; criminal justice personnel are allowed access to electronic evidence for all crimes committed, and that states effectively cooperate with each other in dealing with cyberspace related crime.[69]

Despite the Budapest Convention on Cybercrime being described as "a comprehensive, operational and functional solution" for national and international cybercrime related issues, it is not as holistic as the African Union Convention on Cyber Security and Personal Data Protection which covers three core elements: electronic transactions, personal data protection and cyber security &cybercrime.[70] At the same time, the African Union Convention on Cyber Security and Personal Data Protection is seen as being somewhat unclear in protecting law enforcement officers as it can be interpreted as criminalizing their work; lacks procedural powers compared to its European counterpart; lacks crucial definitions for key terms leaving it open to different interpretations by member states and, lacks "an effective and fully-functional mechanism for international cooperation between State Parties".[71]

---

[66] Yarik Turianskyi, "Cyber Crime and Data Privacy: How Africa Can Up Its Game", *Africa Portal*.

[67] Council of Europe, "Chart of Signatures and Ratifications of Treaty 185 *Convention on Cybercrime* Status as of 19/03/2021", Council of Europe, available at: https://www.coe.int/en/web/conventions/search-on-treaties/-/conventions/treaty/185/signatures?p_auth=GTnGDM2E (accessed 19 March 2021).

[68] Joyce Hakmeh and Allison Peters, "A New UN Cybercrime Treaty? The Way Forward for Supporters of an Open, Free, and Secure Internet", *Council on Foreign Relations*, 13 January 2020. Available at: https://www.cfr.org/blog/new-un-cybercrime-treaty-way-for ward-supporters-open-free-and-secure-internet (accessed 20 February 2021).

[69] Council of Europe, "Comparative Analysis of the Malabo Convention of the African Union and the Budapest Convention on Cybercrime", *Council of Europe*, 20 November 2016. Available at: https://rm.coe.int/16806bf0f8 (accessed 15 December 2020).

[70] Council of Europe, "Comparative Analysis of the Malabo Convention of the African Union and the Budapest Convention on Cybercrime", p. 4.

[71] Council of Europe, "Comparative Analysis of the Malabo Convention of the African Union and the Budapest Convention on Cybercrime", pp. 4–5.

Nonetheless, it is important for policy makers to see both legal frameworks as complementing each other, not opposing each other thus there is a need to adopt both treaties to ensure effective international cooperation on cybersecurity and cybercrime related cases.[72]

In December 2020, Russia succeeded in passing a Russian sponsored resolution on cybercrime that has been criticized as posing human rights concerns, destabilizing as it slows down the uptake of the Budapest Convention and the lack of a valid and convincing explanation by the sponsor on the need for a new resolution.[73] Overall, there is need for the development of national, regional and international legal frameworks to deal with cyberspace related crimes. This will ensure that states cooperate with each other to bring criminals to book so that Africa ceases being a space where they can act freely and with impunity.

POLICY RECOMMENDATIONS

This chapter makes eight recommendations to transform Africa's cybersecurity that incorporate concerted efforts between governments, the private sector and academia.

First, the implementation of African Union Convention on Cyber Security and Personal Data Protection is crucial for Africa to have a "one continent, one law"[74] as in the case of the European Union's General Data Protection Regulation (GDPR). This will ensure that Africa has a standard way of dealing with cybersecurity-related issues which is vital to ensure that the continent starts building a body of legal knowledge on how to effectively define, prosecute and investigate these issues. This sentiment is echoed by Denys Reva who in 2020 stated that "the interconnected nature of cyber security requires a collective approach based on cooperation and harmonization of responses and common standards".[75] Although Reva was writing to explain the nexus between cybersecurity and maritime security on the continent and globally, there is no doubt that by extension, other sectors such as education, healthcare, financial and international trade and travel will greatly benefit from a continental approach to cybersecurity.

---

[72] Council of Europe, "Comparative Analysis of the Malabo Convention of the African Union and the Budapest Convention on Cybercrime", p. 8.

[73] Joyce Hakmeh and Allison Peters, "A New UN Cybercrime Treaty? The Way Forward for Supporters of an Open, Free, and Secure Internet", available at: https://www.cfr.org/blog/new-un-cybercrime-treaty-way-forward-supporters-open-free-and-sec ure-internet (accessed 3 March 2021).

[74] Daniel Castro, "5 Lessons the U.S. Can Learn from European Privacy Efforts", *Government Technology*, July/August 2019, available at: https://www.govtech.com/pol icy/5-Lessons-the-US-Can-Learn-from-European-Privacy-Efforts.html (accessed 3 March 2021).

[75] Denys Reva, "Maritime Cyber Security: Getting Africa Ready", *Institute for Security Studies*, October 2020, available at: https://issafrica.s3.amazonaws.com/site/uploads/ar-29.pdf (accessed 3 March 2021), p. 8.

More African states need to ratify the Malabo Convention as it will ensure that the continent has a standard way of dealing with cybersecurity-related issues.[76] The use of different stakeholders such as private sector, civil society and governments is needed and initiatives like the African Peer Review Mechanism (APRM) and the Open Government Partnership can play a crucial role in this as both institutions have wide membership and are seen as credible.[77] African states need to set tangible targets for themselves on cybersecurity issues, by using global standards such as the Global Cybersecurity Index (GCI) by aiming to move up global rankings within a given period of time as this will force them to prioritize the five key parameters—legal measures, technical and procedural measures, organizational structures, capacity building and international cooperation.[78]

To fast track this process, regional groupings on the continent need to take ownership of this process so as to encourage member states to prioritize cybersecurity issues. Given that the International Telecommunication Union report ranks Mauritius, Kenya and Rwanda highest in their cybersecurity standards based on the aforementioned parameters, other countries need to pick lessons that can be used to replicate similar results elsewhere, but caution must be taken to tailor these "lessons" to the target states as contexts differ.[79]

In line with Kuwali's recommendation in Chapter 13, as African states ratify the convention, there is need to pick the best practices from the European Union's experience with the GDPR. These include ensuring that local, regional and continental cybersecurity legal frameworks: are simple so that even people with limited cybersecurity expertise understand the contents of the law. These efforts should include ensuring that there is adequate information sharing, knowledge on how to effectively conduct investigations so that cases are dealt with quickly to ensure justice for victims and hold individuals accountable for unbecoming cyber behaviour. Next, finding a balance between restraining data collection and innovation by coming up with context-specific laws that suit the needs and interests of different African states. Also reducing compliance costs to encourage the private sector to buy-in and take ownership for the need for a continental approach to cybersecurity issues without fear that high compliance costs could adversely affect their businesses.[80]

---

[76] Denys Reva, "Maritime Cyber Security: Getting Africa Ready", p. 9.

[77] Yarik Turianskyi, "Cyber Crime and Data Privacy: How Africa Can Up Its Game", *Africa Portal*.

[78] International Telecommunication Union, "Global Cybersecurity Index", *International Telecommunication Union*, available at: https://www.itu.int/en/ITU-D/Cybersecurity/Pages/global-cybersecurity-index.aspx (accessed 10 March 2021).

[79] International Telecommunication Union, "Global Cybersecurity Index (GCI) 2018", International Telecommunication Union, available at: https://www.itu.int/dms_pub/itu-d/opb/str/D-STR-GCI.01-2018-PDF-E.pdf, 2019 (accessed 3 March 2021).

[80] Daniel Castro, "5 Lessons the U.S. Can Learn from European Privacy Efforts", *Government Technology*.

To encourage this continental ratification is having a widespread advocacy campaign across the continent that will help key decision makers such as heads of states, ministers of ICT-related ministries and security agencies comprehend the importance of cybersecurity issues to other human and state security aspects.[81] Second, bilateral and multilateral cooperation is required to strengthen Africa's cybersecurity architecture. Depending on the existing diplomatic relations different African states have with each other and with non-African states, efforts should be made to foster cooperation geared towards knowledge transfer of best practices on cybersecurity issues, intelligence sharing and extradition of cybercriminals. For instance, Israel presents a good case study for the steps that Africa need to take to overcome cybersecurity challenges, and position itself as a powerhouse in the cyber domain.[82]

Six points that encapsulate Israel's cybersecurity success are: the central role of the government as the central "coordinator" for all cyber-related issues; recognition by the government of the business potential of the cybersecurity industry thus massive support; leveraging on the country's geostrategic needs such as need for a strong military to set up incubation hubs for specialized training; supporting human capital development through establishing various cybersecurity educational programmes and courses; taking an interdisciplinary approach to cybersecurity issues to integrate the field into various sectors such as agriculture and, shifting from a "reactive" to a "proactive" cybersecurity approach guided by robustness, resilience and defense.[83]

Although most African states do not have compulsory military service like Israel does, African governments need to find innovative ways of integrating cybersecurity incubation hubs through existing frameworks such as integrating the subject in curricula for various levels preferably starting in lower primary school levels all the way till learners enrol for vocational and higher learning. Besides, most African countries have some form of national youth service programmes that can be a great basis for cybersecurity introduction.

Third, given the low number of skilled cybersecurity professionals in Africa, there have been suggestions by some cybersecurity experts that instead of prosecuting young unemployed youth engaged in online criminal activities, African governments need to find ways of innovatively tapping into their talent to reduce their likelihood of engaging in cybercrime as they will get decent

---

[81] Denys Reva, "Maritime Cyber Security: Getting Africa Ready", p. 11.

[82] Dmitry (Dima) Adamsky, "The Israeli Odyssey Toward Its National Cyber Security Strategy", *The Washington Quarterly* (2017) 40(2), pp. 113–127.

[83] Gil Press, "6 Reasons Israel Became a Cybersecurity Powerhouse Leading The $82 Billion Industry", *Forbes*, 18 July 2017, available at: https://www.forbes.com/sites/gil press/2017/07/18/6-reasons-israel-became-a-cybersecurity-powerhouse-leading-the-82-billion-industry/?sh=30c7c69d420a (accessed 20 February 2021).

livelihoods while contributing to the development of their economies.[84] This echoes Dastmalchi who in 2019 asserted that:

> When these talents do not find jobs, they start going the wrong way into 'yahoo, yahoo' activities, but if we are able to manage such talents well, these guys could become cyber security analysts, getting top security jobs in the banks and defending the country against insider and outsider cyber-attacks.[85]

Another way of solving this challenge is to raise awareness on the cybersecurity tools available on the internet that tech-savvy youth can use to sharpen their skills, and get credible certifications for their skills. Such platforms include Cybrary and Coursera. Fourth, the international diffusion of technology products exhibits a hierarchical pattern with most producers of these goods deeming to continent "unprofitable" hence the flooding of the markets on the continent with low quality devices that are vulnerable to cybersecurity-related attacks and threats.[86]

Given that the continent has a high population of youths and an abundance of natural resources, African states need to become self-reliant as far as the production of technological goods is concerned. This is especially critical given the innovation showcased by Africans in the wake of the Covid-19 pandemic where governments were forced to creatively solve challenges such as local production of personal protection equipment (PPEs) and the prediction that in the aftermath of the pandemic, Africa will be forced to be self-reliant as "the West focuses on its own survival".[87] Further, the development of an African technological manufacturing industry will not only provide employment for many young Africans, but will bolster Africa's cybersecurity posture given that whoever builds cyberspace infrastructure controls it, meaning that if non-Africans develop our technology, we allow them access to our sensitive data as they can always find ways to remotely access the information they want, when they want it.

Fifth, patching, hardening networks and monitoring online communication platforms are crucial prevention measures to guard against threat actors such as cybercriminals and script kiddies as some actors publicly share information on the next potential victims. Moreover, there might be crucial information publicly available through open sources that can help cybersecurity researchers get access to malicious codes being used to carry out different types of

---

[84] Business Ghana, "Harness 'Sakawa' to Combat Cyber Security Threats", Business Ghana, 18 March 2019, available at: http://www.businessghana.com/site/news/general/183792/Harness-Sakawa-to-combat-cyber-security-threats (accessed 20 February 2021).

[85] Business Ghana, "Harness 'Sakawa' to Combat Cyber Security Threats".

[86] Nir Kshetri, "Diffusion and Effects of Cybercrime in Developing Economies", *Third World Quarterly*.

[87] David Mwambari, "The Pandemic Can Be a Catalyst for Decolonisation in Africa", *Al Jazeera*, available at: https://www.aljazeera.com/opinions/2020/4/15/the-pandemic-can-be-a-catalyst-for-decolonisation-in-africa, 15 April 2020 (accessed 7 March 2021).

attacks.[88] The establishment of coding camps for pupils and students in various African countries is a great step that should be replicated across the continent and made affordable and accessible even for learners from public learning institutions, as most are only set up in high-end private schools.

Such platforms will expose learners to coding, software development and cybersecurity issues so that they can be safe on the cyberspace, increase innovation and raise a generation of cyber-savvy learners that will transform Africa's cyberspace. Incorporating the private sector to support such efforts through their corporate social responsibility projects is a great way to increase funds directed towards this. Moreover, effective patch management, hardening networks and real-time monitoring of ICT architecture will guard against cybercriminals, cyberterrorists, hackers and insider threats. There should be widespread awareness on the importance of these measures as some are not prioritized by organizations.

Sixth, interdisciplinary collaboration through forums such as the Global Internet Forum to Counter Terrorism (GIFCT) involving stakeholders from the public, private, civil society and academia is needed for continuous surveillance of the cyberspace to facilitate effective responses during cybersecurity-related incidents and promote learning of how to prevent terrorists and extremist groups from using the cyberspace in pursuit of their objectives.[89] GIFCT has been part of numerous research programmes that incorporate academics and cybersecurity experts to support the establishment of best practices using emerging technology to secure the cyberspace from extremist groups.

Furthermore, the institution has funded projects in Africa to support community-based organizations to support their work which ensures evidence-based programming that is context-specific thus more effective compared to a top-down structure that is not inclusive, and sensitive to nuances such as local languages and in-group imagery that artificial intelligence or non-locals would misunderstand. Also, public–private partnerships are crucial to ensure that states safeguard the integrity of election by training electoral personnel and streamlining procurement processes for election-related equipment to increase public trust in the legitimacy of elected government officials.

Seventh, there is need to raise awareness on cybersecurity on effective fact-checking to guard against misinformation, and negligent behaviour that can be costly. One verification initiative that stands out is PesaCheck which began fact-checking statements made by east African leaders, but now has factcheckers working in West Africa and the Sahel too, using multiple

---

[88] Cyber Vista, "Threat Actor Profiles: Script Kiddies", *Cyber Vista*, https://www.cybervista.net/threat-actor-profiles-script-kiddies/, 2 May 2017 (accessed 27 December 2020).

[89] Global Internet Forum to Counter Terrorism, "Preventing Terrorists and Violent Extremists from Exploiting Digital Platforms", GIFCT, available at: https://gifct.org/, not dated (accessed 15 February 2021).

languages.[90] Effective fact-checking will bolster civic education efforts to prepare voters to make informed choices when deciding which electoral candidates to vote for. It will also ensure compliance with practices that improve living standards such as busting myths related to healthcare and income issues. Besides, it will also foster social cohesion as hate speech will be identified easily. All things considered, cybersecurity measures must be taken by all cyberspace users as any weak link exposes everyone else to threats.

CONCLUSION

Increased internet connectivity and phone penetration has considerably increased the number of people in Africa that use the cyberspace; a development that has led to an increase in the number of cyberattacks emanating from the continent as well as those targeting internet users in Africa.[91] At the same time, Africa has suffered vast economic losses due to these cybersecurity threats, that could otherwise have been directed to development projects.[92] This is due to the fact that the continent is seen as an area where various cybersecurity threat actors can act contrary to the law, and without fear of being held accountable.

Unless effective mapping of cybersecurity threat actors is done, policy makers cannot design effective interventions as they would be forced to either use outdated measures, or copy-paste solutions from other regions which might not apply to the African context. This is especially critical now that the COVID-19 pandemic has made more internet users vulnerable to various threats as institutions and individuals have become more reliant on the cyberspace for business, and virtual operations are common as people work from home in a bid to socially distance themselves from others to curb the transmission of the virus from affected individuals. Also, the misuse of the cyberspace by African and non-African actors who engage in online election interference further complicates the situation.

Effective cybersecurity measures on the African continent need to be three-fold-protection of personal data from misuse by private sector actors and criminals; secure with only privileged access to data and, protection of the intellectual data so that African businesses and youth compete fairly with those in other regions. Overall, this can only be achieved through: implementation of a continental legal framework after ratification of the Malabo Convention, increased number of cybersecurity experts on the continent, deliberate prioritization of cybersecurity issues through adequate budgetary allocation and

---

[90] PesaCheck, "About PesaCheck", *PesaCheck*, available at: https://pesacheck.org/about (accessed 25 March 2021).

[91] Nir Kshetri, "Cybercrime and Cybersecurity in Africa", p. 77.

[92] Serianu, "Africa Cyber Security Report 2016", p. 12.

having a bottom-up cybersecurity structure that includes everyone; increased awareness on cybersecurity across various sectors, proactive approach to cyber-security efforts as opposed to being reactive and waiting for threats to emerge.

CHAPTER 11

The Proliferation of Popular Protests and Coups d'Etas in Africa

Prince Bright Majiga

INTRODUCTION

Public protests are a global phenomenon occurring in both developed and developing countries, albeit in varying proportions and intensities.[1] Africa is no exception to this wave. Since the partition of Africa, African nations have been struggling to liberate themselves from one form of bondage or another as discussed by Desire Hakorimana and Gordard Busingye in Chapter 2 as well as Youssef Mahmoud and Chimwemwe Fabiano in Chapter 3. African nations have a history of resistance and this history has manifested itself repeatedly whenever socioeconomic or socio-political conditions within such nations were not encouraging. The history of Africa is a complex one with almost the whole continent, except for Ethiopia and Liberia, having been colonised by European powers. The struggle for independence took different directions in different African nations. For some, independence was peacefully negotiated, while for others independence was realised after bloody bush wars.

[1] Shah, A. (2011). Public Protests Around the World—Global Issues: Social, Political, Economic, and Environmental Issues That Affect Us All, available at: http://www.globalissues.org/article/45/public-protestsaround-the-world (accessed 1 June 2020).

P. B. Majiga (✉)
Mzuzu University, Mzuzu, Malawi

Malawi Defence Force, Lilongwe, Malawi

© The Author(s), under exclusive license to Springer Nature Switzerland AG 2022
D. Kuwali (ed.), *The Palgrave Handbook of Sustainable Peace and Security in Africa*, https://doi.org/10.1007/978-3-030-82020-6_11

181

In the wake of independence, a wave of disillusionment swept across African states because most citizens believed that their expectations had not been fulfilled.[2] The majority of western trained leaders who assumed power were regarded as an extension of the Europeans, and to many citizens' chagrin, what had only been secured was mere "flag independence". As a result of such disillusionment, citizens in different nations started protesting as a way of demanding better socio-political amenities and realities. In different nations, owing to different realities, such demands for improved socio-political conditions took different directions to the extent that while in some countries citizens were protesting on the streets, other countries experienced waves of revolutions, coup d'états and civil wars.

Protests gained particular prominence in the late 1980s and 1990s, and have been credited with helping to bring about a democratic shift across the continent. Between 1989 and 1994, 35 countries in Africa moved from one-party rule to multi-party elections, resulting in changes of leadership in 18 countries (compared to none before 1990, with the exception of South Africa and Mauritius).

Seen in that context, recent protests do not necessarily represent a radically new development for Africa. Rather, they fit into a historical pattern of popular mobilisation to express discontent with the leadership performance of some governments. At their core, they are expressions of unmet and frozen popular aspirations for change and of the inability or unwillingness of many governments to provide a serious response to the grievances which triggered earlier waves of protest.

To compliment the discussion by Tadziwana Kapeni in Chapter 17, this chapter looks at the causes of proliferation of mass protests, the nature of these protests, the implications of such protests since some lead into coups or little change in governance systems. The chapter also examines the role of the African Union (AU) in dealing with popular protests and coups. Finally, the chapter offers some solutions to these issues. It argues that there is need for improved governance structures on the continent, which must simultaneously seek to provide citizens with robust social and economic development in order to avert mass protests and create a conducive environment for the attainment of Agenda 2063.

Causes of Popular Protests in Africa

It is trite that Africa has recently witnessed a proliferation of popular protest, most of which have been characterised by violence. While attention is often

---

[2] See Isaacman, A. (1990). Peasants and Rural Social Protest in Africa. *African Studies Review* 33(2): 1–120; Malila, V., & Garman, A. (2016). Listening to the 'Born Frees': Politics and Disillusionment in South Africa. *African Journalism Studies* 37(1): 64–80.

drawn to events during and after the protests, an examination of the underlying causes of the protest is an imperative that all African states must undertake with particular diligence. It is for this reason that this chapter makes an attempt to not only look at triggers, but analyse the key underlying causes of popular protests in Africa. The expectation is that by confronting the key underlying causes, African states will avert and mitigate any risks associated with popular protests. As it may be appreciated, popular protests are actuated by different reasons, depending on geo-political factors as well as social economic factors prevalent in a particular country or region. Admittedly, there are quite a number of significant causes of popular which may not be exhaustively examined in this chapter. That being the case, the following factors represent causes that generally apply across the continent.

Poor Governance

A common denominator to Africa's popular protests is that they are driven by deep-seated frustration with the economic and political status quo.[3] Popular unrest and mass mobilisation resulting thereof have taken different forms, varied in scale, and occurred both at the local and national level. They include street demonstrations against rising food prices and the cost of living in Chad, Guinea, Niger, strike actions over arrears in wage payments and labour disputes in Botswana, Nigeria, South Africa, Zimbabwe, protests over alleged rigged elections or attempts by leaders to extend their constitutional term limits in Malawi, Burkina Faso, Burundi, the Democratic Republic of the Congo (DRC), Gabon, Togo, student protests in Uganda, South Africa, and outbreaks of unrest over police violence, extortion, corruption and impunity in Ethiopia, Chad, Kenya and, Senegal.[4]

It is beyond argument that unemployment rate among the youth is high in Africa.[5] The continent progressed well in education levels during the last three decades. This socioeconomic situation played an important role in social change especially towards democratisation. History reveals that the nations rich of youth do not fear the uprisings, political aggression and civil clashes. The countries which had young population, had to suffer from civil clashes three times more than the others which had mature population during 1990s.[6]

---

[3] Cilliers, J. (2014). The Future of Democracy in Africa African Futures Paper 19, 15 October 2014.

[4] Sakor, Bintu Zahara, & Soko, Vamo. (2020). Protests, Elections, and Ethnic Tensions in West Africa: What Are the Driving Forces? 24 November 2020, available at: https://blogs.prio.org/2020/11/protests-elections-and-ethnic-tensions-in-west-africa-what-are-the-driving-forces/ (accessed 17 January 2021).

[5] BBC. (2012). A BBC Trust Report on the Impartiality and Accuracy of the BBC's Coverage of the Events Known as the "Arab Spring".

[6] Terrill, D. (2011). The Arab Spring and the Future of U.S. Interests and Cooperative Security in the Arab World. Washington: Strategic Studies Institute.

The continent's average Gross Domestic Product (GDP) has increased by around 5% each year since 2000. However, this has not translated into a substantial reduction in economic inequality, (youth) unemployment, a reliance of large sections of the population on the informal sector and overall poverty. At the same time, data from Afrobarometer, suggests that while there has been an increase between 2002 and 2019[7] in the demand for democracy, there is also a widespread perception that political leaders are failing to deliver. It is due to some of these pressing conditions that protests spring out.

Poor Leadership

The popular North Africa riots can be described from a political economy point of view by discussing the social desire of the people for additional political and civil rights.[8] People and especially youth of the region asked the respective governments to advance their social and economic circumstances with access to education and employment opportunities. However, this was largely ignored and at times, met with indifference by the governments. Consequently, this led to mass protests as last resort.

Apart from the grievances from the governed, protests are further driven by frictions caused by the arbitrariness of state rule and its often-violent interference in the day-to-day lives of people—through the destruction of informal settlements, the dismantlement or relocation of informal markets, daily police harassment and extortion, for instance. This, in turn, impacts on already insecure and precarious economic situations. Recent protest movements in South Africa and Ethiopia offer an illustration of the close intertwining of these different protest dynamics.

Corruption

As further elaborated by Dan Kuwali in Chapter 33, most African states are often weak and inefficient, and most leaders, while no more greedy or self-serving than those elsewhere, tend to extract resources for "safe" investment outside the continent. In this manner "corruption does not grease the wheels of development but pours sand into the system, soaking up oil and clogging things up".[9] Blended with impunity, executive arrogance, this has over time led to discontent and resulted in mass protests against such kind of leadership.

---

[7] Afrobarometer is a pan-African, nonpartisan survey research network that provides reliable data on Africans' experiences and evaluations democracy, governance and quality of life. For more information, visit: www.afrobarometer.org.

[8] Terrill, D. (2011). The Arab Spring and the Future of U.S. Interests and Cooperative Security in the Arab World. Washington: Strategic Studies Institute.

[9] Cilliers, J. (2014). The Future of Democracy in Africa African Futures Paper 19, 15 October 2014, 16.

Poorly-Run Elections

The African Charter on Democracy, Elections and Governance[10] strongly posits the need for free and fair elections goes further to set electoral standards for the continent. This is buttressed by the notion that despite not being necessarily equal to democracy itself, holding of free, fair and credible elections is accepted and recognised as hallmark of accountability and a fundamental component of a normal and functioning democracy.[11] Drawing on 2019/2020 Afrobarometer data from 18 African countries, it appears that "most Africans believe in elections as the best way to select their leaders, popular support for elections has weakened, and only a minority think elections help produce representative, accountable leadership".[12] In agreement with Achiles Bwete and his colleagues in Chapter 21, this may explain growing discontent, which subsequently manifests in protests.

Protests after disputed elections have also emerged as a common trend in the electoralist path to democracy, either through making the regime accept defeat at the polls or leading to negotiations on electoral reform and/or power sharing mechanisms until the next electoral cycle.[13] Thompson attributes an essential role to political protest, arguing that "mass mobilization, not a well-developed civil society, is decisive in democratic revolutions". Between early 2018 and 2021 protests against electoral results were experienced in Malawi, Zimbabwe, Mali, Uganda, DRC, among several African states.[14]

It should be noted that while not being necessarily a cause of protests, the social media has been a key enabler of mass popular protests as indicated by Peter Makossah and Gilbert Mittawa in Chapter 14. The social media has enabled both a rapid and broad social mobilisation while also raising international visibility. Social media has also played an important role in facilitating protests, in line with a wider trend of a growing popularity of hashtag

[10] African Union. (2007). African Charter on Democracy, Elections and Governance.

[11] Lindberg, S. I. (2006). Democracy and elections in Africa. Baltimore, MD: Johns Hopkins University Press.

[12] M'Cormack-Hale, Fredline, & Dome, Mavis Zupork. (2021). Support for Elections Weakens among Africans; Many See Them as Ineffective in Holding Leaders Accountable, 9 February 2021, Afrobarometer Dispatch No. 425, available at: https://www.afrobarom eter.org/blogs/africans-want-elections-fewer-now-believe-they-work (accessed 17 February 2021).

[13] Bratton, Michael, & Van de Walle, Nicolas. (1997). *Democratic Experiments in Africa: Regime Transitions in Comparative Perspective*. Cambridge, UK: Cambridge University Press. Eisenstadt, Todd A. (2004). *Courting Democracy in Mexico: Party Strategies and Electoral Institutions*. Cambridge: Cambridge University Press. Howard, Marc Morje, and Roessler, Philip. (2006). Liberalizing Election Outcomes in Competitive Authoritarian Regimes. *American Journal of Political Science* 50(2): 365–381. McFaul, Michael. (2005). Transitions from Post-Communism. *Journal of Democracy* 16(3): 5–19.

[14] Fredline M'Cormack-Hale and Mavis Zupork Dome, footnote 12.

campaigns like #ThisFlag, #FeesMustFall or #BringBackOurGirls.[15] However, owing to comparatively low level of internet penetration in Africa the mobilising effect of social media continues to be mostly limited to urban areas, while street mobilisation remains reliant on more traditional methods such as leaflet distribution and word-of-mouth information spreading.

THE NATURE AND SCOPE OF POPULAR PROTESTS IN AFRICA

Popular protests in Africa have taken different forms owing to differences in reasons behind the protests. Further to that, some countries have a history of protests while some do not. This affects how protests are organised and even conducted. Consequently, nature of mass protests in Africa tends to range from passive, non-violent protests to active violent protests where everything goes and the streets resemble battlefields.

Two major forms of popular uprisings are noticeable on the continent. The first is a widely supported popular military action that results in regime change. Such actions usually end in coups d'état, which are clearly condemned under AU norms especially the Lome Declaration which condemns unconstitutional changes of government and the African Charter on Democracy, Elections and Governance.

The second form of uprising, however, is a popular mass civilian protest demanding respect for civil, economic and political rights or changes in governance or government. Popular cases in recent times include Egypt, Algeria and Sudan. In Libya, however, clashes resulting from the government's response to mass protests triggered a civil war, setting off a chain of events that ultimately led to the overthrow of the country's leader, Colonel Muammar Gaddafi. While the AU unequivocally rejects regime changes that result from military coups d'état, the organisation's legal and normative frameworks are not clear on whether the removal of sitting governments through popular uprisings constitutes an unconstitutional change of government.[16]

After a paucity in an activity since 2011, albeit followed by lukewarm reception to mass mobilisation movements in between, the 2019 post-election

---

[15] Ojobode, Ayo. (2018). How Bring Back Our Girls Went from Hashtag to Social Movement, While Rejecting Funding from Donors, October 10, 2018, available at: https://oxfamblogs.org/fp2p/how-bring-back-our-girls-went-from-hashtag-to-social-movement-while-rejecting-funding-from-donors/ (accessed 24 December 2020); Mavunga, George. (2019). #FeesMustFall Protests in South Africa: A Critical Realist Analysis of Selected Newspaper Articles. *Journal of Student Affairs in Africa* 7(1): 81–99, 2307–6267, https://doi.org/10.24085/jsaa.v7i1.3694.

[16] Abebe, Adem K. (2020). The African Union's Hypocrisy Undermines Its Credibility, 27 August 2020, available at: https://foreignpolicy.com/2020/08/27/the-african-unions-hypocrisy-undermines-its-credibility/ (accessed 12 December 2020).

protests in Malawi were accompanied by violence.[17] This was in part driven by the heavy-handed tactics employed by the police, which provoked retaliatory violence. Though a hotly disputed assertion, violence, and in particular destruction of public and private property, was seen as an effective means by protestors to force authorities to pay attention to their demands. It was more or less like the protestors were trying to make a Fanon-like statement, that violence is a language that authorities easily understand. Though never explicitly expressed by mass mobilisation leaders, this was the apparent stance as evidenced by their scantly veiled social media posts and loosely guarded behaviour to distance themselves from the looters.

In the two decades since the end of apartheid, South Africa has become one of the most vibrant liberal democracies in Africa. However, despite the transition to formal democracy being praised as peaceful, the post-apartheid political environment has been characterised by ongoing community protests. The gains made in political and civil rights have not adequately extended to the arena of economic freedom for most of the country's citizens, making South Africa one of the most unequal societies in the world.[18] South Africa has also seen an escalation of student protests at universities, which have resulted in the disruption or suspension of academic activity at all major universities, violent confrontations between students and the police and extensive damage to property.

Students initially started protesting against higher student fees, concerned that this would prevent many already disenfranchised youths from accessing education,[19] and the outsourcing of service jobs on campuses. All that said, these movements are yet to link up with social movements beyond campuses, and it is unclear how sustainable the protests will be—also considering the loose organisation of the student movements. All the same, the protests reflect an increased questioning of the hegemony of the African National Congress (ANC) over its failure to address economic disenfranchisement and redress racial and class inequalities.

Ethiopia has also seen some spate of mass protests in recent times. Although the protests began over a land reform measure, grievances run much deeper. They vary between regions and between political parties, but common factors are the opposition to the government, the call for a more democratic political space and a fairer distribution of wealth and jobs, and the fight against corruption. In sum, Ethiopia is confronted with the aspirations of a growing and

---

[17] Cheeseman, Nic. Africa: Repression & Resistance Are Two Key Trends Heading into 2021, 22 December 2020, available at: https://www.theafricareport.com/56131/africa-repression-resistance-are-two-key-trends-heading-into-2021/ (accessed 25 December 2020).

[18] Cable News Network (CNN). South Africa is the World's Most Unequal Country. 25 Years of Freedom Have Failed to Bridge the Divide, 10 May 2019, available at: https://edition.cnn.com/2019/05/07/africa/south-africa-elections-inequality-intl/index.html (accessed 15 June 2020).

[19] Mavunga, George, footnote 15.

increasingly well-educated youth that wants to participate in the political and economic system. In 2016, the protests in Oromia spread to the neighbouring Amhara region.[20] While there are currently no indicators of a formal alliance, a political *rapprochement* between both groups would represent a significant threat to the government and an important shift in Ethiopia's socio-political landscape.

A distinctive feature of Sudan and Algeria's protests calling for an end to injustice, inequity, high unemployment, insufficient housing and health care, epidemic corruption, government repression, unaccountability and unresponsiveness has been the role of the collective outrage and dissatisfaction of the marginalised, discriminated, subjugated and oppressed urban populations to mass mobilise themselves in political defiance.[21] In line with this, it is posited that poor and marginalised people in Africa engage in protests having thought critically about their circumstances, reasoning that their situation is unnatural, their oppression and marginalisation unjust, and thereby start to devise strategies for altering their situation. While this is debatable, considering low education levels in some African countries, it remains valid that conscientisation is a condition that can be attained regardless of peoples' education levels, owing to the pangs that are auxiliary to marginalisation and suffering and repeated exposure to radical messages.

At the heart of these protests have been youth movements. An important aspect of the recent protests is the central role played by youth movements such as *Y'en a marre (We are fed up) in Senegal, and BalaiCitoyen (Citizens' Broom) in Burkina Faso* and *La Lucha* in the DRC.[22] They have been the harbinger of new forms of protest (different from more traditional civil society actions) and are rooted in the development of connections between grassroots activities and national-level protests.

Regime Change Agenda Card

In Sub-Saharan Africa, protest is pointed out as a common trend throughout Africa's transitions in the early 1990s; "[t]ransitions away from one-party and military regimes started with political protest, evolved through liberalization reforms, often culminated in competitive elections, and usually ended with the installation of new forms of regimes". It is based on the realisation of these trends that African most governments look at mass protests as part of

[20] Cheeseman, Nic, footnote 17.

[21] Cilliers, J., footnote 9.

[22] See Amnesty International. Senegal: Right to Peaceful Protest and Freedom of Expression Must Be Respected Amid Crackdown on Dissent, 18 April 2018, available at: https://www.refworld.org/docid/5b3232824.html (accessed 17 February 2021). Amnesty International. DRC: Authorities Must Immediately and Unconditionally Release 10 Youth Activists, 19 January 2021, https://www.amnesty.org/en/latest/news/2021/01/drc-authorities-must-immediately-and-unconditionally-release-10-youth-activists/ (accessed 17 February 2020).

a "regime change" agenda. This claim is a card most African governments flash not only to seek sympathy but also to create a dichotomy and raise a feeling of "us versus them" among their supporters. This narrative is further buttressed by the fact that most civil society organisations are Western funded and appear to be advancing the interests of their handlers. Compounding this are the claims and demands by most mass popular protest leaders who at times overtly state regime change as their end state.

Most governments also use the regime change card to claim that and at times validly so, that mass protests are not necessarily the whole picture but largely part of it. Governments claim that protests are augmented by propaganda, judicial hostility and the involvement of some alternative elite who are no longer in power or want to be in power.[23] While sometimes these claims are dismissed as bordering on paranoia, most governments end up hardening their resolve and set out to reject the demands made through popular mass protests.

"We Shall Meet in the Streets"[24]

As an attendant to the regime change card, most African governments set out to stand in the way of mass protests. Hegemonies by their virtue seek to exclude certain groups from attaining and sharing power and, consequently, very little change is affected by protesters since their struggle against marginalisation seeks inclusion in the hegemonies that marginalise them. Rather than relent to the demands of the marginalised and protesting group, agents of hegemony resist change and engage in violence to maintain their power. This is evident in the brutal force the state security is increasingly using to subdue protesters.[25]

[23] See Kizzi Asala, AFP. CAR: Government Denounces Ex-President's "Coup d'état Attempt, 19 December 2020, available at: https://www.africanews.com/2020/12/19/central-african-government-denounces-president-s-coup-d-etat-attempt// (accessed 26 December 2020); Jeune Afrique. Latest coup d'état attempt in Benin foiled, 30 June 2020, available at: https://www.theafricareport.com/31841/latest-coup-detat-attempt-in-benin-foiled/ (accessed 26 December 2020) and David Phiri in New Africa. Before He Lost at the Polls, Malawi's Peter Mutharika Was Ousted by the Courts, 10 December 2020, available at: https://newafricanmagazine.com/24382/ (accessed 26 December 2020).

[24] "If you continue demonstrating, we shall meet in the streets," Malawi's third President Bingu wa Mutharika warned CSO leaders on July 22 2011 as they planned to hold protests the subsequent month. "This time around, I will follow you to your hiding place and smoke you out." The 20 July 2011 demonstrations were primarily called out of concern for the leader's increasingly-autocratic methods and apparent mishandling of the economy. 20 people killed, with scores injured as the Malawi Police Service opened fire on civilians in several cities in the country. See Travis Lupick The Africa Report, "Malawi's Riots: A Day of Reckoning for President Bingu", 29 July 2011, available at: https://www.theafricareport.com/8485/malawis-riots-a-day-of-reckoning-for-president-bingu/ (accessed 14 February 2021).

[25] Farlam, I., Hemraj, P., & Tokota, B. (2015). Marikana Commission of Inquiry: Report on Matters of Public, National and International Concern Arising Out of the

In Kenya, in the days following the elections of 8 August 2017, police killed scores of people and injured hundreds during repression of protests in opposition strongholds in Nairobi.[26] In August 2017, Togo's civic space deteriorated quickly when security forces used live ammunition to disperse opposition protesters demanding a return of the two-term limit for presidents, leading to several fatal and injuries. Several more died during opposition protests in Togo on 19 October 2017.[27] In the Democratic Republic of the Congo (DRC), between December 2017 and February 2018, several people were killed by security officers who used live ammunition and teargas during a series of after church mass protests to demand the implementation of the Saint-Sylvestre political agreement—an agreement between ruling and opposition parties on the holding of elections without president Kabila seeking a third term—including against civilians seeking refuge in churches.[28]

Worth noting is that the contemporary protest movement represents a qualitatively higher level of social and political activism compared to earlier phases. While previously much of the activism was limited to civil society organisations such as unions and human rights and women's groups led by professionals, their methods of mobilizing did not enable them to reach out to wider communities. However, the present protests are marked by resilience and determination not seen before. Suffice to say that that is happening in the constant face of threats, assaults, abductions and even arrests of protestors.

In the face of this assessment, it can be seen that most African governments seem to have answers to every criticism and even display novel and sometimes, sophisticated methods of dealing with dissent but display embarrassing and depressing incompetence in dealing with issues affecting day-to-day lives of their citizenry. It is sometimes this apparent detachment from realities facing their citizens that attract protracted protests.

Tragic Incidents at the Lonmin Mine in Marikana, in the North West Province. Marikana Commission of Inquiry Pretoria: Government Printers.

[26] Duggan, Briana, Karimi, Faith, & Narayan, Chandrika, CNN. 24 Killed in Post-Election Violence in Kenya, Rights Group Says, August 13, 2017, available at: https://edition.cnn.com/2017/08/12/africa/kenya-elections-protests/index.html (accessed 17 February 2021).

[27] Amnesty International, Amnesty International Report 2017/18—Togo, 22 February 2018, available at: https://www.refworld.org/docid/5a99384b4.html (accessed 17 February 2021).

[28] United Kingdom: Foreign and Commonwealth Office, Human Rights and Democracy Report 2017—Democratic Republic of the Congo (DRC), 16 July 2018, available at: https://www.refworld.org/docid/5b9109c4a.html (accessed 17 February 2021).

Coup d'États in Africa: A Clear and Present Danger

Since independence, *coups d'états* have been experienced on the African continent, some of which have been unsuccessful. While the causes of coups may have changed overtime, the phenomenon is very much alive, with ugly scenes and results as witnessed in Mali.[29]

More than 200 military coups have been staged in Africa since the post-independence era of 1960s, with 45% of them being successful and resulting in a regime change...,[30] While a significant number of successful coups occurred in the immediate post-independence era (during the 1960s), the 1970s and 1980s were marked by a plethora of both successful and failed coup attempts. Of the 39 coups that happened during the 1960s, 27 (or 69%) resulted in the successful toppling of established regimes.[31] The 1990s and 2000s, on the other hand, witnessed a decrease in the number of both successful and failed coups, with about half of African countries being coup free. The reasons for the absence of coups and coup attempts during this period are manifold, ranging from foreign powers guaranteeing stability in some countries, to other nations being caught up in different manifestations of political violence (e.g. civil or interstate wars), or to established regimes being equipped with measures of systemic legitimacy that discouraged praetorian assaults from the armed forces.[32]

Still, Africa remains the world's most coup-prone region, accounting for over half of all coup attempts globally in the last two decades. In 2019, three of five coup attempts occurred in Africa. These recent African coups include a failed coup attempt against Ali Bongo in Gabon, and successful coups against Abdelaziz Bouteflika in Algeria and Omar al-Bashir in Sudan and in Mali.

One reason for the resurgence of this phenomenon is the failure of democracy in Africa.[33] Democracy has been interpreted and applied in different ways throughout the continent according to the whims and caprices of politicians and ruling elites, causing significant discontent among many African people. Democracy, or at least, its mishandling seems to have disappointed many citizens. To the extent that large segments of the population in developing countries remain poor, and faith in the ability of democratic regimes to improve living standards and provide security weakens, memories of the failures of military rule are likely to fade and it will once again become a plausible

---

[29] Mali is not a stranger to coups. Since gaining independence from France in 1960, it has experienced numerous coup plots, five coup attempts and four successful coups.

[30] Ncube, Mnthuli, et al., Economic Brief: Political Fragility in Africa: Are Military Coups d'Etat a Never-Ending Phenomenon? African Development Bank September (2012).

[31] Ibid.

[32] Ibid.

[33] Barracca, S. (2007). Military Coups in the Post-Cold War Era: Pakistan, Ecuador and Venezuela. *Third World Quarterly* 28(1): 137–154.

(and even attractive) alternative.[34] Indeed, a government's inability to design, implement and administer sound public policy—in conjunction with other economic and political weaknesses, such as low economic growth, corruption and lack of institutionalised democratic structures—may motivate soldiers and rebels to take full advantage of the situation and overthrow political leaders with the goal of pursuing corporate or personal interests.

Interestingly enough, some coups, especially the most successful, have rode on the back of mass protests, especially at local level. All the same, this shows the dilemma and lack of options that pits citizens and self-serving, self-perpetuating leaders, especially if the latter has hardened his or her resolve to stay on in power, regardless of the reasonable concerns by the former. In most African states, coups have been organised usually with an explicit aim to restore constitutional order for a limited period of time so as to allow a return to democracy which has supposedly been corrupted by ruling civilian elites/governments. Similar to 1991, Mali's 2020 coup was facilitated in part by months of escalating anti-government mass protest. The June 5 protest movement (M5-RFP) disputed the April 2020 parliamentary election results and decried corruption and government ineptitude.[35] While there may be concerns about failure of democracy which sometimes translates into mass protests, it is interesting that the military, which is supposedly the backbone of state and is under civilian rule, thinks that it has primacy in protecting the Constitution.

In 2019, Africa witnessed two major uprisings that resulted in the toppling of long-term leaders in Algeria and Sudan.[36] Protests and subsequent coup in Mali also pointed to a similar scenario. This leaves the African Union (AU), which has established strong continental norms against unconstitutional changes of government, with a dilemma: should regime changes resulting from popular uprisings be treated as "unconstitutional changes of government" and condemned by the AU, or should they be considered as the popular will of the people and supported? Yet coups in Africa have also shown that the AU and regional blocs have a credibility problem as apparently, they do not necessarily denounce those who flout laws to hold on to power, but complain only when the military seizes it.

---

[34] Aning, K., & Birikorang, E. (2012). Negotiating Populism and Populist Politics in Ghana: 1949–2012, in K. Aning and K. Danso, eds., *Managing Election-Related Violence for Democratic Stability in Ghana*. Accra: Friedrich Ebert-Stiftung.

[35] Chin, John. A 'Good Coup' in Africa? Mali's Latest Military Coup in Perspective, 4 November 2020, Institute for Politics and Strategy, Center for International Relations and Politics, CIRP Journal, cirp-journal-online available at: https://www.cmu.edu/ir/cirp-jou rnal/cirp-journal-online/john-chin-africa-coups.html (accessed 25 December 2020).

[36] Institute for Security Studies, Should Regime Changes Resulting from Popular Uprisings Be Treated as Unconstitutional Changes of Government? News and Press Release, 21 August 2019, available at: https://issafrica.org/pscreport/psc-insights/from-popular-uprisings-to-regime-change (accessed 14 December 2020).

In the aftermath of the coup in Mali, observers also defended the military intervention as a "corrective" or "democratic" coup, with an article in an influential South African newspaper sarcastically wondering if the AU's job was "to protect people from authoritarian regimes or to protect authoritarian regimes from their people?"[37] Thus, certain coups have become romanticised. From Egypt to Mali, the mutineers were seen by many as the legitimate representatives of the people in the face of unlawful governments. In the long run, there appears to be an inherent tension between two key AU principles—the respect for constitutional order in leadership changes and the right of people to oppose an oppressive regime, through peaceful protests.

The institutionalisation of coups in Africa has been caused by those leaders in Africa who have openly supported unconstitutional changes of government. For example, In March 2009, the then Chairman of the African Union, Colonel Muammar Gaddafi, and then Senegalese President Abdoulaye Wade were against sanctions against Mauritania.[38] Thus the resolve of the AU was undermined by some of its own "senior members". However, it needs to be established within the African Union and the general African consciousness that irrespective of the misrule of a constitutionally elected regime, overthrowing the regime through a military coup, or other unconstitutional means is unacceptable. There is no such thing like a "good coup", just like there are "no beautiful graves".

This places greater responsibility on the African Union, regional blocs such as SADC, ECOWAS and other international organisations who monitor elections, to ensure that the elections are genuinely free, fair, credible and a reflection of the people's choice. When flawed elections are passed as free and fair, it leads to contestation within the state, as citizens are left with no choice than to wait another four or five years. This presents an ominous opportunity to some hideous characters in the military or other parts of the government to ride on such genuine waves and organise coups, further complicating a state's political and socioeconomic fortunes.

While it is impossible to predict the onset, incidence or success rate of a potential military coup, yet by addressing some core economic and sociopolitical problems, governments could mitigate the risk of such an event. In other words, good governance and policies that provide economic opportunities for all citizens and that create the enabling environment for poverty reduction may be the panacea to tackle political instability. On its part, the AU needs to find intelligent ways to end its incumbent bias. It must treat all cases of unconstitutionality with the same Pan-African zest and fairness, whether perpetrated by a military junta or an incumbent civilian authority. This would not only allow it to respond to all coups with the firmness and

---

[37] Abebe, Adem K. "The African Union's Hypocrisy Undermines Its Credibility", 27 August 2020, available at: https://foreignpolicy.com/2020/08/27/the-african-unions-hypocrisy-undermines-its-credibility/ (accessed 12 December 2020).

[38] Chin, John, footnote 35.

Silencing the Guns or Muting the Protestors: What Is the Way Forward?

In the course of prevailing and future protests on the continent, there is need to consider some measures that can be adopted in order to protect lives, ensure transparency and enhance trust between the rulers and the ruled. Firstly, CSOs need to draw a key lesson from the democratisation wave of the 1990s in Africa that regime change does not necessarily lead to systemic change. Recent trends in Egypt have shown that the crisis of leadership associated with some "leaderless movements" end up resulting in the inability of the people to agree on a common course of action to take. The consequence of this is usually a disagreement among the disparate groups that make up the movement and the parties that mount the saddle of political leadership[39] Such disagreement builds up and results in a divided group interest, crisis of confidence and struggle for group supremacy, which ultimately brings about the inability of the group to achieve its objective.

A midway point and a possible win–win take for both CSOs and governments is to facilitate a systems change. However, this should be guarded in view of the possibility that some authoritarian political elites rebrand and re-organise themselves as "born-again" democrats that embrace democratic values while continuing to foster repression and control camouflaged/masked/disguised as political and economic reforms.

Kuwali is right in Chapter 13 that African governments need to desist from harassing, attacking and intimidating journalists who cover assemblies of opposition parties or report on issues considered sensitive by the government. Further to that, there is need to stop obstructing live radio broadcasts that involve civil society and members of the political opposition, particularly during elections period. Additionally, governments need to prioritise their engagement with civil society in the formulation and implementation of policies and legislation affecting citizens. There should be regular consultations between different arms of government, particularly the judiciary, security sector and the legislature, on human rights issues and on ways to adhere to constitutional, regional and international human rights obligations.

Further to that, Mark Maxwell is correct in Chapter 24 that there is need to de-politicise and professionalise the military with a view to subordinating military establishment to civilian leadership and authority. Finally, when protests do occur, the issues behind them should be addressed with urgency, so as to reduce the potential for violent manifestations. To deal with this in the long

---

[39] Kirkova, R., & Milosevska, T. (2014). The Success of Democratization in Post Arab Spring Societies. *International Journal of Social Sciences* III(1): 29–40.

term, African governments must ensure that the social, economic and political landscape in their countries caters effectively for peoples' needs.

Preemptively, states need to consider providing equal educational, vocational and economic opportunities for all citizens regardless of their social class, ethnicity, gender or geographical location. Boosting educational and vocational opportunities will help to address the massive youth unemployment challenge currently facing the region, which is alienating youth and creating social disaffection. The need for production of graduates who study demand-driven courses cannot be emphasised. Policies to boost social inclusion and social protection, particularly for those in remote rural areas and in slum settlements in the cities, will help to extinguish the sparks of social unrest which can be politically destabilising and which may open the way to interventions such as military coups.

As can be seen, Agenda 2063's success partly hinges on the elimination of coups. On its part, importantly, the AU needs to move away from backing miscreant incumbents, a tendency that makes it look like an "old boys club" to unequivocally showing no tolerance to leaders who overstay in power, show blatant disregard to human rights and abuse the electoral process.

Conclusion

The protests phenomena have always been part of Africa's history and cannot be wished away without any meaningful interventions at all levels. Addressing popular protests and coup d'états is certainly an endeavour that cannot be attained in fortnight. It requires both the Au and its member states to rethink how both governments and protestors alike perceive mass protests. Popular protests in Africa, therefore, should not necessarily be viewed as vehicles for regime change, even though this may be the declared aim of some of them. Instead, they are to be viewed as a means to press for reform and challenge the state's monopoly of political discourse and action. This calls for strategic interventions that do not just cure the triggers, but address the key underlying causes. The AU needs to maintain a tough stance on coups. Instead of being seen as selectively applying its own rules, the grouping, together with regional blocs, should set out to clear denounce coups.

CHAPTER 12

Countering Violent Extremism in Africa

Dan Kuwali

INTRODUCTION

The kidnapping of 200 girls in Nigeria's Borno State in 2014, the massacre of university students in Kenya following a siege by operatives of the extremist group Al-Shabaab in 2015 and the beheading of at least 50 villagers in Cabo Delgado in Mozambique in 2020, among others, on the African continent have raised concerns whether eradicating extremism is possible.[1] Reports indicate that the battleground for the Islamic State (IS) group has moved away from the Middle East going mainly southwards to Africa, with a 67% increase of total deaths by IS in sub-Saharan Africa between 2019 and 2020 due to

---

[1] See also Correspondent, 'Militant Islamists "behead more than 50" in Mozambique,' *BBC News*, 9 November 2020, available at: https://www.bbc.com/news/world-africa/54877202 (accessed 11 February 2020).

D. Kuwali (✉)
University of Pretoria, Pretoria, South Africa

© The Author(s), under exclusive license to Springer Nature Switzerland AG 2022
D. Kuwali (ed.), *The Palgrave Handbook of Sustainable Peace and Security in Africa*, https://doi.org/10.1007/978-3-030-82020-6_12

197

expansion of ISIS affiliates into sub-Saharan Africa.[2] The Global Terrorism Index indicates that at least seven of the ten countries with the biggest surge in terrorism were in sub-Saharan Africa, namely Burkina Faso, Cameroon, the Democratic Republic of the Congo (DRC), Ethiopia, Mali, Mozambique and Niger.[3]

The African Union (AU) has noted that 'terrorism constitutes a serious violation of human rights and, in particular, the rights to physical integrity, life, freedom and security, and impedes socioeconomic development through destabilization of States'.[4] Violent extremism also weaken States that are weak, further eroding public trust in the ability of state institutions to protect the general welfare of its citizens.[5] Article 1(3) of the AU Convention on the Prevention and Combating of Terrorism defines a terrorist act as:

(a) any act which is a violation of the criminal laws of a State Party and which may endanger the life, physical integrity or freedom of, or cause serious injury or death to, any person, any number or group of persons or causes or may cause damage to public or private property, natural resources, environmental or cultural heritage and is calculated or intended to:

   (i) intimidate, put in fear, force, coerce or induce any government, body, institution, the general public or any segment thereof, to do or abstain from doing any act, or to adopt or abandon a particular standpoint, or to act according to certain principles; or
   (ii) disrupt any public service, the delivery of any essential service to the public or to create a public emergency; or
   (iii) create general insurrection in a State;

---

[2] See Institute for Economics and Peace, 'Global Terrorism Index 2020: Measuring the Impact of Terrorism,' Sydney, November 2020, available at: http://visionofhumanity.org/reports (accessed 11 February 2021). The Global Terrorism Index (GTI) analyzes 'the impact of terrorism for 163 countries covering 99.7 per cent of the world's population' and 'looks at the application of systems thinking to terrorism, using mainly statistical techniques and mathematical models to better understand the dynamics of terrorism and its subsequent impact on society.' Erin Dauphinais-Soo, 'Global Terrorism Index,' Homeland Security Digital Library, 30 November 2020, also available at: https://hsdl.org/c/global-terrorism-index-2020 (accessed 11 February 2021).

[3] As above, p. 2. See also Frank Gardner, 'Is Africa overtaking the Middle East as the New Jihadist Battleground?' *BBC News*, 3 December 2020, accessed at: https://www.bbc.com/new/worl-africa55147863 (accessed 11 February 2021).

[4] OAU Convention on the Prevention and Combating of Terrorism, 1999, Adopted at Algiers on 14 July 1999 Entry into force in accordance with Article 20 Depositary: Secretary-General of the Organization of African Unity.

[5] Geofrey Mugumya, 'Prevention of terrorist Movement and Effective Border Security,' emarks by the Commission of the African Union to the Fifth Special Meeting of the Counter-Terrorism Conference with International, Regional and Sub-Regional organizations, Nairobi Kenya, 29 October 2007.

(b) any promotion, sponsoring, contribution to, command, aid, incitement, encouragement, attempt, threat, conspiracy, organizing, or procurement of any person, with the intent to commit any act referred to in paragraph (a) (i) to (iii)

Article 3(2) of the AU Convention on the Prevention and Combating of Terrorism rejects that 'political, philosophical, ideological, racial, ethnic, religious or other motives shall not be a justifiable defence against a terrorist act'. Extremism and radicalisation have fueled the violence and terrorism that afflict communities around the world today.[6] These scourges are borderless in their effects, and countering them is in the interest of all states. An extremist is emblematic of a person who advocates or resorts to measures beyond the norm, especially in politics, religion or culture. A related term, radicalism, denotes political principles focused on altering social structures through revolutionary means and changing value systems in fundamental ways.

As articulated by Tabitha Mwangi, Tracy Asave and Iretioluwa Akerele in Chapter 10, extremism and radicalisation have fueled violence and terrorism, which are some of the burning problems that affect communities around the world. On the African continent, from Somalia, Al-Shabaab terrorists have launched attacks across East Africa. In Nigeria and neighboring countries, Boko Haram kills and kidnaps innocent men, women and especially, girls and children. Today, the worst terrorist threat in the world is not a meticulously plotted event like the attacks on 11 September 2001 in the United States (US), but rather homegrown citizens who become radicalised on their own or by a foreign terrorist organisation.[7]

Since the attacks of 11 September 2001, the international community has stepped up efforts on how to deal with radicalisation, violent extremism and terrorism. Countering these scourges is in the interest of all states, considering the borderless effects of such criminal acts. The proliferation of violent extremism in Africa has presented the continent with a geopolitical situation that calls for rethinking of security paradigms beyond the sole military or police-based approach, to rather re-examine human security issues that span political and religious spaces, the clash of cultures and other socioeconomic factors that lead to grievances and exclusion of some segments of the society.

The extent of the violence and the trans-national and multifacetted nature of the actors have raised questions on the ability of states to counter extremist messages, which has a reach and agility in social media that far outstrips that of

---

[6] United Nations 'First Report of the Working Group on Radicalisation and Extremism that Lead to Terrorism: Inventory of State Programmes, CounterTerrorism Implementation Task Force,' para 1, available at: http://www.un.org/en/terrorism/pdfs/radicalization.pdf (accessed 5 January 2015). See also Trevor P. Chimimba, 'Defining Terrorism under the United Nations System,' *Zanzibar Yearbook of Law* (2013), pp. 51–94.

[7] See also G. Yoroms, 'Defining and Mapping Threats of Terrorism in Africa,' in W. Okumu & A. Botha (eds) *Understanding Terrorism in Africa: In Search for an African Voice*, Institute for Security Studies (2007), pp. 3–14.

most governments. The relative ease with which extremists recruit and carry out their attacks seems to suggest that governments are being outdone both in terms of amplification strategies and the capability to lead in the battle of ideas. It is generally accepted that military might is only one dimension in tackling extremism and terrorism. Although military force can hypothetically annihilate the entire safe haven for extremists, the ideology and the threat of extremism cannot be eliminated given the massive propaganda they disseminate over social media.

The creation of the Working Group on 'Addressing Radicalisation and Extremism that Lead to Terrorism', by the United Nations (UN) was a response to member states' demand for help in furthering their understanding of what makes a terrorist to be a terrorist and in identifying effective policies and practices to prevent this from happening.[8] The UN Working Group has highlighted the importance of preventive and long-term measures in fighting terrorism, separate from, and additional to, suppressive and coercive action that may involve the use of force.[9] The main focus of the UN Working Group is on non-coercive approaches to violent extremism that rely on engagement with, and winning hearts and minds of, the segments of society that are normally targeted by extremist and radical groups for recruitment, support and funding.[10] Building on the strategies outlined by the UN Working Group and in addition to the measures outlined in Article 4 of the AU Convention on the Prevention and Combating of Terrorism, this chapter seeks to interrogate the rationale behind radicalisation and examine how violent extremism can be eradicated from the African continent.[11] The chapter does so by assessing how an anthropological dimension can be integrated into the prevention of radicalisation in order to eradicate extremism by taking advantage of African cultural, religious and political diversity. This, it is envisaged, would embrace dialogue, address grievances, prevent exclusion and promote tolerance.

THE DRIVERS OF EXTREMISM IN AFRICA

To eradicate extremism, it is key to find out what causes extremism. Without addressing the causes, any strategy purporting to eradicate extremism may only combat or alleviate the symptoms and not the cause. There are various forms of violent extremism bordering on political, religious or cultural realms, with

[8] First Report of the Working Group on Radicalisation and Extremism that Lead to Terrorism: Inventory of State Programmes, CounterTerrorism Implementation Task Force (UNReport), available at: http://www.un.org/en/terrorism/pdfs/radicalization.pdf (accessed 5 January 2015), para 1.

[9] See also UN Working Group Report, footnote 6 above, para 2.

[10] See UN Working Group Report, footnote 6 above, para 2. See also K. Schillinger, 'The role of the international community' in Okumu & Botha (eds) footnote 7 above, pp. 3–14.

[11] See Article 4 4 of the AU Convention on the Prevention and Combating of Terrorism, footnote 4 above.

variety of causes ranging from political, religious or cultural marginalisation, a vacuum of governance and security as well as colonial influences. The diverging ideological influences from the colonial era (Arabic, English and French) in Africa and the clashes between religious models on the continent have resulted in socioeconomic and religious imbalances in several countries. The issue of an ideological confrontation resonated following the appearance of radical ideological groups, terrorist activities and hostage taking in the Maghreb societies and the Horn of Africa. Given the porous borders on the continent, it was inevitable for the phenomenon of extremism to extend to the south of the Sahara. The instability on the continent has been exacerbated by the diverging interests and due to rivalries between both foreign powers and neighbouring countries on a strategic and an economic level, scrambling for abundant oil, cocoa, minerals and energy resources on the continent.[12]

Tadziwana Kapeni and Archiles Bwete and his colleagues in Chapters 17 and 21, respectively, are right that political instability which creates power vacuum, security lapses and ungoverned spaces, discrimination, political marginalisation, discrimination on the basis of religious or such other status, economic crisis including social penury and the proliferation of small arms and light weapons (SALW) and underdevelopment on the continent are some of the key factors that have contributed to the breeding of extremist groups such as Al-Shabaab, Boko Haram and Ansaru Dine, Al-Qaeda in the Islamic Maghreb (AQIM), the Movement for the Oneness and Jihad in West Africa (MOJWA) in North and West Africa, the Lord's Resistance Army (LRA) and the *Movement pour l'Unification et le Jihad en Afrique de l'Quest* (MUJAO) on the continent. The current wave of religious extremism and armed conflicts sweeping through countries such as Syria, Yemen has also contributed to insecurity in Africa.

The infiltration of the terrorist organisation, Islamic State of Iraq and al-Sham (ISIS) in North Africa has caused panic and brought to the fore the search for effective strategies to countering terrorism. Extremist groups are generally amorphous groups or figuratively speaking,—'combatants without borders' who recruit terrorists who are willing to conduct attacks in their home countries and to travel abroad for this atrocious purpose. With steady funding from drug trafficking and hostage taking, the transnational nature of the actors, the porosity of borders along with the reduction of the area through modern means of communication tend to favour the propagation of the extremism on the continent.[13]

Article 4(o) of the AU Constitutive Act calls for 'respect for the sanctity of human life, condemnation and rejection of impunity and political assassination, acts of terrorism and subversive activities', which is underscored

---

[12] See also SM Makinda 'The history and root causes of terrorism in Africa' in Okumu & Botha, footnote 7 above, pp. 15–21.

[13] See generally A Botha 'Africa's vulnerability to terrorism and its ability to combat it in Africa' in Okumu & Botha, footnote 7 above, pp. 23–41.

in the preamble as the need to promote peace, security and stability as a prerequisite for the implementation of Africa's development agenda.[14] The ninth recital of the preamble of the AU Convention on the Prevention and Combating Terrorism notes that 'terrorism constitutes a serious violation of human rights and, in particular, the rights to physical integrity, life, freedom and security, and impedes socioeconomic development through destabilization of States'.[15] Further, the first recital of the preamble of the Protocol to the AU Convention on the Prevention and Combating Terrorism highlights 'the growing risks of linkages between terrorism and mercenaryism, weapons of mass destruction, drug trafficking, corruption, transnational organized crimes, money laundering, and the illicit proliferation of small arms'.[16] While the AU has established an impressive legal framework to address radicalisation and extremism and to combat terrorism, what is needed is not only the political will to implement and enforce the law but also, as this chapter outlines below, a strategy to eradicate the causes of extremism.

Countering Violent Extremism in Africa

Aside from better policing and secure borders, the long-term solution to counter terrorism is the creation of economic opportunities and political stability that eventually dissuade people, especially the youth, from involvement in violence as explained by Mphatso Boti-Phiri in Chapter 25.[17] In an effort to facilitate information sharing among member states, the UN Working Group embarked on a mapping exercise with the objective of creating an inventory of counter-radicalisation and deradicalisation measures implemented by its member states. The Working Group identified eleven key strategic issues (or types of programmes), involving counterradicalisation and deradicalisation measures implemented by some states. These are: (1) engaging and working with civil society; (2) prison programmes; (3) education; (4) promoting

[14] African Union, The Constitutive Act of the African Union, adopted in 2000 at the Lomé Summit (Togo), entered into force in 2001 available at http://www.au.int/en/about/constitutive_act (accessed 10 February 2021).

[15] African Union, African Union (AU) Convention on the Prevention and Combating Terrorism, adopted at the 35th Ordinary Session of the OAU Ordinary Summit held in Algiers, Algeria, in July 1999 available at: http://www.au.int/en/sites/default/files/OAU_CONVENTION_PREVENTION_COMBATING_TERRORISM.pdf (accessed 10 January 2021).

[16] African Union, Protocol to the AU Convention on the Prevention and Combating of Terrorism, available at: http://www.au.int/en/sites/default/files/protocol_oau_convention_on_the_prevention_combating_terrorism.pdf (accessed 10 February 2021).

[17] Nisha Bellinger and Kyle T. Kattelman, 'Domestic terrorism in the developing world: Role of food security,' *Journal of International Relations and Development* (2020), available at: https://doi.org/10.1057/s41268-020-00191-y (accessed 21 February 2021). See also Edward Newman, 'Weak States, State Failure, and Terrorism,' 19(4) *Terrorism and Political Violence* (2007), pp. 463–488, also available at: https://doi.org/10.1080/09546550701590636 (accessed 10 February 2021).

alliance of civilisations and intercultural dialogue; (5) tackling economic and social inequalities; (6) global programmes to counter radicalisation; (7) the internet; (8) legislation reforms; (9) rehabilitation programmes; (10) developing and disseminating information and (11) training and qualifying agencies involved in implementing counterradicalisation policies.[18] Therefore, to address radicalisation and extremism that lead to terrorism on the continent, African States need to build on these measures and integrate an anthropological dimension that capitalises on the diverse cultural, religious and political resources including dialogue, mediation and socialisation on the continent.

Conflict Prevention Through Broad-Based Socioeconomic Development

There is an implicit recognition among many states that economic and social inequalities (real or perceived) fuel discontent and encourage grievances that create conditions conducive to the spread of violent extremism.[19] Although not all individuals who share the same fate of deprivation turn to violent extremism, such abhorrent acts are always the action of a few within the larger group or community. When people—especially young people—feel entirely trapped in impoverished communities, where there is no order and no path for advancement, where there are no educational opportunities, where there are no ways to support families and no escape from injustice and the humiliations of corruption—that feeds instability and disorder, and makes those communities ripe for extremist recruitment.

Therefore, to counter violent extremism, states should confront these socioeconomic grievances. Hence, governments should formulate policies that help young people to forge new collaborations in entrepreneurship and science and technology. In doing so, states should ensure broad-based development that creates growth and jobs, not just for the few at the top, but for the many. Governments should ensure to promote economic growth and development, fighting corruption and encouraging other countries to devote more resources to education, including for girls and women.[20]

There is need to break the cycles of conflict that have become magnets for violent extremism by addressing underlying inequalities which fuel terrorist activity. Causal factors need to be delineated and measures implemented, which allow equal access to resources and sustainability for all people. Such activities empower citizens providing 'freedom from fear' and 'freedom from

---

[18] UN Working Group Report, footnote 6 above, para 9.

[19] As above, para 20.

[20] D. Kuwali, 'Just peace: Achieving peace, justice, and development in post conflict African Countries,' Policy Paper, Africa Peacebuilding Network, New York, Social Science Research Council (2014), 17–18, available at: http://webarchive.ssrc.org/workingpapers/APN_WorkingPapers02_Kuwali.pdf (accessed 10 December 2020).

204   D. KUWALI

want'.[21] For example, The Dutch authorities have undertaken several policies to address discrimination, including in the labour market, as well as to equip the youth with skills they require to find work. They have also provided financial resources for language training and to encourage young people to complete their schooling, and have increased support for parents to help them equip their children to participate in the Dutch society.[22] To promote broad-based growth, the AU has encouraged its member states to ensure the successful implementation of their economic development and poverty alleviation policies and programmes. In this respect, the AU Commission seeks to work with the African Development Bank and the United Nations Economic Commission for Africa, to provide the necessary support to member states.[23]

Countering Extremism with Respect for Human Rights and Humanitarian Law

Oftentimes, counterterrorism programmes trample on human rights. Strategies such as intelligence gathering, using military force, and enforcing the law cannot by themselves solve—and, when misused, can exacerbate—the problem of violent extremism. Such measures should, therefore, be developed and implemented in full compliance with international law—in particular, with international human rights and humanitarian law as well as with the principles and purposes of the UN Charter.[24] At the same time, states should be seen protecting the rights as well as the safety and security of individuals, not just monitoring their religious and political expression.[25]

At the same time, when governments oppress their people, deny human rights, stifle dissent or marginalise ethnic and religious groups, or favor certain religious groups over others, they create an environment that is ripe for terrorists to exploit. When peaceful, democratic change is impossible, that failure feeds into the terrorist propaganda that violence is the only answer available.

---

[21] This can take many forms including the provision of clean drinking water, education, vaccination programmes, provision of food and shelter and protection from violence, military or otherwise. Successful human security campaigns have been characterised by the participation of a diverse group of actors including governments, non-government organisations (NGOs) and citizens.

[22] UN Working Group Report, footnote 6 above, para 21.

[23] See African Union 'Statement delivered by the African Union Commissioner for Peace and Security, Ambassador Smäil Chergui, at the Ministerial Component of the White House Summit to Counter Terrorism,' available at: http://www.peaceau.org/uploads/auc.cps.statement.wh.summit.violent.extremism.19.02.2015.pdf (accessed 10 January 2021).

[24] See also G. Kegoro, 'The effects of counter-terrorism measures on human rights: The experiences of East African Countries,' in Okumu & Botha, footnote 7 above, pp. 51–57.

[25] White House Office of the Press Secretary, 'Statement from the Press Secretary on the White House Summit on Countering Violent Extremism,' 11 January 2015, available at: http://www.whitehouse.gov/the-press-office/2015/01/11/statement-press-secretary-white-house-summit-countering-violent-extremism (accessed 9 March 2015).

Such violations make those communities more vulnerable to being recruited.[26] As violent extremists might seek to destabilise governments and sow internal frictions within societies, it is important that governments uphold and preserve democratic principles, and promote the rule of law to address these challenges. States should behave in a way so that victims of hate crimes and violent extremism know that government agencies are there to protect their rights, safety and security, and not be seen as spineless enforcers of oppressive laws.[27]

Capability of Security Agents to Protect Populations at Risk

Firstly, there is need for security agents to train and attain capacity in countering radicalisation. Such training is crucial to improve the cultural competence of counter-radicalisation agencies, qualify them to do their jobs and equip them with essential knowledge and capability to protect populations at risk. Secondly, security and law enforcement agents should have a deterrent capability including show of decisive force to deter attacks against civilians. This is because deterrence is the best way to stop violent extremism at the lowest cost and risk. As such, the presence of troops (show of force) in areas infested by extremists can have a significant deterrent effect.

The show of force should be accompanied by credible political statements. Thirdly, troops and law enforcement officers should have the capacity to execute arrest of armed extremists. This view arises from the fact that the failure to arrest and punish extremists compromises the protection of civilians and promotes the proliferation of violent extremism. Although the International Criminal Court (ICC) has the jurisdiction to prosecute perpetrators of such atrocities against humanity, The Hague-based court does not have its own police force to arrest suspects for purposes of bringing them to justice.[28] Therefore, troops and law enforcement agents should have the capability to arrest armed extremists and bring them to justice.[29]

---

[26] In Syria for example, Assad's war against his own people and deliberate stoking of sectarian tensions helped to fuel the rise of *Islamic State of Iraq and the Levant* (ISIL).

[27] See also J. Kollapen, 'Human rights, terrorism and the interests of a secure society,' in Okumu and Botha, footnote 7 above, pp. 131–134.

[28] The International Criminal Court (ICC) depends upon the cooperation of states to arrest and surrender those indicted by the Court. Where such support or cooperation is not forthcoming, the perpetrators may go scot-free, thereby defeating the purpose of the establishment of the ICC.

[29] D. Kuwali, 'Humanitarian rights: Enforcement of international humanitarian law by the African Court of Human Rights,' *African Yearbook of International Humanitarian Law* (2011), pp. 174–175.

Community Empowerment to Deter Extremist Groups and Control Borders

Extremist groups may sometimes promise services and food supplies to communities in areas they control in order to win support of the locals. Thus, to prevent people from being susceptible to false promises of extremism, the international community should offer better opportunities and access to social services. To this end, Article 3(1)(a) of the Protocol to the AU Convention on the Prevention and Combating of Terrorism requires States to 'take all necessary measures to protect the fundamental human rights of their populations against all acts of terrorism'.[30] Countering Violent Extremism (CVE) efforts are effective where there are well-informed and resilient local communities. Investing in contacts with local communities not only facilitates and accelerates the process of information gathering, but can also act as an early observation/warning or recognition system of any violent extremist tendencies, hence permitting an early and effective counter strategy.[31] For this reason, states should empower communities to protect themselves from violent ideologies and recruitment through public awareness and provision of policing services. In the United States, for example, several states have embarked on building CVE frameworks by integrating a range of social service providers, including education administrators, mental health professionals and religious leaders, with law enforcement agencies to address violent extremism as part of the broader mandate of community safety and crime prevention.[32]

There is need to explore how development and other relevant foreign assistance could contribute to addressing populations at risk of recruitment by violent extremists and the conditions conducive to radicalisation to violence. More advanced and richer countries should help less advanced and poorer countries to build up their security forces so that they can prevent ungoverned spaces where terrorists find safe haven, and to deter them from committing their atrocious acts. On its part, the UN Working Group Report has recommended the creation of 'Global Programmes to Counter Radicalisation and Build Capacity in Third Countries'.[33] More importantly, governments must take robust measures to monitor and regulate their borders to keep away terrorists and their weapons while welcoming all legitimate travelers and allowing commerce to thrive.

---

[30] African Union, Protocol to the AU Convention on the Prevention and Combating of Terrorism, available at: http://www.au.int/en/sites/default/files/Protocol_Oau_Convention_On_The_Prevention_Combating_Terrorism.pdf (accessed 14 June 2015).

[31] UN Working Group Report, footnote 6 above, para 10.

[32] See generally C. Mayson, 'Engaging religious communities and building partnerships,' in Okumu & Botha, footnote 7 above, pp. 77–80. See also White House Press Statement on Countering Violent Extremism, footnote 25 above.

[33] See also A. du Plessis, 'The role of the United Nations in providing technical assistance in Africa,' in Okumu & Botha, footnote 7 above, pp. 85–92. See UN Working Group Report, footnote 6 above, para 22.

Choking-Off Extremists' Financing

Securing and sustaining funding is at the heart of any extremist or insurgent organisation's success, but it is also its Achilles' heel. It has been observed that skillful financial management is at the heart of the success of any extremist or insurgent organisation. Securing and sustaining funding is the key to moving from fringe radical group to a more planned and organised terrorist organisation. Funding is clearly the lifeblood of such organisations but it is also their Achilles' heels.[34] Generally, terrorist groups can draw on financing in two primary ways: internally, through illegal taxation and trade, as well as proceeds from kidnap and ransom; and externally, from donors sympathetic to their causes.

As observed across northern Syria and Iraq, however, starving extremists of financing is no easy task once they evolve from external reliance to internal self-sufficiency. This is why there is need for concerted efforts by countries and individuals to suffocate extremists from funding through legislative frameworks such as anti-money laundering and other anti-corruption strategies.

Reports that the US Central Intelligence Agency (CIA) paid Al-Qaeda ransom to free an Afghan diplomat are disturbing.[35] To suffocate terrorists groups, the AU Assembly has strongly condemned the payment of ransom to terrorist groups in exchange for the release of hostages, and suggested that the payment of ransom to terrorist groups be considered a crime.[36] Following the AU's suggestion, the UN Security Council adopted Resolution 2133 (2014), which reaffirms earlier Security Council decisions requesting member states to prevent and suppress the financing of terrorist acts and refrain from providing any form of support to entities or persons involved in terrorist acts, as well as to prohibit their nationals or any persons or entities within their territories from making any funds, financial assets or economic resources available for persons and entities involved in the commission of terrorist acts. Resolution 2133 calls upon UN member states to prevent terrorists from benefiting directly or indirectly from ransom payments or from political concessions and to secure the safe release of hostages.[37] Hence, states and individuals need to make concerted efforts to cut extremists off from funding by legislative means,

---

[34] This explains why the United States (US)-led coalition against ISIS has directed a considerable portion of its air strike effort against oil refineries and smuggling routes believed to be the mainstay of the group's financial survival in the belief that disrupting funding sources would precipitate its demise.

[35] G. Korte, 'Report: CIA paid Al-Qaeda ransom to free official,' *USA Today*, 16 March 2015, 2A.

[36] African Union, 'Report of the Chairperson of the Commission on Terrorism and Violent Extremism in Africa at the Peace and Security Council 455th Meeting at the Level of Heads of State and Government, Nairobi, Kenya,' available at: http://cpauc.au.int/en/content/report-chairperson-commission-terrorism-and-violent-extremism-africa-peace-and-security-co-0 (accessed 10 March 2015), para 44.

[37] United Nations, UN Doc. UNSC/RES/2133(2014) adopted on 27 January 2014.

208   D. KUWALI

such as outlawing money laundering, and the use of other anti-corruption strategies, such as condemning the payment of ransom to terrorist groups in exchange for the release of hostages.[38]

Combating Corruption and Promoting the Rule of Law and Good Governance

Lasting stability and real security require democracy. Countries that are emerging and developing should create structures of governance and transparency so that any assistance provided actually works and reaches people. This entails free and periodical elections where people can choose their own future, and independent judiciaries that uphold the rule of law, and police and security forces that respect human rights, and free speech and freedom for civil society groups. And it means freedom of religion—because when people are free to practice their faith as they choose, it helps hold diverse societies together. Governments should step up efforts against corruption, so a person can go about their day and an entrepreneur can start a business without having to pay a bribe. Governments should expand education, including for girls. There is also need to expand opportunities, including for women since there cannot be sustainable development without womens' contributions.

On its part, the UN has central role to play in efforts to address violent extremism and the comprehensive framework that the UN Global Counter-Terrorism Strategy offers for addressing the conditions conducive to the spread of terrorism. In line with the Strategy, the Working Group aims to help identify programmes and initiatives directed at furthering, *inter alia*, the dialogue, respect, tolerance and understanding among civilisations, cultures, peoples and religions; social inclusion of the marginalised; countering incitement to commit terrorist acts and human rights and the rule of law.[39] In line with Article 2(b) of the AU Convention on Prevention and Combating of Terrorism, states should, as a matter of priority, sign or ratify, or accede to, the international instruments condemning terrorism and other forms of extremist violence.

Curbing Extremist Propaganda and Recruitment Through the Internet

With nearly 70% of its population under the age of 30, Africa is a continent with the youngest population in the world. As the youth in Africa are becoming more tech-savvy, extremist groups are taking advantage of poverty and high rate of unemployment among the youth by manipulating them with

---

[38] African Union 'Report of the Chairperson of the Commission on Terrorism and Violent Extremism in Africa at the Peace and Security Council 455th Meeting at the Level of Heads of State and Government, Nairobi, Kenya' para 44, available at: http://cpauc.au.int/en/content/report-chairperson-commission-terrorism-and-violent-extremism-africa-peace-and-security-co-0 (accessed 10 January 2021).

[39] UN Working Group Report, footnote 6 above, para 3.

promises of quick gains. As ably discussed by Peter Makossah and Gilbert Mittawa in Chapter 14, violent extremists have also used the social media as a virtual training camp by establishing various forms of online, private, person-toperson or group communication to exchange experience and knowledge. Violent extremists have successfully turned the brighter side of the internet—low cost, ease of access, lack of regulation, vast potential audience, and fast communication and flow of information—to its darker side by using it as a means to achieve propaganda and attract recruits.[40]

Governments have toiled with the question of how to limit terrorist abuse of the social media. The debate centres around whether governments should intervene through censorship, monitoring and counterpropaganda programmes, or allow the freeflow of online traffic to avoid undermining democratic values such as freedom of expression.[41] As a way forward, mechanisms should be established, in collaboration with internet service providers, to monitor websites that facilitate and encourage violent extremism and recruitment. In this way, internet sites that incite hatred and violent extremism can either be shut down or systematically monitored and investigated in order to counter radicalisation and curb brainwashing and indoctrination.[42]

For example, Nigeria has organised several seminars on combating terrorism through the internet, including the organisation of capacity building and training on law enforcement and digital technologies for all agencies involved in countering radicalisation, as well as the initiation of online projects aimed at undermining the capacity of violent extremists to propagate violent ideologies through the internet.[43] Another example is in the United Kingdom where the government has been using the internet as an instrument to support mainstream voices to articulate a moderate understanding of various religions in the country.[44] In the same vein, the European Commissionsponsored 'Check the Web' project, proposes a common European approach to internet-monitoring based on strengthened cooperation and coordinated monitoring and evaluation of open internet sources.[45]

---

[40] See B. Wilson 'Detection and prevention of terrorist threats' in Okumu & Botha (footnote 1 above) 103–105. See also UN Working Group Report, footnote 6 above, para 24.

[41] UN Working Group Report, footnote 6 above, para 25.

[42] UN Working Group Report, footnote 6 above, para 26. See also S. Lone 'Terrorism, media and the search for an African voice' in Okumu & Botha (eds), footnote 7 above, pp. 123–126.

[43] UN Working Group Report, footnote 6 above, para 24. See also Kollapen, 'Human rights, terrorism and the interests of a UN Working Group Report, footnote 6 above, para 24. See also Kollapen, 'Human rights, terrorism and the interests of a secure society' (footnote 20 above) 131–134.

[44] UN Working Group Report, footnote 6 above, para 24.

[45] See Lone, 'Terrorism, media and the search for an African voice' (footnote 36 above) 123–126. UN Working Group Report (footnote 1 above), para 27.

Counter-Radicalization, De-radicalization Programmes and Disengagement

Extremists are made, not born, and are therefore receptive to de-radicalisation.[46] Deradicalisation involves programmes directed at radicalised individuals to dissuade them from violence and reintegrate them into society through, for example, psychological counseling, vocational education and employment, and by preventing incarceration facilities from becoming breeding grounds for extremists. Counterradicalisation, on the other hand, aims to protect people from extremism by addressing conditions that may propel individuals to become extremists. It involves undermining extremist groups' leadership, challenging ideology, exposing hypocrisy and providing incentives to withdraw from extremist groups.[47]

Political exclusion, religious alienation and social isolation in a community can play a role in how someone becomes radicalised. Usually, extremists tend to brainwash their audiences that some countries, religions, policies or cultures are hostile to others. They use the concept of 'we' versus 'them' often portraying the other entities as 'evil' worth fighting. When people spew hatred towards others because of their faith, race, ethnicity, culture or such other status, it feeds into extremist narratives. If entire communities feel they can never become a full part of the society in which they reside, it breeds a cycle of fear and resentment and a sense of injustice upon which extremists prey. In this way, what propels individuals to join radical groups is the quest for personal significance. For example, when people feel alienated from society or they see the opportunity in gaining significant personal gain such as becoming a hero or martyr; then, they become attuned to those narratives that provide a means to achieve that very goal.[48]

On the one hand, the term counterradicalisation refers to policies and programmes aimed at addressing conditions that may propel individuals down the path of terrorism. In this sense, the term counterradicalisation is used broadly to refer to a package of social, political, legal, educational and economic programmes, specifically designed to deter disaffected (and possibly already radicalised) individuals from crossing the line and becoming terrorists. In other words, counter-radicalisation is the process of preventing and protecting people from radicalisation.[49]

---

[46] Africa Defense Forum (ADF) 'Extremists are made, not born,' *Countering Terrorist Recruitment*, Volume 5, Quarter 2, 45 (Date of publication not known).

[47] See Statement by the AU Commissioner for Peace and Security, Ambassador Smäil Chergui at the White House Summit to Counter Terrorism, footnote 23 above.

[48] See also Stanley O. Ehiane, De-radicalisation and disengagement of the extremist group in Africa: the Nigerian experience,' 6(2) *Journal of African Foreign Affairs* (2019), pp. 123–138.

[49] Africa Defense Forum 'Exiting terror: How government can draw defectors' (footnote 40 above) 45.

The term deradicalisation, on the other hand, is used to refer to programmes that are generally directed at individuals who have become radical with the aim of reintegrating them into society or at least dissuading them from violence.[50] That is to say, re-integration and resettlement of ex-extremists, which is akin to demobilisation, disarmament and reintegration (DDR) processes in post-conflict settings. Such initiatives seek to rehabilitate disengaged extremists and support their reintegration into their communities. Such initiatives are already underway in Somalia and will soon be expanded to other AU member states.[51] Another way to de-radicalise people is to provide psychological counseling and vocational education. Countries such as Germany and Denmark have implemented such programmes, to fulfill the quest for personal significance in a positive way.[52] The programmes aim, for example, at ensuring that ex-extremists have employment and education in order to re-integrate them into society.

Reforms in correctional facilities in several countries have developed special programmes aimed at preventing incarceration facilities from becoming breeding grounds for extremists and a pool for recruitment.[53] Initiatives that promote an alliance of civilisations and foster intercultural understanding to counter radicalisation have been launched in New Zealand through co-sponsorship of the 'AsiaPacific Interfaith Dialogue', which brings together 15 representatives of the major faith and community groups in the Southeast Asian and South Pacific regions.[54] The Swiss Federal Department of Foreign Affairs has made 'religiopolitical conflicts' a special priority and launched the 'Montreux Initiative' in cooperation with Islamic charities and the Graduate Institute of International and Development Studies in Geneva to improve trust and understanding between the Swiss federal authorities and charitable organisations.[55]

Disengagement is a behavioural change to reject violent participation in the activity of a group. In this case, it should be noted that an extremist can disengage from a group without being de-radicalised. For purposes of clarity, deradicalisation is the abandonment of an extremist ideology while disengagement is the cessation of extremist activity. Ehiane has noted that 'the initial physical disengagement by extremists is through apprehension and detainment by the security agencies. This first step segregates the terrorist from his affiliation. Effective deradicalisation and disengagement takes place when there is a strong rehabilitative intervention. The rehabilitation process ultimately prepares the terrorists psychologically for disengagement'.

---

[50] UN Working Group Report (footnote 1 above), para 8.

[51] See Statement by the AU Commissioner for Peace and Security, Ambassador Smäil Chergui at the White House Summit to Counter Terrorism, footnote 23 above.

[52] UN Working Group Report, footnote 6 above, para 8.

[53] As above, para 13.

[54] As above, para 18. See also Mayson, footnote 32 above, pp. 77–80.

[55] UN Working Group Report, para 19. See also Mayson, footnote 32 above.

212 D. KUWALI

Condemning Violence and Correcting Misinterpretations

Usually desperate for legitimacy, extremists manipulate ideologies to justify their violence and recruitment. Categorically condemning all acts of violent extremism and correcting misinterpreted ideologies espoused by extremists is thus imperative. Since extremists brainwash young impressionable individuals, leaders and clerics at all levels, there should be clear and correct understanding of cultural, religious and political diversity, including the principle of unity in diversity, and promote tolerance and cooperation among youths from all quarters of the globe.[56]

It is generally accepted that no political ideology, religion or culture is responsible for violence and terrorism. This is where leaders and clerics at all levels have the duty to counter extremist ideologies by correcting misinterpreted and distorted narratives espoused by extremists to incite people to violence. It is the responsibility of religious and community leaders to exclude from the community and report to the authorities those extremists who pose a danger to the community.

For example, where groups such as Boko Haram [a Kanuri dialect in Nigeria meaning 'Western education is forbidden'] and Al-Shaabab are deliberately targeting their propaganda to Muslim communities, particularly Muslim youth, Imams, clerics and scholars should correct twisted interpretations of Islam and debunk theories of a 'clash of civilizations'.[57] Likewise, Christian clerics should clearly and explicitly reject narratives that Christianity is at war with Islam or that it seeks to suppress Muslims. On a positive note, it is encouraging to see that Muslim clerics have been working for peace with Christian pastors and priests in Nigeria and the Central African Republic (CAR) to put an end to the cycle of hate in those countries. The AU is also engaging the media through the AU created Network of African Journalists for Peace (NetPeace) for it to be an active partner in countering terrorist narratives and delegitimising violent ideologies.[58]

Communication Through Cross- and Intra-cultural, Faith and Political Dialogue

Promoting an alliance of civilisations and encouraging intercultural dialogue are important for cultivating a culture of peace and unity in diversity, as well as for bringing about understanding, respect and tolerance among religious and cultural communities and combating stereotypes and dismantling prejudices on all sides. There is need for a concerted effort to counter extremism to cultivate a culture of peace, tolerance, inclusion and acceptance of the concept of

---

[56] As above.

[57] See generally, S.P. Huntington, 'Clash of civilizations' available at: http://www.hks.harvard.edu/fs/pnorris/Acrobat/Huntington_Clash.pdf (accessed 3 April 2015).

[58] Ambassador Smäil Chergui, footnote 23 above.

'unity in diversity'by amplifying such positive African values, especially online. Promoting an alliance of civilisations and encouraging intercultural dialogue are important tools in promoting understanding, respect and tolerance among religious and cultural communities and combating stereotypes and dismantling prejudices on all sides. As such, there is need to build and bolster bridges of communication and trust to eradicate extremism through dialogue. Beginning and maintaining dialogue may not be easy, however, because extremists are not part of a centralised organisation but rather comprise factions that subscribe to varying degrees of extremism. In the words of King Abdullah:

> [Dialogue] stems the flow of blood and rejects sectarianism, ignorance and extremism; it allows peace to prevail around our world . . . [Teachers] must prepare their students for living in a way that accepts the 'other,' to debate with them in the best way possible. The educational curriculum is a suitable environment for making the student familiar with dialogue, and that any disagreement can be solved with dialogue and debate.[59]

Education as an Enabler/Catalyst in Combatting Terrorism

Thus, schools and other educational establishments can play a crucial role in the development of a resilient community that upholds values of non-violence, peaceful coexistence and tolerance. This is why education features highly in the counterradicalisation programmes developed by most states.[60] To combat extremism, there is a need to find solution to the issue of the duality of education systems, which carry the seed of protest, marginalisation and frustration of the disciples of radicalism that can be exploited by extremists. For instance, efforts to use education as a means to counter violent extremist ideology in the United States have included programmes designed specifically to reach out to youth, as well as to marginalised groups and racial and religious minorities.[61] On its part, the AU has facilitated open discussions and engagement between State authorities and civil society, including religious authorities and women organisations. The AU seeks to use the Nouakchott Process, to engage in outreach campaigns, open fora and consultations to allow communities to air their grievances and contribute actively to efforts to counter extremist ideologies.[62] As such, African States should build and bolster bridges of communication and trust to eradicate extremism through dialogue and amplify positive values, especially online.

---

[59] Asharq Al-Awsat 'King Abdullah: We will eradicate terrorism, religious extremism,' 6 October 2014, available at: http://www.aawsat.net/2014/10/article55337252/king-abd ullah-we-will-eradicate-terrorism-religious-extremism (accessed 20 December 2014).

[60] UN Working Group Report, footnote 6 above, para 15.

[61] As above, para 16.

[62] Ambassador Smäil Chergui, footnote 23 above.

Conclusion

When governments oppress their own citizens and deny their human rights, particularly along sectarian lines or ethnic lines, they sow the seeds of extremism and violence. The horrendous events in the CAR, Egypt, Kenya, Libya, Mozambique, Nigeria and Somalia have brought to the fore the plight of innocent civilians as a result of proliferation of extremism and terrorism on the continent. These cycles of extremism should not be allowed to tear the fabric of African cultural, political and religious diversity. Leaders at all levels should encourage dialogues across and within faiths, cultures, political groupings and across countries. To this end, religious and community leaders should play their role in tackling the root causes of extremism and terrorism, by providing young people with the best examples of how to engage in dialogue with other people and cultures and how to treat them well. Ex-extremists also have the responsibility in debunking terrorist ideologies. Education is one of the most effective tools that can eradicate extremist attitudes.

In addition to the measures outlined in Article 4 of the AU Convention on the Prevention and Combating of Terrorism, there is need for regional cooperation on security including intelligence sharing. Further, governments need a multi-agency approach to formulate targeted policies that undistorted political and religious ideologies can be more widely heard, and thereby remedy the clear lack of alternatives to the radical discourse that is fueled by social injustice and the lack of socialisation frameworks. By working with the civil society and local communities, governments can help counter extremist ideologies and promote peaceful dialogue. As such, there is need for a concerted effort to counter extremism to cultivate a culture of peace, tolerance, inclusion and acceptance of unity in diversityby amplifying such positive African values, especially online.

Violent extremism and terrorism should not be associated with any religion, nationality, civilisation or ethnic group. Some people become extremists, but it is not because of the religion—it is because of themselves as individuals. Instead of being entangled in terminology, dealing with extremism is, in fact, dealing with criminality. Obviously, military might cannot eradicate extremist ideology. At best, military force can temporarily limit the ability of extremists to perpetrate mindless acts of terror.[63] There is need for a shift in approach from predominantly state-centric, military-heavy and territorial counter insurgency concept to people-centric, governance and proactive prevention strategies. Using strategies such as intelligence gathering, military force and law-enforcement alone to curb extremism can exacerbate extremism

---

[63] Military action will come to an end—war cannot be perpetual—and when it does, those who ceased to operate will return with their ideology intact, those who were killed will leave behind loved ones ripe for recruitment and those already in the pipeline being brainwashed will be cited the death and destruction caused by this military action in order to further ingrain them with extremist ideology.

when misused. What is required is a holistic and multi-pronged counter-terrorism policy, which includes soft power mechanisms to win hearts and minds and addresses the core issues that result in the breeding, enablement and enactment of extremism.[64]

There is need for a multi-pronged approach to understand the end-to-end process of extremism, that is to say: the underlying ideology, the agents and locations of radicalisation, the people who are radicalised, the logistics of radicalisation, the people that fight radicals and the capability of state institutions to handle extremism.[65] Most extremists are the youth who find themselves unemployed and face social and political exclusion, and it is no wonder that they resort to extremist violence. Hence, governments should formulate policies that ensure broad-based social and economic growth and development, including creating decent jobs, especially for the youth without discrimination, fighting corruption and equalisation of opportunities and access to social services such as education, especially for girls and women.

Countries and individuals have a responsibility to cut off funding that fuels hatred and corrupts young minds and endangers communities. Poverty, illiteracy and high rate of unemployment among the youth and the general population render them vulnerable to the manipulative messages of terrorist groups and their promises of quick gain.[66] As such, states should also focus more on human security, including prevention of conflicts and political instability as well as combating drug trafficking and other organised crime, which tend to finance terrorists and other extremist organisations.[67]

The 'ten Cs' approach advanced here provides a roadmap for tackling these tasks and eradicating extremism in Africa by way of: (1) conflict prevention through broad-based socioeconomic development; (2) countering extremism with respect for human rights and humanitarian law; (3) capability of security

---

[64] See generally, White House Summit Statement on Countering Violent Extremism, footnote 25 above.

[65] H. Bokhari 'Eradicating extremist ideology,' 30 December 2014 available at: http://pakteahouse.net/2014/12/30/eradicating-extremist-ideology/ (accessed 9 January 2021).

[66] African Union 'Report of the Chairperson of the Commission on Terrorism and Violent Extremism in Africa' (footnote 32 above).

[67] On 8 September, 2006, the General Assembly unanimously adopted the United Nations Global CounterTerrorism Strategy. Member states embarked upon a new phase in their counter-terrorism efforts by agreeing on a global strategy to counter terrorism. The Strategy marks the first time that all member states of the United Nations have agreed to a common strategic and operational framework to fight terrorism. The Strategy forms a basis for a concrete plan of action: to address the conditions conducive to the spread of terrorism; to prevent and combat terrorism; to take measures to build state capacity to fight terrorism; to strengthen the role of the United Nations in combating terrorism and to ensure the respect of human rights while countering terrorism. The Strategy builds on the unique consensus achieved by world leaders at their 2005 September Summit to condemn terrorism in all its forms and manifestations.

agents to protect populations at risk; (4) community empowerment to deter extremist groups and control borders; (5) choking off extremists' financing; (6) combating corruption and promoting the rule of law and good governance; (7) curbing terrorist propaganda and recruitment through the internet; (8) counter-radicalisation and de-radicalisation programmes; (9) condemning violence and correcting misinterpretations and (10) communication through cross- and intra-cultural, faith and political dialogue.

CHAPTER 13

The Future of Violence in Africa

Dan Kuwali

Introduction

The Geneva Conventions have been regulating armed conflicts for the past 72 years. It cannot be disputed that compliance with the Law of Armed Conflict (LoAC) increases prospects of returning to peace by parties to a conflict. However, it is abundantly clear that incidences of conventional warfare have decreased since the Second World War (WWII). Both interstate and intrastate armed conflicts have declined steadily in the past two decades. What is increasing are attacks against vulnerable populations, wildlife and the environment, where LoAC is largely not applicable. The fourth aspiration of a peaceful and secure Africa of silencing the guns by 2020 in the African Agenda 2063 as read with Goal 16 of the Sustainable Development Goals (SDGs) will have a net effect of reducing armed conflicts and, consequently, rendering LoAC to be rarely triggered.

Future wars will continue to be asymmetric against an amorphous enemy on an undefined battlefield. Mwaniki notes that unlike old wars which had a political or ideological agenda, new wars are based on exclusivist identities.[1] Unfortunately, most of the victims will continue to be innocent civilians and not combatants. The use of force will be akin to law enforcement operations

[1]Njuki Mwaniki, "How New Are 'New Wars?'," 1(2), *Contemporary Security in Africa* (2012), pp. 63–78, p. 71.

D. Kuwali (✉)
University of Pretoria, Pretoria, South Africa

© The Author(s), under exclusive license to Springer Nature Switzerland AG 2022
D. Kuwali (ed.), *The Palgrave Handbook of Sustainable Peace and Security in Africa*, https://doi.org/10.1007/978-3-030-82020-6_13

217

218   D. KUWALI

which will need to strike a delicate balance pitching the State's responsibility to ensure security and the concomitant use of force with the right to life, the right to privacy and human dignity. The operations will also involve protection of the health and safety of the population, protection of strategic physical and cyber infrastructure, citizens and the environment, particularly wildlife. It has also been projected that the combined challenge of an increased population, demands on resources and the effects of climate change, particularly drought, on food and water supplies, are likely to lead to tension that could result in conflict in Africa.[2] This chapter seeks to illustrate the future of violence in Africa and how it can be mitigated to protect life, flora and fauna and African countries' strategic interests.

FUTURE USE OF VIOLENCE IN AFRICA AND HOW TO MITIGATE IT

Most countries in Africa are experiencing several emerging challenges. Once in a while there are talks of rising ethnicity in some countries, land wrangles and conflicts over resources. The most predominant threat to peace, safety and security of the population in most African countries is not military in nature but threats to the social and economic well-being of the citizens including deprivation of basic day-to-day needs, social and political marginalization as well as environmental degradation. The trajectory of contemporary violence forecasts that there is very little prospect either of nuclear war or widespread conventional war in the near future, especially on the African continent. Looking at the crystal ball, the trends and nature of future violence can generally be categorized into 10 scenarios as follows:

International Terrorism and Violent Extremism

As can be noted from several incidents in Cabo Delgado province in Mozambique and Nairobi in Kenya, there is a growing number of cases of terrorism and violent extremism on the continent. This has been characterized by a spate of violent attacks against innocent populations in shopping malls, schools, restaurants, among other previously unimaginable places. The root causes of terrorism and the motivation of terrorists are multifarious have been ably discussed in the preceding chapter. However, most of the recent incidents tend to be based on a perception of religious and political marginalization. The proliferation of small arms and ammunition on the continent has contributed to the prevalence of terrorist activities in Africa. The problem is exacerbated by porous borders and socioeconomic exclusion and unemployment. Given the transnational nature of actors and their activities, Africa cannot be said to be immune to possibility of terrorist attacks from these amorphous

---

[2] Ministry of Defence, "Strategic Trends Programme: Global Strategic Trends-Out to 2045," Fifth Edition, 2014, p. xxiii.

combatants without borders.[3] Recruitment by extremist groups is usually done online taking advantage of the curiosity and desperation of the unemployed youth who are later radicalized. The rise in activities of operatives of the extremist groups against innocent civilians raises concerns whether eradicating extremism is possible.

Terrorism is a macabre form of theatre where the real targets are not innocent victims but the spectators.[4] The perpetrators intend this fear to motivate the spectators to react in a manner that furthers the perpetrators' goals. Sometimes perpetrators use terror to provoke a government backlash that ultimately strengthens support for their cause among the victimized population. Unless terrorist activities reach the scale of an armed conflict, terrorism is mainly a criminal activity which has a bearing on human rights of both the victims and the perpetrators. Ensuring the right to equality, non-discrimination and provision of socioeconomic rights can contribute to eradication of terrorism. Used figuratively, violent extremism is not armed conflict properly so called. Like terrorism, violent extremism is a law enforcement and human rights issue.

To eradicate terrorism and violent extremism, there is need for a soft power approach to win hearts and minds, including provision of social and economic rights, non-discrimination and provision of gainful employment to the youth. In other words, African countries need to step up efforts to prevent and counter terrorism by eradicating the root causes of extremism and terrorism. According to Morumbasi, the solutions should "involve political considerations that inform the agendas of the terrorist networks".[5] African States also need to strengthen measures to prevent the possibility of recruitment and use of their countries as a transit route for extremist groups.[6] Sporadic attacks against vulnerable populations are not governed by LoAC. Dealing with lone wolves requires reforming criminal justice systems, mental health therapy, civic education and vigilance by the citizenry as security is now a concern for all.

Invisible Battles: Cybercrime and Cyber Terrorism

On the one hand, digitalisation has transformed way of life with significant social and economic benefits. On the other hand, dependence on technology poses fundamental security risks. Cybercrimes are an emerging security challenge in Africa. Rapid advances in information and communications technologies (ICT) have given rise to cybercrimes which compromise users' data

---

[3] Dan Kuwali, "How to Eradicate Extremism," *Mail & Guardian* (Thought Leader), available at: http://www.thoughtleader.co.za/readerblog/2015/05/06/how-to-eradicate-extremism/ (accessed 7 December 2020).

[4] See generally Thomas R. Mockaitis, "Terrorism, Insurgency and Organised Crimes," in Paul Shemella (editor), *Fighting Back; What Governments Can Do about Terrorism*, Stanford: Stanford University Press, 2011, pp. 11–26.

[5] Kigen Morumbasi, "State Survival and Terrorism in Africa," 3(2), *Contemporary Security in Africa* (2015), pp. 1–15, p. 1.

[6] Kuwali, footnote 3 above.

in the cyberspace. The exponential rise of cybercrimes has been too fast to be arrested by ICT experts, in the absence of a global entity to police the Web. The response to cybersecurity threats by most African governments has not matched the fast-evolving array of digital threats from espionage, critical infrastructure sabotage, organized crime and combat innovation.[7] As discussed by Tabitha Mwangi and Tracy Asava in Chapter 10, the unprecedented threats to cybersecurity are multidimensional, indiscriminate and undermine ICT systems worldwide. Cyber-attacks target individuals, governmental agencies and the private sector, especially financial institutions. Perpetrators of cybercrimes are often also accessories to organised crimes in that they facilitate offences such as money laundering, terrorism, child pornography and identity theft, among others.[8]

Although Africa has relatively slow and lower online connectivity, perpetrators of organized crimes are employing online tools to facilitate diverse illicit activities on the continent.[9] The International Criminal Police (INTERPOL) has reported that online crime is now a major security threat for law enforcement in Africa than ever before.[10] A key factor driving the increase in online crime in Africa is the lack of comprehensive legal, policy and strategic framework to combat cybercrime in most countries on the continent.[11] The other challenge is the complexity in establishing effective defensive measures against cybercrimes and cyber terrorism. Cross-border and the ever-expanding nature of digital technologies complicates the extent and nature of critical cyber dependencies, threats and vulnerabilities.

Cyber terrorism is a paradigm shift from traditional terrorism in that it is not only characterized by attacks against people but also malicious hacking and cybercrime, disruption of public services networks, among others. Cyber terrorism has equalized and neutralized some aspects of which previously only the State used to enjoy monopoly of as it can even be used by militarily weak elements. Cyber terrorism is also used as a tool for fundraising, propaganda and recruitment and radicalization by terrorists and extremists. Thus, cyber terrorism raises questions as to what legal frameworks can be established and how it can be applied in the cyber security realm. Cyber terrorism challenges States to find ways of protecting strategic (information) infrastructure;

---

[7] Nathaniel Allen, Africa's Evolving Cyber Threats, Africa Centre for Strategic Studies, January 19, 2021, available at: https://africacentre.org/spotlight/Africa-evolving-cyber-threats (accessed 22 February 2021).

[8] See also Uchenna Jerome Orji, "The African Union Convention on Cybersecurity: A Regional Response Towards Cyber Stability?," 12(2), *Masaryk University Journal of Law and Technology* (2018), pp. 91–129.

[9] See International Police (INTERPOL), "Online Crime in Africa: A Bigger Threat That Ever Before," 14 August 2020, also available at: https://www.interpol.int/en/News-/2020/online-crime-Africa-a-bigger-threat-then-ever-before-INTETPOL-report-warns (accessed 8 February 2020).

[10] As above.

[11] As above.

how critical vulnerabilities can be mitigated and the most detrimental threats countered.

Apart from finding the right technologies to counter emerging cyber threats, African States should develop effective cyber security legal, policy and strategic frameworks. To ensure cyber security, African States should adopt a comprehensive cyber security strategy and enact legislation to ensure cyber security and prevention of cybercrimes taking to account human rights guarantees of right to privacy and freedom of expression. While the African Union (AU) adopted the Convention on Cybersecurity and Personal Data Protection in 2014, the majority of States have not ratified the Convention.[12] The Convention needs to be ratified by at least 15 member countries to enter into force. At the time of writing, only seven countries had ratified the Convention indicating that cyber security is still not perceived as a necessity by many African countries, a situation which further exacerbates the problem.[13] Unless it escalates to an armed conflict, cyber terrorism involves invisible battles that raise questions relating to respect for human rights in cyber espionage, surveillance and reconnaissance.

Wireless Wars: Artificial Intelligence (AI) on the Battlefield

In light of the proliferation of Unmanned Aerial Vehicles (UAVs), also known as robots or drones, future armed conflicts will invariably be fought with the aid of cyber elements. Such robots, which theoretically incorporate "Artificial Intelligence" (AI), are able to execute missions on their own whether on the ground, on and under water or in space.[14] AI on the battlefield represents a quantum leap in warfare technology.[15] Robotics technology is driven as much by consumer and industrial markets as by military budgets, particularly as it becomes cheaper and simpler to produce and use.

At least 14 African national militaries have acquired intelligence, surveillance and reconnaissance (ISR) drones.[16] The conflict in Libya provides a telling illustration of how AI is influencing modern warfare as drones have

---

[12] African Union, The Convention on Cybersecurity and Personal Data Protection, adopted by the 23rd Ordinary Session of the AU Assembly in Malabo, Equatorial Guinea on 27 June 2014. AU Doc. EX.CL/846(XXV).

[13] As of January 2020. See for example INTERPOL, footnote 9 above.

[14] Artificial Intelligence is the capability of a computer system to perform tasks that normally require human intelligence, such as visual perception, speech recognition and decision-making. See Mary L. Cummings, "Artificial Intelligence and the Future of Warfare," International Security Department and US and the Americas Programme, Research Paper, Chatham House, the Royal Institute of International Affairs, January 2017, p. 2.

[15] As above, p. 1.

[16] Allen, footnote 6 above.

become widely integrated into combat operations by belligerents.[17] Militaries are even contemplating "amoeba warfare" to be waged by swarm squadrons leading to a new kind of Arms Race. In such a scenario, a sophisticated robotic military can theoretically even be operated by a single individual, according that operator unimaginable firepower. If this can be the case, authoritarian regimes can easily threaten to remain in power against the will of the people or internal uprisings. As a force multiplier, the deployment of AI could exponentially amplify the capabilities of small groups of insurgents or terrorists, thereby increasing their ubiquitous threat.[18]

Most of the questions concerning LoAC and Autonomous Weapon Systems (AWS) are concerned with the way those weapons are used, not the technology and its capabilities as such. The key element being that today, human beings are still in active control of the AWS during their missions, albeit from a location far from the battlefield. The question is if an AWS does commit a violation of the rules of war who will be held responsible? The commander who sent the drone or robot into battle or the manufacturer of the software that runs the robot?

The increasing use and efficacy of drones in both military and commercial settings has raised questions as to the legality of these "robotic weapons", "killer robots" or "slaughterbots".[19] The debate centres on whether killer robots should be allowed to execute missions where there is a possibility that any human life could be at stake.[20] Cummings has noted that "while computers and AI can be superior to humans in some skill-and rule-based tasks, under situations that require judgment and knowledge, in the presence of significant uncertainty, humans are superior to computers".[21]

Another issue in the debate over AI on the battlefield is the simultaneous development of commercial drones and military UAVs, as the former are harmless whereas the latter are potentially lethal. This dilemma poses a challenge to ban on autonomous technology for military use given that derivative or superior technologies could well be available in the commercial sector.[22] Further, drones are largely used by NSAGs for intelligence purposes on armed conflicts on the continent. For example, the use of surveillance drones by the Nigerian extremist group Boko Haram, which are reportedly more superior and sophisticated than those used by the Nigerian Armed Forces, have contributed to insurgent's group escalation of violence.[23]

---

[17] The defeat of Khalifa Haftar's Libyan National Army during its 2019 offensive against Tripoli has been widely credited to Turkish intervention, and to Turkey's deployment of superior. See as above.

[18] Ministry of Defence, footnote 2 above, p. xxii.

[19] Cummings, footnote 14 above.

[20] As above.

[21] As above, p. 2.

[22] As above.

[23] Allen, footnote 6 above.

There are calls for regulation, new treaty law and even moratoriums and bans on such weapons. However, what is critical is for States to live up to their obligations under the 1949 Geneva Conventions and their Additional Protocols (AP). Of particular importance here is Article 35 of AP I, which obliges States to ensure that all new weapons systems should comply with the LoAC before they are developed and deployed. Such a weapon would have to be able to distinguish not only between combatants and civilians, but also, for instance, between active combatants and those *hors de* combat, and between civilians taking a direct part in hostilities and armed civilians such as law enforcement personnel or hunters.

Cummings has warned that launching "nascent technologies without comprehensive testing could put both military personnel and civilians at undue risk."[24] Therefore, the onus is on States and developers of AWS. AWS would also have to comply with the rule of proportionality, which requires that the incidental civilian casualties expected from an attack on a military target not be excessive when weighed against the anticipated concrete and direct military advantage. When attacking, it would have to be capable of taking precautions to minimize civilian casualties, as outlined in Article 57 of API. When questions of AI on the battlefield are raised, the solution is in Article 35 of API and the *Martens* Clause, which provides for considerations of humanity. AI also raises ethical questions which cannot be comprehensively answered by the LoAC but by business ethics and professional standards of manufacturers. It is, therefore, imperative for the defence industry to capacity to develop and test safe and controllable AI weapon systems, especially those that fire weapons.[25]

Political Violence: War Against the People

The 2007 post-election violence in Kenya is well documented.[26] The 2016 general elections in Zambia were marred by electoral violence, which threatened the country's democratic fabric.[27] Violence has been a constant feature of Zimbabwe's political landscape with reports of attempted assignation of the incumbent president in 2018.[28] Stories coming from Malawi, Zambia, Zimbabwe and Uganda, among others show a pattern of rising political

---

[24] As above, p. 1.

[25] As above.

[26] See for example, Andrew M. Linke, "Post-Election Violence in Kenya: Leadership Legacies, Demography and Motivations," *Territory, Politics, Governance* (2020), https://doi.org/10.1080/21622671.2020.1757503. See also John Hickman, "Explaining Post-Election Violence in Kenya and Zimbabwe," 28(1), *Journal of Third World Studies* (2011), pp. 29–46.

[27] Kabale Ignatius Mukunto, "Electoral Violence and Young Party Cadres in Zambia," 18(1), *Journal of African Elections*, pp. 129–147.

[28] Michelle Gavid, "Political Violence in Zimbabwe," Council on Foreign Relations, 25 June 2018. Also available at: https://www.cfr.org/political-violence-zeimbabwe (accessed 5 February 2021).

violence in Africa. Prior to May 2019, Malawi was rocked by political violence particularly campaign violence and voter intimidation, which followed post-election violent demonstrations between May 2019 and February 2020 when the High Court in Malawi sitting as a Constitution Court nullified the widely disputed election due to massive irregularities. There has been a repeat of the Malawi scenario in Uganda with the only difference of the security forces clamping down of the citizenry in the latter case.[29] At the time of writing, civil society groups in Chad claimed that some of their leaders were arrested after police fired teargas to disperse protesters against nomination of the incumbent president for a sixth term in office.[30]

In most, if not all cases, the victims are mostly opposition party members beaten by suspected supporters of the ruling party or security forces. Outbreaks of violence have profound and lasting effects that shape future electoral politics. There has also been increased attacks against women, persons with albinism, among other vulnerable groups. In some cases, the violence has been perpetrated by young ruling political party cadres against members of the opposition whereas in other cases there have been running battles of the citizenry and security forces.[31] The violence usually take the form of intimidation of the opposition, molestation, seizure of public property, public disorder, vandalizing of party property, lawlessness and aggressive rhetoric.[32]

Unemployed youths are particularly susceptible to electoral violence as they are abused by political leaders to fan violence at a small fee.[33] The vulnerability is due to negative socioeconomic conditions, leadership manipulation

[29] Travis Curtise, "Soldiers and Police Are on the Streets as Ugandans Prepare to Vote," *The Washington Post*, 13 January 2021, also available at: https://www.washingtonpost.com/2021/01/13/soldiers-police-are-streets-ugandans-prepare-vote-jan-14 (accessed 7 February 2021). See also International Crisis Group, "Uganda: Uganda's Museveni Clings to Power—But Trouble Lies Ahead," also available at: www.crisigroup.org/africa/uganda (accessed 6 February 2021). See also "Malawi: Fears over Rising Political Violence," *Pambazuka News*, 22 August 2002, available at: www.pambazuka.org/human-security/malawi-fears-over-rising-political-violence (accessed 7 February 2021).

[30] France 24, "Chad Police Clash with Protesters after Deby Nominated for Sixth Term," 6 February 2021, available at: https://www.france24.com/en/africa/20210206-chad-police-clash-with-protestors-after-deby-nominatedd-for-sixth-term (accessed 11 February 2021).

[31] See also Makhura Benjamin Rapanyane and Happy Mathew Tirivangasi, "Incidents of Political Violence, Vote Rigging and Post-Electoral Instability: What Is Going on in Malawi?" September 2020, 18(1), *Gender and Behaviour*, September 2020, pp. 15176–15189. See also Catherine Musuva 2009 "Chapter 7: Malawi," in Denis Kadima and Susan Booysen (eds) *Compendium of Elections in Southern Africa 1989–2009: 20 Years of Multiparty Democracy*, EISA, Johannesburg, pp. 235–237.

[32] Mukunto, footnote 27 above. See also Johan Brosché, Hanne Fjeld and Kristine Höglund, "How History Explains Election Violence: Kenya and Zambia Tell the Story," *The Conversation*, 17 February 2020, also available at: https://theconversation.com/how-histiry-explains-election-violenve-kenya-and-zambia-tell-the-story-131405 (accessed 15 February 2021).

[33] Rosemary Fumpa-Makano and Vincent Mbaulu Mukanda, "Participatory Action Research and Prospects for Electoral Conflict Prevention in Zambia," available

and incentives.[34] Nepotistic tendencies in employment has also contributed to lack of employment of the vast majority of educated unemployed youth resulting into a potentially explosive youth bulge. Most of the university graduates remain unemployed as most of the employment opportunities are in the informal sector where most employees are still paid below the minimum wage. Experts have also noted that the politicization of ethnicity and regionalism encourages violence and discrimination.

Further, hate speeches by political elites, the fragility of democracy contributes to intolerance. Political violence relates to rebellion against "democratic peace" emanating from cases where there is failure of accountability mechanisms. Absence of free and fair processes is a recipe for electoral violence.[35] As the youth are the common perpetrators of electoral violence, it is imperative that young party cadres are constructively engaged to desist from violence while addressing the socioeconomic challenges they face.[36] Governments should not, and cannot, wage war against their own people because they have the primary responsibility under international human rights law to protect their own citizens. Under Article IV of the AU Declaration on the Principles Governing Democratic Elections in Africa all countries in Africa have the responsibility to safeguard the human and civil liberties of all citizens including the freedom of movement, assembly, association, expression and campaigning as well as access to the media on the part of all stakeholders, during electoral processes.[37]

More so, Article 25 of the International Covenant on Civil and Political Rights, which African States have ratified, state that States have an obligation to ensure that every citizen has the right and the opportunity to vote and to be elected at genuine periodic elections, which should be by universal and equal suffrage and be held by secret ballot to guarantee the free expression of the will of the electors. Thus, States are obliged to take positive steps to provide a conducive environment for citizens to safely and effectively exercise their voting rights. If elections are to be regarded free, fair and credible in Africa, political violence must end. LoAC does not govern political violence, which can be curbed by strong and independent oversight mechanisms including transparent and credible electoral processes.

---

at: https://www.lindenwood.edu/files/resources/21-46-fumba-makano.pdf (accessed 7 February 2021).

[34] Mukunto, footnote 27 above.

[35] Human Rights Watch, "Malawi: Ensure Free, Fair, Safe Elections," Safeguard Citizens Against Violence during Presidential Rerun Vote, 3 June 220, available at: https://www.hrw.org/news/2020/06/03/Malawi-ensure-free-fair-safe-elections (accessed 7 February 2021).

[36] Fumpa-Makano and Mukanda, footnote 33 above.

[37] African Union, African Union Declaration on the Principles Governing Democratic Elections in Africa, AHG/Decl.1 (XXXVIII), 2002.

Popular Protests: Demonstrations Riots and Insurgency

Demonstrations and riots appear to have become fashionable in Africa, usually spearheaded by the youth. Likewise, Article 11 of the African Charter for Human and People's Rights provides for freedom of assembly.[38] Likewise, the International Covenant on Civil and Political Rights, which African States have ratified, in Article 21 provides for the right to peaceful assembly. Although the right to peaceful assembly is guaranteed by international human rights instruments, in certain cases, some overzealous citizens have been involved in violent protests, sometimes on issues they even have no knowledge about. While some demonstrations have been on legitimate claims, others have been on petty issues that could have simply been resolved through directing the issues to the right people. In agreement with Prince Bright Majiga in Chapter 11 as well as Mwangi and Asava in Chapter 10, to prevent frequent confrontation and violent demonstrations, government officials, law enforcement agencies and leaders of civil society organizations require training in crisis management techniques and dispute resolutions. There is also need to emphasize inclusive and participatory approaches to conflict resolution (multistakeholder approach including media, civil society, youth, women, special interest groups). On their part, African governments are obliged to respect the freedom of peaceful assembly, free speech, liberty and freedom of movement as enshrined in the Banjul Charter.[39]

Another threat to peace and security in Africa is insurgency by rebellious groups of individuals. Insurgency is an organized movement aimed at overthrowing a lawfully constituted government through use of subversion and armed conflict. One of the longest running insurgency in Africa, which started in 1987, is waged by the Lord's Resistance Army (LRA) who seek to overthrow the Ugandan government and establish a theocratic state based on the Ten Commandments and Acholi tradition.[40] The ongoing insurgency in Cabo Delgado province of Mozambique which started in October 2017, is a contemporary example of the growing threat of insurgency in Africa. The hostilities involve mainly jihadists seeking to establish an Islamic state in the region who are pitted against Mozambican security forces. Unfortunately, the insurgents known as Ahlu Sunnah Wal Jammah (ASWJ), and aligned with the so-called Islamic State have targeted and beheaded civilians in the local communities.[41] There is a danger that the hostilities could spill over to surrounding provinces in northern Mozambique and eventually spread to

---

[38] African (Banjul) Charter on Human and Peoples' Rights (Adopted 27 June 1981, OAU Doc. CAB/LEG/67/3 rev. 5, 21 I.L.M. 58 (1982), entered into force 21 October 1986).

[39] See the Banjul Charter, Articles 11, 9, 6 and 12, respectively. As above.

[40] Ruddy Doom and Koen Vlassenroot, "Kony's Message: A New Koine? The Lord's Resistance Army in Northern Uganda," 98(390), *African Affairs* (1999), pp. 5–36.

[41] Philip Kleinfeld, "Mozambique's Cabo Delgado: Militants Advance as aid Access Shrinks," *The New Humanitarian*, 21 December 2020.

neighbouring countries.[42] At the same time, the Boko Haram insurgency by the self-declared affiliate of Al-Qaeda who abhor Western education, keep on accelerating the frequency of attacks and lethality in Nigeria while there is no end in sight to the convoluted insurgency in the Central African Republic.[43]

Looking at the recruitment reservoirs of the insurgents consisting of marginalized youth unable to benefit from natural resources exploited by local elites and foreign corporations, marginalization may be one of the root causes of insurgency.[44] Sometimes insurgency is supported by foreign powers or by disgruntled citizens and diaspora such as the insurgent groups in Libya. If the current trajectory persists, Africa is likely to experience increasing insurgency, if the marginalization of the youth continues and narratives of jihadist revolt and terrorist technologies remain uncensured. Where an insurgency reaches the threshold of a non-international armed conflict (NIAC), the LoAC applies. Where a government is unable or unwilling to protect its populations, then it becomes the responsibility of the international community to protect (R2P) and Article 4(h) intervention. Adherence to principles of human rights, good governance and respect for the rule of law can assist preventing insurgencies.

Green Violence: Environmental Degradation and Climate Change

As rightly noted by Mphatso Boti-Phiri in Chapter 9, most countries in Africa are prone to different types, frequencies and magnitudes of disasters, which can be attributed to adverse effects of climate change. Several countries in Africa have faced a variety of devastating natural disasters, including cyclones, cyclical drought, earthquakes, flash floods, severe storms and pest infestations. Flash floods have killed thousands of people in Africa including farm animals. The devastating floods have also damaged property including crops. Most countries in Africa are prone to different types, frequencies and magnitudes of disasters, which can be attributed to adverse effects of climate change. In addition, vulnerable populations experience recurring food insecurity. It is advisable that African countries should put in place legal, policy and institutional frameworks for disaster management, preparedness and response including disaster risk management.

Most African countries have also seen an increase in green violence in form of wanton deforestation and poaching where poachers with automatic rifles have exchanged fire with armed forces. In Botswana, Malawi and Zambia the military has been called upon to protect the flora and fauna in their countries. Several individuals have been arrested for smuggling rhino horns, ivory,

---

[42] As above.

[43] See also Richard Joseph, "Insecurity and Counter-Insurgency in Africa," in *Foresight Africa: Top Priorities for the Continent in 2012, Africa Growth Initiative, the Brookings Institution*, available at: https://www.brookings.edu/wp-content/uploads/2016/06/01_insecurity_country_insurgency_joseph.pdf (accessed 10 February 2021).

[44] Kleinfeld footnote 41 above.

228   D. KUWALI

pangolins and other protected flora and fauna products. Illegal fishing and disposal of toxic waste, especially in the Gulf of Guinea is another challenge as is deforestation and smuggling of wildlife products in countries such Kenya, Malawi, Tanzania and Zambia. Pursuit of poachers cannot be regarded as an armed conflict. It is a law enforcement and human rights issue, which requires striking a delicate balance between human rights and the use of force and firearms. At the same time, developing countries stand to be adversely affected by climate change due to little or no resilient capacity and adaptability than developed economies. Therefore, there is an urgent need for policy tools for sustainable environment and disaster preparedness by putting in place strategies for mitigation, adaptation and resilience to climate change as well as strengthening disaster preparedness, response and recovery.

Organized Crime

There has been an increased occurrence of organized crime in Africa including fraud, money laundering, human trafficking, drugs (narcotics) smuggling, banditry, sexual and gender-based violence, armed robbery and other violent crimes including marketing body parts, especially of people with albinism. Africa is perceived as a weak link for traffickers smuggling ivory and other illicit goods endangering the continent and the region's wildlife. Porous borders, weak legislation on corruption in border posts and airports may have contributed to this abhorrent phenomenon. As illustrated by Mlowoka Noel Kayira in Chapter 18, those criminals who commit organized crimes in Africa are not organised groups in the form of classic Mafia syndicates but are rag-tag gangs although they are active throughout the continent and operate on multiple fronts with focus on diverse crimes, both misdemeanors and felonies alike.[45]

Generally, "organised crime" are criminal activities that are planned and controlled by powerful groups and carried out on a large scale. There are many elements of organized crime, which might not occur in every case, and might also change over time, making a specific consensus definition difficult.[46] Organized crimes exist as transnational, national and local groupings of highly centralized enterprises. The determinant feature in the term organised crime is that it involves a number of people working as a system in doing criminal activities. The groupings include family ties, mafia-type organization, gang-type organization, "mixed" models and participation of non-members and

---

[45] Ja Banda, "Institutional Responses to Organised Crime in Malawi," in Charles Goredema, *Organised Crime in Southern Africa: Assessing Legislation*, Institute for Security Studies, pp. 46–54.

[46] United Nations, United Nations Office on Drugs and Crime, available at: www.unodc.org/e4s/en/organised-crime/module-1/key-issues/definition-in-Convention.html (accessed 10 February 2021).

cells and complex networks (the use of internet).[47] Transnational organized crimes involve those criminal activities that are done across borders.

The 2000 United Nations Conventions against Transnational Organized Crime, also known as the Palermo Convention was adopted to address such practices and gives states guidance in coming up with legislation.[48] The key to curbing organised crimes in Africa, lies on states' seriousness and determination in dealing with such crimes decisively. The seriousness of states is a collective action demonstrated by enacting laws that criminalize organized criminal activities at a continental level. The challenge for Africa is that there is no clear legal definition of what constitutes organized crime is, hence countries choose what activities constitute organized crimes in their context. The lack of a generally accepted definition at continental level affects enforcement of laws in transnational organized crimes. It is an established principle in Criminal Law that a crime has to have clear definitional elements as to what is the prohibited conduct, who is the perpetrator and the victim. Law of Armed Conflicts (LoAC) does not govern organised crime, which is dealt with by International Treaties, especially Human Rights, Refugee Law, Financial Crimes, among others.

To address this challenge, the African Union should consider adopting a continental convention to define and regulate organised crimes, which will pave way to a uniform understanding of such offences by member states and enhance the African jurisprudence with regard to combating organised crimes. Currently, the regulation leans on adopting the Palermo Convention, which is broader and does not recognize African practices exhaustively. Hence the enactment of the convention will facilitate continent-wide enforcement and judicial cooperation against organized crimes in Africa. The assumption is that joint determination by African States in dealing with organized crimes, will close all the loopholes for perpetrators of organized crimes on the continent.

Resource Conflicts

Natural resource extraction by mining (including oil, diamonds, copper and cobalt) has tremendous positive economic potential for states. However, as comprehensively discussed by Godard Busingye in Chapter 19 and George Chipembere Lwanda in Chapter 30, these resources can also do more harm than good if used towards ulterior motives including corruption, unequal distribution of wealth and to fuel violence. Valuable resources can both fuel violence through competition for territorial control, promoting looting and

---

[47] United Nations Office on Drugs and Crime, Digest of Organised Crime Cases (A Compilation of cases with Commentaries and lessons Learned), New York, 2012.

[48] See Article 3 of United Nations Conventions against Transnational Organised Crime, G.A. Res. 25, annex I, United Nations GAOR, 55th Session, Supp. No. 49, at 44, U.N. Doc. A/45/49 (Vol. I) (2001), entered into force on 29 September 2003.

230   D. KUWALI

rent-seeking, as well as sustaining violence through financing conflict.[49] It is axiomatic to argue that most conflicts in Africa have a symbiotic relationship with resources.[50] Rebel groups used profits from conflict diamonds to finance civil wars in Angola, DRC and Sierra Leone.[51]

Scarcity of resources and increased demand of precious resources such as minerals, water and pastoral land are also causes of instability. Incessant conflicts that are fueled and caused by resources may create vulnerability of national unity. It may antagonize others due to viewing themselves as resource-less, thereby causing resource-based hostility, rivalry and antagonism.[52] This has manifested by convoluted land disputes in Burundi,[53] the Rwandan genocide and the war in the Darfur region of Sudan have been traced back to water conflict.[54] The Liberian conflict which lasted for decades is a textbook example of resource-based conflict.[55] The resource-related conflict in Nigeria revolves around oil just like in South Sudan. Scramble for resources continues to be a source of conflicts. Unless the tension escalates to an armed conflict, resource conflicts can be avoided if states stick to the principle of *uti possidetis juris* and adoption of policies for equitable use of resources and resource governance. Mediation is considered a viable option for resolving resource disputes, since it tends to be less time-consuming and is easily accessible to beneficiaries in comparison with the courts.[56]

Xenophobic Attacks

There has been a growing pattern of nationwide attacks against foreigners in South Africa. The genesis of xenophobia can be traced from the transition from apartheid to democratic government in 1994 when independence and

[49] See also Sheriff Ghali Ibrahim, Sadeeque Abba and Farouq Bibi, "Resource Based Conflicts and Political Instability in Africa: Major Trends, Challenges and Prospects," 1(9), *International Journal of Humanities Social Sciences and Education*, September 2014, pp. 71–78. Roudabesh Kish, "Resource-Related Conflict in Africa," ACLED, 19 November 2014.

[50] See also Jeff Sponen, "Conflict over Natural Resources," World History Project, available at: khanacademy.org/humanities/whp-1750/xcabef9ed3fc7da7b:unit-9-global izatin/xcabef9ed3fc7da7b:a-b-the-environment-in-an-age-of-intense-globalization/a/read-conflict-over-natural-resources (accessed 9 February 2021).

[51] Amnesty International, "Oil, Gas and Mining Industries," 19 May 2017, available at: https://amnestyusa.org/themes/business-human-rights/oil-gas-mining-industries (accessed 9 February 2021).

[52] Ibrahim et al., above footnote 49.

[53] Jenny Theron, "Resolving Land Disputes in Burundi," 1 *Conflict Trends* 2009, pp. 3–10, pp. 8–9.

[54] James Tulloch, "Water Conflicts: Fight or Flight?" Allianz, 26 August 2009, also available at: https://archive.vn?20080829171957?http://knowledge.allianz.com/en/globaliss ues/climate-change/natural-disasters/water-conflict.html (accessed 9 February 2021).

[55] Ibrahim et al., footnote 49 above, p. 73.

[56] Theron, footnote 53 above, pp. 8–9.

freedom came with the ideology that the country must be protected from foreigners. Naturally, the "government wanted to put its citizens first in line for transformation and change. The closed-door migration policies, sluggish development and increase in poverty and inequality" provided a fertile ground for xenophobia. Xenophobia is exacerbated by high unemployment rates and poverty.[57] With an influx of armed conflict refugees from Angola, the Democratic Republic of the Congo and economic refugees from countries such as Malawi, Zambia and Zimbabwe, South African citizens faced stiff competition over employment and related socioeconomic activities in their own yard. South Africa's policy responses to migration failed to focus on specific issues and important linkages between issues such as brain drain phenomenon, increasing inequality among citizens, employment and HIV and AIDS.[58]

If South Africa is to fulfil its constitutional mandate, as well as international and regional agreements to pursue migration assistance through pro-poor policies, it must make greater efforts to lead the region in providing policies for free movement and the protection of people to encourage livelihoods and discourage further xenophobic reactions. Bilateral and regional agreements have the potential to manage migration between neighbouring countries, and provide protection for the movement of people between them. National and regional social policies can only truly be effective when they begin to address emigration as well as areas such as remittances, HIV/AIDS, entry into labour markets and social protection services.[59]

Policies that focus on the protection of migrants provide a rights-based approach (upon which South Africa's Constitution is founded) and open doors to further discussion of xenophobia within the region. They also have the capacity to create an environment that will peacefully enhance the economic potential of thousands of migrants who are already within South Africa's borders. Creative policies and dialogue that recognize and accept migration as a continued phenomenon are needed within southern Africa. The South African government must remain relevant to the changing form of migration and realize that, in this globalized economy, migration has become a means for both country and an individual to overcome poverty. The response from leaders and departments—more specifically, the Presidency and leading political—have the influence to either encourage or discourage xenophobia. Government has the mandate and the ability to provide safety and protection for those within its borders, even for non-citizens.[60]

---

[57] Christy McConnell, "Migration and Xenophobia in South Africa," 1 *Conflict Trends* 2009, pp. 38–45, p. 40.

[58] As above, p. 42.

[59] As above, pp. 43–44.

[60] As above, pp. 45–46.

The Threat of Weapons of Mass Destruction

The issue of Weapons of Mass Destruction (WMD) in Africa has been discussed at length by Charitable Tusiime and her colleagues in Chapter 23. There are estimated 40,640 nuclear warheads on planet earth. The risk of accidental nuclear-weapon detonation remains a very real danger. Even if a nuclear weapon were never again exploded over a city, there are intolerable effects from the production, testing and deployment of nuclear arsenals that are experienced as an ongoing personal and community catastrophe by many people around the globe. The International Committee of the Red Cross (ICRC) has noted that: "until the last nuclear weapon is eliminated, more must be done to diminish the immediate risks of intentional or accidental nuclear detonations."

Unlike chemical weapons, biological weapons, anti-personnel landmines and cluster munitions, nuclear weapons are the only weapon of mass destruction not explicitly and comprehensively prohibited in a universal manner under international law today.[61] The African Nuclear Weapon Free Zone Treaty, also known as the Treaty of Pelindaba establishes a Nuclear-Weapon-Free Zone (NWFZ) in Africa.[62] In general terms, the Pelindaba Treaty prohibits the research, development, manufacture, stockpiling, acquisition, testing, possession, control or stationing of nuclear explosive devices inside the designated territory and the dumping of radioactive wastes in the African zone by Treaty parties.[63] The establishment of NWFZs is an invaluable interim measure to promote peace and stability at the regional and international level.[64]

The 1968 Non-Proliferation Treaty (NPT) contains only partial prohibitions, and nuclear-weapon-free zone treaties prohibit nuclear weapons only within certain geographical regions. It is, therefore, a cause for concern for African States in the NWFZ that the continued existence of nuclear weapons present an imminent danger to the environment, international peace and security.[65] Therefore, prohibiting and completely eliminating nuclear weapons is

[61] Article 36 and Reaching Critical Will, "Filling the Legal Gap: The Prohibition of Nuclear Weapons," April 2015.

[62] The treaty was signed in 1996 and came into effect with the 28th ratification on 15 July 2009.

[63] The Treaty also prohibits any attack against nuclear installations in the zone by Treaty parties and requires them to maintain the highest standards of physical protection of nuclear material, facilities and equipment, which are to be used exclusively for peaceful purposes.

[64] As of October 2018, the Treaty has been ratified by 41 States and the Sahrawi Arab Republic and entered into force on 15 July 2009. Twelve countries are yet to ratify the Treaty, namely: Central African Republic, the Democratic Republic of the Congo, Djibouti, Egypt, Eritrea, Liberia, Morocco, São Tomé and Príncipe, Sierra Leone, Somalia, Sudan and Uganda.

[65] See United Nations General Assembly, "Addressing Nuclear Disarmament: Recommendations from the Perspective of Nuclear-Weapon-Free Zones," 11 May 2016, UN Doc. A/AC. 286/WP.34/Rev.1, paras. 4 and 5.

the only guarantee against their use.[66] Despite the recognition of catastrophic humanitarian consequences of any use of nuclear weapons the nine NAS have continued modernization of nuclear weapons[67] suggesting that their role in security policies is not being reduced.

A humanitarian case has been made for the elimination of nuclear weapons considering their catastrophic consequences, which would be indiscriminate and borderless.[68] As experienced in Hiroshima and Nagasaki in Japan, the effects of radiation on human beings would cause suffering and death long after the initial explosion.[69] Similarly, from a security point of view, nuclear weapons pose a direct and constant threat to global security. The military efficacy and strategic utility of nuclear weapons in war is also in doubt.[70] Likewise, the theory that nuclear deterrence is the reason why there has not been a war between NWS since 1945, is considered anachronistic as far from keeping the peace, they breed fear and mistrust among States and are actually a cause for national and global insecurity.[71]

As a matter of fact, nuclear weapons are useless in addressing contemporary threats to security such as terrorism, climate change, extreme poverty, overpopulation and diseases.[72] From an environmental standpoint, nuclear weapons would have "catastrophic consequences for human health and the environment."[73] From an economic perspective, nuclear weapons programmes divert public funds from vital social services. It has been reported that funding allocated to disarmament efforts is far less than the money spent by nuclear powers to maintain and modernize their nuclear arsenals.[74]

In light of the catastrophic consequences of nuclear weapons, the NPT States Parties adopted the 2017 Treaty on the Prohibition of Nuclear Weapons (TPNW), or the Nuclear Weapon Ban Treaty, to comprehensively prohibit

---

[66] The International Committee of the Red Cross (ICRC), "Eliminating Nuclear Weapons," 2015 Review Conference of the Parties to the Treaty on the Non-Proliferation of Nuclear Weapons, 27 April to 22 May 2015, Statement of the ICRC, 1 May 2015, available at: https://www.icrc.org/en/document/nuclear-weapons-conference (accessed 1 February 2021).

[67] See also above.

[68] As above.

[69] As above.

[70] James E. Doyle, "Why Eliminate Nuclear Weapons?," 55(1), *Survival: Global Politics and Strategy* (February–March 2013, pp. 7–34, also available at: http://www.iiss.org/en/publications/survival/sections/2013-94b0/survival--global-politics-and-strategy-february-march-2013-3db7/55-1-02-doyle-a88b. See also John Mueller, *Atomic Obsession: Nuclear Alarmism from Hiroshima to Al-Qaeda*, Oxford: Oxford University Press, 2010.

[71] Doyle, footnote 69 above.

[72] The International Campaign to *Abolish Nuclear Weapons (ICAN)*, Arguments for nuclear abolition, available at: http://www.icanw.org/why-a-ban/arguments-for-a-ban/ (accessed 10 January 2021).

[73] See also ICRC, footnote 61 above.

[74] ICAN footnote 71 above.

nuclear weapons, with the ultimate goal being their total elimination.[75] In this way, the Nuclear Weapon Ban Treaty fills the legal gap in the existing international regime governing nuclear weapons.[76] The drawback is that the Treaty was concluded without the participation of the NAS.[77] The Treaty also provides for a time-bound framework to nuclear armed states for negotiations leading to the verified and irreversible elimination of its nuclear weapons programme.[78]

Although, the Nuclear Weapon Ban Treaty does not contain the legal and technical measures required for elimination of nuclear weapons, it may help "stigmatize" nuclear weapons, and serve as a catalyst for eventual elimination.[79] The benefits of eliminating nuclear weapons on the face of the earth would include a world free of the environmental, economic, social, psychological and spiritual horror of a thermonuclear Armageddon or terrorist threat or attack."[80] As such, it is in the interest of the very survival of humanity that nuclear weapons are never used again under any circumstances. Although NAS bear the ultimate responsibility to completely eliminate their nuclear arsenals, it is a shared responsibility of all States to prevent the humanitarian impact and effects related to these weapons of mass destruction.[81] All States should reassess nuclear weapons in both legal and policy terms, towards eliminating them as there is no valid legal, military or economic justification for nuclear weapons.[82]

---

[75] The Nuclear Weapon Ban Treaty prohibits the development, testing, production, stockpiling, stationing, transfer, use and threat of use of nuclear weapons, as well as assistance and encouragement to the prohibited activities. The Treaty was adopted on 7 July 2017, opened for signature on 20 September 2017, and entered into force on 22 January 2021. The treaty passed on schedule on 7 July with 122 in favour, 1 against (Netherlands) and 1 official abstention (Singapore).

[76] United Nations General Assembly, "Open-Ended Working Group Taking Forward Multilateral Nuclear Disarmament Negotiations Geneva 2016," 4 May 2016. UN Doc. A/AC.286/WP.36.

[77] Sixty-nine (69) States did not vote, among them all of the nuclear weapon States and all NATO members except the Netherlands.

[78] See United Nations General Assembly, "Addressing Nuclear Disarmament: Recommendations from the Perspective of Nuclear-Weapon-Free Zones," 11 May 2016, UN Doc. A/AC. 286/WP.34/Rev.1.

[79] Ray Acheson, Thomas Nash, and Richard Moyes, "Treaty Banning Nuclear Weapons Developing a Legal Framework for the Prohibition and Elimination of Nuclear Weapons," Article 36 and Reaching Critical Will May 2014. See also Article 36, "Banning Nuclear Weapons Without the Nuclear Armed States," Briefing Paper, October 2013. See also. Doyle, footnote 69 above.

[80] UNESCO, see footnote 63 above.

[81] See United Nations General Assembly, "Addressing Nuclear Disarmament: Recommendations from the Perspective of Nuclear-Weapon-Free Zones," 11 May 2016, UN Doc. A/AC. 286/WP.34/Rev.1, paras. 4 and 5.

[82] UNESCO, 'Making the World Safe', available at: http://www.unesco.org/education/tlsf/mods/theme_a/interact/www.worldgame.org/wwwproject/what17.shtml (accessed 2 February 2021).

Emerging Global Pandemics and Epidemics

The gravity of epidemics and pandemics in Africa has been well exposed by Chikondi Mandala and John Phuka in Chapter 16. While the scale of HIV and AIDS has significantly decreased on the continent, the epidemic still threatens a significant number of people in Africa. The rate of the HIV/AIDS prevalence on the continent is among the highest globally, with the sub-Saharan Africa, being the worst hit region by the scourge in the world.[83] The HIV epidemic has significantly contributed to reduced life expectancy.[84]

In November 2019, an unprecedented and deadly Corona virus spread in Wuhan, Hubei Province in China. This highly contagious virus causes Corona Virus Disease (Covid-19), characterized by severe acute respiratory syndrome.[85] The virus has spread globally, infecting over 102.2 million people and killing at least 2.2 million others worldwide, as of February 2021.[86] At the time of writing, Africa alone had over 3.5 million affected cases with at least 88 thousand reported deaths and about 2.9 million recoveries.[87] The World Health Organization (WHO) declared Covid-19, which has a mortality rate in excess of three per cent, as a pandemic.[88]

The "the alarming levels of spread and severity" led WHO to ask governments to take urgent and aggressive action to stop the spread of this virus.[89] Currently, there is no vaccine to prevent Covid-19, and no specific medical treatment for it, other than management of the symptoms.[90] The only way is to contain, manage and prevent the spread of this deadly and highly infectious

---

[83] UNAIDS, "Turning Point for Africa: An Historic Opportunity to End AIDS as Public Health Threat by 2030 Launch a New Era of Sustainability," 20 April 2018, available at: www.unaids.org/en/resources/presscentre/featurestories/2018/april/turning-point-for-africa (accessed 11 February 2018).

[84] For example, see World Health Organization (WHO), 'Malawi Country Statistics', available at: http://www.who.int/countries/mwi/en/ (accessed 12 January 2018).

[85] World Health Organization, "Coronavirus Disease (COVID-19) Pandemic," available at: https://www.who.int/emergencies/diseases/novel-coronavirus-2019 (accessed 4 February 2020). See also Centers for Disease Control, "Corona Virus Disease 2019 (COVID-19)," available at: https://www.cdc.gov/coronavirus/2019-ncov/symptoms-testing/symptoms.html (accessed 20 June 2020).

[86] See also Africa Union, "Coronavirus Disease 2019 (COVID-19): Latest Updates on the COVID-19 Crisis from Africa CDC," available: https://africacdc.org/covid-19/ (accessed 4 February 2021). See also WHO, "WHO Coronavirus Disease (COVID-19) Dashboard," available at: https://covid19.who.int/ (accessed 4 February 2021).

[87] See African Union (AU), "Coronavirus Disease 2019 (COVID-19)," available at: https://africacdc.org/covid-19/ (accessed 20 June 2020). See also Africa News, "Coronavirus in Africa: 209,380 cases; 5689 deaths; 95,084 recoveries," available at: https://www.africanews.com/2020/06/11/coronavirus-in-africa-breakdown-of-infected-virus-free-countries/ (accessed 12 June 2020).

[88] WHO, footnote 85 above.

[89] As above.

[90] But see Michelle Roberts, "Coronavirus: Dexamethasone Proves First Life-Saving Drug," https://www.bbc.com/news/health-53061281 (accessed 20 June 2020).

virus. For this reason, governments are challenged in seeking to protect their populations from Covid-19. The second wave of this virulent virus emerged in January 2021 together with new variants that ravaged even more people worldwide, causing unprecedented society and economic disruption.[91]

This has led to the regular functioning of society not able to be maintained, particularly in implementing the main protective measure to contain the virus, which is confinement. These protective measures have inevitably encroached on human rights, which are an integral and necessary part of a democratic society governed by the rule of law.[92] Besides the health implications associated with inadequacy in the healthcare system, the pandemic has also been accompanied by human rights violations including fears regarding increased government surveillance, misinformation, job losses and increased poverty governments have failed to consistently uphold human rights obligations in their responses to the Covid-19 pandemic by limiting access to information and implementing restrictions in discriminatory or arbitrary ways.[93] Respect for human rights across the spectrum, including economic and social rights, and civil and political rights, is fundamental to the success of the public health response to this global pandemic. Human rights violations mutate, rather than facilitate, responses to Covid-19 and undercut their efficiency.[94]

The unprecedented public health emergency emanating from Covid-19 pandemic, has forced governments to take drastic measures to contain its transmission. In view of the exceptional situation and to preserve life, countries have adopted extraordinary measures, which inadvertently infringe upon human rights and personal freedoms, with far-reaching consequences for economic, social and political lives of the people.[95] This impact comes from the disease itself but also from the measures necessary to combat it coming up against underlying factors like inequalities and weak protection systems. It falls disproportionately on some people, often those least able to protect themselves. The Covid-19 situation shows more striking example of the interconnectedness and the indivisibility of human rights.

[91] Peter Mwai, "Coronavirus: Africa's Second Waves Sees Rising Death Rate," *BBC News*, 3 February 2021, available at: https://www.bbc.com/news/world/Africa-531 815555 (accessed 4 February 2021).

[92] Council of Europe, "Respecting Democracy, Rule of Law and Human Rights in the Framework of the COVID-19 Sanitary Crisis: A Toolkit for Member States," SG/Inf (2020)11, 17 April 2020.

[93] United Nations (UN), "Covid-19 and Human Rights: We Are All in this Together," April 2020, available at: https://www.un.org/sites/un2.un.org/files/un_policy_brief_on_human_rights_and_covid_23_april_2020.pdf, p. 5 (accessed 13 June 2020).

[94] Amnesty International, "Explainer: Seven Ways the Coronavirus Affects Human Rights," 5 February 2020, available at: https://www.amnesty.org/en/latest/news/2020/02/explainer-seven-ways-the-coronavirus-affects-human-rights/ (accessed 13 March 2020).

[95] UN Office of the Human Rights Commissioner, "Covid-19 and Human Rights," available at: https://www.ohchr.org/EN/NewsEvents/Pages/COVID19andHR.aspx (accessed 14 February 2021).

In other cases, governments have ordered cessation of social and economic activity, except essential services. Such measures have inadvertently affected people's livelihoods and security, their access to health care, food, water and sanitation, work, education, including leisure. Response to Covid-19 have also occasioned human rights violations including censorship, discrimination, arbitrary detention, xenophobia. With the large informal sector and people who survive on a subsistence in most countries coupled with a limited welfare system and poor data, most governments have been unable to provide sufficient social support. The lack of social determinants of health has also rendered many in the informal sector more vulnerable due to the absence of social safety nets.[96] Therefore, it is crucial that effective measures should be taken to mitigate any such unintended consequences in response to the pandemic.

While Covid-19 remains a highly infectious pandemic of worldwide proportions requiring urgent attention to protect populations, its management must not be used to infringe upon the human rights. Given the effects of Covid-19 on the people, economy and its impact on the enjoyment of human rights, there is a critical need for a human rights-based approach (HRBA) to responding to the Covid-19 pandemic. Thus, governments should put human rights at the centre of the pandemic response by applying the principles of non-discrimination, participation, empowerment and accountability needed to be applied to all health-related policies including in accessing health care, services and life-saving treatment. The pandemic has also highlighted and exacerbated systemic inequalities. Many governments' responses to Covid-19 have had devastating effects on people in poverty, persons with disabilities, older persons and women. Therefore, special attention should also be paid to disease surveillance, prevention and control of epidemics, pandemics as well as intermittent diseases. Governments should also provide access to reliable and accurate information and the protection of the right to privacy, including in the use of technologies to track the spread of the virus.

RETHINKING THE AU COMMON DEFENCE ON SECURITY

Faced with continued insecurity, persistent poverty and deteriorating socioeconomic conditions caused by conflicts in several countries on the continent, the AU prioritized the promotion of peace, security and stability into its objectives in Articles 3 and 4 of the AU Constitutive Act.[97] In 2004, African States adopted a Common Defence and Security Policy for Africa (CADSP) as a

---

[96] Cheluchi Onyemelukwe, "The Law and Human Rights in Nigeria's Response to the COVID-19 Pandemic," 4 June 2020, available at: https://blog.petrieflom.law.harvard.edu/2020/06/04/the-law-and-human-rights-in-nigerias-response-to-the-covid-19-pandemic/ (accessed 5 July 2020).

[97] See Omar A. Touray, "The Common African Defence and Security Policy," 104(417) *African Affairs* (2005), pp. 635–56, also available at: http://www.jstor.org/stable/3518810 (accessed 10 February, 2021).

238   D. KUWALI

conceptual framework for achieving peace, security and stability on the continent.[98] The CADSP is based on a common African perception of collective responsibility to find African solutions to Africa problems by ensuring that common defence and security interests and goals are safeguarded in the face of a common threat to the continent. Thus, the CADSP serves as a tool for the simultaneous enhancement of defence cooperation between and among African States, and the consolidation of national defence.[99]

The CADSP progressively expands the horizon of a common vision of defence and security in Africa by defining the concept of security to go beyond the security of the state and threats to the state, to include threats to the well-being of the citizens of a state.[100] The CADSP duly recognizes that "security of each African country is inseparably linked to that of other African countries and the African continent as a whole."[101] The concept of defence also follows the same approach that incorporates the concept of human security together with the traditional definition of defence, implying both military and non-military aspects for the protection of national sovereignty, territorial integrity, the environment and its people, including their political, social and economic values.[102]

Among others, the CADSP promotes initiatives that will enhance peace and development in Africa, ensures a collective response to threats to Africa and establishes a threat deterrence and containment capacity within the AU, protects Member States from internal and external threats, encourages Member States to conclude and ratify non-aggression pacts between and among African States and to harmonize such agreements; provides a framework for post-conflict peace-building and reconstruction, and promotes peaceful co-existence among Member States and emphasizes the peaceful means of conflict resolution. Several number of defence and security frameworks existing in Africa at the continental, regional/sub-regional levels, will constitute the Actors or the Organs for implementing the Common Defence and Security Policy for the whole African continent. At the continental level, these include the Assembly of the African Union, the Peace and Security Council provided for under the Protocol relating to it and the peace and security mechanisms of the regional economic groupings.

The CADSP views common security threats as those that may be deemed to pose a danger to the common defence and security interests of the continent. Although the CADSP has comprehensively taken into account the relevant

---

[98] Melkamu Aboma Tolera, *Common African Defence and Security Policy: A Study of the African Union Common African Defence and Security Policy: Challenges and Opportunities for Implementation*, LAP LAMBERT Academic Publishing, 2012.

[99] Clause 13(c) of the Common African Defence and Security Policy (CADSP), African Union, Addis Ababa, 2004.

[100] Clause 6, CADSP, footnote 99 above.

[101] As above.

[102] Clause 5, CADSP, footnote 99 above.

interstate and intrastate security threats, it did not factor in some contemporary and emerging security threats as outlined above such as cyber terrorism, cybercrimes, green violence, political violence, pandemics and xenophobia. This may be an oversight in that the contemporary and future threats are out of the radar of the continental organization. It is, therefore, critical that a review conference established under Clause 36 of CADSP to review the state of peace and security on the continent should factor in the new and emerging threats to peace and security on the continent and adopt the relevant legal, policy and institutional frameworks to counter them.[103]

CONCLUSION

The trajectory of contemporary violence in Africa does not include the possibility of the prospect either of nuclear war or widespread conventional interstate conflict in the near future. The evolving threat to peace, safety and security of the population on the continent is not military in nature but human security in the sense of threats to the social and economic well-being of the citizens including social and political marginalization as well as environmental degradation. Future hostilities will continue to be asymmetric against an amorphous enemy on an undefined battlefield. Unfortunately, most of the victims will be innocent civilians and not combatants. These hostilities will mainly involve law enforcement operations governed by human rights law.

International terrorism and violent extremism, invisible battles in the form of cybercrime and cyber terrorism, wireless wars characterized by AI on the battlefield, political violence resulting from, popular protests and insurgency in some extreme cases, green violence involving destruction of flora and fauna, environmental degradation and climate change, organized crime, resource conflicts, xenophobic attacks, the threat of weapons of mass destruction as well as ravaging global pandemics and epidemics with virulent viruses killing masses of people, are continent-wide security threats as they pose a danger to the common defence and security interests of the continent.

While LoAC obliges States to ensure that all new weapons systems are lawful, developers of AI also have an ethical duty not to delegate the decision to kill to a machine. Likewise, the destruction of the environment is not only an issue of legality but also an ethical question of the future of the Planet. The emergence of these hostilities presents novel challenges, with which some well-established arrangements may not fully address. Therefore, for LoAC to continue to be relevant to regulate future hostilities, practitioners should not deal with the law in isolation but rather in conjunction with other multinational peace initiatives such as the Common Defence and Security Policy for Africa, African Agenda 2063 and UN SDGs 2030.

---

[103] Clause 36 of CDSPA provides for regular conferences, every six months, between the Peace and Security Council and the conflict resolution mechanisms of the various regional organizations, to review the state of peace and security on the whole continent.

African States face challenges that undermine their ability to provide security and prevent conflict such as failed leadership, corruption, fragile democracies, unemployed youth bulge and weak law enforcement framework, among others. African States should also ratify the relevant treaties such as the 2014 Convention on Cybersecurity and Personal Data Protection and Palermo Convention, among others in order to curb common contemporary threats to pace and security on the continent. The African Peace and Security Architecture should also actively engage States to adopt mediation to resolve disputes and eradicate marginalization, especially of the youth as well as promoting socioeconomic well-being of their citizens indiscriminately.

The CADSP progressively expands the definition of security from state security to include human security.[104] Nonetheless, most of these contemporary and emerging security threats were not foreseen at the time of crafting the CADSP in 2004 such as cyber terrorism, cybercrimes, green violence, political violence, pandemics and xenophobia. This may be an oversight and render such contemporary and future threats to be out of the radar of the continental organization. As such the CADSP review conferences should critically project such threats if African States are to effectively overcome them.[105] A long-term strategy to overcome threats to peace and security in Africa should involve addressing security and good governance challenges, focus on the link between security and development and redesigning a functional continental defence and security strategy.[106]

---

[104] As above.

[105] See Clause 36 of CDSPA, footnote 99 above.

[106] Njuki Mwaniki, "Security Challenges Facing the Great Lakes Region," 3(2), *Contemporary Security in Africa* (2015), pp. 70–85, p. 70.

CHAPTER 14

Social Media, Peace and Security in Africa

Peter Makossah and Gilbert Mittawa

INTRODUCTION

It may not be disputed that communication, through any means is an integral part of human life in the modern dispensation. It is also true to say that Social media has become an important part of everyday life in the world and in Africa in particular. It is quick, easy, spontaneous and faster and has changed the way we access information and express opinions on a wide range of issues. Over the years, social media has been so critical in preventing and responding to violence perpetuated largely by political and sometimes religious intolerance.[1] There is a lot of excitement about the role of the social media in non-violent change and democratisation.[2] The United Nations (UN) has described Information and Communication Technology (ICT) as a double-edged sword.[3]

---

[1] Joseph Bock, *The technology of non-violence*. Cambridge, MIT Press 2012; and Peacebuilding in information age, sifting hype from reality, ICT4Peace Foundation 2011.

[2] Larry Diamond and Marc Plattner (eds) Liberation technology, Baltimore, Johns Hopkins University Press 2012.

[3] Kate Cox and others, "Social Media in Africa: A double-edged sword for security and development", RAND Europe and UNDP, p. 1.

P. Makossah (✉) · G. Mittawa
Blavatnik School of Government, University of Oxford, Oxford, UK

© The Author(s), under exclusive license to Springer Nature
Switzerland AG 2022
D. Kuwali (ed.), *The Palgrave Handbook of Sustainable Peace
and Security in Africa*, https://doi.org/10.1007/978-3-030-82020-6_14

241

This assertion could be particularly true if one considers the role of Social Media in Africa. While it has promoted social, political and economic development, it has also been used to perpetrate violence and other illegal activities. For example, it has been noted that "[t]oday, al-Shabaab, Boko Haram, ISIL and other violent extremist groups in Africa use Twitter, Facebook, YouTube and other social media channels to broadcast their messages, inspire followers, and recruit new fighters to unprecedented levels".[4] It may therefore, be argued that if not well managed, Social Media, can be used as catalyst for insecurity in Africa with the prospect of undermining Africa's aspirations to silence the guns.

It is on the above premises that this chapter examines the role that social media plays in Africa's peace and security. The Chapter will discuss the social media revolution in Africa, drawing particular inspiration from the way social media was used by protesters during the Arab Spring. The chapter further proceeds to discuss how social media can be utilised in upholding peace and security in Africa particularly in post-conflict peace building, reconstruction and recovery?

The Nature and Forms of Social Media

Social media refers to websites, applications and other online communications channels that enable users to create and share content or to participate in social networking. It involves the confluence of online social networking and user-generated content (UGC), which refers in part, to the platforms for content generation and consumption. Social media allows for dissemination of content in a peer-to-peer rather than unidirectional manner. Rather than a revolution, social media has been an evolution having almost inevitably replaced traditional media also known as main stream media.

A number of reasons can be attributed to the surge in Social Media. Unlike main stream media mostly uses portable devices such as mobile phones and tablets. These devices are easily accessible by most Africans, including those in rural areas. These devices can also produce high quality signals and images for recording and processing of data. Thus, a person can, using a mobile phone or tablet record a video or take pictures and transmit them to millions of people within seconds. Social media does not require any mastery of technology and techniques. It is a process that does not necessarily require any special technical know-how or creative thinking which is some of the key elements in the main stream media. As a result, Social Media has become a very popular and attractive mode of communication worldwide.

The roots of social media go deeper than what many might imagine. The earliest methods of communicating across great distances used to be written

---

[4] Cox K and others, "Social Media in Africa: A double-edged sword for security and development".

correspondences delivered by hand.[5] Two important discoveries happened in the last decade of 1800s: the telephone in 1890 and the radio in 1891. Both technologies are still in use today, although their modern versions are very much more sophisticated than their predecessors. However, the use of Social Media came into prominence in 1997 with the first ever social media platform called Six degrees.[6] It lasted only until 2001, and somehow, laid the foundation for the present Social Media platforms.[7]

MySpace is first ever social media platform to be released in the early 2000s, and at that time, its users seemed to love the idea of being able to communicate with each other and personalise their profiles with pictures and colours. At the time MySpace was getting underway, LinkedIn was also created as a social network for business professionals. MySpace eventually lost credence and popularity and has since become a social network for musicians while LinkedIn remains popular with its original format to this very day.

Facebook is another social media platform that gained popularity in the early 2000's. It was created by Mark Zuckerberg and his Harvard University roommates with a sole purpose of helping American college students "rate" one another's attractiveness.[8] By December 2005, Facebook had six million users.[9] As of February 2011, Facebook had become the largest online photo host.[10] In December, 2009 Facebook hit a major milestone with 350 million registered users and 132 million unique monthly users. In July 2009 Facebook registered 500 users and the following year in November 2010 Facebook was valued at a staggering US$41 billion. Facebook continued to grow and there was no sign of progress slowing. In June of 2011, there was another huge milestone as Facebook reached 1 trillion page views. In the third quarter of 2012, the number of active users surpassed 1 billion people, making it the first social media network to have ever achieved that feat. With roughly 2.8 Billion active users as of the fourth quarter of 2020, Facebook is biggest social media network worldwide.[11] Facebook has been largely used to mobilise people for protests against regimes and social media revolution.

Twitter is another important social media platform which was initially designed in a way that people could convey their ideas, with either images or text messages that were 140 characters long, which leads to a lot of grammatical and spelling innovation. Twitter, an American micro-blogging and social networking platform was created by Jack Dorsey and others in March 2006

---

[5] As above.

[6] As above.

[7] As above.

[8] Carlson Nicholas, At last—The Full Story of How Facebook was founded; Business Insider (5 March 2010).

[9] Mark Zuckerberg, Lecture by Mark Zuckerberg—YouTube (7 December 2005).

[10] Sarah Kessler, Facebook Photos By the numbers (14 February 2011).

[11] H Tankovska, Global social networks ranked by number of users 2021 (9 February 2021).

and launched in July of that very same year. By 2012, Twitter had more than 100 million users who together posted over 340 million tweets a day, and the service handled an average of 1.6 search queries per day. Just like Facebook, Twitter has for the past years been used for a multiplicity of purposes in Africa.

For example, Twitter was used in North Africa during the Arab Spring to organise protests and mobilise people to join demonstrations, sometimes referred to as "Twitter Revolutions". It has also been used in Xenophophic protests in South Africa and presidential elections dispute demonstration in Malawi. It use during elections has proved to be significant for especially for politicians who have a reciprocal engagement with the electorate. It has been observed for example that "political candidates that use twitter to communicate with their electorate will receive more preferential votes than those who do not". [12]

Today, there are many new social media platforms being introduced that all seem to be breaking down the idea of social media into endless small niches. Over the past few years, the growing number of social media options for users means that social media platforms are starting to develop dedicated target audience. This makes it easier for marketing experts to formulate social media marketing plans that are effective and target oriented. This idea seems to be the central theme behind the creation of Instagram. The popularity of images on Twitter helped to spur the creation of a series of social media platforms around the year, 2010.

Flickr and Instagram got their start at the very earliest point of image-centric social media platforms, and both are still very popular today. Instagram, popularly known as "Insta" and commonly abbreviated as IG is an American instant photo and video social network sharing utility and owned by Facebook, was born in San Francisco as a Burbn, a mobile check-in app created by Kelvin Systrom and Mike Krieger on October 6, 2010.[13] Just like any other social media utility, Instagram is used for variety of reasons including fighting social injustice. It can be used as a quicker means to mobilise people for a revolution. In 2018 Instagram was the second most downloaded free app on Apple-store and had over 1 billion users by 2019.

THE IMPACT OF SOCIAL MEDIA ON AFRICA'S PEACE AND SECURITY

The use of social media as a medium of communication has brought with it serious security and privacy concerns, including new vectors for cyber-attack that African governments and their security agents cannot ignore. Criminal

---

[12] Sanne Kruikemeier, How political candidates use Twitter and the ipact on vote, Computers in Human Behaviour, Vol. 34 (2014) p. 132.

[13] Erica Edwards, Esposito, Jennifer (2019) Reading social media intersectionally; Intersectional Analysis as a method to analyse Popular Culture: Clarity in the Matrix.

gangs, terrorist organisations, non-state actors with bad intentions and subversive elements including Al-Shabaab, Boko Haram and ISIL are using social media to recruit, radicalise and coordinate their operations. Individuals use social media to send alarming messages, hate messages and false information to the public regarding state of national security affairs.

Most of the social media users remain unanimous and cannot be easily traced by law enforcement agencies and subsequent prosecution. States therefore, are now confronted with a new security challenge as tracking, monitoring and containing the use and misuse of social media is not easy. Africa's security mechanisms demand a strategy such as monitoring conversations and content shared on Social Media, arranging effective methods to counter adversaries' propaganda and interferences, improving governmental agencies and institutions' performances, strengthening a state's geopolitical position and its international credibility. However, such initiatives require sophisticated technologies which are very complex, costly by third world countries. The result is that most states are unable to deter security threats driven by social media, hence undermining Africa's peace and security.

Africa has experienced continuing violence, insecurity and instability since the outbreak of the various uprisings in Tunisia spread out in Egypt, Algeria and Morocco.[14] These uprisings, while desired to bring justice, peace and good governance, were characterised by the threat of or use of violence. Social Media played a critical role in the organisation and execution of these uprisings. Evidence shows that during the Arab revolution of 2011,[15] social media networks such as Face Book, Twitter, YouTube and weblogs played a great role in facilitating uprisings in Egypt, Tunisia and Syria. It was observed that the usage and growth of social media in the Arab region played a great role in mass mobilisation of protestors, empowerment, shaping of opinions and influencing change. To date such Arab countries have witnessed constant conflicts and political instability, coupled with widespread social unrest affecting negatively on broader sets of economic, social and political factors.[16] It can therefore, be argued that social media is not in itself a cause of insecurity but an important catalyst for insecurity.

Political crises associated with transitions and the challenge of state and nation building is still the main sources of (un)peace and (in) security on the African continent. Most episodes of violence in Africa in the last few years are associated with conflict over political power at the highest level. Violence appears to be one of the tools in the battles to access power or keep it.[17] While

[14] Oxfam policy brief, *women, peace and Security: Keeping the promise.*

[15] Maha Taki and Lorenzo Coretti, The roe of social media in the Arab uprisings-Past and Present, Wesminister Papers in Communication and Culture, Vol. 9:2 (2013) p. 1.

[16] W Ghonim, Revolution 2.0: The Power of the People is Greater Than the People in Power. Houghton Mifflin Harcourt, Boston (2012) p. 30.

[17] Institute of Security Studies; *Armed Conflict in Africa—Real-time Analysis of African Political Violence.*

social media plays a significant role, as a mass media medium, in promoting peace and security in Africa, it is also a serious threat to security and peace in Africa. The growing of social media in Africa has increased citizens' awareness of political events, changing perceptions both nationally and internationally.

For example, increasing Twitter use in Kenya is said to be linked to citizens' interest in challenging misrepresentation by the international mainstream media in terms of how violence and election campaigns are reported.[18] Similarly, in Nigeria, social media activity has reportedly been encouraged as a result of the Nigerian's mainstream media's reluctance to critique the conduct of the Nigerian government top officials or powerful corporations.[19]

Apart from popular protests, the problem of terrorism has also worsened to unprecedented levels with the regional expansion of the Islamic State and Al-Shabaab, among others.[20] According to the 2020 Global Terrorism Index, it is noted that seven of the ten countries with the largest increase in terrorism were in sub-Saharan Africa. Nigeria and Somalia are among the top five countries impacted by terrorism. The largest increase in deaths from terrorism occurred in Burkina Faso, where deaths rose from 86 to 593, representing a 590 per cent increase. These statistics show the extent of terrorism in Africa.[21] While this state of affairs is largely attributed to existing armed conflicts in Africa,[22] it is also important to note the role that Social Media has played in facilitating the spread of terrorism. Social Media is used by terrorists as a tool to enlist, train, coordinate and communicate with followers and potential recruits remotely. Terrorists in Africa have been using Twitter, Facebook, YouTube and other social media channels to broadcast their messages, inspire followers and recruit new fighters to unprecedented levels.[23]

It is noted, for example, that Al-Shabaab has established itself as one of the more technologically advanced jihadist groups worldwide through early adoption of the Internet as a strategic tool for promoting its operations.[24] Al-Shabaab uses social media, particularly on Twitter to share propaganda, recruit followers, coordinate activities and access funding. In 2011, Al-Shabaab used Twitter to report its 2013 attack on the Westgate shopping mall in Nairobi, Kenya, in real time. This demonstrates a concerted effort to become the core

---

[18] Nyabola (2017), for example, *there are several thousands of Kenyans on Twitter*.

[19] Jacobs et al. (2017); *The power of social media in Nigeria*.

[20] Human security Report for International Conflict Research (2015) *Conflict Barometer 2015 N0. 24*.

[21] Institute for Economics and Peace, Global Terrorism Index 2020: Measurig the impact of Terrorism, 4 https://www.visionofhumanity.org accessed 11 March 2021.

[22] Institute for Economics and Peace, Global Terrorism Index 2020: Measurig the impact of Terrorism.

[23] Cox K and others, "Social Media in Africa: A double-edged sword for security and development" p. 12.

[24] Cox K and others, "Social Media in Africa: A double-edged sword for security and development" p. 13.

narrator of the event, divert attention from official reporting by the Kenyan government, and attract international media attention. This strategy was twice repeated in 2015, both in the Al-Shabaab attack on Lido Beach, Mogadishu, in January, and the Maka alMukarama hotel attack in March.[25]

Similarly, as observed by Dan Kuwali in Chapter 12, in Nigeria Boko Haram has been employing Social Media as a tool to share its propaganda, recruit and coordinate its activities using You Tube, Twitter and Facebook. It has been rightly noted that "Boko Haram's use of social media has been influenced by a number of contextual factors, including rapidly growing Internet access in Nigeria in recent years". Boko Haram's popularity grew after its pledge of allegiance to ISIL and associated expansion of its social media strategy, which positively shaped youth perceptions of the group.[26]

In agreement with Tabitha Mwangi and Tracy Asava in Chapter 10, the use of social media by Boko Haram operatives, followers and potential recruits can be attributed to a number of socialeconomic factors including easy accessibility of social media owing to an increase in Internet access especially among the youth. It is also important to note that so far, it has been very difficult to have meaningful censorship and control over social media. For example, individuals can own several social media accounts using fake identities. With no proper technology to trace and track such individuals, it becomes practically difficult to exercise meaningful censorship and control over social media. As a result, social media is easily abused for illegal activities in Africa, such that instead of being a tool for social economic development, it has become a vehicle for insecurity.

Social Media, Peace and Security in Africa: Addressing the Challenges

Dealing with the adverse impact of social media has become a huge challenge for both governments in Africa and beyond. One key issue revolves around the respect for individual rights, especially the right to privacy. For instance, there is continued debate and conflict as to what should take precedence between Human Rights and Security. Most Human Rights activists and other Non-Governmental organisations advocate for enhanced right to privacy that protects against tracing and tracking social media users. On the other hand, government authorities and security agents seek more transparency in the use of social media and other online platforms. Thus, striking a balance between the regulation of online space and protecting individuals' freedom of expression has become a key stumbling block to regulating social media thereby affecting Africa's peace and security. It should be appreciated however, that

[25] As above.
[26] As above, p. 33.

"all human rights are universal, indivisible, interrelated, interdependent and mutually reinforcing".[27]

To suggest that only a certain category of rights requires priority over the other may be misleading. For example, it is trite that the right to privacy, if exercised irresponsibly can result in violent activities which may undermine the right to life. This position was buttressed by the 2006 United Nations (UN) General Assembly resolution establishing the Human Rights Council which reaffirmed that "all human rights are universal, indivisible, interrelated, interdependent and mutually reinforcing, and that all human rights must be treated in a fair and equal manner, on the same footing and with the same emphasis."[28]

Thus, it is imperative to appreciate that "these rights condition each other, with the human person as 'the central subject and 'beneficiary' of the rights".[29] With that in mind, there is need to exercise caution when priotising the right to privacy or due process rights over an individual's security. In any event, the right to privacy is not absolute such that its limitation would be permissible where there is breach or likelihood of breach of security or where it may undermine other fundamental rights.

Another challenge is the increased high levels of encryption protecting users' communication on social media and messaging services, which makes it difficult to design and deliver interventions to counter online radicalisation. While social media companies can be quick to take down extremist content online, resource limitations can often constrain their ability to build counter-narratives or continuously monitor social media content.

African governments have been deploying a number of strategies and mechanisms to deal with peace and security issues propagated by social media. There have been efforts to curb social media abuse by installing soft wares that monitor hate speech and act on information gathered. These efforts are complimented by taking firm action through legislation, interception and censorship, taking punitive measures against social media abusers. There have also been efforts to coordinate and cooperate with hosts of social media platforms to monitor and shut down sites deemed to be propagating criminal activities. There is also constant monitoring of misuse of social media, coming up with policies to guard against abuse of social media, having necessary laws to control people on how to use social media, mechanisms to trace social inciters in place, teaching the public about the use of social media without hate speech, block sources of threat in the social media.

While all these efforts are recommendable, the continued abuse of social media is an indication that the fight is far from over. If not addressed, social media abuse will continue to undermine Africa's pace and security and thus,

---

[27] Theo Van Boven, 'Categories of Rights' in Daniel Moeckli et al. (eds), *International Human Rights Law* (OUP, 2018) 140.

[28] As above.

[29] As above.

affect the successful implementation of Agenda 2063. It should be noted that most of the efforts so far have not focused on innovative technological approaches utilised by the perpetrators. As a result, the perpetrators are always ahead and advanced. In view of the above, there is also need to develop strategic engagement and partnership with local communities and NGOs to capacitate them in fighting insecurity perpetrated by social media abuse. This must focus on training the communities NGOs and religious associations to enable them understand how they can develop effective counter-narratives to social media abuse and extremist narratives. Particular focus must be placed on the youth who are often times both targets and perpetrators.

Having recognised the potential and actual impact of social media on peace and security, the question arises as to how best can Africa flip the coin and use the same social media to promote peace and security. Social media should be utilised to spread messages about peace, encouraging dialogue among people from different ethnic backgrounds and nationalities. With its fast-reaching effect, social media can easily change perceptions and promote tolerance and mutual understanding. It is also important to realise the effect of social media in weakening the control of authoritarian regimes over information content.

To this end, social media can be used to provide objective critique and oversight on poor governance. It may be argued that there is a fundamental difference between promoting violence and extremism on the one hand, and providing objective and balanced information, on the other hand. The latter is compatible with the desire and aspirations to have an informed society that can hold its government accountable. Thus, it would be ideal to use social media to encourage, among others universal values such as security of the person, political participation, human rights including women's rights, and uncorrupt free economies without professing violence.

Social media can also be used as an important tool for resource mobilisation to enhance Africa's social economic development. It has been demonstrated that through the use of social media, one can reach out to millions of people within a short period of time. It is also easy to send attractive content by using either videos or pictures that appeal to the audience. Recently, social media has proved useful in most African states where individuals launched online campaigns to contribute resources towards mitigating the impact of Covid-19. In Malawi, for example, some citizens of goodwill established a movement called "Covid Response Private Response". The objective of the movement was to mobilise resources to help buy equipment to mitigate the effects of Covid-19.

The response from both private citizens and business entities was overwhelming and within a short period, they managed to buy and supply equipments such as oxygen cylinders, gas and other personal protective equipment. This demonstrates a classic example of how social media can be utilised to promote Africa's aspirations in line with Agenda 2063 framework. Further efforts can be put to use social media to report and locate victims during public emergencies such as floods. By using applications such as Google map, communities can be encouraged to report actual locations of victims or hotspots to enable rescue teams carry out its operations. Similar approach can be taken during public protests to aid security agents respond in a timely and effective manner. It is argued that by promoting these positive faces of social media, communities will stop focusing on using social media as a tool for destruction.

Apart from taking the above strategies, African states need to prioritise developing robust policies and legislation on data protection and privacy. Where there is already legislation in place, efforts must be towards improving such legislation. The focus should not only be to address privacy issues, but eliminate threats to Africa's peace and security cultivated through social media. In agreement with recommendations made by Mwangi in Chapter 10 and Kuwali in Chapters 12 and 13, the AU should play an advisory and coordination role to ensure harmonisation of policies and laws aimed at curbing social media abuse. African states must share best practices in dealing with social media threats as well as share information and intelligence on any potential and emerging threats. All these measures require constant monitoring and evaluation to assess their effectiveness and where they are deemed lacking, take appropriate measures to enhance their effectiveness. However, in order to realistically silence "social media guns" there is need for political will from all African governments. Such political will should include commitment of necessary financial and human resources towards dealing with social media threats.

Conclusion

There is hope for peace and security in Africa. However, this hope is attainable only if we use and utilise social media well and positively. Africa appears to be getting peaceful and secure in what can be described as a long-term perspective. The amount of conflict and resultant deaths has been steadily decreasing for decades, now. Social media has to a greater extent contributed to Africa's insecurity by propagating and promoting violence. This has a likelihood of undermining Africa's peace and security efforts and the desired targets of Agenda 2063. If Africa is to realistically "silence the guns" there is need to silence negative use of social media through both legal and institutional mechanisms.

Admittedly, such mechanisms may not be effective if there is no mindset change from the users of social media, particularly the youth. To this end, deliberate strategic interventions need to be deployed both at domestic and continental level to promote and reap the positive side of social media. There is also an urgent need to evaluate the strengths and weaknesses of social media as a tool for conflict prevention and peace building; to analyze the contribution of regulatory mechanism of social media in promoting peace building;

to examine the potential role of social media in generating social and political tensions that might result into violence and to identify the early warning social and political signals through social media and conflict prevention. It is hoped that through these interventions, Africa will have realistic chances of silencing "social media guns" and thus, promote the continents social economic development.

CHAPTER 15

Emerging Epidemics and Pandemics in Africa

Chikondi M. Mandala and John C. Phuka

INTRODUCTION

The increasing frequency of epidemics, pandemics and natural disasters in Africa is a major threat to peace. Putting together peace instruments, frameworks and strategies requires dialogue and painstaking implementation. However, peace agreements and enforcement measures, like security oversight interventions, are disrupted by natural catastrophes. Over the past decade, the world has faced catastrophes with increasing frequency and intensity: Covid-19 most recently, Cyclone Idai in 2019[1] and severe Ebola Virus Disease (EVD) from 2014 to date.[2] It is instructive that Ebola has not caused a breakdown in governance leading to social chaos, nor wider security crises. Even more worrying is when multiple catastrophic events happen together or when the catastrophes present with evolving complexities. Unlike natural disasters like earthquakes, floods and cyclones that usually hit once, a disease may be there

---

[1] World Vision, 2019 Cyclone Idai: Facts, 'FAQs and how to help' https://www.worldvision.org/disaster-relief-news-stories/2019-cyclone-idai-facts (accessed on 29 December 2020).

[2] World Health Organisation, 'Ebola Virus Disease' 10 February 2020 https://www.who.int/news-room/fact-sheets/detail/ebola-virus-disease (accessed on 29 December 2020).

C. M. Mandala (✉) · J. C. Phuka
Zomba, Malawi

© The Author(s), under exclusive license to Springer Nature Switzerland AG 2022
D. Kuwali (ed.), *The Palgrave Handbook of Sustainable Peace and Security in Africa*, https://doi.org/10.1007/978-3-030-82020-6_15

253

for a long time with recurring surges and new variants with challenging properties.[3] Covid-19 clearly represents a threat to human security in that it has the potential to affect both the person and his or her ability to pursue life and other interests. In addition to threatening the health of an individual, the spread of the disease can weaken public confidence in government's ability to respond, have an adverse economic impact, undermine a state's social order and catalyse regional instability.

As alluded to by Dan Kuwali in Chapter 13, Covid-19 has brought global societal upheaval and halted most socio-economic activities. World statistics showed an ever-increasing number of cases with close to 80 million cases occurring in the first 12 months. As if the numbers are not shocking enough, the disease also presented with new strains with higher virulence and properties to spread faster. Associated death was correspondingly alarming at over 1.7 million in the same period.[4] Unlike poverty-related diseases, these catastrophes do not discriminate between high-income and low-income countries—if anything high-income countries have been hit the hardest by Covid-19.[5] Although at lower levels than high-income continents, Africa also suffered from the disease with over 1.7 million confirmed cases,[6] over 56,000 deaths[7] and slowing down of industries, including the hospitality sector.

Low-income countries like Malawi also struggled with the disease. At the end of the first 12 months in the history of Covid-19 and eight months occurrence of the disease in Malawi, the country had registered over 6000 cases with 190 deaths.[8] Between December 2020 and February 2020, Malawi had seen a fivefold increase in the number of cases and deaths. As of 11 February 2021, Malawi had registered a total of 28,270 cases and 914 deaths.[9] Malawi is classified as a low-income economy that struggles with inadequate resources. At the time the pandemic struck, the last amendment made to the Public Health

---

[3] James Gallagher, 'New coronavirus variant: What do we know' 20 December 2020 https://www.bbc.com/news/health-55388846 (accessed on 29 December 2020).

[4] World Health Organisation, 'Coronavirus Disease (COVID-19) Dashboard' 22 December 2020 https://covid19.who.int (accessed on 23 December 2020).

[5] Steve Baragone, 'Why COVID-19 Hit High-Income Countries Harder' 26 April 2020 https://www.voanews.com/covid-19-pandemic/why-covid-19-hit-high-income-cou ntries-harder (accessed on 29 December 2020).

[6] World Health Organisation, 'Coronavirus Disease (COVID-19) Dashboard' 22 December 2020 https://covid19.who.int (accessed on 23 December 2020).

[7] Saiffaidin Galal, 'Coronavirus deaths in Africa as of December 14, 2020, by country' 15 December 2020 https://www.statista.com/statistics/1170530/coronavirus-deaths-in-africa/ (accessed on 29 December 2020).

[8] Government of Malawi, Press Statement: Covid-19 Situation Update as of 29 December 2020.

[9] Government of Malawi, Press Statement: Covid-19 Situation Update as of 11 February 2021.

Act was in 1992 and as rightly then listed infectious diseases such as Smallpox, Yellow fever and Blackwater fever, among others.[10] The pandemic also struck at a time when there was an upcoming fresh election that had followed months of protests. As we contextualise pandemics and peace and security, Malawi is particularly intriguing for the multiplicity of factors that existed when crafting the Covid-19 response.

Although Malawi underpins a country to reflect on, other countries suffered multiple burdens during the Covid—19 pandemic, especially those experiencing armed conflict. Since March 2020, warring parties in Libya have escalated fighting,[11] Boko Haram insurgents launched attacks in Chad[12] and abducted school children in Nigeria,[13] Al-Shabaab continued daily attacks on civilian populations in Somalia[14] and Islamic militants committed brutal attacks in Mozambique.[15] Despite the Secretary-General of the United Nations' appeal to all warring parties that there be a global ceasefire so that all attention, energy and resources could be directed towards fighting the pandemic,[16] fighting continued unabetted in most parts of the continent.

The recent challenges arising from the Covid-19 pandemic have tormented various actors for a while and are complex events that threaten peace and its related frameworks and instruments. As early as the 1990s, the relationship between pandemics and security was clearly recognised and appreciated for the impact that international disease outbreaks have on societies, political systems and economies.[17] According to the UN Peacebuilding Commission:

[10] Section 11 of the Public Health Act Number 12 of 1948, Laws of Malawi [Cap 33:05].

[11] UN Office for the Coordination of Humanitarian Affairs, Libya Situation Report 29 April 2020, 29 April 2020 https://reliefweb.int/report/libya/libya-situation-report-29-april-2020 (accessed on 1 January 2021).

[12] The Guardian, 'Boko Haram kills 92 Chadian soldiers in seven-hour attack' 24 March 2020 https://www.theguardian.com/world/2020/mar/24/boko-haram-kills-92-chadian-soldiers-in-seven-hour-attack (accessed on 1 January 2021).

[13] BBC News, 'Nigeria school attack: Hundreds of boys return home after kidnap ordeal' 18 December 2020 https://www.bbc.com/news/world-africa-55364394 (accessed on 1 January 2021).

[14] Mary Harper, 'Somalia conflict: Al-Shabab "collects more revenue than government"' 26 October 2020 https://www.bbc.com/news/world-africa-54690561 (accessed on 1 January 2021).

[15] BBC News, 'Militant Islamists "behead more than 50" in Mozambique' 9 November 2020 https://www.bbc.com/news/world-africa-54877202 (accessed on 1 January 2021).

[16] Daniel Dickinson "COVID-19: UN chief calls for global ceasefire to focus on 'the true fight of our lives'" UN News, 23 March 2020 https://news.un.org/en/story/2020/03/1059972 (accessed on 25 December 2020).

[17] Sara E Davies, "National Security and Pandemics", UN Chronicle https://www.un.org/en/chronicle/article/national-security-and-pandemics (accessed on 5 November 2020).

Peacebuilding involves a range of measures targeted to reduce the risk of lapsing or relapsing into conflict in countries emerging from conflict by strengthening national capacities at all levels, address key causes of conflict and lay the foundations for sustainable peace and development. These measures include, for example, security sector reform, elections and human rights monitoring and institutional capacity development.

Therefore, this chapter aims at reviewing the risk that pandemics pose to peace and security. It is likely that in countries with weak institutions and legacies of political instability, pandemics can increase political stresses and tensions.[18] This chapter will specifically describe Malawi's experience as a demonstration for the Covid-19 response during the time of the re-election.

Natural disasters and disease have devastating effects on countries. Societies are fractured, economies are affected and rule of law may be compromised or strengthened. Despite the integrated nature and complexity from these events, we mostly see vertical planning in governments and Africa leadership forums that makes it difficult to be responsive to these complex challenges. Therefore, this chapter further aims to review how different jurisdictions responded to Covid-19 and to map out best lessons.

As the world has progressed to high dependence on digital communication, it still is a question whether this could serve as an alternative to interpersonal dialogues. Exploring the feasibility of this alternative is extremely important. Therefore, the chapter also explores virtual approaches as an alternative to peace keeping through the fight of pandemics. Digital communication channels suffer from potential leakage of data and information as well as abuse through disinformation and misinformation. Reliance on virtual platforms for peace keeping negotiations interacts with increasing abuse and mistrust of electronic communication.[19] This is twofold: peacekeeping discussions occur during the times of tension in environments of doubt and mistrust. On the other hand, virtual sessions are easy to infiltrate.

The complexity of infectious diseases means that they present themselves as 'threats without enemies'[20] with sources internal rather than external to the political order that the concept of 'national interest' has traditionally represented to states. This greatly affects citizens and eventually the state itself. In order to appreciate this, we will look at how the concept of 'Human Security' is inextricably connected to the issue of infectious diseases and state survival.

---

[18] Nita Madhav, Ben Oppenheim, Mark Gallivan, Prime Mulembakani, Edward Rubin, and Nathan Wolfe "Pandemics: Risks, Impacts and Mitigation" in Jamison DT, Gelband H, Horton S, et al. (eds.), *Disease Control Priorities: Improving Health and Reducing Poverty. 3rd edition* (Washington DC, The International Bank for Reconstruction and Development / The World Bank, 2017) https://www.ncbi.nlm.nih.gov/books/NBK525 302/ (accessed on 25 December 2020).

[19] Ibid.

[20] Abshire, "US Foreign Policy in the Post Cold War Era," pp. 42–44; Dalby, "Security, Intelligence, the National Interest and the Global Environment," p. 186.

State of Disease—Epidemics and Human Security

The key idea behind human security is the focus on the individual as the primary object of security.[21] More specifically, human security recognizes that an individual's personal preservation and protection emanate not just from safeguarding the state as a single political unit but also from ensuring adequate access to welfare and quality of life.[22]

As Thakur observes, this has a dual aspect:

> Negatively, it refers to freedom from: want, hunger, attack, torture, imprisonment without a free and fair trial, discrimination on spurious grounds, and so on. Positively, it means freedom to: the capacity and opportunity that allows each human being to enjoy life to the fullest without putting constraints upon others engaged in the same pursuit. Putting the two together, human security refers to the quality of life of the people of a society or polity. Anything which degrades their quality of life—demographic pressures, diminished access to or stock of resources, and so on—is a security threat. Conversely, anything which can upgrade their quality of life—economic growth, improved access to resources, social and political empowerment, and so on, is an enhancement of human security.[23]

The argument that epidemics pose a threat to human security rests on the simple proposition that it seriously threatens both the individual and the quality of life that a person is able to attain within a given society, polity or state. The COVID-19 pandemic is transforming into a multidimensional crisis that threatens to stress and erode, in particular, the social contract between individuals and communities with the states that represent, govern and protect them. The phenomenon is world-wide and is increasing the risk of violent conflict and instability. This is especially the case in developing and conflict-affected contexts where the indirect 'downstream' impacts on mortality and humanitarian needs because of Covid-19 may far exceed the immediate impact of the virus itself. Specifically, this occurs in at least five ways.

First and most fundamental, disease kills—far surpassing war as a threat to human life. Covid-19 alone is expected to have killed over 2 million people by January 2021. Second, if left unchecked, disease can undermine public confidence in the state's general custodian function, in the process eroding a polity's

---

[21] Tow, "Linkages Between Traditional Security and Human Security," in William Tow, Ramesh Thakur, and In-Taek Hyun, eds., Asia's Emerging Regional Order: Reconciling Traditional and Human Security, Tokyo: United Nations University Press, 2000, p. 19.

[22] George McLean, "The United Nations and the New Security Agenda," available at http://www.unac.org/canada/security/mclean.html (accessed on 16 January 2021). See also Keith Krause and Michael Williams, "From Strategy to Security: Foundations of Critical Security Studies," in Keith Krause and Michael Williams, eds., Critical Security Studies, Minneapolis: University of Minnesota Press, 1997, p. 43.

[23] Thakur, Ramesh, "From National to Human Security," in Stuart Harris and Andrew Mack, eds., Asia–Pacific Security: The Economics-Politics Nexus, Sydney: Allen and Unwin, 1997, pp. 53–54.

overall governing legitimacy as well as undermining the ability of the state itself to function. When large-scale outbreaks occur, such effects can become particularly acute as the ranks of first responders and medical personnel are decimated, making it doubly difficult for an already stressed government to respond adequately.

Third, disease adversely affects the economic foundation upon which both human and state security depends. The fiscal burden imposed by the HIV/AIDS and Covid-19 epidemic provides a case in point. Given the challenges that many African countries face with weak health systems, the implications of Covid-19 pandemic on public health, peace and security on the continent is dire.

Fourth, disease can have a profound, negative impact on a state's social order, functioning and psyche. Epidemics may also lead to forms of post-traumatic stress. A number of analyses have been undertaken to assess the long-term psychological effects on those who have been continually subjected to poor sanitary conditions and outbreaks of disease. The studies consistently document the extreme emotional stress suffered by these people and the difficulty of integrating them back into 'normal society'.[24]

Fifth, the spread of infectious diseases can act as a catalyst for regional instability. Epidemics can severely undermine defence force capabilities (just as they distort civilian worker productivity). By galvanising mass cross-border population flows and fostering economic problems, they can also help create the type of widespread volatility that can quickly translate into heightened tension both within and between states.

LEGAL INTERVENTIONS/INSTRUMENTS: THE LAW IN FACE OF THE PANDEMIC

As part of strategies to fight the disease, countries closed schools, reduced numbers of expected crowds and only ran essential services. Legal instruments were the basis upon which prevention and containment measures were made and states scaled up the use and enforcement of law as an implementing tool for public health interventions, to varying degrees with varying results. We hereby discuss the legal instruments as categorised below.

In South Africa, the Covid-19 response was based on the Disaster Management Act[25] that mandates the Minister to declare a national state of disaster. The national state of disaster may be in place for a renewable period of three months, the renewal can be for no more than one month at a time.[26] A State of Disaster was declared in late March 2020 and is still in place to date. Among

---

[24] Chalk, Non-Military Security and Global Order, pp. 113–114; D. W. FitzSimons and A. W. Whiteside, "Conflict, War and Public Health," Conflict Studies, Vol. 276, 1994, p. 28.

[25] Disaster Management Act Number 57 of 2002.

[26] Disaster Management Act Number 57 of 2002 section 27(5).

other things, it allows 'the release of personnel of a national organ of state for the rendering of emergency services [...] the regulation of the movement of persons and goods to, from or within the disaster-stricken or threatened area'.

On 29 December 2020, South Africa amended its regulations and imposed an 'Adjusted Alert Level 3' that imposed a curfew between 9 p.m. and 6 p.m., that made the wearing of face masks in public mandatory and restricted attendance to social and faith-based gatherings and political events. Failure to follow the specified prescriptions attracted either a fine or six months imprisonment or both.[27]

Likewise, Kenya has published a series of regulations, rules and guidelines including curfew orders,[28] declarations of infected areas and restrictions of movement,[29] and regulations and subsidiary legislation detailing response measures.[30] The Public Health Act[31] and the Public Order Act[32] have been the primary vehicles for the expression of executive powers during the pandemic. Kenya has criminalised: exposing others to the virus, breaching curfew, failing to wear a mask in public (includes your private car), failing to maintain social distancing and escaping from isolation or quarantine.

On 18 March 2020, the Namibian President declared a state of emergency 'on account of the outbreak of the coronavirus disease'.[33] The declaration of the state of emergency was made following powers granted to the President to declare a state of emergency in circumstances where there is a national disaster, state of national defence or a public emergency threatening the life of the nation or the constitutional order.[34] A state of emergency further allows the president to suspend operation of any rule of common law, statute and fundamental right or freedom protected by the Constitution. The Namibian President can make this declaration and have it in place for at least 30 days without approval of the National Assembly or it can be in effect for a renewable period of six months at a time with a two-thirds majority of the National Assembly's approval.

---

[27] Disaster Management Act, 2002: Amendment of Regulations Issued in terms of section 27(2), Government Gazette of 29 December 2020.

[28] The Public Order (State Curfew) Order, 2020 Legal Notice. Number 36.

[29] The Public Health (COVID-19 Restriction of Movement of Persons and Related Measures) Rules, 2020 Kenya Gazette Supplement Number 41 of 6 April 2020.

[30] The Public Health (Prevention, Control and Suppression of Covid-19) Rules, 2020, Kenya Gazette Supplement Number 39 of 3 April 2020.

[31] The Public Health Act, 2012, Chapter 242 of the Laws of Kenya.

[32] The Public Order Act, 2012, Chapter 56 of the Laws of Kenya.

[33] Proclamation by the President of Namibia, Government Gazette of the Republic of Namibia Number 7148, 18 March 2020.

[34] Article 26 (1) of the Constitution of the Sovereign and Independent Republic of Namibia.

On 20th March 2020 the Malawian President declared a state of disaster pursuant to Disaster Preparedness and Relief Act[35] that allows the President to declare that a state of disaster exists in an area where it appears that:

> [A]any disaster is of such a nature and extent that extraordinary measures are necessary to assist and protect the persons affected or likely to be affected by the disaster in any area within Malawi or that circumstances are likely to arise making such measures necessary.[36]

The President is required to inform the National Assembly of this declaration at their next meeting.[37] A state of disaster may be distinguished from a state of emergency in that a state of emergency can be declared under circumstances of war or threat of war and/or widespread natural disaster.[38] A state of disaster may be in place for three months and can be extended for three months at a time by way of notice in the gazette. In March 2020 the Minister of Health promulgated subsidiary regulation on the containment and prevention of Covid-19.[39] Subsequently, the Minister of Health has promulgated subsidiary legislation on 9 April 2020, 7 August 2020[40] and 18 January 2021.[41]

STORM AND STRESS—SELECTED COUNTRY EXPERIENCES

Africa's Covid-19 crisis should be seen, not as a generalised pandemic but as different national and subnational epidemics that will play out differently depending on demographic and social factors, which is why understanding individual national epidemics is so important.

Most African countries have used the police and military to help enforce Covid-19 containment measures. As early as April 2020, the United Nations human rights chief lamented that there have been 'toxic lockdown cultures' in some countries and cited numerous countries where police officers were being investigated for causing deaths in implementing lockdowns, using rubber

---

[35] Disaster Preparedness and Relief Act Number 27 of 1991 [Cap 33:05 of the Laws of Malawi].

[36] Section 32 of the Disaster Preparedness and Relief Act Number 27 of 1991 [Cap 33:05 of the Laws of Malawi].

[37] Section 33 of the Disaster Preparedness and Relief Act Number 27 of 1991 [Cap 33:05 of the Laws of Malawi].

[38] Section (46) (4) (b) of Republic of Malawi (Constitution) Act.

[39] Public Health (Corona Virus Prevention, Containment and Management) Rules, 2020, 9 April 2020, Malawi Government Notice Number 5.

[40] Public Health (Corona Virus and Covid-19) (Prevention, Containment and Management) Rules, 2020, 7th August 2020, Malawi Government Notice Number 48.

[41] Public Health (Corona Virus and Covid-19) (Prevention, Containment and Management) (Amendment) Rules, 2021, 18 January 2021, Malawi Government Notice Number 2.

bullets, tear gas, water bombs and whips to enforce social distancing as well as rape, use of firearms and corruption.[42] The disruption to peace by the disease is not from disease alone, it can be compounded by other factors such as fear, political processes and the relationship between the state and society. Some of these factors will be discussed below.

Malawi registered its first Covid-19 case on 2 April 2020. At the time, then opposition parties had successfully challenged in court the results of a presidential election held in May 2019 for having too many irregularities. Hence, this was right in the middle of the court mandated 150 days for the preparation of the fresh presidential elections. The government then applied that implementation of the Court Order be stayed in light of the rising number of Covid-19 cases. The Courts ruled that the re-run ought to happen regardless. Although Malawi has been a multiparty democracy with constitutionally guaranteed rights since 1994, the country has faced low levels of economic growth and rising inequality, rampant allegations of corruption and nepotism and affronts to the rule of law.

Other than in Malawi, the Covid-19 pandemic found countries like Ghana, Burundi, Tanzania, Ethiopia and Burkina Faso as they prepared for elections. Like all other governance systems, the electoral systems in these countries suffered and needed quick adaptation to deliver the expected else creating a huge risk to continuity of democracy in many countries.

Ghana's preparations for its December 2020 presidential and parliamentary elections were impeded by Covid-19. Despite legal challenges and public protests that pre-election voter registration could expose registrants to Covid-19 infection, the National Electoral Commission went forward with the registration exercise. Since then, reports of overcrowding and lack of adherence to Covid-19 protocols at voter registration centres, and politically motivated violence in some locales, have raised concerns of a spike in Covid-19 infections. Although the government begun to ease pandemic-related lockdown measures, it kept restrictions on mass political rallies and gatherings. While Ghana has a solid record of election fidelity, some observers were concerned that the incumbent government was exploiting Covid-19 mitigation measures to disadvantage the opposition in the lead-up to the December elections.[43]

Before the general elections in Burundi in May 2020, the Burundi government announced a 14-day quarantine requirement for any observers

---

[42] Aljazeera, 'UN raises alarm about police brutality in COVID-19 lockdowns' 28 April 2020 https://www.aljazeera.com/news/2020/4/28/un-raises-alarm-about-police-brutality-in-covid-19-lockdowns (accessed on 1 January 2021).

[43] Ossei Baffour Frimpong, Rigobert Minani Bihuzo SJ and Richmond Commodore, "The COVID-19 Pandemic in Africa: Impact, Responses, and Lessons from Ghana, the Democratic Republic of the Congo, and Rwanda" *Wilson Center—Africa Program Occasional Paper* (2020) https://www.wilsoncenter.org/sites/default/files/media/uploads/documents/The%20COVID-19%20Pandemic%20in%20Africa%20-%20Impact%20Responses%20and%20Lessons.pdf (accessed on 25 December 2020).

entering the country due to the coronavirus pandemic. Consequently, election observers were not able to follow up the electoral process because the quarantine period would elapse two days after the elections were held.[44]

Also, in Guinea a referendum was held in a context of general unrest. The constitutional change referendum was believed to be a way for the President to seek more presidential mandates even though he has already served twice. Opposition parties boycotted the election and independent election observers were absent.[45]

The Covid-19 response has also met a citizenry that does not trust that the government response to the pandemic is adequate, nor do they trust the credibility of the information being provided by their respective governments. In August 2020, the sitting President of Mali was overthrown in a military coup. The coup occurred following calls for the resignation of the president and accountability for the resources allocated to the Covid-19 response. There was a strong belief that, in order to receive more international Covid-19 support from development partners, the number of Covid-19 cases was being bloated.[46]

In Uganda, citizens, in conjunction with opposition leaders, believe that the State is unable to manage the Covid-19 response. As a result, there have been widespread demonstrations against the government's Covid-19 response.[47] The demonstrations have been marred with arrests and allegations of police brutality against protestors.[48] In Malawi, the pandemic tested, largely unused, legal instruments that caused inconsistencies in application of their provisions during a political climate that garnered societal mistrust to both public health and the associated legal interventions.

As the prevalence of Covid-19 became imminent in Malawi, with neighbouring countries registering increasing numbers of infections, the State

[44] Roos Haer and Leila Demarest, "Covid-19 in Africa: Turning a Health Crisis into a Human Security Threat?" (2020) https://openaccess.leidenuniv.nl/bitstream/handle/1887/136599/%5b15548597_-_Peace_Economics%2c_Peace_Science_and_Public_Policy%5d_COVID-19_in_Africa__Turning_a_Health_Crisis_into_a_Human_Security_Threat_.pdf?sequence=1 (accessed on 25 December 2020).

[45] Roos Haer and Leila Demarest, "Covid-19 in Africa: Turning a Health Crisis into a Human Security Threat?" (2020) https://openaccess.leidenuniv.nl/bitstream/handle/1887/136599/%5b15548597_-_Peace_Economics%2c_Peace_Science_and_Public_Policy%5d_COVID-19_in_Africa__Turning_a_Health_Crisis_into_a_Human_Security_Threat_.pdf?sequence=1 (accessed on 25 December 2020).

[46] The New Humanitarian, 'What's behind the mass protests in Mali?' 10 July 2020 https://www.thenewhumanitarian.org/news/2020/07/10/Mali-protests-Keita-Dicko (accessed on 4 January 2021).

[47] Halima Athumani, 'Uganda's main opposition Leaders Unite, Call for Peaceful Protests' 15 June 2020 https://www.voanews.com/africa/ugandas-main-opposition-leaders-unite-call-peaceful-protests (accessed on 4 January 2021).

[48] BBC News, 'Bobi Wine protests: Shoot to kill defended by Uganda minister' 20 November 2020 https://www.bbc.com/news/world-africa-55016519 (accessed on 4 January 2021).

President declared a state of disaster on 20 March 2020. On 9 April 2020, the Minister of Health promulgated subsidiary legislation for the containment of Corona virus that among other things, allowed the Minister of Health/ President to impose a lockdown which restricted the movement of persons, imposed maximum numbers of people to attend public gatherings and imposed a curfew.[49] Prior to commencement of the lockdown, private individuals and civil society organisations obtained an injunction from the High Court in Malawi preventing implementation of the lockdown due what they claimed were inadequate social and economic measures to protect the citizenry from the impact of the lockdown.[50] The High Court, sitting as a Constitutional Court, later found that the rules as promulgated were unconstitutional.[51] On 7 August 2020, the Minister of Health, promulgated yet another subsidiary legislation for the prevention, containment and management of Covid-19.[52] Again, this was challenged and on 24 December 2020, the High Court granted an injunction to musicians who challenged the restrictions on numbers for public attendances.

In Kenya, Libya and Nigeria there are widespread beliefs that Covid-19 does not exist or that the statistics are being inflated in order to allow for embezzlement of public funds. In Libya specifically, the government's attempts at dispelling the belief have been met with scorn and have concretised the belief that members of the government are abusing public funds and are inept.[53]

Despite the ongoing public awareness campaigns on Covid-19 in some African states, doubts have been raised on many aspects of the Covid-19 response. Questions have been raised on the efficacy of masks, stay at home orders, curfews and social distancing.[54] The doubt being shed on public health interventions is exhibited through non-compliance with the regulations. As

---

[49] Public Health (Corona Virus Prevention, Containment and Management) Rules, 2020, 9 April 2020, Malawi Government Notice Number 5.

[50] The State (on application of Esther Cecilia Kathumba, Monica Chang'anamuno, Church and Society Programme the Livingstonia Synod of the Church of Central Africa Presbyterian & Prophet David F Mbewe) v President of Malawi, Ministry of the Malawi Government Responsible for Health, Inspector General of the Malawi Police Service, Commander of the Malawi Defence Force, Attorney General & Malawi Council of Churches -High Court of Malawi, Constitutional Reference Number 1 of 2020.

[51] Ibid.

[52] Public Health (Corona Virus and Covid-19) (Prevention, Containment and Management) Rules, 2020, 7 August 2020, Malawi Government Notice Number 48.

[53] Mercy Corps, 'Advancing Peace in A Changed World: Covid-19 effects on conflict and how to respond' September 2020 https://reliefweb.int/sites/reliefweb.int/files/resources/Advancing_Peace_COVID-19_and_Conflict_Sept-2020_0.pdf (accessed on 3 January 2020).

[54] Klaus Dodds, Vanesa Castan Broto, Klaus Detterbeck, Martin Jones, Virginie Mamadouh, Maano Ramutsindela, Monica Varsanyi, David Wachsmuth and Chih Yuan Woon, "The COVID-19 pandemic: Territorial, political and governance dimensions of the crisis" *Territory, Politics, Governance* (2020) 8(3), 289–298.

a result, there have been allegations of heavy handedness by state security agents in enforcing Covid-19 response measures. It is also worth noting that most Covid-19 prevention and containment measures bear penal sanctions. Enforcement of adherence to the rules has been placed in the hands of the police and/or the military.

Unfortunately, some jurisdictions have seen increases in human rights injustices and/excesses by the police and/or the military due to the criminalisation of non-adherence to Covid-19 response measures.[55] Deaths and injuries resulting directly from actions by State security personnel have been reported in a number of African countries including Nigeria, Zimbabwe, Kenya and South Africa.[56] Social scientists warned that these measures carry with them societal ramifications including spikes in domestic violence, child abuse and mental health crises.[57]

Despite these statistics, the military is best placed to mobilise quickly and has both the personnel and machinery to set up setting up relief centres and to monitor compliance to Covid-19 response measures. This is likely to be extended to orderly distribution of the vaccine as well. One of the factors contributing to the successful containment of the 2014 West African Ebola outbreak was cohesive international relations and diplomacy, combined with military assistance.[58]

On the other hand, armed groups may also capitalise on the existence of the pandemic to scale up operations. While it might be harder for cross-border recruitment for armed groups, it might have been easier to recruit and radicalise vulnerable people during the Covid-19 response. Pandemics may contain regional expansionism, generate new military roles or force countries to turn inward, they also have dramatic impacts on other aspects of international relations and security. For example, in August 2020, the military coup that took place in Mali following protests against the management of Covid-19 were

[55] News Wires, "Security forces use violent tactics to enforce Africa's coronavirus shutdowns," France24, April 1, 2020 https://www.france24.com/en/20200401-security-for ces-use-violent-tactics-to-enforce-africa-s-coronavirus-shutdowns. (accessed on 16 January 2021).

[56] News Wires, "Security forces use violent tactics to enforce Africa's coronavirus shutdowns," France24, April 1, 2020 https://www.france24.com/en/20200401-security-for ces-use-violent-tactics-to-enforce-africa-s-coronavirus-shutdowns (accessed on 16 January 2021).

[57] Klaus Dodds, Vanesa Castan Broto, Klaus Detterbeck, Martin Jones, Virginie Mamadouh, Maano Ramutsindela, Monica Varsanyi, David Wachsmuth and Chih Yuan Woon, "The COVID-19 pandemic: territorial, political and governance dimensions of the crisis" *Territory, Politics, Governance* (2020) 8(3), 289–298.

[58] Sebastian Kevany, Deon Canyon, Michael Baker and Robert Ostergard "The Nexus Between the Covid-19 Pandemic, International Relations, and International Security" Security Nexus: Daniel K. Inouye Asia–Pacific Center for Security Studies (2020) doi:10.2307/resrep24856, https://www.jstor.org/stable/resrep24856 (accessed on 23 December 2020).

intertwined with protests demanding the resignation of the President.[59] The unrest in Mali spilled over to neighbouring states of Burkina Faso and Niger, causing unrest to the entire region.[60]

THE CHALLENGES OF MAINTAINING PEACE DURING PANDEMICS AND EPIDEMICS

A development that we are currently seeing in some African countries is that the Covid-19 crisis has disrupted registration, campaigns and other activities related to elections. While some countries have held elections amid the pandemic, others postponed them.[61] Between February and June 2020, 64 countries postponed national and subnational elections, 21 countries postponed national elections and referendums and 30 countries held national or subnational elections as planned, 14 of these held national elections or referendums.[62] In Africa, 11 countries—Botswana, Chad, Ethiopia, Gabon, Gambia, Kenya, Liberia, Nigeria, South Africa, Uganda and Zimbabwe—postponed their elections, while Burundi, Malawi, Benin, Guinea, Cameroon and Mali held theirs as originally scheduled.[63]

The postponement of elections has significantly shaped Ethiopian politics. Two weeks after the first case of Covid-19 was detected, the Ethiopian authorities declared a state of emergency, and parliamentary elections to elect the Prime Minister, initially scheduled for August 2020, were postponed until 'the pandemic is over'.[64] There are escalating tensions between political factions, and regions that threatens to reverse significant democratic gains that the country has recently made.

[59] Mercy Corps, 'Advancing Peace in A Changed World: Covid-19 effects on conflict and how to respond' September 2020, https://reliefweb.int/sites/reliefweb.int/files/resources/Advancing_Peace_COVID-19_and_Conflict_Sept-2020_0.pdf (accessed on 3 January 2020).

[60] VOA, 'West Africa Mediator Urges End to Mali Protests' 11 August 2020 https://www.voanews.com/africa/west-africa-mediator-urges-end-mali-protests (accessed on 4 January 2020).

[61] Roos Haer and Leila Demarest, "Covid-19 in Africa: Turning a Health Crisis into a Human Security Threat?" (2020) https://openaccess.leidenuniv.nl/bitstream/handle/1887/136599/%5b15548597_-_Peace_Economics%2c_Peace_Science_and_Public_Policy%5d_COVID-19_in_Africa__Turning_a_Health_Crisis_into_a_Human_Security_Threat_.pdf?sequence=1 (accessed on 25 December 2020).

[62] Institute for Democracy and Electoral Assistance, Impact of COVID-19 on Elections (May 2020), 5 June 2020 https://www.idea.int/news-media/media/infographic-global-overview-covid-19-impact-elections-may-2020 (accessed on 25 December 2020).

[63] Hela Slim, "Electoral process in Africa: The impact of COVID-19 and challenges for the EU" *European View* (2020) 19(2), 212–221.

[64] Roos Haer and Leila Demarest, "Covid-19 in Africa: Turning a Health Crisis into a Human Security Threat?" (2020) https://openaccess.leidenuniv.nl/bitstream/handle/1887/136599/%5b15548597_-_Peace_Economics%2c_Peace_Science_and_Public_Policy%5d_COVID-19_in_Africa__Turning_a_Health_Crisis_into_a_Human_Security_Threat_.pdf?sequence=1 (accessed on 25 December 2020).

In electoral contexts, outbreak response measures such as quarantines have sparked violence and tension between states and citizens.[65] In the Democratic Republic of Congo, the Ebola Virus Disease (EVD) outbreak roused suspicion of electoral tampering and caused discontent in certain circles of the country.[66] This led to distrust, leading to attacks on EVD support personnel and facilities. It is also worth noting that EVD spread reduced peacekeepers' presence through patrols, leading to loss of valuable intelligence, apart from allowing illegal armed groups to recuperate and later roam almost freely in the North Eastern part of that country. EVD was on rampage in 2014 when it found Liberia in an election year. At the time, the country was war-torn and facing a political and security crisis.[67]

Overall, Covid-19 measures were heavily politicised, militarised and legalised.[68] This created a protectionist international order that affected diplomatic relations, international travel and weakened inter-state relationships.[69] Additionally, some countries were rated to be more infectious than others, and travel bans were effected for countries with higher numbers of Covid-19 cases. Even within countries, doubts were cast on State responses to the pandemic as bearing motives other than disease control. Further, there is increased stigmatisation across groups and violent attacks against healthcare workers, immigrants and citizens suspected of being infected with the virus.[70]

[65] Nita Madhav, Ben Oppenheim, Mark Gallivan, Prime Mulembakani, Edward Rubin, and Nathan Wolfe "Pandemics: Risks, Impacts and Mitigation" in Jamison DT, Gelband H, Horton S, et al. (eds.), *Disease Control Priorities: Improving Health and Reducing Poverty. 3rd edition* (Washington, DC, The International Bank for Reconstruction and Development / The World Bank, 2017) https://www.ncbi.nlm.nih.gov/books/NBK525 302/ (accessed on 25 December 2020).

[66] Roos Haer and Leila Demarest, "Covid-19 in Africa: Turning a Health Crisis into a Human Security Threat?" (2020) https://openaccess.leidenuniv.nl/bitstream/han dle/1887/136599/%5b15548597_-_Peace_Economics%2c_Peace_Science_and_Public_Policy%5d_COVID-19_in_Africa__Turning_a_Health_Crisis_into_a_Human_Security_Thr eat_.pdf?sequence=1 (accessed on 25 December 2020).

[67] Hela Slim, "Electoral process in Africa: The impact of COVID-19 and challenges for the EU" *European View* (2020) 19(2), 212–221.

[68] Klaus Dodds, Vanesa Castan Broto, Klaus Detterbeck, Martin Jones, Virginie Mamadouh, Maano Ramutsindela, Monica Varsanyi, David Wachsmuth & Chih Yuan Woon (2020) "The COVID-19 pandemic: Territorial, political and governance dimensions of the crisis" *Territory, Politics, Governance* 8(3), 289 298, 10.1080/21622671.2020.1771022.

[69] Sebastian Kevany, Deon Canyon, Michael Baker and Robert Ostergard "The Nexus Between the Covid-19 Pandemic, International Relations, and International Security" Security Nexus: Daniel K. Inouye Asia–Pacific Center for Security Studies (2020) doi:10.2307/resrep24856, https://www.jstor.org/stable/resrep24856 (accessed on 23 December 2020).

[70] Mercy Corps, 'Advancing Peace in A Changed World: Covid-19 effects on conflict and how to respond' September 2020 https://reliefweb.int/sites/reliefweb.int/files/resour ces/Advancing_Peace_COVID-19_and_Conflict_Sept-2020_0.pdf (accessed on 3 January 2020).

The travel bans make it increasingly difficult for consultations and discussions that would normally be the case in peace negotiations. In June 2020, two months before the military coup, the Economic Community of West African States (ECOWAS) sent a delegation to Mali to negotiate with the sitting president and opposition leaders. Those discussions were not successful and eventually the coup took place in August 2020. Thereafter, the ECOWAS delegation was in constant negotiation with the military leaders and this resulted in the transition of power from the military leaders to a civilian leader. Social cohesion is disrupted by the threat of the disease that prohibits travel for in-person discussions. As was seen in Mali, the importance of in-person discussions for peace negotiations cannot be overemphasised.

The Covid-19 pandemic could also potentially worsen existing group tensions. Especially marginalised groups, such as migrants and refugees, may be the victims of stereotyping and become characterised as being the main carriers of the disease.[71] In Nigeria, restrictions on movement as a Covid-19 response mechanism has increased pressure on and competition for land and water. There has been escalated violence between pastoralists and farmers who both believe that the other is spreading Covid-19.[72]

In the DRC, pandemic crisis management has become a field for political competition. Competing political actors within the ruling coalition are using the crisis to weaken each other, resulting in contradictions within the national response and sparking internal political wrangling. This, together with Covid-related food price hikes and border closures, could further aggravate the country's fragile stability.

Other conflict-affected or post-conflict African countries, including Burkina Faso, Mali, Niger, Nigeria, Cameroon, Libya, Somalia and South Sudan, have all reported cases of Covid-19. Should these governments redeploy their troops to deal with public health crises as a result of the coronavirus, disruptions are likely to occur with respect to counterterrorism activities and contribution of troops to peacekeeping missions.

Another concern is the possibility of troop deployment becoming another channel for transmitting Covid-19 within countries and across borders. This factor lends itself to the need for a regional African approach to address the pandemic.

As the numbers of persons infected and affected by Covid-19 grew, countries curtailed civil and political rights such as the right to move, to assemble,

---

[71] Roos Haer and Leila Demarest, "Covid-19 in Africa: Turning a Health Crisis into a Human Security Threat?" (2020) https://openaccess.leidenuniv.nl/bitstream/han dle/1887/136599/%5b15548597_-_Peace_Economics%2c_Peace_Science_and_Public_ Policy%5d_COVID-19_in_Africa__Turning_a_Health_Crisis_into_a_Human_Security_Thr eat_.pdf?sequence=1 (accessed on 25 December 2020).

[72] Mercy Corps, 'Advancing Peace in A Changed World: Covid-19 effects on conflict and how to respond' September 2020, https://reliefweb.int/sites/reliefweb.int/files/resour ces/Advancing_Peace_COVID-19_and_Conflict_Sept-2020_0.pdf (accessed on 3 January 2020).

to demonstrate and to attend religious services.[73] Most of these measures were met with strong public support following advice from both public health and legal experts. Some quarters, however, expressed concern on the severity of the measures, the accompanying implementation measures and the lack of predictability on the time periods that the measures would be in effect.

It is important to note that in most countries states of emergency/states of disaster cannot be in effect for unspecified periods without parliamentary approval. For parliaments where the one political party holds a majority, there is a huge risk that a state of emergency/disaster can last for too long a period and become the new norm.[74] The use of states of emergencies and/or disaster could potentially be used by opportunistic governments to tame the populace by withholding fundamental rights and freedoms. It has been acknowledged that direct and indirect responses to Covid-19 feed into and trigger pre-existing patterns of inequality and exclusion. At its heart, Covid-19 presents challenges to human rights both in the relationships between states and their citizens, and in the horizontal relationships between citizens and groups in affected societies.

There is potential for emerging conflict on one hand, and of greater justice and human rights on the other. The pandemic and the specific risks associated with the transmission and contagion of the virus forces a constant, fraught and competing balance between rights and norms. Parliamentary democracies, therefore, ought to think about how and when they recalibrate the relationship between the executive and legislature as not doing so could result in permanence of declarations of emergencies/disasters which could be permanence in curtailed rights and freedoms.

In East Asia, Europe and North America, lockdown policies are designed with one of the three exit strategies in mind: 'hold' which consists of reducing transmission to near zero; 'build' which is buying time to build up hospital capacity to cope with a second wave of infections and 'shield' which is developing methods for protecting vulnerable populations from infection when restrictions are lifted.[75] African countries may not have determined which exit strategies are best, how to implement them and the implications of success or failure in their exit plans.

---

[73] Klaus Dodds, Vanesa Castan Broto, Klaus Detterbeck, Martin Jones, Virginie Mamadouh, Maano Ramutsindela, Monica Varsanyi, David Wachsmuth and Chih Yuan Woon, "The COVID-19 pandemic: Territorial, political and governance dimensions of the crisis" *Territory, Politics, Governance* (2020) 8(3), 289–298.

[74] Klaus Dodds, Vanesa Castan Broto, Klaus Detterbeck, Martin Jones, Virginie Mamadouh, Maano Ramutsindela, Monica Varsanyi, David Wachsmuth and Chih Yuan Woon, "The COVID-19 pandemic: Territorial, political and governance dimensions of the crisis" *Territory, Politics, Governance* (2020) 8(3), 289–298.

[75] Alex de Waal, "Governance Implications of Epidemic Disease in Africa: Updating the Agenda for COVID-19" Conflict Research Programme. Research Memo (April 2020) London school of Economics and Political Science.

FEATURES OF PEACE RESILIENCE DURING PANDEMICS

Below are some of the factors that may help maintain peace, law and order in the face of a ravaging pandemic of natural disaster.

Regional Coalitions

The importance of regional coalitions is especially important during pandemics for numerous reasons, it provides a governance mechanism for stability and neutrality in the region. As was seen in Mali, mediation was undertaken by ECOWAS and when that failed, discussions continued through the military coup to the transfer of power to a civilian government. The involvement of ECOWAS also brought peace to the region. Additionally, regional coalitions are necessary for social and economic factors such as continued movement of essential goods and services such as medication and relief packages as well as repatriation of citizens who might be facing xenophobia in foreign territories.

Provision of Socio-Economic Support

A recurring theme in this discussion has been the lack of social and economic provision. In low-income economies, it is likely that pandemic response measures will not be adhered to where social and economic measures have not been but in place to consider an economy that has slowed down. The rationale for poor people's behaviour is that they need to earn a daily income, so they would rather take their chances with the lottery of infection than surrender to the certainty of hunger. It is, therefore, important to ensure that citizens have access to healthcare, food, water and shelter. Where these are not provided for, it is unlikely that response measures to pandemics will be adhered to and it is likely to breed resentment and eventually uprising in a populace.

Transparency and Good Governance

The common thread that can be seen is that many citizens do not trust officials in power. Even historically, colonial governments' policies of enforcing quarantine (to control cholera or relapsing fever) or population relocation (for example, away from tsetse-infested areas) were deeply resented, as were the medical screenings imposed by South Africa's mining companies on migrant labourers. There have been lamentations that Covid-19 is being used as an excuse to circumvent democratic processes, to embezzle public funds, to shield the incompetence of public officials and to stop certain religious practices. This needs to be aligned with Agenda 2063 which advocates for entrenched democratic values, practices and respect for universal principles of human rights, justice and the rule of law.[76]

Legal mechanisms have been at the fore of the Covid-19 response with countries either employing states of emergencies or declaring states of disaster. The speed at which subsidiary legislation has been promulgated and enforced has similarly been astounding. States would therefore have better cooperation from their citizenry if there were more transparent about the use of resources, and the thought processes behind the measures employed. This would help reduce perceptions that governments are trying to repurpose emergency powers just to perpetuate their grip on power. Decisions that are made with the involvement of the citizenry, through active engagement and not rubberstamping, are more likely to succeed in their implementation.

Covid-19 policy responses call for unique changes to traditional roles of security actors threatening increased state-sponsored violence. Whether it is the armed services, UN peacekeeping, public law enforcement, border guards or custom authorities or civil defence groups or private security providers, different security actors have assumed or been given some new and unfamiliar roles during the crisis.[77] In contexts where authorities have or will declare states of emergency or martial law, the prevailing quality of security sector governance and the trust of the population in their various security providers will largely influence the levels of trust and/or conflict between the state and society. This is particularly acute in situations where there is already active conflict or where the levels of trust in security services is low.

The Importance of Embedding Trust in Health Responses

Trust is rooted simultaneously in the issues of legitimacy, accountability and equity or fairness on one hand and in the quality of services on the other. This is as true of state health systems as it is of criminal justice systems. Lessons from Ebola epidemics in West Africa (2014–2016) and in the Democratic Republic of Congo (2018 to present) show the consequences of failure to integrate trust into health responses.

Peacebuilding approaches need to be embedded into technical health responses as well as broader socio-economic responses to Covid-19. This is key to both their technical effectiveness but also to mitigating potential broader conflict and ensuring security. This is aside from specific and relevant peacebuilding work that may work on sources of misinformation surrounding the

---

[76] African Union, Agenda 2063 Framework Document "The Africa We Want" September 2015.

[77] Geneva Centre for Security Sector Governance (DCAF), 'Impact of COVID-19 on Security Sector Governance' (DCAF 2020) https://dcaf.ch/sites/default/files/publications/documents/Covid19_BN_DCAF_0.pdf (accessed on 15 January 2021).

pandemic and addressing lack of trust of health care providers through trusted local intermediaries.

Since the state is often the central provider of health care, and often distrusted in many conflict-affected settings, the integration of peacebuilding approaches into technical health responses in order to realise greater trust is important. If trust is not embedded into health responses, there is a significant risk of coercive measures that are poorly understood or delivered with little sensitivity to local customs and needs resulting in social unrest in turn which can undermine the effectiveness of the technical health response and spread the epidemic further.

Conclusion—Adaptation for Peace Resilience and Effective Response Mechanisms

The pandemic's impact is a factor compounding the existing stresses on Africa's governing institutions. It is unlikely that the illness and death caused by Covid-19 will in themselves be a cause for governance disruption or state crisis. More concerning is that the fear of social breakdown or governance collapse will cause governments to enact repressive measures aimed at regime survival. The economic recession, fiscal crises and especially the squeeze on regime political funding are likely to intensify transactional survival politics at the expense of public goods.

Conflict and violence are the single biggest impediments to development and to the fulfilment of the Sustainable Development Goals (SDGs) and Agenda 2063. If tensions over scarce food, a breakdown in civic trust, or rumours about the virus fuel inter-ethnic violence, the core efforts to stem the spread of the virus will be undermined, and progress towards the SDGs will be reversed. This not only calls for parallel and continued investment in peacebuilding efforts and approaches as prevention but also requires the response efforts in all sectors to go beyond being 'conflict sensitive' and to become more proactively and systemically 'peace responsive'.

The Covid-19 pandemic brought Africa's major confrontation between public health laws and a public health crisis. This was coupled with numerous societal factors that made reception of and implementation of Covid-19 responses difficult and in some cases deadly. We believe the policy directions suggested above would allow states to better prepare for pandemics without affecting long-negotiated peace or losing any gains made in trying to achieve it.

The Africa Centre for Disease Control and Prevention (Africa CDC) is well positioned to provide technical tools and measures that can be adapted to ensure that the contextual dynamics in individual African countries are taken into account in all Covid-19 mitigation responses to address its adverse effects on populations already facing severe socio-economic inequalities.

PART IV

Perennial Problems to Peace and Security in Africa

CHAPTER 16

Protection of Human and People's Rights in Africa

Gloria David Phiri and Chikondi M. Mandala

INTRODUCTION

As a direct

reaction towards events leading up to and occurring during the Second World War, the Charter of the United Nations (UN) and the Universal Declaration of Human Rights (UDHR) were adopted in 1945 and 1948, respectively. These documents formed the basis of the international human rights movement and systems we know today.[1]

Prior to this, human rights were affairs between an individual and the state often attracting administrative sanctions against the offending state. The UN Charter and UDHR shifted the focus as the world acknowledged cruel acts against humanity done in the Second World War.[2] The international community came together and vowed never to allow the atrocities conducted in this

---

[1] Manfred O Hinz, "Human rights between universalism and cultural relativism? The need for anthropological jurisprudence in the globalizing world" in Anton Bosl & Joseph Diescho (eds), Human Rights in Africa: Legal Perspectives on their Protection and Promotion (Macmillan Education Namibia, 2009), pp. 3–32.

[2] Kabange Nkongolo Christian-Junior, "Protection of Human Rights in Africa: African Human Rights in a Comparative Perspective", Droit Congolais, n.d., available at https://www.leganet.cd/Doctrine.textes/DroitPublic/DH/ProtectionofHR.Kabange.htm (accessed 12 January 2021).

G. D. Phiri (✉) · C. M. Mandala
Lilongwe, Malawi

© The Author(s), under exclusive license to Springer Nature
Switzerland AG 2022
D. Kuwali (ed.), *The Palgrave Handbook of Sustainable Peace and Security in Africa*, https://doi.org/10.1007/978-3-030-82020-6_16

275

war to be repeated. The UN Charter was put in place to function as a road map to ensure the upholding of human rights to all people in the world.

Most current members of the UN were not present during the drafting of the Charter due to the yoke of colonialism.[3] More so, the adoption of the Charter did not stop Apartheid in South Africa that was operational and thriving during the enactment of both the UN Charter and the UDHR and eventually ended in 1992. The UN Charter and UDHR had no effect on the genocide in Rwanda in 1994, the abduction of Chibok schoolchildren by the Boko Haram in Nigeria in 2014, terrorist attacks in Kenya between 2011 and 2014 and Mozambique insurgency from 2017.

As early as 1963, African leaders noted that the international human rights framework did not support Africa's issues, such as freedom from European colonial rule. The Organisation of African Unity (OAU) proposed an intergovernmental continental organisation of African nations for the 'promotion of solidarity among African states, improved quality of life for Africans, a promise to defend the sovereignty of African states, and eradication of colonialism in all its forms'.[4]

Unfortunately, the OAU was considered vague, had limited reference to human rights and focussed more on sovereignty, welfare, socio-economic concerns, African unity and internal affairs. There was limited mention of human rights and therefore a lack of accountability and effort to exalt human rights between, often autocratic, heads of state and systematic human rights violations by regimes.[5]

These deficiencies led to the creation of the African Union (AU) in 2001 which is focussed on the union of African peoples as opposed to African leaders as was the OAU. The AU has a comprehensive governance structure that puts both civil and political rights, and socio-economic rights, at the fore. This is the basis of Africa's current human rights protection framework.

---

[3] Manfred O Hinz, "Human rights between universalism and cultural relativism? The need for anthropological jurisprudence in the globalizing world" in Anton Bosl & Joseph Diescho (eds), Human Rights in Africa: Legal Perspectives on their Protection and Promotion (Macmillan Education Namibia, 2009), pp. 3–32.

[4] Alys Beverton, 'Organization of African Unity (1963–2002)', Blackpast, 10 May 2009, available at: https://www.blackpast.org/global-african-history/organization-african-unity-1963-2002/ (accessed 23 March 2021).

[5] Kabange Nkongolo Christian-Junior, "Protection of Human Rights in Africa: African Human Rights in a Comparative Perspective", Droit Congolais, n.d., available at: https://www.leganet.cd/Doctrine.textes/DroitPublic/DH/ProtectionofHR.Kabange.htm (accessed 12 January 2021).

HUMAN RIGHTS DEFINED

Human rights are rights one has because they are a human being.[6] Human rights are rights inherent to all human beings, regardless of race, sex, nationality, ethnicity, language, region or any other status.[7] There are a myriad of human rights issues prevalent in our world, from domestic violence, terrorism, the suppression of religion and freedom of conscience, child trafficking and prostitution, police brutality and state sanctioned abuse that remain at the fore of our discussions.

The protection of human rights is enhanced when two conditions are met, namely: victims can seek remedies when their human rights have been violated and individuals and organisations are able to advocate, campaign or speak on behalf of victims and survivors of human rights violations.[8]

As we delve into the discussion of the protection of human rights in Africa, this chapter will set out the human rights landscape in Africa, discuss contemporary human rights issues affecting Africa and potential solutions and will conclude by making recommendations on how to strengthen human rights protections in Africa.

THE HUMAN RIGHTS LANDSCAPE IN AFRICA

The African continent has a comprehensive human rights system based on the African Charter on Human and Peoples' Rights (the Banjul Charter) that is interpreted by the African Commission on Human and People's Rights, and whose judicial seat is the African Court on Human and People's Rights.[9]

CONTINENTAL HUMAN RIGHTS INSTRUMENTS

The main international human rights instrument spanning the continent is the African Charter on Human and Peoples' Rights (the Banjul Charter). It came into force in October 1986[10] as a direct response to widespread despotic

---

[6] Jack Donnelly, *Universal Human Rights in Theory and Practice*, Cornell University Press, 2013, JSTOR, available at: www.jstor.org/stable/10.7591/j.ctt1xx5q2 (accessed 14 March 2021).

[7] United Nations, 'Human Rights' https://www.un.org/en/global-issues/human-rights (accessed 23 March 2021).

[8] Remy N. Lumbu, *Compendium on the Legal Protection of Human Rights Defenders in Africa* (Pretoria: Pretoria University Law Press, 2018).

[9] African Union, Protocol to the African Charter on Human and Peoples Rights - Establishment of an African Court on Human and Peoples Rights, (1998) available at: https://au.int/en/treaties/protocol-african-charter-human-andpeoples-rights-establishment-african-court-human-and (accessed 22 November 2021).

[10] African Union, "African Charter on Human and Peoples Rights", October 1986, available at: https://www.achpr.org/legalinstruments/detail?id=49 (accessed 23 March 2021).

regimes across the African Continent, specifically those of Idi Amin and Jean-Bedel Bokassa.[11]

The Banjul Charter aimed to consolidate the Universal Declaration of Human Rights in its promotion and protection of human and peoples' rights and freedoms that would also encompass the preservation of African tradition and identity and would be specifically tailored for the legal and political cultures of African states.[12]

The Banjul Charter has been criticised for its focus on social and economic rights at the expense of civil and political rights. For example, the Charter does not expressly recognise the right to privacy and its provisions on the right to fair trial[13] and political participation[14] do not meet international standards.

The Banjul Charter forms the basis for other specialised and focussed protocols and charters that cater to specific areas of concern. For example, the Protocol to the African Charter on Human and Peoples' Rights on the Rights of Women in Africa (Maputo Protocol) stems from Article 4(1) of the Constitutive Act of the African Union that enshrines gender equality as one of the principles to be followed to ensure its functionality.[15] This was an amendment to the AU's functional principles made pursuant to the adoption of the Maputo Protocol in 2003.[16] The Maputo Protocol contains articles that are relevant to the protection and promotion of the rights of women, such as providing for the rights to life, integrity and security of the person; access to justice and equal protection of the law, the right to participation in the political and decision-making process; the right to peace and the protection of women in armed conflicts.[17]

---

[11] C. Anno, "The African Charter on Human and Peoples' Rights: How Effective is this Legal Instrument in Shaping a Continental Human Rights Culture in Africa", Le Petit Juriste, 21 December 2014, available at: https://www.lepetitjuriste.fr/the-african-charter-on-human-and-peoples-rights-how-effective-is-this-legal-instrument-in-shaping-a-continental-human-rights-culture-in-africa/ (accessed 23 March 2021).

[12] Ibid.

[13] Article 7 of African Union, "African Charter on Human and Peoples Rights", October 1986, available at: https://www.achpr.org/legalinstruments/detail?id=49 (accessed 23 March 2021).

[14] Article 13 of African Union, "African Charter on Human and Peoples Rights", October 1986, available at: https://www.achpr.org/legalinstruments/detail?id=49 (accessed 23 March 2021).

[15] African Union, "Constitutive Act of the African Union" available at: https://au.int/sites/default/files/pages/34873-file-constitutiveact_en.pdf (accessed 5 November 2019).

[16] African Union, "Protocol to the African Charter on Human and People's Rights on the Rights of Women in Africa", 2003, available at: < https://www.un.org/en/africa/osaa/pdf/au/protocol_rights_women_africa_2003.pdf (accessed 5 November 2019).

[17] Articles 4, 8, 9, 10, and 11 of the African Union, "Protocol to the African Charter on Human and People's Rights on the Rights of Women in Africa", 2003, available at: https://www.un.org/en/africa/osaa/pdf/au/protocol_rights_women_africa_2003.pdf (accessed 5 November 2019).

Similarly, there are several other declarations, principles, guidelines, charters and conventions that supplement the general principles contained in the Banjul Charter. One of them is the Declaration of Principles on Freedom of Expression and Access to Information adopted in 2019 that enshrines the right to freedom of expression as a fundamental human right and as a cornerstone of democracy. The other one is The Principles and Guidelines on the Right to a Fair Trial and Legal Assistance in Africa whose name is self-explanatory. It was adopted in 2003. Another interesting one was the Malabo Protocol that was adopted in 2014, it extended the jurisdiction of the African Court on Human Peoples Rights to include international and transnational organised crimes.

It was agreed that an African Criminal Court be created for the prosecution of international crimes in response to what was seen as the unfair targeting of African leaders by the International Criminal Court (ICC). The African Court would technically have an overlapping mandate with the International Criminal Court. The AU Convention on Preventing and Combating Corruption was also adopted in 2003 as a move towards fighting rampant political corruption on the continent.

As can be evidenced, while the continent has various legal instruments that provide the basis for the protection of human rights, it is quite stark that there is a heavy focus on socio-economic rights. However, the African Court on Human and Peoples' Rights (the African Court) offers some recourse for victims and survivors of state infractions on civil and political rights. The African Court is a continental court that ensures protection of human rights of African peoples and makes the provisions of the Banjul Charter justiciable.[18]

Regional Blocs' Human Rights Interventions and Mechanisms

African countries efforts towards regional integration have been piecemeal, and often focussed on geographical location such as the East African Community (EAC), Common Market for Eastern and Southern Africa (COMESA), Southern African Development Community (SADC) and Economic Community of West African States (ECOWAS). Some progress has been made on the Tripartite Free Trade Area among the EAC, COMESA and SADC. As can be seen, most regional groupings in Africa have been centred on economic integration, easier movement and improved trade relations. There are different unions across the continent for this purpose. However, some attempts to have human rights instruments have been made.

Ordinarily, these regional agreements are African models for integration for various purposes such as trade and development, and women's peace and

[18] African Court of Human and Peoples' Rights, "Welcome to the African Court" available at: https://www.african-court.org/wpafc/welcome-to-the-african-court/ (accessed 23 March 2021).

security. Regional Agreements are designed to reflect the needs of the countries involved. For example, the Common Market for Eastern and Southern Africa (COMESA) aims: 'to co-operate in the promotion of peace, security and stability among the member states to enhance economic development in the region'. The member states further agreed by Article 6 to be governed by fundamental principles such as: (e) recognition, promotion and protection of human and peoples' rights in accordance with the provisions of the African Charter on Human and Peoples' Rights and (i) the maintenance of regional peace and stability through the promotion and strengthening of good neighbourliness.[19] Another example is the Southern African Development Community (SADC) which is a Regional Economic Community comprising 16 Member States. Established in 1992, SADC is committed to regional integration and poverty eradication within Southern Africa through economic development, peace and security.

A similar arrangement in West Africa manifested in the Dakar Declaration where all countries committed to adopt, as soon as possible, a national action plan for the implementation of United Nations Security Council Resolution 1325. The Declaration sets out clear commitments made by government ministers in charge of gender issues in West Africa, ECOWAS, the Mano River Union (MRU), the African Union (AU), civil society and the UN to accelerate the implementation of resolution 1325 both at national and regional level.

NATIONAL HUMAN RIGHTS MECHANISMS

There are also national mechanisms for human rights protections such as human rights commissions and ombudspersons. For countries faced with great conflict, such as civil war and/or recovery from autocratic regimes, in addition to the local court structures for accessing redress for gross human rights violations, truth and reconciliation commissions and specialised courts have also been instituted. These will be discussed in turn below.

Governmental Human Rights Institutions

Democratisation from authoritarian, often military, regimes in Africa in the early 1990s came with the advent of governmental human rights institutions (GHRIs) in African states.[20] In 1989 only one African country had a governmental human rights institution. By 1999, 23 more had been instituted.[21]

---

[19] African Union, "African Charter on Human and Peoples Rights", October 1986, https://www.achpr.org/legalinstruments/detail?id=49 (accessed on 23 March 2021).

[20] Michael Fleshman, 'Human rights move up on Africa's agenda' Africa Renewal, July 2004, available at: https://www.un.org/africarenewal/magazine/july-2004/human-rights-move-africas-agenda (accessed 23 March 2021).

[21] Mary Ellen Tsekos, "Human Rights Institutions in Africa", *Human Rights Brief* (2002) 9(2), pp. 21–24.

These GHRIs often take two forms: human rights commissions and ombudspersons. The ombudsperson is dedicated solely to watching government entities for human rights abuses, while the human rights commission may also check private entities and individuals in addition to government entities. Neither of the two are judicial in nature nor do they have law-making abilities.[22]

The challenge with these institutions is that they are state-funded, hence their operations may be crippled by lack of resources, sometimes deliberately, by the state. They may also be seen as barking dogs with no bite in that victims and survivors of violations might not get the remedies they looked for due to limited enforcement mechanisms.

Truth Commissions

Truth commissions are temporary state sanctioned bodies investigating large-scale human rights violations committed over a period.[23] Truth-seeking processes assist post-conflict and transitional societies to investigate past human rights violations and are undertaken by truth commissions, commissions of inquiry or other fact-finding missions.[24]

Given that nationalist myth-making based on historical distortion, has fuelled both interstate and intrastate wars, efforts to prevent the instrumentalisation of facts and history are needed to prevent a return to violent conflict.[25]

A truth commission is considered a means 'to engage and confront all of society in a painful national dialogue, with serious soul-searching, and attempt to look at the ills within society that make abuses possible'. Furthermore, civil society produces a sense of public ownership in this process, so that this dialogue actually leads to something. Otherwise, a country has merely a nice history lesson, destined for the bookshelf.[26]

Some governments have formed commissions of inquiry charged with the task of establishing the truth about what happened under previous regime(s). Some commissions have produced thorough reports complete with detailed recommendations for future human rights protection[27] such as the Sierra

---

[22] Ibid.

[23] Stan L and Nedelsky N (ed) 'Truth Commissions' (2013) *Encyclopaedia of Transitional Justice: Volume 1* 99.

[24] United Nations (2010) 8.

[25] Fischer M (2011) 410.

[26] Kritz, Neil J 'Policy Implications of Empirical Research on Transitional Justice' in van der Merwe H, Baxter V and Chapman AR (eds). *Assessing the Impact of Transitional Justice: Challenges for Empirical Research* (2009) 18.

[27] Benomar (2004) 34.

Leone Truth Commission. Yet still, others have lacked independence, impartiality, sound methods and ample resources needed to do their job such as Uganda's Commission of Inquiry into Violations of Human Rights.[28]

Specialised Courts

The prosecution of suspects and subsequent punishment of the guilty is one of the central transitional justice mechanisms for dealing with past violations.[29] Bringing violators to justice sends a clear message to all that human rights violations will not be tolerated or allowed to continue.[30]

On its own, prosecution is perceived as necessary for a wide range of different, but interconnected, reasons: it is morally correct; it individualises guilt; it will have a deterrent effect for future crimes and it is a prerequisite for (re)establishing the rule of law and strengthening democratic practises.[31]

At the same time, states emerging from years of conflict or repressive rule may be unable or unwilling to conduct effective investigations and prosecutions. In such situations, international and hybrid criminal tribunals may exercise concurrent jurisdiction, for example, in Rwanda the local *Gacaca* courts and the International Criminal Tribunal for Rwanda that was headquartered in Arusha Tanzania exercised concurrent jurisdiction for crimes committed during the genocide. The establishment of these various criminal tribunals represents a historic achievement in seeking accountability for international crimes. When establishing an international or hybrid criminal tribunal, it is essential that priority consideration is given to their legacy in the country concerned as well as to the exit strategy.[32]

CONTEMPORARY HUMAN RIGHTS ISSUES IN AFRICA

While Africa has a comprehensive human rights system, human rights violations abound. There are numerous social, economic and political factors that influence incidences of human rights abuses such as political instability, migration, sexism and discrimination and religious intolerance, just to mention a few. The fundamental shift that has occurred over the years is the shift from

---

[28] Commission of Inquiry into Violations of Human Rights is still operational. It was instituted in 1986 to cover human rights violations between December 1962 and January 1986 and was commissioned by the President. Some claim that the commission serves only to legitimize the current government and promote the image of human rights with no intention of publishing a report.

[29] Stan L and Nedelsky N (ed) 'Prosecute and Punish' (2013) *Encyclopaedia of Transitional Justice: Volume 1* 57.

[30] Benomar (2004) 41.

[31] Stan L and Nedelsky N, note 29.

[32] United Nations 'Guidance Note of the Secretary General: United Nations Approach to Transitional Justice' (2010) available at: https://www.un.org/ruleoflaw/files/TJ_Guidance_Note_March_2010FINAL.pdf (last accessed 24 April 2018).

mainly state sanctioned/state-imposed violence to the extension to human rights abuses by corporations, individuals and between and among individuals.

ARMED CONFLICT

Armed groups continually cause insecurity in Burkina Faso, Cameroon, Central African Republic, the Democratic Republic of Congo, Mali, Nigeria, Somalia and elsewhere. Both attacks and responses of security forces involve violations of human rights and international humanitarian law. Both states and international peacekeepers alike face challenges in preventing atrocities and protecting civilians from human rights abuses committed by armed groups such as rape, disappearances, torture and murder.[33]

Mozambique has a history of armed conflict caused by political and socio-economic discontent resulting in the death of many, injuries and displacements of many civilians often.[34] In eastern DRC, local police and nearby UN peacekeepers stayed in their camps, while armed groups killed at least 70 civilians in Beni during November 2019.[35]

Al Shabaab, a Somali terrorist group, rooted in political ideology has its victims in Somalia and Kenya. Kenya borders Somalia but is on the terrorist group's cross-hairs the terror group attacks because of its affiliation to the United States of America and intervention in Somalia. In January 2019, Kenya experienced its second terrorist attack from the terror group at Dusit Hotel, as a form of retaliation from the belief that Kenya is trying to control Somalia through its military intervention. Victims of armed conflicts and terrorism are people present at the terror attacks, their families and the majority of citizens in the country due to the perception of fear and insecurity.[36]

NATURAL DISASTERS

Natural disasters have caused numerous international human rights concerns. For example, in Somalia over 300,000 people were internally displaced in 2019 due to droughts and floods. This also had a significant impact on delivery and access to humanitarian aid.[37]

---

[33] Amnesty International, "Africa 2019" available at: https://www.amnesty.org/en/cou ntries/africa/report-africa/ (accessed 25 March 2021).

[34] Ibid.

[35] Ibid.

[36] Brendon J Cannon et al. "Why al-Shabaab targets Kenya and how to stop the attacks", Quartz Africa, 16 January 2019, available at: https://www.google.com/amp/s/qz. com/africa/1525710/nairobi-hotel-attacks-why-al-shabaab-targets-kenya/amp/ (accessed 25 March 2021).

[37] Amnesty International, "Africa 2019" https://www.amnesty.org/en/countries/afr ica/report-africa/ (accessed 25 March 2021).

Refugees, Migrants and Displaced People

The increase in migration (forced and voluntary) across the region is exacerbated by natural disasters, civil unrest and protracted conflict. In these situations, there are humanitarian crises where a scramble for basic resources is prevalent as well human rights violations perpetrated on the most vulnerable. This forces thousands and thousands of people to flee from their homes if they still have them, or to seek refuge in neighbouring countries, cities and towns in hopes of building a new life. In some instances, refugees are welcomed but in others it only lays the basis for further human rights abuse.

Women's Rights Violations and Abuse

Women's rights are still some of the most commonly abused rights. As an illustration, in 2019, over a hundred women were arrested on suspicion of being commercial sex workers in Nigeria. These women faced physical and verbal abuse, sexual violence and financial extortion. They were tried by mobile courts, where they were denied legal representation. Nigeria aside, women still face prejudice in their everyday lives as injustice against them is still dominant in most parts of Africa. Despite the advent of, and attempts to entrench democracy on the continent, women are still viewed as deplorable and incompetent in most parts of rural Africa.

Gender-based violence remains one of the most prevalent forms of oppression in Africa. There was shown to be a large increase in the number of abuses, disappearance, murders and rape cases of women in South Africa. In 2020, Malawi also saw a soaring increase in the number of gender-based violence related cases during the Corona virus disease (Covid-19) pandemic, as most people were working from home. It is unclear to say that whether there has been an increase in gender-based violence, or just an increase in reporting.

Equatorial Guinea, Sierra Leone and Tanzania continue to exclude pregnant girls from public schools. There was some push back against this in Sierra Leone and in December 2019 the Economic Community of West African States' (ECOWAS) Court of Justice rejected Sierra Leone's 2015 ban on pregnant girls from seating for examinations and attending mainstream school as amounting to discrimination.

On a positive note, Ghana introduced an Affirmative Action Bill seeking a 50 per cent representation of women in public positions of power. In 2020, Sudan's transitional government repealed restrictive public order laws governing women's presence in public spaces.[38]

[38] Ibid.

Children's Rights

Prevailing and interconnected issues of child trafficking, prostitution and pornography are rampant on the continent. The ease with which children can travel has exacerbated these abuses. This has been compounded by some childrens' desire to seek better futures and to support their families, which sometimes results in situations where they are taken advantage of by various entities.

An example is child prostitution that is defined as 'the travel to a different locale for the purposes of engaging in sexual acts with minors'.[39] In Africa, Kenya is seen as a country with a growing market for child prostitutes. About 55 per cent of children in Kenya are in the industry out of their self-will and are considered to have given consent.[40] This newly found market accommodates both male and female minors. According to Kenyan law, consent begins at age of 18; and according to the Sexual Offences Act, No. 3 of 2006, a person who commits an act which causes penetration with a child is guilty of defilement. This is because children are considered a vulnerable group and consent given by a child is considered invalid, and therefore engaging in sexual acts with children results into a violation of their human rights. Kenya shows an alarming rise in the practise of child prostitution, especially in coastal Kenya.

LGBTQ+-

The definition of sexual orientation encompasses all person's capacity for profound emotional, affectional and sexual attraction to, and intimate and sexual relations with, individuals of a different gender or the same gender or more than one gender.[41] While the definition of gender identity alludes to deeply felt internal and individual experience of gender,[42] sexual orientation and gender identity are universal struggles that every single person deals with, including heterosexual, cisgender people. All people are on a spectrum between heterosexual and homosexual as well as cisgender and transgender. The existence of this spectrum universalizes the issues and warrants the need for urgent protection.

[39] Wikipedia, "Sex Tourism", Wikipedia, available at: https://en.m.wikipedia.org/wiki/Sex_tourism (accessed 25 March 2021).

[40] Sara C Jones, "The extent and effects of sex tourism and sexual exploitation of children on the Kenyan Coast", 19 December 2006, available at: http://lastradainternational.org/lsidocs/418%20extent_n_efect_1007.pdf (accessed 28 January 2021).

[41] International Commission of Jurists, The Yogyakarta Principles—Principles on the Application of International Human Rights Law in Relation to Sexual Orientation and Gender Identity, available at: https://www.refworld.org/docid/48244e602.html (accessed 15 December 2018).

[42] International Commission of Jurists, *supra* note 7, at 6.

Interestingly though, 32 of the 72 countries worldwide that criminalise homosexuality are in Africa.[43] Half of the countries in Africa outlaw homosexuality and in four of these countries (for example, Mauritania and Sudan), homosexuality attracts the death penalty.[44] The criminalisation of homosexuality often leads to infringement of other civil liberties and exposes members of the LGBTQ+- community to arbitrary arrests, humiliating intimate searches, insecurity and threats to life.

In 2018, the Tanzanian government announced the creation of a surveillance squad to track down members of the LGBTQ community.[45] Hundreds of LGBTQ+ activists went into hiding as a result and members of the LGBTQ+ community were forced to hide their sexual orientations for fear of being found out and punished.[46] In 2018, during a police raid on a Lagos hotel, 47 men were arrested and charged with offences related to public displays of affection with the same sex.[47] In 2019, two men were imprisoned to 15 years imprisonment for consensual same-sex sex in Zambia after being found in a hotel room. In July 2020, 20 LGBTQ+- persons filed a lawsuit against Ugandan authorities after being arrested for 'doing an act likely to spread infection of disease' while in a shelter on the outskirts of Kampala. They were held for 50 days during which they were denied access to sanitary facilities, medical care and food. For 42 of the 50 days, it is alleged that they were also denied any access to legal representation.[48]

These are a few examples of the impact that criminalisation of same-sex sex can have on security. Most recently, Botswana de-criminalised its homosexuality laws on the basis that they were a colonial import and no longer served its people.[49] Prior to colonialism, African countries did not show any

[43] Kaitie Hairsine, "Why is homosexuality still taboo in many African countries?" DW, 4 December 2019, available at: https://www.dw.com/en/why-is-homosexuality-still-taboo-in-many-african-countries/a-51528737 (accessed 23 March 2021).

[44] Leah Buckle, "African sexuality and the legacy of imported homophobia", Stonewall, 1 October 2020. Available at: https://www.stonewall.org.uk/about-us/news/african-sexuality-and-legacy-imported-homophobia (accessed 23 March 2021).

[45] BBC News, "Tanzania: Anti-gay crackdown in Dar es Salaam", 31 October 2018, availale at: https://www.bbc.com/news/world-africa-46048804 (accessed on 23 March 2021).

[46] Jason Burke, "Hundreds in hiding as Tanzania launches anti-gay crackdown", The Guardian, 5 November 2018, available at: https://www.theguardian.com/world/2018/nov/05/tanzania-gay-people-in-hiding-lgbt-activists-crackdown (accessed on 23 March 2021).

[47] Kaitie Hairsine, see note 49.

[48] Alice McCool, "We were beaten': 20 LGBTQ+ Ugandans file lawsuit over alleged torture", The Guardian, 22 July 2020, available at: https://www.theguardian.com/global-development/2020/jul/22/we-were-beaten-so-badly-20-lgbtq-people-file-torture-law suit-in-uganda (accessed 23 March 2021).

[49] Leah Buckle, "African sexuality and the legacy of imported homophobia", Stonewall, 1 October 2020 https://www.stonewall.org.uk/about-us/news/african-sexuality-and-leg acy-imported-homophobia (accessed on 23 March 2021).

hard lines against same-sex activity or gender fluidity. Accounts are given of Niankhkhnum and Khnumotep of Egypt whose tomb was excavated, and they (two men) were found in a lovers' embrace, even in death. Deities were often memorialised as women with erect penises such as Mut and Sekmeht, and King Mwanga the second of Buganda (present-day Uganda) was openly gay. In the Yoruba and Igbo tribes of Nigeria, gender was not assigned at birth but later in life after a manifestation of the child's character. And finally, the Dagaaba people of present-day Ghana determine gender by a child's character and not anatomy.[50]

While the importation of colonial laws affected Africa's feelings of sexual orientation and gender identity, it also infringed the rights to find and form a family, freedom of expression and association and stripped members of the LGBTQ+ community of their chosen identities. Worse still, it can be an offence punishable by death and may lead to other infringements of rights such as freedom from arbitrary arrest and detention, and the right to liberty.

CIVIL LIBERTIES

Freedom of Association and Peaceful Assembly

In over 20 African countries, citizens were denied their right to peaceful protests—through unlawful bans, use of excessive force and harassment and arbitrary arrests. Use of excessive force and other abusesto disperse peaceful protests resulted in deaths, injuries and unlawful arrests in several countries.[51] For example, in 2019, Malawians took to the streets to express discontent with apparent fraudulent elections. The state responded by sending out the police service to stop protests by using excessive force and teargas on civilians. The Malawi Defence Force stepped in to protect civilians from the abuse of the state under police service after the High Court and Supreme Court confirmed the civilian right to protest.

Freedom of Expression

According to Amnesty International, in at least 25 African countries, media freedom was curtailed and journalists faced criminalisation for exercising their freedom of expression against regimes in 2020. Somalia has had the most intense media restrictions and abuse. Journalists are repressed by the government and Al Shabaab, and face beatings, despotic arrests and threats. The state's abuse of media limitation was most prevalent in south central Somalia. The insurgent group Al Shabaab targeted journalists during an attack in Kismayo in 2019.

[50] Leah Buckle, see note 50.

[51] Amnesty International, see note 39.

Socio-Economic Rights

Right to Education

Access to education in countries affected by armed conflicts has been particularly problematic.[52] This has been exacerbated by the Covid-19 pandemic where preventive measures and regulations require schools to be closed for extended periods. In Burkina Faso armed groups attacked schools, staff and students, leading to the closure of 2087 schools.[53] In Mali, 920 schools were closed by June 2019 after attacks on teachers and facilities. In Cameroon's conflict-ridden north-west and south-west, by December 2019 just 17 per cent of schools were functional and just 29 per cent of teachers were able to work.[54]

Right to Adequate Housing

Forced evictions abound in some countries including Eswatini, Nigeria, Uganda and Zimbabwe. In 2019, thousands of people were evicted without due process, compensation or other remedy.[55]

In 2000, two ministers in Zimbabwe occupied Haydon farms to develop it for commercial and residential use. This resulted in the forced evictions of 116 people, who were originally located at the Haydon farms. The evicted people were given land to settle at Zvimba Rural district council. There have been court orders to have the settled evicted from the land as well. This move has been challenged by the courts of Zimbabwe, awaiting judgement from the Supreme Court.[56]

Conclusion and Recommendations

The Banjul Charter is the backbone of the human rights framework in Africa, and is the basis upon which added, specialised, conventions, charters and protocols are adopted to prevent human rights abuse and to protect human rights in Africa. At national level, there are organisations and tools that also form part of this framework for the same purpose.

Despite the comprehensive human rights framework that exists, human rights violations persist on the continent. In considering the myriad of issues, the chapter singled out a few mechanisms that can be put in place to counter the prevalence of human rights abuses.

---

[52] Amnesty International, "Africa 2019" https://www.amnesty.org/en/countries/africa/report-africa/ (accessed on 25 March 2021).

[53] Ibid.

[54] Ibid.

[55] Ibid.

[56] Ibid.

Strengthening Compliance—as can be seen from the discussion above, there is a comprehensive, often overlapping, human rights system in Africa. This may pose a challenge to enforcement mechanisms, for example, the decisions of the African Court on Human and People's Rights. Further, compliance with decisions of regional bodies in Africa is still low. Member states often aim to undermine the regional bodies' independence and autonomy and simply do not cooperate when required to. Only a handful of countries have submitted state party reports to the African Commission on Human and Peoples' Rights (ACHPR) and the African Committee of Experts on the Rights and Welfare of the Child (ACERWC).[57] Hence, compliance to the existing systems would assist in entrenching human rights and ending impunity on the continent.

Protection of Human Rights Defenders and Activists—Activists are often targeted by States to repress dissent. There is need for their protection and an expansion of the civic space for the purpose of objective reports on violations of human rights. By extension, free reporting by the media will supplement this to ensure objective and unbiased media narratives that will promote and protect human rights.

Civic Education—most victims of human rights violations are vulnerable persons, either due to age, sex, creed, sexual orientation and gender identity and/or disability. There is, therefore, a need to strengthen their voice and to provide all vulnerable groups with the agency required for them to input their voices in national human rights agendas. More so, to engage the public to raise awareness on the specific human rights issues and their complexities when society confronts them.

[57] Amnesty International, Ibid.

CHAPTER 17

The Governance Conundrum in Africa

Tadziwana Kapeni

INTRODUCTION

Governance is a term which covers many aspects related to concepts, theories and practices that help in running the affairs of an organization and or a state.[1] Governance is multifaceted and encompasses a lot of elements. According the to World Bank, the elements include transparency, inclusiveness, participation, integrity and accountability.[2] Leadership, as understood in governance, plays an instrumental role in making sure that the elements in governance are enacted. Thus, failure in governance is to a certain degree accredited to poor leadership. The failure of leadership in governance as alluded to earlier has posed a threat to peace and security in many African countries.

Governance and leadership are intertwined concepts, one depends on and regulates the other.[3] While governance institutes processes, configurations and establishments for outlining, safeguarding and implementing and evaluating

---

[1]Steven L. Wartick and Philip L. Cochran *The Academy of Management Review.* Vol. 10, No. 4 (October 1985), pp. 758–769.

[2]The World Bank. *Governance: The World Bank's Experience.* International Bank of Reconstruction and Development (1994). Available at: http://www.worldbank.org/ (accessed on 5 August 2020).

[3]Bevir, Mark, Governance: A very Short Introduction. Oxford, UK: Oxford University Press (2012).

T. Kapeni (✉)
Lilongwe, Malawi

© The Author(s), under exclusive license to Springer Nature Switzerland AG 2022
D. Kuwali (ed.), *The Palgrave Handbook of Sustainable Peace and Security in Africa*, https://doi.org/10.1007/978-3-030-82020-6_17

collective desired aspirations of a people, leaderships sets out the priorities and the directions in tasking and resource allocation for the realization of the fashioned aspirations.[4] Understanding this collaboration is, therefore, critical in every governance and leadership discourse.

In recent years certain governance attributes have become known to facilitate effective collective leadership than others. These include participation and representation, responsiveness, openness and transparency, rule of law, competency and capacity and accountability among others. Scholars contend, for example, "that government is legitimate and democratic in a positive sense when the government is installed by the people through institution arrangements that are put in place by the people and when the performance of the [leader] is adjudge good and accepted by the people and when the people have no [arbitrary] power to remove the leader in case of grievous offence."[5]

Since time immemorial, nations have made strides in governance, political economy, social justice and peace and security because of leadership. Scholars have argued that true leadership manifests itself in time of adversity. Thus, crises have produced great men and women. Their response in time of adversity really built and shaped what their nations are today. Today, we would not be talking of United Nations (UN) in the absence of the World Wars. Alluding to current political trends in some African countries, it is evident that leadership failure in governance can bring chaos than one can fathom. Today, we are talking of massive plunder of public resources in many countries because of poor leadership or leadership failure. South Africa, for example, under the Jacob Zuma regime has seen massive plunder of public resources. Malawi somewhat shares this plate with South Africa either subtle or in clear manifest. It must be understood that political choices and the processes through which those choices are made have consequences. Any country's state of affairs is as a result of a political choices that the citizens made either willingly or unwillingly.

This chapter will look at three major forms of leadership as espoused by Morton in her article "Political leadership and global governance." The chapter will look side by side in relation to leadership as to how the former affected the latter in the African context. Thus, this chapter will look at how the absence of good leadership in governance brought many African countries at the brink of economic chaos, political instability and insatiability and lapse of peace and security.

[4] Bevir, Mark, Governance: A Very Short Introduction. Oxford, UK: Oxford University Press (2012).

[5] Young, Oran R. 1991. "Political Leadership and Regime Formation: On the Development of Institutions in International Society". *International Organization* 45(3): 281–308 (Summer).

According to Morton, leadership can be categorized into charismatic, structural and collaborative leadership.[6] Citing Rudolf Sohn, Morton described a charismatic leader as one endowed with extraordinary traits. A charismatic leader is mission oriented. He or she has inner determination and inner restraint. This type of leadership was seen in Bingu wa Mutharika, the former President of Malawi. His leadership was much emphasized on his individual qualities rather than the context in which he showed his leadership. However, this exposes how the context in which he operated failed him as a leader to a certain extent. This notion is expounded in the subsequent discussion of the same chapter. The question to ask is in what context does a charismatic leader thrive or flourish?

Collaborative or Entrepreneurial leadership are alleged to be big thinkers whose strength lie in innovation and flexibility.[7] There are more fluid in their approach to issues and they rely on discourse with employees, colleagues and a number of stakeholders. The late Dr. John Pombe Magufuli, the then President of the Republic of Tanzania, can be given as a good example on this type of leadership. According to Morton, these leaders are risk takers and their visions are long term. As such, this type of leadership requires patience on the part of the led. These leaders are accountable and bear responsibility of failures.

Nevertheless, this type of leadership looks at the bigger picture and as such may lose focus along the way because they may neglect smaller details of the process. This statement can never be far from how Magufuli handled the Covid-19 pandemic in his country. The country stopped recording the cases and is on record of planning to refuse the vaccine. This choice will in the long run have consequences. Whether the leadership is right or wrong, it must be put on record that there will be consequences and all these will hinge on leadership likewise any country which decides to take a different path in as far as tackling the pandemic is concerned.

It is worthwhile to note that leaders may exhibit various forms of leadership. It is the situation that may determine a switch from one form to the other. Hence, leaders must be flexible enough to conform to the current situation and act accordingly. Having looked at various forms of leadership, let us look at how leaders fail. Leadership failure and poor governance has often rendered efforts to silence the guns in Africa somewhat a fanciful dream. In this part of the chapter, how leaders get into power is looked into with further analysis into what makes leaders stick to power even when they are not delivering according to people's expectations.

---

[6] Morton, Katherine. (2017). "Political Leadership and Global Governance: Structural Power Versus Custodial Leadership". *Chinese Political Science Review* 2: 477–493. 10.1007/s41111-017-0089-4.

[7] Morton, Katherine. (2017). "Political Leadership and Global Governance: Structural Power Versus Custodial Leadership". *Chinese Political Science Review* 2: 477–493. 10.1007/s41111-017-0089-4 (accessed on 5 August 2020).

Usually when the populace elect people into various leadership positions, there are expectations that the people place on them. Failure to meet these expectations has often been seen as a failure in leadership. Most often than not, most African states have failed somewhat to meet the expectations of the people due to greed, corruption, failure to heed advice, lack of vision/direction and entertainment of mediocrity on the part of supporters of the government in place. Corruption is the cancer that has so far being regarded as part of the DNA of governments in the African continent. In Nigeria, for example, coupled with ineffective leadership, corruption has had a negative impact on democratic stability and her economic development as has clearly been demonstrated by Dan Kuwali in Chapter 33.[8]

Good governance promotes authority whose leaders are elected in an open and unprejudiced manner.[9] It promotes fairness where all capable men and women are given a chance to show and pursue their interests for leadership and public positions. Additionally, democratic governance provides for the need of holding regular, free and fair elections in order for the majority to decide the type of leader they so desire. Among other things, regular free and fair elections provide room for the majority to confirm their choice in the elected leaders (those they have already tried after serving for number of years) or gives them a chance to seek alternative leadership in other capable aspirants having proven that the chosen leadership failed to deliver on the promises they made.

Although most African countries run-through regular elections, nonetheless, the election process—from the nomination of candidates, the preparations of elections, to the announcement and swearing ceremony of the elected leaders,—smells of rambling and severe undemocratic susceptibilities.[10] In Chapter 21, Archiles Bwete and his colleagues have eloquently presented the challenges presented by elections in Africa. Gichuki argues that "for the first 30 years after independence, the number of African presidents who were elected in free and fair democratic elections was few and far between. Only a third of one hundred and two political successions between 1963 and 1998 were regulated."[11] It can be concluded that most leaders in Africa still get hold of power by bullet/gun, rigging or giving power to handpicked successors. President Emerson Mnangagwa, for example, became president after the ouster of Robert Mugabe by Zimbabwe Defence Force. Yoweli Museveni, President of Uganda won the 2021 general elections amid rigging claims and flawed electoral process.

---

[8] Joseph C. Ebegbulem. (2012). "Corruption and Leadership Crisis in Africa: Nigeria in Focus". *International Journal of Business and Social Science* 3(11), June.

[9] Mohammed Yimer. (2015). "Governance and Leadership Challenges in Africa". *International Journal of Political Science and Development* 3(3): 129–137, March.

[10] As above.

[11] Gichuki Douglas. (2014). *Leadership in Africa and the Role of Youth in the Leadership Milieu.* https://minds-africa.org/ (accessed on 7 August 2020).

In many illustrations, the African elections are a sheer parade of the process and not an authentic expression of the electorate. The undemocratic ascension to power has often made the said leaders to lead in constant fear of being toppled. The consequence has been leaders' total concentration on consolidating allegiance, propagating ideas for longer office tenancy and silencing any opposition.[12] In many instances the voter is unswervingly deprived of change through having in position of influence people who have no serious regard of his/her welfare. Change for the ordinary African remains a political lullaby. Hence, there are always disputes after elections like the cases of Kenya in 2007 and 2013, Gambia in 2016, Gabon in 2016, Sao Tome and Principe in 2016 and the Democratic Republic of the Congo in 2019.

Malawi held general elections in May 2019, which were marred by massive irregularities. This forced the Constitutional court to invalidate the results of the disputed Presidential elections and order a rerun. The way the 2019 elections were held proved that poor leadership regulated the process and determined the outcome. The current leader of the Malawi's Electoral Commission, Justice Dr. Chifundo Kachale had limited time to plan and execute credible elections with time as a limiting factor. However, his leadership style paid the dividends. Thus, both the judges at the constitutional court and the Chairperson are acclaimed to have done a great job. It can be concluded, therefore, that leadership and governance in the courts enhanced peace and security in Malawi. The landmark ruling echoed the fragrance of Kenya's 2018 general elections.

Democratic governance promotes performance-based legitimacy to governance.[13] A leader's legitimacy to govern is relative to his/her commitment to fulfillment of collective intentions. The leaders who stay true to their promise are rewarded with another chance to govern for another term as is a case of many African leaders. Bingu wa Mutharika did well in his first term as the President and as such the electorate gave him another five years which because of loss of focus, messed up. His second term was marred with shortages of fuel, dictatorial tendencies and massive demonstrations which led to the killing of some innocent protestors. Recently, Zimbabwe's Emmerson Mnangagwa seems not to sustain the power he has. Once adorned as Africa's food basket, Zimbabwe has seen the worst economic war in recent history even after the death of Mugabe who was a darling of the East. Recently, the citizens in diaspora took to the streets to demand for his resignation as President.

Despite under performance, non-performance or expiry of their term of service, African leaders continue to exercise their dominance over the electorate. Africa has seen many leaders clinging to power and only a few have left

---

[12] Mudacumura, Gedeon and Morçöl, Göktuğ (Editors). (2014). *Challenges to Democratic Governance in Developing Countries*. Springer, New York.

[13] Afegbua, Salami Issa and Adejuwon, Kehinde David. (2012). "The Challenges of Leadership and Governance in Africa". *International Journal of Academic Research in Business and Social Sciences September* 2(9).

voluntarily. Kofi Annan, former United Nations Secretary General, called on African leaders to step down after the expiry of their terms. Annan observed that the only resolve that people have when a leader clings to power is through a coup or taking to the streets in massive demonstrations for change both of which have the ability to destabilize states.[14] It is also on record that several African leaders have on several occasion attempted constitutional changes and amendments to extend their mandate on the populace. This stance was taken in Malawi by the former President of Malawi Bakili Muluzi who sought to bulldoze a Constitutional change to allow him to run for a third term. Guinea's ruling party is on record to have urged President Alpha Conde to seek a third term in elections in 2020. These efforts to stick to power eventually end up threatening a country's peace and security.

People of Burkina Faso, for example, stormed Parliament in 2014 to prevent President Blaise Compaore from extending his 27-year-old rule. Although some leaders succeed in clinging to power, this has often made these leaders leading a deeply acrimonious nation.

Having looked at how Most African leaders get into power and how they maintain their grip on it, let us look at what makes them fail. Most of the failure is attributed to lack of employment of elements of good governance and good leadership as espoused by different scholars. There are elements that leaders do not employ or only half-heartedly employ in their pursuit of governance. A society sets goals for a government to achieve in the time and space the society has allowed the government to govern. As cogently argued by Bright Prince Majiga in Chapter 11, if government fails to take necessary or appropriate measures to achieve those goals, the society labels that government as ineffective.[15]

Summarizing attributes of a democratic governance the Council of Europe's European Label of Governance Excellence (ELoGE) outlines 12 key principles of good governance. Relatable to the African situation under discussion are the principles of participation, responsiveness, openness and transparency, ethical conduct, competence and capacity, sustainability and long-term orientation and accountability.

Lack of inclusiveness is a notable and significant problem of African governance. History indicates that the struggle for independence was won on grounds of wider participation, that men and women, the young and old participated relatively squarely in the liberation and freedoms of the African people from the colonial masters.[16] In Malawi, a lot people participated in the demand for change by taking to the streets or subtlety by adding their voices

---

[14] Kofi Annan speaking at a Forum on *Security in Africa* in Addis Ababa in Ethiopia on April 22, 2016.

[15] Frank Cunningham. (2002). *Theories of Democracy, A Critical Introduction.* Routledge, London.

[16] Gichuki Douglas. (2014). *Leadership in Africa and the Role of Youth in the Leadership Milieu.* Available at: https://minds-africa.org/ (accessed 7 August 2020).

through social media platforms. The then ruling party was accused of lack of inclusivity with most matters of the state and access to resources confined to selected few.

Youth participation has become a new concept in African politics and governance. According to Gichuki, "African youth were both the intellectual and ground forces in the nationalist and pan-African movements."[17] The subject of youth participation in political affairs is an elephant in the room as the African continent has a young population, most of whom are unemployed. Malawi saw the youth including university students rallying behind and advocating ideas of certain political parties. Despite having a demonstrated capability, however, not many of the youth that support political parties have been given a chance to run the affairs of the State after the ascendency to power of those particular political parties. Elsewhere in Africa, discontented youth join insurrections against governments which often leads to chaos and lapse of peace and security. Some go as a far as bearing armaments to destabilize governments. This was evident in Burundi and recently Central African Republic.

Many African leaders need to revisit the current tendency of engaging the youth through manipulation and start perceiving them as important interested party. The African woman has not seen the full representation on governance and political spheres. The struggle continues for them to find political podium to fully express and fulfill their aspirations and political thought.[18] Nonetheless, a continued number of countries are recognizing the benefit of incorporating the female person in the affairs of the communities and country at large. For example, in 11 African countries, women hold almost one-third of parliament seats, more than in Europe and the United States.

Recent times have also seen women rising the political ladder to lead nations as elected presidents. Ellen Johnson Sirleaf served as the 24th President of Liberia from 2006 to 2018. Sirleaf was the first elected female head of state in Africa. Dr. Joyce Banda was the first female President of Malawi after the demise of Professor Bingu Wa Mutharika in 2012. In addition, countries continue to take thoughtful actions such as quotas in representation in parliament, ministerial posts and other governance institutions. Governments in Africa have had this quest also as part of good governance and respect of human rights declarations. However, financial hardships, cultural beliefs, low education and religion continue to pose a challenge to effective female participation in these realms.[19]

---

[17] As above.

[18] Gichuki Douglas. (2014). *Leadership in Africa and the Role of Youth in the Leadership Milieu*. Available at: https://minds-africa.org/ (accessed 7 August 2020).

[19] See Amundsen, Inge, Kayuni, Happy; Chasukwa, Michael, Chikadza, Kondwani, et al. (Editors). (2016). *Women in Politics in Malawi*.

Citizens of any country have expectations and needs. Government must ensure that its vision or developmental goals, legislation it is advocating and procedures thereof must be in tandem with these needs and expectations to ensure good governance.[20] Government must ensure timely delivery of public services, timely response to disasters and requests. Governments that respond within a reasonable time frame receives positive ratings from the people they govern. Responding to adversities in a timely manner have rendered leaders to be held in high acclaim and the opposite is true. Responsiveness entails responsibility and the duty leaders have over their people. Many leaders have failed because they failed to respond in a timely manner. The consequences for such lack of responsiveness has afflicted the citizenry, most of the times leading to, at the minimum, discontent and protest and the maximum, removal or attempts at removal of leaders.

Openness and transparency as attributes of good governance ensure that decisions are taken and enforced in accordance with rules and regulations. They also necessitate that information on decisions, complementation of polices and results is made available to the public in such a way as to enable it to follow and contribute to the work. Lack of openness or transparency has been seen as the breeding ground for corruption. Many leaders in Africa and beyond have failed to satisfactorily enhance transparency and openness. This has also affected the efforts of silencing the guns in Africa by leaders who do not strive to follow the rule of law. Many African leaders miss this aspect which has proven to be a breeding ground for corruption. Efforts of silencing the guns in Africa require concerted efforts ranging from advocacy to participation. If leaders are not open enough to the people they are governing, they end up attracting dissent.

African leaders must undertake measures to enhance transparency and openness as continued citizens' trust in the government is largely premised on these attributes. Lack of openness and transparency has led to many African leaders gather resources for individual gains than to better the lives of the governed. A number of priority areas suffer because corruption undermines efficacy as time and money are wasted through corrupt activities. Competence and capacity ensure that only those that have the requisite knowledge and relevant skills are hired to carry out governance issues and that professional competencies and skill of such individuals are continuously maintained and strengthened in order to improve output and impact. However, African leaders tend to employ people to carry out governance issues not based on their competence and knowledge but rather as a token of appreciation. The people are appointed based on their loyalty to the leader and times on tribalistic or nepotistic grounds. This leads to situation whereby the ruling elite is made up of "yes men" who rarely question leadership but only seek to advance their selfish interests at the expense of the citizenry.

---

[20] European Label of Governance Excellence. Good Governance Benchmark. Council of Europe. Available at: https://bacid.eu (accessed on 11 February 2021).

Issues of competence and capacity come to the fore when it comes to averting or resolving conflict issues in Africa. The sounds of guns and mortars, the reek of burning tires in the streets cannot be silenced or extinguished with leadership that survives on cronyism. That is so because cronyism, among other auxiliary vices is part of the problem. It is thus important that African leaders go beyond instincts of political survival and place primacy of the state and citizens as a priority. Hiring or maintaining of competent professionals would ensure that leadership is supported by individuals who are experienced in various fields and just to seek self-glorification.

Africa is well known for its cultural multiplicity with a number of ethnic groups inhabiting it. However, instead of using this cultural diversity to enhance its systems and processes, cultural diversity in Africa has been a source of factionalism that has led to party-political schism.[21] It has become a norm among African leaders to use the tribal tags to further selfish political agendas. People are commonly becoming ethnically affiliated to a particular tribe to reap significant political and financial returns. No wonder it is becoming increasingly difficult for political parties or political candidates to accept electoral results since elections results are seen as victory for tribal coalitions or powerful clans. This mindset has led to political violence, visionless loyalty and sluggishness in development agenda since appointments and development projects are offered as token of gratitude for own people. Less likely is again the ability of a people who consider the leader their son or daughter to offer meaningful constructive criticism.

According to Gichuki communities that promote good governance will ensure that "the needs of future generations are sincerely taken into account in current policies" and that "decisions [adopted] strive to internalize all cost and not transfer problems and tensions, be they environmental, structural, financial, economic, social, [and political] to the future generations."[22] Malawi developed and adopted the erstwhile Vision 2020 ideas and concepts in the recent past. However, due to leadership issues surrounding its implementation, the plan was not successfully supported and implemented another plan has been developed termed Vision 2063. Interestingly though, Rwanda reportedly borrowed a leaf from the Malawi's Vision 2020 concepts and ideas and the fruits thereof are being felt and exhibited. Policies and or ideas must be sustainable and must relate to the long-term orientation that the government has. Leaders in Africa tend to consider the plans or ideas of their immediate past regime as nonsensical even if they made sense in extreme cases. That spirit has killed a number of ideas that would propel a nation to greatness.

Issues of sustainability and long-term planning have a bearing in achieving peace that goes beyond absence of armed conflict. Haphazard and myopic

---

[21] Gichuki Douglas. (2014). *Leadership in Africa and the Role of Youth in the Leadership Milieu*. Available at: Retrieved from https://minds-africa.org/ (accessed on 7 August 2020).

[22] As above.

policy planning tend to reverse gains that otherwise good policies may have achieved. When the aspect that most conflicts in Africa have their roots in socio-economic issues, the role of long-term, sustainable planning cannot be undermined. It is thus imperative that African leaders take issues of planning seriously as lack of planning, implementation of unstainable and fire-fighting policies translate into poor service delivery, continued inequalities, among other state and peace threatening scenarios.

African leaders despite many attempts are having difficulties to revolutionize the people's lives. They have failed to position the masses in the path to reap maximum benefits from technology. It is an undeniable fact that many African leaders have been struggling to provide their citizens with electricity and other basic technological needs. The excuses for this attitude ranges from lack of maintenance of generating plants, environmental changes and increased population. In essence the failure has been due to lack of focused investment in the technological sector as well as the growing tendency to use such corporate institutions as golden cow for milking public funds to finance political campaigns and personal projects.[23] The ultimate victim in all this remains the average poor masses who have no choice but to accept the circumstances as natural.

The other notable area where African leadership has been slothful is in agricultural mechanization. Agriculture remains a core economic activity in many African countries. Regardless, the field of agriculture remains largely undeveloped technologically. Most of the farming activities are being done using the ordinary means thereby compromising on quantity and quality of the produce and increased production time.

Conclusion

Poor leadership often leads to poor governance. African leaders have failed in governance somewhat also because of the people that surround the leaders. The nagging presence of incompetent, boot leaking aides or associates has to an extent contributed to leadership fiascos, year in, year out. The need to develop home-grown ideas and adopt concepts that could stand the test of time with the future generations in mind cannot be emphasized. Notwithstanding the current political landscape and geopolitics, leaders ought to embrace change and enhance full participation of youth and women in governance and leadership. It must be borne in the minds of African leaders that their citizens expect more from them in regards to maintenance of peace and security in the continent. Contact and dialog is one policy that can help to

---

[23] Elin Falguera, Samuel Jones and Magnus Ohman. (2014). (Editors). *Funding of Political Parties and Election Campaigns: A Handbook on Political Finance.* International Institute for Democracy and Electoral Assistance, Stockholm.

enhance peace and security. It is on record that dialog championed by the regional bodies fail to effect authentic engagement among factions because of hidden agenda that leaders may have if such engagements are put in action. Failure to silence guns may be connected to leadership failures, to such an extent that improvements in leadership through the election of capable leaders and visionary leaders/reforms would go a long way in achieving deafening silence of guns in Africa.

CHAPTER 18

Organized Crime in Africa

Mlowoka Noel Kayira

INTRODUCTION

Organized crime remains one of the most complex, multi-dimensional and evolving forms of crime across the globe.[1] Africa remains a huge source, conduit as well as one of the biggest markets and beneficiary of organized crime.[2] Organized crime takes a number of forms such as trafficking in persons, drugs, wildlife, forest products and firearms.[3] As the term connotes, organized crime is usually committed by well-organized and complex groups of criminals.

[1] Vyaccheslav Afanasyev. (1994). Organized Crime and Society. Institute of Sociology of Academy of Sciences of Russia. Demokratizatsiya, pp. 426–441, 426, available at: https://demokratizatsiya.pub/archives/02-3_Afanasyev.PDF (accessed 18 March 2021). Channing May. (2017). Transnational Crime and Developing World. Global Financial Integrity Report, available at: https://secureservercdn.net/45.40.149.159/34n.8bd.myftpupload.com/wp-content/uploads/2017/03/Transnational_Crime-final.pdf (accessed 15 January 2020), p. 1.

[2] The United Nations Office on Drugs and Crime (UNODC), Organized Crime and Instability in Central Africa: A Threat Assessment, available at: https://www.unodc.org/documents/data-and-analysis/Studies/Central_Africa_Report_2011_web.pdf (accessed 10 February 2021), p. 15.

[3] Institute for Security Studies and Interpol. Organized Crime Index Africa Report, Pretoria, South Africa, 2019, p. 28. See also May note 1 above, p. 1.

M. N. Kayira (✉)
Ramsey, USA

© The Author(s), under exclusive license to Springer Nature Switzerland AG 2022
D. Kuwali (ed.), *The Palgrave Handbook of Sustainable Peace and Security in Africa*, https://doi.org/10.1007/978-3-030-82020-6_18

Organized crime groups continue to operate in Africa through very complex chain of networks.[4] The groups employ a variety of means which are influenced by corruption of state machinery, private sector, weak governance institutions and fragile states in most instances.[5] Through corruption, organized crime groups have managed to infiltrate both the private and public sector. Organized crime groups often times use force and intimidation to protect their operations.

Despite efforts to combat the organized crime at national, bilateral and multilateral levels, the transnational nature of the scourge continues to pose a huge challenge to the peace, security, governance, tourism, political, health, economic and human development on the African continent.[6] The flourishing of organized crime in Africa poses a huge potential of undermining the AU Agenda 2063. It is on the above premise that this chapter proceeds to analyse the problem of organized crime in Africa in order to ascertain strategies for addressing the same. The paper focuses on the extent and impact of organized crime on Africa's social-economic development. This is followed by a discussion of the challenges associated with fighting organized crime in Africa which include corruption, weak governance institutions as well as fragile states. As a way forward, the chapter propose key strategic interventions that can be employed to deal with organized crime in Africa.

WHAT IS ORGANIZED CRIME?

Organized crime remains one of the most notoriously difficult concepts to define.[7] Despite the term being very popular and in use among law enforcement agencies and scholars, it remains poorly defined. Even the United Nations Convention Against Transnational Organised Crime (UNTOC) of 2000 has no proper definition of organized crime. Instead, the UNTOC simply defines organized crime groups. One analyst currently has the count at 160 different definitions of organized crime and is still counting.[8] It has thus, become a norm that when discussing organized crime, the focus has been on what constitutes organized crime and how different it is from other forms of crime. Thus, any attempt to define the phenomenon has often times ended at defining the characteristics of the concept. Challenges to have a harmonized

---

[4] Mark Shaw and Tuesday Reitano. (2013). The evolution of organised crime in Africa: Towards a new response. Institute for Security Studies. Paper 224, available at: https://media.africaportal.org/documents/Paper244.pdf (accessed 10 February 2021), p. 4.

[5] As above, p. 2.

[6] Institute for Security Studies, Organized crime Index, note 3 above, p. 8; UNODC. (2005). Crime and Development in Africa, p. 10, available at: https://www.unodc.org/pdf/African_report.pdf (accessed 12 January 2021).

[7] Institute for Security Studies, Organized Crime Index Africa 2019 note 3 above, p. 27.

[8] Shaw and Reitano, note 4 above, p. 8.

definition of the term organized crime are acerbated by the complex nature in which organized crime manifests itself.

Prior to the promulgation of the UN Convention against Organized Crime,[9] attempted to define organized crime as follows:

> those serious criminal offences committed by a criminal organization which is based on a structured association of more than two persons acting in concert over a prolonged period of time in pursuit of both their criminal objectives and profits.

The definition by Gastrow remains one of the attempts to define organized crime in absolute terms. This paper, considers organized crime in light of both the UNTOC and Gastrow's definitions. From the preceding definitions, one common denominator comes out, that is to say the element of organized criminal groups. Art 2 (a) of the UNTOC states that an organized criminal group is a 'structured group of three or more persons, existing for a period of time and acting in concert with the aim of committing one or more serious crimes or offences established in accordance with this Convention, in order to obtain, directly or indirectly, a financial or other material benefit'. The Convention under Art 2 (b) goes further to define 'structured group' as a group that is not randomly formed for the immediate commission of an offence and that does not need to have formally defined roles for its members, continuity of its membership or a developed structure or any hierarchy.

THE EXTENT OF ORGANIZED CRIME IN AFRICA

Organized crime takes place across all countries in Africa and takes a variety of forms. However, the discussion in this chapter is limited to trafficking and smuggling of human beings, trade and trafficking in wildlife, trafficking of firearms as well as trafficking in drugs. These four are among the most deep-rooted forms of organized crime in Africa.

TRAFFICKING AND SMUGGLING OF HUMAN BEINGS

Trafficking and smuggling of human beings are among the fastest-growing Transnational Organized Crimes (TOC). Human trafficking involves movement and subsequent exploitation of men, women or children in different forms such as forced labour, commercial sexual exploitation, organ harvesting, domestic servitude and exploitation in other licit and illicit labour markets,

---

[9] Peter Gastrow. (1998). Organized crime in South Africa: An assessment of the nature and origins. *ISS. Monograph Series No. 28*. Pretoria, p. 6, available at: https://issafrica.org/research/monographs/monograph-28-organised-crime-in-south-africa-an-assessment-of-its-nature-and-origins-by-peter-gastrow (accessed 4 August 2020), p. 6.

while human smuggling involves the provision of a service such as transportation or fraudulent documents to an individual who voluntarily seeks to gain illegal entry into a foreign country.[10] There is a clear distinction between these types of illegal migration made in the UN Protocols on the Trafficking in Persons and Smuggling in Migrants—in the former the victim is the individual, while in the latter it is the country where someone has illegally entered that is a victim. It is possible the crime may start out as human smuggling but quickly turn into human trafficking.

According to the 2019 Africa Organised Crime Index, p. 15, human trafficking constitutes one of the highest criminal markets on the African continent and attracts a wide variety of illicit actors, from Organized Crime Groups (OCGs) to terrorist organizations, operating both within and outside the continent. The report further indicates that human trafficking is influenced by a number of factors including heavy profits and weak penalties for perpetrators. The prevalence of human trafficking on the continent is largely due to its composite nature, encompassing crimes ranging from labour and sexual exploitation, ferrying drugs, to kidnapping for ransom and forced begging and marriage.[11]

Labour and sexual exploitation remain key forms of human trafficking and smuggling world over.[12] Annually millions of women, male and female children are trafficked and smuggled across the borders to work as labourers and sex slaves.[13] Traditionally labour exploitation is not a priority for law enforcement activities and often remains undetected.[14] Labour, domestic servitude, forced marriages and sexual exploitation are driven by either lack of reporting or under-reporting of such cases.[15]

People are also trafficked to ferry drugs across international borders. Popularly known as 'drug mules', the victims are made to swallow balloons containing illicit drugs and are then transported across borders.[16] Once they have reached their destination, these balloons are retrieved from the victim's

---

[10] Ella Cockbain and Kate Bowers. (2019). Human trafficking for sex, labour and domestic servitude: How do key trafficking types compare and what are their predictors? Crime, Law and Social Change (2019) 72(9–34), p. 10, available at: https://doi.org/10.1007/s10611-019-09836-7 (accessed 18 March 2021).

[11] Peter H. van der Laan, Monika Smit, Inge Busschers and Pauline Aarten. (2011). Cross-border Trafficking in Human Beings: Prevention and Intervention Strategies for Reducing Sexual Exploitation. Campbell Systematic Reviews, p. 5. https://doi.org/10.4073/csr.2011.9, available at: https://onlinelibrary.wiley.com/doi/pdf/10.4073/csr.2011.9 (accessed 16 February 2021).

[12] As above, p. 5.

[13] Cockbain and Bowers, note 10 above, pp. 10–11.

[14] Van der Laan et al., note 11 above, p. 8.

[15] As above, p. 8.

[16] UNODC, World Drug Report. United Nations publication, 2018, p. 29, available at: https://www.unodc.org/wdr2018/prelaunch/WDR18_Booklet_5_WOMEN.pdf (accessed 10 February 2021).

body. For example, on 8 January 2021, a court in Malawi convicted and sentenced a Nigerian national, Alex Ojuku to ten (10) years imprisonment with hard labour for trafficking a 20-year-old girl who later died in Brazil as a result of the drugs she had swallowed.[17] And recently on 9 March 2021, a court in Hong Kong, China, sentenced a Malawian woman Estina Mukasera to 24 years imprisonment with hard labour after she was found guilty of trafficking 2.2 kilograms of cocaine.[18] These examples simply show how deed rooted illicit drug trafficking has become.

According to Coluccello and Massey, the main causes of human trafficking and people smuggling from North and Sub-Saharan African across national borders is motivated by a variety of factors but predominately economic betterment, discrimination and political instability as well as the effects of globalization.[19] For example, the political instability in Libya has made it very easy for traffickers and people smugglers to conduct their trade across the Mediterranean without much disturbances.[20] Additionally, economic hardships and poverty have made many Africans susceptible and easy targets of people and human smugglers. Furthermore, globalization has made communication and transportation very easy from any place to any destination. Human trafficking and people smuggling is further compounded by weak law enforcement institutions, weak governance and corruption among both government and private sector in most African states.

WILDLIFE TRAFFICKING

According to the Organized Crime Index Africa,[21] wildlife (fauna and flora) crime is ranked the second highest form of organized crime on the African continent with the Democratic Republic of Congo and the central Africa region as the main source of wildlife trafficking. It is an illegal industry that some estimate is worth $5–23 billion USD annually; it occurs in over 120 countries around the world and involves multiple taxa of species, including mammals, corals, reptiles, bony fishes and birds.[22] Evidence shows that wildlife trade and trafficking remain a key threat to biodiversity and is often associated

---

[17] (*The Maravi Post*).

[18] Ibid.

[19] Salvatore Coluccello and Simon Massey. (2007). Out of Africa: The human trade between Libya and Lampedusa. Trends in Organized Crime, 10 (4): 77–90, p. 78, available at: http://dx.doi.org/10.1007/s12117-007-9020-y (accessed on 13 March 2021).

[20] As above, p. 84.

[21] Saba Kassa and Baez-Camargo, Claudia and Costa, Jacopo. *Corruption and wildlife trafficking: Exploring drivers, facilitators and networks behind illegal wildlife trade in East Africa*. Working Paper, 30 (2019), p. 15, available at: https://edoc.unibas.ch/75261/ (accessed 18 February 2021).

[22] Helen Agu and Meredith Gore. (2020). Global Ecology and Conservation. Volume 23, p. 1, available at: https://doi.org/10.1016/j.gecco.2020.e01166 (accessed 11 March 2021).

with illicit arms deals, trafficking of people and drug smuggling.[23] The inclusion of marine species as part of wildlife crimes has made the crime far more prevalent across the continent than if distinct markets for land and sea species had been presented.[24]

Kassa et al. indicate that the main drivers and facilitators of illegal wildlife trade (IWT) diverse.[25] These include poverty and need, corruption as a cross cutting facilitator, weak governance and security institutions, inadequate livelihoods for the communities that live around protected areas and globalization which provides easy communication and transportation of such contraband.[26] The problem of IWT is further compounded by availability of criminal networks that operate in a well-coordinated manner, and availability of lucrative illicit markets for wildlife products that span across the world.[27] Such networks extend over several countries and hence beyond the jurisdiction of any one law enforcement authority making investigations and prosecution a complex venture. In some cases, political instability and civil wars exacerbate illegal wildlife trade and trafficking. Huge profits and greed are yet another key push factor for wildlife crime in Africa.[28]

The high demand for wildlife, animal parts, plants and plant material around the world has resulted in criminal activities on a large scale. Considerably cheaper than legally sourced material, the illegal trade in fauna and flora offers opportunities to reap significant profits. Gaps in domestic and international control regimes, difficulties in identifying illegal commodities and secondary products, along with intricate trafficking routes make it difficult to effectively curtail the trade. Although several international and non-governmental organizations have launched initiatives aimed at bringing international attention to the problem of wildlife trafficking, political commitment and operational capacity to tackle this phenomenon are not commensurate to the scale of the problem. There is, to date, no universal framework to prevent and suppress this crime type and there is a lack of critical and credible expertise and scholarship on this phenomenon.[29]

---

[23] Timothy C. Haas and Sam M. Ferreira. (2015). Federated databases and actionable intelligence: Using social network analysis to disrupt transnational wildlife trafficking criminal networks. *Secur Inform* 4, 2, p. 2, available at: https://doi.org/10.1186/s13388-015-0018-8 (accessed 10 December 2021).

[24] ISS, Organized Crime Index of 2019, note above 3, p. 15.

[25] Kassa, et al., note 21 above, p. 2.

[26] As above.

[27] Haas and Ferreira, note 23 above, p. 3.

[28] See for example, Kofi Ernest Abotsi, Paolo Galizzi and Alena Herklotz. (2016). *Wildlife Crime and Degradation in Africa: An Analysis of the Current Crisis and Prospects for a Secure Future*, 27 Fordham Environmental Law Review, p. 394.

[29] Gian Andrea Ege and Georgina Howe. (2020). *Criminalisation of Wildlife Trafficking*. In: Ege, Gian Andrea; Schloenhardt, Andreas; Schwarzenegger, Christian. Wildlife Trafficking: The illicit trade in wildlife, animal parts, and derivatives. Illegaler Handel mit

Despite the actual and potential scale of the scourge, wildlife trafficking often remains overlooked and poorly understood by many governments. As a result, preventing and suppressing the illegal trade in wildlife, animal parts, and plants is presently not a priority in many countries. Wildlife and biodiversity related policies, laws, and their enforcement have, for the most part, not kept up with the changing levels and patterns of wildlife trafficking. Poorly developed legal frameworks, weak law enforcement, prosecutorial and judicial practices have resulted in valuable wildlife and plant resources becoming threatened.

Evidence shows that illicit wildlife trade and trafficking impacts on the global and ecosystem order in myriad ways. For example, the increased demand for bushmeat has contributed greatly towards degradation of wildlife. Additionally, wildlife crimes lead to the proliferation of guns in areas that would be gun free. The tourism industry continues to be heavily affected with the degradation of wildlife, particularly in National Parks and Game Reserves of countries such as Zambia, Kenya and South Africa.

To deal with wildlife crimes it requires consented efforts. There is need for African countries to develop and implement continental strategies and action plans to deal with the scourge. The other novel way of dealing with illegal wildlife trade and trafficking is to develop a federated database that would help to overcome disjointed information kept in different databases by independent.[30] Through such a database intelligence and any kind of information on criminal networks is readily available under one database, making it easy for law enforcers to search for criminals from anywhere in the world. There is also a need to conduct joint social network analyses that can provide law enforcers with targeted responses that can maximally disrupt these criminal networks. Through such social network analysis, it is easy to identify key players and predicts player succession in the IWT. There is also need for African states to continue sharing information on criminal activities surrounding wildlife trade and trafficking.

ILLICIT ARMS TRADE AND TRAFFICKING

The illicit trade in small arms and light weapons (SALWs) in Africa remains a huge problem and is one of the greatest sources of armed conflicts in the continent since the departure of the colonialists in the 1960s.[31] With the rise of globalization and unprecedented changes in the production of weapons of mass destruction and ammunition, Africa has remained the destination of

---

Tieren, Tierbestandteilen und Tierprodukten. Berlin: Carl Grossmann Verlag, 245–270 (available at: https://www.zora.uzh.ch/id/eprint/192201/ (accessed 13 January 2021).

[30] Haas and Ferreira, note 23 above, p. 2.

[31] Waziri Adisa, Arms Proliferation, Boko Haram Extremism and Insecurity in Nigeria. Internal Security Management in Nigeria, 2019, p. 307, available at: https://doi.org/10.1007/978-981-13-8215-4_15 (accessed 9 March 2021).

a large cache of arms and ammunition sold and smuggled to the conflict-ridden societies in the continent. Illicit trade and trafficking in small arms and light weapons remain the third highest form of organized crime in Africa, with Sudan, Chad, the Central African Republic and the Democratic Republic of Congo as the highest hot spots for the scourge.

The problem of small arms is compounded by difficulties in identifying illegally manufactured arms since, it is the legally manufactured arms that have often ended up in illegal markets thereby making it difficult to identify and trace their illegality.[32]

Studies show that proliferation of Small Arms and Light Weapons (SALW) is caused by many factors such as permanent political instability in most of the highly affected countries, emanating from the short-term policy of the former colonial powers and later on solidified by a series of violent power changes, arms races, direct sale from manufacturers; weak governments and porous borders.[33]

For example, due to political instability, Chad has been marked by a division of the country along ethnic and religious lines since as far back as the colonial period. Arms traffickers take advantage of political instability to corrupt government officials and traffic illegal arms into Chad and across the countries. The lack of trust between the various ethnic groups of the population has led to the high demand for illegal arms in order to compete for exclusive control over the state machinery and mineral resources.[34]

Arms race is another contributing factor to proliferation of small arms in Africa. War-torn countries believe that the only way to retain advantage over their opponents and competitors is by maintaining huge stocks of firearms. Arms continue to spread in Africa and the world over because countries would want to ensure their national security and, of course, maintain supremacy over their opponents.[35]

In certain instances, like in Sudan, trafficking of arms is made possible through several sources such as the government, military representatives, distributors, terrorists, multinational corporations, smugglers and covert government agencies who engage in secret deliveries of firearms to different armed groups.[36] In Sudan, arms also reach Sudanese opposition forces

---

[32] Philip K. Chebbet. (2002). A Security Problem in the Greta Lakes Region and the Horn of Africa: Proliferation of Small Arms and Light Weapons. Strategy Research Project. Carlisle Barracks, Pennsylvania 1701 3, p. 5, available at: https://www.hsdl.org/?view&did=439549 (accessed 10 March 2021).

[33] Patrick Berg. (2008). The Dynamics of Conflict in the Tri-Border Region of the Sudan, Chad and the Central African Republic, p. 8, available at: http://www.moncamer.ch/DRDC2/images/DRDC/StudiesAndResearch/The_Dynamics_of_Conflict_in_the_Tri Border_Region.pdf (accessed 27 February 2021).

[34] As above, p. 9.

[35] As abobe, p. 241.

[36] Curtis Burton Managing and Christopher LaMonica. (2012). *Africana*, 6 (1), p. 220, available at: www.africanajournal.org (accessed 9 March 2021).

through an informal smuggling network within Africa that stretches as far south as Mozambique and Angola.[37] Thus, direct sales of firearms from weapon manufacturers to foreign governments or private entities remain quite common in most war-torn or politically unstable countries.

Cold war era surplus stock is another source of small arms and light weapons supply in the central and western war-torn countries. After the cold war, the US military has given away or sold at discount vast quantities of excess assault rifles, carbines, 45 calibre pistols, machine guns and grenade launchers and these weapons continue to traffic into and across Africa, where they are used to various forms of crimes including terrorism.[38]

When it comes Democratic Republic of Congo (DRC), in addition to above causes, the migration of the Hutus from Rwanda also contributed to proliferation of small arms in DRC.[39] When fleeing their country, these migrants carried with firearms. These arms continue to be smuggled and trafficked across several countries in the west, central and southern Africa.

Weak government structures and porous borders in the conflict zones make it impossible for governments to have control over the movement of SALW.[40] For example, the porosity of Nigerian borders has given the Boko Haram arms smugglers an opportunity to use different methods to move arms into the country.[41] Boko Haram members often conceal arms in sacks, trucks and at the back of camels and donkeys to avoid being arrested by Nigerian security forces as they cross porous borders from different exporting countries. Once trafficked into an African country, illicit SALW circulate in war-torn and conflict zones. Thus, a small arm that was initially trafficked from Liberia to Sierra Leone, may find its way into to Côte d'Ivoire, and then to Guinea. In the same way, weapons from Chad have been used in Darfur, while weapons in Somalia have originated from Djibouti, Ethiopia, Egypt, Eritrea and Libya, Uganda and Yemen crossing the porous borders with much ease.[42]

---

[37] As above, p. 222.

[38] As above, pp. 220–222.

[39] Temesgen Thomas Halabo. (2020). Conflicts in the Democratic Republic of Congo: Dynamics, Trends and Challenges for Peace. PJAEE, 17 (9) (2020), p. 10,093, available at: file:///C:/Users/LENOVO/AppData/Local/Temp/6336-Article%20Text-12335-1-10–20,210,204.pdf (accessed 9 March 2021).

[40] As above, p. 10,095.

[41] Adisa note 31 above, p. 314.

[42] Rachel Stohl and EJ Hogendoorn. Stopping the Destructive Spread of Small Arms: How Small Arms and Light Weapons Proliferation Undermines Security and Development. Centre for American Progress, 2010, p. 6, available at: www.americanprogress.com (accessed 10 March 2021); Nancy Annan. (2014). Violent Conflicts and Civil Strife in West Africa: Causes, Challenges and Prospects. Stability: International Journal of Security & Development, 3(1): 3, pp. 1–16, 9, available at: http://dx.doi.org/10.5334/sta.da (accessed 9 March 2021).

ILLICIT DRUG TRAFFICKING

Africa has historically held a peripheral role in the transnational illicit drug trade, but in recent years has increasingly become a locus for drug trafficking, particularly cocaine and counterfeit drugs.[43] Cannabis Sativa, Cocaine, Heroin and a number of other synthetic narcotics are the main types of dangerous drugs that are commonly trafficked by organized criminal syndicates in and across Africa.[44] UNODC further reports that drug trafficking data collected in the World *Drug Report 2020* also show that between 2013 and 2017, 20 per cent of all global *seizures* of cannabis herb and resin were made in Africa. This observation buttresses previous UNODA reports which indicated that seizures in Africa had increased from under 1 metric tonnes per year in the 1998–2002 period to 15 metric tonnes in 2006, and that during the three years from 2005 through 2007, officials seized at least 33 metric tonnes of cocaine bound for Europe via West Africa.[45]

It has been observed that most of the drugs trafficked in Africa are obtained from outside the continent.[46] On the West African coast, Ghanaian and Nigerian drug barons obtain their consignments of cocaine from Colombia and the Latin America. In the horn and part of East Africa, drugs are trafficked from South and South West Asia. Recently, the East African coast has now been identified by anti-narcotics agencies as a major transit point for hard drugs.[47]

Most of the illicit drugs that pass through East Africa originate from India and Thailand and are destined for Southern Africa and Europe. More recently, drug cartels have established contacts with Asian and Far Eastern producers to use South Africa as a conduit for smuggling Cannabis, Heroin and Opium to Europe and the US. It has been observed, for example, that many female victims of human trafficking are used as 'drug moles' across international borders, in particular, between West Africa and Latin America and West Africa and South Africa.[48] This means West Africa is also a huge source, conduit and great beneficiary of drug trafficking.

In the area of counterfeit drugs, International Criminal Police Organization (INTERPOL) reports that Africa has recently become the hub of counterfeit drug production and trafficking. For example, during Africa's Operations code-named Afya and Heera II, which were conducted and coordinated by INTERPOL between the months of March and May in 2018, the Tanzania's Food and Drug Administration seized US$8300 worth of counterfeit medical products, including antibiotics, anti-malarial tablets, ferrous sulphate

---

[43] Liana Sun Wyler, Illegal Drug Trade in Africa: Trends and U.S. Policy. Congressional Research Service, 2010, p. 1, available at: www.crs.gov.R40838 (accessed 10 March 2021).

[44] UNODC 2018, note 16 above, pp. 25–30.

[45] As above, pp. 20–28.

[46] Sun Wyler note 43 above, p. 1.

[47] UNODC 2018, note 16 above, pp. 29–30.

[48] As above.

and analgesics. The Zimbabwe Republican Police seized 5700 tablets of counterfeit pharmaceutics and 250 kg of skin lotions smuggled from Zambia. In Western Africa, Operation Heera II saw the identification of smuggling transit routes including one where a counterfeit brand of antalgic tablet was being distributed to western African countries by road after importation to Benin, Ghana and Togo seaports. At Niger's Makalondi Border Crossing Point, police intercepted 29 tonnes of counterfeit medicines in two trucks thought to be travelling from Ghana.

Impact of Organized Crime on Development in Africa

Organized crime gas explicitly been integrated on the global development agenda. In the Sustainable Development Goals (SDGs), which set a universal global agenda, Traget 16.4 aims to 'significantly reduce illicit financial and arms flow, strengthen the recovery return of stolen assets and combat all forms of organized crime'.[49] Likewise, the African Union's Agenda 2063, which is the principal framework for the achievement of Africa's development priorities, identifies organized crime as key threat to Africa's development.

Organized crime poses a huge threat to the promotion of economic growth; reduction of poverty and the rule of law, to peace and stability. It also threatens the general maintenance of global bio-diversity and sustainable environments; the building of safe and inclusive societies; the promotion of public health and people's well-being; and even the orderly management of migration. The inclusion of organized crime in the SDGs and AUs Agenda 2063, therefore, emphasises how deep-rooted organized crime is at global as well as continental level and the urgent need for countries to address the vice. Every society is now affected by of organized crime in one or the other. Many of the development challenges that Africa faces are associated with high crime rates, which threaten the achievement of African Union development blue-print; Agenda 2063 as a cross cutting-issue.

The impact of organized crime on the African continent is devastating and has a bearing on several fronts of development. Economically, organized crime has both positive and negative impacts. For example, in war-torn countries like DRC, organized crime through its illegal deals can be a source of livelihoods, a resilience strategy for the poor and vulnerable and, in some aspirational markets, a genuine means for achieving development. That is through organized crime, illicit goods are able to reach those communities that otherwise could not have managed to afford them. There is also a development paradox at play where the illicit economy may present the best possible development returns for certain communities or for the life chances of individuals.

---

[49] Tuesday Reitano and Marcena Hunter, The crime-development paradox / Organised crime and the SDGs, ENACT, Continental Report 2, February 2018, available at: https://enact-africa.s3.amazonaws.site/uploads/2018-02-20-continentalreport-crimedevelopment.-paradox.researchpdf (accessed 17 March 2021).

314   M. N. KAYIRA

On a negative note, most organized crime groups engage in predatory acts of crime such as armed robberies and bank frauds and kidnappings. Organized criminal groups may also get involved in fraud and commercial crimes such as counterfeit currency. In states where governments are weak and fragile, organized crime gangs are involved in arms smuggling, smuggling of mineral resources that could help in the economic development of those countries. Example of this development include what happened in Angola in late 1980s and the DRC in late 1990s, where the UN found that large amounts of precious minerals and other resources were smuggled from areas under 'rebel' control and sold outside the country. Such trade is a huge negative effect on economic development of most African countries. In the area of world-trade, organized crime has the power to destabilize international economies. For example, smuggling of oil in major resource producing countries like Nigeria results in the increase of oil and other oil products across Africa.[50] Adverse changes in the price of oil affects the fortunes of so many countries.

In the area of peace and stability, the sale and transfer of illicit small arms and light weapons have exacerbated tensions, threatened democracy and destabilized nations causing untold hardships, atrocities and deaths to many people that are already ravaged by extreme poverty.[51] It is estimated that 500,000 people die every year from violent conflicts worldwide, the majority of who are from Africa and other developing countries.[52] Reports also indicate that uncontrolled arms transfer has deepened armed violence in many poverty-stricken African countries such as Central African Republic, Mali, Libya, Democratic Republic of Congo, Congo, Kenya, Somalia Lake Chad Basin, Sudan, South-Sudan, Nigeria and Cameroon.[53]

On the human capital front, crime erodes Africa's social and human capital. That is when crime rates are high in a country, both skilled and unskilled workers migrate overseas in fear of being victimized. In the same connection, crime also drives business away from Africa. Organized crime is bad for investor confidence. Both foreign and domestic investors see crime in Africa as sign of social instability. According to World Bank Investment Climate survey data from nine African countries, over 29% of business people in Africa reported that crime was a major constraint on investment, about 50% more than the global average.

For organized crime to thrive in Africa, corruption is its lubricant. Organize crime groups and syndicates usually indulge in corruption and bribes to achieve their goals. For organized crime groups to move goods across the

---

[50] Charles Goredema, Organised crime and terrorism: Observations from Southern Africa, ISS Paper 101 • March 2005, p. 6, available at: https://files.ethz.ch/isn/99194/PAGER151.pdf (accessed 18 March 2021).

[51] Adisa note 31 above, p. 308.

[52] Adesoji Adeniyi, The Human Cost of Uncontrolled Arms in Africa: Cross-national research on seven African countries, Oxfam Research Report 2017.

[53] Adisa note 31 above, p. 308.

borders, they have to corrupt or bribe law enforcement and tax officials. Such malpractice erodes the tax base of a country which regresses economic development. Bribe-seeking officials fuel inequality and increase informality making people lose trust in government systems. When people lose confidence in government systems, they may engage in vigilantism, which further undermines the state. Bribe-seeking official also drive up the cost of doing business in Africa. As a result, investors shy away from corrupt countries, thereby reducing competition in the market because the buyers have less choices from the market. The World Bank says corruption is the single greatest obstacle to development globally.

Organized crime also has negative impacts on governance in Africa. In most cases organized crime involves bribing of the bureaucracy and law enforcement authorities to buy passage and operate in specific countries. Once the bureaucrats have been bribed, they can no longer carry out their duties impartially. The community loses trust the state and its agencies. As a result, crime thrives, thereby undermining peace and security in Africa. The organized crime curtails are able to operate freely and infiltrate both the private and public sectors, thereby weakening the governance system in most African states.

The Africa's tourism industry has also suffered the blunt effects of organized crime. Transnational organized crime has led to annihilation of some of the rarest species that attract tourists thereby bringing revenue to African countries. Rare species such as rhinos, elephants, tigers, buffaloes and pangolins which attract tourism remain endangered and are lost to wildlife crime. Killing of rare species makes the tourism industry less attractive resulting in reduced revenue collection from the tourism industry.

Additionally, organized crime leads to saturation of counterfeit products on the market. Consumption of counterfeit products such as food, drugs and cigarettes have huge negative impacts on human health. Counterfeit products cause ailments thereby reducing human participation in social and development activities in their countries. Poor health resulting from consumption of counterfeit products also drains resources allocated to public hospitals.

Lastly, organized crime has devastating effects on the health and wellbeing of women and children particularly in war-torn countries and countries infiltrated by armed insurgents such as Democratic Republic of Congo (DRC), Somalia and Nigeria. In these countries armed groups fighting to control illegal trade in minerals, drugs and firearms perpetually commit sexual violence such as gang rape, genital mutilations, abduction, defilement against tens of thousands of women and girls and expose them to sexual slavery.[54] For example, Boko Haram insurgents abducted several Chibok girls from their secondary school in August of 2016 who were exposed to various forms

[54] James Cockayne and Daniel Pfister. (2008). Peace Operations and Organised Crime. Geneva Papers. The Geneva Centre for Security Policy (GCSP). International Peace Institute. Geneva 1, Switzerland, p. 27, available at: https://www.files.ethz.ch/isn/57279/gen eva_paper_2.pdf, available at: accessed 24 February 2002.

316   M. N. KAYIRA

of sexual violence including rape, defilement, sexually transmitted diseases and early pregnancies.[55] Armed groups also employ a lot of child soldiers in Africa's war-torn countries. Hard drugs like cannabis sativa and cocaine contribute towards increased case of mental health and drug disorders in Africa.[56]

CHALLENGES IN COMBATING ORGANIZED CRIME IN AFRICA

The war against organized crime faces many challenges to be won not only in Africa but globally. These challenges include the complex nature of organized crime itself and the way it is committed, inadequate resources to implement initiatives and strategies to fight organized crime, improved communication technology and definitional dilemmas.[57]

By nature, organized crime is generally sophisticated and complex and requires people with adequate skills and knowledge to be executed. Another key challenge in the fight against organized crime is the sophisticated and complex nature in which organized criminal groups and networks operate.[58] Unlike conventional criminals, organized criminal groups take time to learn their business and master their tricks. Often times organized crime offenders are the more seasoned criminals who might even have a long judicial history. In terms of modus operandi, different forms of organized crime follow different modus operandi. Most organized criminals such as drug traffickers have more connections to the criminal underworld. Owing to this complex and sophisticated nature in which organized crime is committed, it is clear that ordinary methods or interventions used in fighting conventional crimes are not as sufficient and as effective to deal with the scourge. Additionally, the complexity of organized crime requires huge intelligence and logistical support to be trailed and busted. Fighting organized crime requires a certain level of intelligence among law enforcers and specific organizational skills sets.[59] Otherwise, efforts in the fight against organized crime becomes moot. Basic policing knowledge and skills to combat organized crime at local police station and national level cannot cope in the fight against organized crime.

The complex nature of organized crime has created difficulties in collecting statistics concerning some categories of organized crimes such as wildlife trafficking, drug trafficking and arms trafficking. Available statistics are only the

---

[55] Adisa note 31 above, p. 312.

[56] UNODC. (2020). World Drug Report 2020 (United Nations publication, Sales No. E.20.XI.6), p. 15, available at: https://wdr.unodc.org/wdr2020/field/WDR20_BOO KLET_1.pdf (accessed 10 March 2021).

[57] Shaw and Reitano note 4 above, p. 6.

[58] Van Koppen, M. V., de Poot, C. J. and Blokland, A. A. J. (2010). Comparing Criminal Careers of Organized Crime Offenders and General Offenders. *European Journal of Criminology*, 7 (5), pp. 356–374, available at: https://doi.org/10.1177/147737081037 3730 (accessed 18 March 2021).

[59] As above.

ones concerning reported cases or where law enforces have managed to arrest the culprits.[60] Otherwise, statistics on cases that are not reported are not included in any reports.

Another major obstacle in the fight against organized crime is lack of resources to implement initiatives and strategies to fight organized crime. Law enforcement officials in many African countries are poorly trained and ill equipped to mount aggressive attacks on organized crime. In many instances, African countries rely donor support for advanced training in criminal matters. Similarly, most African countries have not made significant investment in developing infrastructure to facilitate the fight against organized crime. Many African countries lack technological, scientific and human capacity to conduct covert or undercover operations and investigations. African states have inadequate aerial and maritime resources to conduct surveillance of organized crimes and criminal networks involved in illegal wildlife trafficking, firearms, human and drug traffickers as well as criminal networks involved in the scourge. There is need for massive technological and human resource investment if the fight against organized crime is to remain meaningful in Africa. Such investment will require huge amount of finances, which most African do not have.

Another factor that contributes to challenges in holistically dealing with organized crime emanates from the definition dilemma. So far there appears to be no clear and single definition of the phenomenon.[61] The Southern Africa Development Community (SADC) has attempted to define the phenomenon. In its definition, SADC recognizes organized crime as illegal criminal activities carried out by a criminal group or group of persons, however loosely or tightly organized. However, this definition has not yet been accepted at African Union level nor has it been embraced in any domestic legislation in any member state of the African Union. This dilemma has created confusion to develop harmonize strategies and legislation in responding to the scourge among African states. For example, African states including Malawi, Zambia, Zimbabwe, South Africa and Rwanda do not recognize organized crime as a specific criminal offence in their domestic legal frameworks.[62] Each African country has its own definition. Lack of a single definition pauses further challenges when it comes to prosecuting and extraditing criminals who jump borders.

---

[60] William Robert Avis. (2017). Criminal networks and illicit wildlife trade: Knowledge, Evidence and Learning for Development. K4D Helpdesk Report, p. 5, available at: https://assets.publishing.service.gov.uk/media/5975df3ded915d59ba00000a/150-Illicit-Wildlife-Trade.pdf. Accessed March 10, 2021 (accessed 18 March 2021).

[61] Cockayne and Pfister, note 54 above, p. 12.

[62] Stephen Ellis and Mark Shaw. (2015). Does organized crime exist in Africa? *African Affairs*. 114. adv035. 10.1093/afraf/adv035.

318   M. N. KAYIRA

FIGHTING ORGANIZED CRIME IN AFRICA

Like any other scourge that has devastating effects, organized crime needs a holistic approach to be dealt with in Africa. There is need for African States and the international community to develop collective and comprehensive responses in preventing, detecting and prosecuting offences bordering on organized crime. A successful response in the fight against organized crime requires efforts from everyone, ranging from members of the community to multinational companies and state institutions. International corporations investing in Africa must partner with governments in developing interventions against organized crime.[63] Some of the key strategies that can be deployed in the fight against organized crime are discussed below.

At national level, African countries must be encouraged to adopt best practises such as establishing of specialized units to gather information and investigate activities concerning organized crimes. In South Africa, such specialized units include, among others, the organized crime units of the South African Police Service (SAPS), South African Narcotics and Alcohol Bureau (SANAB), the Commercial Branch, Vehicle Theft Units, the Endangered Species Unit, the Diamond and Gold Branch, SAPS Anti-corruption units, SAPS Internal Security (formerly Security Branch), the National Intelligence Agency (NIA), Military Intelligence (MI) and the South African Secret Service (SASS). Similar units have also been established in many African security agencies. Other countries like Nigeria, Malawi have also embraced similar best practises. And the effects of such units are evident from the many cases that are detected and prosecuted.

Developing adequate and effective legislation and policy frameworks to combat organized crime is another key approach that all African countries need to embrace. African countries need to come up joint efforts to develop adequate, strong and effective legal and policy frameworks that are capable of deterring organized criminal groups from operating and using African countries as sources, transit routes and markets for contraband. African states must strive at harmonizing international legal frameworks such as the extradition treaties to ensure that fugitives involved in organized crime do not find safe heavens across the borders particularly in countries where such formal arrangements exist. Domestic legislations alone are not sufficient to win the battle against the scourge. In many instances, domestic legislations are so weak in many African states and makes it convenient and easy for organized criminal groups to operate and transit through such countries. Weak legislations include provisions for weak penalties for organized crimes such as drug trafficking.[64]

---

[63] Reitano and Hunter, above note 49.

[64] Ellis and Shaw, note 62 above.

For example, penalties for convictions for possession of Dangerous Drugs in most southern African countries are mostly fines.[65]

The fight against organized crime in Africa can also be enhanced by increasing the number of police officers in most African countries. According to Mutume, Africa has far fewer police per citizen than other regions.[66] He contends that there are only 180 police per 100,000 people on the continent, while in Asia there are 363. Furthermore, when police officers are underpaid and government officials are susceptible to corruption, it is suggested that the increase in number of police officers must be accompanied by supplying the police and other law enforcement agencies with relevant and modern training, adequate and modern equipment such as vehicles and communication equipment. African countries must be encouraged to deploy more technologically advanced equipment such as Unmanned Aerial Vehicles (UAVs) and thermo-imagery sensors in the fight against organized crime.

African countries must also be encouraged to provide adequate support to regional and continental institutions and agreements established by regional blocs to fight transnational crime. There are several regional and continental institutions established under various economic and political blocs aimed at fighting cross-border crime such as firearms trafficking, drug trafficking, human trafficking and wildlife crime. Through regional blocs and INTERPOL, states and international organizations are able to share and exchange information, intelligence and strategies to fight crime and criminal syndicates. As the world's largest police organization, and with a mandate to share and process criminal information globally, African countries and regional bodies need to harness the benefits accrued by working with from INTERPOL in the fight against organized crime.

Joint trans-border exercises among African countries is also another key strategy that African countries can deploy to combat transnational crimes. Studies show that countries like Malawi, South Africa, Zambia and others in southern Africa have always promoted joint cross-border activities to combat arms smuggling, car thefts, drug trafficking and wildlife crimes (Small Arms Survey, 2010).

Another effective strategy in the fight against organized crime in Africa and across the world is by conducting coordinated 'Operations' targeting specific forms of cross-border crimes. Such operations which are usually coordinated by INTERPOL and regional blocs such as Southern Africa Regional Police Chiefs Cooperation Organization (SARPCCOO) yield overwhelming results. For example, between 30 November and 6 December 2020, INTERPOL and the United Nations Office on Drugs and Crime (UNODC) jointly coordinated a seven-day operation codenamed Operation KAFO II that saw law

---

[65] Gumisai Mutume. (2007). Organized crime targets weak African States. Africa Renewal, 2007, available at: https://www.un.org/africarenewal/magazine/july-2007/organized-crimetargetsweak-africanstates (accessed 7 June 2020).

[66] As above.

enforcement officers intercept illicit firearms, ammunition and explosives and disrupt the trafficking networks used to supply terrorists across West Africa. The operation mobilized 260 officers from police, gendarmerie, national commissions for the control of small arms and light weapons, customs and anti-trafficking airport units and border and prosecution services in all four countries in West Africa and recovered several firearms, ammunitions and other offensive weapons (INTERPOL website).

To win the battle against organized crime, African states must also strive at modernizing their border management capabilities and infrastructure. Long, porous borders and weak border control, including undermanned ports and numerous secondary airports, accord organized criminal groups free movement across African borders. Remoteness and uneven terrain of most borders make it extremely difficult to be accessible by law enforcement agencies, thereby limiting their action in combating organized crime. Sadly, most African countries lack well-trained law officials to man the borders. To ensure proper border management, law enforcement institutions must enhance their skills through proper training. States must also ensure they have modern border management infrastructure including drones, maritime and other aerial surveillance mechanisms. Additionally, African states must encourage international cooperation in particular sharing of crime information among countries that share common borders. Though this approach requires time and willing partners to be effective, it is effective in preventing the free movement of criminals and illegal goods across the borders. For example, to curb the growing presence of illicit drugs in South Africa, the country may consider tightening border security by among others; intensifying border patrols and surveillance along the borders (Organized Crime Index Africa, 2019, p. 9).

Conclusion and Way Forward

Organized crime continues to grow and flourish across the African continent, presenting diverse threats to sustainable development and achievement of Agenda 2063. From the discussion in this chapter, human trafficking and human smuggling are the most widespread forms of organized crime in Africa with Libya and Eritrea as the greatest hotspots for the scourge. Wildlife crime is the second most predominant forms of organized crime in Africa with Democratic Republic of Congo and the central African region being the most highly affected. Arms trafficking remain the third highest form of organized crime in Africa with Sudan, Chad, the Central African Republic and the Democratic Republic of Congo as the highest hot spots for the scourge. Drug Trafficking, in particular cannabis remains the fourth most prevalent form of organized crime in Africa. Morocco, Tanzania and Sudan are key countries involved in the production, distribution and use of cannabis.

The devastating impacts of the scourge continue to compromise peace and security in most African countries in particular those countries ravaged by civil wars. Social and economic development of African countries has also been retarded to organize crime. Skilled and unskilled human resource continue to migrate from Africa. Foreign investment is heavily affected by corruption. The tourism sector also continues to suffer low patronage in Africa due to depletion of wildlife. Counterfeit products which include fake drugs and vaccines also keeping taking tall on human health. Women and children continue to suffer from the effects of organized crime through sexual exploitation and being used as child soldiers.

Considering the complex nature of organized crimes, it is apparent that no country can singlehandedly successfully confront the scourge. It is, therefore, prudent that any response mechanisms to the problem must be interlaced into both national and global security, political, economic, social and legal strategies. Politically, African states must strive at ensuring that there is peace and stability in all African countries. Peace and stability drive away criminal gangs that take advantage of weak and corrupt governance institutions and bureaucracies to thrive. Security wise, African states must ensure that law enforcement institutions promote cross-border cooperation as well as sharing of information. Economically, African states must encourage economic development of African societies so that their livelihood improves, thereby reducing the reliance on illegally obtained products. Improved livelihood also reduces the propensity for individuals to indulge in organized crime. Thus, impairing the demand side of illicit goods. The technological aspect of organized crime calls for African states to embrace new and emerging technologies to keep pace with increasing sophistication of organized criminal groups. This can be achieved by acquiring modern surveillance equipment to monitor cross-border activities at all times. Finally, African states must develop comprehensive national and international legal frameworks that would facilitate smooth investigation, prosecution and extradition of transnational organized criminals.

CHAPTER 19

Resource Conflicts in Africa

Godard Busingye

INTRODUCTION

Conflicts over natural resources in Africa, among other causes, stem from lack of democratic management of natural resources in some States, corruption and greed for political power in others. It also stems from the insatiable interest of external actors in Africa's politics and natural resources. To tame the problem, the African Union (AU) came up with a guiding vision on silencing guns, under the general theme of Agenda 2063.[1] Under this framework, Africans set milestones to be achieved and by which dates. It was anticipated that by 2020, guns would be silent on the continent. All wars and civil conflicts, gender-based violence and violent conflicts would equally have ended.

The African continent would then be working toward stabilizing the continent and preparing it to move to another level of economic development. It was also hoped that by 2023, all inter and intra national conflicts would have ceased and the target of silencing of all guns on the continent would have been attained. Local and national mechanisms for conflict prevention and resolution would be entrenched and functioning for the cause of peace. Unfortunately, 2020 came to pass before much of the desired targets had been achieved.

[1]African Union Commission, Agenda 2063, The Africa We Want, A Shared Strategic Framework for Inclusive Growth and Sustainable Development First Ten-Year Implementation Plan 2014–2023, September 2015.

G. Busingye (✉)
Kampala International University, Kampala, Uganda

© The Author(s), under exclusive license to Springer Nature Switzerland AG 2022
D. Kuwali (ed.), *The Palgrave Handbook of Sustainable Peace and Security in Africa*, https://doi.org/10.1007/978-3-030-82020-6_19

323

There is still hope for building on the progress so far made so that the targets under Agenda 2063 for the year 2023 are met.

As agreed by George Chipembere Lwanda in Chapter 30, the African continent is richly endowed with natural resources, which if harnessed and proceeds therefrom are utilized well, can significantly contribute to poverty reduction efforts in many countries. The problem starts when these natural resources are exploited and conflicts begin over who takes what portion of the proceeds therefrom. In some cases, such as the Democratic Republic of the Congo (DRC), nationals would be better off, at least for now, without the available natural resources being exploited. Unfortunately, some of the citizens of the DRC live in abject poverty, amidst abundant natural resources. The same trend is true for some other African States. Burnley considers that conflict-prone societies such as the DRC present even more complex challenges given the underlying political and historical reasons for the conflicts.[2]

In support of this view, Fiott avers that "[N]atural resources such as precious metals and stones, oil, food, water and timber and conflict make for an unusual and complex relationship."[3] This position is reinforced by Kiiza et al., who consider that abundance of natural resources on the African continent is a curse, not a blessing.[4] The phenomenon of a resource curse is well articulated in the African Development Report, 2007. The Report conceptualises a resource curse as a situation whereby a country has an export-driven natural resources sector that generates large revenues for government but leads paradoxically to economic stagnation and political instability.[5] In extreme cases, the resource curse culminates into conflicts, which sometimes are violent in nature. This paradoxically becomes the unintended outcome of greed and poor natural resources management on the African continent.

Undoubtedly, the problem of conflict of interest over natural resources is not about to be resolved. Conflict of interest prevents African leaders from utilizing the abundant natural resources to improve the well-being of their nationals. In turn, the disgruntled nationals, resort to resolve their grievances with the political heads using the gun. To an African, silencing the guns,

[2] Clementine Burnley, Natural Resources Conflict in the Democratic Republic of the Congo: A Question of Governance? Sustainable Development Law and Policy, Article 5, Volume 12, Issue 1, Fall 2011.

[3] Daniel Fiott, Natural Resources and Conflict in Africa, European Union, Technical Report, October 2009.

[4] Julius Kiiza, Lawrence Bategeka, and Sarah Ssewanyana, Righting Resource-Curse Wrongs in Uganda: The Political Economy of Oil Discovery and the Management of Popular Expectations Published in Mawazo: The Journal of Humanities and Social Sciences, Makerere University, Volume 10, Isuue 3, September 2011, pp. 183–203, accessed at: https://Righting_Resource-Curse_Wrongs_in_Uganda%20(1).pdf, on 12 December 2019.

[5] African Development Bank, African Development Report: Africa's Natural Resources: The Paradox of Plenty, 2007, Chapter 4, accessed at: https://www.afdb.org/fileadmin/uploads/afdb/Documents/Publications/(E)%20AfricanBank%202007%20Ch4.pdf, on 6 December 2019.

therefore, is not an option, if the continent must develop based on its abundant natural resources. The reason why the theme of silencing the guns was adopted by the African Union must not be side-lined at any cost. Once natural resources-linked rocking guns are silenced on the African continent, it will be possible for the continent to be a conflict-free Africa, prevent genocide, make peace a reality for all and rid the continent of wars, violent conflicts, human rights violations, and humanitarian disasters.[6]

Silencing the guns on the African continent, therefore, is a move that must be embraced by all States of the African continent if the continent is to take a leap from its present poverty levels. African leaders anticipate that within a conflict-free environment, majority of the continent's population shall have moved to at least the lower middle-income levels by 2063.[7] The African continent, however, is not a single country with homogeneous features, similar aspirations and even natural resource endowments. It is a continental bloc of several countries with different socio-economic, cultural and political backgrounds. This mosaic and inter-play of features mean that African States cannot, at the continental level, readily agree on the modus operandi of exploiting the continental natural resources.

Each of the 55 sovereign States has its national interests, which it desires to protect, much as the African Union outfit cannot be wished away, because of the need to protect continental interests by all African States. In this respect, Broadman asserts that: "Africa is not a monolith; African countries are not homogeneous, the African continent is currently comprised of 55 countries. Needless to say, Africa's countries all differ from one another—many starkly so—along a variety of dimensions: location, square area, topography, coastal vs. landlocked, population size, resource endowment, ethnic composition, diversity of religious practices, languages spoken, colonial heritage, political make-up, and so on."[8]

When considered as a single bloc, however, the African continent is rich with non-renewable mineral resources. Unfortunately, these resources are not fully harnessed, and their exploitation is not driven by the national or continental needs, but largely by those of the former imperial colonial powers. Foreign multinational companies, in some cases with the support of their Governments, take the lead in exploitation of Africa's natural resources. Some of these companies have been on the ground as far back as the countries in which they operate in were still under colonial domination. Unfortunately,

---

[6] Ziporah Musau, Silencing the Guns Campaign Kicks Off in 2020, Africa Renewal, December 2019–March 2020, accessed at: https://www.un.org/africarenewal/magazine/december-2019-march-2020/silencing-guns-campaign-kicks-2020, on 22 February 2021.

[7] African Union Commission, Silencing Guns in Africa: Building a Roadmap to a Conflict-Free Continent, Durban, 2014, accessed at: https://au.int/en/newsevents/201 40429, on 12 December 2019.

[8] Harry G. Broadman, Africa, The Continent of Economic Misperceptions, 2016, accessed at: https://www.forbes.com/sites/harrybroadman/2016/03/31/africa-the-con tinent-of-economic-misperceptions/#3b9dd77e6c54, on 12 December 2019.

the post-colonial African State has not been able to successfully take over the resources' exploration and exploitation drives on its own. It still calls for the former colonial masters' hand to sustain the exploitation of the resources. In cases where the colonial masters were totally kicked out their former colonies, the exploitation levels have gone down or the ventures closed down.

The Problem

Exploitation of natural resources on the African continent is largely undertaken by foreign governments and companies. The major foreign powers with investments in natural resources on the African continent are largely the former colonial powers, namely: The United Kingdom (UK), France, Belgium, Netherlands, Germany, and lately the United States of America, and China. The major companies especially in the oil and gas sector include Total and Shell, in other sectors, Coca Cola, an American registered Company, and the British American Tobacco. Indeed, today, multinational companies hold enormous economic and political power in post-independence African countries.[9]

Very few African Governments have the capacity to invest hefty resources in the exploration, exploitation, and marketing of the abundant natural resources on the continent. Worst of all, many African Governments have not invested heavily in the development of the necessary technologies to conserve, or sustainably utilize the continental abundant natural resources. Moreover, some of the natural resources are illegally exploited, and smuggled out of the continent, hence benefits derived therefrom cannot be accounted for. In a number of cases, such as in the DRC, Sierra Leone, Angola, Libya, and South Sudan, rebel groups in their held territories exploit natural resources which they sell to sustain their fight against Governments.[10]

Lack of accountability by political leaders to their nationals of the benefits or even losses incurred as a result of harnessing the natural resources raises suspicion as to what actually happens when those resources are exploited. Suspicion and lack of trust in political leaders by their nationals culminate into conflicts, starting as low-level violence, sometimes graduating into high-intensity armed conflicts. Examples, include the Lord's Resistance Army (LRA) armed conflict which devastated much of the northern and north Eastern Uganda and also spread to the Central African Republic, South Sudan, and the Democratic Republic of Congo.

[9] Kieron Monks, Why the Wealth of Africa Does Not Make Africans Wealthy, 2018, accessed at: https://edition.cnn.com/2016/04/18/africa/looting-machine-tom-burgis-africa/index.html, on 11 December 2019.

[10] Ian Bannon and Paul Collier (Eds), Natural Resources and Violent Conflict: Options and Actions, The World Bank, Washington, DC, 203, accessed at: http://documents.worldbank.org/curated/en/578321468762592831/pdf/282450Natural0resources0violent0conflict.pdf, on 18 December 2019.

The ongoing South Sudan internal strife between the Government of President Salvar Kirr and his former Vice President, Riak Machar, the Boko Haram terrorist group in Nigeria and neighboring countries, and several armed groups in the East of the Democratic Republic of the Congo (DRC) demonstrates the problematic nature of conflicts stemming from existence of abundant natural resources on the continent. Within the current political dispensations on the African continent, there is little hope that the resource curse can be overcome, soon.

This is largely because some African leaders themselves are hostages of both latent and overt foreign interest in the continent's natural resources. Such leaders are unable to vehemently protect the interest of Africans. Moreover, the zeal expressed by the post-colonial African leaders to deal with political issues afflicting their nations does not match the low-ebb exhibited when it comes to protecting their countries' natural resources from foreign interests. Even the seemingly benevolent latter post-colonial leaders, fall into the same cyclic trap of self-aggrandisement and corruption that befell their predecessors, which aggravates the already worse situation.

There is also a problem of engendering the management of resources on the African continent where men, not women, make important decisions as whether or not to exploit the resources. Men also determine what to do with the proceeds derived from the sale of the resources, as women watch helplessly. Suffice to note that women are agents and reliable allies for development but remain excluded from decision-making arenas concerning their existence. When pressed to the no survival corner, women can take up guns and fight for those rights. In the case of Uganda, one Alice Lakwena commanded a spirited armed rebellion against the National Resistance Movement (NRM) Government for a number of years until her forces were defeated and she ran into exile in a neighboring country. Unfortunately, she died in exile, but her body was returned and buried in Uganda. Queen Nzingha of Angola defended her kingdom against the Portuguese for 40 years and defeated them.

In her youth, Nzingha was strongly favored by her father, who allowed her to witness as he governed his kingdom, and who carried her with him to war. She participated in all the intense training for warriors. Nzingha grew up in a world normally suited for males. She was educated in the fields of hunting and archery and in diplomacy and trade.[11] Examples of such women warriors show that if given an opportunity, women are good defenders of the citizens' rights, but it would be farfetched to surmise that the status quo is about to change so that they take up a lead role in protection of the continent's resources. The future still looks gloomy for Africans, with the gun not about to be silenced soon.

---

[11] Patricia C. McKissack, Nzingha: Warrior Queen of Matamba, Angola, Africa, 1595 Hardcover—September 1, 2000, accessed at: https://www.amazon.com/Nzingha-Warrior-Matamba-Angola-Africa/dp/0439112109/ref=sr_1_1?ie=UTF8&qid=1363641719&sr=8-1&keywords=nzingha, on 1 December 2019.

Causes of Resources-Linked Conflicts

There are a number of causes attributable to the problem of rocking guns over natural resources on the African continent. A number of writers have advanced opinion as to how guns can be silenced on the African continent. Nillesen and Bulte consider that: "Natural resource stocks may represent a prize worth fighting for, and trading resources thus gained may be used to finance (ongoing) conflict. They further attribute the problem of rocking guns on the African continent to mismanagement or theft of resource rents, or environmental damages caused by large-scale resource extraction by the political leaders."[12] Following closely on such views leads to an understanding that guns on the African continent can be silenced if the continental natural resources are properly managed, and in the interests of the majority of the population.

In order to provide a candid analysis of Africa's problem of conflict over natural resources, one must first provide a historical context which informs the current political dispensations on the continent. For example, Burnley avers that "violent and nonviolent conflicts linked to the use of its natural resources have historically prevented the DRC from fully utilizing its resources to generate revenue and improve quality of life for its citizens."[13] The historical political trends in the DRC, for example, with much of the country's territory under constant armed conflict, which are fueled from without the country shows how the country is not about to emerge out this problem. The vast lands of the DRC, which have never been brought under effective control of the State equally demonstrate how colonial powers wished the country to remain long after attaining its political independence.

It is noteworthy that the historical problem of armed conflict over natural resources in Africa is widespread across the continent, and not limited to a particular group of countries. The Great Lakes Region countries of Africa, Nigeria, Libya, and Cameroun, however, remain epicenters of natural resources-linked armed conflict. In each of these examples, it is clear that an amalgam of causes to the conflict over natural resources exists. Some of them are endogenic, while others remain exogenic to the African continent. None of these causes can be tackled without tackling the other, which permeates a hard-to-deal with scenario for the Africans. The next subsection highlights the major natural resources of the African continent, the bait for the gun-wielding exploiters.

[12] Eleonora Nillesen and Erwin Bulte, Natural Resources and Violent Conflict, Annual Review of Resource Economics, Volume 6, 2014, pp. 69–83.

[13] Clementine Burnley, Natural Resources Conflict in the Democratic Republic of the Congo: A Question of Governance? Sustainable Development Law and Policy, Article 5, Volume 12, Issue 1, Fall 2011.

Major Natural Resources of the African Continent

The African continent is richly endowed with good climate, fertile soils, abundant mineral wealth, water resources, and natural vegetation. Africa has varied climatic patterns, largely suitable for agriculture and other human-based activities. According to the World Weather Atlas "most of Africa is in the tropics, and except for the peaks of mountains in the Great Rift Valley, it never freezes. The continent's northern half is primarily desert or arid, while its central and southern areas contain both savannah plains and very dense jungle (rainforest) regions."[14]

Overall, the continent experiences good weather conducive for agriculture and other human-based activities. The continental weather supports the soil fertility reinforcing systems to make Africa a suitable continent capable of producing enough food for all the people on the continent. This has not been possible because of several strands of conflicts over natural resources exploitation and extraction on the continent. In regard to soils, Appiah states that the African continent has fertile soils which, if well harnessed can maximize crop yields.[15] This position is further supported by Nkonya of the International Food Policy Research Institute, who considers that for most of its history, sub-Saharan Africa has been short of people, not land and that "Africa is the future breadbasket of the world.[16]

African continent is equally endowed with abundant water resources. There are a number of all year-round flowing rivers and lakes whose water levels rarely go down all the year around. The River Nile flows from the central plateau, a region popularly referred to as the Great Lakes Region of Africa through a number of countries before joining the Mediterranean Sea at the Port of Alexandria in Egypt. In regard to potential conflict over the Nile waters, Fadel et al., observe that disputes over the utilization of Nile waters by the riparian States, coupled with regional political instability and internal armed conflicts within the majority of the involved countries further amplifies the problem of rocking guns on the continent.[17] Reinforcing this position, Veilleux, observes that: [T]he Nile River has been the setting for recent tensions and conflict over control of the water rights between upstream Ethiopia's construction of

[14] World Atlas, Africa Weather, 2018, accessed at: https://www.worldatlas.com/web image/countrys/afweather.htm, on 13 December 2019.

[15] Bernard Appiah, Africa's Soil Diversity Mapped for the First Time, Guardian Development Network, Global Development, 2013, accessed at: https://www.theguardian.com/global-development/2013/may/23/africa-soil-diversity-mapped, on 12 December 2019.

[16] Ephraim Nkonya, Farming in Africa, International Food Policy Research Institute, Washington, DC. In the Economist, Middle East and Africa, April 28, 2018, Edition, accessed at: https://www.economist.com/middle-east-and-africa/2018/04/28/africa-has-plenty-of-land-why-is-it-so-hard-to-make-a-living-from-it, on 13 December 2019.

[17] M. El-Fadel, Y. El-Sayegh, K. El-Fadl, and D. Khorbotly, The Nile River Basin: A Case Study in Surface Water Conflict Resolution, Journal of Natural Resources and Life Sciences Education, Volume 32, 2003, accessed at: https://www.agronomy.org/files/jnr lse/issues/2003/e02-15.pdf, on 13 December 2019.

the Grand Ethiopian Renaissance Dam and downstream Egypt and Sudan's almost total dependence on Nile River water resources.[18]

Fortunately, conflicts over usage of the Nile waters by the Nile Basin countries have never escalated to the level of armed conflict. Negotiations about the equitable utilization of the Nile waters have been going on for over a century, and there is a ray of hope that due to scientific research undertaken, no country may use the waters to the total disadvantage of the other. Such information enables the riparian States to de-escalate their drives toward armed or any conflicts, at all over the Nile waters. The latest discussions about the equitable utilization of the Nile waters, within the Framework of the Nile Basin Initiative have so far led to the drafting of the Comprehensive Cooperation Framework Agreement (CAF) for the Equitable Utilization of the Nile waters.

The CFA is a framework agreement to strengthen cooperation and govern relations among the basin countries with regard to the Nile River Basin. CFA is intended, among others, to promote integrated management, sustainable development, and harmonious utilization of the water resources of the Basin, as well as their conservation and protection for the benefit of present and future generations.[19] The CFA, however, does not seek to prevent any Nile Basin Country from utilizing the waters of the Nile, rather it seeks to promote integrated management and utilization of the Nile waters. The CFA outlines principles, rights, and obligations for cooperative management and development of the Nile Basin water resources, which if adhered to, can avert any possible conflict over the waters of the Nile.[20]

Apart from the CFA, there are other cooperation arrangements providing for sustainable management of waters of other major transboundary Rivers. These include the Zambezi, The Niger River, and the Congo River Basin agreements.[21] In regard to Lakes, the discussion centers on Lake Victoria,

---

[18] Jennifer C. Veilleux, Water Conflict Case Study—Ethiopia's Grand Renaissance Dam: Turning from Conflict to Cooperation, 2015, accessed at: https://www.researchg ate.net/publication/281641708_Water_Conflict_Case_Study_-_Ethiopia's_Grand_Renaiss ance_Dam_Turning_from_Conflict_to_Cooperation, on 13 December 2019.

[19] Nile Basin Initiative Secretariat (Nile-SEC), Entebbe, Uganda, 2015, accessed at: https://www.nilebasin.org/index.php/nbi/cooperative-framework-agreement, on 13 December 2019.

[20] Nile Basin Initiative Secretariat (Nile-SEC), Entebbe, Uganda, 2015, accessed at: https://www.nilebasin.org/index.php/nbi/cooperative-framework-agreement, on 13 December 2019.

[21] See Christine J. Kirchhoff and Jonathan W. Bulkley, Sustainable Water Management in the Zambezi River Basin, The Journal of the International Institute, Volume 15, Issue 2: The Africa Issue, Spring 2008, accessed at: http://hdl.handle.net/2027/spo. 4750978.0015.208, on 13 December 2019; Inger Andersen, Ousmane Dione, Martha Jarosewich-Holder, and Jean-Claude Olivry in Katherin George Golitzen (Ed.), The Niger River Basin: A Vision for Sustainable Management, The World Bank, Washington, DC, 2005, accessed at: https://www.Natural%20resources/Niger_River_Basin_Vision_Sus tainable_Management.pdf, on 13 December 2019; Benjamin Ndala, Congo River Basin: Congo River Basin: Challenges and Current Initiatives, International Commission of the International Commission of the Congo Congo-Oubangui Oubangui-Sangha Basin Sangha

the biggest Lake in the heart of Africa to show how conflicts over the waters of this lake have been managed. The main agreements governing the Lake Victoria Basin fall under the institutional umbrella of the East African Community (EAC), a regional intergovernmental organization comprised of Burundi Kenya, Uganda, Tanzania, Rwanda, and South Sudan.[22] Tensions over the sustainable utilization of the Lake Victoria waters, such as the Uganda-Kenya tensions over the ownership of the Migingo Islands are resolved in sisterly manner under the umbrella of the EAC Treaty.[23]

The African continent is equally endowed with a number of very important minerals. According to Aljazeera Interactive, besides oil and gas, Africa is rich in precious minerals, which include Diamonds, Gold, Nickel and Uranium, Pozzolana, Titanium, Graphite, Iron Ore, Phosphates, Aluminum, and Cooper.[24] Oil and gas and other minerals such as uranium, gold, and diamonds are closely linked with violent armed conflicts on the continent. There is strong evidence, for example, that oil increases the risk of conflict.[25] An examination of the natural vegetation cover shows that the African continent is richly endowed with rare tree species.[26]

In DRC, some of these rare species have been illegally exploited by armed rebels, especially in the Eastern part of the country, to finance their activities. An overview of the natural resources of the African continent reveals that these many and varied species require a strong legal framework to protect them, especially since many of them transcend national boundaries. Even then, the

---

Basin, 5th World Water Forum 5th World Water Forum—Italian Side Event Italian Side Event" "the Po Valley Compares Itself the Po Valley Compares Itself with Big International Basins, accessed at: https://www.riob.org/IMG/pdf/03_CICOS-PO.pdf, on 13 December 2019.

[22] The Treaty for the Establishment of the East African Community (EAC) was originally signed by Kenya, the United Republic of Tanzania and Uganda in 1999. The Republic of Burundi and the Republic of Rwanda acceded to the Treaty in 2005, while the Republic of South Sudan is the latest Partner State to the EAC.

[23] See for example, Charles Etukuri, Uganda, Kenya Agree on Migingo Island, The New Vision Newspaper, 2016, accessed at: https://www.newvision.co.ug/new_vision/news/1433591/uganda-kenya-agree-migingo-island, on 13 December 2019.

[24] Aljazeera, Mapping Africa's Natural Resources: An Overview of the Continent's Main Natural Resources, 2018, accessed at: https://www.aljazeera.com/indepth/interactive/2016/10/mapping-africa-natural-resources-161020075811145.html, on 13 December 2019.

[25] Philippe Le Billon, Natural Resources, Armed Conflicts, and the UN Security Council Paper presented at the Seminar on Natural Resources and Armed Conflicts United Nations Headquarters, Liu Institute Working Paper 07–001, New York, 21 May 2007, accessed at: http://liu.xplorex.com/sites/liu/files/Publications/30May2007_Natural_Resources_Armed_Conflicts_UNSC07-001.pdf, on 13 December 2019.

[26] See Global Forest Atlas; Congo Basin Forest Ecology, accessed at: https://globalforestatlas.yale.edu/congo/ecoregions/congo-basin-forest-ecology, on 13 December 2019; Shashank Nakate, A List of Endangered Plants It's Time to Be Concerned About, Gardenerdy, accessed at: https://gardenerdy.com/endangered-plants-list, on 13 December 2019.

332   G. BUSINGYE

possibility of conflicts emanating from the use of these resources, both by the nationals, all Africans, and the entire world remains eminent. In fact, many of the armed conflicts on the continent are in countries richly endowed with these natural resources.

CONTEXTUAL AND CONCEPTUAL ASPECTS

Conceptually, "resources" connote a broad description of human made and naturally existing phenomena. Conflicts over resources in Africa, therefore, refer to conflicts over both the human and natural resources, which might derail this discussion. The discussion, however, deliberately refocuses itself on the narrow concept of "natural resources," which humans fight to control, exploit, and modify or otherwise harness for a living. The current egocentric philosophy of control of natural resources of the African continent is a function of the violent colonial history African countries went through while under colonial dominion and in some cases, at the time of the exit of colonial masters.

A span through the continent shows that most post-independence leaders had to violently overthrow the colonial regime, or the regimes that came on board at the time of independence. The first form of conflict that existed at that time spanned around whether or not natural resources, particularly minerals, had a bearing on politics of any post-colonial State. The next phenomenal form of conflict came up when the post-colonial leaders discovered the value of the abundant resources at their disposal. Some of them celebrated because they had discovered means of entrenching themselves in the newly attained political positions. The third category, and the most significant causal link between natural resources and violent conflicts on the African continent comes up when African charismatic leaders attempted to deny the former colonial masters' access to the natural resources. The latter view is demonstrated by examining a few examples of African States' violent regime changes.

In the case of Algeria, war was wedged between Algerians and the French from 1954 to 1962, when the country became independent; in the case of Kenya, the Mau Mau rebellion against the British colonial leaders lasted between 1952 and 1964. In the case of Rwanda, the Social Revolution of 1959 saw many Rwandans of Tutsi origin killed and others fleeing for safety in neighboring countries. The Hutu majority, supported by the Belgian former colonizers toppled the Tutsi minority and took revenge against their former masters, the Tutsis. The cyclic bloody events in Rwanda went on until the 1990 genocide, where thousands of Rwandans of Tutsi minority and moderate Hutus were killed.[27]

---

[27] Marc de Miramon, Maggie Calt, Brutal from the Beginning: The Truth About Everyone's Strongman, Harper's Magazine, December 13, 2019, accessed at: harpers.org/archive/2, on 13 December 2019.

After the genocide, Rwandan Government pursued the genocidaires in the neighboring DRC, where to date, there have been skirmishes between the Rwandan Patriotic Army (RPA) and the former genocidaires in the Province of Kivu in the DRC.[28] The Rwandan former genocidaires are able to survive in the foreign country largely because they are able to illegally extract valuable natural resources in the Eastern DRC, and sell them to foreign markets. In this case, one cannot surmise that the gun in Eastern DRC is about to be silenced until or unless the last genocidaires either denounce the genocide ideology and hand themselves to the Rwandan authorities, or die off, either naturally or at the battlefield.

In the case of DRC, the period 1960–1966 was one of violent turmoil, which saw Mobutu seize power from the Belgians. Laurent Kabila was a President of the DRC from 1997 after he violently overthrew Mobutu. Laurent Kabila was assassinated in 2001 and succeeded by his son, Joseph Kabila. The years 1966–1970 saw the bloody period in Nigeria when the South-Eastern State declared its independence and named itself Biafra. To attain her independence, Zimbabwe fought the British rule until an African Government led by the late Robert Mugabe took over the political leadership of the country. On their part, South Africans fought the Apartheid regime till Africans gained independence; Benin was under military dictatorship after Mathieu Kérékou, who seized power in a military *coup d'état.*

The story of Sudan and South Sudan, formerly one State, but divided after South Sudan gained independence from Sudan in 2011, shows historical ties between the two States in the management of the oil and gas reserves. The richest oil and gas reserves are either in the Republic of South Sudan, or in the disputed territories between the two States. There are a number of armed groups fighting for independence from Sudan, but who do not wish to become part of South Sudan. These groups' armed activities are largely funded by proceeds from illegal exploitation of the oil and gas and other mineral resources in the region. The ongoing armed conflict in South Sudan is largely linked to the inequitable distribution of the benefits got from extraction of oil and gas reserves in the country.[29]

The story of the Uganda's unconstitutional changes of governments, dating to the colonial period, also shows how struggle for control of natural resources has been characterized by the rocking gun. The cyclic violent events using the gun started with the British brutally taking over the country and directing their effort to natural resources exploitation. The British fought Omukama (King) Kabalega of Bunyoro Kitara Kingdom in the oil and gas rich Albertine region for close to 30 years until they overpowered him and established their rule

---

[28] Marc de Miramon, Maggie Calt, Brutal from the Beginning: The Truth About Everyone's Strongman, Harper's Magazine, December 13, 2019, accessed at: harpers.org/archive/2, on 13 December 2019.

[29] Human Rights Watch, South Sudan: Events of 2018, World Report, 2019, accessed at: https://www.hrw.org/world-report/2019/country-chapters/south-sudan, on 13 December 2019.

334   G. BUSINGYE

over his kingdom.[30] The Kilembe Copper Mines in the South Western district of Kasese, now in disuse state, were the main focus of the British colonial government in Uganda.

Immediately after the country attained Independence in 1962, Dr. Apollo Milton Obote violently overthrew Sir Edward Mutesa, who was the Kabaka of Buganda and the First President of the independent Uganda. The coup d'état took place in 1966. Dr. Apollo Milton Obote was overthrown in a military coup d'état by General Idi Amin in 1971; Amin was later overthrown by Ugandans exiled in the diaspora, who used the United Republic of Tanzania as a ground to launch a decisive attack that led to the collapse of Amin's regime in 1979. The gun was not silenced in the country until recently after the NRM Government defeating the last strongest insurgent group, the Lord's Resistance Army (LRA) led by Joseph Kony.

The hasty and unwilling departure of the colonial masters, without leaving behind strong legal and institutional frameworks to take care of the management of natural resource being harnessed created a very precarious situation for the post-colonial African leaders. Those leaders could only hazard on what to do with the resources, hitherto exploited by the colonial State. Some chose to use them for self-enrichment. Talton (undated) reinforces this narrative thus: "[T]hrough the process of decolonization that began, in most African territories, at the close of World War II, African leaders gained greater political power under European rule. Some worked against the challenges of continued European cultural and political hegemony, while others worked with European powers in order to protect their interests and maintain control over economic and political resources."[31]

In the case of Angola, an OXFAM Reports states that "Angola could be one of the richest countries in the developing world. It has great wealth in natural resources, particularly oil. Properly managed, the money from oil, diamonds and other natural resources could, in the short term, respond to Angola's humanitarian crisis. In the long term, these resources could bring prosperity and development to Angola's population for decades to come. Instead, the bulk of the money goes to fight Angola's 26-year old war."[32]

In the case of the Democratic Republic of Congo (DRC), for example, there was no fundamental change in the stealing of the country's natural

[30] Faustin Mugabe, Kabalega Attacks British Army Base, Sparks War with Colonialists, The Daily Monitor, Ugandan Newspaper, Sunday, June 30, 2019, accessed at: https://www.monitor.co.ug/Magazines/PeoplePower/Kabalega-attacks-British-army-base-sparks-war-colonialists/689844-5177238-g4g0wcz/index.html, on 20 December 2019.

[31] Benjamin Talton, The Challenge of Decolonisation in Africa, undated, accessed at: http://exhibitions.nypl.org/africanaage/essay-challenge-of-decolonization-africa.html, on 8 December 2019.

[32] OXFAM, Global Policy Forum, Angola's Wealth: Stories of War and Neglect, 2001, accessed at: https://www.globalpolicy.org/component/content/article/198/40272.html, on 10 December 2019.

resources when DRC became independent. The project of blaming colonial rule in order to cover up acts of post-colonial leaders can, therefore, not be sustained any longer. Lucy (undated) asserts that the stunted growth of African States is largely due to the large-scale corruption perpetrated by their leaders. She states, in respect to the DRC, "King Leopold of Belgium and the Belgians stole the national patrimony of the country, and after Congo was declared a self-governing status, their own leaders continued with the brazen festival of thievery and steal while the citizens wallow in abject poverty and untold hardship."[33]

In order to regain their sovereign over natural resources, Congolese had to take up guns, fight and overthrow their hitherto Post-Independence hero, Mobutu, who fled into exile where he died, still living a luxurious life over the resources he plundered from his country. Unfortunately, the war over natural resources of the DRC is not about to end. There are over 70 armed groups each fighting to have uncontested control over the country's natural resources.[34] Some of these armed groups, such as the Allied Democratic Front (ADF) and Lord's Resistance Army (LRA), unfortunately are non-Congolese. They only illegally exploit the DRC natural resources using the gun, in the "ungoverned" territory of the country, and use the proceeds to fight wars back home in Uganda. Bhattacharyya asserts that "[a]ccess to an oil rig or a mine could provide lucrative financial opportunities to rebel leaders to build and sustain rebel organizations which would encourage armed conflict."[35]

The case of DRC, which is the largest natural resource-rich country in Africa, paints a pathetic for the rest of the African continent. The country's government has not been able to exert strong political authority over its vast territory. African countries, who together formed the African Union, have not been able to come to the aid of sister country to uproot the gun from the country. That could be done, if there was good will to do so. For example, in the case of Uganda, a Ugandan–Tanzanian led National Liberation Army overthrew the dictatorial regime of Idi Amin in 1979, thus freeing the country from a bloody regime. The Frontline States, led by Late Mwalimu Julius Nyere of Tanzania liberated most of the South African Region and consolidated their efforts into the Southern African Development Cooperation (SADC), which has helped to democratize the region.

[33] LuciPost, How Mobutu Sese Seko Plundered Congo's Resources, 2018, https://www.lucipost.com/2018/12/how-mobutu-sese-seko-plundered-congos-resources/, on 6 December 2019.

[34] Paul Nantulya, A Medley of Armed Groups Play on Congo's Crisis, African Centre for Strategic Studies, Elsa Buchanan, Battle for Control of the DRC: Who Are the Armed Groups Killing for Land, Resources, and Ethnicity? 2017, accessed at: https://www.ibtimes.co.uk/battle-control-drc-who-are-armed-groups-killing-land-resources-ethnicity-1526317, on 2 December 2019.

[35] Sambit Bhattacharyya, Natural Resources and Conflict in Africa: Isolating Facts from Fiction, Centre for the Study of African Economies, 2015, accessed at: https://blogs.csae.ox.ac.uk/2015/11/natural-resources-and-conflict-in-africa-isolating-facts-from-fiction/, on 2 December 2019.

In support of this narrative, Azikiwe avers that "[F]rom the earliest days of independence, Tanzania under TANU served as a base for various liberation movements fighting against colonialism and settler-colonialism." Tanzania became a focal point where various movements received training and organizational support for ongoing political activities. The Organization of African Unity Liberation Committee was based in Tanzania. This body supplied material aid to various mass organizations and independence movements.[36] Unfortunately, the case of Tanzania's support to sister African countries has not been emulated to silence guns in other parts of the continent, thus letting the rocking guns shout unabated in the armed conflict-prone territories on the continent.

Worst of all, wherever natural resources such as oil and gas and diamonds have been exploited and extracted, there has been no evidence to show tangible benefits to the local communities. This is the case, for example, in the South Africa. To date, Soweto is still a poor district in the gold, diamond, and other mineral rich country; Nigerians in the oil rich parts of the country are among some of the poorest people in the country, and lastly, in the DRC, nationals in the rich Eastern part of the country are poor and guns rock in that part of the country largely over ownership and management of the abundant natural resources. In support of this narrative, Ahmadov and Guliyev assert that natural resource production can fuel local conflict and violence by increasing the perceived marginalization of local communities.[37]

Reversing foreign interests over African resources has been realized too late, and any forceful ejection of foreign interests from the continent to pave way for African solutions to African problems has been responded to by the gun. Moreover, local Governments and communities have not been able to agree on how to utilize the benefits derived from the resource exploitation. Maphosa observes that despite lack of consensus on the underlying relationship between natural resources and conflict, it is understandable that the struggle over access to and control over natural resources constitutes considerable grounds for tension and conflict. He recommends that where natural resources have been the main driver of social violence, they need to be treated as crucial dimensions of conflict prevention that could unlock the economic potential of building

---

[36] Abayomi Azikiwe, (Editor), Pan-African News Wire; Julius Nyerere: Pioneer in the liberation of Africa: Reviewing the Tanzanian Experience 10 Years Since the Passing of Mwalimu, 2009, accessed at: https://www.workers.org/2009/world/julius_nyerere_1 105/, on 12 December 2009.

[37] Anar Ahmadov and Farid Guliyev, Tackling the Resource Curse: The Role of Democracy in Achieving Sustainable Development in Resource-Rich Countries, International Institute for Democracy and Electoral Assistance, 2016.

peace in fragile societies.[38] On his part, Gapa notes that [W]orldwide, countries whose economies are highly skewed toward a dependence on the export of non-renewable natural resources such as oil, diamonds, and uranium, have been among the most troubled, authoritarian, poverty-stricken, and conflict-prone; a phenomenon widely regarded as the "resource curse." The resource curse phenomenon explains the varying fortunes of countries based on their resource wealth, with resource-rich countries faring much worse than their resource-poor counterparts.[39]

KEY INITIATIVES FOR SILENCING GUNS ON THE AFRICAN CONTINENT

Silencing resource linked guns on the African continent is an obligation of everyone and every State in the world. This is spearheaded under the continental framework of Agenda 2063. This form of jurisprudence stems from the Charter of the United Nations, 1945. First and foremost, the Charter seeks to prevent future scourges of World Wars as had been witnessed in the First World War, 1918–1919, and the Second World War, 1939–1945. It is possible that the purpose of the Charter has been achieved, because not such World War has ever been fought after its coming into force. Unfortunately, there have been, and continue to be a number of armed conflicts, inter-state and increasingly intra-state in nature in many parts of the world.

The root causes of these wars have been highlighted in the foregoing subsections of this chapter. A reflection on the mandate of the United Nations regarding maintenance of international peace and security resonates well with the African Union theme of silencing the guns.[40] The United Nations works collectively to prevent and remove threats to international peace. It is also mandated to suppress acts of aggression or other breaches of the peace, and to bring about by peaceful means.[41] A clear understanding of the working relations between the UN and the regional blocs, such as the African Union points to the fact that Africa is moving in the right direction toward silencing guns linked to natural resources harnessing on the continent. Undoubtedly, the desired goals of Agenda 2063 cannot be achieved without the blessing and material support from the United Nations, which is mandated to maintain international peace and security.

[38] Sylvester Bongani Maphosa, Natural Resources and Conflict: Unlocking the Economic Dimension of Peace-Building in Africa, Africa Institute of South Africa Briefing No. 74, March 2012, accessed at: http://www.ai.org.za/wp-content/uploads/downlo ads/2012/04/No.-74.-Natural-Resources-and-Conflict.-Unlocking-the-economic-diment ion-of-peace-building-in-Africa.pdf, on 12 December 2019.

[39] Gapa, Angela, Escaping the Resource Curse: The Sources of Institutional Quality in Botswana, 2013. FIU Electronic Theses and Dissertations. Paper 1019. http://digitalco mmons.fiu.edu/etd/1019.

[40] See The Charter of the United Nations, 1945, Preamble.

[41] Charter of the United Nations, 1945, Article 1 (1).

The Security Council is the global watch-dog over all matters relating peace and security, which embody silencing guns as a key component. The United Nations Security Council works closely with other sister organs of the UN like the United Nations Environment Programme (UNEP), which has concerns that global natural resources such as water, soil, trees, and wildlife are being damaged and destroyed at alarming rates, especially during armed conflict.[42] Indeed, natural resources in armed conflict areas may not only be exploited to fund conflict but they are also equally wantonly destroyed by the activities of the armed groups, State and non-state actors alike. In execution of its mandate, the United Nations Security Council (UNSC) has taken an unprecedented number of measures to tackle links between natural resources and armed conflicts over the past decade. Billon observes that the UNSC has been able to limit wartime resource exploitation to benefit the population after the conflict, rather than belligerents during the conflict; and to reform resource sectors to prevent conflicts and consolidate peace.[43]

One other important measure undertaken by the UNSC to curtail access to resources-based revenues to finance armed conflicts has been to blacklist "blood diamonds." In regard to blood diamonds, Barnes observes that "[W]ar diamonds (alias 'blood diamonds') have received their name because they are being mined in war or conflict areas. This is the case of blood diamonds in Africa which are sold financially to support wrong causes such as armies and warlords."[44] The United Nations Security Council imposes sanctions on individuals, States, and groups of non-state actors, believed to be illegally exploiting natural resources to foment conflict, or, if legally extracted, in the case of a State, used to finance violation of human rights. Currently, some officials in the Government of South Sudan even in the Opposition armed groups are under UNSC sanctions because of their involvement in natural resources-linked armed conflict.[45]

Much as sanctions are believed to be effective tools to prevent resource linked guns and violation of human rights, sanctions-busters do evade national regulations by smuggling the list resources to neighboring countries for sale

---

[42] UNEP, Protecting the Environment During Armed Conflict: An Inventory and Analysis of International Law, 2009.

[43] Philippe Le Billon, Natural resources, armed conflicts, and the UN Security Council Paper presented at the Seminar on Natural Resources and Armed Conflicts United Nations Headquarters, Liu Institute Working Paper 07–001, New York, 21 May 2007, accessed at: http://liu.xplorex.com/sites/liu/files/Publications/30May2007_Natural_Resources_Armed_Conflicts_UNSC07-001.pdf, on 13 December 2019.

[44] Oscar Barnes, All There Is to Know About the Blood Diamonds in Africa, The Diamond Authority, 2016, accessed at: https://www.thediamondauthority.org/blood-diamonds-in-africa/, on 14 December 2019.

[45] See for example, UNSC Resolution 2428 (2018), Security Council Extends Sanctions on South Sudan, accessed at: https://reliefweb.int/report/south-sudan/adopting-resolution-2428-2018-security-council-extends-sanctions-south-sudan, on 14 December 2019.

on world markets.[46] This is a negative aspect of the United Nations system which does not have a law enforcement institution of its own, that would be deployed in such cases to enforce its resolutions. In its Preamble, the AU Constitutive Act, inter alia recognizes the fact that the scourge of conflicts in Africa constitutes a major impediment to the socio-economic development of the continent. It, therefore, underscores the need to promote peace, security, and stability as a prerequisite for the implementation of the continental developmental and integration agenda.

Key objectives of the African Union as clearly laid down in the Constitutive Act of the AU include promotion of peace, security, and stability on the continent and popular participation and good governance. Under Article 4 and in order to tame the problem of armed conflicts on the continent, the Constitutive Act provides for establishment of a common defense policy for the African Continent and the right of the Union to intervene in a Member State pursuant to a decision of the Assembly in respect of grave circumstances. Such circumstances include commission of war crimes, genocide, and crimes against humanity on the continent.

Sadly, the good intentions of the AU under this Act are watered down by the weak nature of its principal organs such as the General Assembly, which is required to take decisions on the implementation of the Act. For example, the Assembly is expected to take its decisions by consensus or, failing which, by a two-thirds majority of the Member States of the Union.[47] This aspect of consensus and two-thirds majority, coupled with lack of self-funding mechanisms for the Union has crippled the Union especially in matters of peace and security on the continent. No decision may be readily adopted if it will involve financing large-scale operations on the continent without first seeking donor and development partners' consent and support. The latter is not readily obtainable. In any case, the AU handles matters of peace and security on behalf of the UN Security Council, which must be informed of the intended actions in regard to restoring peace and security by the Union prior to implementing it. This bureaucratic process, disabled the Union from taking actions to silence the guns in the Republic of Burundi, in the most desired circumstances.

As persuasive argued by Kuwali in Chapter 4, the African Stand by Force, the Defence and Security Policy and the African Peace and Security Architecture in general are expected to contribute toward the preservation and maintenance of peace in the continent.[48] Unfortunately, there are still no clear indications that guns linked to the rich African resources are about to be silenced. The internal strife in South Sudan, the armed conflict in the

---

[46] Michael Fleshman, Conflict Diamonds Evade UN Sanctions, African Renewal Magazine, 2001, https://www.un.org/africarenewal/magazine/december-2001/conflict-diamonds-evade-un-sanctions, on 14 December 2019.

[47] The Constitutive Act of the African Union, Article 7.

[48] African Union Commission, Agenda 2063, The Africa We Want, A Shared Strategic Framework for Inclusive Growth and Sustainable Development First Ten-Year Implementation Plan 2014–2023, September 2015; Aspiration No. 4.

disputed territories between South Sudan and Sudan, the internal strife in Nigeria and neighboring countries where Boko Haram is causing mayhem, and in the Eastern DRC, where there are more than 70 armed groups, each acting under a different command are examples to augment the position taken in this paper. Suffice to note that the African Union acts through Regional Economic Communities (RECs) and other regional blocs on the continent to achieve much of its set goals.[49] RECs and other regional arrangements equally, are not able, without support from the AU to silence natural resources-linked rocking guns without the support of the AU. Unfortunately, the latter, too, lacks capacity, much as it has the will to resolve this problem.

AU RECs which are the pillars of peace and security on the continent are: Arab Maghreb Union (UMA), Common Market for Eastern and Southern Africa (COMESA), Community of Sahel–Saharan States (CEN–SAD), East African Community (EAC), Economic Community of Central African States (ECCAS), Economic Community of West African States (ECOWAS), Inter-governmental Authority on Development (IGAD), and the Southern African Development Community (SADC).[50] In addition to these traditional arrangements, the International Conference for the Great Lakes Region (ICGLR) was specifically formed to resolve the problem of rocking natural resources-linked guns in the Great lakes Region of the continent.[51] Unfortunately, even within this framework, resources-linked guns are still rocking high and are not about to be silenced as anticipated under Agenda 2063 of the African Union.

CONCLUSION

The reasons as to why guns still rock over natural resources in Africa are many, complex, but interrelated. Political background, especially the colonial history plays a big role in influencing which natural resources are harnessed and for what purpose. Lack of democratic management of Africa's natural resources in some States, greed for political power, and insatiable interest of external actors in Africa's natural resources continue to fuel armed conflicts on the continent. In sum, Africa is fraught with persistent armed conflicts related to exploitation of the continental natural resources. This is because the post-colonial African leaders have not been able to disentangle their countries from the cord of the former colonial masters.

---

[49] African Union, A Guide for Those Working with and Within the African Union, African Union Handbook, 2019.

[50] African Union, A Guide for Those Working with and Within the African Union, African Union Handbook, 2019, p. 17.

[51] ICGLR, Regional Initiative Against the Illegal Exploitation of Natural Resources, 2014, accessed at: http://www.icglr.org/index.php/en/natural-resources, on 13 December 2019; members of the ICGLR are: Angola, Burundi, Central African Republic, Republic of Congo, Democratic Republic of Congo (DRC), Kenya, Rwanda, South Sudan, Sudan, United Republic of Tanzania, Uganda and Zambia.

The latter still wish to have space in the political governance of the continent, which they achieve through, among others, unstable political entities on the continent. Foreign intervention, therefore, cannot be ruled out in the several cases where natural resources-guns related armed conflicts have not been silenced. It is, therefore, clear from the foregoing that poor governance, coupled with lack of accountability by leaders to their citizenry, still breeds discontent in some African countries. The marginalized, sometimes, with the help of foreign interests, take up the gun to resolve their political wrangles with those in power, who they accuse of greed and self-aggrandisement, at the expense of the ordinary citizens.

Marginalization based on gender has been cited as yet another cause of dissent and subsequent taking up arms to fight for denied rights. Equally important is the fact that exclusion of particular genders from directly participating in decisions concerning governance in particular countries denies them an opportunity, for instance, to have a holistic approach to the problems at hand. In the result, the powerful and mighty take up guns to resolve their grievances, which could have been resolved on table, if an all-inclusive platform had been adopted.

In terms of the legal framework, a lot remains to be desired. The United Nations, which is clothed with an unlimited mandate to address matters of peace and security globally lacks its own enforcement mechanisms to execute its mandate. Implementation of its resolutions, for example, sanctions, depends on the good will of sovereign States, which sometimes is lacking. Regional mechanisms such as the African Union frameworks are equally weak. The African Union in particular functions largely on donor and development partners' funding, which may not be forthcoming at the exact time when they are needed to solve an urgent problem. The need to seek authorization from the United Nations Security by regional mechanisms such as the African Union defeats the letter and purpose of silencing the gun in a timely and most appropriate manner on the continent. This problem coupled with inadequate logistical support at the regional level exacerbates the already worsening situation on the ground.

In the premises, the following is suggested as the way forward. African governments should resolve their governance issues by themselves by adopting and entrenching an all-inclusive governance system in their countries. Dissenting and minority views should be accommodated in the natural resources governance structures and always listened to. African Governments should utilize the available natural resources to address welfare problems in their countries, instead of using them to satisfy their insatiable greed for power interests. African governments should not be enticed by foreign interests to harness their resources if there is no local capacity available to do so, they should instead utilize the readily available resources and build capacity for their nationals to be the ones to exploit the rich resources in future.

CHAPTER 20

Combating Piracy in African Waters

Prince Bright Majiga

INTRODUCTION

In recent years, piracy has emerged as a growing problem in Africa, more especially the Gulf of Guinea. The gulf has, in the past years, witnessed a sharp rise in pirate attacks. Alarmingly, both the frequency of piracy attacks and the level of physical violence against seafarers have increased in recent years. There are also indications of links in the area between piracy and other types of organised crime such as oil bunkering and drug trafficking. The problem has thus become a recent source of concern for the international community of nations.

In general parlance, piracy is robbery at sea. Legally, it refers to certain acts of violence committed either on the high seas or in an exclusive economic zone (EEZ).[1] Although piracy has come to the frequent attention of the international community in recent times, it is not a new phenomenon or trend. In this regard, the international legal framework in which issues on piracy arise relies on rules that codify international customary law and are reflected in the United Nations Convention on the Law of the sea (UNCLOs) of 10 December 1982, which replicate those contained in the Geneva Convention on the High seas of

[1] The concept of an exclusive economic zone (EEZ) refers to the area of sea that extends maximally 200 nm from a state's coastal baseline. UNCLOS defines it as an area beyond and adjacent to the territorial sea in which states have full sovereignty to explore and exploit natural resources.

P. B. Majiga (✉)
Mzuzu University, Mzuzu, Malawi

© The Author(s), under exclusive license to Springer Nature Switzerland AG 2022
D. Kuwali (ed.), *The Palgrave Handbook of Sustainable Peace and Security in Africa*, https://doi.org/10.1007/978-3-030-82020-6_20

343

20 April 1958. In particular, under Article 101 of UNCLOs piracy is defined as an illegal act of violence or detention, or an act of depredation, committed for private ends by the crew or passengers of a private ship and directed against another ship or aircraft or against persons or property on board, but which has to take place on the high seas or in a place outside the jurisdiction of any state.

Although piracy on the high seas has been a persistent feature of seafaring commerce for centuries, the number of reported acts of piracy began to dwindle in the nineteenth and twentieth centuries; however, in the last few decades of the twentieth century, the rate of piratical attacks sharply increased worldwide. The sharp spike in pirate attacks in the Gulf of Aden and off the coast of East Africa over the last three years has renewed international interest in the suppression of maritime piracy. The Indian Ocean, the Arabian Sea, the Horn of Africa and the Gulf of Guinea are indeed high strategic arena for those states whose economies are strongly interlinked with these zones.

The history of piracy suggests that it has changed in nature and location. Piracy varies by region in terms of frequency, violence, tactics, level of organisation, distance from the shore, time of day and the ship's position. Regarding the location of piracy incidents, piracy in Asia tends to occur close to coasts, while piracy in East African waters has generally been further from shore, most often in international waters. Further, the most common piracy practise of kidnapping, followed by pirates throughout ages, has been replaced by a variety of business models, including hostage taking of crews for ransom, theft of vessels and/or their cargo and the looting of valuables from vessels in quick raids.[2] This changing nature of modern-day piracy, its increasing link with other illegal maritime activities and its mounting economic costs (for example, the cost of ransom, piracy insurance premiums, naval deployment in piracy infested areas and piracy prosecution) have given a new dimension to the piracy phenomenon.

Although piracy is common in particular geographic regions of the world, there are certain similarities and differences as regard the crisis in each region. The identical causal factors include weak governance, unfunded law enforcement and security systems and common geographic features. Differences include the typology of the attacks. It is argued that "the differences in political and economic landscapes influence how pirates embed their operations across territory, and thus how they carry out their operations".[3] Yet, in most cases, the motivation for piracy is similar: it is linked to economic deprivation. For example, Somali pirates have claimed that they are fighting to defend their local fishing sector, while Nigerian pirate groups point to the unequal sharing of oil resources to justify their actions. However, the models

---

[2] See J.M. Shane, E.L. Piza, and M. Mandala, "Situational Crime Prevention and Worldwide Piracy: A Cross-Continent Analysis", *Crime Science* 4 (21): 1–13 (2015), available at: http://dx.doi.org/10.1186/s40163-015-0032-7 (accessed 14 January 2021).

[3] Christian Bueger, "Learning from Piracy: Future Challenges of Maritime Security Governance", *Global Affairs* 1 (1): 33–42 (2015), available at: http://dx.doi.org/10.1080/23340460.2015.960170 (accessed 14 January 2021).

of piracy and typologies of attack in different regions do differ in nature. Given this, it is clear that actions taken to repress piracy need to reflect the realities of the piracy in a given region. It is important to understand the threats and challenges of piracy in view of the socio-economic, political, cultural and geographical dimensions of the regional states concerned. Apart from international efforts to combat piracy through international cooperation, success in combating piracy largely depends on the continuation of national efforts and regional initiatives.

Over the last few years, states and various organisations have embarked on national, regional and international initiatives aimed at preventing and controlling piracy. Nationally, states have been focussing on policing their waters. Regional stakeholders have aimed at building regional capacity through information sharing and a reporting system. At the international level, counter-piracy efforts have largely focussed on the military response to piracy. Despite these initiatives, maritime piracy remains a matter of serious concern, as it is a growing threat to the security and safety of shipping.[4] The intertwining of piracy creates substantial risks for global markets, as the bulk of international maritime commercial transport is carried on through many of these pirate-infested regions.[5]

While international efforts to curb piracy in the region have met with some success, a permanent solution requires that local governments take primary responsibility for its suppression. Superficially, the situation in East Africa shares a number of characteristics with a spate of pirate attacks perpetrated roughly a decade ago on vessels traversing the Strait of Malacca. The scope of the problem in Somalia, combined with the relative weakness of regional governments, suggests that a successful regional cooperation agreement will require international legal and financial support. Mozambique has a long coastline with a rich diversity of resources which occupy a very relevant national social and economic impact and an important role regionally. Currently, piracy in this area is operating between the Gulf of Aden and the Kenyan border along the Indian Ocean, but they can extend their illegal acts.[6] There remains a possibility that these acts extend to other Indian Ocean waters. This would include Kenyan waters, Tanzania Madagascar even Mozambique waters along the Mozambique Channel. This would destabilise a larger region, with further socio-economic consequences.

---

[4] Ruijie He, "Coast Guards and Maritime Piracy: Sailing Past the Impediments to Cooperation in Asia", *The Pacific Review* 22: 667 (2009).

[5] Nong Hong and Adolf K.Y. Ng, "The International Legal Instruments in Addressing Piracy and Maritime Terrorism: A Critical Review", *Research in Transportation Economics* 27 (1): 51 (2010).

[6] Izildo Roque Rangel Ferreira Developing, "An Integrated Ocean Policy for Mozambique". The United Nation-Nippon Foundation Fellowship Programme 2008–2009 Division for Ocean Affairs and the Law of the Sea Office of Legal Affairs, The United Nations, New York, 2009.

Causes of Piracy in Africa

In the meanwhile, extensive piracy studies literature provides a good understanding of which factors trigger the outbreak of piracy.[7] Studies on the purported "root causes" of piracy and on the regional variations of piracy operations and their sophistication have elaborated various factors. The nature of piracy is unique. Firstly, it is the oldest crime against the entire society; this firm belief has become increasingly rooted in history and has led the response to piracy to be universally recognised by international law as an indisputable collective need. Even though it is intrinsically dangerous, piracy remains a profitable activity and worth the risk for thousands of unemployed people living in desperately poor and often instable countries. Several triggers can be condensed from the literature: conflict and disorder, geography; weak law enforcement; economic dislocation; maritime insecurity, cultural acceptability and access to small and light weapons (SALW).

Conflict and Disorder

Piracy is a product of failed or weak states. It usually flourishes in areas with either a fragile or non-existent governing authority. Somali piracy is often attributed to being a land-based problem of lawlessness that manifests itself at sea.[8] For example, the collapse of the Somali state in 1991 and the civil war thereafter led to the spread of chaos in the country that eventually contributed to the development of piracy in the Gulf of Aden. It can also be argued that the collapse of the Somali state and the weakness of local authorities means that they are too weak to protect their coastal waters or enforce maritime law and, as a result, pirates have taken advantage of this situation.[9] Pirates in Somali waters have access to sophisticated arms as a result of their proximity to armed conflicts and the proliferation of small arms in the region.[10] A study of maritime kidnapping in West Africa finds that awareness of the Nigerian political situation is key to understanding the kidnapping threat in the Gulf

[7] C. Bueger, "Piracy Studies: Academic Responses to the Return of an Ancient Menace", *Cooperation and Conflict* 49: 406–416 (2014); S.P. Menefee and M.Q. Mejia, "A Rutter for Piracy" in 2012. *WMU Journal of Maritime Affairs* 11 (1): 1–13 (2012); and L. Seay, "Understanding Somali Piracy", *The Journal of Modern African Studies* 51 (1): 169–175 (2013).

[8] S. Percy and A. Shortland, "The Business of Piracy in Somalia", *Journal of Strategic Studies* 36 (4): 541–578 (2013), available at: http://dx.doi.org/10.1080/01402390.2012.750242 (accessed 11 February 2021).

[9] A.A. Elmi, l. Affi, W.A. Knight, and S. Mohamed, "Piracy in the Horn of Africa Waters: Definitions, History, and Modern Causes", *African Security* 8 (3): 147–165 (2015), available at: http://dx.doi.org/10.1080/19392206.2015.1069118 (accessed 11 February 2021).

[10] K. Clark, "The (Un)importance of Somali Piracy", *Crime Law and Social Change* 63: 269–280 (2015), available at: http://dx.doi.org/10.1007/s10611-015-9565-7 (accessed 11 February 2021).

of Guinea, as the majority of kidnappings occur in Nigerian waters, and if outside, there is almost always a significant Nigerian connection.[11]

Geography

Geography firstly refers to the obvious fact that regions with close proximity to waterways tend to have piracy. The geographical condition of the Gulf of Guinea plays an important role in allowing pirates to execute attacks for various reasons. First, the region occupies a vast area of largely unsecured coastline, giving pirates a wide area to exploit. This provides pirates the flexibility to conduct attacks without fear of naval retribution. Second, the maritime area occupies a strategic location of high economic importance for its large reserves of natural resources, notably oil and gas. The major economic powers have invested heavily in the oil sector, making the region one of absolute economic and strategic necessity for the global community. Third, the transport requirement of moving this oil necessitates that ships, particularly tankers, come nearer to the coast. Proximity to major lanes of transportation and major ports renders piracy more lucrative and hence increases the likelihood of piracy. Geography also refers to the existence of hideouts, that is coastal strips or islands which are difficult to reach or control.[12] Hideouts are necessary for preparing a piracy operation and for the case of ransom piracy to anchor the vessel. Piracy dens require basic infrastructure, such as roads or nearby villages to ensure the logistics needed for an operation. In principle piracy operations can also be launched from ports, especially if they are weakly governed and surveilled.

Economic Dislocation

Rightfully piracy has often been described as a business model and seen as an activity that is primarily economically motivated. While piracy promises considerable revenues, a direct causal link between poverty or lack of employment opportunities and piracy cannot be constructed. Rather than poverty per se, the crucial factor is economic dislocation. The oil industry in the Niger Delta has created poverty, conflict and despair for the majority of people in the oil-producing areas.[13] Communities that tend to engage in piracy are

---

[11] Oceans Beyond Piracy (OBP). (2016). Kidnap for Ransom Piracy Trending Higher in Gulf of Guinea. OBP, available at: http://oceansbeyondpiracy.org/sites/default/files/attachments/2016%20GOG%20Trends.pdf (accessed 11 February 2021).

[12] R. Marchal, "Somali Piracy: The Local Contexts of an International Obsession", *Humanity* 2 (1): 31–50 (2011), available at: http://dx.doi.org/10.1353/hum.2011.0004 (accessed 30 December 2020).

[13] UK P&I CLUB, UK War Risks, Hellenic War Risks, & Terra Firma Risk Management. (2016). Risk Focus: Kidnap and Ransom—Anatomy of West African Maritime Kidnapping—A Guide for Seafarers, available at: http://www.ukpandi.com/fileadmin/uploads/

348 P. B. MAJIGA

those which have been economically marginalised, have been put at a disadvantage by economic developments and globalisation processes or are not allowed to participate in sources of wealth. In light of the recent discoveries of considerable amounts of gas in the EEZs of Tanzania and Mozambique, the region may now be the locus for a growing number of state and non-state counter-piracy actors.

Cultural Acceptability and Skills

Piracy has also a considerable cultural dimension. Piracy has a tendency to flourish in areas where it is culturally accepted. In order for piracy to prevail it requires some sense of legitimacy. Foot soldiers have to be recruited and convinced that to engage in piracy is a legitimate activity and the majority of piracy operations are dependent on support from local communities, which provide shelter, food and other supplies. In the case of Somalia cultural acceptability has mainly been provided through the prevalence of a narrative which justifies piracy as a legitimate response to maritime insecurity. In this "coast guard narrative" piracy is projected as a legitimate, almost state-like practise of protecting coastal waters against outside threats such as illegal resource exploitation or environmental crime. This narrative of the benevolent protective character of piracy has been a crucial factor in recruitment as well as for ensuring the support of local communities.

This is what may make it difficult for piracy to thrive in the Mozambican channel. However, this could be offset by the prevalence of skills considering that the terrorist group is made up of fighters from countries where piracy is almost normal.

Thus, another cultural dimension is the availability of skills required for piracy among the populace. Such skills include navigation, boarding, weapon handling or negotiation skills. Skills necessary to perform piracy are widespread in Somalia and form part of a traditional cultural repertoire. This includes the navigation skills of fishermen and dhow traders, or the negotiation skills provided by a society governed by customary law and informal governance processes. Skills such as the handling of weapons have been learned in decades of civil war; others, such as the handling of navigation devices or boarding skills, have been learned in attempts at setting up coast guards.

Access to Small and Light Weapons

There is an increasing nexus between the growth of piracy and the proliferation of illegal arms in the Niger Delta. Since the 1990s, inter-communal and ethnic conflicts over resources have fuelled an arms race across the region that has

uk-pi/Latest_Publications/Circulars/2016/UK_Kidnap10-2.pdf (accessed 30 December 2020).

indirectly led to an increase in piratical activities. The prevalence of small and light weapons in the region is a worrying factor.

Weak Law Enforcement

The UNCLOS definition of piracy limits piracy to an act occurring on the high seas and is silent on the legality of such acts occurring within territorial waters. This gap in the definition suggests that such acts are jurisdictionally the problem of the state in whose territorial waters they occur.[14] To date, piracy in the Gulf of Guinea has largely been confined to territorial waters. In this sense, very few of the attacks satisfy the definition of piracy. Further, law enforcement officials face jurisdictional complications in chasing pirates into the territorial waters of neighbouring states. Despite piracy being a common threat to the coastal countries of the region, states are reluctant to allow external coastguards and navy to operate in their waters.

The factor of weak law enforcement stresses that the lower the risk of getting caught and punished for piracy, the higher the likelihood that piracy occurs. This concerns various levels of law enforcement stretching from coast guard and naval capabilities by which coastlines and the sea are patrolled and surveilled, to policing, intelligence and prosecution capabilities on land, as well as the efficiency of the judicial sector allowing for the prosecution of piracy. As shown in various studies the prevalence of official corruption is a further major factor impacting the likelihood of piracy, since pirates do not always operate outside the law but often in collaboration with law enforcement agencies. Finally, also the quality of regional inter-state collaboration in maritime security matters has to be considered. Pirates operate across (maritime) borders and efficient collaboration mechanisms are needed to allow for hot pursuit of perpetrators as well as the sharing of intelligence and evidence between national agencies.

Maritime Insecurity

A factor closely related to weak law enforcement is the degree to which the maritime environment of a region is insecure and prone to violence. Piracy tends to occur in seas in which there is a host of other illegal activity, such as trafficking, smuggling and illegal fishing. This is not only related to the question of coast guarding and law enforcement at sea but also in how far violence and insecurity at sea is considered to be the norm. The more the maritime environment is securitised and it is, for instance, normal to carry weapons at sea, the higher the likelihood of piracy. This is compounded by

---

[14] Martin N. Murphy, "The Troubled Waters of Africa: Piracy in the Africa Littoral", *Journal of the Middle East and Africa* 67 (2011).

IMPACT OF PIRACY

the limited maritime security capability of the coastal states has contributed significantly to the steady rise and growth of piracy, as most of the countries of the Gulf of Guinea have little or no resources to fight piracy.

The effects of piracy are widespread and felt throughout the Gulf of Guinea. The growing threat of piracy in the region imposes a substantial burden on regional governments and the maritime industry, which have to take steps to protect against pirate attacks. There are also implications for the regional economy and stability, regional security and the global economy. The expansion of piracy in the Gulf poses a serious threat to the local economies of the region. It is estimated that the economies of the countries in the region lose approximately $2 billion in annual revenue due to piracy. The impact on the state economies of the Gulf is clear as port revenue forms a major part of their national income. For example, the fees raised from the port of Cotonou of Republic of Benin generate 80 per cent of the income for that country's national budget.[15] Since the first pirate attack off Benin's coast, the country has experienced a catastrophic drop-in activity in the port of Cotonou. The number of vessels availing the port facility has decreased by 70 per cent, causing revenue to fall.

The adverse effect on the local economy may affect stability in the region. Pirates have been reported to use the profits accruing from piracy to arm rebel groups (for example, in the Niger Delta of Nigeria).[16] If true, this practise would directly impact the stability of affected countries. Uncontrolled piracy may also hamper development in the sense that trading companies will search for safer alternative trading routes, avoiding the territorial waters and ports of affected countries. This will disrupt the flow of foreign investment and trade. This has a potential to perpetuate the same conditions that led to piracy in the first place.

Piracy also affects local and regional security. The coastal states have to devote significant sums as military expenditure for countering piracy. To improve maritime security, regional military forces spend money on piracy in the form of procuring vessels and conducting patrols, training and military exercises. Currently, Chief of Naval Staff of Nigeria illustrated, engaging eight ships at sea for one week of exercises costs about $3.8 million.[17] Piracy related naval expenditures are likely to grow for the regional countries while the threat persists. This is likely to have an impact in regions like SADC where

---

[15] United Nations Assessment Mission Report, Piracy in the Gulf of Guinea, Security Council Doc. S/2012/45 (7–24 November 2011), 11.

[16] SC Rep 1, "Emerging Security Threats in West Africa" (May 2011).

Funso Ajewolw, "Navy Can Secure Nigerian Waters", The Daily Times NG (online), 17 November 2012, available at: http://www.dailytimes.com.ng/article/navy-can-secure-nigerian-waters-%E2%80%93-ezeoba#.UKe5dVTC79Q (accessed 26 January 2021).

[17] As above.

the regional hegemony, South Africa bears most of the blunt. The negative implications of piracy in the Gulf could well spread far beyond Africa, with probable complications for the wider global economy, and the US in particular. The nations off the coast of the Gulf of Guinea—namely, Angola, Nigeria, Ghana, Ivory Coast, Democratic Republic of Congo and Gabon—produce over 3 million barrels of oil daily, largely for North American and European markets.[18]

All seafarers transiting through the Gulf of Guinea have to deal with increased fear and uncertainty. The anticipatory concern over the high rate of violence used in pirate attacks makes these seafarers worried about working in the region. For those seafarers held captive or attacked by pirates, there is the potential for long-term physical and psychological trauma. This could lead to "clinically significant consequences"[19] and have serious negative implications for seafarers and their families.

Interventions in Curbing Piracy in Africa

UNCLOS and SUA are the key international legal instruments that govern piracy. The piracy rules as embodied in these instruments contain some loopholes and are therefore inadequate to address the problem. The inadequacies have led to an imbalance between counter-piracy goals and the expected result. In the context of the Gulf of Guinea, the vast majority of pirate attacks occur within the territorial seas of the coastal states. The piracy provisions as contained in UNCLOS apply only on the high seas and exclude territorial waters.[20] Hence, very few of the incidents in the Gulf of Guinea qualify as piracy under UNCLOS. Therefore, the piracy regime under UNCLOS appears to be weak for preventing and suppressing attacks on ships in the region.

The SUA Convention "creates the prospect for a more committed and coherent cooperation amongst nations" in the fight against piracy. However, the utility of the Convention depends on its being widely ratified in the piracy-affected region. The usefulness of the international legal instrument in the Gulf of Guinea region is limited due to the low number of states that ratified the Convention. Nigeria is the only country that has ratified the Convention (in 2004). The country is presently in the process of domesticating the Convention by considering enactment of the "Piracy and Other Unlawful Acts at Sea Bill".[21] Togo, Benin, Cameroon, Ghana, Sao Tome and Principe

[18] United Nations Assessment Mission Report, footnote 15.

[19] Seamen's Church Institute, "The Psychological Impact of Piracy on Seafarers", 6 (2012), available at: http://www.seamenschurch.org/sites/default/files/sci-piracy-study-report-web_0.pdf (accessed 31 January 2021).

[20] H.E. Jose Luis Jesus, "Protection of Foreign Ships against Piracy and Terrorism at Sea: Legal Aspects", *International Journal of Marine and Coastal Law* 18: 386 (2003).

[21] Michael I. Igbokwe, "Recent Developments in Nigerian Maritime Law and Practice: Piracy and Unlawful Acts at Sea". Paper presented at the 12th Maritime Seminar for Judges, Abuja, 5–7 June 2012, 8.

352 P. B. MAJIGA

acceded to the Convention but have not yet passed any legislation to implement their obligations under the Convention. Cameroon and Côte d'Ivoire are not yet parties to the Convention.

Continental and Regional Strategic Initiatives

Against this backdrop, regional cooperation has produced some beneficial results in combating piratical acts in piracy-affected regions. Regional anti-piracy agreements have offered the best opportunity for regional cooperation in this regard. The establishment of the Regional Cooperation Agreement on Combating Piracy and Armed Robbery against Ships in Asia ReCAAP and the Djibouti Code of Conduct concerning the suppression of piracy and armed robbery of ships in the Indian Ocean and Gulf of Aden, respectively, have made a major contribution to the fight against piracy in those regions. Both agreements anticipate a higher degree of cooperation between regional states in implementing their obligations towards security on the high seas and in their territorial waters. Thus, regional codes may serve as a useful tool to avoid the disadvantages of multilateral negotiations like UNCLOS and SUA by specifically targeting regional circumstances.

The Brenthurst Foundation postulates that maritime security is a key component of collective security which directly affects economic prosperity.[22] Kornegay similarly states that the range of maritime security challenges and its international implications should focus the attention on a continental and regional approach to address the interregional and continental maritime challenges around the coast of Africa.[23] No one country can thus tackle maritime security on its own. What is needed in this regard is continental and specifically regional direction and cooperation.

Africa's Integrated Maritime Strategy 2050 (AIMS 2050)

During 2010, the African Union (AU) opted to pursue an integrated African maritime strategy (briefly known as AIMS 2050) that signifies further progress.[24] AIMS 2050, adopted by the African Union (AU) in 2012, recognises the vast potential for wealth creation in the maritime domain for the continent, that all member states have common maritime challenges,

---

[22] S. Stead, K. Chitiyo, J. Potgieter, and G. Till, "Maritime Development in Africa: An Independent Specialists' Framework". Brenthurst Foundation Discussion Paper 2010/3. Johannesburg: The Brenthurst Foundation, 2010, 8.

[23] F.A. Kornegay, "A New Approach to Africa's Maritime Security", Africa Up Close, 13 December 2018, available at: https://africaupclose.wilsoncenter.org/a-new-approach-to-africas-maritime-security/ (accessed 13 February 2021).

[24] African Union, "AU's Commitment to Improve Maritime Security and Safety". Press Release No. 46/2010, 5 April 2010; African Union, "Maritime Security and Safety in Africa: Moving from Talking to Taking Concrete Action". Press Release No. 47/2010, 6 April 2010.

opportunities and responsibilities, requiring the requisite political will for implementing a common strategy. An AIMS 2050 Task Force was created in 2011 with the task of establishing a Department of Maritime Affairs (to develop and coordinate all policy implementation). Each regional economic community (REC) within the AU is also required to have a focal point and to establish a steering committee as well as develop an evaluation and monitoring tool.[25]

AIMS 2050 further charges the RECs to "develop, coordinate and harmonise policies and strategies and improve African maritime security and safety standards as well as the African maritime economy".[26] However, Africa's contribution to dominium over its seas, thus, remains limited and compromises good order at sea.[27]

In addition to the AIMS 2050 declaration, the Brenthurst Discussion Paper No. 3 of 2010 outlines a comprehensive NGO (non-governmental organisation) view on an Africa-informed maritime strategy.[28] At the sub-regional level, the 2011 Heads of State Summit of the Southern African Development Community (SADC), Luanda accepted a maritime strategy to fight piracy along the African eastern and western shores respectively.[29] African navies also play a role since 2005 through the biennial Sea Power for Africa symposia to sensitise their governments and ultimately the AU through resolutions emphasising Africa's oceans, its resources, those who live from the oceans and thus the need to protect the seas.[30]

The Djibouti Code of Conduct

The East African states have made several attempts to cooperate on maritime security. On 29 January 2009, the Djibouti Code of Conduct was adopted at a meeting convened by the IMO in Djibouti. The Code is the first regional agreement between Arab and African countries against acts of piracy.[31] It

---

[25] African Union, 2050 Africa's Integrated Maritime Strategy. Version 1.0. Addis Ababa, 2012.

[26] As above, p. 10.

[27] Francois Vreÿ, "Turning the Tide: Revisiting African Maritime Security", *Scientia Militaria, South African Journal of Military Studies* 41 (2): 1–23 (2013) available at: https://doi.org/10.5787/41-2-1065 (accessed 13 February 2021).

[28] Brenthurst Foundation, "Maritime Development in Africa: An Independent Specialists' Framework". Brenthurst Discussion Paper No. 3, 2010, 7.

[29] United Nations, United Nations Convention on the Law of the Sea, 1982, p. 10.

[30] South African Government Communication and Information System (GCIS). "International Cooperation, Trade and Security". GCIS Media Briefing, 13 September 2011, available at: http://www.gcis.gov.za/newsroom/releases/briefings/2011/110913.htm (accessed 26 December 2020).

[31] The Code was signed by the representatives of Djibouti, Ethiopia, Kenya, Madagascar, Maldives, Seychelles, Somalia, the United Republic of Tanzania and Yemen.

354   P. B. MAJIGA

primarily focusses on the creation of mechanisms to promote enhanced cooperation between the participant states. The main objective of the Code is to enhance the effectiveness of the prevention, interdiction, prosecution and punishment of persons engaged in piracy and armed robbery against ships.[32]

The SADC Maritime Security Strategy

While a lack of maritime domain awareness increases the likelihood of piracy incidents, the notoriously rough seas and inhospitable coasts in the SADC area of operations inhibit such incidents.[33] Incidents of piracy or attempted piracy and armed robbery at sea are, however, not new to SADC waters. This is clearly illustrated by the 2010 attacks on two fishing vessels close to the coast of Mozambique as well as reported failed incidents off the coast of Beira.[34] This has also been compounded by an insurgency in Cabo Delgado in Mozambique.

The SADC maritime security strategy to counter maritime insecurity in SADC's Indian Ocean region focusses the strategy on the elimination of piracy in the SADC's Eastern Indian Ocean. The strategy has not yet been released publicly but cites three priorities: the eradication of Somali piracy in Southern Africa; securing the west coast of Southern Africa; and securing Southern Africa's vast rivers and lakes.[35] Due to its geographical position on the Cape sea route linking the Atlantic and Indian oceans, the South African economy relative to that of other SADC states, its maritime infrastructures and its capacity to deal with maritime security challenges, make the country the ideal candidate for taking the initiative in responding to challenges to good order at sea within the SADC region. South Africa, therefore, took the lead in developing an SADC maritime security strategy, endorsed by the SADC Organ on Politics, Defence and Security[36] on 14 June 2011.

---

[32] The sub-regional meeting to conclude agreements on maritime security, piracy and armed robbery against ships for the states from the Western Indian Ocean, Gulf of Aden and Red Sea areas held in Djibouti, 26–29 January 2009. The meeting was attended by 17 (out of the 21) states in the region. In addition, 12 states from outside the region attended the meeting as observers.

[33] H. Fouché, "Piracy: The African Experience". In T. D. Potgieter and R. Pommerin (eds), Maritime Security in Southern African Waters. Stellenbosch: Sun Press, 2009, 84–86.

[34] J. Germishuys, "SO1 Maritime Planning at the South African Joint Operations HQ in Pretoria". Personal interview, 7 April 2014 in Sayed Mohammed Mohiuddin Hasan "The adequacies and inadequacies of the piracy regime: A Gulf of Guinea perspective" A thesis submitted for the degree of Master of Laws School of Law University of Western Sydney, Australia, 2014.

[35] JPB Coelho, African Approaches to Maritime Security: Southern Africa. Maputo: Friedrich-Ebert-Stiftung Mozambique, 2013, 13.

[36] SADC, Towards a Common Future, 2012, available at: https://www.sadc.int/sadc-secretariat/directorates/office-executive-secretary/organ-politics-defense-and-security/ (accessed 6 March 2020).

The strategy could be seen as "South Africa-driven" and reflects mostly South African interests while highlighting the country's dichotomy in the region—balancing South Africa's geo-strategic motives as self-appointed rescuer in the region while not adequately addressing domestic challenges in respect of other maritime security issues, such as trafficking, IUU fishing, environmental protection and disaster response.[37] Although the SADC maritime security strategy is titled "maritime security strategy", it does not adequately address the whole ambit of maritime insecurity and may thus be insufficient to deal with the holistic concept of good order at sea.[38] The execution of the strategy resulted in the formation of a SADC maritime task force (Operation Copper), which focussed almost exclusively on anti-piracy operations.[39]

Code of Conduct to Combat Piracy in West and Central Africa

The Economic Community of Central African States (ECCAS), the Economic Community of West African States (ECOWAS) and the Gulf of Guinea Commission[40] developed this Code of Conduct, with the assistance of the International Maritime Organisation. It was formally adopted in 2013 and is modelled on the Djibouti Code of Conduct. It commits to cooperation in the prevention and repression of piracy and armed robbery against ships, transnational organised crime in the maritime domain, maritime terrorism, illegal, unreported and unregulated fishing and other illegal activities at sea.[41]

Maritime Organisation of West and Central African States (MOWCA)

Twenty coastal and five landlocked states form part of MOWCA,[42] and the most significant contribution stems from attempts to establish a sub-regional

---

[37] As above, p. 14.

[38] The SA Navy hosted members of the SADC from 23 to 25 July 2019 to review the strategy and to draft an integrated maritime security strategy, which now has to be ratified by SADC organisation.

[39] L.N. Sisulu, "Address at the SADC Extraordinary Meeting on Regional Anti-Piracy Strategy". Government Communication and Information System, 2013, available at: https://www.gov.za/address-l-n-sisulu-mp-minister-defence-and-military-veterans-sadc-extraordinary-meeting-regional (accessed 18 July 2014).

[40] This institution is driven by oil producing states, all of whom are affected by the problem of piracy.

[41] R. Asariotis, A. Premti, J. Lavelle, and H. Benamara, Maritime Piracy Part II: An Overview of the International Legal Framework and of Multilateral Cooperation to Combat Piracy. UNCTAD, 2014b, available at: http://eprints.soton.ac.uk/368255/1/dtl tlb2013d3_en.pdf (accessed 15 February 2021).

[42] By the middle of 2013, both MOWCA and the GGC participated in the growing efforts by ECCAS and ECOWAS (resulting in the Yaounde Declaration) to cooperate in response to the steep rise in attacks upon shipping (oil tankers in particular) in the Gulf of Guinea.

coastguard, a regional maritime fund and communications centre. In cooperation with the IMO, MOWCA aims to create cooperative networks to enforce standing international arrangements better, to counter threats such as piracy, robberies and pollution and to promote safety at sea through existing conventions.[43] MOWCA represents the largest maritime security grouping in the region and as such acts as an umbrella organisation for a range of maritime actors and interested parties.[44]

WHITHER PIRACY? ASSESSMENT OF NATIONAL AND REGIONAL RESPONSES IN AFRICA

The primary responsibility for eradicating piracy rests with the states concerned. The building of national capacities—that is, enacting anti-piracy legislation, prosecuting and imprisoning pirates and enhancing naval, judicial and law enforcement capacities—is of crucial importance for combating piracy. Considering the adverse effects of piracy, the countries in various region have followed state-centric policies, such as tightening border security and deploying Special Forces to piracy prone areas. Most states have also responded to the threat by strengthening national initiatives by entering into partnerships with a view to promote a regional approach to maritime security through joint efforts to patrol the waters. However, these efforts must be seen in light of the assertion and reality that "the challenges of governing ocean spaces can be daunting if handled unilaterally".[45]

The declarations and conventions mentioned above show that the legal framework is in place in order for states to conduct their maritime security, and there is specific emphasis on the fact the regional cooperation is critical for successful maritime security. Overall, in an African context, there is a seemingly sufficient framework, both normatively and legally, to support regional cooperation within the maritime domain. States may freely enter into bilateral or multilateral agreements in order to enhance their limited capacity. Despite various national, regional and international initiatives taken by African countries to combat piracy, there are clear indications of increased pirate activity on the continent.

Given the financial, legal and logistical limitations, the national responses to piracy by countries have been met with mixed success. The efforts have proved insufficient to deter piracy because of the limited naval capacity of individual states on the continent. Most of states have limited maritime capacity and seriously lack in infrastructure, equipment and legal framework. In many cases,

---

[43] J. Raidt and K. Smith, "Advancing US, African and Global Interests: Security and Stability in the West African Maritime Domain", *Atlantic Council* 9, 30 November 2010.

[44] See MOWCA detail on members, partners and projects at: http://www.mowca.org/new%20design/about-mowca.html (accessed 25 January 2021).

[45] P.M. Wambua, "Enhancing Regional Maritime Cooperation in Africa: The Planned End State", *African Security Review* 18 (3): 51 (2009).

pirates have been found to be better equipped than naval patrols. Pirates have been able to exploit this weakness and stage attacks without fear of government intervention. The lack of effective maritime policies, especially among the Gulf of Guinea states has also allowed pirates to operate successfully. Most of these states have inadequate policies on maritime security and lack adequate anti-piracy legislation authorising the enforcement of legal actions against piracy and the prosecution of pirates. At the bilateral level, efforts have primarily focussed on improving security in the region. However, most of these efforts have not been sustained in the long run.

Despite continued efforts to foster maritime cooperation, the formulation of a successful maritime regime in Africa is limited by the sensitive issue of national sovereignty. Many states on the continent are strongly protective of their sovereignty and are usually unwilling to approve any cooperative activities that might compromise their sovereign rights. This emphasis on sovereignty makes regional integration in security matters particularly difficult. Weaker countries are particularly cautious about their stronger neighbours' (especially Nigeria and South Africa's) ability to project influence in the regions. The relations between regional neighbours are also affected by political problems such as international territorial disputes (such as between Nigeria and Cameroon) and maritime border disputes (such as between Ghana and Côte d'Ivoire). Such tense relationships hamper the exchange of information.

Sharing of information related to maritime security is affected by some tense relationships between neighbouring countries. The continuing maritime border dispute between Ghana and Côte d'Ivoire, the sovereignty dispute between Equatorial Guinea and Gabon over islands in Corisco Bay and the tensions between Cameroon and Equatorial Guinea over an island at the mouth of Ntem River[46] make maritime security cooperation more difficult within the subregion. In addition, the region's naval forces have different types of communication systems and cultures of confidentiality, hampering the exchange of information.

Despite enhanced national and bilateral efforts to address the scourge, it is evident that the ongoing regional initiatives are critical to comprehensively address piracy. If piracy is to be reduced, a region-wide strategy should be put in place. Efforts so far by regional governments to mitigate piracy are commendable but insufficient. Until recently, there has been a comparatively low level of cooperation between regional institutions. As the regional institution responsible for peace and security in the region, ECOWAS has made little progress in formulating any regional response to maritime insecurity.

To date, the regional organisations operating in the Gulf of Guinea and SADC region have shown highly unequal implementation capacities in dealing with the piracy problem. Pooling together of available resources remains a

---

[46] International Crisis Group, "The Gulf of Guinea: The New Danger Zone". Africa Report No. 195, International Crisis Group, 2012.

challenge.[47] Blended with indifference and divisive tendencies among the leaders of the community progress in articulating a coherent regional response to maritime insecurity has been seriously hampered. Throughout the SADC region, states score high in terms of their participation and commitment with regard to global agreements, such as UNCLOS and various other international treaties.[48] The picture changes, however, once the focus narrows to continental agreements where only five out of the 16 SADC countries have signed the Lomé Charter.[49] None of them have ratified the Charter. At a regional level, Angola has signed the Yaoundé Declaration[50] and only six out of the 16 SADC countries have signed the Jeddah Amendment. This is summed up by a think-thank that posits:

> We concluded then, and now, that the SADC leadership is rhetorically committed to full integration in both the socio-economic and security arenas (and to the eventual merging of the two into one, human security, agenda). The practice reveals the maintenance of a stable (but not always efficient) institution, used by members to behave in a disaggregated manner, driven by the overriding demands of national interest and sovereignty.[51]

The regional cooperation in the East Africa region has been marked by unlinked and uncoordinated policies and activities. The regional approaches to combating piracy indicate poor coordination and planning. Many of the efforts suffer from lack of coordination and tend to address only maritime security issues.[52] As the Code was not the result of initiatives by East African nations, the level of political support for the Code has been weak.[53] This has led the IMO to become the central forum for debating the future of the instrument. The Code has also been criticised as overly ambitious, as it tries to bring a host of countries in the region together in a common forum that does not have a successful legacy of political cooperation. This is reinforced by the fact that the states could not agree on one single information sharing centre under the Code.[54]

[47] Tim Walker, "Pursuit of Maritime Security in a Region Lacking Regionalism", June 2020, available at: 10.5787/47-2-1283.

[48] Stable Seas, available at: https://stableseas.org/issue-areas/international-cooperation#1 (accessed 13 August 2019).

[49] As above.

[50] As above.

[51] SADC Policy Analysis and Dialogue Programme SADC Think-Tank Meeting SADC Regional Think Tank, 11 August 2012.

[52] Christian Bueger and Mohanvir Singh Saran, "Finding a Regional Solution to Piracy: Is the Djibouti Process the Answer?" In Christian Bueger and Mohanvir Singh Saran (eds), Piracy Studies (18 August 2012), available at: http://piracystudies.org/author/christian-bueger-and-mohanvir-singh-saran/ (accessed 14 February 2021).

[53] As above.

[54] As above.

Way Forward in Fighting Piracy in Africa

Piracy is in many ways not only the most visible maritime security challenge but also a paradigmatic one. There are several issues that need to be considered in fighting piracy. It should be noted, however, the problem cannot be solved by exclusively relying on a military-based approach. Seeking such a solution may render piracy purely as a security problem rather than as a symptom of more serious governance problems onshore. Thus, the military approach needs to be operationalised hand-in-hand with a non-military approach to address critical issues, most of which are root causes piracy on the continent.

The Military-Based Approach

Historically, the principal defense against piracy has been through military intervention. Over the centuries, the model of international cooperation to suppress piracy has been through aggressive international enforcement.[55] The international community has primarily responded to the threat by following an armed strategy of deterring and combating. For example, to counter piracy in the Gulf of Aden and other waters of the Indian Ocean, there has been heavy patrolling by joint maritime forces of several nations, including European Union (EU) and North Atlantic Treaty Organisation (NATO)-led fleets. These international military efforts and strategies have proven effective to a certain extent in containing the number of successful attacks but have not eradicated piracy itself.

Coastal states having maritime enforcement capability usually control piracy by naval action. However, the Gulf of Guinea and SADC countries have limited maritime capacity and little capability to counter the threat effectively through these means. They also lack the unity required to allow for sustained surveillance and security in their regional waters. Consequently, weak naval enforcements have done little to prevent pirates from attacking merchant vessels with impunity. Realising the complexity of the situation, the following options may be invoked by African countries.

Build Regional Maritime Capacity

Piracy in the Gulf of Guinea occurs mostly in the territorial seas of coastal states. In this sense, the primary responsibility to suppress piracy lies with the national security forces of the regional countries. Notably, the growth of piracy in the region is due mainly to the inability of the coastal states to defend their territorial seas. Therefore, it is in their strategic interest to develop local maritime capacity. The states need to ensure that they are better equipped to

---

[55] Eugene Kontorovich, "Piracy and International Law", *e-Law Journal: Global Law Forum* (8 February 2009), available at: http://jcpa.org/article/piracy-and-international-law/ (accessed 13 February 2021).

tackle piracy. This can be achieved by strengthening the local maritime forces and their operational capabilities.

It is important to note that the introduction of an international naval force in the coastal waters of the Gulf of Guinea as has occurred off the coast of Somalia may be problematic. While the majority of pirate attacks in Somalia take place on the high seas, most of the attacks in the Gulf of Guinea occur within territorial waters. Given the broad regional sensitivities concerning external interference, the presence of foreign vessels in jurisdictional waters is likely to be considered by many states as unwarranted. Further, the possibility of foreign warships being a target of attack by pirates may undermine the usefulness of any such deployment.[56]

Improve Collective Military Cooperation

One possible option for a systemic solution to piracy could be the creation of a regional cooperative maritime security approach. Such an approach would make maritime safety and security a shared responsibility and enable regional states to conduct cross border patrols and share law enforcement intelligence. Implementation of the approach would require building a regional maritime security partnership among the regional countries. This would significantly improve the efficient coordination of information and assets among all the naval forces of the region. The objective of such a task force would be to create a centre for law enforcement cooperation to facilitate the building of a sustainable regional capacity and capability.

Enhance Maritime Domain Surveillance

Successful suppression of piracy can be accomplished by the collective vigilance of the maritime domain of regional countries. Progress in this regard can be achieved through a joint anti-piracy operation with all the navies of the region. The countries of the region can establish a common surveillance procedure and develop joint operational coordination capabilities in this regard. This would facilitate an effective maritime security intervention through a regional security system. It is expected that coordinated anti-piracy patrols would have deterrent effects on piracy.

However, it is important to note that the technology is just part of a solution. To emphasise the importance of functional cooperation does not imply that technology is the single most important component in addressing maritime security. Much emphasis has been placed in East Africa on developing maritime surveillance capacities (maritime domain awareness) and information sharing platforms. One needs to keep in mind that given the nature and "unruliness" of maritime space, surveillance capacities will never be able

---

[56] United Nations Assessment Mission Report, Piracy in the Gulf of Guinea, Security Council Doc. S/2012/45 (7–24 November 2011), 15.

to give a full real-time depiction of what happens at sea. Moreover, data on movements and incidents, even if they are accurate and adequately shared, are only meaningful if the political will and the capabilities exist to act upon this knowledge. Hence, technological infrastructure is only one part of the broader spectrum of measures that are required for maritime security.

Consider the Use of Private Military Security Companies

Ship owners operating in the region may consider the use of privately contracted armed guards. The presence of armed players in the Indian Ocean has been effective in reducing the number of successful hijackings in the region.[57] While this solution may create new problems, the perceived success of private armed guards in protecting ships against Somali-based piracy may encourage the coastal states in the Gulf of Guinea and ship owners to consider this option. States willing to permit the use of Privately Contracted Armed Security Personnel need to establish a suitable national framework governing this.

It is recommended that the use of private armed guards should be considered by Gulf of Guinea governments as an absolute last choice. It is uncertain whether the presence of armed guards in the Gulf of Guinea would have the same effect as off the coast of Somalia. It is believed that due to previous armed conflicts in the region, the Nigerian pirates have access to more sophisticated weaponry than those in Somalia. Moreover, the pirates seem to be less hesitant to employ violence against crews. This being the case, it may be risky to allow private armed guards to operate in the territorial waters of the region. Moreover, such as deployment may lead to international disputes, as carriage of armed personnel has legal implications for coastal and port states.

NON-MILITARY MEANS TO SUPPRESS PIRACY

To fight and eradicate piracy, the African states need to address the main causes of the problem. The rise of piracy in the region is due mainly to lack of good governance practises. The failure of the countries to maintain effective command over their land and sea territories has contributed to the growth of piracy. Furthermore, poverty, crime and corruption have created conducive conditions for piracy to thrive. As explicitly stated, "there is a legitimate causal connection between [1] combating piracy and [2] rendering Africa in general economically viable and economically stable".[58]

---

[57] James Brown, "Pirates and Privateers: Managing the Indian Ocean's Private Security Boom" (2012). Lowy Institute for International Policy, 3.

[58] Parliamentary Monitoring Group (PMG), "Hansard: Debate on Budget Vote no. 22—Defence and Military Veterans". National Assembly, 23 May 2013, available at: https://pmg.org.za/hansard/18377/ (accessed 6 February 2021).

It is important to understand and appreciate that piracy is situated in a security development nexus. Piracy highlights that maritime security threats have a security as well as a development dimension. Factors such as corruption, economic dislocation, cultural acceptability or skills emphasise that development policies are crucial in addressing maritime insecurity. This includes awareness campaigns, reintegration programmes as well as vocational training or infrastructure measures which are beneficial to marginalised coastal populations.

Moreover, as already evidenced, maritime threats such as piracy have significant economic consequences. The benefits of a country's ports, coastline and exclusive economic zone can only be realised in the realm of good maritime governance. This calls for a close coordination between security and development policies and actors. Yet, as other studies of the security–development nexus have shown, coordinating or even integrating security and development policies and actors is very intricate. Therefore, addressing the root causes of piracy on the continent requires the adoption of long-term policies actively focussing on improving economic governance and ensuring the socio-economic welfare, more especially of coastal communities.

Improve Economic Governance

Poor economic governance in the Gulf of Guinea has seen the region become characterised by crude oil theft, drug trafficking and illegal fishing. These illegal activities have in turn fostered widespread corruption and criminality in the region. The Gulf of Guinea piracy is thus largely the result of poor governance. Notably, the massive organised oil theft business has enabled certain corrupt groups to become rich, leaving the mainstream populations poor. Such economic inequality has led to the growth of maritime crimes along the coast. The development of piracy tends to coincide with economic marginalisation as the vast majority of piratical incidents are motivated by poverty.

This serves as a reminder that maritime insecurities are interdependent. Piracy develops in a larger context of maritime insecurity. If coastlines, exclusive economic zones or the international sea are weakly governed, host a broad range of illegal activities, maritime violence is naturalised or sea transport militarised, threats such as piracy are more likely to occur. Different illegal activities re-enforce and trigger each other. Maritime threats should hence be seen as interdependent and the goal has to be to address the full spectrum of maritime insecurities. The Gulf of Guinea, East Africa and SADC states should thus focus on removing opportunities for corruption and ensure that the proceeds from oil revenue benefit the poor.

Increase Development on the Coast

Piracy is largely driven by poor economic opportunities. Lack of sources of livelihood may compel coastal communities to resort to maritime crimes, including piracy. This is very much true in the Niger Delta and Cabo Delgado, respectively, where the local residents lost their fishing-related and farming related livelihood structures to environmental pollution and construction caused by the oil industry. The solution to piracy in this regard lies with the creation of alternative forms of economic activity along the coast. African states should focus on boosting coastal state governance by introducing improved employment opportunities for the coastal population. This reconstruction effort will help to drive prospective pirates away from piracy.

Formalise and Operationalise Custody and Prosecution Arrangements

The African states should have a common agreement or arrangement in place to facilitate expeditious investigation, prosecution and punishment for any captured pirates. The effectiveness of the agreement could be further enhanced by prescribing a mechanism for suspects transfer agreements between the apprehending state and the prosecuting state. The agreement must provide procedures for the extradiction and transfer of suspects and the conditions under which this may take place.

Enhance Regional Cooperation

Regional cooperation and the coordination of all states within various regional blocs would aid in the prevention and suppression of piracy. As the majority of incidents of piracy occur within the respective jurisdictional sea areas of the countries, improved regional cooperation is required within the territorial seas. To this end, the countries must establish a regional mechanism for piracy suppression. The countries in the region need to adopt legal and policy frameworks for suppressing piracy and focus on enhancing cooperation and coordination in law enforcement and intelligence sharing. This needs to be encouraged, especially among "landlocked countries". To counter the symptoms and causes of piracy, the countries need to improve regional dialogue on the issue.

Another take home in the fight against piracy is that good law does not imply good law enforcement. A powerful lesson drawn from Somali piracy ably demonstrates this point. While UNCLOS provided a sufficient legal framework to address a threat such as piracy, the problem that the international community faced was how to enforce the law. This includes implementation challenges such as how to work across different legal regimes, for instance, in transferring suspects. Hence, even if it is important that states improve their legal codes to respond to maritime security challenges, this does not necessarily or directly translate into good law enforcement.

Conclusion

Although piracy is only one of the several other maritime security threats, it can be considered as a paradigmatic one. Piracy illustrates that maritime security threats tend to be sticky. Once they emerge, they are difficult to eradicate. Hence, prevention strategies and mechanisms are crucial. If threats cannot be prevented it is important to have early warning and early response mechanisms in place in order to avoid escalation. Maritime security threats are moreover asymmetric. They cannot be addressed by military might or firepower alone. Seeking such a solution may render piracy purely as a security problem rather than as a symptom of more serious governance problems onshore. They require complex and coordinated responses and tactical innovation. Somali piracy moreover forcefully reveals how apparently local problems can have considerable global effects.

The problem of piracy has led to a fundamental re-evaluation of the importance of maritime security for the African continent, and indeed there is a strong international consensus to act and support regional actors to tackle maritime security challenges. In this sense, piracy has opened a window of opportunity to re-organise maritime security governance and build sustainable institutions. With the decline of Somali piracy there is, however, the risk that the momentum could get lost soon and that the window of opportunity may close. It is vital that the international community starts learning from piracy, countries should restructure their maritime sector and ensure that sufficient resources are made available for implementing programmes that tackle maritime insecurity.

What is required is nothing less than fundamental reforms of the maritime security sector on national and regional levels. Further a mainstreaming of maritime security concerns across international donor policies will be needed. If maritime insecurity breeds threats, then the long-term goal has to be employed to work towards de-securitising the maritime and building regional maritime security communities. This, in the end, might be the core paradox of current strategies: in order to achieve a de-securitisation of the sea in the long run, what is first required is a securitisation, that is, the recognition for the serious impact that maritime threats have on economies, livelihoods and national and international security interests.

CHAPTER 21

Post-Electoral Violence in Africa

*Archiles A. Bwete, Leonard Hatungimana,
and Wilson N. Parsauti*

Introduction

Africa comprises of 54 independent countries,[1] with a population of approximately 1325 million,[2] and a total land area of 11,724.000 square miles.[3] Africa suffers from a curse inflicted in one of Europe's most famous and cosmopolitan cities: Berlin. The Berlin Conference of 1884–1885, under the supervision of Germany's Chancellor Otto von Bismarck, carved up Africa into territories that reflected compromises struck between avaricious European imperialists to

---

[1] Countries in Africa, available at: http://www.worldometers.info/geography/how-many-countries-in-Africa (accessed on 28 December 2019).

[2] African Population, available at: http://www.worldometers.info/world-population/africa-population/ (accessed on 27 December 2019).

[3] Africa Continent, available at: https://www.britannica.com/place/Africa (accessed on 3 January 2020).

A. A. Bwete (✉)
Kampala, Uganda

L. Hatungimana
National Defense Force, Bujumbura, Burundi

W. N. Parsauti
Moi University, Mombasa, Kenya

© The Author(s), under exclusive license to Springer Nature
Switzerland AG 2022
D. Kuwali (ed.), *The Palgrave Handbook of Sustainable Peace
and Security in Africa*, https://doi.org/10.1007/978-3-030-82020-6_21

365

wit, Britain, France, Portugal, Belgium, Spain, and Germany rather than the political, social, and economic interests of Africa.[4]

No Africans were invited to attend the Berlin Conference of 1884, either as participants or as observers.[5] The colonial boundaries are still exalted on the continent as a matter of 'sovereignty' which is injurious to African Unity and Prosperity. The election process must be purveyed through a legitimate and well-structured procedure where agreed regulatory frameworks are put in place to elect representatives of the people. As such, the electoral process is a system for ascendancy to political power where institutions are imbued with the primary responsibility of guaranteeing that the process does not sow discord within the society.

The African context of electoral processes has attracted immense attention moving its gravitation towards violence. While a majority of African states have transitioned from single-party dictatorship to multi-party democracy, violence has been marked as a resultant phenomenon. In 2010, the presidential election in Ivory Coast resulted in political turmoil, leading to over 1000 deaths and displacement of over 500,000 people. More recently, the candidacy of the then Burundian President Pierre Nkurunziza for a third term triggered a violent political crisis in Burundi, resulting in hundreds of deaths and about 200,000 refugees who fled to neighbouring countries.

In Angola, the 1992 elections led to a ten (10) year civil war. In the May 2005 election, Ethiopia held the third competitive multi-party election in that country. Although the pre-election and the Voting Day were remarkably peaceful, the post-election period was marred by electoral violence that led to the death of more than 193 people and the detention of more than 40,000 people.[6] We posit that post-election violence manifests in the 'first world' as it does in Africa thus there is nothing African about it. Following the election victory of the 45th United States (US) President Donald Trump, quite a number of American citizens went to the streets to protest and riot against the victory of Donald Trump.

Post-election violence is largely the breaker of peace and tranquillity in Africa. To cure the African continent against post-election violence, there is a need to understand its nature. Countries that have experienced post-election violence include Cameroon, the Democratic Republic of the Congo, Liberia, Equatorial Guinea, Gambia, Guinea, Kenya, Madagascar, Malawi, Sierra Leone, Senegal, Burundi, and Uganda among others. While electoral violence is pervasive in Africa, its causes and dynamics remain poorly understood.

---

[4] Adekeye Adebajo, The Curse of Berlin: Africa's Security Dilemmas Page 1, available at: https://library.fes.de/pdf-files/id/ipg/03044.pdf (accessed on 24 September 2020).

[5] John Reader, Africa—A Biography of the Continent, p. 543.

[6] Wondwosen Teshome, Electoral Violence in Africa: Experience from Ethiopia. World Academy of Science, Engineering and Technology. *International Journal of Humanities and Social Sciences* Vol. 3, No. 7, 2009, p. 4.

There is little consensus on the causes of post-electoral violence in Africa. In this chapter, the causes shall be categorised into cardinal, minor, and cognate causes. It must be reiterated that there is no thin line separating the causes of post-election violence and an attempt to do so is an exercise in futility. On the contrary, its causes are intertwined, each leading to the other. The cure for post-election violence in Africa is interestingly within our reach to wit: Federation of African States, Promotion of Democracy and Rule of Law, Education and Sensitisation of all stakeholders.

CAUSES OF POST-ELECTION VIOLENCE IN AFRICA

In our view, the Cardinal causes of post-election violence in Africa are threefold and intertwined. These include neo-colonialism, sectarianism, and economic factors.

Neo-Colonialism

Kwame Nkrumah observes that neo-colonialism of today represents imperialism in its final and perhaps most dangerous stage. The essence of neo-colonialism is that the state which is subject to it, is in theory independent, and has all outward trappings of international sovereignty. In reality, its economic system and thus its political policy is directed from outside.[7]

Immediately after independence of most African States, their former colonial masters continued to remote control the political trajectory of the former colonies. In the Democratic Republic of the Congo (DRC), following the powerful Independence speech of the then Prime Minister Patrice Lumumba, the Congolese applauded warmly, but Belgians were deeply shaken and regarded the speech as an insult.[8] There are strong indications that foreign intelligence agents planned and in collaboration with some locals assassinated the Congo's first Prime Minister.[9]

Kamanda contends that the United States, China, and many European states have a great presence in Africa. This is manifested by a volume of multinational companies which inject foreign capital in legal and illegal political activity.[10] In South Sudan, for instance, Chinese peacekeepers engaged in a standoff with South Sudanese rebels in 2018. The Chinese companies and government support the current government in South Sudan.[11]

---

[7] Kwame Nkrumah, Neo-Colonialism: The Last Stage of Imperialism, PANAF, London, p. ix.

[8] John Reader, pp. 650–651.

[9] Ibid., p. 644.

[10] Interview with Mr. Godfrey Kamanda on 29 November 2019.

[11] Austin Bodetti, How China Came to Dominate South Sudan's Oil, available at: https://thediplomat.com/2019/02/how-china-came-to-dominate-south-sudans-oil/ (accessed on 24 September 2020).

The emergence of China's interests on the African continent for markets and raw materials is likely to hit on a collision path with the interests of the United States. With these economic interests at loggerheads, African Head of States will elect to either pay homage to the Chinese or the United States for regime survival; however, no matter their choice, the opposing imperial power will resort to support political opponents, which will be deemed as an alternative. With the United States and China being the two superpowers, the rest of the world would be forced to take sides, and the conflict would be ideologically charged.[12] It is apparent that the conflict predicted by Eric Posner and John Yoo is already in our midst. Africa is the playing field for the scramble of raw materials by the Chinese and United States with her western allies. Drazen Jorgic argues that China is swapping its reserved diplomacy for a hands-on approach to help resolve a more than five months of rebellion in South Sudan that threatens Beijing's oil investments.[13]

The scramble for African resources is responsible for causing post-election violence in Africa with a competing imperial power supporting opposing political groups. It follows, therefore, that violence is an inevitable phenomenon. Evidently, in many parts of Africa where even when elections are free and fair, post-election violence follows to push for power-sharing deals whereby competing imperial powers or their proxies in the name of losing local political players strive to secure a win–win result.

In 2008, Kenya and Zimbabwe saw power-sharing deals introduced after contested election results that escalated into post-election violence. Following sham elections in Nigeria in 2007, the new president proposed an all-inclusive government.[14] As already stated neo-colonialism is not a standalone phenomenon but is interrelated to other cardinal causes of post-election violence.

Sectarianism

This is at times referred to as politics of identity. These identities are a tool of mobilisation by crafty politicians in Africa. Sectarianism as a cause of post-election violence is twofold: ethno-politics and faith politics.

Firstly, the word ethno-politics comes from two English words which are Ethnicity and Politics. Ethno-politics is, therefore, politics of ethnicity. Hashmi and Majeed opine that in the developing world, ethnio-politics is one of the

---

[12] Eric A. Posner, John C. Yoo, International Law and the Rise of China 2006, University of Chicago Law School.

[13] Drazen Jorgic, China Takes More Assertive Line in South Sudan Diplomacy, available at: https://www.google.com/amp/s/mobile.reuters..com/article/amp/idUSKBNOEG00 320140605 (accessed on 28 December 2019).

[14] Anna K. Jarstad, The Prevalence of Power-Sharing: Exploring the Patterns of Post-Election Peace, p. 42, available at: https://journals.sagepub.com/doi/pdf/10.1177/000 203970904400303 (accessed on 24 September 2020).

main reasons of internal instability.[15] Lutaaya argues that given the fact that most African countries are heterogeneous Nations, there exists a multiplicity of ethnic groups in one country. Politicians who belong to particular ethnic groups charge their social groupings with the propaganda of 'us versus them' and call for civil disobedience in the event a candidate who hails from their ethnic group losses the elections.[16]

Suffice to note, the first political parties in several African countries were formed on ethnic grounds usually but not necessarily to propel ethnic goals. Prominent among them are Buganda Political Organisation called *Kabaka Yekka* (King Alone) formed in Uganda to elevate the interests of the people of Buganda[17] and the Muhutu Social Movement (MSM) in Rwanda formed to promote the objectives of the Hutu Manifesto,[18] the Orange Democratic Movement in Kenya whose grassroots campaign turned the election into a contest of 'forty-one tribes against one' and 'Kenya against the Kikuyu tribe' highlighting Kikuyu domination of government and the commanding heights of the economy, and blaming Kikuyu success for marginalisation suffered by other groups.[19] Ravinder Joshi observes that political cleavages became based on ethnic identity, but initially, they were more precisely drawn along political class lines.[20]

Politics of ethnicity is a recipe for disaster in Africa evident from the lessons drawn from the 1994 Rwandan Genocide where over 100,000 people lost their lives and hundreds of thousands were displaced. History tells us that the African people and leaders are quick to forget or ignore our troubled past of ethnic violence. After Rwanda, no one expected recurrences of ethnic violence at gigantic proportions until the 27 December 2007 elections in Kenya which sprouted into post-election violence.

Peter Kagwanja and Roger Southall contend that after the controversial declaration of Mwai Kibaki as the winner by the Electoral Commission of Kenya on 30 December 2007, violence erupted in strongholds of the Orange Democratic Movement.[21] The effects of the post-election violence were disastrous on the New Year's Day, when 39 people, mainly women, children, and disabled were burnt to death by marauding ethnic supporters of Orange

---

[15] Rehana Saeed Hashmi, Gulshan Majeed, Politics of Ethnicity: A Theoretical Perspective. *A Research Journal of South Asian Studies* Vol. 30, No. 1, January–June 2015, p. 319.

[16] Interview with Mr. Richard Lutaaya on 29 November 2019.

[17] Apolo Robin Nsibambi, National Integration in Uganda 1962–2013, Fountain Publishers, p. 30.

[18] Ravinder Joshi, Genocide in Rwanda: The Root Causes. *East African Journal of Peace & Human Rights* Vol. 3, No. 1, 1997, p. 59.

[19] M. Chege, Kenya: Back from the Brink? *Journal of Democracy* Vol. 19, No. 4, 2008, pp. 125–139.

[20] Supra, Ravinder Joshi.

[21] Peter Kagwanja, Roger Southall, Introduction: Kenya—A Democracy in Retreat? *Journal of Contemporary African Studies* Vol. 27, No. 3, July 2009, pp. 259–277.

370 A. A. BWETE ET AL.

Democratic Movement who set ablaze a church in Eldoret where the former had taken asylum.[22] By the time the violence subsided in April 2008, it had left 1000–2000 people dead, 600,000 displaced, and costed the economy over 100 billion shillings.[23]

Professor Apolo R. Nsibambi poses the question that if there is a major conflict between the demands of a nation and the demands of an ethnic group, does the nation command the ultimate loyalty?[24] No African post-independence leader has ever been put on the loyalty scale to choose between the interests of his ethnic group and those of his country than the First President of Uganda who doubled as the King of Buganda Sir Edward Mutesa. In his capacity as President of Uganda, Mutesa refused to sign the instrument relocating the lost counties to Bunyoro Kindgom.[25] He reasoned that he would be ceding part of his Kingdom to a traditional rival Bunyoro.[26] In essence, the then President of the Republic of Uganda portrayed that loyalty to his Kingdom of Buganda superseded that of the country he presided over as President.

The card of ethnicity is played by many political opportunists to swing numbers to their side in order to win elections at whatever level. It is quite surprising that a country like Tanzania, which comprises of 126 ethnic groups her politics, is not based on ethnicity and yet Rwanda and Kenya comprising of 3 and 42 tribes respectively, are know for practising politics of ethnicity.

Kenyan politics has, predictably, revolved around ethnic coalitions to win competitive national elections. The Kikuyu-Luo detente swept KANU to victory in 1963 elections. Actually, three Kenyan Presidents from 1963 to 2007 ascended to power through strong coalitions of two or more of the four 'political tribes'.[27] Micheal Wrong contends that given Kenya's political tradition of ethnic patronage, a Raila Presidency would surely mean new jobs, fresh investment, new roads, hospitals, and schools for Luos, just as it had been for Kikuyu under Kenyatta and Kalenjin under Moi.[28] Thus, as they queued to cast their ballots on 27 December 2008, Kisumu's residents had a clear sense of what was their 'due'. 'We're voting for change', was the politically correct formula, but many quietly added, 'It's our time'.[29]

It follows that ethnicity in politics plays a major role in causing post-election violence, since people of a particular ethnic group hope to reap satisfactorily on the national cake when their own (tribesmen) are in political office. With such

[22] Ibid.

[23] Ibid.

[24] Supra, Apolo Robin Nsibambi, p. 9.

[25] Ibid., p. 35.

[26] Onek C. Adyanga, Modes of British Imperial Control of Africa: A Case Study of Uganda, C. 1890–1990, p. 159.

[27] Supra, Peter Kagwanja, Roger Southall.

[28] Michela Wrong, It's Our Turn to Eat, HarperCollins (2010), p. 220.

[29] Ibid.

ethno-politics, the ultimate goal is either own victory or defeat of their opponents. Their slogan is and shall always be 'we win or they lose'. Conceding defeat is never on the table and the losing coalition calls for protests to force a power-sharing deal thus making post-election violence inevitable. Ethnicity is also intertwined to other causes of post-election violence like religion and economic factors.

Faith politics comes from two English words which are Faith and Politics. This is politics based on religious beliefs. In Africa, many political parties were formed based on religious leaning. This is well illustrated in Uganda, where the Democratic Party was formed with a leaning on Roman Catholic Religion and Uganda People's Congress leaned on Protestant's faith. The Islamic Party for moslems in Kenya. Al Jama-ah Party for Muslims and African Christian Democratic Party for christians in South Africa. Religion is a tool that has been used by politicians to manipulate voters, for instance, Butambala district in central Uganda, Northern Nigeria, Coastal areas of Kenya, and North Eastern Kenya regions are areas which are predominately occupied by Muslim communities. Inevitably the political leaders that hail from those regions subscribe to the moslem faith. This is also the case in areas which are dominantly occupied with christians, the leaders are interestly of christian faith.

Oriku opines that religion is a social fabric of African society that affects the relations of those who practice similar religious beliefs. In event of elections, those casting votes want to have an identity or inclination that propels them to vote for a particular person and religion is one of those elements that are largely taken into consideration. It is expected that violence will arise if an elected candidate is not from the popular religious group.[30]

Cheeseman writes that 2007 was the first time in Kenyan elections that religion turned into a mobilising issue, manipulated by both ODM and PNU in their attempts to win the hearts of both Muslims and Christians.[31] Kenga writes that in the run-up of the 2007 general elections, churches were openly partisan along ethnic lines depending on their leaders' ethnic backgrounds. Prominent church leaders gave conflicting 'prophesies' on who would emerge victorious in the elections and even anointing them in public to signify that God had chosen them for Presidency.[32]

In the aftermath of the elections, many church buildings were burnt down in the violence while church leaders' efforts in stopping and meditating in the conflict were largely unsuccessful as the public no longer viewed them as

---

[30] Interview with Ms. Brenda Oriku on 27 September 2019.

[31] N. Cheeseman, The Kenyan Elections of 2007: An Introduction. *Journal of Eastern African Studies* Vol. 2, No. 2, 2008, pp. 166–184.

[32] Catherine Kenga, The Role of Religion in Politics and Governance in Kenya. Research Paper submitted in partial fulfilment of the Degree of Masters of Arts in International Studies, University of Nairobi, p. 6.

neutral arbitrators because of their previous political stands in supporting or opposing various politicians.[33]

In Africa, religion/faith matters in all aspects of life including politics. Gandhi notes that those who say religion has nothing to do with politics do not know what religion is.[34] In their unguarded hour, the African electorates would truthfully say that 'I have voted for so and so because we profess the same religion, go to the same church, call God by one name and my religion must win'. This is evident from the observation of statistics from different African countries which conduct regular elections.

Generally, African countries with predominately Moslem populations have Moslem presidents, for instance, Egypt, Tunisia, Somalia, Libya, and Algeria. On the other hand, countries with predominately Christian populations have Christian heads of States like South Africa, Zimbabwe, Kenya, and Angola. It is of cardinal importance to stress that there are few exceptions like Tanzania where the presidence is not a census of religions. It follows that victory or threat by a candidate from a minority religious group makes post-election violence inevitable. It should, however, be noted that religion is intertwined with all other forms of sectarianism and other cardinal causes of post-election violence.

Economic Factors

In most African countries, political office is sought as an employment placing—thus making the route to Parliament, Senate, or Presidency a matter of life and death. Some Parliamentary hopefuls usually go to the extent of mortgaging their assets with financial institutions and also seek loans from money lenders to fuel their campaigns all the way to Election Day. The money invested to procure victory at all costs makes post-election violence inevitable since only through victory can the resources so invested be recovered from the national basket. It should be noted that the state is the first line of resources in a given country and having executive powers in Africa, means the power to divide and distribute the national cake at one's discretion.

Gaining political power in most African countries is an opportunity to amass wealth and protect the same. Therefore, incumbents will not easily concede even a genuine political defeat which may enrage the electorate and culminate into post-election violence.[35] This is one driving force to post-election violence in Africa. Politicians usually hide under the veils of religion and ethnicity to manipulate the electorate to bring them into power either through the elections or post-election violence.

[33] Ibid.

[34] Uwazie Earnest, Conflict Resolution and Peace Education in Africa, Lanham, Boulder (2003), p. 56.

[35] Interview with Mr. Blaise Aryatuha Kiiza on 3 November 2019.

Electoral violence is mostly fuelled by poverty and unemployment in Africa. Africa today boasts of the youngest population in the world. Poverty in Africa is very alarming and this gives room for the youth who are usually unemployed to be manipulated to perpetuate all forms of violence. People are not able to meet the basic necessities of life and unscrupulous politicians use it for their personal and political gain. They manipulate the youth, luring them with money and alcohol during political campaigns and meetings. When the economic hardship becomes too unbearable, the propensity for violence increases and jeopardizes African democracies and stability. This explains the looting during the post election violence. In summation, we reiterate that there is a nexus between neo-colonialism, sectarianism, and economic factors in causing post-election violence.

Minor and Cognate Causes of Post-Election Violence

Be that as it may, there are minor and cognate causes of post-election violence to wit: maladministration of elections and weak government institutions.

Maladministration of Elections

Articles 3(4) and 17 of the African Charter on Democracy, Elections and Governance (2007/2012) require state parties to hold regular, transparent, free, and fair elections. According to a report by Human Rights and Peace Centre, the vote should be protected from any acts of rigging. Actual or perceived acts of rigging may not only trigger violence but also have potential to demoralise voters and result in prolonged voter apathy.[36]

A classical illustration of mal-electoral administration is Kenyan presidential election of 2007. Peter Kagwanja and Roger Southhall argue that within minutes of the announcement of Kibaki's victory, he was sworn in for a second five-year term at a hastily organised ceremony at State House before a handful of guests (excluding diplomats) and the Kenya Broadcasting Corporation, despite calls for a recount by the opposition and international observers. This fostered a widespread perception that the count of the presidential election was codified in favour of Kibaki.[37]

In Uganda, the electoral commission has been faulted for maladministration in two Presidential election petitions preceding the 2001 and 2006 Presidential elections. In both instances, the Supreme Court roundly condemned the process of election as having been riddled with irregularities and unfair practices. Among other things, the Electoral Commission was criticised for

---

[36] The Road to 2016 Citizens' Perceptions of Uganda's Forthcoming Elections. A Synthesis Report. Human Rights and Peace Centre (HURIPEC) of the School of Law Makerere University and Kituo Cha Katiba: Eastern Africa Center for Constitutional Development (KcK).

[37] Supra, Peter Kagwanja, Roger Southall.

374   A. A. BWETE ET AL.

incompetence.[38] However, the Supreme Court of Uganda held that the irregularities and malpractices committed had not affected the elections in a 'substantial manner'.[39]

We posit that no general election in the world has ever been conducted devoid of any irregularities or non-compliance with the electoral laws. Upon this background, the substantial test has been embraced in many jurisdictions and codified into law. Section 59(6)(a) of the Presidential Elections Act, 16 of 2005 of Uganda reads that the election of a candidate as President shall only be annulled if to the satisfaction of the Court the non-compliance with the provisions of this Act and the non-compliance affected the result of the election in a substantial manner.

It must be emphasised that maladministration of the electoral process in Africa is usually a trigger to post-election violence; however, even in cases where there is genuine victory by a given candidate, the opponent(s) usually never concede defeat. This is a custom that has obtained in Africa and it is a matter of extreme rarity for an opponent to concede election defeat. Democracy and electioneering in Africa are marred with accusations and counter-accusations by both the government in power and the government in waiting. There is completely erosion of character and integrity among most political players.

In Ethiopia, for instance, the opposition parties accused the government of trying to steal the votes through ballot-rigging. On the other hand, the ruling party accused the opposition parties of photocopying ballot papers for multiple uses, ballot and stopping women from voting in two regions.[40] Maladministration of elections is intertwined with weak institutions and other cardinal causes (neo-colonialism, sectarianism, and desire to control resources) of post-election violence in Africa.

Weak Governance Institutions

In our view, weak government institutions entail: a partial judiciary, inadequate capacity of security forces, and unregulated media reporting.

Firstly, with regards to a partial judiciary, Article 14 of the International Covenant on Civil and Political Rights of 1966 provides that everyone shall be entitled to a fair and public hearing by a competent, independent, and impartial tribunal established by law. Article 32(3) of the African Charter on Democracy, Elections and Governance (2007/2012), Fortifies this position

[38] J. Oloka-Onyango and Christopher Mbazira, Befriending the Judiciary: Behind and Beyond the 2016 Supreme Court Amicus Curiae Ruling in Uganda, p. 11.

[39] Judgment of Justice BJ Odoki in Col (Rtd) Dr. Kizza Besigye Versus Electoral Commission and Yoweri Kaguta Museveni Election Petition No. 1 of 2006 {2007} UGSC 24, p. 152.

[40] Supra, Wondwosen Teshome, p. 5.

by saying that State Parties shall strive to institutionalise good governance through an independent judiciary.

Without a strong and independent judiciary, the population resort to taking the law into their own hands through civil disobedience or armed struggle. After elections, any dispute ought to be channelled to the grand arbiter for adjudication and as a matter of law, the need for an impartial Court or tribunal is unquestionable. In most African countries, however, the judiciary is faced with a lot of challenges thus making impartiality of the Court illusionary. Lack of trust in the courts by the electorate is likely to induce them to seek electoral justice by other means, leading to a situation that may culminate into post-election violence.

Secondly, with regards to inadequate capacity of security forces, it must fore mostly be noted that freedom of expression is guaranteed by Article 19(2) of the International Covenant on Civil and Political Rights 1966 and Article 11 of the African Charter on Human and Peoples' Rights 1981/1986. This freedom has been observed in the breach than in the observance by various national police and other security forces in several African countries. The struggle to realise this fundamental freedom has occasioned authorities to suppress these efforts thus culminating to post-election violence. All the same, some national courts as custodians of justice and human rights have stood tall to protect this freedom and right. The Constitutional Court of Uganda held that:

> Citizens of this country are free to walk, demonstrate, shout or otherwise express their discontent with politics, actions or laws or lack of them at any time. It does not matter that those doing so are members of political parties in opposition or ordinary citizens by whatever name called. The rights enjoyed by members of the ruling party and its supporters are the same ought to be enjoyed by the rest of the population. One of the key tenets of democracy is that those with dissenting and or minority opinions must be allowed to express them within the law. Whilst doing so they commit no offence. Criminalising dissent is therefore unconstitutional.[41]

Given that there are distinctive roles played by numerous security agencies in any given state, the role of mitigating law and order is the domain of the police. All the same, Terry D. Gill and Dieter Fleck observe that, in the practice of military operations, military forces are often called upon to carry out law enforcement and maintenance of order functions. For instance, military forces can be involved in quelling riots.[42] In States where the security forces are inadequate in capacity in terms of manpower, equipment, and tactics, post-election violence is inevitable. The violence is orchestrated mainly by the use

---

[41] Judgment of Justice Kenneth Kakuru, JCC. Col. (Rtd) Dr. Kiiza Besigye vs Attorney General, Constitutional Petition No. 33 of 2011, pp. 15–16.

[42] Terry D. Gill and Dieter Fleck, The Handbook of the International Law of Military Operations. Second Edition. Oxford University Press. Please indicate year of publication.

of brutal force which provokes the population in the aftermath of the elections and the insufficient capacity by the forces to maintain law and order.

Thirdly, as regards unregulated media reporting, paragraph 10 of the Declaration on Principles Governing Democratic Elections in Africa (2002) requires that in covering the electoral process, the media should maintain impartiality and refrain from broadcasting and publishing abusive language, inciting hate, and other forms of provocative language that may lead to violence. In many African countries, the media is misused by politicians to mobilise the population by sowing seeds of violence. We emphasise that the media was used in Kenya by politicians and leaders to spit venom escalating the massacre of thousands in the aftermath of the 2007 general election. This was evidenced when vernacular radio stations, which broadcast in local languages rather than English or Swahili, were used as a platform to incite violence with hateful messages. Some radio hosts allowed callers to use coded language to incite others. Radicalised opinion leaders also incited their communities on air.[43]

Prescription for Curbing Post-Election Violence in Africa

To immunise Africa against post-election violence, there is a need to prescribe the following antidotes namely: federation of African States, promotion of democracy and rule of law, and education and sensitisation of stakeholders.

Federation of African States

Harelimana defines a federation as a form of Government or country where there is a territorial distribution of power between one central or a common government and subordinate or lower Governments. Elements of a federation, therefore, include shared powers and responsibilities defined by law and practice.[44] Federation is permissible and in tandem with International Law. Its legality is derived from the right to self-determination. Common Article 1(1) of the International Covenant on Civil and Political Rights 1966 and the International Covenant on Social, Cultural and Economic Rights 1966 provides that all peoples have the right of self-determination. It follows, therefore, that provided the peoples of the different African states opt to unite into one successor state, the successor state would emerge at the international plane.

The principle of sovereign equality of states under Article 2(1) of the United Nations Charter is a mockery to African states. For illustration

---

[43] Sharon Anyango Odhiambo, The Role of the Media in Promoting Peace During Elections in Africa: Lessons from Kenya (2017), Research Paper No. 17, p. 1.

[44] Hon. Abdulkarim Harelimana, Paper on "The East African Political Federation: Addressing Fears, Concerns and Challenges". Presented at The Symposium of EALA 10th Anniversary on 2 June 2011, Arusha Tanzania, p. 1.

purposes, it is bewildering to imagine, how a country so tiny both economically and geographically like Djibouti can reasonably negotiate with China on equal terms. With all due respect to its people, Djibouti comprises of a population of 988,000,[45] land area of 23,180 per km^2,[46] and a GDP of US$2923 million.[47] That is in comparison to China which boasts with a population of 1,436,601,518,[48] landmass of 9,706,961 km^2,[49] and a GPD of US$25.27 trillion. Further, comparing the statistics we find that most African countries are weak, poor, and have no negotiating capacity to deal with these gigantic imperial countries. Such powers handpick or show preference for some leaders for Africa and indirectly control these poor and weak countries, thus consolidating their proxy leaders' power base while making them unpopular at the ballot hereby fanning and escalating post-election violence.

We posit that Africa's salvation is Federation of the different countries into one single bloc as envisaged by an early Pan-Africanist leader Kwame Nkurumah. In 1963, at a meeting of 32 African Heads of State and Government in Addis Ababa, Nkurumah decreed that:

> Our objective is African union now. There is no time to waste. We must unite now or perish. I am confident that by our concerted effort and determination, we shall lay here the foundations for a continental Union of African States. On this continent, it has not taken us long to discover that the struggle against colonialism does not end with the attainment of national independence. Independence is only the prelude to a new and more involved struggle for the right to conduct our own economic and social affairs; to construct our society according to our aspirations, unhampered by crushing and humiliating neo-colonialist controls and interference.[50]

Through federation, Africa stands to realise her potential. Federation in this context means a large market, unshakable negotiating power with the rest of the world, joint defence, and security. This shall enable Africa to fend off all forms of neo-colonialism that are the cause of post-election violence and all forms of war. We emphasise that until then the guns shall still haunt us to our backyards. To realise this African dream, the process must move in two phases of federation. The first phase being the regional integration from the North

---

[45] African Countries by Population (2020), available at: https://www.worldometers.info/population/countries-in-africa-by-population/ (accessed on 3 January 2020).

[46] Ibid.

[47] Djibouti GDP—Gross Domestic Product, available at: https://countryeconomy.com/gdp/djibouti (accessed on 3 January 2020).

[48] China Population (Live), available at: https://www.worldometers.info/world-population/china-population/ (accessed on 3 January 2020).

[49] Largest Countries in the World (by Area), available at: https://www.worldometers.info/geography/largest-countries-in-the-world/ (accessed on 3 January 2020).

[50] Centre for Conscientist Studies and Analyses (CENCSA), Dr. Kwame Nkrumah Speaks in Addis Ababa in 1963, available at: https://consciencism.wordpress.com/history/dr-kwame-nkrumah-speaks-in-addis-ababa-in-1963/ (accessed on 3 January 2020).

African States to the Southern African States and the East African States to the Western African States. As reality can tell, however, Africa has stagnated at this stage one for now over 50 years.

Further, the second and final stage is the creation of one single federation, the United States of Africa as Mwalimu Julius Nyerere called it. He declared way back in 1963, that our goal must be United States of Africa. Only this can give Africa the future her people deserve after centuries of economic uncertainty and social oppression. The national boundaries inherited from the colonial era are a serious threat to African unity.[51]

Promotion of Democracy and Rule of Law

Democracy is a process of political participation based on meaningful and extensive competition highly inclusive of all adult individuals and major groups in the selection of leaders and policies through regular and fair elections.[52] Few concepts have been as captivating as the rule of law. Its genius lies in the subordination of rulers to the law and due process. Modern democracy is not possible without the rule of law.[53] Democracy and Rule of Law, therefore, entail credible and impartial institutions including the legislature, judiciary, and executive. Constitutional institutions like the electoral commission ought to adhere to the electoral laws in the election process.

Article 4(1) of the African Charter on Democracy, Elections and Governance (2007/2012) provides that State parties shall commit themselves to promote democracy, the principle of rule of law, and human rights. It follows, therefore, that the most democratic African countries like Mauritius, Cape Verde, Botswana, Ghana, and Lesotho have had no or negligible forms of post-election violence. It must be emphasised that adherence to democracy and rule of law can cure post-election violence on the continent. We posit that without democracy and rule of law, post-election violence is the opted destination sooner or later. According to Duya, post-election violence can be curbed through setting up institutions that will reduce impunity. The need for respect of rule of law in Africa cannot be overemphasised.[54] There are two institutions that stand out in safeguarding against post-election violence. These are namely: the electoral commission (electoral administrators) and an independent judiciary.

---

[51] Supra, John Reader, p. 659.

[52] G. Mesay Berhanu. Introduction to African Studies_Final Paper (20 June 2017), The Challenges of Democracy in Africa: The Case of Ethiopia. Available at: https://www.academia.edu/36105744/The_Challenges_of_Democracy_in_Africa_the_case_of_Ethiopia (accessed on 4 January 2021).

[53] Makau Mutua, Africa and the Rule of Law, p. 2.

[54] Interview with Ms. Elizabeth Duya an Advocate of the High Court of Kenya and Uganda on 20 November 2019.

Firstly, the Electoral Commissionis usually a constitutional body with the mandate to organise the elections. Article 2(3) and (13) of the African Charter on Democracy, Elections and Governance (2007/2012) places primacy on the promotion of the holding of regular free and fair elections, and promotion of best practices in the management of elections for purposes of political stability and good governance. To operationalise this aspiration, the African Charter on Democracy, Elections and Governance (2007/2012) under Article 17(1) further requires state parties to establish and strengthen independent and impartial national electoral bodies responsible for the management of elections. Elections being a process rather than an event, it is incumbent on the electoral commission to ensure transparency and integrity of the process before, during, and after the elections.

First and fore most before elections, trust should be built between all stakeholders to set the rules of the competition, meaning that the legal framework, which ensures the integrity of the electoral process. The actions to be taken at this stage include the consensual establishment of a body responsible for organising the election. The consensual registration of the voters or updating voters registers, gazetting or publishing polling stations, the transparent production, and actual distribution of voters' cards were applicable among others.

Secondly, transparency should prevail in all electoral operations during elections stage which runs from the electoral campaign to the announcement of the results. At this stage, the electoral administers among others ought to adhere to timelines, the counting of votes must be as open as possible to the voters, supported by the display of election results at respective polling stations. Further, credible dispute resolution arrangements must be in place to timely address complaints as they emerge.

Lastly, after elections, the electoral administrative body ought to be open and accessible to all candidates and voters. Dispute resolution and administrative procedure must be in place to ensure not only transparency but perception of transparency as well. At this stage requests for recounting votes and cognate complaints may emerge thus a need for a mechanism or authority to timely address issues.

Secondly, an independent judiciary as an element of rule of law is laid down under Article 14 of the ICCPR 1966. Further, Articles 2(5) and 15(2) of the African Charter on Democracy, Elections and Governance (2007/2012) require state parties to promote and protect the independence of the judiciary. Lack of adequate conflict resolution mechanism has also been cited as the key reason that may spark post-election violence.

An honest and independent arbiter in any dispute is most vital, particularly because whichever party that may feel its concerns have not been judiciously addressed, might seek redress from the law of the jungle. Oloka Onyango stresses that when faced with excesses by the Executive such as detention-without-trial, arbitrary administrative action, or human rights abuse, it was more likely to be the case that the judiciary succumbed to the authority which was backed by military power.[55]

Museveni stresses that where a population that has lost hope in peaceful ways of resolving problems, the issue of popular support for the armed resistance was guaranteed and overwhelming.[56] Indeed, where the electorate has lost faith in the judiciary for its partiality, post-election violence becomes the next recourse. It must be emphasised that ensuring judicial independence curbs post-election violence as it has been stated earlier.

Education and Sensitisation of Stakeholders

For this purpose, stakeholders in elections include candidates, the electorate, media, and security forces. Law does not exist in a vacuum. Nor can law and rights language by themselves transform society.[57] Rethinking the curbing of post-election violence shall require the use of tactics other than the enactment of new electoral laws and regulations. The lawgiver shall not legislate that 'thou shall not follow tribal or religious sentiments when casting your vote'. We posit that the need for education and sensitisation is paramount in curbing post-election violence.

The need for sensitising the public on the benefits of unity, tolerance and the dangers of sectarianism is significant in curbing post-election violence. This can be done by introducing or boosting compulsory National Service to all young people before either joining Advanced or college level. We posit that teaching curriculums should entail a country's or Africa's strategic interests including fighting neo-colonialism, strategic defence, eradicating poverty and disease, and achieving the African Federation.

Journalists need training to improve their capacity to report profession-ally and neutrally.[58] There is need to promote peace in elections by the media. For instance, in the 2017 Kenyan elections, the media served as a plat-form to broadcast messages of peace during the election period. The media condemned hate speech uttered by politicians.[59] Reforms to improve the lives of ordinary citizens and provide alternative socio-economic assurance to those in power are required to move beyond simply establishing formal 'constitutional' democracy.[60]

The African population should be inspired by the story of their militaries to eradicate sectarianism. In military life, during war or military training your

[55] Joe Oloka Onyango, Professor of Law. Ghosts and the Law: An Inaugural Lecture 12 November 2015.

[56] Yoweri Kaguta Museveni, Sowing the Mustard Seed. The Struggle for Freedom and Democracy in Uganda. Second Edition, p. 153.

[57] Supra, Makau Mutua, p. 12.

[58] Supra, Sharon A. Odhiambo.

[59] Ibid.

[60] Nordic African Institute, Electoral Violence in Africa, Policy Notes 2012/3, p. 4.

tribe or faith does not matter, what matters, however, are the comrades in your section, platoon, company, or battalion. Your lives depend on each other and each other is all you have. The friendship and bonds that are forged in war or training can never be shaken by tribe or religion. At a regional level, the conflict in Somalia has buttressed the brotherhood of the African armies (Somalia, Burundi, Kenya, and Uganda armies among others) since they conduct joint operations to secure the area.

CONCLUSION

There is no Mexican wall between the economic desires of an individual, political party, and foreign imperial power in the affairs of a given country. If there was a marathon of the causes of post-election violence in Africa, economic factors would certainly emerge triumphantly. Individuals and States can never be safe against violence from each other, and this is evident from the consideration that every one of his own will naturally do what seems good and right in his own eyes, entirely independent of the opinion of others.[61]

States, like individual, act in their own best interests or desires. The struggle for resources is as old as humanity. As observed above, African politicians appeal to the electorate covertly relying on patronage, tribalism, religion, and any other form of sectarianism. These sentiments are so dear to people in that elections have turned out as census of different tribes and religions in a given African society. History reminds us that such electioneering is disastrous to a country or a people.

Be that as it may, understanding the real causes of post-election violence equips us with lasting solutions to neatly address the problems. Failing to understand the real causes is tantamount to a physician prescribing mebendazole to treat malaria. In summation the 'silver bullets in silencing the guns' of post-electoral violence in Africa comprise of Federation of African States, Promotion of Democracy and Rule of Law, and Education and sensitisation of the African people.

[61] Immanuel Kant, The Philosophy of Law, p. 163.

CHAPTER 22

Illicit Small Arms and Light Weapons in Africa

Gilbert Mittawa

INTRODUCTION

The proliferation of Small Arms and Light Weapons (SALW) in various parts of the globe continues to pose a threat to long-term social and economic development of many nations, particularly those in Africa. There is a consensus that Africa has become a centre of armed violence dominated by intra state conflicts. The conflicts have resulted into human suffering with women and children as the most vulnerable. At the centre of this suffering is the use of illicit Small Arms and Light Weapons (SALW). It has been suggested that "While small arms and light weapons do not of course, cause conflicts, they soon become part of the conflict equation by fuelling and exacerbating underlying tensions, generating more insecurity, deepening the sense of crisis, and adding to the number of casualties".[1]

The conclusion therefore would be that SALW play a great role in fuelling conflict and making it more lethal at every level, from criminal activity to

[1] Comfort Ero and Angela Ndinga-Muvumba, "Small Arms and Light Weapons", in West Africa's Security Challenges: Building Peace in a Troubled Region (ed) Adekeye Adebajo and Ismail Rashid (London: Lynne Rienner Publishers, 2004) 224.

[2] Taya Weiss, "A Demand-Side Approach to Fighting Small Arms Proliferation", Africa Security Review 12, No. 2 (2003) 4.

G. Mittawa (✉)
Blavatnik School of Government, University of Oxford, Oxford, Oxfordshire, United Kingdom

© The Author(s), under exclusive license to Springer Nature Switzerland AG 2022
D. Kuwali (ed.), *The Palgrave Handbook of Sustainable Peace and Security in Africa*, https://doi.org/10.1007/978-3-030-82020-6_22

383

full-fledged war, in both developed and developing countries.[2] The United Nations Security Council (UNSC) agrees that:

> The destabilizing accumulation and uncontrolled spread of small arms and light weapons in many regions of the world increases the intensity and duration of armed conflict, undermines the sustainability of peace agreements, impedes the success of peace building, frustrates efforts aimed at the prevention of armed conflict, hinders considerably the provision of humanitarian assistance and compromises the effectiveness of the Security Council discharging its primary responsibility for the maintenance of international peace and security.[3]

SALW are convenient and attractive to rebel/illegal armed groups and dissidents that characterize the African landscape because they are widely available, very cheap, deadly, easy to use, and easy to transport and smuggle. Unlike heavy conventional arms, such as artillery pieces and tanks, which are typically acquired by government forces, small arms transcend the dividing line between government forces, police, soldiers, and civil populations.[4] It may therefore be argued that the abundant presence of SALW has significantly contributed to Africa's insecurity which has the likely effect of undermining the potential success of Agenda 2063.

The question of illicit SALW has been a stricken issue and has eaten deep into the survival of most African states, particularly those engulfed in conflict or still recovering from it. The effects of SALW are devastating, regardless of age, gender, religion, or ethnicity. The proliferation of illicit SALW in Africa is increasingly threatening Africa's social economic development. It has increased criminality, youth violence, hostage taking, and cross boarder crimes. It may generally be agreed that Africa has not yet developed the required resilience to deal with the dangers posed by the illicit SALW.

There is, therefore, need for a holistic approach to deal with the question of SALW in Africa. This chapter, therefore, examines the extent and impact of SALW in Africa and their relationship to Africa's security challenges. The chapter proceeds to proffer ways and means by which African states and regional organizations can deal with the question of SALW as a prelude to creating a safe and secure Africa. The aspiration is that if Africa can effectively deal with the question of SALW, it will create conditions for the realization of its social economic goals, within the framework of Agenda 2063, for the betterment of its people.

---

[3] United Nations, Program of Action to Prevent, Combat and Eradicate the Illicit Trade in Small Arms and Light Weapons in All Its Aspects, New York, March 2002, 31.

[4] Jeffery Boutwell and Michael T. Klare, "A Scourge of Small Arms", American Academy of Arts and Science 282, No. 6 (June 2000) 1.

The Extent and Impact of Small Arms and Light Weapons in Africa

Data from selected African countries demonstrates the extent of proliferation of SALW on the African continent. According to the 2019 Small Arms Survey (SAS) and the African Union (AU) study, it is estimated that 80% of Africa's SALW are in the hands of civilians. Civilians, including rebel groups and militias, hold more than 40 million SALW while government-related entities hold fewer than 11 million.[5] It is noted that cross-border trafficking by land is the most prominent type of illicit arms flow affecting countries on the continent. The weapons trafficked comprise both those sourced from within the continent—such as legacy weapons recycled from earlier conflicts and weapons diverted from national stockpiles—as well as arms sourced from other parts of the world, including embargo-breaking transfers from the Middle East and Eastern Europe.[6]

It is estimated that in 2017, civilians in the DRC held a total of 946,000 guns (both licit and illicit). However, the number of registered guns in the DRC was reported to be only 216 in 2017. The defence forces of the DRC are reported to have 161,100 firearms and police forces in the DRC reported to have 46,000 firearms.[7] The Human Rights Watch (HRW) and the New York University-based Congo Research Group reported in August 2019 that in the Kivu provinces alone, 1900 civilians were killed and 3300 others were kidnapped between 2017 and 2019.[8] The trend is similar in South Africa where it is estimated that 90 per cent of gun owners are civilians. In Zambia, it was estimated that civilians held a total of 158,000 firearms (both licit and illicit) in 2017. In Malawi the total number of SALW in civilian hands by 2017 was 47,000 while the military had 24,480 and law enforcement agents held 6400.[9]

Homicide cases associated with SALW by 2016 in Malawi were 272 while suicide cases were 669.[10] In Nigeria, it was reported that there were between 1,000,000 and 350,000,000 unregistered and illicit SALW contributing to

---

[5] Zipporah Musau, Silencing the Guns in Africa by 2020: African Union's 2020 Campaign to Achieve Peace and End Conflict, Extremism, Crime, Africa Renewal E-Magazine (December 2019) https://www.un.org/africarenewal/magazine/december-2019-march-2020/silencing-guns-africa-2020 accessed 30 December 2020.

[6] Francis Wairagu, Nicolas Florquin, and Sigrid Lipott, Weapons Compass: Mapping Illicit Arms Flows in Africa, African Union and Small Arms Survey Report (2019) http://www.smallarmssurvey.org/fileadmin/docs/U-Reports/SAS-AU-Weapons-Compass.pdf accessed 13 December 2020.

[7] The UN Office on Drugs and Crime (UNODC).

[8] Misser, Francois, "Rivers of Arms", The Journal of Good Governance in Africa, 52 (2020).

[9] Malawi-Gun Facts, Figures and the Law https://www.gunpolicy.org/firearms/region/malawi accessed 29 December 2020.

[10] Aaron Karp, "Civilian Firearms Holdings, 2017", *Estimating Global Civilian-Held Firearms Numbers*. Geneva: Small Arms Survey, the Graduate Institute of International

over 30,000 deaths per year.[11] As for Uganda, as of 2017 civilians owned over 300,000 SALW against about 200,000 for Government Forces. The illicit SALW contributed to an estimated 200 deaths per year.[12] As can be seen from the above data, most SALW in Africa are in the hands of either civilians or illegal armed groups. This increases risk of abuse as they are used for illegal purposes being it commission of homicide, suicide, and criminality and in worst case scenario, terrorist activities.

Most of the weapons in Africa are imported. Official military expenditure in Africa stood at around US$40.2 billion in 2018, with North Africa spending US$22.2 billion and sub-Saharan Africa US$18.8 billion.[13] The top arms suppliers to Africa between 2014 and 2018 were Russia, China, Ukraine, Germany, and France, and the largest recipients were Egypt, Algeria, and Morocco, according to a study by the Stockholm International Peace Research Institute (SIPRI), an independent international institute dedicated to research into conflict, armaments, arms control, and disarmament. The SIPRI Arms Transfers Database provides information on all international transfers of major arms (including sales, gifts, and production under license) to states, international organizations, and non-state groups.

Twenty-two African countries also manufacture various kinds of small arms and light weapons. Home-made artisanal weapons production is also prevalent on the continent, with those weapons reported to be fuelling criminality in some countries. While African countries can control the purchase of legal arms, it is difficult to track the illegal trafficking and flows on the continent. Porous borders and long coastlines also enable traffickers to smuggle small arms between countries with considerable ease. There are also concerns about how well some national arms stocks are managed to ensure that the weapons do not end up in the wrong hands.

The UNSC observed that "SALW do not only make easy the taking and maiming of lives, but also kill economies and the social bonds on which every kind of collective institution and progress rely".[14] The UNSC further notes that denial of education and health, criminality, illicit plundering of natural resources, decreased trade and investment, violence against women and girls, gang violence, and the collapse of the rule of law are facilitated by widespread access to the weapons. It is estimated that there are over a billion SALW in circulation globally, with most small arms belonging to the private sphere. Their illicit proliferation contributes to the increase in global armed violence

and Development Studies, Geneva. 18 June 2018 www.gunpolicy.org/firearms accessed 29 December 2020.

[11] https://www.gunpolicy.org/firearms/region/nigeria accessed 10 January 2020.

[12] https://www.gunpolicy.org/firearms/region/uganda accessed 10 January 2020.

[13] Zipporah Musau, Silencing the Guns in Africa by 2020.

[14] United Nations, Human Cost of Illicit Flow of Small Arms, Light Weapons Stressed in Security Council Debate, UNSC 7442 Meetings Coverage and Press Releases, SC/11889 (13 May 2015) www.un.org/sc/meetingscovereage accessed 20 December 2020.

and insecurity. The accumulation of SALW also has destabilizing effects within a country region or continent. SALW have contributed to much of Africa's human suffering both in and out of conflict and hence a major obstacle to achieving sustainable human development.[15]

Just like Dan Kuwali in Chapter 13, the International Red Cross Committee (ICRC) suggests that the proliferation of SALW contributes to the prolongation of conflicts, the violation of international humanitarian and human rights law, and to a culture of violence that persists even after the end of conflicts.[16] Similarly, the UNSC submitted that the "illicit transfer, destabilizing accumulation and misuse of SALW pose threats to inter-national peace and security, cause significant loss of life, [and] contribute to instability and insecurity".[17] The UNSC has also recognized that (illicit) SALW "fuel conflicts and have a wide range of negative human rights, humanitarian, development and socio-economic consequences, in particular on the security of civilians in armed conflict, including the disproportionate impact on violence perpetrated against women and girls".[18] A 2017 study by Oxfam, The Human Cost of Uncontrolled Arms in Africa, estimates that at least 500,000 people die every year and millions of others are displaced or abused as a result of armed violence and conflict.[19]

Illicit SALW constitute a serious threat to safety, security, and stability in Africa. Equally, small arms and light weapons have long been considered the primary tools and enablers of violence throughout the history of conflict in the continent. In conflict situations, small arms are often used to commit a wide range of human rights and humanitarian law violations, including mass killings, forced displacements, gender-based violence, and attacks on peacekeepers and humanitarian workers. Outside the immediate context of armed conflict, illicit small arms aggravate both inter-communal conflict and competition over natural resources and facilitate a broad spectrum of criminal activities.

The impact of SALW can best be understood from a human security point of view. In this context, it is security of the people from various threats as opposed to the protection and guarding of territorial integrity from external aggression. The problem of illicit SALW causes destruction and the decline of physical infrastructure and agricultural production, respectively. It affects families and their children, leading to reduced school enrolment. There is

---

[15] UNICEF, "A Programme of Action to Address the Human Cost of SALW", Inter-Agency Standing Committee, Unicef www.unicef.org accessed 19 November 2020.

[16] International Committee of the Red Cross (ICRC), Statement on the implementation of the UN Programme of Action on Small Arms and Light Weapons (June 2014) www.icrc.org/en/doc/resources/documents/statement/2014/06-19-arms-availability accessed 16 October 2020.

[17] Carmen-Cristina Cîrlig, Illicit Small Arms and Light Weapons, International and European Union Action, European Parliamentary Research Service (July 2015) 8.

[18] Carmen-Cristina Cîrlig, Illicit Small Arms and Light Weapons.

[19] Zipporah Musau, Silencing the Guns in Africa by 2020.

also foreign and domestic investment decreases, resulting in loss of domestic revenue. In Africa, particularly in conflict zones such as DRC and Somalia, children are increasingly exposed to guns, coming to believe that weapons are essential instruments for protection and survival. This ultimately leads to gun dependency, gun glorification, and a culture of violence, fear, and hopelessness. Conflict has resulted in the forced migration of millions of people. This further inhibits development and leads to restriction of basic needs such as food, clothing, and shelter.

Illicit SALW have also contributed to most of Africa's insecurity through forced displacement of millions of people, particularly women and children combined with the use of sexual violence as a weapon of war and the phenomenon of child soldiers. It is reported that there are over 3 million refugees and 5 million internally displaced persons in Africa. These people combined with stateless people brings the total number of forcibly displaced people to over 11 million.[20] This results in poor socio-economic development of not only the individuals affected but also the continent at large. Most refugees hardly engage in developmental activities as they have limited resources and freedom of association. For instance, Malawi entered reservation on the right to free movement under the Refugees Convention.

This means that those with refugee status in Malawi are at most confined to a designated geographical area. This in turn reduces the refugee's ability to interact and contribute meaningfully to socio-economic activities within the country. Another second order effect is that governments are forced to use their limited resources to cater for the refugees. This places an economic burden on most governments thus affecting their economic security. The presence and proliferation of SALW also leads to diversion of already scarce resources away from critical development agendas. For instance, fuelled by SALW, the prolonged periods of conflict in Angola, Mozambique, Sudan, and DRC resulted in significant resources directed to war efforts. Similarly, it has been noted that Africa's regional and sub-regional organizations, the OAU/AU, and the Regional Economic Communities (RECs), dedicated much of their efforts on peace and security issues at the expense of pursuing their primary mandates of accelerating the continent's economic development and integration.[21]

The abuse of SALW have also led to the damage, destruction of important state infrastructures such as schools, hospitals, places of work, markets, residential areas, buildings, and areas of religious and cultural significance, as well as to a breakdown in basic services.[22] There are also increasing threats posed

---

[20] Joseph Dube, "The Africa We Want: Silencing the Guns", International Action Network on Small Arms (2019) 9   www.iansa.org/briefing-papers accessed 20 December 2020.

[21] Joseph Dube, The Africa We Want: Silencing the Guns, 10.

[22] Amnesty International, How an Arms Trade Treaty Can Help Prevent Armed Violence, Amnesty International and International Action Network on Small Arms

by emerging transnational crimes such as terrorism and violent extremism, drug trafficking, piracy, illicit arms proliferation, human trafficking and smuggling, and money laundering. The case of abuse of SALW by Boko Haram in Nigeria provides a classic example. It is reported that commercial activities in the northeast part of Nigeria have been reduced because of attacks by Boko Haram. Banks, markets, and shops do not open regularly due to fear of attacks. Human capital and investors flight is hampering economic development due to the attacks on banks, markets, parks, and government departments.[23]

The attacks on these commercial areas have also led to the migration of people to other parts of the country. The economy of the northeast is seriously affected because foreign citizens who contributed significantly to the development of the northeast are sent back to their countries of origin. Consequently, the persistent presence of Boko Haram in the region has created an economic dichotomy between the north and southern parts of Nigeria. The poverty profile released by the National Bureau of Statistics illustrates that there is the prevalence of poverty in the north as compared to the south.[24] Thus, if the status quo remains development of the region will be static and the material inequality between the north and south will widen.

The social effects of Boko Haram in Nigeria are also enormous. Churches, schools, markets, clinics, mosques, and recreational centres are potential targets for Boko Haram attacks. Attacks on these social places have prevented people from going to these places for social gatherings. As it may be recalled, in April 2014, a federal government girls' college was attacked which resulted in the abduction of over 250 female students. Due to incessant attacks on schools, some students have stopped attending school, while others have moved to the southern part of the country to continue their schooling. Likewise, Christians are afraid to attend worship in the churches due to the fear of being attacked by the sect.

The UN addressed the relationship between SALW and violent extremism. A study on firearms by the UN Office on Drugs and Crime (UNODC) published in 2015 established intricacies relating to transnational organized criminal networks that interweave Africa and the other parts of the world.[25] The study confirms the existence of smuggling routes between Europe and Africa facilitating the flow of illicit weapons.[26] Most of these weapons end up

---

(2011) https://aser-asso.org/wpcontent/uploads/2017/03/How-an-Arms-Trade-Treaty-can-help-prevent-Armed-Violence-IANSAAmnesty-International-Fevrier-2011.pdf accessed 10 December 2019.

[23] Kubiat Umana, Effect of Boko Haram in Nigeria, 16 January 2019 https://researchc yber.com/effect-impacts-boko-haram-nigeria accessed 20 December 2019.

[24] As above.

[25] Joseph Dube, The Africa We Want: Silencing the Guns, 15–16.

[26] United Nations Office on Drugs and Crime (UNODC), Study On Firearms: A Study on the Transnational Nature of and Routes and Modus Operandi Used in Trafficking in Firearms (Vienna, UNODC, 2015).

in the hands of extremist groups who abuse them in conducting terrorist activities. Due to illicit SALW, Africa continues to experience the threat of terrorist attacks. In January 2019, the Somali armed group Al-Shabaab carried out a deadly attack on a Nairobi hotel and office complex in retaliation to the US President Trump's declaration of Jerusalem as Israel's capital.[27]

The attackers used guns and explosives, claimed the lives of at least 21 people in the massive complex, which includes a 101-room hotel, spa, restaurant, and offices. Again, before dawn on a Sunday 5 January 2020, the Al-Shabaab extremists overran a key military base used by US counterterrorism forces in Kenya, killing at least three American Department of Defence personnel and destroying several US aircraft and vehicles before they were repelled.[28] The recent terrorist/Jihadist attacks in Mozambique's restive Cabo Delgado province,[29] which are also spreading towards Tanzania clearly shows the extent of access and abuse of SALW by extremist groups.

MECHANISMS TO CURB ILLICIT SMALL ARMS AND LIGHT WEAPONS IN AFRICA

Controlling the illicit proliferation, circulation, and trafficking of SALW has been at the heart of the African Union's efforts to prevent conflicts, mitigate their adverse impact, and consolidate peace. Over the past decades important policy and legal instruments have been adopted at the continental level in response to the proliferation of SALW with significant progress being made in their implementation. While gaps are still visible, the adoption of the African Union (AU) Master Roadmap of Practical Steps to Silence the Guns in Africa by 2020 offers a window of opportunity for renewed and serious efforts to deal with the problem of illicit small arms. African States have participated in the development of several international instruments, including the United Nations Convention on Certain Conventional Weapons (1980) and its various Protocols, the UN Basic Principles on the Use of Force and Firearms by Law Enforcement Officials (1990), the Mine Ban Treaty (1997), the Protocol against the Illicit Manufacturing and Trafficking in Firearms, Their Parts and Components and Ammunition (Firearms Protocol) (2001) supplementing the Convention Against Transnational Organized Crime, the UNPoA (2001)

---

[27] Middle East Eye, "Al-Shabab Claims Nairobi Attack Was Retaliation for Trump's Jerusalem Move", available at: https://www.middleeasteye.net/news/al-shabab-claims-nairobi-attack-was-retaliation-trumps-jerusalem-move accessed 17 November 2020.

[28] Voice of America News (VoA), "US Embassy's Move in Israel Draws Criticism from Around the World", footnote 4 above.

[29] Steven Brown, ISIS Behead More Than 50 Men and Boys in Horrific Attack in Mozambique, The Express, 10 November 2020 https://www.express.co.uk/news/world/1358426/isis-news-mozambique-beheading-women-kidnapped-terror accessed 20 November 2020. See also Pamela Geller, Bloody Jihad in Mozambique Spread to Tanzania, 300 Muslim Attackers Slaughter Dozens, Geller Report, 20 November 2020 https://gellerreport.com/2020/10/tanzania-jihad.html/ accessed 20 November 2020.

supplemented by the International Tracing Instrument (2005), the Cluster Munitions Convention (2008), and the Arms Trade Treaty (2013).

African States have also established their own binding regional instruments. In Africa, the binding regional instruments are the Protocol of the Southern African Development Community (SADC) on the control of Firearms, Ammunition and Other Materials (2001); the Nairobi Protocol for the Prevention, Control and Reduction of Small Arms and Light Weapons in East Africa, the Great Lakes and the Horn of Africa (2002); the Convention of the Economic Community of West African States (ECOWAS) to Combat and Eradicate the Illicit Trade in Small Arms, Light Weapons, their Ammunition and Other Related Materials (2006); and the Central African Convention for the Control of Small Arms and Light Weapons, Their Ammunition and All Parts and Components That Can Be Used For Their Manufacture, Repair and Assembly (Kinshasa Convention) (2010). Together, these binding instruments form a common framework of obligations and guidelines to initiate and sustain concerted action by African governments. Building national capacity for such action evidently requires more dedicated international assistance and cooperation in many countries.

International and African regional instruments have provided an essential basis for preventing the proliferation and misuse of SALW in Africa. So too, AU instruments and decisions about peace, security, and governance provide a solid framework to address challenges to peace and security. Notwithstanding these efforts, there still exist gaps that African states and organizations must consider seriously. One of the gaps relates to the sharing of information on the successes and failures of efforts on the ground. As rightly noted by the AU and the Small Arms Survey (SAS), this area is still sub-optimal, and it consequently hampers the provision of lessons learned and the development of practical guidance for expanding the most promising initiatives.[30] Further, there is need for coordinated implementation of all initiatives including development partners' agendas. Lack of coordination is likely to result in disjointed efforts whereby some types of illicit SALW arms flows may be tackled while others may be left out.

It is also important to note that the culture of implementation of these instruments and decisions among African countries is still seriously lacking.[31] There is, therefore, a need for conscientious and systematic implementation of instruments and decisions adopted by AU and RECs policy organs. It is also imperative to establish a common legal and policy framework to develop consistent strategies and actionable plans to stem proliferation of SALW and their abuse. Besides legal implementation gaps, implementation may also be hampered by lack of political will beyond ratification of agreements, actuated by regional political dynamics. States may shy away from international and

---

[30] Francis Wairagu, Nicolas Florquin and Sigrid Lipott, Weapons Compass: Mapping Illicit Arms Flows in Africa, 15.

[31] Joseph Dube, The Africa We Want: Silencing the Guns.

regional legal instruments for fear of diluting their sovereignty, among others. However, such fears undermine the common aspirations driven by Agenda 2063. To this end, it is suggested that African states must ratify the binding instruments and domesticate them with relevant modifications to suit their respective local context.

THE QUESTION OF ILLICIT SMALL ARMS AND LIGHT WEAPONS: WHAT IS THE WAY FORWARD?

While acknowledging the tremendous efforts and progress on the control of illicit SALW in the world and in Africa to be specific, it is important to note the gaps which have arguably contributed to the continued presence of SALW. If unaddressed, it is assessed with a high degree of confidence that these gaps will continue to facilitate the proliferation of SALW on the African continent and thus undermining Africa's peace and security both in the medium and long term. Consequently, the unprecedented human suffering caused by the proliferation of SALW demands an urgent need to find effective measures to control their use and limit their impact. There is need to manage SALW through national action, implementation of treaties, and strengthened international cooperation.

The obvious question, therefore, is what can be done to address the issue of SALW and their associated threat towards attainment of Agenda 2063. The ICRC has poignantly suggested that the humanitarian consequences of the widespread availability of SALW can be reduced by controlling the availability of such weapons and ensuring that those who obtain weapons will use them in a manner that respects the rules of International Humanitarian Law.[32] It is with such aspirations that this paper proceeds to proffer some measures that can be adopted to address the question of illicit SALW. These measures can be undertaken by states, RECs, and the AU and other stakeholders in a synchronized manner.

In 2001, the first UN conference to address the availability of small arms and light weapons adopted a Global Programme of Action to "prevent, combat and eradicate the illicit trade in small arms and light weapons in all its aspects".[33] While not legally binding, the Programme of Action commits governments to take a variety of measures to control the availability SALW. For example, the Programme of Action calls for secure management of national

[32] ICRC, Statement on the implementation of the UN Programme of Action on Small Arms and Light Weapons.

[33] The UN Role and Efforts in Combating the Proliferation of Small Arms and Light Weapons www.un.org accessed 19 December 2019.

stocks of arms, regulation of arms brokering activities, and collection and destruction of surplus small arms and light weapons after conflicts.[34]

Following the Global Programme of Action, the UN General Assembly adopted the Arms Trade Treaty (ATT), which establishes the highest possible common international standards for regulating the international trade in conventional arms. The ATT entered into force on 24 December 2014 (UN GA A/Res/67/234)[35] with one of its explicit purposes being the reduction of human suffering. This new international legally binding instrument established a global norm to prevent arms transfers when there is a manifest risk that war crimes or serious violations of human rights will be committed. The treaty sets out standards that States must apply when authorizing transfers of arms, ammunition, and parts and components. Under the treaty, a country cannot transfer these items if it knows that the weapons would be used to commit genocide, crimes against humanity, or certain types of war crimes. Even short of such knowledge, a country must assess the risk of the weapons being used to commit serious violations of IHL or human rights law, and the country must deny arms exports if the risk is overriding.

Given the correlation between SALW proliferation and the commission of atrocities, it is critical that the international community take steps to curtail the flow of SALW from one conflict zone to another. Implementation of the Arms Trade Treaty is, therefore, crucial in this regard. It can ensure states achieve more effective stockpile management, improve physical security, record keeping, reporting, and other national and international measures to prevent diversion of arms through illicit channels. It is imperative, therefore, that states should adopt policy and legislative measures to give effect to the ATT, adopt legislative measures criminalizing illegal manufacturing, possession, stockpiling, and trade of SALW or establishing national coordination bodies to guide, research, and monitor the eradication of the illicit trade of SALW. These measures will ensure that SALW do not end up in the wrong hands and thus contribute towards the realization of Africa's peace and security. Further, there must be awareness at all levels, including local communities on the dangers associated with the proliferation of SALW and armed violence. States must strengthen the capacity of security institutions and communities to enhance safety and most importantly encourage voluntary weapons surrender/collection in return for community-based development projects.[36]

---

[34] B. Heger, *Arms Availability*, ICRC, 2013 https://www.icrc.org/eng/war-and-law/weapons/small-arms-availability/overview-small-arms-availability accessed 26 January 2015.

[35] For a full text, see https://www.icrc.org/applic/ihl/ihl.nsf/Treaty.xsp?document.

[36] *Ecowas, EU and UNDP to Boost Fight Against Proliferation of Small Arms in Ecowas Sub-Region.* The programme was launched on 16 September 2014, in Abuja, Nigeria in order to enhance the global fight against the illicit proliferation of Small Arms and Light Weapons http://www.ng.undp.org/content/nigeria/en/home/presscenter/pre ssreleases/2014/09/16/eu-allocates-5-56m-to-boost-fight-against-proliferation-of-small-arms-in-ecowas-sub-region accessed 12 April 2015.

The aspiration to silence the guns can be given its true meaning if states join efforts towards successful Disarmament, Demobilization, and Reintegration (DDR) especially in transitional environments. One of the problems associated with DDR programmes is the blind eye given to the active role of women and children in conflict. Women are often given a blind eye during DDR process due to a mischaracterized narrative featuring women as perpetual victims of systemic sexual violence and male rebel groups as perpetrators. Experience has shown that women and girls are the most groups used in smuggling arms and ammunition as they are least suspected and therefore not subjected to vigorous search or scrutiny compared to males.

In Eastern DRC, for example, women are used to move arms in flour baskets, and are able to pass through check points unnoticed.[37] Institutions involved in transitional processes have neglected the presence of female combatants as active participants during conflict, and thus failed to determine how women and girls who have abandoned traditional gender roles to become combatants can reclaim their identities as members in communities reluctant to welcome them back in their midst. As a result, the women "ex-combatants" usually maintain their roles of supplying arms and ammunition for their day-to-day survival. It is such misconceptions and characterization that has resulted in failures to engage in effective and sustainable DDR.[38] In view of the above, redefining gender should become an integral part of any DDR process to achieve its intended long-term social and economic impact. The AU, Donors, and NGOs involved in designing DDR programmes ought to consider enhancing capacity building in advocacy efforts on behalf of, and call for a focus on, female combatants, as well as for an expansion of the scope of financial grants allocated for women's programmes.

Today, weapons are easily accessible to a wide variety of groups or individuals that may have no knowledge of or respect for International Human Rights Law (IHRL) and International Humanitarian law (IHL). It is, therefore, imperative to identify measures to close all loopholes for irresponsible trade or transfer of small arms and light weapons, including ammunition. These, among others, ought to include adequate training including Skill at Arms and International Human Rights and Humanitarian Law. Considering that uncontrolled spread of small arms and light weapons constitute a threat to peace and security, it is pertinent to further address the menace and illicit supply of small arms, which have largely contributed to the commission of atrocities against civilians. It is argued that the protection of civilians is a humanitarian, political, and legal imperative that recognizes the inherent dignity and worth of every

---

[37] The information was obtained by the author during his tour of duty in DRC under MONUSCO from 2014 to 2015.

[38] M. Houngbedji, R. Grace, and J. Brooks, *The Impact of Gendered Misconceptions of Militarized Identities on Disarmament, Demobilization, Reintegration and Humanitarian Assistance in the Democratic Republic of the Congo*, ATHA http://www.atha.se/themat icbrief/impact-gendered-misconceptions-militarized-identities-disarmament-demobilization accessed 17 December 2020.

human being. It is for this reason that the responsibility for ensuring civilian protection should be respected by both state and non-state actors.[39]

It cannot be disputed that both the AU and its member states have demonstrated strong political will to tackle the scourge of illicit SALW. The practical steps identified in the AU Roadmap, notably capacity building for states in the areas of stockpile management, record keeping and tracing, and the destruction of illicit firearms, can contribute to reducing the threat posed by SALW. However, significant challenge lies in prioritizing, coordinating, and implementing these commitments and initiatives. AU member states' participation in international information-sharing platforms that can help to provide critical weapons-trafficking intelligence has been very limited to date.[40] Prioritizing this area has the potential to provide the continent with timely and actionable information on new and emerging trends in illicit firearms trafficking. The continent has hosted innovative interventions, notably in the areas of weapons collection in (post-)conflict settings, joint border initiatives, and end-user controls, such measures demand further dissemination and development into practical guidelines.

There is also a greater need to enhance national efforts in the fights against illicit SALW. This is particularly true considering that regional and international arrangements are complimentary to national efforts. If illicit SALW are addressed at national level, it will be easier for international and regional organizations to coordinate the efforts. On the above premises it is proposed that national capacity-building efforts must be prioritized so that they can adequately address the needs expressed by national authorities. There is need to harmonize national legislation with international instruments to ensure that national legislation addresses the issues of craft production and imitation firearms. There is also need for national authorities to seriously address implementation and enforcement of arms embargoes which will help stem flow of illicit SALW.

States must adopt deliberate policies and plans to conduct training and provide technical assistance to law enforcement agencies to combat the land and sea-based trafficking of SALW, this should include developing the capacities of national forensic institutions to identify, track, and seize illicit SALW. Boarder control and use of advance technology such as drones should be considered whenever conducting such training. To accelerate action against illicit SALW, the AU launched a continent-wide campaign on "Silencing the Guns" to mobilize all stakeholders to prioritize efforts on peace and effective socio-economic development. Challenges that lead people to violent conflicts, including poverty, historical injustices, inequality, unemployment,

---

[39] UN Security Council, Report of the Secretary-General on the protection of civilians in armed conflict, 28 October 2007, S/2007/643<https://www.securitycouncilrep ort.org>accessed 20 November 2021.

[40] Francis Wairagu, Nicolas Florquin and Sigrid Lipott, Weapons Compass: Mapping Illicit Arms Flows in Africa, 18.

climate change, illegal financial flows, and corruption should be addressed too for the guns to be silenced. To this end one would be compelled to agree with the words of Bience Gawanas who poignantly submitted that "[f]or me, I see silencing the guns in two ways. It's the physical dropping of the guns, which is very important. But I believe that we must also focus on development, let us invest in our people to be able to silence the guns".[41]

CONCLUSION

The proliferation of illicit SALW in Africa presents a serious security threat that undermines Africa's socio-economic development under Agenda 2063. The social, economic, and human/psychological effects associated with abuse of SALW necessitate collective action by African states, Regional Organizations, and the AU to find meaningful solutions. To this end, it has been suggested that there is a need for African states to adopt coherent international and regional strategies for the control of both lawful and unlawful transfer of small arms, light weapons, and ammunition. This is particularly true considering that without a coordinated regional approach, efforts of any one country to control the presence of arms on its territory could easily be undermined. Thus, regional efforts to limit arms availability are needed and deserve the support of the entire international community. Supported by civil society and citizens, implemented by governments concerned/affected and backed up by governments from outside the region, the arrangement will form the cornerstone of effective strategies to develop norms for the transfer of arms and ammunition and to put an end to illicit transfers. Such strategies would not only alleviate the plight of civilians caught up in armed conflict but would also bring major benefits in terms of economic development, promoting national and regional stability and ensuring respect for human rights.

[41] UN Under-Secretary General and Special Adviser on Africa.

CHAPTER 23

Weapons of Mass Destruction in Africa

Godard Busingye, Sarah Mukashaba, and Christable Tusiime

INTRODUCTION

International law, customary and treaty law, does not have a blanket definition of what constitutes weapons of mass destruction (WMD). WMD are varied and have different effects on the targets or the unintended objectives. Each category of a WMD is, therefore, handled separately, sometimes under a separate legal regime. WMD are governed by the general body of international law, but specifically, international criminal law, international humanitarian law (IHL), and human rights law. It suffices to note, however, that these bodies of law were not developed specifically to address WMD.[1] There are, however, in any branch of international law, prohibitions, and in some instances, penalties for violations of restrictions put in place to regulate the use of WMD. From a human rights-based approach, a total ban on the production of WMD would be the most appropriate course of action to be taken by any right-thinking member of society. That, however, need not be the approach to WMD, because the same technologies and compositions that are used as

[1] Advisory Opinion, Legality of the Use of Force by a State of Nuclear Weapons in Armed Conflict, ICJ Reports 66 (1996), available at: http://www.icj-cij.org/icj www/icases/iunan/iunanframe.htm (accessed on 2 January 2020).

G. Busingye (✉) · S. Mukashaba
Kampala International University, Kampala, Uganda

C. Tusiime
Uganda Peoples' Defence Forces, Kampala, Uganda

© The Author(s), under exclusive license to Springer Nature
Switzerland AG 2022
D. Kuwali (ed.), *The Palgrave Handbook of Sustainable Peace and Security in Africa*, https://doi.org/10.1007/978-3-030-82020-6_23

WMD can be used for development of non-violent uses and applications. For example, the medical arena uses X-rays to treat ailments such as cancer or detect deformities in human bodies. Manufacturing or possession of WMD may also be a useful tool to deter their use by an opposing force, either ideologically or wantonly. A human rights-based approach is a conceptual framework for the process of human development that is normatively based on international human rights standards and operationally directed to promoting and protecting human rights.[2] A human rights-based approach, is an appropriate dimension for assessing the problem of WMD in Africa and the world over. It is not blind to the fact that WMD can be used for development of non-violent uses and application. For example, the medical field uses X-rays to treat ailments such as cancer or detect deformities in the human bodies, yet such rays may be used as WMD. Manufacturing or possession of WMD may also be a useful tool to deter their use by an opposing force, either ideologically or wantonly.[3]

CONCEPT AND CLASSIFICATION
OF WEAPONS OF MASS DESTRUCTION

The term "weapons of mass destruction (WMD)" is not clearly defined in any available literature. WMD are difficult to succinctly define because they are many in number, and varied in composition. They are also amenable to change because of changes in time and space where they are used. For that reason, there is no treaty or body of customary international law that contains an authoritative definition of WMD.[4] In some instances, they are broadly defined as "those devices capable of extensive destruction when deployed in a manner intended to destroy large numbers of people. Weapons of mass destruction can be high explosives, nuclear or radiological devices, chemical or biological weapons, or any other device, even those not yet developed or disclosed, that are intended to kill large masses of people."[5] Sometimes, each category of a WMD is handled separately, often under a separate treaty much as a general conceptualization, though they are given a generic name—WMD.

The fact that some WMD are not yet developed or disclosed gives room for admission of more weapons on the list of WMD. Expansion of the list may

---

[2] UNICEF, Human Rights-based approach programming, 2016, available at: https://www.unicef.org/policyanalysis/rights/index_62012.html (accessed on 4 January 2020).

[3] Advisory Opinion, Legality of the Use of Force by a State of Nuclear Weapons in Armed Conflict, ICJ Reports 66 (1996), available at: http://www.icj-cij.org/icjwww/icases/iunan/iunanframe.htm.

[4] David P. Fidler, Weapons of Mass Destruction and International Law, *American Society of International Law*, Volume 8, Issue 3 (2003), available at: https://www.asil.org/insights/volume/8/issue/3/weapons-mass-destruction-and-international-law (accessed on 2 January 2020).

[5] HG Legal resources, WMD Law—Weapons of Mass Destruction Law, available at: https://www.hg.org/weapons-mass-destruction.html (accessed on 2 January 2020).

depend on legal, political, ideological, or any other inclination. On his part, Seth considers that "the phrase WMD is an amorphous one, changing meaning according to the whims of the speaker. That, however, does not imply that when viewed by experts in the field, or when used, one cannot tell that they are such weapons. Raising the specter of WMD is more a way by which politicians assign blame or take a stand on seemingly objective moral standards than a way by which they assess a particular weapons system".[6] A key ingredient in the definition of WMD is that of their capability to "destroy people". This is an odd formulation implying physical destruction in addition to morbidity and mortality. It also seems to imply exclusion of chemical and biological (CB) weapons, if they cannot destroy a person, but only incapacitate him or her.[7]

From Seth's definition, it is possible that political and ideological inclinations may influence what one calls a weapon of mass destruction—the criteria being killing or destroying people massively. Such criteria increase the ambiguity in the definition of an endless list of weapons capable of destroying or killing people in masses. Mauroni on the other hand, considers that "there is a great deal of debate on the proper legal, military, and diplomatic definition of what WMD really are". For example, the original definition crafted by the United Nations in 1948 to address the new class of weapons was good enough for the Cold War, but after Aum Shinrikyo's use of nerve agent in Tokyo's subway in 1995, that changed. The threats of Chemical, biological, radiological and nuclear (CBRN) terrorism, pandemic disease outbreaks, and radiological incidents caused policymakers to use "WMD" in different forms.[8]

According to the United Nations (UN) Office for Disarmament Affairs, WMD constitute a class of weaponry with the potential to, in a single moment, kill millions of civilians, jeopardize the natural environment, and fundamentally alter the world and the lives of future generations through their catastrophic effects. In this case, what UN Office for Disarmament Affairs does, is merely to describe the undesirable effects of WMD, but not to succinctly define what they are. The term WMD, therefore, seems to be amenable to adjustments depending on the existing knowledge of what WMD are, and their effects, at a particular point in time. It is also to be accepted depending on where they are used, and by who. An understanding of what WMD are, may equally be

---

[6] W. Seth Carus, Defining "Weapons of Mass Destruction", Occasional Paper 8, Revised and Updated, Center for the Study of Weapons of Mass Destruction National Defense University, USA, available at: https://wmdcenter.ndu.edu/Portals/97/Documents/Pub lications/Occasional%20Papers/08_Defining%20Weapons%20of%20Mass%20Destruction. pdf (accessed on 22 December 2019).

[7] W. Seth Carus, Defining "Weapons of Mass Destruction", Occasional Paper 8, Revised and Updated, Center for the Study of Weapons of Mass Destruction National Defense University, USA, available at: https://wmdcenter.ndu.edu/Portals/97/Documents/Pub lications/Occasional%20Papers/08_Defining%20Weapons%20of%20Mass%20Destruction. pdf (accessed on 22 December 2019).

[8] Al Mauroni, War Books: What Are Weapons of Mass Destruction, Anyway? Modern War Institute, USA, 2019, available at: https://mwi.usma.edu/war-books-weapons-mass-destruction-anyway/ (accessed on 15 December 2019).

influenced by developments in science and technology, and also the political and ideological landscape of the time.

As narrated by Tabitha Mwangi and Tracy Asava in Chapter 10, the emergence of the Internet Revolution has increased challenges regarding the exact definition of WMD. Cyber technology has brought on board yet another element of WMD—cyber-attacks (weapons), whose effects may be more or comparable to those caused by biological, chemical, or nuclear weapons.[9] Another newcomer on the scene of WMD, especially on the African continent, is the broad category of improvised explosives (IEDs), which are largely in the hands of terrorists. These, too, have the capacity to destroy people in the same manner as they already identifiable WMD do. It is probable that the present-day COVID-19 pandemic, attributable to a virus, which is a biological substance, is yet another form of WMD, if the criteria of "destroying people massively" is taken as the correct one. The reason being that it is not clear, whether the destruction of people envisaged under the broad definition of WMD must be instantaneous or gradual, depending on the purpose for which WMD would have been deployed.

The foregoing discussion demonstrates that WMD are many, and of different categories depending on the purpose and actual effects on the ground. They, however, may be categorized under two broad headings: those that are industrially manufactured by the civilized society, and those that are improvised and largely used by terrorists. Industrial manufacture in this case implies that WMD have an industrial application protected under intellectual property law.[10] The industrially manufactured WMD can easily be regulated under international law, because their production is either in the hands of States or State-licensed Companies. IEDs, on the other hand, are largely used by frustrated non-state actors, experimenting or excluded persons, largely to terrorize States. These cannot be directly regulated by international law, but their use remains under the general province of international law. When arrested, makers or users of IEDs cannot escape the wraths of the law, simply because they are not specifically catered for in the existing legal frameworks. The destruction caused by IEDs would definitely be categorized using another criterion, well-defined and recognized under both international law, and municipal law of some States. In cases of ambiguity in the law, resort shall be made to the circumstances under which they were used so that perpetrators qualify as war criminals or genocidaires, or become amenable to be arraigned in court for committing crimes against humanity.

---

[9] See Michael N. Schmitt (ed.), *Tallinn Manual on the International Law Applicable to Cyber Warfare*, International Group of Expert at the Invitation of NATO Cooperative Cyber Defence Centre of Excellence, Cambridge, 2013.

[10] See Arya Mathew, Protection of Intellectual Property Rights Under the Indian & International Laws, ALTACIT GLOBAL, available at: https://www.altacit.com/public ation/protection-of-intellectual-property-rights-under-the-indian-and-international-laws/ (accessed on 2 January 2020).

Moving to particular categorization, chemical weapons are defined under Article II (1) of the Chemical Weapons Convention to mean the following, together or separately: (a) Toxic chemicals and their precursors, except where intended for purposes not prohibited under this Convention, as long as the types and quantities are consistent with such purposes; (b) Munitions and devices, specifically designed to cause death or other harm through the toxic properties of those toxic chemicals specified in subparagraph (a), which would be released as a result of the employment of such munitions and devices; (c) Any equipment specifically designed for use directly in connection with the employment of munitions and devices specified in subparagraph (b).[11]

Chemical weapons, therefore, are activated when their characteristics are subjected to other processes which activate them to either explode or behave in a harmful manner. Article II (2) defines "Toxic chemicals" to mean "any chemical which through its chemical action on life processes can cause death, temporary incapacitation or permanent harm to humans or animals." This includes all such chemicals, regardless of their origin or of their method of production, and regardless of whether they are produced in facilities, in munitions, or elsewhere.[12] Radiological Weapons are those that disperse radioactive agents to inflict injury or cause contamination or damage. A dirty bomb using a conventional explosion to disperse radioactive contaminants is one such type of weapon, but this could also encompass other ways to disperse nuclear contaminates, such as through a food or water source.[13]

Biological WMD on the other hand, are defined in the Convention as (1) "microbial or other biological agents, or toxins whatever their origin or method of production, of types and in quantities that have no justification for prophylactic, protective, or other peaceful purposes; (2) Weapons, equipment or means of delivery designed to use such agents or toxins for hostile purposes or in armed conflict".[14] This broad definition of biological WMD is unique and intended to capture a wide spectrum of violators of the law—it includes means as a violation of the law, making the holder of the means, not the actual WMD amenable to criminal prosecution.

A cyber-attack (weapon) is defined as a "cyber operation, whether offensive or defensive, that is reasonably expected to cause injury or death to persons

---

[11] The Convention on the Prohibition of the Development, Production, Stockpiling and Use of Chemical Weapons and on Their Destruction, 1993, Article II (1).

[12] The Convention on the Prohibition of the Development, Production, Stockpiling and Use of Chemical Weapons and on Their Destruction, 1993, Article II (2).

[13] IRMI, Radiological Weapon, available at: https://www.irmi.com/term/insurance-definitions/radiological-weapon (accessed on 5 January 2020).

[14] The Convention on the Prohibition of the Development, Production and Stockpiling of Bacteriological (Biological) and Toxin Weapons and on their Destruction (usually referred to as the Biological Weapons Convention, abbreviation: BWC, or Biological and Toxin Weapons Convention, abbreviation: BTWC) was the first multilateral disarmament treaty banning the production of an entire category of weapons, adopted signed on April 10, 1972, came into force on March 26, 1975, Article 1.

or damage or destruction to objects."[15] Unlike other forms of WMD, cyber WMD may be employed to attack systems upon which life-supporting systems depend. That would not be a direct attack on the victims, but deployment of such would qualify if the effect criterion of "destruction of people" is adopted. For example, if the navigational system upon which a pilot depends to steer an airplane is attacked using cyber weapons and the plane crushes, killing its occupants, the initiators of the attack would have squarely brought themselves within the purview of the law, and would be punished.

On the other hand, improvised explosive devices are defined as "a device placed or fabricated in an improvised manner incorporating destructive, lethal, noxious, pyrotechnic, or incendiary chemicals and designed to destroy, incapacitate, harass, or distract. It may incorporate military stores, but is normally devised from non-military components."[16] This definition is both political and ideological in a sense that it is not intended to compare the industrially manufactured WMD to those whose formula is not known to the public. That, however, does not mean that the craters cannot make similar weapons, following the same steps used before.

The foregoing discussion attempts to define what each of the discussed categories of WMD does but does not succinctly bring out the exact meaning for each of them. It is loaded with legal, political, and generally ideological contestations that blur the exact picture of what actually WMD are or are not. At best this is an attempt to describe what they are or what effects they have once deployed. Anderson and Moodie observe that "chemical, biological, radiological, or nuclear weapons each pose differing challenges to international peace and security, often leading scholarly publications to focus on one category of WMD and one discrete aspect (such as the proliferation of relevant materials) of the challenge posed by the weapons and delivery systems within this category."[17] These definitions, though not so clear, are, relied upon and used in this chapter, for want of better definitions.

Background to the Threats Posed by WMD on the African Continent

From a historical perspective, the term WMD seems to have appeared in the realm of modern knowledge during and after the Second World War. There is no doubt, however, that WMD, of the kindred known to humanity today, were used during the First World War or long before that event. Indeed,

[15] Michael N. Schmitt (ed.), *Tallinn Manual on the International Law Applicable to Cyber Warfare*, International Group of Expert at the Invitation of NATO Cooperative Cyber Defence Centre of Excellence, Cambridge, 2013, Rule 30, p. 106.

[16] FARLEX, The Free Online Dictionary, 2005, available at: https://www.thefreedicti onary.com/improvised+explosive+device (accessed on 5 January 2020).

[17] Justin Anderson, Amanda Moodie, Weapons of Mass Destruction, Oxford Bibliographies, 2017, at: https://www.oxfordbibliographies.com/view/document/obo-978019997 43292/obo-9780199743292-0221.xml (accessed on 18 December 2019).

Rhodes affirms that they were widely used during the First World War.[18] The term WMD, however, came up about the year 1937, when it was used to describe massed formations of bomber aircraft.[19] At that time, these high-flying battleships of the air were used in the Second World War to bomb cities such as Hamburg in Germany, and London in the United Kingdom. Tens of thousands of civilians died in a single night.[20] Anderson and Moodie consider that the term "WMD" was first expressly defined by the UN in 1948 as "atomic explosive weapons, radioactive material weapons, lethal chemical and biological weapons, and any weapons developed in the future which have characteristics comparable in destructive effect to those of the atomic bomb or other weapons mentioned above."[21]

The 1948 UN definition permits inclusion of future developments and expansion of the list of WMD, depending on the purpose for which the inclusion shall be required to serve. During the Cold War, the United States, the Soviet Union, and other major powers built up enormous stockpiles containing tens of thousands of nuclear bombs, missile warheads, and artillery shells so many that the military and diplomatic standoff of that era was sometimes described as a "balance of terror."[22] It is clear that even then, no African country was involved in the so-called balance of terror. That, however, does not mean that Africa would be spared of the effects of the WMD if they had been used. The African continent was unsafe as much as any other part of the world. Moreover, the 1948 UN definition was intended for global purposes, without any exclusions of where they would be deployed from or used.

The historical documentation of WMD captured largely those WMD in the hands of State actors or the peace-loving people, but did not in any way take into account the role of non-state actors, who could use WMD to destroy State structures and people who support them. Today, the worry about WMD is no longer because they are available in the hands of States or their agencies, but rather because they may be used by non-state actors to destroy the States. State-held WMD are controlled by treaty, and even customary international law entrenched into the minds of the States long before 1948. When disaggregated, however, WMD pose a greater threat to humanity and the environment,

---

[18] Richard Rhodes, World War I and the Mordant of History of Weapons of Mass Destruction, *The Washington Post*, 2015, available at: https://www.washingtonpost.com/opinions/world-war-i-and-the-mordant-history-of-weapons-of-mass-destruction/2015/02/27/5875dbfc-a339-11e4-903f-9f2faf7cd9fe_story.html (accessed on 4 January 2020).

[19] Encyclopedia Britannica, Weapon of Mass Destruction, available at: https://www.britannica.com/technology/weapon-of-mass-destruction (accessed on 12 December 2019).

[20] Conrad C. Crane, *Bombs, Cities, and Civilians: American Airpower Strategy in World War II*, University Press of Kansas, Lawrence, 1993.

[21] Justin Anderson, Amanda Moodie, Weapons of Mass Destruction, Oxford Bibliographies, 2017, available at: https://www.oxfordbibliographies.com/view/document/obo-9780199743292/obo-9780199743292-0221.xml (accessed on 18 December 2019).

[22] Conrad C. Crane, *Bombs, Cities, and Civilians: American Airpower Strategy in World War II*, University Press of Kansas, Lawrence, 1993.

than when they are identified as a single concept, the latter giving them a less threatening face. For example, Biological weapons have been identified in literature to "contain natural toxins or infectious agents such as bacteria, viruses, or fungi; sprayed or burst over populated areas, they might cause limited but severe outbreaks of such deadly diseases as anthrax, pneumonic plague, or smallpox."[23]

Biological weapons have not been used in modern war since the Japanese spread plague-infected lice in areas of China during Second World War.[24] They nevertheless, remain available, and may be used contrary to the law. Nuclear weapons are essentially explosive devices whose destructive potential derives from the release of energy that accompanies the splitting or combining of atomic nuclei. The discussion in this chapter, however, does not specifically address itself to the scientific effects of WMD, rather it concentrates on the legal and to some extent policy and ideological considerations for use of WMD. In terms of scope, the discussion is limited to the presently known classes of WMD, chemical, nuclear, radiological, biological, cyber, and IEDs.

In order to prohibit WMD on its land, the African continent took a stand to demand that every State in the world supports a world free of abhorrent and indiscriminate biological, chemical, and nuclear weapons (WMD). In this regard, a Common African Defence and Security Policy (CADSP) was adopted by the Second Extraordinary Session of the Assembly of the Union, held in Sirte, Libya, on 28 February 2004. For Africans, WMD were identified as a common threat facing all member states, which should be addressed in a collective manner.

The Problem

Prohibition of manufacturing, possession, stockpiling, transfer, or use of weapons of mass destruction (WMD) is global and historical. It has remained an elusive aspect of the global peace and security architecture.[25] Ideally, the world should be free of any WMD or the threats they pose to humanity. Humanity, however, cannot be judged from one perspective. The need for existence equally brings on board the need to protect and defend oneself. In a bid to protect oneself, humanity has developed weapons, which deter the actual and perceived enemy threats from destroying the world of the self, and the innocent.

---

[23] Don Bosco School, Siliguri, Bosco Model United Nations 2017, Study Guide, General Assembly—Disarmament and International Security Committee, available at: http://boscomunsiliguri.com/pdf/GA%20DISEC.pdf (accessed on 12 December 2019).

[24] As above.

[25] Hellenic Republic, Ministry of Foreign Affairs, Non–Proliferation and Disarmament (Weapons of Mass Destruction), Saturday, 4 January 2020, available at: https://www.mfa.gr/en/foreign-policy/global-issues/decommissioning-weapons-of-mass-destruction.html (accessed on 4 January 2020).

The cyclic relationship created through the lenses of the existentialist ideologists, then, creates a problem—life becomes a function of suspicions, which necessitates wearing the strongest available armor of protection. WMD seem to provide that armor. Humanity has developed so much that it is no longer a question of possessing the technical know-how, only that matters, but also how the technology available can be put to use to defend the self and the defenseless. Due to advancements in science and technology, new inventions such as cyber weapons have been developed and added to the list of WMD.

The ideology of exclusion and global politics based on existentialist ideals create the friends and foes paradigm; with the latter category of politicians and ideologists being regarded as terrorists. Terrorists rely heavily on improvised explosive devices (IEDs) to keep governments at bay, because they do not have access to State resources and even stable grounds to develop industrially manufactured WMD. A wide range of WMD is, therefore, in existence, both in the hands of the peace-loving members of society and of the perceived enemies.

The dual-purpose use of the same material and composition of substances used in the production of WMD and peaceful and developmental needs of humanity equally poses a danger to humanity. Yudin, using the example of nuclear energy, problematizes this situation. From the onset of nuclear age, the challenge has been to facilitate the peaceful use of nuclear energy while inhibiting the proliferation of nuclear weapons. The close technical parallelism and interrelation of the peaceful and military (weapons) applications of atomic energy make countering nuclear proliferation an especially difficult task.

At the heart of the problem is an overlap between civilian and military (meaning for weapons use) applications of nuclear energy, which both depend essentially on the same key ingredient, fissile materials. These materials can undergo fission to release significant amounts of energy, which can be harnessed to generate electricity or used to produce tremendous explosive force.[26] Indeed, other materials and programs for development of WMD do have a dual purpose just like the ingredients for nuclear energy. For example, cyber technology is good for human development and also as a weapon of mass destruction. The analogy made using these examples shows how difficult it shall be for the African continent to get rid of WMD through prohibitions, only.

Lack of goodwill, largely by the developed Western World, to put in place a strong legal framework for a total ban of WMD remains a potential threat to the African continent, which has always been at the receiving end of technologies developed in the Western World. Current international law only regulates the manufacture, possession, stockpiling of otherwise disposing off WMD. It

---

[26] Yury Yudin, Multilateralization of the Nuclear Fuel Cycle: The Need to Build Trust, The United Nations Institute for Disarmament Research (UNIDIR), Geneva, Switzerland, 2019, p. 1.

accommodates their regulated manufacture, possession, and use.[27] The emergence of the Internet Revolution, which has brought on board cyber weapons, and the easy technology for making IEDs, equally poses a great danger to humanity, especially on the African continent. The last two categories are not easily regulated under international law, at best they could be regulated by destroying their sites, which is also not possible. Attempts to destroy the sites of WMD on the African continent, for example, in Libya and Somalia have escalated the problem.

Non-state actors, who must exist, because they are human beings with the same brains and capacity to defend themselves, have escalated the level of use of IEDs to levels well beyond the precincts of international regulation.[28] Worst of all, when released from their "homes," WMD can spread uncontrollably to the near and far areas. Proximity in terms of the destructive capacity of WMD is not the only criteria to be focused on when discussing WMD. Regarding prohibition of WMD on the African continent, the devil, therefore, lies in the conscience of those who manufacture, or handle WMD in any way or capacity to ensure that the rest of humanity is not put at a great risk of destruction by such weapons. WMD are manufactured by those with the technology, just like any other goods and sold on market, *albeit* under international condemnation and unenforceable legal restrictions to those who proliferate them to the intended end users. Due to the multiplicity of armed conflicts on the continent, there are several non-state actors in possession of IEDs on the African continent. In any case, the impact of IEDs may not be totally different from that of industrially manufactured WMD. For example, Al Shabaab and other Al Qaeda-linked terrorist groups such as Boko Haram and Allied Democratic Forces (ADF) on the African continent craft, possess, and frequently use IEDs.[29]

THE LEGAL FRAMEWORK ON PROHIBITION OF WEAPONS OF MASS DESTRUCTION IN AFRICA

Various branches of international law attempt, tacitly to regulate the use of WMD For example, international humanitarian law (IHL) limits the means and methods of warfare that cause unnecessary suffering to victims or have

[27] See the Advisory Opinion, Legality of the Use of Force by a State of Nuclear Weapons in Armed Conflict, ICJ Reports 66 (1996), available at: http://www.icj-cij.org/icjwww/icases/iunan/iunanframe.htm.

[28] Keeley, Robert, Improvised Explosive Devices (IED): A Humanitarian Mine Action Perspective, *Journal of Conventional Weapons Destruction*, Volume 21, Issue 1 (2017), Article 3. Available at: https://commons.lib.jmu.edu/cisr-journal/vol21/iss1/3 (accessed on 3 January 2020).

[29] See for example, AFP, Al-Shabaab Militants Claim Huge Mogadishu Bomb Attack, 30 December 2019, available at: https://www.thisismoney.co.uk/wires/afp/article-7838201/Al-Shabaab-militants-claim-huge-Mogadishu-bomb-attack.html (accessed on 3 January 2020).

long-lasting effects on the environment.[30] International human rights law broadly prohibits infliction of cruel, inhuman, or degrading treatment to fellow human beings.[31] International criminal law criminalizes and punishes violations such as grave breaches of the Geneva Conventions, which are related to violations caused inter alia by WMD.[32] It suffices to note, however, that these branches of international law were not developed specifically to address WMD; they may, however, in cases of grey areas in the law, be relied upon to punish violators.[33]

Laws regarding WMD are created through international treaties and agreements and generally enforced through organizations like the UN and by the military power of other nations.[34] The legal framework for the prohibition of WMD in Africa follows the global framework and is as diverse as there are categories of WMD. At the international level, customary and treaty law and State practice guide the handling of WMD in terms of manufacture, sale, stockpiling, and proliferation. Prohibition of manufacturing, possession, stockpiling, transfer, or use of weapons of mass destruction (WMD) is the desired goal for each and every peace-loving African. This, however, remains a wish that is too far to be reached because the manufacturers are far from Africa. Suffice to note that only industrially manufactured WMD are regulated and monitored under the law. IEDs, are regulated in terms of prohibition of use, but not regarding their manufacture, stockpiling, transfer or use. The global legal framework emanates from the statement of the purpose of the UN.

This is spelt out in the Charter of the UN, in Article 1, which mandates the UN to maintain international peace and security, take effective collective measures for the prevention and removal of threats to the peace, and for the suppression of acts of aggression or other breaches of the peace, and to bring about by peaceful means, and in conformity with the principles of justice and international law, adjustment or settlement of international disputes or situations which might lead to a breach of the peace. The Charter further obliges all members of the UN to refrain in their international relations from the threat or use of force against the territorial integrity or political independence of

---

[30] Additional Protocol I to the Geneva Conventions, 1949; Article 35; see also The Convention on the Prohibition of Military or any other Hostile Use of Environmental Modification Techniques (ENMOD Convention), 1976, which is an instrument of international disarmament law specifically intended to protect the environment in the event of armed conflict. It prohibits hostile use of the environment as a means of warfare.

[31] See, for instance, the United Nations Convention Against Torture and Other Cruel, Inhuman or Degrading Treatment or Punishment, adopted by the United Nations General Assembly at New York on December 10, 1984.

[32] The Rome Statute of the International Criminal Court, 2002, Article 8.

[33] Advisory Opinion, Legality of the Use of Force by a State of Nuclear Weapons in Armed Conflict, ICJ Reports 66 (1996), available at: http://www.icj-cij.org/icjwww/icases/iunan/iunanframe.htm.

[34] HG Legal resources, WMD Law—Weapons of Mass Destruction Law, available at: https://www.hg.org/weapons-mass-destruction.html (accessed on 2 January 2020).

any state, or in any other manner inconsistent with the Purposes of the UN. These pronouncements of the global body were directed at member States, or States in general terms. For the non-members and non-state actors, the Charter under Article 1(6), gives authority to the UN to ensure that such non-member States, and by necessary implications, non-state actors are compelled to abide by the principles set forth in the Charter. To that end, it can be rightly stated that the UN Charter binds the members and any other non-members, in so far as actions of the non-member affect the mandate of the UN.

In order for there to be peace proscribed under the Charter of the UN in 1945, a special organ, the Security Council was created to be the overseer of all global aspects of peace and security. It is noteworthy, that WMD had been used prior to the creation of the Security Council, and therefore, it is correct to state that the Security Council is clothed with mandate to prohibit all aspects of WMD, if they constitute a threat to international peace and security. The key function of the Security Council as stated in Article 24 (1) of the Charter is to ensure prompt and effective action by the UN in the maintenance of international peace and security. Moreover, in doing so, the Security Council acts on all members of the UN.

In order for the African continent to attain a total prohibition of WMD, therefore, the Security Council of the UN must be ready and willing to execute the noble task assigned to it under the Charter. It should among others, ensure that WMD are not manufactured on the African continent, or are not prolif-erated onto the continent or used thereon. This, however, is an uphill task, which the UN Security Council may not be well prepared for. It is possible to argue that prohibition of WMD on the African continent is a regional matter, which the African Union, should, through its established channels handle because the UN Charter under Article 52 empowers regional arrangements or agencies to effectively handle matters relating to maintenance of international peace and security.

Prohibition of WMD on the African continent is, however, totally outside the purview of the African Union because, apart from IEDs, much of the industrial manufacturing of WMD is done outside the continent. At best, the African Union can lobby the UN Security Council to effectively exercise its mandate and ensure that Africa is free from WMD. The question posed here is: considering the composition of the Security Council and the polarization that has gone on unbated since the creation of this organ, would it be foreseen that it can prohibit any member country from manufacturing, and possessing such weapons? In case it is able to monitor these aspects, is it in position to ensure non-proliferation of the same? The authors' view is that these answers attract only negative answers. Moreover, an examination of the efforts undertaken by the Security Council raises no hope that the African continent is about to reach near to a point of prohibiting WMD on its land. For example, while adopting its Resolution 2325 (2016), the Security Council, and in anticipation of an open debate on WMD in the hands of terrorists "called for intensified efforts to ensure the development of a secure international framework for that purpose in the face rapid technological advances and increasingly ambitious malefactors. Unanimously adopting resolution 2325 (2016), the UN Security Council called on all States to strengthen national anti-proliferation regimes in implementation of resolution 1540 (2004). This Resolution seeks to keep non-state actors from acquiring nuclear, biological, and chemical weapons of mass destruction, which, however, is not possible. True, proliferation is prohibited under the law, but there are no clear mechanisms under this legal regime to ensure that illicit transfer of such weapons, or their components and technology is not let into the hands of prohibited persons., Finally, Resolution 2325 (2016) calls for greater assistance for building State capacity in the drive to prevent illicit use of WMD. The success of this call largely depends on the willingness of member states and other stakeholders, including the civil society and academia.[35]

Indeed, this and several other Resolutions have been adopted by the Security Council, but still, the threat posed to the African States about the use of WMD still stands. Fortunately, some of those Resolutions have culminated into negotiation and adoption of international treaties on WMD. The UN Security Council Resolution 1540 (2004) requires members states to develop and enforce appropriate legal and regulatory measures against the proliferation of chemical, biological, radiological, and nuclear weapons and their means of delivery, in particular, to prevent the spread of weapons of mass destruction to non-state actors.[36] Still, the language used in this resolution is not robust to guarantee that what it requires has to be done. Member states, especially on the African continent do not have the requisite resources, human, capital, and technology to ensure compliance with the normative demands of this Resolution.

Several African countries have stood out in terms of the efforts they have made to implement Resolution 1540, effectively. The African continent has historically, however, been an arena for testing the western superior hegemonic power of rule of law. Power is right and power makes law. The formerly colonized African States remain disempowered under this paradigm and cannot dictate what pace of technological and political development takes place in the developed western world. In the same vein, regulation of WMD remains a preserve of the western developed world, which use a lack of capacity by African countries to regulate WMD as a tool for denying them the requisite technology for the industrial manufacture of WMD. Without the requisite technological know-how to manufacture WMD, African countries cannot know-how to regulate their use or diffuse them when used on the continent. The problem of WMD on the African continent then ceases to be only of

---

[35] United Nations Security Council, 7837th Meeting, SC/12628, 15 December 2016.

[36] The UN Office for Disarmament Affairs (UNODA), UN Security Council Resolution 1540 (2004), available at: https://www.un.org/disarmament/wmd/sc1540/ (accessed on 4 January 2020).

410 G. BUSINGYE ET AL.

their perceived effect once used, but also how to diffuse them if used on the continent.

Prohibition of WMD in Africa must, therefore, be understood within the broader perspective of global peace and security architecture, where sovereign States are equal and under the notion of equality of States, but do not have an equal right to state what is right or wrong. African countries participate in international fora discussing prohibition of WMD, merely as invitees, since they do not have capacity either to industrially manufacture them or control their manufacture. The discussion of self-defense in the Advisory Opinion on the use of nuclear weapons demonstrates how those countries that already possess them or technology to manufacture them will continue to pose a threat to the African continent.[37] Any attempt by an African country to manufacture WMD will, in the eyes of the Western World be viewed as a threat to their peace, and may be replied with their use in the identified African States.

Not so much, has, however, been achieved toward ridding the world of WMD, and hence the African continent may have to wait much longer before it achieves its goal of prohibiting WMD on its land. Sadly, like the UNSC Resolutions, International Conventions intended to prohibit WMD appear to be permissive to their retention by those States which already had them at the time when those treaties were negotiated. For example, in the Nuclear Tests Cases, Court failed to pronounce itself on the question whatever or not the use of nuclear weapons is prohibited in any circumstances. It left the world to guess when and who would be entitled to use such weapons when it allowed their use only in self-defense.[38]

Permissive language is expressly used in the Nuclear Ban Treaty under Article I, which requires each nuclear-weapon State Party to the Treaty to undertake not to transfer to any recipient whatsoever nuclear weapons or other nuclear explosive devices or control over such weapons or explosive devices directly, or indirectly. The treaty equally prohibits nuclear-weapon State parties from assisting, encouraging, or inducing any non-nuclear-weapon State to manufacture or otherwise acquire nuclear weapons or other nuclear explosive devices, or control over such weapons or explosive devices. There seem to be no legal means, within this treaty of ensuring that a nuclear-weapon State Party complies with such a call.

By implications, if no such undertaking is done, then only the soft language of condemnation can be used against such a Party. Within the purview of this Treaty, there is a category of countries, the nuclear-weapon States, which are permitted to keep nuclear weapons, and for the purposes for which they were manufactured, and there is another class, the non-nuclear weapons States which in no circumstances are allowed to acquire them. On its part, the Biological Convention under Article I requires "each State Party to undertake never in any circumstances to develop, produce, stockpile or otherwise

[37] *Nuclear Tests Case (Australia V. France) (Interim Protection) Order of 22 June 1973.*
[38] *P.C.I.J., Series A, No. IO*, pp. 18 and 19.

acquire or retain."[39] The same problem of lack of enforceability of the treaty provisions defeats the purpose for which it was negotiated and adopted.

Lack of authoritative position on their total ban has, however, not deterred international and even national action to continue looking for a solution to tame them. Fidler observes that "the dominant international legal activity on WMD has been the negotiation and implementation of arms control treaties." The arms control approach reflected three objectives-to deter the use of WMD by States. For example, nuclear arms control treaties between the United States and the Soviet Union prohibit the emplacement and testing of WMD in certain areas such as the orbit or on the sea-bed or ocean floor.[40] The foregoing discussion demonstrates how difficult it is to regulate industrially manufactured WMD not only on the African continent, but globally. By necessary implications, it also demonstrates a more problematic case on the attempts to regulate WMD in the hands of non-state actors, especially on the African continent. Within such circumstances, the only viable means of regulating the use of WMD in the hands of non-state actors would be to win the hearts and minds and convince them to abandon their activities. Short of that, States must be prepared to use all the legal means available to them and bring them to order, or else, defeat them militarily.

It is possible that a change of attitude by Governments toward democracy, by adopting all-inclusive policies would minimize political dissent and hence reduce the prevalence of terrorism on the African continent. Failure to win the hearts and minds of the terror groups or defeat them militarily means that the problem of availability and use of IEDs remains a thorn in the flesh, wherever terrorists exist. Even in the case of industrially manufactured WMD, regulation is not an outright concept for the African continent. WMD may be smuggled out of the normal channels of distribution and fall into the hands of non-state actors. Worst of all, they may not be easy to identify by African governments which may not have the technological know-how to detect such WMD when they are being proliferated across the continent.

To complicate the problem, the desire to annihilate all terrorist groups on the African continent, in a bid to stop the use of WMD, even with the support of the western countries as of now, has not been successful as shown by the example of Al Shabaab and Boko Haram and other Al Qaeda-linked terrorist groups. A question posed here is: do States have control over terrorists, or do they have, especially the African States, capacity to stop terrorism, well aware that in the case of the Democratic Republic of Congo, in Nigeria,

---

[39] The Convention on the Prohibition of the Development, Production and Stockpiling of Bacteriological (Biological) and Toxin Weapons and on their Destruction, commonly known as the Biological Weapons Convention (BWC) or Biological and Toxin Weapons Convention (BTWC), opened for signature in 1972 and entered into force in 1975.

[40] David P. Fidler, Weapons of Mass Destruction and International Law, *American Society of International Law*, Volume 8, Issue 3 (2003), available at: https://www.asil.org/ins ights/volume/8/issue/3/weapons-mass-destruction-and-international-law (accessed on 2 January 2020).

and in Somalia terrorist claim territories, and keep State machinery off such territories? Most importantly, are States ready to identify with terrorists and accommodate them in their Governments so that terrorism stops, and hence have a relief against WMD being used against them? The second viable option to take in a drive to prohibit WMD on the African continent is by States building the necessary capacity required to ensure due compliance with the law by all, without exception. That, however, may breed dictatorial regimes that can be opposed, leading to a cyclic problem of conflict where IEDs are the major tools in the hands of the oppressed.

From the foregoing discussion, it is clear that strict regulation of all aspects of WMD within the purview of States, right from manufacture, sale, possession, or use is not possible, much as it is the desired goal. The laws in place remain weak and almost unenforceable. Laufer reinforces this position by observing that the law of weapons is among the oldest of the laws of armed conflict, yet one of the least effective ones. As weaponry advanced rapidly in the twentieth century, the law struggled to keep up with these developments. The emergence of modern lethal weapons requires States to achieve the right balance between their military interests and legal obligations more than ever before.[41] Due to weak laws to regulate WMD in all aspects, the United Nations framework has been rendered a mere watchdog, without the capacity to bite those who violate the law. Moreover, the technology for manufacturing WMD does not necessarily reside within the purview of the UN or State actors only. Non-state actors may also have such technology and indeed manufacture the same for the obvious purpose of terrorizing sovereign States.

The African continent is basically a victim of a weak international legal framework regarding prohibition of manufacture, transfer, and use of WMD. Unfortunately, the voice of the African continent to have a world free of WMD cannot be listened to, largely due to historical reasons associated with the colonized and the colonizers paradigm. The African continent is a non-nuclear-weapon continent. Invitation of African States to participate in international fora discussing prohibition of WMD is intended to inhibit their capacity to engage in the development of WMD, but not to discuss their regulation. For example, the permitted use of WMD in self-defence by those States that possess them is intended to be a tool to permanently keep African States on their knees begging for mercy so that WMD are not used against them.

In any case, international law allows possessors of WMD to use them in self-defense, without prescribing which force they should be responding to. The language used by the International Court of Justice when adjudicating disputes regarding nuclear tests is not authoritative as to amount to a pronouncement condemning manufacture, possession, and use of nuclear

---

[41] Helin M. Laufer, War, Weapons and Watchdogs: An Assessment of the Legality of New Weapons Under International Human Rights Law, *Cambridge International Law Journal*, Volume 6, Issue 1, pp. 62–74.

weapons.[42] Such permissive language in the most serious circumstances attracts criticism from the purview of a human rights-based perspective. Essentially, the prohibition of WMD in Africa remains a fallacy, and a desire far-fetched—they may be used on the continent without any one African State preventing their use, apart from complaining to the UN Security Council, but of course without a hope for any viable remedy.

CONCLUSION

The African continent promotes and supports implementation of measures relating to non-proliferation of WMD on the continent. The continent, is however, unable to prohibit WMD on its land. There are a number of reasons attributed to this problem, namely: lack of expert knowledge to identify and detect the presence of WMD, since Africa is not a WMD-producing continent. Prohibition of WMD requires different approaches because WMD are not similar; they belong to several categories—nuclear, radiological, chemical, and biological weapons, and their components or agents, cyber weapons, and IEDs. Worst of all, the dual-use purpose nature of substances and technologies for WMD and peaceful means creates dilemma in their prohibition. There is less incentive for African countries that do not possess any such weapons capabilities to prioritize reporting and implementation of provisions of treaties in place.

There, is, however, no country in the world that can consider itself immune from the threat of an attack involving WMD or from having its territory exploited by non-state actors attempting to produce, acquire or transfer WMD, or their components. This, therefore means that, countering the threats of international terrorism and WMD proliferation requires efforts at national, regional, and international levels. The biggest challenge is that most African states lack the capacity and knowledge to make any real progress on implementing resolutions to prohibit weapons of mass destruction, and as a result, progress on the continent has been slow. In spite of important breakthroughs, African States are still facing important human, technical, organizational, and financial difficulties in building their non-proliferation capacities.

Lastly, the yearned for prohibition of WMD on the African continent may be achieved if: the African continent adoptions a coordinated continental approach to the non-proliferation of WMD onto or within the continent. African governments prioritize implementation of the UN framework demands for prohibition of WMD by setting aside funds for that purpose. African governments must be ready and willing to adopt all-inclusive democracies that will take care of each and every citizen of the continent, and hence reduce political dissent which is a fertile ground for breeding terrorists. African

---

[42] *Nuclear Tests Case (Australia V. France) (Interim Protection) Order of 22 June 1973.*

governments must strive and continue pressing to be heard in the UN fora, so that their interests are taken care of just like is done for the rest of the world.

African governments should set aside funds for research on the dangers of WMD and avail those funds to the research institutions, individual academicians, and their militaries who should strive to find better ways of taming the problem of WMD on the continent. WMD possessing countries should act in good faith in favor of all humanity, and not seek to use the western-established UN framework to sideline the less developed continents like Africa. The International community should adopt a human rights-based approach to the whole saga of WMD so that these weapons are not produced anymore, those in stock are destroyed or converted into peaceful uses.

PART V

Strategies for Sustaining Peace and Security in Africa

CHAPTER 24

Securing a Path to Security and Peace: Building a People's Trust in the Military

Mark D. Maxwell

Introduction

Although Africa's promise is boundless, peace and security are elusive and even nonexistent in many sectors of the continent. In the hope of finding the right prescription for achieving peace and security, nations have tried multiple strategies ranging from economic and international initiatives to cultural and informational efforts. In this chapter, the road map to security, which is a precondition for peace, is shown to start with the professionalization of a nation's military.[1] This does mean that military and security are synonymous, but they are inextricably linked. The measures to improve the military discussed in this chapter are not exclusive to achieving peace and security. Numerous factors play into a nation's ability to establish security, for example, geography, natural resources, population, and historical influences. But one factor directly in the hands of its leaders is governance. Within governance is a recognition of what capacity and capability exist within the military vis-à-vis its

[1] The use of nation and state are interchangeable in this article, even though the author recognizes there is a legal distinction.

The views expressed in this chapter are those of the author's and not necessarily those of the U.S. Department of Defense and/or the U.S. Africa Command.

M. D. Maxwell (✉)
U.S. Africa Command, Stuttgart, Germany
e-mail: majormaxwell@aol.com

© The Author(s), under exclusive license to Springer Nature Switzerland AG 2022
D. Kuwali (ed.), *The Palgrave Handbook of Sustainable Peace and Security in Africa*, https://doi.org/10.1007/978-3-030-82020-6_24

418   M. D. MAXWELL

ability to transform the military into a force that is professional and accountable to its people. Put differently, what are the nation's "ways" and "means" to make the military an agent of security and peace for its people?

Peace and security are a tall order for any country. The competing interests of governance make this extraordinarily complex and challenging. A nation must have three things to achieve a professional military: the capability (the means); the capacity (the ways); and the political will (the ends).[2] The ways and means of every country will vary, but the real Achilles' heel is political will. Without it, any reform of the military that promotes peace and security is aspirational, at best.

Road Map

Just like Tadziwana Kapeni suggested in Chapter 17, political leaders of every state should pursue three lines of effort to demonstrate political will. These three lines of effort to lay the foundation for security and ultimately peace are: first, advancing a soldier's accountability; second, ensuring commanders' adherence to the rule of law; and third, building professionalism within the military ranks. These efforts are essential and can be accomplished by enforcing rules and discipline, even for those nations whose capability and capacity have limitations.

In agreement with the passionate plea by Dan Kuwali in Chapter 27, accountability is the lynchpin to a military that serves its people. Many states around the globe have compartmentalized their security sector, and the results are militaries that fail to interface with the other governmental sectors within society. Although the security sector is integral to a nation's survival, the judicial sector must also interface with the security sector. This is imperative because the military must know how and when to hold soldiers accountable for crimes that they commit. In other words, both the security and judicial sectors are part of ensuring justice.

But the degree of justice is only as strong as the military leaders who are in charge of those soldiers. The chapter will then discuss those military leaders: commanders. Commanders make life-and-death decisions on behalf of the State. The advice they receive about what the law requires is critical to making the right and lawful decisions. The military structure should incorporate military lawyers as legal advisors to commanders. These professionals help the commander with both the law and the tone of the command.

Having access to legal expertise allows the commander to measure his command actions. It also enhances accountability because legal advisors can assist the commander with what is appropriate and acceptable behavior of

---

[2] "Strategies and tactics must be fashioned that create a match—not a mismatch—between aims and the means available for acting on those aims." Dennis Ross, Statecraft and How to Restore America's Standing in the World, Farrar, Straus and Giroux (2008), p. 22. In other words, every state will have different ways and means to accomplish the means desired.

subordinates. Holding someone accountable only triggers after tragedy has occurred. Making a lawyer part of the commanders' team will help inform the commander of what the law requires and, in the process, avoid tragic decisions and set a positive tone within the command.

Setting a positive tone to ensure soldiers follow the rule of law should be inculcated into every military's ethos. The third part of this chapter will discuss the most important aspect of any military formation: a soldier's professionalism. Soldiers must understand their role in society. Soldiers are not only individual actors; they are part of a proud profession. This profession is tethered to both human rights law and the law of war. The soldier has a unique profession: the soldier can use force, to include lethal force, on behalf of the State. This is both a privilege and a burden. Professionalization through education and training helps the soldier to balance both, resulting in adherence to the rule of law.

Through the lens of accountability, competent commanders, and professionalization, a nation can build the trust of its people, and with trust comes security, and with security comes peace. In the end, nations must create militaries its people run to, not run from.[3]

Accountability: The Interface Between the Judicial and Security Sectors

In many states across the globe, the interaction between the state's security sector and its judicial sector is minimal. The profession of arms and the profession of law are seen as disparate. It goes to the essential belief: in war, there is no law. This conclusion, of course, is profoundly wrong. There is law in conflict and more essentially, there is right and there is wrong. When soldiers do something wrong, like intentionally kill an innocent person or rape someone, they must be held accountable. If the soldier is not held to account, then there is no justice and there will be a tone within the ranks that this type of grotesque behavior is acceptable.

The military not only protects the nation, it is a reflection of its people. Therefore, when a soldier commits a crime, there should be a process in place to try the soldier for that transgression. This requires the participation of legal professionals. They must investigate the crime; prosecute the crime; defend the crime; and adjudicate the crime. Once a soldier commits a crime, an entirely different sector of society is triggered—the judicial sector.[4] This sector must be independent, transparent, and fair. The decision of the military to try a soldier for allegations of serious crimes like murder and rape must be informed and

---

[3] This phrase and concept are "stolen" from Ambassador Alexander M. Laskaris, formerly the Deputy to the U.S. Africa Commander for Military Engagements.

[4] The judicial sector could exists within the ministry of defense, like the United States, but the rules and oversight are monitored and dictated by the norms within the ministry of justice. In other words, the rights of a soldier parallel those of a civilian defendant.

420   M. D. MAXWELL

assisted by the judicial sector. The format of how that is executed is country-specific; that is, it will look different from country to country, but in the end, it is crucial that these two sectors work together to ensure the allegations are addressed and if credible, the state holds the soldier accountable.

Many countries within Africa have not yet enacted comprehensive military justice codes.[5] Every country has codified the crimes of murder and rape and other serious crimes, but this civil legislation focuses on its civilian population, not its soldiers. Therefore, when a soldier commits a crime—for example, a soldier murders someone during a peacekeeping operation—the crime has the potential to go unpunished. The two most common scenarios are: in some countries, it is considered a military matter outside the purview of the civil judicial sector; that is, the judicial sector allows the security sector to handle the crime; and in other countries, the judicial sector fails to have the authority to handle the case; that is, there is no jurisdiction. Either scenario is troubling and falls short in advancing the rule of law. Without legislation expressly outlining how a soldier is to be tried, then what is left is, at best, a patchwork fix, or at worst, impunity.

Every country should have legislation that ensures soldiers are held accountable; however, the process for soldiers accused of a crime must be fair. Fairness is advanced by four factors, namely: the soldier receives a transparent and open trial that allows the soldier a defense; the victims and witnesses understand the process and receive an opportunity to participate in the process; the domestic courts have jurisdiction to hear cases involving soldiers (regardless of the location of the allegation); and the public interest is served in a transparent and efficient manner. Drafting legislation that creates a comprehensive military justice system is difficult and time consuming. It does require a country's capacity and capability to build a military justice system that will be fair and just. Every African nation has the ways and means to draft legislation involving its military and judiciary. The real impediment is political will.

For the United States (US), as an example, the political will to create a functioning and fair military justice system took many years. No real substantive changes were made to the American military justice system between the Articles of War, dating back to the American Revolutionary War in the 1700s, until after World War II. In December 1941, when the American military went to war, the Articles of War still set out the punishable offenses applicable to soldiers, the procedures for holding them accountable, and potential penalties. During the course of World War II, about 1.7 million courts-martial were convened, over 100 capital executions were carried out, and over 45,000 soldiers were imprisoned.[6] At the end of the war, numerous veterans' groups

---

[5] The author has data of which states have enacted a military justice code and which have not. The purpose of this article is establish a roadmap—not to call particular states out; therefore, the data is not part of this article.

[6] Bills to Improve the Administration of Justice in the Armed Services: Hearing Before Subcommittee on Constitutional Rights of the Senate Committee of the Judiciary and a

raised genuine concerns about the fairness of the military justice system. There had been "accountability," but veterans decried the lack of transparency and the unfairness to the soldiers.

After World War II, the American public started to debate the fairness and effectiveness of the Articles of War. This debate raged on for over six years and it was not until 1951 when the United States enacted the Uniform Code of Military Justice (UCMJ).[7] The UCMJ not only contained provisions subjecting soldiers to the jurisdiction of the code worldwide for offenses committed on and off duty, on and off post, and against military and non-military individuals, but also outlined and guaranteed the rights of each soldier suspected of a crime. This code has evolved, and reforms over the years have strengthened the rights of soldiers, while ensuring soldiers are accountable to the law.

Each country needs to consider how to handle military cases. The American model is not the only way to handle military cases. Some countries use their civilian system to handle these types of cases. Some countries using the civilian courts have carved out military-specific laws that assist the civil courts to process crimes committed by its soldiers. Regardless of the form, the legislation that is enacted sets in motion the process for how soldiers are to be tried in a court of law. For legislation to be effective, it must grapple with six issues.

First, the legislation must identify the judges who will handle military cases.[8] Determining the number of military judges sufficient to preside over the trials of soldiers accused of crimes will be a function of the volume of military cases. Related training would then be required, but the training would be a function of how the nation's code of military justice is drafted. Second, the code must identify prosecutors handling military cases. Like judges, prosecutors will need to be trained in accordance with the nation's code of military justice.

Third, the code must establish a soldier's right to counsel and with that right, an independent defense counsel bar. The critical determination will be the degree of autonomy accorded defense counsel supporting military personnel accused of criminal offenses. The legislation must outline what is acceptable: use "in house" defense counsel for accused soldiers; use members of the national defense bar who would be retained to provide counsel; or for more minor offenses, use non-lawyers, trained in the process, to defend

---

Special Subcommittee of the Senate Committee on Armed Services, 89th Congress 713, 714 (1966) (discussing the evolution of the Uniform Code of Military Justice in the late 1940s).

[7] 10 United State Code Chapter 47.

[8] In the end, criminal offenses must be handled by a court—but not necessarily by the same court—so long as there is accountability somewhere. Some countries have all offenses by military members handled in a civilian forum, but other countries have military offenses in military courts and all else in civilian courts.

soldiers. Fourth, the code should outline procedures for disciplinary infractions and minor offenses, such as disrespect to a superior officer and failure to show up for duty. The procedures set forth the offenses covered, who can adjudicate these infractions, and the penalties for these types of disciplinary offenses.

Fifth, the code should identify court personnel to support the prosecution of cases. In a manner similar to the policy determinations made on independence of defense counsel to support the military justice process, the code should outline the requirements for court personnel to support the prosecution of military cases; such as, court-reporters and clerks of court. Lastly, the courts that adjudicate offenses committed by military members, whether civilian or military fora and whether civilian or military offenses, must be open to the public and the proceeding must be transparent. This will allow the military to design a public information campaign to disseminate information about prosecutions of individuals within the military. This outreach would explain how the military justice system works; for example, there could be press releases at the conclusion of a pending case announcing the result, with some comment on the basis for the conclusions reached—no matter the result, such as an acquittal, a conviction, or a dismissal.

These recommendations are not exhaustive. There are two competing interests at work—holding the soldier accountable for what he or she did, on one end, and ensuring the process is fair to the soldier, on the other. That balance is difficult for any nation, but there must be recognition that both are important and complementary. There is a tone within the ranks that wrong behavior will be dealt with—creating a deterrent to such behavior in the future; while knowing that if you are accused of a crime as a soldier, you will be treated fairly and given rights to defend yourself—creating confidence in the judicial system. This balance is the essence of a military that possesses good order and discipline within its ranks.

THE COMMANDER'S MILITARY LAWYER

Giving a commander confident and disciplined soldiers is essential to effective military operations. It will be the commander who gives those soldiers orders to execute a mission; the commander will tell his subordinates potentially to use violence to accomplish a military mission. A commander of soldiers has enormous power. The state has entrusted the commander to use violence, if necessary, to win armed conflicts. There is no other profession like it. The state allows the commander to kill innocent civilians—not intentionally, of course, but to accomplish a concrete military objective. The commander, like the soldiers they command, enters into a world that is unlike any other. The rule of law morphs and the law that the commander must follow is very different from the peacetime law left behind. There are laws that control the conduct of the commander in war, but the average citizen does not appreciate this world. The laws that apply to soldiers during armed conflict are so different from the laws that apply to citizens in their own capital. These two paradigms of law are important to understand.[9]

THE LAW-ENFORCEMENT PARADIGM

The law-enforcement paradigm triggers when the agent of the state—this could be a soldier, a police officer, a marshal, or just a citizen of that country—responds to a threat, normally in a domestic context. This paradigm, also known as the human rights paradigm, assumes that the preference is not to use lethal force but rather to arrest a criminal suspect and then to investigate and try the suspect before a court of law.[10] The presumption in a law-enforcement paradigm is that the use of lethal force by an agent of the state, such as a police officer or soldier, is not justified unless necessary to meet an unlawful threat to human life. Necessity assumes that "only the amount of force required to meet the threat and restore the status quo ante may be employed against [the] source of the threat, thereby limiting the force that may be lawfully applied by the state actor."[11] The taking of life is only justified "when lesser means for reducing the threat were ineffective."[12]

Professor Geoffrey C. Corn makes this point by highlighting that a law-enforcement officer could *not* use deadly force "against suspected criminals based solely on a determination an individual was a member of a criminal group."[13] Under the law-enforcement paradigm, "a country cannot target any individual in its own territory unless there is no other way to avert a great danger."[14] It is the individual's *conduct* at the time of the threat that gives the state the right to respond with lethal force. The law-enforcement paradigm

---

[9] The law of war, known as International Humanitarian Law (IHL) and the law of human rights, known as International Human Rights Law (IHRL), are two distinct bodies of law but can be complementary. Both are concerned with the protection of the life, health, and dignity of individuals. The law of war applies in armed conflict—both international and non-international—while human rights law always applies (in peacetime as well as in times of war). The main difference is in the focus of their application: human right law protects the individual citizen from the state while the law of war dictates to the state who on the battlefield takes a protected status.

[10] Judgment, Public Committee Against Torture in Israel v. Israel, HCJ 769/02, [2005] ISrSC, at para. 22.

[11] Geoff Corn, "Mixing Apples and Hand Grenades: The Logical Limit of Applying Human Rights Norms to Armed Conflict," *Journal of International Humanitarian Legal Studies*, Vol. 1, number 52, 85 (2010) [herein, Corn's Human Rights Article].

[12] Ibid., p. 78.

[13] Ibid., p. 77.

[14] Gabriella Blum and Philip Heymann, Law and Policy of Targeted Killing, Laws, Outlaws, and Terrorists: Lesson from the War on Terrorism (Boston: MIT Press 2010), p. 10.

attempts to "minimize the use of lethal force to the extent feasible under the circumstances."[15]

This is the state of the law in most nations around the globe. It is tethered to an individual's human rights. The most basic of those is the right to life. The focus of the law-enforcement paradigm is individual citizens and their protection. The focus of the law of war paradigm is the scope of authority given the state's agents—a soldier—to conduct armed conflict; that is, war. In the African context, this paradigm faces challenges since some militaries face enormous pressure from politicians to suppress civilians that they are duly supposed to protect. It thus requires independent military leadership and judicious military lawyers to clearly set out a path that the military must undertake as was seen in Malawi in 2019 following disputed election results.

Law of War Paradigm

The soldier goes through a dramatic legal conversion once armed conflict begins. The soldier morphs from a civilian legally indistinguishable from any other concerning the use of force to a new type of legal entity authorized by the world community to use deadly force. In war, the rules of when an individual can be killed are starkly different than in peacetime. Minimal force is not the legal standard in war. What applies in war is the law of war paradigm, known as the Law of Armed Conflict (LoAC) or International Humanitarian Law (IHL) paradigm. Once the enemy is declared hostile, enemy soldiers are now targetable because of their *status* as enemy soldiers.

Unlike the law-enforcement paradigm, the law of war paradigm requires neither a certain conduct by the enemy nor a reasonable amount of force analysis to engage belligerents. In armed conflict, it is wholly permissible to inflict "death on enemy personnel irrespective of the actual risk they present."[16] Armed conflict does not consider the law-enforcement presumption that lethal force against an individual is justified only when necessary. If an individual is an enemy, then "soldiers are not constrained by the law of war from applying the full range of lawful weapons."[17] The commander, through the state, tells the soldier that an enemy is hostile and the soldier may engage that individual without any consideration of the threat currently posed.

There are limitations to what the commander and his soldier can do in conflict. Those rules have evolved primarily through custom. Modern treaties, such as the four Geneva Conventions and its Additional Protocols, have acted to codify rules evolved from core principles developed by the practice of

[15] Philip Alston, "Report of the Special Rapporteur on Extrajudicial, Summary or Arbitrary Executions: Study on Targeted Killings," UN General Assembly, Human Rights Council, 28 May 2010, p. 23 [herein, Alston UN Report].

[16] Corn's Human Rights Article, p. 94.

[17] W. Hays Parks, "Direct Participation in Hostilities Study: No Mandate, No Expertise, and Legally Incorrect," *New York University Journal of International Law and Politics*, Vol. 42 (Spring 2010), p. 780.

professional warfighters over centuries.[18] These principles include Distinction, Military Necessity, Proportionality, and Humanity.

THE PRINCIPLE OF DISTINCTION[19]

At the center of the Geneva Conventions and its Additional Protocols is its "cardinal"[20] rule, the principle of distinction: "The parties to the conflict must at all times distinguish between civilians and combatants."[21] This principle provides that attacks against civilians are prohibited.[22] Civilians are defined in the negative as "all persons who are not members of State armed forces or organized armed groups of a party to the conflict are civilians and, therefore, entitled to protection against direct attack unless and for such time as they take a direct part in hostilities."[23] States are obligated never to make civilians the object of attack, thereby restricting the use of lethal force by the armed forces of any State.

THE PRINCIPLE OF MILITARY NECESSITY[24]

Distinction clarifies what one must do to qualify for the privilege of being authorized to use force, and military necessity identifies what violent powers a soldier is granted. In a nutshell, the principle of military necessity authorizes the combatant to do acts of violence against the enemy military that are needed to bring about the complete submission of that enemy and an end to the war.[25] Military necessity justifies actions, such as destroying and seizing

---

[18] The Lieber Code is often cited as the first documentation of the modern laws of war. This code was not a creative work, but rather the result of Francis Lieber working on a committee of military professionals to codify existing customary practice that had been developed over centuries.

[19] DoD Law of War Manual, para. 2.5 (2015).

[20] Advisory Opinion on the Legality of the Threat or Use of Nuclear Weapons, ICJ Reports 1996, 226, 257.

[21] The Public Committee Against Torture in Israel v. Israel, Judgment of the Supreme Court, A. Barak for the Court (December 11, 2005), para. 23.

[22] Protocol Additional to the Geneva Conventions of 12 August 1949, and Relating to the Protection of Victims of International Armed Conflicts, art 51(2), Dec. 12, 1977, 1125 U.N.T.S. 3 [herein Protocol I]; Protocol Additional to the Geneva Conventions of 12 August 1949, and Relating to the Protection of Victims of Non-International Armed Conflicts, art 13(2), Dec. 12, 1977, 1125 U.N.T.S. 609 [herein Protocol II]. The additional protocols have not been ratified by the United States, but the articles discussed in this paper are considered customary international law.

[23] Nils Melzer, International Committee on the Red Cross, Interpretive Guidance on the Notion of Direct Participation in Hostilities under International Humanitarian Law, adopted on February 26, 2009, International Review of the Red Cross, Vol. 90, Number 872 (December 2008), p. 1002. [ICRC Guidance].

[24] See DoD Law of War Manual, para. 2.2 (2020).

[25] Ibid.

persons and property. But military necessity does not allow the commander to depart from the law of war.

THE PRINCIPLE OF PROPORTIONALITY[26]

The principle of proportionality requires the anticipated result of an attack to bring about a military advantage exceeding the collateral damage to civilians and civilian property.[27] For example, a soldier blows up the enemy commander's car, purposefully killing him and knowingly killing his son who is riding with him, the attack would be legal under the law of war if the concrete military advantage gained by the commander's death outweighed the death of the innocent bystander. The soldier could never target the son, but under the principle of proportionality, his collateral death could be legally acceptable. Like military necessity, this concept of legally acceptable collateral damage is limited to the soldier.

THE PRINCIPLE OF HUMANITY[28]

This principle mandates that the soldier should not inflict unnecessary suffering, referred to as gratuitous violence, on the enemy. Although there is no definitive definition of unnecessary suffering, violence is forbidden if the infliction of suffering, injury, or destruction is unnecessary to accomplish a legitimate military purpose. In other words, this principle is inextricably linked to the principle of military necessity.

These four principles work together to allow a commander to execute the war within the confines of these customary and obligatory norms. The Principle of Military Necessity is authorizing, while the other three principles are constraining. The interface between these four principles can be difficult and challenging for even the most experienced commanders. The reality is that members of the public will second-guess commanders on the amount of force they use in conflict. There will be those who do not think enough force was used because the enemy escaped; while others will think too much force was used because there were civilian casualties. The considerations of how much force to use and when to use it are extremely complicated and require intelligence, training, and instinct. In the end, the subjective aspect of warfare is a reality, even in today's age of technology and precision.

The commander will be guided by experience and knowledge of the enemy. There is no substitute for good judgment. That judgment must be informed, however, by what the law requires and an understanding of the tactical and strategic risks of a particular course of action. Military lawyers are essential in today's asymmetric battlefield; they help the commander understand what

[26] Ibid., para. 2.4.

[27] Additional Protocol I, art. 52.

[28] DoD Law of War Manual, para. 2.3.

his legal responsibilities are and how to mitigate risks. This advice could be as varied as the appropriateness of targeting an individual; the use of certain munitions; the scope of a soldier's right of self-defense; the appropriate application for the rule of engagement; to the handling of a captured enemy belligerent.

In today's battlefield, one of the first questions commanders ask is: what are my legal authorities to use force against an enemy? The question is much more nuanced than one would think. It is not straightforward. Nevertheless, the baseline is the requirements set out in the law of war and its four principles. The biggest fault line in today's battlefields line is when the status of an individual is unknown—that is, the commander is not certain whether the encountered force has been declared an enemy, even though their conduct is hostile. What laws apply in this asymmetric setting?

This is no truer than when forces are deployed in peacekeeping operations. Does the commander use a human rights law-centered approach, which centers on the individual and would result in constraining the use of force, even though his soldiers would be at risk? Alternatively, does the commander use the law of war-centered approach, which centers on the state and would result in potentially expanding the use of force, even though civilians could be harmed? Professor Corn articulates the tension between these two bodies of law:

> Because th[e human-rights law] presumption is inconsistent with the underlying presumptions related to the use of force against operational opponents that qualify as lawful military objectives, human rights standards for the employment of force cannot be relied upon to define what constitutes an arbitrary deprivation of life inflicted upon such opponents.[29]

Which law you use can produce disparate outcomes. This reality plagues modern military forces on countless occasions. The commander must understand the applicable body of law. Many times, the determination is the *conduct* of the opposing forces in question. These real-time and evolving life-and-death decisions can be grounded by the advice of a military lawyer, who knows the law and can help the command apply it. This acknowledgment is reflected in Article 82, Additional Protocol I, which mandates that "the Parties to the conflict in time of armed conflict, shall ensure that legal advisors are available, when necessary, to advise military commanders at the appropriate level on the application of the Conventions and this Protocol and on the appropriate instructions to be given to the armed forces on this subject."[30]

The landscape of war is treacherous. States must always begin from the perspective that everyone is a civilian. The burden is on the commander, on behalf of the State, to establish if an individual is targetable; that is, in

[29] Corn's Human Rights Article, p. 104.
[30] Additional Protocol I, art. 82.

international-law speaking, a member of a hostile armed group; normally this can be as certained through a pattern of hostile conduct. A scenario best teases out the complexity of this decision. Assume the commander has been deployed to a peacekeeping operation in a hostile area. Only a hill separates the peacekeepers and the hostile force. There is an elder of the local town that appears to be a lookout for the hostile forces on the other side of the hill. What can the commander do? If the only intelligence that the commander has received is that the elder was once a lookout, without any other indicia of hostility toward the State's forces, the reasonable option for the commander is to resort to the law-enforcement paradigm, meaning the elder could be arrested, but he cannot be targeted.

If, on the other hand, the commander now learns that the elder's lookout function is continuous, then there is a greater degree of certainty that the elder could be targeted. If intelligence further shows the elder is informing the hostile group of the location of the state's military, then more evidence exists to target the elder. If you can establish that the elder is a member of the hostile group or at least receives instructions from the group on what to do next, then the commander can definitively conclude that the elder is targetable—the elder is an enemy; that is, a member of the hostile armed group.

Yet this is not the end of the analysis. At the time of using force, if the elder's conduct is hostile, then the commander must consider the four principles of the law of war.

- Is the elder targetable—distinction? Yes, if there is evidence that the elder is taking direct participation in hostilities. This will be based on the conduct of the elder and the intelligence received about the elder's intent.
- Is the use of force required to accomplish a lawful mission—military necessity? Yes, if the elder is conducting hostile acts or demonstrating hostile intent toward the commander's forces.
- Is the "the anticipated loss of life and damage to property incidental to attacks not be excessive in relation to the concrete and direct military advantage expect to be gained"—proportionality? This will depend on the surrounding environment and the military advantage to be gained. What if the elder is surrounded by children? A commander could get "yes" on targeting the elder, but the commander's proportionality decision is difficult and subjective. The commander, with the advice of his counsel, knows he cannot intentionally attack the children—that is forbidden by the law of war. But what is excessive and how will this one-act help bring the end to the war?
- Finally, is the act of violence by the commander inflicting gratuitous violence on the enemy—Humanity? The fact that there are children in the area might make the commander consider other options, but that assumes those options exist.

The commander makes many extremely important decisions—having a military legal advisor helps inform those decisions. There is an endless number of vignettes that could be proffered to show that warfare and the law are inextricably linked. As one commander quipped in Afghanistan, "going to war without a lawyer is like going into battle without a rifle."[31] War is violent and seems lawless, at times, but it is driven by legal principles that aspire to make a better and more lasting peace. Put differently, the law is steeped into warfare and, in turn, governs the amount of force a commander can use to accomplish a military mission. When the commander follows the law and can articulate how the law was applied, especially when results were less than optimal, like when there is a civilian casualty, then the commander's actions garner credibility. This credibility translates into confidence by the nation's citizenry. The results might not have always been ideal, but the fact that legal considerations and counsel were part of the decision made by the commander, makes the military more transparent and trusted.

The other function performed by a legal advisor on the commander's staff is assisting the commander with the good order and discipline of the forces. If the nation creates a code for military justice, then there will need to be ways to preserve evidence and ensure the accused soldier receives a fair trial. The military lawyer can advise the commander on how to deal with transgressions and if the decision is to send the soldier to trial, then the military lawyer is in a position to help the prosecutor with collecting evidence and ascertaining facts in the case. This investigative stage of any prosecution is the most prone to error—evidence is lost or tampered with; witnesses are unavailable; and forensic testing is not done because the crime occurred on foreign soil. There are other challenges with assembling a case against a soldier deployed on foreign soil, but having a military legal advisor to assist the command with making sure the command is not the impediment to a successful prosecution in itself.

PROFESSIONALISM: TRAINED SOLDIERS ARE ESSENTIAL

A structure both to ensure soldiers are held accountable and to allow commanders to have access to legal advice in some of the most difficult mission sets imaginable is necessary, but these initiatives will fail if the very members of the military are not professionals. Most countries in the African Union require training before deploying as part of an African Union (AU) or United Nations

---

[31] This quote was said by one of the author's senior commanders during a planning conference in 2013 when the author was a Staff Judge Advocate in Afghanistan. There is an excellent article about judge advocates in conflict: Steven Keeva, Lawyers in the War Room, American Bar Association Journal, December 1991, p. 52. In the article, General Colin Powell, the then-Chairman of the Joint Chiefs of Staff says when talking about Desert Strom (the campaign to remove Iraq from Kuwait in 1991), "Decisions were impacted by legal considerations at every level... Lawyers proved invaluable in the decision-making process."

(UN) task force for peacekeeping operations. Countries need to train soldiers on the basic building blocks, such as the law of war; that is, International Humanitarian Law, the law of human rights; that is, International Human Rights Law, and what it means to be a soldier; that is, professionalism. These foundational requirements need to be institutionalized from the highest level to the newly inducted private. It must be part of a military's culture. Without it, the military is nothing more than a cadre of individuals with weapons. In fact, some militaries shun this type of training or provide it to their senior ranks but not their rank-and-file foot soldier. The training to be a member of the profession of arms is as much a requirement of a private as it is for a general.

The reason is simple: civil–military relations. This relationship hinges on how civilian authority is established and maintained over the military. There must be an understanding within the ranks that there are legal, moral, and ethical restrictions on the military. In the United States, this relationship rests on professionalism. In Professor Samuel P. Huntington's landmark book, *The Soldier and The State*, Huntington posits that the military is professional because it possesses three characteristics: expertise in the use of violence, a sense of responsibility to the country's citizenry, and a sense of unity as soldiers.[32] The driving force behind professionalism stems from the soldier's central skill on behalf of the state: the management of violence. This professionalism begins with trust.

Trust is the bedrock of the profession of arms.[33] It must be inculcated in soldiers that their task is unique and the training they receive must incorporate the three characteristics outlined by Huntington. Trust manifests itself in two interrelated but distinct ways. First is the trust within the ranks—trust for the soldier's fellow soldiers, as well as trust of the soldier's commander. Second is the trust soldiers hold between themselves and the public they serve. It is the core to the public's legitimacy of the military.

The training received by a soldier throughout his or her career is critical to transform him or her from a civilian to a member of the profession of arms. The tactical training received by a soldier will range from how to shoot a weapon to how to build a fighting position to how to evade an enemy. The tactical level training that makes a civilian into a soldier is critical and gives the soldier expertise in the use of violence. But a soldier's sense of responsibility to the nation served, along with a sense of unity and pride to be a soldier, is strategic training.

The tactical training goes to how to be a soldier and to use force under the rules imposed by the state; the strategic training goes to why the individual is a soldier and whom the soldier is defending and why the soldier is committed

---

[32] Samuel P. Huntington, The Soldier and The State: The Theory and Politics of Civil-Military Relations (Belknap Press, 1957), Chapter 1.

[33] Charles D. Allen and William G. Braun, Trust: Implication for the Army Profession, Military Review, September–October 2013, p. 73.

to following the state's-imposed proscriptions on your use of force. It is, to some degree, a transformation. This transformation is accomplished, in part, by education and training. Underpinning any transformation is leadership by superiors. For the front-line soldier, this transformational training should be developed to concentrate on three areas: the soldier's role in society, the law of war, and the law of human rights.

Role of the Soldier

Every soldier needs training at the ground level of what the soldier's purpose is within society. This sounds basic, but numerous non-military personnel have the same conclusion: the average soldier's mindset is that he or she serves a particular militia, and not the nation as a whole. There is no way to give tangible evidence of this conclusion—since every nation/state is different— but the soldier must be inculcated with the notion that he or she is part of the nation's military. The training and education must emphasize that soldiers serve a unique role: on behalf of the state, they are given the unique authority to use force, and on occasion, lethal force. This license to use force, however, comes with heavy responsibilities. Outlining those responsibilities is critical. Those responsibilities can be bifurcated into two bodies of law: the law of war and the law of human rights.

The Law of War

Every military needs robust training in the law of war. This law is a compact the soldier has with the nation—it is not a compact between the soldier and the enemy, which is why the soldier must follow it even when the enemy does not. This training is not merely a PowerPoint presentation. This requires vignettes and case study-based instruction on the legal responsibilities of a soldier when he or she dons a uniform. Part of the training is why there are four principles behind the law of war and how these principles promote a meaningful peace at the end of conflict.

Acting within the law is a baseline for every soldier and is central to the soldier's professional ethos. American soldiers have annual training in law of war; this training needs to be based on real-life situations. It must be tailored to the missions that await the soldier. For example, if the soldier is about to deploy on a peacekeeping mission, the soldier should be trained on scenarios to help him decipher the complex environment he is about to enter. This is a model that African militaries may need to consider adopting and adapting to their respective situations while maintaining the spirit behind such training.

Law of Human Rights

Gloria Phiri and Chikondi Mandala have ably outlined the imperative to protect human and peoples' rights in Africa in Chapter 16. Along with the law of war, soldiers need to understand the law of human rights and what obligations the soldier has vis-à-vis civilians. The law is particularly important when soldiers are conducting operations internal to their State'sborders. These obligations and the responsibilities of what rights the individual citizen possesses should be taught interactively and, like the law of war instruction, made clear through vignettes and case studies. Soldiers must be taught that they are a reflection of their nation. Their conduct is magnified by every departure from what the law of human rights mandates. This training can also help exposesoldiers to how they can be held accountable for their transgressions.

These three areas are not an exclusive list; quite the contrary, there are many areas of training and education that can make the soldier better understand his profession. But as a guidepost, if the training focuses on the soldier's expertise in the use of violence, sense of responsibility to the country's citizenry, and sense of soldierly unity, then the first steps to professionalism have begun.

CONCLUSION

As stated at the outset, and also confirmed by Prince Bright Magiga in Chapter 11 and Kuwali in Chapter 27, a nation with a professional military, whose soldiers are accountable and whose commanders are properly advised, does not mean there will be peace and security. Without these three prongs, however, peace and security are simply not attainable. If these three prongs are addressed, they start to build a military that garners the trust and confidence of its citizens. The military is a protector, not a predator, because its soldiers are professionals and the public knows that if the soldier does something wrong, then the soldier will be held to account. Equally important are the actions of commanders who deploy on behalf of the State. If their actions are grounded in international legal norms, then they promote confidence in the rule of law.

The profession of arms is truly unique. For most nations, it is essential to their survival. In some nations, the military is respected; in others, it is feared. If one was to chart whether a state has (1) a form of a military justice code; (2) legal advisors for commanders; and (3) a promotion of professionalism, the continuum would go from respect (for those states that have each) to fear (for those that do not). You would also see the continuum of a military where its citizens run to its soldiers vice run from them. That African militaries need to seek to be trusted and respected is an issue that should go beyond rhetoric but be pursued with vigorous will by military leadership and embraced with passion by soldiers.

As a norm, in those states that respect their military, the degree of peace and security is higher than in those states that fear their military. Again, the recommendations in this chapter are not a panacea for peace and security, but they are a start if the political will is present.

CHAPTER 25

Addressing Youth Unemployment in Africa

Mphatso Jones Boti Phiri

INTRODUCTION

According to a UN Report on the youth global situation, 75 per cent of the world's one billion youth live in developing countries.[1] The African continent has a youth population of over 400 million aged between the ages of 15–35 years, according to the African Union report.[2] This youthful population calls for an immediate attention to ensure the achievement of peace, security, and socio-economic development within African states. The UN-Habitat's State of Urban Youth Report indicates that the youth demographic explosion in Africa has led to massive youth migration into urban areas, most of whom lack jobs and facilities to absorb the demographic shift.

---

[1] United Nations, *World Population Prospects 2019—Volume II: Demographic Profiles*. Produced by the Department of Economic and Social Affairs, Population Division. Sales No. E.20.XIII.8, p. 10. Available at: https://population.un.org/wpp/Publications/Files/WPP2019_Volume-II-Demographic-Profiles.pdf, see also United Nations World Youth Report 2020: Youth Social Entrepreneurship and the 2030 Agenda. Available at: www.un.org/development/desa/youth (Accessed 20 March 2021). The UN defined youth as all persons between the ages of 15 and 24 years.

[2] See: https://au.int/en/youth-development.

M. J. Boti Phiri (✉)
The Malawi Parliament, Lilongwe, Malawi

© The Author(s), under exclusive license to Springer Nature
Switzerland AG 2022
D. Kuwali (ed.), *The Palgrave Handbook of Sustainable Peace
and Security in Africa*, https://doi.org/10.1007/978-3-030-82020-6_25

The majority of the unemployed people in Africa are aged 15–24.[3] The lack of employment opportunities for youth has triggered underemployment, inequality, and marginalisation with these posing potential as significant security and development challenges in Africa. This chapter contends that the youth bulge provides a motivating factor for creativity and innovation. Furthermore, it provides an opportunity for growth and socio-economic development in developing countries. For instance, supporting entrepreneurship and agriculture in post-conflict countries can lead to peacebuilding and economic development. It is, however, noted that if youth unemployment is not addressed, the unprecedented high rates of youth unemployment have the potential to fuel extremism and political instability in the continent.

THE YOUTH CHALLENGE

A 2012 UN global population report predicts that the global population will grow to 9.6 billion people by 2050. The UN Economic Commission for Africa report indicates that, over 70 per cent of Africa's population is under the age of 30, and is expected to continue to grow younger for the next 20 years. Global estimates indicate that young people between 15 and 24 years of age are about 1.21 billion and account for 15.5 per cent of the global population. Projections further suggest that by 2030 the youth population will hit 1.29 billion (15.1 per cent of the world total) and almost 1.34 billion (13.8 per cent of the overall population) by 2050.[4]

The Sub-Saharan Africa has the youngest age distribution in global terms. With an average growth of 2.3 per cent annually from 2015 to 2020, "the total population of the least developed countries is growing 2.5 times faster than the total population of the rest of the world".[5] This indicates that the youth bulge will keep increasing posing global challenge that comes with youth unemployment. Research shows that most of the growing youth population are flowing into cities and it is estimated that African cities are absorbing 18 million people every year.[6] The number of young people in the continent is growing faster

---

[3] African Development Bank, *Enhancing Capacity for Youth Employment in Africa: Some Emerging Lessons*, Vol 2(2), December 2011.

[4] United Nations, *World Population Prospects 2019—Volume II: Demographic Profiles*. Produced by the Department of Economic and Social Affairs, Population Division. Sales No. E.20.XIII.8, p. 10. Available at: https://population.un.org/wpp/Publications/Files/WPP2019_Volume-II-Demographic-Profiles.pdf, see also United Nations World Youth Report 2020: Youth Social Entrepreneurship and the 2030 Agenda. Available at: www.un.org/development/desa/youth (Accessed 20 March 2021).

[5] United Nations, *World Population Prospects 2019: Highlights*. Produced by the Department of Economic and Social Affairs, Population Division. Sales No. E.19.XIII.4. Available at: https://population.un.org/wpp/Publications/Files/WPP2019_Highlights.pdf (Accessed 20 March 2021).

[6] Africa Center for Strategic Studies Report, UN-Habitat report on the state of African cities.

than anywhere else in the world.[7] The urban population in Sub-Saharan Africa has expanded by 600 per cent in the last 35 years, and this expansion shows no sign of shrinking.[8] At the same time, African cities have not developed necessary structures and institutions to accommodate this youth migration thereby creating a myriad of challenges.

The youth challenge has appealed to both global and continental interventions. Several tools have been developed at the continental level to accelerate inclusive youth development. One of them is the African Youth Charter. The African Union Heads of States and Governments endorsed the African Youth Charter (AYC) in 2006. The Charter is a political and legal document which serves as the strategic framework that gives direction for youth empowerment and development at continental, regional, and national levels. The AYC gives priority to youth development on the African Union's development agenda.

In 2009, the Assembly of Heads of States and Governments of the African Union declared the years 2009 to 2018 as the "Decade on Youth Development in Africa". An in-depth discussion on the African youth development decade is done later in the chapter. Another tool is the African Union Demographic Dividend (AUDD) Roadmap. The demographic dividend is the accelerated economic growth that may result from a decline in a country's birth and death rates and the subsequent change in the age structure of the population.[9] Through the AUDD, the African Union Commission (AUC) identified key pillars for increasing investments in youth, driving policy change, and setting member states on a path towards a prosperous future.[10]

The four AUDD pillars are: employment and entrepreneurship; education and skills development; health and well-being; rights, governance, and empowerment. An assessment of the cross-cutting issues from these four pillars indicates that African countries need to holistically address youth development by evaluating interrelated policies and programmes that may be based on comparative advantages at the national, regional, and continental level. From this backdrop, addressing African youth challenges require members states not to operate in isolation but pool resources together and rely on evidence-based solutions from across the continent.

While most African countries have made efforts to involve young people in political and decision-making processes through national youth parliaments, national youth councils, and youth appointments in executive positions, there is little evidence of strengthened and consolidated continental and regional

---

[7] Mohamed, A. (2014) Youth Unemployment: A Global Security Challenge. *Harvard International Review*, Vol. 36, No. 1 (Summer 2014), pp. 13–17. Available at: https://www.jstor.org/stable/43649240 (Accessed 22 November 2020).

[8] Ibid., p. 14.

[9] Definition provided in the policy brief distilled from the Status of African Youth Report (SoAYR) released in 2019 by the African Union Commission Data-driven policies.

[10] African Union Commission and Population Reference Bureau (2019). This report was jointly published by the African Union Commission (AUC), Department of Human Resources, Science and Technology and the Population Reference Bureau (PRB).

partnerships that have led to policy and programmes implementation that promote the youth lives and enhance their contribution to socio-economic development of the African countries.

The youth remain the poorest population globally and the problem is further exacerbated in conflict and post-conflict countries. For instance, in Somalia, the UNDP Human Development report of 2012 indicates that 67 per cent of youth in the country are unemployed, and in South Central Somalia, 87 per cent live in abject poverty. According to UNICEF, of the world's one billion slum dwellers, over 70 per cent are under the age of 30. Similarly, according to a World Population report, 72 per cent of urban residents in Sub-Saharan Africa live in slums. It is argued that young people are three times more likely to be unemployed than adults, and those working are often in low-skill jobs, underemployed, and in insecure jobs.[11] Most youth population lack the required qualifications, skills, or training to enable them get jobs in secure and formal sectors. Due to inadequate skills, most African youth engage in the informal sector, which accounts for 90 per cent of the jobs created in the African continent.[12] Research data indicates that globally, 300 million youths are classified as working poor with low wages.[13]

The Youth and Radical Political Mobilisation

Research has shown that global violent activities, crimes, drug use, and recruitment of drug traffickers and militias are rampant in slums and among the youth.[14] Security concerns resulting from youth bulges and related demographic factors are evident in contemporary conflicts.[15] As shown above, the high concentration of unemployed, disenfranchised youth in African in both rural and urban centres is a threat to peace and security. Explosive conditions such as bad governance already exist in most African countries that can cause political crisis, instability, and violent conflicts.

Many youth slum dwellers are marginalised, and their lives are characterised by uncertainty and despair often leading to gang violence and instability. The

[11] Ibid., 15, See also Peter Kenyon, "Partnerships for Youth Employment. A review of selected community-based initiatives," *International Labour Office, Youth Employment Programme*, 2009. Available at: http://www.ilo.org/public/libdoc/ilo/2009/109B09_97_engl.pdf.

[12] African Development Bank, *Enhancing Capacity for Youth Employment in Africa: Some Emerging Lessons*, Vol 2(2), December 2011, p. 3.

[13] International Labour Organisation (ILO) (2016) World Employment Social Outlook; Trends for Youth 2016. See also International Labour Organisation (2020) Global Employment Trends for Youth 2020: Technology and the Future of Jobs.

[14] Mohamed, A. (2014) Youth Unemployment: A Global Security Challenge. *Harvard International Review*, Vol. 36, No. 1 (Summer 2014), pp. 13–17. Available at: https://www.jstor.org/stable/43649240 (Accessed 22 November 2020).

[15] LaGraffe, Dan (2012) The Youth Bulge in Egypt: An Intersection of Demographics, Security, and the Arab Spring. *Journal of Strategic Security*, Vol. 5, No. 2 (Summer 2012), pp. 65–80.

African youth bulge coupled with political marginalisation and despair paints a grim picture of African peace, stability, and development. Scholars have shown that political opinions of the unemployed youth tend to significantly support radicalisation and revolutionary political ideas.[16] Additionally, there is an increasing lack of political trust among the youth.[17] From this backdrop, youth unemployment has significant implications to peace and security and economic development.

CONSEQUENCES OF YOUTH UNEMPLOYMENT ON DEMOCRATIC CONSOLIDATION IN AFRICA

It has been argued that unemployed people are often frustrated with political elites and as a result tend to develop negative views on how democracy and capitalist societies work.[18] Unemployment in Africa is mainly caused by low-level industrialisation, governments remain the biggest employers in African economies. The remaining significant population is engaged in peasant rain-fed agriculture or other forms of informal economy. As a result of this, a huge population depends on the state, thereby creating a powerful manipulative government leading to a toxic political cycle of hope, elections, and frustration. Additionally, such economies have exacerbated the culture of African patronage politics that has painted an unattractive picture of democracy.

From this background, there has been an increasing support for welfare state in most in the African continent. While some studies have found a positive link between unemployment and public support for welfare policies,[19] most governments in Sub-Saharan Africa have been architects and supporters of such policies, mostly with the aim of manipulating voters and winning elections. It is, however, important to note that most African economies have small tax base to support welfare policies due to limited industrial development and high unemployment. Consequently, political elites have crafted a cartel built on corruption, intimidation, and limited political space for effective democracy. The manipulative political agenda setting has contributed to high youth unemployment levels and disenfranchised societies. In this light, the lack of democratic consolidation has significantly led to youth unemployment and limited space for constructive political engagement.

[16] Bay, A.H. and Blekesaune, M. (2002) Youth, Unemployment and Political Marginalization. *International Journal of Social Welfare*, Vol. 11, No. 2, pp. 132–139.

[17] Afrobarometer Round 7 survey in Malawi: State of the nation: Malawians' reflections on political governance. Available at: https://afrobarometer.org/online-data-analysis (Accessed 26 March 2021).

[18] Bay, A.H. and Blekesaune, M (2002) Youth, Unemployment and Political Marginalization. *International Journal of Social Welfare*, Vol. 11, No. 2, pp. 132–139.

[19] Blekesaune, M. (2007) Economic Conditions and Public Attitudes to Welfare Policies. *Europe Sociological Review*, Vol. 23, No. 3, pp. 393–403. See also Blekesaune, M. and Quadagno, J. (2003) Public Attitudes Towards Welfare State Policies: A Comparative Analysis of 24 Nations. *European Sociological Review*, Vol. 19, No. 5, pp. 415–427.

The Role of Governments in Addressing African Youth Unemployment

African Youth Decade 2009–2018 Plan of Action under the theme; "Accelerating Youth Empowerment for Sustainable Development" clearly appreciates the emergent youth bulge and calls for their integration in order to fully realised its demographic advantage. The Plan of Action appeals for mobilisation and empowerment into peace and development agenda of African states. It recognises the youth as an essential pillar in creating a strong and accountable governance structure anchored on participation and youth investment. The Youth Decade Plan of action is one of the important documents that require further scrutiny in order to appreciate the continental approach to youth unemployment and the role of African member states.

The objectives of the Youth Decade Plan of Action are[20]:

- *To serve as a road map on the accelerated implementation of African Youth Charter (AYC);*
- *To mainstream and operationalize the implementation of the AYC with a youth perspective in financing and monitoring African development goals and indicators;*
- *To establish a benchmark of standards, indicative criteria and accountability in design, implementing and monitoring of youth development policies, programmes and activities in Africa.*

These objectives are further followed by clear expected outcomes which are:

- *Enhanced capacity of member states to develop and implement comprehensive, integrated and cross-sector Youth development policies and plans;*
- *Youth perspectives are effectively mainstreamed in the design, implementation and monitoring of sustainable development goals and priorities;*
- *Increased investment in youth development programmes and activities linked to the assessment of development targets;*
- *Resource requirement and mobilization for Youth development at all levels is based on evidence and results;*
- *The Youth Decade Plan of Action is adopted as framework for funding and evaluation of youth empowerment and development policies, programmes and activities on the continent.*

The implementation of the Youth Decade Plan of Action requires comprehensive research-based solutions. The need for evidence-based approaches in designing youth development initiatives has been stressed by the AUC through the Status of African Youth Report 2019 (SoAYR). Such approaches will assure that young people in Africa enjoy quality education, good health,

[20] African Union Commission 2011. See more at: www.africa-youth.org; www.au.int.

financial independence, and political participation. By doing this, the African member states will directly address governance deficits, reduce the negative consequences of youth unemployment and contribute to stability, peace, and security on the continent.

Data from the Status of African Youth Report 2019 indicates a mixed bag of progress and decline of youth status in Africa. The data is significant for policy decisions in peace and security as it reflects on the employability of the youth on the job market. As shown above, research indicates that in 2015, 75 per cent of the total African population were the youth ages 15–24. With such a large population of young people, the political, peace and security landscape of Africa will likely be determined by how the youth are utilised. From this backdrop, supportive policies and programmes for youth development are critical in addressing African security challenges. It is argued "that investing in young people will not only transform their lives but also transform communities, nations, and the continent—helping to break intergenerational poverty, address inequalities, and create a stable, peaceful, and prosperous Africa".[21]

Policy brief on Africa's Future Youth and the Data adopted from the SoAYR indicates that at the continental level, youth employment and entrepreneurship in Africa showed improvement from 2013 to 2017. This positive outlook suggests improving quality of life for young Africans. A rapidly growing youth workforce in Africa needs targeted interventions for high-quality job growth and economic opportunities. Available indicators show that regions across Africa have made substantial improvements in offerings for youth education and skills development. Youth enrolment in technical and vocational education and training (TVET) increased from 2012 to 2017, rising from 1.4 to 2.4 per cent.[22]

This optimism is, however, curtailed by the worsening trends in the rate of youth unemployment and the rate of youth not in education, employment, or training (NEET). From 2013 to 2017, the total rate of unemployed youth across Africa increased from 16.8 to 17.4 per cent. Among youth not in education, employment, or training, the continental rate increased significantly from 19.4 to 27.7 per cent from 2013 to 2017.[23]

These continental trends on the rate of youth unemployment and NEET are a significant concern to peace and security and governance policymakers.

[21] African Union Commission and Population Reference Bureau (2019) *Policy Brief Africa's Future Youth and the Data Defining Their Lives*, September 2019, p. 4. See also Office of the Special Advisor on Africa (OSAA), "Youth Empowerment," accessed at: https://un.org/en/africa/osaa/peace/youth.shtml.

[22] World Bank, "Databank: Education Statistics," available at: https://databank.worldbank.org/source/education-statistics-%5E-all-indicators/Type/TABLE/preview/on (Accessed 24 March 2021). See also *Policy Brief Africa's Future Youth and the Data Defining Their Lives*, September 2019. Across regions, Central Africa attained the highest combined rate of young people enrolled in TVET programmes over time, averaging 3.8 per cent from 2012 to 2017.

[23] African Union Commission and Population Reference Bureau (2019) *Policy Brief Africa's Future Youth and the Data Defining Their Lives*, September 2019, p. 4.

While the regional data illuminate differences between Regional Economic Communities (RECs)[24] there are common trends of underemployment resulting in increased number of working poor youth.

Challenges in Addressing Youth Unemployment

An assessment of the status of the youth in African members states indicates that they still face a lot of challenges in the areas of education, entrepreneurship, skills development, sustainable livelihoods, and youth unemployment, participation in decision-making, health, gender inequalities, migration, and conflicts. While several policy decisions on education and employment have been undertaken to address the problem, they have not been affectively implemented.[25]

In Sub–Saharan Africa structural barriers make it difficult to improve the youth employment and entrepreneurship opportunities. Slow economic development, inequality, and political instability undermine economic and social prospects for youth. The persistent and wide-ranging challenges facing the African youth necessitate out of the box strategies in addressing this problem. The African way of life and culture provides a significant social capital that can be explored. The youth social entrepreneurship has been suggested as a valuable part.[26] The core elements of social entrepreneurship, drawn from Bidet and Spear (2003),[27] indicates that these are initiatives that are launched formally and informally by individual(s) and team(s) with a central social mission that explicitly aim to benefit the community, and with limited profit distribution among the teams or individuals of the enterprise.

Internal processes such as decision-making and human resource practices are not based on capital ownership but form an integral part of the social value proposition. An example of such initiatives has been the community

---

[24] The AU has several subregional groups or RECs, some of which have developed their own subregional peace and security arrangements. These include Arab Maghreb Union (UMA); Intergovernmental Authority on Development (IGAD); Community of Sahel-Saharan States (CEN-SAD); the East African Community (EAC); Economic Community of West African States (ECOWAS); Southern African Development Community (SADC); and the Economic Community of Central African States (ECCAS). See *Policy Brief Africa's Future Youth and the Data Defining Their Lives*, September 2019, p. 5. For example, in 2017 West Africa had the lowest youth unemployment rate at just over 8 per cent but the highest rate of youth working poor (42.6 per cent). Furthermore, West Africa and Central Africa had the highest rates of child labour in 2017, at more than 30 per cent. In contrast, Southern Africa and North Africa had the highest rates of youth unemployment in 2017, at 32.3 per cent and 30.5 per cent, respectively. In 2017, Southern Africa had the highest rate of NEET youth (35.6 per cent), and North Africa had the highest rate of long-term youth unemployment (64.0 per cent).

[25] African Union Commission 2011. See more at www.africa-youth.org; www.au.int.

[26] United Nations 2020. Youth Social Entrepreneurship and the 2030 Agenda. Available at: www.un.org/development/desa/youth (Accessed 20 March 2021).

[27] Bidet, Eric and Roger Spear (2003) The Role of Social enterprise in European labour markets. EMES Network Working Paper No. 03/10.

carpentry workshops and construction companies that train youth people and provide entrepreneurship opportunities.[28] It is proposed that African member states should put deliberate policies that can accelerate the implementation of youth social entrepreneurship as a way of reducing youth unemployment. Research indicates that most African economies are characterised by excessive dependence on primary commodity exports, subsistence agriculture, and capital-intensive extractive industries, all of which have low potential for job creation for the youth.[29] Investing in the construction industry and most labour-intensive food crops such as fruits and vegetables would be one way of alleviating youth unemployment.

Resource mobilisation remains a key challenge in the implementation of appropriate initiatives and programmes in addressing youth unemployment in Africa. African states should give the necessary and pragmatic modalities for the funding initiatives such as youth fund at national, regional, and continental levels. The prevailing and emergent global challenges like Corona Virus disease (COVID-19) and other trends in international relations continue to affect level of support from Development Partners and stakeholders in youth pragmas funding. Additionally, the continuing funding fatigue from the donor community requires African member states to have political will and build capacity to support local result-based youth development programmes and activities and youth-serving organisations.

The growing interest by African states in developing and implementing strategies and mechanisms for a strengthened Public–Private-Partnership (PPP), provides an opportunity for eradicating youth unemployment on the continent. Growing the indigenous private sector growth that would create youth employment and youth-focused human capital development within the PPP arrangement would provide domestic solutions to youth unemployment.

Literature shows that employment provides economic and social well-being and the lack of it can lead to a vicious cycle of exclusion, poverty, and ill-health.[30] As indicated above, African governments have traditionally been significant economic actors and the largest providers of employment in construction industries and public service. In this light, African governments need to bear the burden of not only providing conducive environment for foreign direct investments, but also adopting deliberate policies that alleviate the liabilities of youth unemployment.

As noted above, many young people lack relevant skills, and most of them are unskilled. However, technical training centres for the youth skills

---

[28] United Nations 2020. Youth Social Entrepreneurship and the 2030 Agenda. Available at: www.un.org/development/desa/youth (Accessed 20 March 2021).

[29] ILO, 2011. Global Employment Trends, International Labour Organization.

[30] Tor Jakobsen, G. and Listhaug, Ola (2012) Issue Ownership, Unemployment and Support for Government Intervention. *Work, Employment & Society*, Vol. 26, No. 3 (June 2012), pp. 396–411.

remain low in Southern Africa compared to West Africa.[31] The technical colleges require necessary technology to provide relevant skills that match the demand in the labour market. It is noted that weak institutional capacity and lack of adequate infrastructure (including Information and Communication Technologies), have hampered the creation of jobs for the youth.[32] Malawi, for instance, has significantly lugged behind in technical training with few technical colleges developed since 1980.

The African Peace and Security Architecture (APSA) established in 2002 and the subsequent institutions such as an African Standby Force (ASF) have mainly occupied the AUC activities than youth unemployment. Additionally, the Continental Early Warning System (CEWS) has been biased to military component without much focus in addressing root causes of conflicts that include youth unemployment. It is argued in this chapter that youth unemployment should be added to the more "classical threats" to peace and security in the continent.

Youth unemployment in Africa presents deeper structural challenges that can proliferate instability through terrorism, violent extremism, and organised crime. The disenfranchised youth are easily recruited into terrorist organisations causing significant threats to security.[33] A comprehensive approach to peace and security in Africa requires a broad regional policy framework that addresses different aspects of youth unemployment. Conflict prevention in Africa must take into account the pressing issue of youth unemployment. Although the AUC has developed tools aimed at addressing youth unemployment, thereby addressing peace and security threats, most of its attention has been on reactive instruments for peace and stability.

CONCLUSION

The problem of youth unemployment is multifaceted and structural in nature and hence requires government strategic efforts. It is argued that youth employment should be treated as a core strategic objective of development policy and be reflected in usual strategic planning processes such as poverty

---

[31] For instance, in Malawi most technical colleges have not expanded for the past 40 years and those that were functional then are not utilised to their full potential and lack any new technology. Instead new community technical colleges have emerged but are largely ill-equipped for twenty-first century job requirements and technology.

[32] ILO, 2011. Global Employment Trends, International Labour Organization. See also African Development Bank, *Enhancing Capacity for Youth Employment in Africa: Some Emerging Lessons*, Vol 2(2), December 2011, p. 4.

[33] There is significant evidence on the linkages between youth unemployment and recruitment in terrorist organisations like Al Shabab in Somalia and Boko Haram in Nigeria.

reduction strategy papers, national security strategy, and overall country strategy papers.[34]

Issues affecting youths are diverse and cannot be addressed in isolation. African member states need innovative, multisectoral approaches that holistically address youth experiences—across the employment, education, health, and governance sectors by creating an enabling environment. Several implementation challenges have been highlighted and includes lack of resources and capacity, limited commitment by Governments and other stakeholders, lack of existence of such initiatives and lack of an effective follow-up mechanism for implementation, monitoring, and evaluation.

The loose connection between the African Union Commission and African Member States is one of the biggest challenges in the implementation of the AU frameworks. The African continent still lacks an integrated, interrelated, and coherent implementation and follow-up at national, regional, and continental levels of Summit Decisions. The AU Member States and Regional Economic Communities have the primary responsibility to ensure implementation. However, their relationship with the African Union Commission has at times been marred with needless unproductive competitive supremacy.[35] This makes it difficult for the African Union Commission to play an important role in reviewing progresses in the implementation of its tools at all levels including the youth charter.

---

[34] African Development Bank, *Enhancing Capacity for Youth Employment in Africa: Some Emerging Lessons*, Vol 2(2), December 2011, p. 3.

[35] See Boti-Phiri, M.J. (2018) *Leadership, regionalisation of peace operations and conflict mediation: African Union and Southern African Development Community in perspective.* PhD Thesis, Coventry University.

CHAPTER 26

Increasing the Role of Women in Peace and Security in Africa

Thomasin Tumpale Gondwe and Laika Nakanga

INTRODUCTION

It has been almost 20 years since the adoption of the landmark Resolution 1325 on women, peace, and security by the UN Security Council. UN Resolution 1325 brought an awareness and enlightenment on the significance of the involvement of women in peace and security-related matters. It explicitly stresses the role of women in preventing, resolving conflict, and peacekeeping. It therefore particularly expressed the Council's willingness to incorporate a gender perspective into peacekeeping missions. Twenty years ago this was a progressive step in ensuring peace and security in the whole world and of particular interest Africa cognizant of the fact that Africa is a continent which has been mostly affected by both internal and international armed conflict.[1]

These conflicts adversely affect women in many ways calling for the need to view enhancing peace and security through a gender-based lens. Since the landmark Resolution 1325, several resolutions have been passed to ensure that more angles tackling women, peace, and security are addressed. The aim is to ensure that women are not left behind in the quest for peace and security. Whether it is protecting women whose rights are affected by the conflicts or

[1] Dan Kuwali, Catherine Nakirya and Grace Amuge, "Protection from Sexual and Gender-Based Violence in Africa", in Dan Kuwali and Frans Viljoen (eds.), *Africa and the Responsibility to Protect: Article 4 (h) of the African Union Consitutive Act* (London: Routledge, 2014), pp. 167–184.

T. T. Gondwe · L. Nakanga (✉)
Chancellor College, University of Malawi, Zomba, Malawi

© The Author(s), under exclusive license to Springer Nature Switzerland AG 2022
D. Kuwali (ed.), *The Palgrave Handbook of Sustainable Peace and Security in Africa*, https://doi.org/10.1007/978-3-030-82020-6_26

445

involving women in effecting peace and security the underlying principle is the involvement of women.

It must not be forgotten that women have a role to play in conflict as agents of peace or wagers of war. Recognizing that women have a role to play in peace and security, this chapter takes a special focus on the role women play in peace operations in Africa. The discussion analyzes the role of women peacekeepers, female engagement teams, and military gender advisors. It further examines the challenges encountered and proposes the best practices, recommendations on increasing the role of women in ensuring peace, and security in Africa.

LEGAL FRAMEWORK ON WOMEN, PEACE, AND SECURITY

In order to ensure that women are involved in implementing peace and security, the United Nations (UN) and the African Union (AU), and other regional groupings have developed a legal framework consisting of legal instruments directly dealing with issues affecting women but at the same time ensuring that women are used as agents of peace through their involvement at different levels, be it decision-making down to the female peacekeeper on the ground.

The ground for women involvement was first laid down through the 1979 Convention on the Elimination of all Forms of Discrimination Against Women (CEDAW) by the UN General Assembly. This treaty provided for rights for women and called for all the 189 states that ratified to recognize and implement the rights of women as well as their involvement in different matters that affect them. This was followed by the 1995 Beijing Declaration and Platform for Action which was built on CEDAW and formalized obligations on Women's rights. There are ten resolutions that make up the Women, Peace, and Security Agenda in the UN Security Council beginning with Resolution 1325 (2000) which has framed the agenda for the past twenty years.

UNITED SECURITY COUNCIL RESOLUTION 1325 (2000)

This resolution on women, peace, and security, in particular, expresses the Council's willingness to incorporate a gender perspective into peacekeeping missions, calling on all parties to protect women and girls from gender-based violence and to put an end to impunity for such crimes. The resolution recognized the urgent need to mainstream a gender perspective into peacekeeping operations.[2] It is the first resolution adopted by the UN Security Council which dealt specifically with gender issues and women's experiences in conflict and post-conflict situations and the central role of women in conflict prevention and peacebuilding.[3] For this reason, UN Security Council Resolution

[2] S/RES 1325 (2000), Resolution 1325 (2000), adopted by the Security Council at its 4213th meeting, on 31 October 2000, para. 8.

[3] Implementation of the Women, Peace and Security Agenda in Africa, African Union December 2019, p. 1.

(UNSCR) 1325 is considered the pinnacle of the global women, peace, and security (WPS) agenda.

Resolution 1325 is the focal point for galvanizing worldwide efforts of dealing with many challenges that women face in situations of conflict. It established four pillars of prevention, participation, protection, and peace-building and recovery enabling women to be used as tools for peace sustainment.[4] The important role of women involvement was further stressed through this resolution calling for equal participation and full involvement of women in the maintenance and promotion of peace and security all over the world.

United Security Council Resolution 1820 (2008)

This resolution addressed sexual violence in conflict and post-conflict situations, asked the Secretary-General for a report on the systematic use of sexual violence in conflict areas and proposals for strategies to minimize the prevalence of such acts with benchmarks for measuring progress.

United Security Council Resolution 1888 (2009)

This resolution strengthened efforts to end sexual violence against women. This resolution urged member states, UN bodies, donors, and civil society to ensure that women's protection and empowerment are taken into account during post-conflict needs assessment and planning and children in armed conflict.

United Security Council Resolution 1960 (2010)

This resolution established monitoring, analysis, and reporting mechanism on conflict-related sexual violence, called upon parties to armed conflict to make specific, time-bound commitments to prohibit and punish sexual violence, and asked the Secretary-General to monitor those commitments.

United Security Council Resolution 2106 (2013)

This resolution focused on accountability for perpetrators of sexual violence in conflict and stressed women's political and economic empowerment.

United Security Council Resolution 2122 (2013)

This resolution addressed the persistent gaps in the implementation of the women, peace, and security agenda.

---

[4] S/RES 1325 (2000), Resolution 1325 (2000), adopted by the Security Council at its 4213th meeting, on 31 October 2000, para. 5.

United Security Council Resolution 2422 (2015)

This resolution addressed women's roles in countering violent extremism and terrorism. Considering the changing landscape and emerging conflicts in the past years, this addresses the roles women can play in preventing and countering violent extremism and terrorism.

United Security Council Resolution 2282 (2016)

This resolution reaffirms the important role of women in peacekeeping and takes note of the substantial link between women's full and meaningful involvement in efforts to prevent, resolve, and rebuild from conflict. It further stresses the importance of women's equal participation in all efforts for the maintenance and promotion of peace and security and the need to increase women's role in decision-making with regard to conflict prevention and resolution and peacebuilding. This resolution gives a broad spectrum in which women's presence is supposed to be recognized for enhancement of peace and security. It calls for women's involvement at prevention level, resolving of the conflict as well as rebuilding level after the wreck of conflict.

Implementation of Resolutions on Women Peace and Security

The UN Security Council Resolutions which have been adopted since 2000 that is UNSCR 1325 (2000), 1820 (2008), 1888 (2009) 1889 (2010), 1960 (2011), 2106 (2013), 2122 (2013), 2242 (2015), 2282 (2016), 2467 (2019), and 2493 (2019) are referred to as the Women, Peace, and Security Agenda. These form a path to a more inclusive process of women in peace and security globally. Implementing Women, Peace, and Security Agenda through National Action Plan and other means is a responsibility of UN member states. Therefore, member states are called to develop policies that provide guidance on how to best raise issues affecting women such as women's participation, sexual and gender-based violence to mention a few. It is however observed that the lack of women's meaningful participation in peace processes presents a major challenge to global efforts to resolve violent conflicts. Despite the states committing themselves and urging others to ensure that women are included in peacemaking, evidence shows that calls for women's meaningful participation frequently go unanswered.

It was noted that in 2015, despite 15 years since the adoption of Resolution 1325 more than half of the peace agreements continued to make no mention of women, UN military peacekeepers remain 97 percent male and 2 percent of aid to peace and security in 2014 targeted gender equality as a principal objective. Four years down the lane not much significant change has been made. According to the S/2019/800, Women and Peace and Security

Report of the Secretary-General women still make up only 4.2 percent of military personnel in the UN peacekeeping missions, fewer than 20 percent of all Security Council Resolutions in 2018 contained references to the importance of and the need to ensure fundamental rights and freedoms for civil society, women's groups and women human rights defenders and in 2018 only 28 percent of humanitarian needs overviews articulated the differentiated impact faced by women and girls in crises.[5]

What is worse is the fact that despite the sound international framework with regards to inclusion of women, the progress is so slow and being championed by member states with less numbers adopting national action plans on women and peace and security and providing less funding to such causes. It was observed that only 41 percent of member states have adopted national action plans targeting women and peace and security and just 22 percent of all plans included a budget for the implementation thereof at the time of the adoption.[6] Eighty countries worldwide have adopted national actional plans and of these, about 24 are African countries including Central Africa Republic, South Sudan, Democratic Republic of the Congo, and Ivory Coast representing about 30 percent. The adoption of national action plans while a step in the right direction, has a tendency to be mere window dressing for the international community and does not reflect the attitudes of various countries in relation to the WPS agenda. It remains a fact that many countries remain patriarchal with women being denied access to leadership roles in peace times and being marginalized during conflict and the peacebuilding process. The absence of meaningful women participation in the peacebuilding process should not be overlooked especially when it is considered that peace talks and treaties have a higher chance of success when there is active participation of women during peace negotiations.[7]

In Africa, over the past 20 years, inter-state armed and violent conflicts have significantly diminished. Nonetheless, the continent also continues to witness intra-state conflicts and new security threats with spate of violence that have undoubtedly increased in historic levels and impacted women in disproportionate ways.[8] With this going on it is sad to note that women remain significantly underrepresented in the peace process. According to the UN Secretary-General's Report on WPS for 2018, between 1990 and 2017, women comprised only 1 percent of mediators, 8 percent of negotiators, and 5

[5] S/2019/800, Women and Peace and Security, Report of the Secretary General, on 9th October 2019, para. 4.

[6] S/2019/800, Women and Peace and Security, Report of the Secretary General, on 9th October 2019, para. 4.

[7] Data from UN Women Facts and Figures: Peace and Security accessed 30 September 2020.

[8] Implementation of the Women, Peace and Security Agenda in Africa, African Union December 2019, p. 2.

percent of witnesses and signatories. There is a lack of recognition of women's involvement and contribution at all levels of conflict prevention.

Despite the existence of strong, progressive, and articulated African Continental policies, strategies, and action plans on women, peace, and security, women and girls continue to bear the blunt of conflicts in Africa and remain victims of sexual violence and other forms of abuses and are still unrepresented in peace processes of all levels; local, national and continental.[9] A growing body of evidence shows that perhaps the greatest and most underutilized tool for successfully building peace is the meaningful inclusion of women.

Collectively, the UN, member states, regional organizations, and other actors supporting peace processes are not on track to attain sufficient concrete progress in the area of women and peace and security agenda.[10] One may argue that implementation is curtailed by some practical challenges including entrenched patriarchal attitudes in the national attitudes especially with regard to the participation of women in the political arena which automatically make it difficult for women to be participants at peace negotiation meetings, grassroot peace solutions, and at international levels. Another practical challenge is a lack of resources for advancing the WPS agenda, lack of systems in most post-conflict societies for example judicial systems and accountability mechanisms to ensure that perpetrators of sexual violence are held to account.

In the absence of a robust civil society, governments may not be held accountable to implement the resolutions. Conflicting priorities between non-state actors and governments concerning the implementation of the WPS agenda remain a problem. In post-conflict societies governments tend not to treat the WPS agenda as a priority preferring infrastructure restoration and development and reviving economies over continuing gender-based and sexual violence against women and girls this coupled with a shortage of operational ideas on how to adopt and implement the WPS agenda impede the attainment of peace. There is a need to address the lack of women's inclusion in conflict prevention, crisis management, and post-conflict reconstruction.

WHAT IS THE ROLE OF WOMEN IN PEACE AND SECURITY PROCESS?

In line with the WPS Agenda, women are to be included, have equal participation and full involvement in all efforts for prevention of conflicts, promotion of peace, and security with the end result of maintaining peace. In referring to security, one takes notice that security deals with human intent and actions to intentionally cause harm, acts of violence are the consequence of security threats that stem from armed conflict, terrorism, violent civil unrest,

---

[9] As above.

[10] S/2019/800, Women and Peace and Security, Report of the Secretary General, on 9th October 2019, para. 14.

and crime.[11] It is the call to African States as member of the UN to ensure increased representation of women at all decision-making levels in national, regional, and international institutions and mechanisms for the prevention, management and resolution of conflict.[12] The inclusion of women in dialogue, negotiation, and peace process is important because women are differently embedded in society than men. More inclusive processes can contribute to more comprehensive agreements that better integrate and reflect the concerns of the broader society.

ROLE OF WOMEN IN PREVENTION OF CONFLICT: MEDIATION AND NEGOTIATION PROCESS

The inclusion of women in the peace process should be from the very onset of a conflict brewing. Sadly, this has not been the case. An analysis of women's roles in major peace processes worldwide conducted between 1992 and 2017 found that women comprised only 3 percent of Chief Mediators, 3 percent of witnesses and signatories and 9 percent of negotiators.[13] This is hardly surprising considering that peace negotiation teams comprise high-ranking political and military officials and women are systematically excluded from such spaces. Unless governments make deliberate policies to include women in the political sphere through quotas and other such inclusion policies women will remain at the margin of peace mediations and solutions.

The inclusion of women in government at positions of influence ensures that women voices are heard and laws and policies are put in place to better serve the education, protection, and empowerment of women to the benefit of the WPS agenda. This is because laws and policies are streamlined to include a gender mainstreaming component and deal with pertinent issues faced by women. This is not to say men are incapable of implementing policies and laws which advance the WPS agenda, however, male champions while aware of the challenges faced by women and do their best to alleviate these challenges are still privy to male privilege and cannot fully understand the experiences of marginalization, abuse, and second class treatment of women.

A look at the traditional sequence of process in which a cease-fire is negotiated first, followed by negotiation on a political settlement, one is likely to observe that women will unlikely be involved. Most are the cases whereby cease-fires are negotiated by arms-bearing groups and military expertise of which most women do not partake since they have not risen that far in rank to be considered experts and even where women have risen in rank there is

[11] Carlos Alberto dos Santos Cruz Report: Improving Security of United Nations Peacekeepers: We need to change the way we are doing business, 2017, p. 2.

[12] S/RES 1325 (2000), Resolution 1325 (2000), adopted by the Security Council at its 4213th meeting, on 31 October 2000, para. 11.

[13] UN Women, Council on Foreign Relations, "Women's Participation in Peace Process", www.cfr.org.

still inequality between men and women of the same rank with most women being entrusted to administrative rather than combat roles even where they have undergone the same training as men.

Further, in most militaries, women have been recently recruited into the military as late as 1999 in the case of Malawi and 2006 in the case of Israel. Consequently, women hardly find influence and footing in such scenarios. This is despite the fact that women have often played militant roles in various armed conflicts. There is a need to stop viewing women merely as victims in armed conflict and acknowledge the combative, advisory, and strategic roles that women play in the military. Unfortunately, the narrative of women as victims is deeply entrenched in the psyche of most societies and unless there is a deep reset in the attitudes of society this will continue to be the case to the detriment of durable and sustainable peace.

It is observed that women mostly tend to be involved in discussions relating to humanity, economic, social but are rarely engaged in security or political negotiations or mediations. For example in the Central African Republic, the peace and reconciliation process has been marked by a low rate of women's participation that the joint advocacy of the United Nations Multidimensional Integrated Stabilization Mission in the Central African Republic, the African Union, and other partnerships had to push for the inclusion of women leaders for the first time in the direct peace talks between the Government and non-state armed groups, which were led by the African Union in Khartoum in February 2019.[14] One way of ensuring that women are involved during mediation is by increasing women advisors to the mediators and also encouraging them to take a direct part in the mediation process. This is very important because due to the higher power and influence of mediators to the extent that if women are not involved in talks, there is a higher likelihood, at, the minimum, of downplaying and at the maximum, ignoring the issues that affect women in the course of the mediation.

Only 18 percent of peace agreements signed between 1990 and 2015 make reference to women.[15] This shows that the inclusion of gender perspective in peace process is still lacking. Thus, in order to ensure a gender perspective is included in peace agreements, this should form the part of the negotiation and feed into the conflict analysis stage and in the early phases of negotiation.

There is a need for women's meaningful participation in formal and informal peace negotiations. When women are involved at the mediation level, it ensures gender diversity in the peace process thereby enhancing sustainable outcomes due to the fact that diverse needs of the population are considered and taken into account. Women's meaningful participation in negotiations

---

[14] S/2019/800, Women and Peace and Security, Report of the Secretary General, on 9th October 2019, para. 20.

[15] Bell, Christine "Text and Context: Evaluating Peace Agreements for Their Gender Perspective" UN Women, 2015. https://wps.unwomen.org/pdf/research/Bell/EN.pdf.

entails having a good representation of women at negotiating tables, establishing links to women's peace-building activities, and gender mainstreaming negotiations. This allows for more perspectives to be brought into the management and prevention of the conflict. Women are known to have leverage in their communities on disputing parties, and are often able to intervene informally and have impact. A study investigating 82 peace agreements in 42 armed conflicts between 1989 and 2011 found that peace agreements with women signatories are associated with durable peace.[16]

All the same, this paper argues that it is not sufficient to only focus on increasing the number of women at peace negotiation and mediation tables, but also it is necessary to integrate a gender perspective by ensuring men are aware of what gender mainstreaming is all about because surely not all women have a gender perspective and not all men lack it. Therefore, the best strategy is to increase gender expertise of the teams involved in the negotiations and mediation through training and coaching. Enhancing gender-sensitive mediation at the international, regional, and national level is a progressive step in the Women, Peace, and Security Agenda.

Role of Women in Peace Keeping

Women's participation in peacekeeping has been recognized as a critical component of mission success—leading to greater credibility of the forces, more effective protection efforts to mention a few. UNSCR 1325 calls for an expansion on the role and contribution of women in field-based operations. It is observed that women only make up 4.2 percent of military personnel in the United Nations peacekeeping Missions.[17] In 2019, women comprised 15.1 percent of military observers and staff officers and just 4.4 percent of military contingents, 26.8 percent of individual police officers, 27.0 percent of justice and corrections personnel.[18] This is despite the fact increasing women's participation would allow for a better understanding of underlying structural, sociological, cultural, and historical factors that shape conflicts and also allow for the women to be agents of peace in conflict situations.

Military Operations Planning and Tactical Level

In line with the call of rapidly increasing the number of senior female civilian personnel in peace support operations in all relevant Headquarters departments, including DPKO, and in the field, member states have been asked

---

[16] Implementation of the Women, Peace and Security Agenda in Africa, African Union December 2019, p. 3.

[17] S/2019/800, Women and Peace and Security, Report of the Secretary General, on 9th October 2019, para. 4.

[18] Baldwin Gretchen and Taylor Sarah, "Uniformed Women in Peace Operations: Challenging Assumptions and Transforming Approaches" June 2020 (International Peace Institute).

to increase the number of women in their military and civilian police forces who are qualified to serve in peace support operations at all levels, including the most senior.[19] The presence of female military personnel brings a lot of positive outcomes in the mission area. These women ensure that adequate attention is paid to the vulnerable members of the population including the elderly, pregnant women, apart from the fact their presence boosts protection and response strategies as local women and children may more readily confide in female peacekeepers. Deployment of female military peacekeepers may also have a role-modeling impact on the local women to facilitate increased recruitment to the national security forces.

Another important role uniformed women play is through monitoring and verification tasks including patrolling, investigation, and information operations. It was highlighted in the Santa Cruz Report[20] that it is important for troop-contributing countries to provide personnel with the capabilities of tactical intelligence in order to make it possible to prevent attacks and identify attackers. Women provide such intelligence through their communication with local women as they easily interact. This then facilitates situational awareness and also assists in providing early warning of any danger that threatens peace.

In the course of planning various operations, an important factor of women and men having access to different kinds and sources of information relating to security risks and threats in the area of operation should be considered. This is where women are to be fully involved for example the military gender focal point or gender specialist can facilitate the inclusion of local women's perspectives in information analysis and assessments which will, in turn, inform the Commander's planning and execution of mandated tasks.[21]

The role of women in military operations planning encompasses a thorough use of gender specialists drawing perspectives of both women and men in order to draw a comprehensive picture of the security environment. Through this gender issues are also taken on board during strategic military plans, future planning, and implementations of the plans.

GENDER ADVISOR

The role of the gender advisor is to support the gender-sensitive approaches to the implementation of the mission's mandate, drawing on the provisions of the Security Council resolutions on women peace and security. The gender advisor coordinates gender mainstreaming, analysis, and reporting in the substantive work of the mission, while supporting efforts to promote the participation

---

[19] S/2000/693, The Windhoek Declaration and the Namibia Plan of Action on Mainstreaming a Gender Perspective in Multidimensional Peace Support Operations.

[20] Carlos Alberto dos Santos Cruz Report: Improving Security of United Nations Peacekeepers: We need to change the way we are doing business, 2017, p. 14.

[21] DPKO/DFS Guidelines: Integrating a Gender Perspective into the Work of the United Nations Military in Peace Keeping Operations, 2010, p. 12.

of women in mission mandated activities.[22] The gender adviser works at a strategic mission level. The military gender adviser works under the leadership of the Force Commander. Her role is to support operational and tactical level implementation of mandates on women, peace, and security, within the framework of the broader peacekeeping mandate. She also works under the guidance of the mission gender adviser. Specific tasks include among others provide advice to Force Commander and senior military leadership on strategies for effective implementation of existing mandates on women, peace, and security within the military component, monitor, and support delivery of gender training for all military peacekeepers, monitor and support disaggregated data to facilitate planning for military operations, monitor and advise on operational requirements for female personnel at the operational and tactical level and provide guidance and support to military gender focal points at the tactical level.[23]

Gender Focal points are responsible for supporting and implementing mandates on women, peace, and security at the tactical level activities of military peacekeepers. Their specific task includes among others providing advice to the Commanding Officer to advance implementation of mandates on women, peace, and security in tactical level military peacekeeping tasks, raise awareness of gender issues at battalion level and advocate for inclusion of a gender perspective in military activities to enhance operational effectiveness, consult regularly with local women to identify specific security risks facing women and girls and support identification and implementation of CIMIC projects targeting women and girls.[24]

Despite a willingness to incorporate a gender perspective in field operations where possible as envisaged by Resolution 1325, there is still a long way to go in terms of gendered approach at tactical level. Gender Focal Points are usually not allocated the necessary support and financing required to carry out their activities and are often bundled together with CIMIC. There is still a prevalent attitude of tokenism when it comes to the participation of women in operational planning and analysis. Gender Focal Points are rarely trained before deployment and as a result, the troops are also not trained in gender.

Female Engagement Teams

Female Engagement Teams (FET) are tactical sub-sub-units meant to gather information and gain access to populations by directly engaging host communities. FET tasks are often framed as responding to the gendered needs of

---

[22] https://unmil.unmissions.org/advisor-raises-consciousness-mission-personnel-gender.

[23] DPKO/DFS Guidelines: Integrating a Gender Perspective into the work of the United Nations Military in Peacekeeping 2010.

[24] supra.

those communities.[25] FETS were first used by international military forces in Iraq and Afghanistan and have been deployed on an ad hoc basis to several UN missions in recent years. FETs are particularly prevalent in the missions with robust POC mandates for example under MONUSCO in the Democratic Republic of the Congo. There is no official UN policy on them and due to this, there is no clarity on the structure and lots of debates regarding the role of these teams in community engagement, especially as community engagement has emerged as an increasingly important aspect of peacekeeping.[26] Through deployment of FETs, it is a considered opinion that women are being involved in most duties that were only deemed for male peacekeepers such as foot patrols, security tasks just to mention a few and there is a positive change in being able to serve the local women better who feel at ease with fellow women despite that they are in uniform.

The deployment of female peacekeepers is deemed essential because women tend to establish a good relationship with the conflict-affected community and in particular local women and civil societies. Women are seen as able to open the hearts and minds of people. Having women in uniform ensures collaboration with locals specifically women who have a more defined sense of security through engaging with female peacekeepers than male peacekeepers.

The female peacekeepers have patrol duties to protect the women who pursue outdoor activities in their normal day-to-day routines such as fetching water, firewood. These outdoor activities may expose them to specific security dangers, such as attacks, kidnapping, and rape. Having foot patrols along routes frequented by women and girls by FET is a useful strategy to enhance protection of women and girls and to expand outreach to the local population.

FET is also engaged at checkpoints and roadblocks, where military peacekeepers are engaging with women at checkpoints, it is important that only females interact with women to dispel any mistrust and also guard against fears of sexual exploitation and abuse. FET is also engaged to screen female ex-combatants and also ensure that screening procedures respect the privacy of women and girls. Through the use of FET there is a progressive interaction with local women organizations that enhance implementation of the mandate as per the mission.

Role of Women in Countering Terrorism

Terrorism has a negative impact on the world at large and Africa has not been left out. Countries such as Kenya, Somalia face the terror of Al-Shabaab, while Nigeria and the is reeling from effects of Boko Haram. These violent

---

[25] Baldwin Gretchen and Taylor Sarah, "Uniformed Women in Peace Operations: Challenging Assumptions and Transforming Approaches" June 2020 (International Peace Institute), p. 6.

[26] Baldwin Gretchen and Taylor Sarah, "Uniformed Women in Peace Operations: Challenging Assumptions and Transforming Approaches" June 2020 (International Peace Institute), p. 6.

extremist groups conduct activities that aim at the subjugation of women, violate women's and girl's rights including their basic human rights. The violent extremist groups work to eradicate women's agency, in both public and private spheres, and to subordinate women's existence in order to achieve their agendas.[27] In the rise of terrorism, women have a significant role to play considering that this has a negative effect on women and girls.

Women peace builders around the world continue to call for women's participation, underlining that it is an essential factor in ensuring the effectiveness of counterterrorism and of efforts to prevent and counter violent extremism, and in ensuring that such legislation and efforts to counterterrorism are not used as a means to supress their decades-long activism, peacebuilding, and rights advocacy.[28]

RECOMMENDATIONS

Having recognized that there is a strong need to increase the role of women in the peace and security process the following are some recommendations that can be considered.

Most societies around the world are patriarchal. This is the case even in matrilineal societies where women in leadership positions continue to advance the patriarchal agenda. Women are treated as second-class citizens with no or limited roles in the political space. Men are expected to lead, to provide for their families, to choose leadership, and make decisions as heads of households while women play the supportive role of keeping the house, raising the children, growing food, drawing water, and other such chores around the homestead. This division of gender roles has made it hard for women to breakthrough in leadership and decision-making roles.

Women are rarely in positions of power and this inequality in the balance of power relations in society is exacerbated during times of armed conflict when access to courts, security agencies and local government is highly restricted and the institutions themselves are barely functional. This preconceived bias about gender plays a big role in peace-making and peacebuilding as women are excluded from the peace process. Changing the social perspective of women involvement in peace-building is essential. It is quite obvious that the way societies perceive women involved in official peace process plays a major role in either motivating or deterring the engagement of women in peacebuilding.

Where there is a negative perception, some women may want to distance themselves hence the need to build legitimacy of the role of women in peace process, encourage ownership and create a conducive environment to spur the growth of women inclusiveness and involvement. This can be better

---

[27] S/2019/800, Women and Peace and Security, Report of the Secretary General, on 9th October 2019, para. 70.

[28] S/2019/800, Women and Peace and Security, Report of the Secretary General, on 9th October 2019, para. 73.

achieved by building the capacity of women at all levels to converse, understand, evaluate, and articulate issues which affect them so that they are capable of effectively participate in peace mediation and negotiations like the joint African Centre for the Constructive Resolution of Disputes (ACCORD)/UN Development Fund for Women (UNIFEM) training of women in conflict management, negotiation, and facilitation skills which were a positive factor in ensuring effective participation of women in the peace process in Darfur and Sudan.[29] Capacity building should extend to women in civil organizations, non-state actors, activists, and the armed forces to ensure holistic and organic growth and support for the advancement of the WPS agenda from the grass root, to national and international levels.

Women should be included in negotiations and mediation and should not be viewed as irrelevant because they do not have technical languages or the military knowledge that is deemed required. The women should be encouraged to directly involve themselves as moderators, facilitators, advisors in the peace processes. It should be the States through their Action Plans that ensure that gender perspectives are always taken on board and gender mainstreaming is enhanced at all levels. There is need for governments to provide deliberate opportunities to increase women's representation in the security field which broadens the pool of women security experts available for peace assignments. The normative framework exists, it just requires political will to initiate national policies, laws, strategies, and action plans to ensure the implementation of the WPS agenda.

Governments should allocate resources for the implementation of the WPS agenda. This has been emphasized by S/RES/2282 (2016) as it calls upon national ownership and leadership in peacebuilding, whereby the responsibility of sustaining peace is to be broadly shared by the Government and all other national stakeholders. Women at grass-roots levels should be educated on resolution 1325 and its sister resolutions as well as CEDAW. These women should drive the process of developing and validating National Action Plans to ensure that these policy documents reflect the reality on the ground. Women in the security forces should have the opportunity to be actively involved in this process as well as experts in the field. This will lead to the ownership of the process by the women ensuring that they effectively participate in the peace process.

Awareness of the resolutions by women will put them in a position to demand accountability from perpetrators of abuse and sexual violence. The formation of women groups where such issues can be discussed and disseminated will give women the confidence and numbers to effect real lasting change and consequently durable peace in their communities. Governments

---

[29] Resolution 1325 in 2020: Looking forward, Looking Back a report based on a High-level Seminar organised by ACCORD, together with the African Union Peace and Security Council, at the International Conference Centre, Durban, South Africa on 8 and 9 October 2010.

need to act swiftly through the relevant systems to ensure that perpetrators of conflict-related sexual violence crimes are punished in order to end the impunity with which such crimes are committed. This calls for governments to take deliberate measures to ensure that tough penalties are awarded to perpetrators to ensure the protection of women.

CONCLUSION

The women, peace, and security agenda is impossible to achieve without the effective participation of women pre-conflict, during conflict, and the post-conflict peacebuilding process. Governments must take advantage of the existing normative framework and take deliberate action to initiate and complete the implementation of Resolution 1325 and other related resolutions to advance the women peace and security agenda by educating women at all levels and building their capacity and skills to contribute meaningfully to the WPS agenda, ensuring that women participate in the political arena where necessary devising laws and imposing quotas to ensure such participation and appointing women in influential positions to ensure durable peace.

CHAPTER 27

Respecting the Law of Armed Conflict in Africa

Dan Kuwali

INTRODUCTION

The majority of armed conflicts being fought on the African continent are classified as non-international armed conflicts, and are characterized by the presence of non-state armed groups (NSAGs), multinational peacekeeping forces, and a rising number of civilian victims in volatile contexts. This phenomenon raises specific questions on how to ensure greater respect for Law of Armed Conflict (LoAC) in the region. In recent years, Africa has witnessed numerous instances of grave violations of LoAC in the course of armed conflicts fought on its soil. A reflection on strategies on generating respect for LOAC in Africa should necessarily consider such actors in addition to States as well as the volatility of the battlefield. In light of the concern that the LoAC is increasingly being violated, and in the absence of effective enforcement mechanisms on the continent, there is a pressing need to find ways to ensure greater compliance with, and effective implementation of, LoAC in Africa.

As poignantly pointed out by Mark Maxwell in Chapter 24, the principle of protection of civilians and non-combatants lies at the core of the Geneva Conventions of 1949 and the Additional Protocols of 1977, and indeed, is fundamental to all LoAC. While the protection of civilians is a state responsibility, often it is the government itself that perpetrates abuses. However, governments are not the only violators, noting that many abuses occur in

D. Kuwali (✉)
University of Pretoria, Pretoria, South Africa

© The Author(s), under exclusive license to Springer Nature
Switzerland AG 2022
D. Kuwali (ed.), *The Palgrave Handbook of Sustainable Peace and Security in Africa*, https://doi.org/10.1007/978-3-030-82020-6_27

461

462   D. KUWALI

rebel-held territory to which the government has no access. Abuses persist despite the existence of LoAC that govern the conduct of parties to the conflict, thereby indicating that the mere existence of laws does not guarantee their adherence. Greenwood is lucid in putting the problem in context:

> The most difficult question to answer about the laws of armed conflict is how States can be brought to comply with them. There can be no denying that the enforcement machinery of international law in general is comparatively weak and that it lacks most of the features found in national law. There is no international police and no network of courts with compulsory jurisdiction. Moreover, it is probably true to say that there is no area of international law in which the deficiencies of enforcement are so apparent as the laws of armed conflict.[1]

Juxtaposing these concerns on the African Union (AU) set up, the AU Peace and Security Architecture (APSA) need a comprehensive approach in its enforcement mechanism of human rights and LoAC by combatants. How can one ever explain the fact that the 1949 Geneva Conventions and the 1977 Additional Protocols thereto have been ratified by almost all African States, only to find them dishonoured in breach?[2] How can one explain that laws against war crimes and laws that embody universal jurisdiction are still not part of the legislative fabric of several countries at the epicentre of the maelstrom of armed conflicts in Africa? How can one ever explain the dilemma in application of LoAC in internationalized armed conflicts in Africa and the obstacles in implementation of LoAC by NSAGs who are the protagonists in these conflicts? These concerns underscore the need to devise strategies that would enhance the protection of civilians in armed conflict and the prevention of violations.

The implementation mechanisms of human rights and humanitarian law can be classified into three, i.e., preventive measures to be taken in peacetime; mechanisms to ensure respect during armed conflicts; and mechanisms to repress violations *post facto*.[3] Although, the twenty-first century is the century of prevention, the regime for the protection of human rights and LoAC has largely been reactive and event-driven to specific threats or acts of repression, yet prevention is more effective and cheaper than reacting after the fact.[4]

---

[1] Christopher Greenwood, 'The Law of War (International Humanitarian Law),' in Malcom D. Evans (ed.), *International Law*, Oxford: Oxford University Press, pp. 798–823, p. 817.

[2] Somalia has ratified the 1949 Geneva Conventions but is not a State Party to both 1977 Additional Protocols. Given that République Arabe Sahraoue Démocratic (Western Sahara) is still an unrecognised State in UN terms, it is unable to sign or accede to treaties.

[3] Marco Sassòli, 'The Implementation of International Humanitarian Law: Current and Inherent Challenges,' in 10 *Yearbook of International Humanitarian Law* (2007), pp. 45–73, p. 46.

[4] Manfred Nowak, *An Introduction to Human Rights Regime*, Leiden: Martinus Nijhoff Publishers, 2003, p. 2.

Given that observance of the law in prospect is worthwhile for the victims than punishment of perpetrators in retrospect, this discussion will examine the following issues: (a) how to ensure compliance of human rights and humanitarian law by belligerents in an armed conflict; and (b) how to protect civilians in an ongoing armed conflict by deterring potential perpetrators of violations. Since the challenges revolve around the implementation and enforcement of human rights and humanitarian law in the current legal regime and considering the numerous armed conflicts on the continent, the discussion explores new and better strategies to further increase respect for LoAC in contemporary armed conflicts.

TRENDS IN CONTEMPORARY ARMED CONFLICTS IN AFRICA

Considering the changing and dynamic nature of armed conflicts in Africa, it is crucial to develop mechanisms to ensure that all actors involved are taking their respective responsibilities seriously and that proper oversight is exercised. In mapping current trends in African conflicts, the following trends can be identified: multinational peacekeeping forces; non-state armed groups, increasing asymmetric nature of conflicts; presence of international humanitarian agencies; attacks on civilians and non-combatants, volatility of the battlefields, presence of child soldiers, sexual and gender-based violence, among others. Below is a synopsis of these disturbing trends.

Non-State Armed Groups

Africa has seen a proliferation of NSAGs in the armed conflicts on the continent. There are well over 100 NSAGs involved in the war in the Democratic Republic of the Congo (DRC), including Allied Democratic Forces (ADF), the Democratic Forces for the Liberation of Rwanda (FDLR), and the Mai Mai militia.[5] Boko Haram has been prominent in Nigeria just like Al Shabaab has been a menace in Somalia.[6] In the war in the Central African Republic, there are several ex-Séléka militia groups, Muslim self-defence groups, and anti-Balaka groups, consisting of local protection militias who have split along

---

[5] DRC: A mapping of Non-International Armed Conflict in Kivu, Kasai and Ituri, RULAC/Geneva Academy, available at: https://www.rulac.org/news/democratic-republic-of-the-congo-a-mapping-of-non-international-armed-conflict (accessed 14 February 2021). See also Relief Web, Security Challenge: Non-state Armed Groups—Recommendations for Work in the DRC in the Context of the Ebola Emergency Response 2019–20, *Insecurity Insight*, 14 February 2020, available at: https://reliefweb.int/report/democraticrepubliccongo/security-challenge-non-state-armed-groups-recommendations-work-drc (accessed 14 February 2021).

[6] See generally, Caroline Varin and Dauda Abubakar (eds.), *Violent Non-State Actors in Africa: Terrorists, Rebels and Warlords*, Palgrave Macmillan, 2017.

different, but fluid lines—tribal, local power structures, and over the control of economic resources.[7]

Self-defence, need for security, and fear of attack, territory, authority, and religion are some of the primary motivations for members of non-state armed groups to be involved in the conflict. Armed conflict involving non-state armed groups without the direct involvement of the state government has also been a common phenomenon in African conflicts. In some cases, there has been violence between armed gangs, rebel groups, or communal militias.[8] The DRC and Sudan, for example, have witnessed convoluted inter-rebel clashes. The brutality of these NSAGs demands an urgent action to fashion a "new weapon" to fight a war that in all intents and purpose is far from conventional.[9] The question, therefore, is how to compel States and NSAGs to comply with obligations under human rights and humanitarian law, especially in an ongoing armed conflict?[10]

Marauding "Child Soldiers"

There has been an increased use of boys and girls often referred to as "child soldiers", especially by NSAGs in armed conflicts in Africa. The phenomenon of child soldiers refers to the military use of children under the age of 18 by belligerents. Article 2 of the African Charter on the Rights and Welfare of the Child defines a *child* as every human being below the age of 18 years. Further, Article 22 of the African Charter on the Rights and Welfare of the Child requires the State to "take all necessary measures to ensure that no child shall take a direct part in hostilities and refrain in particular, from recruiting any child". The standard set by the African Charter on the Rights and Welfare of the Child is higher than that set by the Convention on the Rights of the Child in Article 38.[11]

Typically, this classification includes children serving in non-combatant roles such as cooks, spies, or messengers, as well as those serving in combatant roles. It is believed that there are more than 120,000 children under 18 years of age are currently participating in armed conflicts across Africa, some as young as

---

[7] Felix Colchester, Caesar Poblicks and Teresa Dumasy, 'Perspectives of Non-State Armed Groups in the Central African Republic,' Briefing Paper, Conciliation Resources, December 2016, p. 2.

[8] von Uexkull and Pettersson, above.

[9] Francis Jegede, Kelvin Bampton and Malcom Todd, 'State vs Non-state Armed Groups—A Political Economy of Violence,' p. 5, available at: https://core.ac.uk/download/pdf?46557197.pdf (accessed 12 February 2021).

[10] Greenwood, note 1, p. 817. See also Churchill Ewumbue-Monono, 'Respect for International Humanitarian Law by Armed Non-State Actors in Africa,' 88(864) *International Review of the Red Cross* (2006), pp. 905–924.

[11] See African Union, 'African Charter on the Rights and Welfare of the Child,' available at: https://au.in/en/treaties/african-charter-rights-and-welfare-child (accessed 16 February 2021).

seven years. The countries most affected by this problem are: Algeria, Angola, Burundi, Congo-Brazzaville, the DRC, Liberia, Rwanda, Sierra Leone, Sudan, and Uganda. It is reported that the Ethiopian government forces engaged in an armed conflict against Eritrea, and the clans in Somalia, have both included under-18-year old in their ranks.[12]

Further to the concerns presented by Mphatso Boti Phiri in Chapter 25, there are several factors that lead children to become part of an armed force or group. While others join the belligerents for survival or to protect their communities, some are abducted, threatened, coerced, or manipulated by fighters while others are driven by socioeconomic factors especially poverty which forces them to fend for their families. No matter their involvement, the recruitment and use of children by armed forces is a grave violation of child rights and international humanitarian law.[13]

Children recruited to fight face much more challenges in addition to the risks for all combatants. Usually, the children are drugged and become fearless. Coupled with their immaturity and naivety, they often take excessive risks as they may look at fighting as a game. As armed groups regard the children as dispensable force multipliers, they are usually not trained to fight before being deployed to the front line where they are usually massacred.[14] The use of children as soldiers is the result of either deliberate action or deliberate inaction in some cases. Many African countries effectively protect children against military recruitment and use them as soldiers. Therefore, African States should play a leading role in ensuring that the minimum age of recruitment set at 18 is universally adopted as per the standard set by the AU. Both the state's armed forces and NSAGs need to respect the law.[15]

Volatility of the Battlefields

Today's wars have no frontiers. Villages are the battlefronts. Cities have become scenes of unfathomable atrocities. Civilians are deliberate targets. Children are warlords as well as victims. Rape is a weapon of war such that it is now even more dangerous to be a woman than a soldier in contemporary armed conflicts. Human rights and humanitarian law violations are committed in armed conflicts by insurgents as well as government troops. For example, in DRC, the most visible threat to the human rights of civilians are government soldiers. The inevitable trend is that battlefields have been commonplace

[12] Stuart Maslen, 'The Use of Children as Soldiers in Africa: A Country Analysis of Child Recruitment and Participation in Armed Conflict,' available at: https://reliefweb.int/states/reliefweb.in/files/resources/c157333FCA91F573C1256 C130033E448-childsold.htm (accessed 14 February 2021).

[13] United Nations Children Education Fund (UNICEF), 'Children Recruited by Armed Forces,' available at: https://www.unicef.org/protection/children-recruited-by-armed-forces (accessed 14 February 2021).

[14] Maslen, note 12 above.

[15] As above.

on civilians in contemporary warfare in Africa. Yet, the principle of distinction, which seeks to protect civilians and non-combatants in armed conflicts, is the centrepiece of the 1949 Geneva Conventions and the 1977 Additional Protocols. It is, therefore, urgent to ensure compliance of human rights and humanitarian norms by belligerents in contemporary hostilities.

Attacks on International Humanitarian Agencies

The increase in demand for deploying humanitarian workers to conflict-affected areas has come with an expanded risk of violent attacks against staff in insecure field settings.[16] For example in DRC, suspected Mai-Mai elements conducted targeted attacks against Ebola Response Teams (ERTs) on several occasions in Mambasa territory in Ituri Province, especially in 2019.[17] Humanitarian aid workers and peacekeepers have also been abducted and murdered by unscrupulous belligerents in conflict situations such as CAR, DRC, Sudanese Darfur, and Somalia. According to Aid Worker Security Database, at least 483 relief workers were attacked: 125 were killed, 234 wounded and 124 kidnapped, in 277 separate incidents. This was an 18 per cent increase in the number of victims compared to 2018.[18] There are several reasons that explain the exponential rise in attacks on aid workers.

One explanation is the changing role of humanitarian engagement in conflict, where they are working much more extensively in remote field settings, and undertaking a much wider variety of development tasks. This has required international humanitarian agencies to employ new strategies to attempt to reduce operational risk by collaborating with national partners, presenting a less visible local profile, and increasing staff security mechanisms. The relationship between humanitarian agencies and development partners in the Global South and the business-like actions of humanitarian agencies may erode the principle of neutrality of humanitarian space. To an extent, this approach places aid workers at greater risk, and increasing institutional politicization and deeper ties with governments and/or militaries are considered a key factor motivating violence against humanitarian workers.[19]

---

[16] Kristian Hoelscher, Jason Miklian and Håvard Mokleiv Nygård, Understanding Attacks on Humanitarian Aid Workers, 6 *Conflict Trends* (2015).

[17] Lieutenant General Carlos Alberto dos Santoz Cruz, 'United Nations, Independent Assessment Report on the Protection of Civilians and Neutralization of Armed Groups in Beni and Mambasa Territories in the Democratic Republic of the Congo' ("Dos Santos Cruz Report"), 15 January 2020, p. 3.

[18] Aid Worker Security Database, available at: https://aidworkersecurity.org/incidents/reports (accessed 14 February 2021).

[19] Hoelscher et al., note 17 above.

Attacks Against Peacekeepers

Peacekeepers have, time and again, been abducted and murdered by rebels in the armed conflicts in Africa, particularly in the CAR, Chad, Darfur, Sudan, and Eastern DRC. It has been reported that at least 20 UN peacekeepers were injured in a major attack on base for United Nations Multidimensional Integrated Stabilization Mission in Mali (MINUSMA) in Mali on 10 February 2021.[20] This attack followed another attack almost a month earlier, on 14 January 2021, when four peacekeepers in the same mission in Mali were killed and five others wounded in an attack by unidentified armed elements. The peacekeepers' convoy was struck by an improvised explosive device (IED), and the troops then came under attack by unidentified gunmen in the vast Timbuktu region.[21] The attack against MINUSMA peacekeepers took place the same day as another attack where a Rwandan peacekeeper was killed in the UN peacekeeping mission in the CAR, which is known by its French acronym, MINUSCA.[22]

On 23 June 2020, suspected ADF rebel militias attacked a blue helmets patrol convoy in the UN Stabilization Mission in the DRC (MONUSCO), which left one Indonesian peacekeeper dead.[23] On 8 December 2017 there was a worst attack in UN history when at least 15 MONUSCO peacekeepers were killed and 53 others wounded by suspected ADF rebels in North Kivu province in Eastern DRC, which followed another attack in December 2016 where 7 blue helmets were also killed.[24] Such has been the disturbing trend of malicious attacks on blue helmets. It should be remembered that attacks on peacekeepers constitute war crimes under the Rome Statute of the International Criminal Court (ICC). Further, peacekeepers are bound by LoAC when engaged in armed conflict. Moving forward, it is imperative that at the operational level, necessary measures to ensure greater compliance with the law, such as: clarity in mandates, a preventive approach to violations, the assessment of existing compliance mechanisms that ensure all actors respect their obligations are placed under adequate oversight.

Killing of Innocent Civilians

Today, civilians constitute the bulk of casualties in armed conflicts, often deliberately targeted rather than merely caught up in the fighting. For example, in

---

[20] United Nations, 'Mali: Around 20 UN Peacekeepers Injured in Major Attack on MINUSMA Base,' available at: https://news.un.org/en/story/2021/02/1084342 (accessed 15 February 2021).

[21] As above.

[22] As above.

[23] As above.

[24] See United Nations, 'DR Congo: UN Peacekeepers Killed in Attack in North Kiv,' *BBC News*, 8 December 2017, available at: https://www.bbc.com/news/worl-africa-422 85871 (accessed 15 February 2021).

2002 the UN determined that women and children constituted the majority of casualties in contemporary armed conflicts. The Rwandan genocide in 1994 resulted in an estimated 500,000 women and children being raped by marauding militias and soldiers, while the conflicts in Sierra Leone, Liberia and Darfur have all exposed high rates of sexual violence. About 85 per cent of the refugees, asylum-seekers, and internally displaced persons who are victims of conflicts are women and children.

At least 260 civilians were killed by suspected ADF rebels between 30 October and 31 December 2019 in DRC. Many more have been killed over the years in DRC and other armed conflicts on the continent.[25] More than 2 million children worldwide have been killed in situations of armed conflicts, at least 6 million have been permanently disabled or injured and over 14 million children have been displaced within and without their home countries due to armed conflicts.[26] Given their limited mobility and vulnerability, the elderly, and people with disabilities are even more exposed to the brutalities of warfare. The failure to protect civilians in armed conflicts under the watch of peace-keepers sends a wrong signal to warring factions as well as the populations they are supposed to protect. This growing trend also raises disturbing questions both about the political will, capability, and capacity of military forces in the protection of civilians in armed conflicts.

The protection of civilians in armed conflicts is the confluence between international human rights and humanitarian law and the broader human security agenda. International human rights and humanitarian law prohibits all means and methods of warfare that fail to discriminate between combat-ants and non-combatants. The coexistence of human rights and humanitarian law provides windows of opportunity for the effective protection of civilians in armed conflicts. While the protection of civilians is a responsibility of the State, often it is the government itself that perpetrates abuses. However, governments are not the only violators, considering that many abuses occur in rebel-held territory to which the government has little control or no access. Nevertheless, States have responsibility to protect populations at risk and prevent violations by non-state actors. The challenge is how to move away from fragmented, ad hoc approach into the direction of a more comprehensive and effective approach to protect civilians from abuse, to mitigate the impact of warfare, and to alleviate their suffering.

[25] Lieutenant General Carlos Alberto dos Santoz Cruz, 'United Nations, Independent Assessment Report on the Protection of Civilians and Neutralization of Armed Groups in Beni and Mambasa Territories in the Democratic Republic of the Congo' ("Dos Santos Cruz Report"), 15 January 2020, p. 2.

[26] See United Nations, 'Impact of Armed Conflict on Children—Twenty Years of Action Following the Publication of Graça Machel Report to the General Assembly,' Office of the Special Rapporteur of the Secretary-General for Children and Armed Conflict, 25 August 2016, available at: https://childrenandarmedconflict.un.org/2016/08/graca-machel-rep ort-2016 (accessed 15 February 2021). See also Cephas Lumina, '*Child Soldiers*: War Criminals or Pawns in a Deadly Game?' *African Yearbook on International Humanitarian Law* (2007), pp. 76–104.

While the UN, the African Union (AU) and other regional organizations have been developing doctrines and operational capacities to meet such challenges, the protection of civilians on the ground remains a matter of political will and a lot of work needs to be done. There is a need for policymakers to take steps towards filling the gap that exists between reporting situations of the plight of civilians in armed conflicts and the necessary action of bringing appropriate responses. Forward planning for the African Standby Force (ASF) is needed for a comprehensive doctrine for protection of civilians, rules of engagement, and better training of troops to protect civilians. The ASF needs to have a deterrent effect, credible action, actionable intelligence, counter-intelligence capability, and operational security, among others, to be able to adequately protect civilians in contemporary armed conflicts. MONUSCO has developed effective protection responses to attacks against civilians in terms of protection by presence in urban areas (robust patrolling) and protection by projection in remote areas (rapid deployment of temporary bases and long-range patrols).[27]

Sex and Gender-Based Violence

As Thomasin Gondwe and Laika Nakanga have lamented in Chapter 26. sex and gender-based violence (SGBV) is prevalent in contemporary armed conflicts in Africa. SGBV can be understood as "violence that is directed against a person on the basis of gender or sex. It includes acts that inflict physical, mental or sexual harm or suffering, threats of such acts, coercion and other deprivations of liberty".[28] While women, men, boys, and girls can be victims of SGBV, the overwhelming majority of the victims/survivors of SGBV are women and girls.[29] SGBV has been branded "the most pervasive yet least recognized human rights abuse in the world". Accordingly, the Vienna Human Rights Conference and the Fourth World Conference on Women gave priority to this issue, which jeopardizes women's lives, bodies, psychological integrity, and freedom. The Vienna Declaration of Human Rights posited that human rights are universal, inalienable, indivisible, interconnected, and interdependent.[30]

[27] Lieutenant General Carlos Alberto dos Santoz Cruz, "United Nations, Independent Assessment Report on the Protection of Civilians and Neutralization of Armed Groups in Beni and Mambasa Territories in the Democratic Republic of the Congo" ("Dos Santos Cruz Report"), 15 January 2020, p. 8.

[28] United Nations, UN General Assembly Declaration on the Elimination of Violence against Women (1993) UN Doc 48/104, Articles 1 and 2 and Recommendation 19, paragraph 6 of the 11th Session of the CEDAW Committee.

[29] Ibid. See also United Nations High Commissioner for Refugees, Sexual and Gender Based Violence Refugees, Returnees and Internally Displaced Persons; Guidelines for Prevention, 2003, p. 15.

[30] United Nations, Vienna Declaration and Programme of Action, *World Conference on Human Rights*, UN Doc A/CONF.157/23, 12 July 1993. Available at: http://www.unh chr.ch/huridocda/huridoca.nsf/(symbol)/a.conf.157.23.en (accessed 5 January 2021).

Rape in conflict must be understood as an abuse that targets women for political and strategic reasons. Sexual violence is increasingly a strategic tool of war, especially in conflicts driven by identity politics.[31] Organized campaigns of mass rape and sexual assault are sometimes organized by troops in order to punish a group of civilians for perceived sympathies with armed insurgents, and to demonstrate the soldiers' domination over civilians. Rape acts as the ultimate weapon of "ethnic cleansing", dehumanizing the victim, intending to terrorize populations into flight, and sometimes forcibly impregnating women to force their ethnicity onto their victims in societies where "male descent" defines identity. This was overwhelmingly used by the Hutu against the Tutsi in Rwanda in 1994 and is prevalent in the war in DRC.[32]

The terrible trauma of rape is not the only crime committed against victims of sexual assault. In most cases, a second wound is inflicted by the fact that perpetrators usually commit sexual offences with impunity, especially in times of war where impunity for rapists is more common. Both international and non-international armed conflicts are normally characterized by a breakdown of state structures and authority. Judicial systems are often among the first casualties. In many cases, countries where widespread SGBV occurs, have not had a functioning or incorruptible judiciary before the onset of conflict.[33]

Proliferation of Weapons

In agreement with Gilbert Mittawa in Chapter 22, the uncontrolled spread of small arms and light weapons (SALW), due to their accessibility, widespread availability, and ease of use, plays a significant role in the mass atrocities committed in armed conflicts on the African continent.[34] The misuse of SALW has also contributed to protracted armed conflicts. SALW are the tools of the trade for terrorists, rebels, and criminal gangs and their spread in Africa has generally gone unregulated.[35] To curb the menace of SALW that has contributed to mass atrocities on the continent, African states should ratify and implement treaties that regulate and control their spread to, and within, the

---

[31] Dorothy Thomas and Regan Ralph, from the Human Rights Watch Women's Rights Project (*Rape in War: Challenging the Tradition of Impunity*) (Undated).

[32] When sexual violence is a planned part of the military campaign, it is highly unlikely that authorities will prosecute their own troops for acts which they enjoined soldiers to commit in the first place. IRIN Global, 'Our Bodies, Their Grounds,' available at: http://www.irinnews.org/InDepthMain.aspx?InDepthId=20&ReportId=62823 (accessed 12 February 2021).

[33] As above.

[34] Paul Salopek 'Lost in the Sahel,' *National Geographic*, available at: http://ngm.nat ionalgeographic.com/2008/04/sahel/paul-salopek-text/3 (accessed 11 March 2013).

[35] Mike Bourne, 'The Proliferation of Small Arms and Light Weapons,' in E. Krahmann (ed.), *New Threats and New Actors in International Security*, Elke Krahmann, 2005.

continent.[36] Further to the promulgation of these treaties should be deliberate political will to curb the movement and sale of SALW across the continent.

Increasing Use of Improvised Explosive Devices

IEDs have in recent years become the weapon of choice for NASGs in armed conflicts on the continent, as they are cheap and relatively easy to construct anywhere from literally everything that can have a lethal impact upon explosion. For example, on 14 January 2021 a patrol convoy of peacekeepers was hit by an IED in Timbuktu region in Mali.[37] The impact of IED attacks is far-reaching in that they not only hinder the political, social, and economic development of a country but also block life-saving humanitarian aid.

Given their very nature as a weapon of asymmetric warfare, IEDs are produced entirely outside of government oversight rendering regulation to be a particular challenge. Currently, there is no comprehensive approach to address the challenge posed by IEDs apart from the piecemeal international cooperation against the rapid and widespread transfer of knowledge on IED design. However, within the framework of the UN Convention on Certain Conventional Weapons, experts have developed guidelines and best practices aimed at addressing the diversion or illicit use of materials which can be used for IEDs.[38] Further, the UN General Assembly unanimously adopted Resolution 70/46, which calls for the consistent collection of data, awareness-raising, options for the regulation of components, international technical assistance and cooperation, and victim assistance. This requires *strengthening vigilance and national controls on* IEDs and enhancing information sharing on IEDs. UN General Assembly Resolution 70/46 also reiterates the need for increased assistance, better training, and improved international coordination in arresting the menace of IEDs.[39]

THE OBLIGATION TO RESPECT AND ENSURE RESPECT OF THE LoAC

Article 1 common to the Geneva Conventions provides for the obligation to respect and to ensure respect for the 1949 Geneva Conventions. Article 1 common to the four Geneva Conventions reads as follows: "[t]he

---

[36] See also United Nations (2005) op. cit., note 6, paras. 92–96.

[37] United Nations, note 20 above.

[38] Expert Group under Convention on Certain Conventional Weapons (CCW) Amended Protocol II, available at: http://www.unog.ch/80256EE600585943/(httpPages)/393 40DE9A9659E5CC1257CF400344B35?OpenDocument (accessed 15 February 2021).

[39] The International Ammunition Technical Guidelines (IATG), mandated by the General Assembly, provides guidance measures on how to secure conventional ammunition stockpiles (A/RES/63/61, A/RES/66/42). See also See the UN Guiding Principles on Business and Human Rights: Implementing the United Nations "Protect, Respect and Remedy" Framework (A/HRC/17/31).

High Contracting Parties undertake to respect and to ensure respect for the present Convention in all circumstances". Common Article 1 takes the form of an obligation of due diligence, which implies that States must make every lawful effort in their power to prevent LoAC violations, regardless of whether they attain the desired result or not. From the letter and spirit of the provision, it is clear that the obligation in Common Article 1 applies in international and non-international armed conflicts.

Common Article 1 also obliges States to avoid LoAC violations taking place in the future. It does so by creating a framework whereby States not party to a particular armed conflict must use every means at their disposal to ensure that the belligerents comply with the Geneva Conventions and the First Additional Protocol (API), and arguably with the whole body of LoAC. Common Article 1 does not only constitute a basis for action but also imposes upon third States an international legal obligation to ensure respect in all circumstances.

Even more important in contemporary conflicts in Africa is the duty of third States, clearly included in Common Article 1, not to encourage persons or groups engaged in an armed conflict to act in violation of the Geneva Conventions, nor to knowingly aid or assist in the perpetration of such violations. It further includes an obligation to put an end to ongoing LoAC violations. These questions on the application of Common Article 1 may arise where the High Contracting Parties engage in operations conducted by the forces of two or more States within the framework, or under the command and control, of an international or regional organization such as the UN or the AU.

The problem of LoAC violations will not be solved by creating more law: the existing rules of LoAC are sufficient and adapted to the situations they are meant to regulate. Rather, compliance with existing rules seems to be the main hurdle to limiting the effects of armed conflict and adequately protecting persons who are not or are no longer participating in hostilities. This is why underscoring the preventive component of the legal obligation established by Article 1 common to the Geneva Conventions is of paramount importance. The obligation to ensure respect encompasses the duty to prevent breaches of LoAC from occurring in the first place. In view of the ongoing non-international armed conflicts on the African continent and developments in the bodies of law applicable to such conflicts, the AU has an increasing role to play in complementing the role of the International Committee of the Red Cross (ICRC). Considering the numerous armed conflicts on the continent, the AU should explore new and better strategies to further increase respect for LoAC in non-international armed conflicts.

GENERATING RESPECT FOR LoAC IN AFRICA

The protection of civilians in armed conflict affects not only the war-torn countries directly, but the region and the international community at large. At the same time, the responsibility for ensuring civilian protection should be respected by both state and non-state actors. Implementation of human rights and LoAC through permanent, preventive, and corrective scrutiny in the field is more appropriate than a posteriori prosecution of violators.[40] Therefore, in order to enhance the mechanism for compliance with LoAC and the protection of civilians taking into account the unique nature of armed conflicts in Africa, there is a need to consider the following jurisprudential developments. The idea is to construct a legal regime that is able to prevent atrocities against civilians before they occur by deterring potential perpetrators.

The Role of National Courts and LoAC Committees

National or domestic courts have an important role to play in generating respect for, and compliance with, LoAC. Aside from ensuring their impartiality and independence, training of judges in LoAC is important to improve capacity of national courts to promote respect for LoAC. National LOAC committees are complementary to national courts and also play an influential role in generating respect for the law. The ICRC encourages the creation of such bodies because they have proven useful in assisting States to fulfil their obligations under the Geneva Conventions of 1949 and the Additional Protocols, as well as other LoAC instruments. It should be noted, all the same, that the Geneva Conventions do not require the creation of such committees. The decision to do so is solely the prerogative of the government concerned. Nor is there a standard format or structure. As a result, National Committees across different countries vary in composition and in the way they work. A national committee composed of external, influential experts to make these mechanisms particularly effective. Malawi provides a good example of National LoAC committees by, for example, supporting the implementation LoAC legislation and dissemination of LoAC to the military and civilians alike. Within this framework, National Committees within the same geographical region would benefit from peer-to-peer cooperation, to share their expertise to enable a free exchange of experience and knowledge.

The Evolving Role of the UN Human Rights Council

In March 2006, the UN General Assembly established a new and more authoritative human rights body, the Human Rights Council, to replace the Commission on Human Rights as the principal human rights body of the UN. The UN General Assembly established the Human Rights Council as its subsidiary and stipulated that the work of the Council shall be "guided by the principles of universality, impartiality, objectivity and non-selectivity, constructive international dialogue and cooperation, with a view to enhancing

---

[40] Sassòli, note 3 above.

474   D. KUWALI

the promotion and protection of all human rights".[41] International humanitarian law is one of the basis for consideration of the human rights record of member states in the universal periodic review (UPR), which is the most innovative mechanism of the Council. Nevertheless, others argue that it might not be fully appropriated that Human Rights Council, as a body with a specific mandate in the field of human rights, to extend its action to the related but well-differentiated sector of humanitarian law.[42] The argument goes that if the Human Rights Council does not meet the requisite conditions to address international humanitarian law situations, it may "run the risk of losing its authority and credibility".[43]

On the other hand, however, the counterargument is that "given the complimentary and mutually interrelated nature of international human rights law and international humanitarian law, the reference to 'applicable international humanitarian law' as a basis when undertaking the universal periodic review is a correct one does and not cause any confusion".[44] In this way, the recourse to LoAC is necessary "to ensure that a government cannot escape scrutiny by announcing a state of emergency".[45] One reason to use LoAC is the fact that LoAC is the *lex specialis* in armed conflicts. In this way, it would be possible for human rights bodies to constructively use LoAC to determine whether there was a violation of human rights law, without regard to the question of derogation.[46] The Council may make a finding based on LoAC and expressed in the language of human rights law.[47] Importantly, the Council can engage with all relevant actors, both states and non-state actors for purposes of ensuring observance of relevant international human rights and humanitarian law.

Protection of civilians has been one of the subjects of specific recommendations of the Council.[48] It is possible for the Council to apply both human rights and LoAC, for example, since the manner in which investigations for

[41] K. Kemileva et al., 'Expertise in the Human Rights Council: A Policy Paper Prepared Under the Auspices of the Geneva Academy of International Humanitarian Law and Human Rights,' Geneva, June 2010, p. 5.

[42] M. Lempinen and M. Scheinin, The New Human Rights Council: The First Two Years,' Åbo Akademi University, Institute for Human Rights, 2007, p. 5.

[43] Ibid., p. 5.

[44] Ibid.

[45] Ibid.

[46] See for example, the Inter-American Commission and Court of Human Rights, *Abella* v. *Argentina*, Case 11. 137, Report No. 55/97, OEA/Ser. L/V/II.95 Doc. 7 rev., 271 (1997); and *Bámaca Velásquez* Case, Judgment of 25 November 2000 (Ser. C) No. 70 (2000).

[47] Hampson, *supra* note 40, p. 559.

[48] See for example, Report of the Office of the High Commissioner, *supra* note 36, p. 14.

violations are conducted is more or less similar for all mechanisms, irrespective of whether they are humanitarian law or human rights law violations.[49] The simultaneous application of international human rights and LoAC by the Human Rights Council reflect the complimentary nature of the two regimes and may lead to the benefit of the civilians that need protection. The Council may need to train its internal expertise in LoAC or to use external LoAC experts when faced with situations relating to protection of civilians in armed conflicts. On their part, states need to recognize their obligation, stemming from the UN Charter, to cooperate with all appropriate organs of the UN, including the Human Rights Council as well as its special procedures, in their efforts to promote and protect the rights of civilians in armed conflicts.[50]

Adoption of Universal Jurisdiction

Under the Geneva Conventions, any State has the jurisdiction to try perpetrators of war crimes, irrespective of where the crime was committed and whether the State exercising jurisdiction was a party to the armed conflict in which it occurred. All States Parties to the Geneva Conventions have a duty to search for perpetrators of war crimes and bring them to justice.[51] Further, jurisdiction over other types of war crimes is by customary international law and it is also universal in that any State may exercise jurisdiction.[52] Therefore, universal jurisdiction is a useful tool that is available to ensure compliance with human rights and LoAC and bring the perpetrators to justice regardless of where the offence was committed. In principle, the prospect that one may be prosecuted anywhere on the planet in respect of a violation of LoAC or for mass atrocity crimes should act as a serious deterrent to potential perpetrators.

Gross violations of human rights and LoAC are of legitimate concern to the international community, and give rise to prosecution under the principle of universal jurisdiction.[53] The principle of universal jurisdiction recognizes that certain acts are so heinous and widely condemned that any State may prosecute an offender once custody is obtained. The principle of universal

---

[49] Lempinen and Scheinin, note 40 above, p. 5.

[50] As above, p. 29.

[51] *Cf. Geneva Convention for the Amelioration of the Condition of the Wounded and Sick in Armed Forces in the Field*, 75 U.N.T.S. 31, *entered into force* October 21, 1950 ['Geneva Convention I]; *Geneva Convention for the Amelioration of the Condition of Wounded, Sick and Shipwrecked Members of Armed Forces at Sea*, 75 U.N.T.S. 85, *entered into force* October 21, 1950 ['Geneva Convention II]; *Geneva Convention relative to the Treatment of Prisoners of War*, 75 U.N.T.S. 135, *entered into force* October 21, 1950 ['Geneva Convention III]; and *Geneva Convention relative to the Protection of Civilian Persons in Time of War*, 75 U.N.T.S. 287, *entered into force* October. 21, 1950 ['Geneva Convention IV].

[52] See Greenwood, *supra* note 1, p. 817.

[53] Africa Legal Aid, Cairo-Arusha Principles on Universal Jurisdiction in Respect of Gross Human Rights Offences: An African Perspective, 20 October 2002, Principle 6.

476   D. KUWALI

jurisdiction does not require establishment of any link between the criminal and the prosecuting State. All that is required is universal condemnation of the offence. Universal jurisdiction is a useful tool that is available for the international community to ensure compliance with human rights and LoAC treaties and bring the perpetrators of mass atrocities to justice regardless of where the offence was committed. Therefore, one viable means to enhance the protection of civilians is to promote widespread adoption of the principle of universality as the legal basis for prosecutorial jurisdiction. The grave human rights situation in conflict regions deserves international scrutiny and accountability within multilateral processes.

Most States have accepted the principle of universal jurisdiction by becoming parties to instruments which provide for universal jurisdiction over war crimes, genocide, and crimes against humanity. These crimes are also espoused in the 1949 Geneva Conventions, the 1948 Genocide Convention and the 1984 Convention against Torture. However, many States have not ensured that their courts can exercise jurisdiction in respect of mass atrocity crimes on the basis of universal jurisdiction. To ensure that perpetrators of serious violations of human rights and LoAC are brought to justice, States need to "adopt measures, including legislative and administrative, that will ensure that their national courts can exercise universal jurisdiction over gross human rights offences, including, but not limited to, those contained in the Rome Statute".[54] The same is echoed in Principle 11 of the Princeton Principles on Universal Jurisdiction, that states should enact national legislation to enable the exercise of universal jurisdiction.[55]

However, there are problems relating to the normative content of universal jurisdiction. Firstly, universal jurisdiction merely authorizes rather than obliges States to prosecute and punish offenders. International law does not import a mandatory obligation upon States to undertake prosecution. Secondly, there exists no systematic or general rule of law conferring an obligation, or even a right, upon States to prosecute and punish perpetrators of war crimes, genocide, and crimes against humanity, in general. Apart from the problems in the normative content of universal jurisdiction, the legal status of universal

[54] Ibid.

[55] Principle 11 of the Princeton Principles on Universal Jurisdiction. Although it is easy to argue that the Princeton Principles on Universal Jurisdiction are not positive law, and therefore not legally binding nor enforceable, it cannot be disputed that these Principles are an authoritative and persuasive exposition of evolving international law on the subject of universal jurisdiction and can advance the application of the principle of universal jurisdiction in national legal systems. Princeton Principles on Universal Jurisdiction, Princeton: Princeton University Press, 2001 ['Princeton Principles']; see also Principles 20, 23 and 27 of the Updated Principles on Impunity for the protection and promotion of human rights through action to combat impunity [the 'Updated Principles on Impunity'], E/CN.4/2005/102/Add.1, 8 February 2005; see also D. Orentlicher, Report of the Independent expert to update the Updated Principles on Impunity to combat impunity, E/CN.4/2005/102, 18 February 2005 ['Orentlicher Report'].

jurisdiction as a norm of international law is still questionable. State practice regarding the application of universal jurisdiction has been neither general nor consistent; thus, universal jurisdiction is far from universal.[56] This gives room for perpetrators to escape prosecution and punishment because some States may be willing to provide a fugitive of justice safe haven. The questionable status of universal jurisdiction in international law exposes the need for systematic extradition, prosecution, and punishment of perpetrators of mass atrocities.

While not all states recognize the application of the theory of universality, few states have enacted national legislation needed to prosecute perpetrators of mass atrocity crimes. Surely, if more states would recognize and apply this theory of universal jurisdiction, national criminal justice systems would have the competence to exercise their jurisdiction for such crimes. The fact that mass atrocity crimes such as genocide, war crimes, and crimes against humanity are subject to universal jurisdiction indicates that such crimes "are universally repulsive, uniformly condemned, and subject to universal prosecution by any government, anywhere, at any time".[57] As such, universal jurisdiction is an important tool to end impunity and prevent violations of human rights and LoAC in order to protect civilians.

States should ensure the effectiveness of the assumption of universal jurisdiction through reforms in criminal justice, prosecutions, and collection of evidence. States must ensure that they fully satisfy their legal obligations in respect of international and internationalized criminal tribunals. This requires States to enact domestic legislation that enables them to fulfil obligations that arise through their adherence to the Rome Statute of the International Criminal Court (ICC) and other binding instruments, including implementation of applicable obligations to apprehend and surrender suspects and to cooperate in respect of evidence. Institutionalizing universal jurisdiction will spread the web of jurisdiction to fill any jurisdictional vacuum and diminishing safe havens for perpetrators of mass atrocities. The legitimacy of international justice, coupled with the greater accessibility of domestic justice, can facilitate the internalization of accountability in the political culture.[58]

The crimes in Article 5(1) of the Rome Statute of the ICC are highly political and often involve government machinery. As such, there is a great possibility that a territorial state may not be capable of effectively prosecuting and punishing such crimes. As such, there is a need for a legal framework that attributes a right and, even more so, an obligation upon states to exercise universal jurisdiction over mass atrocity crimes, if authors of atrocities are to

---

[56] L.S. Sunga, *International Responsibility in International Law for Serious Human Rights Violations*, Dordrecht: Martinus Nijhoff Publishers, 1992, p. 114.

[57] C.C. Joyner, 'Arresting Impunity: The Case for Universal Jurisdiction in Bringing War Criminals to Accountability,' 59(4) *Accountability for International Crimes and Serious Violations of Fundamental Human Rights* (1996), pp. 153–172, p. 169.

[58] P. Akhavan, 'Beyond Impunity: Can International Criminal Justice Prevent Future Atrocities?' 95(7) *American Journal of International Law* (2001), pp. 7–31, p. 22.

be deterred from committing such heinous crimes. While there is a growing recognition for the exercise of universal jurisdiction for mass atrocity crimes, in the absence of treaty law or an authoritative judicial decision, the basis for a national court to exercise universal jurisdiction may be contested. Hence States should enact legislation unequivocally providing for universal jurisdiction.

It is, therefore, recommended that States should review their laws and policies to ensure arrest, extradition, and prosecution of suspected perpetrators of mass atrocities. Through a concerted effort to facilitate the extradition and trial of perpetrators of mass atrocities, the international community can take positive steps towards ending the culture of impunity. There has been a gap in the practice of some States to deport or deny entry to foreign nationals who are suspected to have committed atrocities, but have not acted to ensure that these individuals are prosecuted abroad. The European Union (EU) has narrowed this gap through decisions establishing a "European Network of Contact Points" in respect of persons responsible for genocide, crimes against humanity, and war crimes and requiring mutual assistance in investigation of such crimes. This is a model that can be emulated to ensure that there is no safe haven for perpetrators of violations of human rights and humanitarian norms in Africa. This view is supported by Principle 12 of the Princeton Principles on Universal Jurisdiction which urges that in all future treaties, and in protocols to existing treaties, concerned with mass atrocity crimes, states shall include provisions for universal jurisdiction.[59]

The Potential Role of the African Court of Justice and Human Rights

The African Union (AU) has established the African Court of Justice and Human Rights (ACtJHR or the "African Court"). An important catalyst for recourse to the African Court is, *inter alia,* Article 28(d) of the ACtJHR Statute which provides that actions may be brought before the Court on the basis of any question of international law. An obvious example would be the interpretation of the often politico-legal penumbra issue of whether or not genocide has been committed in a given situation, as in the Darfur scenario. Further, according to Article 53(1) of the ACtJHR Statute, the African Court may give an advisory opinion on any legal question at the request of any of the organ of the AU or any other organ of the AU as may be authorized by the AU Assembly.

Although not yet operational, the generous jurisdiction of the African Court provides wide latitude to engage the African Court to deal with cases of mass atrocity crimes to change behaviour of repressive States and individual perpetrators.[60] The African Court can also provide legal clarity, for instance,

---

[59] Principle 12 of the Princeton Principles on Universal Jurisdiction, *supra* note 84.

[60] A. de Hoogh, *Obligations Erga Omnes and International Crimes: A Theoretical Inquiry into the Implementation and Enforcement of the International Responsibility of States*, The Hague: Kluwer Law International, 1996, p. 404.

on the dilemma in cases of trade-off between peace and justice in post-conflict settings and the often one-sided victor's justice for war crimes. Furthermore, according to Article 31 of the ACtJHR Statute, the African Court is mandated to apply as sources of law any relevant human rights instrument ratified by the State in question, including the general principles of law recognized universally or by African States. In other words, the African Court could become the judicial arm of panoply of human rights agreements to which AU States are parties as well as the Geneva Conventions and Additional Protocol thereto and the ICC Statute.[61]

Experience has shown that mass atrocity crimes are committed under the hand of the State or those who wield state-like power.[62] This fact begs the difficult question of who will try the perpetrators of war crimes, genocide, or crimes against humanity. Apart from the ICC and ad hoc penal institutions, the African Court may also be a possible forum for bringing such cases. Although the African Court cannot actually prosecute perpetrators of human rights violations, its involvement in cases relating to them can serve far-reaching goals. Given the inter-State complaint procedure and the limited NGO access to the African Court, its judgement can put pressure on governments to comply with extraterritorial obligations such as the *aut dedere aut judicare* principle and duty to cooperate with efforts to bring perpetrators of atrocities to justice. The African Court can also establish an authoritative factual record and adjudicate state responsibility for violations of fundamental human rights and LOAC, which may provide psychological support to victims. The African Court may provide opportunity for parties to initiate cases relatively quickly and inexpensively since its work will not require apprehension of offenders.

To this end, the African Court may serve the most useful purpose as an adjunct to other mechanisms of individual accountability. Such legal suits may clarify international obligations concerning arrest, prosecution, extradition, or judicial assistance and encourage recalcitrant States to comply with them. For example, if a State has custody of an 'indictee' and refuses requests for extradition to a competent national or international tribunal, a case may be brought to induce that State to extradite the indictee.[63] By the same token, if a State refuses to investigate abuses or grants an amnesty to perpetrators in violation of its international law obligations to prosecute them, a suit might be brought against that State to restrain it from doing so.

The African Court has a potential to be a single most powerful engine for the enforcement of the human rights and LoAC commitments by AU States

---

[61] Project on International Courts and Tribunals, African Court of Human and Peoples' Rights, available at: www.pict-pcti.org/courts/ACHPR.html (accessed 12 July 2009).

[62] W.A. Schabas, 'Genocide Convention at Fifty,' *Special Report*, Washington, DC: United States Institute of Peace, 1999, p. 4.

[63] S.R. Ratner and J.S. Abrams, *Accountability for Human Righhts Atrocities in International Law: Beyond the Nuremberg Legacy*, 2nd edn, Oxford: Oxford University Press, 2001, pp. 225–227.

480 D. KUWALI

and the prevention of mass atrocity crimes against civilians. Given that the 'Single Protocol', which established the African Court, allows African governments and inter-governmental organizations (IGOs) as well as the African Commission to bring cases before the African Court, these institutions should closely coordinate in pursuing delinquent States beyond borders and bring them to justice through the African Court. It is, thus, important that African judicial institutions need to be strengthened, and an emphasis placed on the creation of credible enforcement mechanisms that will back up the judgements of the African Court.[64] Therefore, the stakeholder community, AU States, civil society, the AU, and indeed the international community should intensify efforts to urge States to ratify the "Single Protocol", and that AU States should make the declaration allowing for individual petitions.[65]

The Case for an African Continent-Wide Committee on LoAC

The most important means of ensuring compliance with LoAC is scrutiny by, and pressure from, third parties. A State engaged in an armed conflict will often be heavily dependent upon the goodwill of neutral States, which may well be put in jeopardy by allegations of atrocities. Such allegations can also have a major effect upon public opinion in the belligerent States themselves. Pressure of this kind operates outside the law itself, since the law makes no express provision for it.[66] It is in such areas where "pressure operates outside the law" where regional organizations need to intervene to fill the compliance gap. This argument is validated by the fact that the diminishing impact of the "protecting power" system has shifted the burden to the ICRC to assume the humanitarian functions.[67]

Given that the fact that armed conflicts are the major contributors to the suffering of civilians, to protect civilians in armed conflicts, the AU may need to establish a continent-wide committee to oversee the compliance with LoAC to compliment the ICRC—to do at regional level what the ICRC does on the international plane. Such a regional LoAC committee should: ensure that States in the region should make a declaration pursuant to Article 90 of Additional Protocol I recognizing the competence of the International Fact-finding

---

[64] D. Mepham and S. Ramsbotham, *Safeguarding Civilians: Delivering on the Responsibility to Protect in Africa*, London: Institute of Policy Research, 2007, p. 33.

[65] According to Article 30(f) of the ACtJHR Statute, individuals and NGOs accredited to the AU or to its organs can only submit cases against States if the State concerned has made a declaration accepting the competence of the African Court to do so under Article 8 of the 'Single Protocol.' Article 8 of the 'Single Protocol' as read with Article 30(f) of the ACtJHR Statute provides for an additional declaration to be signed by a State Party upon ratification of the 'Single Protocol', accepting the competence of the African Court to hear cases from NGOs and individuals.

[66] Greenwood, *supra* note 1, p. 820.

[67] Ibid., pp. 820–821.

Commission[68]; ensure that countries at war declare a state of emergency pursuant to Article 4 of the ICCPR or else there can be no derogations of fundamental human rights. Recommendation of such a committee should be binding on States in the region. The idea of establishing regional LoAC committees is not to overlook the important role of the ICRC but rather to complement it since monitoring the implementation of LoAC cannot be the sole role or the exclusive domain of the ICRC.

To the extent that human rights law applies in armed conflicts, it covers much the same ground as LoAC. It is generally accepted that although human rights law is applicable in armed conflicts LoAC takes precedence as *lex specialis*. However, since LoAC is based on completely different historical roots, it has been considered mutually exclusive. According to the *Nuclear Weapons* Advisory Opinion, LoAC is tailored for extraordinary situations of an armed conflict and for the protection of the respective interests of the (State) parties, while human rights deal with limitations on regular governmental activities vis-à-vis the individual.[69] The separation has also been institutionally motivated. For example, the ICRC, which is mandated to deal with *jus in bello*, has wanted to keep its neutrality and its distance from the politicized organs of the UN. The UN, while emphasizing on the *jus contra bellum*, does not deal with the "laws of war". The ICRC has been unwilling to approach human rights, which were seen as an emanation of political agendas in the UN. However, the scope of application of human rights is extended to war times in Article 4(1) of the ICCPR.[70]

The omission to include an LoAC body within the framework of the AU does not come as a surprise given that it has generally considered that the UN, for instance, which is an organization for peace and security, should not deal

---

[68] Article 90 of Protocol I provides for the establishment of an International Fact Finding Commission to inquire into alleged violations of the Geneva Conventions and Protocols. While the International Fact Finding Commission's jurisdiction is limited and it has no power to impose any kind of penalty, the publicity which its findings would have may prove a potent weapon. See Greenwood, *supra* note 153, p. 821.

[69] *Legality of the Threat or Use of Nuclear Weapons,* Advisory Opinion of 8 July 1996, *ICJ Reports 1996 (i),* para. 24.

[70] H. Krieger, 'A Conflict of Norms: The Relationship between Humanitarian Law and Human Rights Law in the ICRC Customary Law Study,' 11(2) *Journal of Conflict & Security,* (2006), pp. 265–291, pp. 266–267; see also The European Convention for the Protection of Human Rights and Fundamental Freedoms, 213 U.N.T.S. 222, *entered into force* Sept. 3, 1953, *as amended by* Protocols Numbers 3, 5, 8, and 11 *which entered into force* on 21 September 1970, 20 December 1971, 1 January 1990, and 1 November 1998 *respectively* [the 'European Convention on Human Rights' or 'ECHR'], Art. 15(2).

482   D. KUWALI

with questions relating to armed conflicts.[71] This is punctuated by the International Law Commission (ILC), which decided at its first meeting in 1949 not to include the law of war among the subjects with which it concerns itself. However, in view of more than 250 armed conflicts that have occurred, and more than 40 ongoing, the argument would lose its relevance and credibility. In a similar tone, others argue that LoAC would be politicized if the UN had direct responsibility. However, progressive scholarship suggests that while this argument seems valid, it should be seen as an argument in favour, because LoAC is also a political issue.[72]

Humanitarian instruments in force form part of international law and are interlinked with the system of international security, whether for arms control or for peaceful settlement of conflicts. In *Legal Consequences of the Construction of a Wall in the Occupied Palestinian Territory (Israel Wall* Case), even the ICJ has confirmed that human rights law continues to apply in situations to which LoAC is applicable.[73] The Human Rights Committee has also affirmed that in situations of armed conflict, "both spheres of the law are

---

[71] However, in 1968, the UN General Assembly affirmed the need in all armed conflicts to apply 'basic humanitarian principles,' in its resolution on respect for human rights in armed conflicts (General Assembly Resolution 2444 (XXIII), Respect for human rights in armed conflicts, 19 December 1968). Another resolution was adopted in 1970 on the basic principles for the protection of civilian populations in armed conflicts. The Assembly reiterated the principle of distinction and the prohibition of attacks on the civilian population as such, and added new principles, *inter alia*, the continued full application of fundamental human rights in armed conflicts and the principle of precaution (General Assembly Resolution 2675(XXV)). The Security Council has also taken steps to address issues of LOAC. In 1992 the Council condemned the violations of LOAC taking place in the territory of Somalia and demanded the parties to that conflict to 'immediately cease and desist from all breaches of [LOAC]'; (S/RES/794 (1992). In 1995 the Council recognised the importance of the parties to the conflict in Georgia to abide by the rules of LOAC; (S/RES/993 (1995). With regards to the conflict in Sudan the Security Council, acting under Chapter VIIof the Charter, in 2004 established an international commission of inquiry for the purpose of investigating violations of human rights and LOAC in Darfur; (S/RES/1564 (2004). In a subsequent resolution the Council condemned all violations of LOAC and stated that all the parties to that conflict must show respect for LOAC. In this context the Council demanded both the government and the armed groups to 'ensure that their members comply with [LOAC]'; (S/RES/1574 (2004)). The Council has referred the situation in Sudan and Darfur to the ICC; (S/RES/1593 (2005)). The UN Commission on Human Rights and the UN High Commissioner on Human Rights has also considered questions involving LOAC. (Commission on Human Rights, Report of the United Nations High Commissioner for Human Rights and Follow-Up the World Conference on Human Rights, Situation of Human Rights in the Darfur Region of the Sudan, E/CN.4/2005/3, 7 May 2004). The Human Rights Committee has stated that the ICCPR supplements LOAC in armed conflicts (General Comment No. 31, Nature of the General Legal Obligation Imposed on States Parties to the Covenant, CCPR/C/21/Rev.1/Add.13, 26 May 2004).

[72] See G. Melander, 'The Relationship between Human Rights, Humanitarian Law and Refugee Law,' Lund: Raoul Wallenberg Institute (Undated), p. 33.

[73] *Legal Consequences of the Construction of a Wall in the Occupied Palestinian Territory*, Advisory Opinion, 9 July 2004, General List No. 131, paras. 107–112.

complimentary, not mutually exclusive".[74] This underscores the suggestion that LoAC should be highlighted in the general context of international peace and security, and the AU peace and security agenda in particular.[75]

Towards this end, while highlighting the need for an institution to oversee the implementation of LoAC within the framework of the AU, the AU human rights institutions as well as the UN human rights mechanisms, particularly the Human Rights Council with its Special Procedures should be allowed to investigate, monitor and publicly report on the human rights situation on the continent. It thus becomes imperative that AU Members should establish national and regional mechanisms to ensure accountability in order to end impunity and prevent mass atrocity crimes on the continent.[76]

There is need to emphasize on reporting and monitoring compliance with LoAC and human rights by NSA groups. Nonetheless, due to the traditional confidential approach of the ICRC, there may be need to establish a distinct body providing comments with regard to the LoAC and human rights performance of an armed group and publishing the group's allegations about its performance. It is on this basis that the AU should consider establishing a legal framework that should include a mechanism for enforcing the compliance of international human rights and humanitarian law by armed non-state groups on the battlefield in Africa. The crucial point would be to provide a mechanism where recommendation of such a committee would be binding on AU States.

In addition, the AU needs to encourage the ratification and implementation of the ICC Statute by AU States and promoting effective operation of the ICC, internationalized penal institutions. Additional mechanisms should be explored to enhance the observance of LoAC and incorporating a "Code of Conduct" on human rights and LoAC into the training of all armed forces in the region, including the ASF and the sub-regional standby forces of the AU, which should have a deterrent effect.[77] On their part, AU Member States should develop appeal mechanisms at national and regional levels for the redress of grievances relating to failures to protect civilians in armed conflict. This will help to enhance the protection of civilians in armed conflicts,

---

[74] United Nations, Human Rights Committee, General Comment No. 31 on The Nature of the General Legal Obligation on the States Parties to the International Covenant on Civil and Political Rights, CCCPR/C/21/Rev.1/Add.13, 26 May 2004, para. 11.

[75] M. Veuthey, 'International Humanitarian Law and the Restoration and Maintenance of Peace,' available at: www.iss.co.za/Pubs/ASR/7No5/InternationalHumanitarian.html (accessed 15 February 2021).

[76] See General obligations of States to take effective action to combat impunity, Principle 1 of the Updated Principles on Impunity for the protection and promotion of human rights through action to combat impunity [the Updated Principles on Impunity], E/CN.4/2005/102/Add.1, 8 February 2005.

[77] Lieutenant General Carlos Alberto dos Santoz Cruz, "United Nations, Independent Assessment Report on the Protection of Civilians and Neutralization of Armed Groups in Beni and Mambasa Territories in the Democratic Republic of the Congo" ("Dos Santos Cruz Report"), 15 January 2020, p. 3.

484   D. KUWALI

ensure punishment of violators, and lay a solid foundation for containment and prevention of conflict and mass atrocity crimes.

In armed conflicts, redress to the victims is central such that regional organizations may need to develop appeal mechanisms for the redress of victims' grievances and ensure punishment of violators. Enforcement of LoAC in non-international armed conflicts is difficult under the current legal regime, such that regional mechanisms may need to formulate a comprehensive legal framework for all armed conflicts without distinction. As initiated by the ICRC, regional organizations may need to harness the customary laws applicable to armed conflicts which should bind both State and non-State armed groups. On their part, States should also develop appeal mechanisms at national and regional levels for the redress of grievances relating to failures to protect civilians in armed conflict.

This will help to enhance the protection of civilians in armed conflicts, ensure punishment of violators, and lay a solid foundation for containment and prevention of conflict and mass atrocity crimes. To this end, human rights and humanitarian NGOs within the regional framework should encourage and support governments to review all international instruments and agreements with relevance to protection of civilians in armed conflicts and reform national legislation to be in accord with the regional arrangements. The Common African Defence and Security Policy commits the AU to provide a framework to ensure implementation of LoAC on the continent. AU States have the legal basis, through Article 4(h) as well as the ASF as continental police and with universal jurisdiction to offer perpetrators of war crimes no refugee on the continent. This may mechanism may deter potential perpetrators of violations of LoAC.

CONCLUSION

The protection of civilians in armed conflict in Africa touches not only the war-torn countries directly, but the continent as a whole and beyond. At the same time, the responsibility for ensuring civilian protection should be respected by both State and non-state actors. The absence of a consistent legal framework or useful reporting mechanism can deter victims from reporting abuses and therefore, the norm of protection will remain at the level of rhetoric. Yet, under the Geneva Conventions, any State has the jurisdiction to try perpetrators of war crimes, irrespective of where the crime was committed and whether the State exercising jurisdiction was a party to the armed conflict in which it occurred. All States Parties to the Geneva Conventions have a duty to search for perpetrators of war crimes and bring them to justice.[78]

---

[78] Cf. *Geneva Convention for the Amelioration of the Condition of the Wounded and Sick in Armed Forces in the Field*, 75 U.N.T.S. 31, *entered into force* October 21, 1950 ['Geneva Convention I]; *Geneva Convention for the Amelioration of the Condition of Wounded, Sick and Shipwrecked Members of Armed Forces at Sea*, 75 U.N.T.S. 85, *entered into force* October 21, 1950 ['Geneva Convention II]; *Geneva Convention relative to the Treatment*

Further, jurisdiction over other types of war crimes is by customary international law and it is also universal, in that any State may exercise jurisdiction.[79] Therefore, universal jurisdiction is a useful tool that is available for the AU to ensure compliance with LoAC and bring the perpetrators to justice regardless of where the offence was committed. AU Member States have the legal basis, through the ASF, to act as continental police and with a network of courts with compulsory jurisdiction to offer perpetrators of war crimes no refugee on the continent. In principle, the prospect that one may be prosecuted anywhere on the continent (or even in the world) in respect of a violation of LoAC or for mass atrocity crimes should act as a serious deterrent to potential perpetrators.

Given the limited functions of the present implementation regime of human rights and LOAC in armed conflicts, there is need for the AU to fill in the gaps. For example, the AU should consider establishing a committee within its machinery to oversee the implementation of LoAC in their respective regions as a complimentary to the ICRC. To this end, the UN Special Representative for the Promotion of Protection of Civilians in Armed Conflicts has a monumental task to play in encouraging States to make declarations pursuant to Article 90 of the Additional Protocol I recognizing the competence of the International Fact-finding Commission.[80] The Special Representative should also ensure that countries at war declare state of emergency pursuant to Article 4 of the ICCPR to prevent derogations of fundamental human rights.

More so, there should be no amnesty for atrocities against civilians. On their part, States should domesticate the principle of universal jurisdiction in order to offer violators of human rights and LoAC no safe haven. The prospect that one may be prosecuted by any state worldwide, in respect of serious human rights and LoAC violations may be a serious deterrent to potential perpetrators.[81] To this end, African States that have not yet ratified the Rome Statute should be encouraged to do so and those that have ratified should not only implement the Rome Statute but also cooperate with the ICC to arrest and prosecute offenders. The ICC alone may not be the best tool to deter or end the commission of mass atrocities on the continent. Therefore, instead of focusing on criminal prosecution as curative medicine after the victims have already suffered, the international community should help Africa address the urgent political, social, and economic problems that spark the conflicts that

---

of Prisoners of War, 75 U.N.T.S. 135, *entered into force* October 21, 1950 ['Geneva Convention III]; and *Geneva Convention Relative to the Protection of Civilian Persons in Time of War*, 75 U.N.T.S. 287, *entered into force* October 21, 1950 ['Geneva Convention IV].

[79] See Greenwood, note 1 above, p. 817.

[80] See Greenwood, note 1 above, p. 821.

[81] As above, p. 821.

486   D. KUWALI

lead to the crimes that impel the ICC to hunt for perpetrators in the first place.[82]

On the part of African States, more attention could be paid to the obligation established by Common Article 1 of the Geneva Conventions to respect and to ensure respect for the Geneva Conventions. In particular, there could be more room to explore how AU member states could ensure respect for, and compliance with, LoAC in non-international armed conflict. In this respect, national courts and LoAC committees are two effective instruments for ensuring compliance with the law. All in all, it is the responsibility of governments and international organizations alike to prevent and respond to violations of LoAC, and to protect against their grave humanitarian consequences. The absence of effective controls on the transfer of small arms, light weapons, and anti-personnel landmines along with their low cost and easy availability to untrained combatants has facilitated the commission of mass atrocity crimes.[83] This fortifies the need for a continent-wide moratorium on small arms and light weapons on the continent.

Africa, probably more than any other continent, needs to establish an institution to oversee the implementation of international humanitarian law on the continent. The myriad armed conflicts and the incessant assaults on civilians in Africa justify the need for such an institution to compliment the Geneva-based ICRC. To ensure respect for, and compliance with, LoAC, the AU should consider to: establish a committee within its machinery to oversee the compliance with LoAC to compliment the ICRC. Recommendation of such a committee should be binding on AU States; ensure that AU States should make a declaration pursuant to Article 90 of the Additional Protocol I recognizing the competence of the International Fact-finding Commission; ensure that countries at war declare state of emergency pursuant to Article 4 of the ICCPR or else there be no derogations of fundamental human rights; create a standing police capacity for the ASFthat will ensure that perpetrators of war crimes are brought to justice.

Needless to say that peacekeepers should not only have a capability to protect but also a coherent strategy to protect civilians in armed conflicts. Since the problems surrounding the implementation and enforcement in non-international armed conflicts are manifold and not easily dealt with under the current legal regime, a solution to this problem would be to formulate a comprehensive legal framework for all armed conflicts, as opposed to the current division between international and non-international armed conflicts. To do this, the AU can collate and collect the customary laws applicable to armed conflicts encompassing human rights and LoAC obligations which should bind both State and non-state armed groups. In armed conflicts, redress to the victims is central, and therefore, the AU should develop appeal

---

[82] See Obasi Okafor-Obasi 'The International Criminal Court and Human Rights Enforcement,' 12 *ILSA Journal of International & Comparative Law* (2005), pp. 87–97.

[83] Ibid., para. 23.

mechanisms within its framework for the redress of victims' grievances and ensure punishment of violators.

Enforcement of LoAC in non-international armed conflicts is difficult under the current legal regime, such that the AU may need to formulate a comprehensive legal framework for all armed conflicts without distinction. The AU should harness the customary laws applicable to armed conflicts which should bind both State and NSAGs. The AU should encourage the ratification and implementation of the Rome Statute by AU States and ensure training in LoAC by armed forces on the continent. Implementation through permanent, preventive, and corrective scrutiny in the field is more appropriate than a posteriori penalization of violations.[84]

No doubt, LoAC regulates and contributes to the containment of violence and the preservation of fundamental standards of humanity in the midst of conflicts. For practical, policy, and humanitarian reasons, LoAC applies the same for both belligerents, without any adverse distinction based on the nature or origin of the armed conflict or on the causes espoused by, or attributed to, the Parties to the conflict.[85] Therefore, LoAC is an important component in maintaining peace and its very nature shatters the dangerous illusion of unlimited force or total war; creates areas of peace in the midst of conflict; imposes the principle of common humanity and calls for dialogue.[86] This explains why LoAC is increasingly becoming part of global thinking on security issues at the national, regional, and international levels. The inclusion of LoAC complements the current concept of human security that the implementation of LoAC should form part of a culture of conflict prevention for the twenty-first century. It is for this reason that the Common African Defence and Security Policy commits the AU to provide a framework for humanitarian action to ensure that LoAC is applied during conflicts between and among African States.[87]

---

[84] Sassòli, note 3 above.

[85] See the Preamble to the *Protocol Additional to the Geneva Conventions of 12 August 1949, and Relating to the Protection of Victims of International Armed Conflicts [Additional Protocol I]*, 1125 U.N.T.S. 3, *entered into force* December 7, 1978.

[86] Veuthey, note 73 above.

[87] African Union, *Draft Framework for a Common African Defence and Security Policy*, January, available at: www.iss.co.za/AF/RegOrg/unity_to_union/oaukey.html , p. 11; see also G. Puley, The Responsibility to Protect: East, West, and Southern African Perspectives on Preventing and Responding to Humanitarian Crises, *Working Paper, Project Ploughshares 05–5*, 2005, pp. 12–13, p. 16.

CHAPTER 28

Promoting Peace and Reconciliation in Africa

Ibrahim Mohammed Machina and Lawan Cheri

INTRODUCTION

Africa has witnessed increased armed conflicts such as civil war, violent extremism, and political violence in the last three decades. These have remained a significant challenge to peace and security in Africa and a major setback to Africa's aspirations for peaceful and prosperous societies by 2063. Thus, despite quests for a 'peaceful, integrated, and prosperous Africa' by 2063, achieving peace and security remains elusive in the continent. The end of the Cold War in the 1990s and the triumph of liberal democracy following the collapse of the Soviet Union significantly reduced the threat of inter-state military confrontation in Africa.

However, the supposed liberal-peace dividend has evolved the nature and dynamics of (in)security in Africa a fact which has been proven true by Desire Hakorimana and Godard Busingye in Chapter 2 as well as Youssef Mahmoud and Chimwemwe Fabiano in Chapter 3.[1] While in general African states have

[1] Gary King and Christopher Murray, Rethinking Human Security, *Political Science Quarterly* (2002) 116 (4).

I. M. Machina (✉)
Department of Political Science, Federal University, Gashua, Nigeria

L. Cheri
Public Administration Department, Federal Polytechnic
Damaturu, Damaturu, Nigeria

© The Author(s), under exclusive license to Springer Nature
Switzerland AG 2022
D. Kuwali (ed.), *The Palgrave Handbook of Sustainable Peace and Security in Africa*, https://doi.org/10.1007/978-3-030-82020-6_28

489

made significant efforts towards strengthening peace, security, and democratic ideals, this has been slow and fragile such as in Democratic Republic of the Congo (DRC) and South Sudan.[2] In addition, despite reduction in the number of major armed conflicts in Africa from eleven in 1990 to one in 2007 in Somalia, yet the intensity and impact of these conflicts are greater than before.[3]

Thus, the most pressing threats against peaceful coexistence and social cohesion in many countries in Africa are arguable internal in nature. These threats are referred by terms such as intrastate conflict, civil and uncivil war, fragile or weak states. They breakdown existing social relations and bonds and undermines social cohesion which are the base of societal security and peaceful coexistence.[4] These internal threats are caused mainly by failure and challenges of societies to manage societal fault lines such as differences and diversity.[5]

However, it is worth noting that these societal fault lines which include diversity, ethnicity, or religious differences are not problematic in themselves. It is the failure to manage them that has seen a rise to grievances which manifest across ethnic, religious, and regional divisions. Coupled with socioeconomic factors such as poverty, weak economies and institutions, poor governance, socioeconomic injustices/structural violence, pre and post colonialism disparities, these have led to the myriad of conflicts bedevilling the African continent today because armed conflict thrives and escalates particularly in fragile or deeply divided societies.

To end protracted conflicts and internecine wars in Africa, there is need to develop varieties of measures and strategies to address the conditions that lead to conflict or conflict relapse after peace-making. There is need to strengthen societal capacities to manage diversity and differences and pursue sustainable peace and development. Current approaches to build peace in Africa focuses on state-centric approach using hard power military approach while neglecting programmes to build harmonious relationship between individuals, groups, and their institutions. That is why these peacebuilding efforts have been inadequate and struggle to effectively 'silence the guns by 2020'. Thus, to effectively prevent conflict and ensure sustainable peace in Africa, reviving harmonious relationship between individuals or groups of people in African states is now considered essential in the promotion of peace and stability.[6]

---

[2] Tony Karbo, Introduction: Towards a New Pax Africana, in Tony Karbo and Kudrat Virk (eds), *The Palgrave Handbook of Peacebuilding in Africa* (Switzerland: Palgrave Macmillan).

[3] Rafael Grasa and Oscar Mateos, Conflict, Peace and Security in Africa: An Assessment and New Questions After 50 Years of African Independence, ICIP WORKING PAPERS, 2010/08.

[4] Peter Wallensten, *Understanding Conflict Resolution: War, Peace and the Global System* (London: Sage Publications, 2002).

[5] As above.

[6] H. Haider and C. Mcloughlin, *State-Society Relations and Citizenship in Situations of Conflict and Fragility: Topic Guide Supplement* (Birmingham: GSDRC, 2016).

This highlights the importance of adopting a dynamic and multifaceted approach to addressing the issue of (in)security in Africa. Thus, there is a need to focus on promoting reconciliation and social cohesion as a key goal in peacebuilding. A cohesive society promote and value constructive coexistence of diverse groups with divergent values and lifestyle.[7] Promoting reconciliation and social cohesion is an integral determinant of coexistence and prosperous societies. This creates strong social relations and bonds within and across diverse groups in a given society. This, in turn, leads to high level of trust among the people and between the people and their local institutions. Thus, promoting reconciliation and social cohesion should be an important part of government and civil society engagement in countries in the African continent where people from diverse backgrounds are sharing scarce resources and geographic space. It is even more crucial in deeply divided societies or conflict-affected societies where there is high level of mistrust between the citizens and their institutions.

However, there is limited evidence on effective ways to reestablish trust and dialogue between diverse groups in deeply divided societies or conflict-affected societies in Africa. Against this background, this chapter examines three inter-related approaches; coexistence, reconciliation, and social cohesion as strategies to achieve peace and security at various levels of societies in Africa. These three concepts are relevant dimensions of the conflict resolution spectrum and peacebuilding and they all play an important role in rebuilding war-torn, deeply divided societies or countries in post-conflict stage. The chapter relies on the secondary method to obtain data through desk study. This chapter will provide evidence-based policy recommendations that will guide decision-makers and policymakers on how to build strong and cohesive societies in Africa and pursue sustainable peace, stability, and development, more especially in fragile and post-conflict societies. This chapter argues that strengthening social cohesion should be an integral part of peacebuilding efforts in Africa where most countries have multiple and diverse identity groups sharing scarce resources and geographic space. This, in turn, will support societal resilience and strengthen strong state-society relations in societies in Africa and build lasting and durable peace.

This chapter is structured into six different sections to examines strategies to achieve peace and security at various levels of societies in Africa. The second section following this introduction conceptualises the three key approaches; coexistence, reconciliation, and social cohesion. The third section discusses the imperatives of promoting peaceful coexistence in Africa and the fourth section analyse strategies to foster reconciliation in fragile and post-conflict societies in Africa. The fifth section examines social cohesion as a strategy to promote convergence across groups in Africa and the final section concludes this chapter.

---

[7] Peter Wallensten above note 4.

Conceptualising Coexistence, Reconciliation, and Social Cohesion

Coexistence refers to the capacity of people from diverse backgrounds to live together in harmony, manage diversity and resolve conflict and differences through nonviolent ways. It is evident in relationships across diverse groups in a given community that are built on 'mutual trust, respect, and recognition, and is widely understood as related to social inclusion and integration'.[8] The word reconciliation on the other hand is derived from the Latin word *concili-ates* which means coming together. It literally connotes the process of reviving harmonious relationship between individuals or groups in a given society. This involves reestablishing social relations and dialogue between diverse groups in post-conflict situations and in deeply divided or conflict-affected societies.

Reconciliation is conceptualised in this chapter as the process of restoring social cohesion in societies devastated by conflict and investing in local and national capacities to heal past wrongs and traumas. This includes among others measures to address the root causes of the grievances that fuel conflict, search for justice, truth, forgiveness, and accommodation between conflicting groups and among people in a given society. By rebuilding trust and social relationships, conditions for nurturing social cohesion both as a means to prevent conflict and to consolidate a durable peace will be created. This, in turn, leads to peaceful coexistence in a given society between individuals, groups, and their institutions. Social cohesion is both a means of preventing conflict and a tool for laying the foundation for sustainable peace and coexistence by enabling societies to resolve conflict by pursuing reconciliation.[9]

This is an integral indicator of a peaceful, democratic and prosperous society. It is the 'glue' that bonds society together by promoting a sense of belonging, harmony, community, and increases the degree of commitments by its members to pursuing a shared goal. It is defined as 'a state of affairs concerning both the vertical and the horizontal relationship among members of society as characterised by a set of attitudes and norms that includes trust, a sense of belonging and the willingness to participate and help, as well as their behavioural manifestations'.[10] The United Nations Development Programme (UNDP) defined social cohesion as the 'extent of trust in government and within society and the willingness to participate collectively toward a shared vision of sustainable peace and common development goals'.[11]

---

[8] Coexistence International Focus Paper, What Is Coexistence and Why a Complimentary Approach? Available at: http://www.coexistence.net/.

[9] SEEDS, Social Cohesion and Reconciliation, retrieved from *Social Cohesion and Reconciliation—Seeds of Peace*, 2020, 23/10/2020.

[10] Fletcher D. Cox and Timothy D. Sisk, *Peacebuilding in Deeply Divided Societies Toward Social Cohesion?* (London: Palgrave Macmillan, 2017).

[11] Timothy Sisk, *Strengthening Social Cohesion: Conceptual Framing and Programming Implications* (New York: UNDP, 2020).

Promoting social cohesion is framed in this chapter as the process of strengthening harmonious relations and peaceful coexistence between and among diverse groups, institutions, and state authorities in a given society. This creates positive relationships and trust that binds members of society and promotes intergroup relations and collective action that in turn builds strong, resilient, and socially cohesive societies. 'Social cohesion is present when individuals and groups with different cultures, values, beliefs, lifestyles, and socioeconomic resources have equal access to all domains of societal life and live together without conflict'.[12] Cohesive societies tend to be more inclusive and take care of the well-being of all its members, address marginalisation, and offer its members the opportunity of upward mobility.

PROMOTING PEACEFUL COEXISTENCE IN AFRICA

Promoting peaceful coexistence in Africa is often approached in two ways. The international community that intervenes to support peacebuilding often focuses on national governments spending huge amounts to support democratisation, electoral processes, national institutions, and the military. Another approach is what is called the local turn where peacebuilding initiatives target mitigating and containing major causes of armed conflict between communities with focus on local environments and conflict parties.[13]

The former is usually pursued with the hope of trickle-down effect based on the notion that improved democratic credentials and strong national institutions will improve the capacity of people to resolve differences through nonviolent means. The proponents of this perspective assume that democratic societies establish acceptable methods of sharing resources and allocating benefits to communities and early warning signs are easily contained by strong national institutions. The local approach on the other hand recognises the African cultural traditions of resolving issues through the collective responsibility of families, villages, and communities.

Decoloniality theorists questions the efficacy of Western-inspired peacebuilding initiatives as built on the assumptions of colonial masters without due reverence accorded to the African traditional methods of peacebuilding and peaceful coexistence and replacing it with pursuit of peace that seeks to maintain colonial links with western powers including neocolonialism, imperialism, and overdependence.[14] The formation of African Union (AU) in 2002 resulted in improvements over the years in the processes of preventing conflict

---

[12] David Shiefer and Jolanda van de Noll, The Essentials of Social Coehsion: A Literature Review, *Social Indicators Research: An International and Interdisciplinary Journal for Quality-of-Life Measurement* (2016) 127 (1).

[13] Giulia Piccolino, Local Peacebuilding in a Victor's Peace. Why Local Peace Fails Without National Reconciliation, *International Peacekeeping* (2019) 26 (3), pp. 354–379.

[14] J. Sabelo Ndlovu-Gatsheni, Decoloniality in Africa: A Continuing Search for a New World Order. The Australasian, *Review of African Studies* (2015) 36 (2), pp. 22–50; Ramon Grosfoguel, A Decolonial Approach to Political-Economy: Transmodernity, Border

at international and intranational levels especially through the formation of relevant agencies that work on peace. Prominent among the agencies and commissions is the Peace and Security Council (PSC) that works with national governments and their representatives to detect early warnings and mitigate them before it translates to skirmishes.

The indigenous African approach to peacebuilding and peaceful coexistence emphasises the essentiality of participation rooted in the tradition of village meetings where everyone participates in decision-making in the spirit of solidarity called Ubuntu. The philosophy of Ubuntu centred on interdependence and collectivism where sense of collective responsibility, participation, and sharing guide actions, inactions, and reactions in social relations.[15] The Ubuntu culture is widely practiced in Eastern, Southern, and Central African societies and most of its tenets are observed in western and Northern Africa as well. However, Ubuntu and other African perspectives must be synthesised with western democratic ideas such as gender equality and child rights in order to prevent conflict and encourage peaceful coexistence among all divisions.

Many studies have argued that sociocultural diversity and religious differences are potential threats to social cohesion because it erodes shared cultural values, beliefs, and practices and negatively impacts trust and social networks. However, this view is critique by the argument that it is not so much the actual degree of diversity or differences that is discussed in relation to social cohesion, but rather the way societies manage it. Thus, liberal scholars argued that it is not diversity per se but rather exclusion and socioeconomic status that undermines cohesion by eroding the ties between people.[16]

It is worth noting that failure and challenges of societies to manage societal fault lines such as differences and diversity in addition to socioeconomic factors such as poverty, poor governance, and socioeconomic injustices/structural violence give rise to grievances and eventually lead to conflict which manifests across ethnic, religious, and regional divisions.[17] Furthermore, the ability of people to share resources and facilities regardless of power parity across all divisions—ethnic, regional, historical, linguistic, or religious—and their capacity for tolerance in the face of infringements and anger determines the level of peaceful coexistence among people.

Communities across boundaries have been living in such states long before the colonial rule and must rise to institutionalise such cultures once again in order to promote peaceful coexistence. Border communities at the borders of Nigeria, Benin, and Niger Republic have been sharing facilities regardless

---

Thinking and Global Coloniality, Kult 6 – Special Issue: Epistemological Transformation (2009) Fall, pp. 10–37.

[15] T. Murithi, African Approaches to Building Peace and Social Solidarity, *African Journal on Conflict Resolution* (2006) 6 (2), pp. 9–34.

[16] David shieffer and van der noll above note 12.

[17] Peter Wellensteen above note 4.

of which side of the border provides the facility.[18] Communication is critical to peace promotion among African communities. Media coverage of violent scenes has been portraying the continent as rather hostile place where violence is everywhere from religious extremist groups in Western Africa to the Al-Shabab and pirates in the East, from Xenophobic attacks in the Southern part to Maghreb crisis in the North. New communication channels should devise means of making the many peaceful scenes available to watch in order to encourage thinking about peace and acting towards attaining same.[19] Related to that, developing nonviolent communication skills among youth fosters peaceful coexistence as effective communication remains the cornerstone of conflict prevention, dialogue, and mediation.

The frequency of herders-farmers conflict is another scary issue especially in the West African societies. Addressing such concerns requires concerted efforts at mending fences and promoting peaceful coexistence and mutualism. Establishment of pastoral codes as well as review, enactment and implementation of national and regional laws relating to transhumance remains important in ensuring peaceful coexistence and mutualism. Emphasis on the interlinkages between the two groups in the agriculture value chain creates understanding, tolerance, and trust as interdependence eventually leads to indispensability. Making the two groups come to terms with this symbiotic reality is a step in fostering peaceful coexistence between pastoralist engaged in transhumance and the sedentary farmers along the routes.[20]

Poverty and food insecurity impedes peaceful coexistence. In most African societies, poverty plays significant roles in underpinning crisis and violence as regions with the highest incidence of poverty often slides to violence. Anger, aggression, and animosity prevails where the belly is empty with no hope in sight to provide for basic needs. Attempts at fostering peaceful coexistence must focus on alleviating poverty through economically sustainable approaches that reflect the African environments..[21] Poverty alleviation approaches are mostly copying Euro-American styles and pasting in African environments making it difficult to sustain and the fruits impossible to reap. Encouraging acceptance and sympathy towards the internally displaced persons especially along the Manor river, the Great Lake region, and the Lake Chad is another milestone towards peaceful coexistence.

---

[18] Shuaibu Shittu Isyaku, A Legacy of Peaceful Coexistence: Historico-Political and Economic Perspectives of Nigeria-Benin Relations, *International Journal of Arts and Humanities*. Bahir Dar University, Ethiopia (2017) JAH 6 (1).

[19] Konye Obaji, How to Build Peaceful Coexistence in a Religiously Tensed Nigeria. The Africa Report. 28 January, 2014. https://www.theafricareport.com/4836/how-to-build-a-peaceful-coexistence-in-a-religiously-tensed-nigeria/.

[20] UNOWAS, Pastoralism and Security in West Africa and the Sahel: Towards peaceful coexistence. United Nations Office for West Africa and the Sahel August, 2018.

[21] L. Cheri and A. Kahn, An Examination of Poverty as the Foundation of Crises in Northern Nigeria (2016). A paper published by Insight on Africa Journal. Association of India SAGE publications. 2016.

The fact that most displaced individuals and communities are relying on agrarian resources such as forests, water bodies, and farmlands puts them at odds with host communities which eventual changes their hosting relationship to hostility. However, concerted efforts towards cooperation rather than competition between the hosting and displaced communities usually lead to peaceful coexistence and sustainable management of the resources.[22]

FOSTERING RECONCILIATION IN FRAGILE AND POST-CONFLICT SOCIETIES

Reconciliation is an essential step that is central to the restoration of peace in fragile societies. The fragility of post-conflict societies especially in Africa is rooted in broken social cohesion and the inability of existing institutions to restore trust, confidence, and reassuring conviction that people can live in harmony without resorting the violence. Reconciliation does not presuppose tolerance but rather tries to promote it through communication, understanding, and dialogue.[23] This is because it sounds unrealistic to discuss about restoring mutual trust in the aftermath of violent confrontation between two or more groups when the memories of the atrocities are still fresh in the minds of the actors. More so, if intergroup relationship does not exist prior to the conflict, then it is impossible to talk about restoring harmonious relationship. In most cases, this is usually achieved through 'top-down' approaches such as larger social-political processes like setting up truth and reconciliation commissions at the national level.

For example, the Truth, Justice and Reconciliation Commission (TJRC), and Darfur Internal Dialogue (DIDC) were established after the conflict in Darfur to seek truth and justice and promote reconciliation among communities. This was aim at promoting reconciliation by bringing perpetrators of violence to public awareness through confession and truth-telling so that they are punished through retribution and rule of law or through apology and forgiveness. This, in turn, enables a society or community transitions from a divided past to a shared future. The restoration of social cohesion and amicable settlement of disputes must be preceded by renewal of friendly relations and mutual trust among conflicting communities.

---

[22] Cheri Lawan, From Hosting to Hostilities: Managing Post Boko Haram Displacements in Northeastern Nigeria. A paper presented at the 2nd Canadian International Conference on Humanities and Social Sciences at the University of Toronto, Toronto, Canada from 13–14 July, 2019. The conference is organised by Unique Conferences Canada in partnership with International Center for Research and Development, Sri Lanka. The presentation slides are can be found at https://www.slideshare.net/theicrd/lawan-cheri.

[23] Krishna Kumar, Promoting Social Reconciliation in Post-Conflict Societies: Selected Lessons from USAID's Experience, USAID Program and Operations Assessment Report No. 24, 1999.

Effective reconciliation is only attainable when diversified to cover all segments of society especially the vulnerable groups including women, youths, minority groups, migrants, and those living with disability. Depending on the nature and type of conflict, critical members of the communities such as religious leaders, tribal warlords, tribal leaders, unionists, local warriors, and security experts must be involved to spearhead the process of reconciliation. Involvement of traditional authorities will complement formal structures and make the process reflect the environment.[24] Involvement of critical stakeholders in the community will create the needed will and resolute commitment to reconcile. The assumption is that when people are encouraged to take part in decisions either as individuals or groups, they will willingly support the process of dialogue, mediation, and reconciliation. This has been proven true in the discussion by Prince Bright Majiga in Chapter 11.

The imperative of acceptance by disputants lies in the parties' ownership of the entire process thereby making them to consider every effort as their own and therefore working to ensure the success and sustainability of the exercise. The engagement will also serve as capacity building avenue for stakeholders because bringing them together fosters mutual understanding and build tolerance and peaceful coexistence. The overall goal is to create conducive situation for the resolution of conflict or at least managing conflict to reduce its impact on the communities and establish the possibility of replacing chaos with normalcy through and with the community members. Guaranteeing open access to reconciliation, fairness, and justice is imperative in winning confidence of parties. Nonviolent communication channels are critical instruments for achieving cooperation and making parties to open up and share feelings.

As a transitional justice mechanism, reconciliation in post-conflict societies is better proposed and handled by actors external to the conflict. International communities or organisations within the country that are neither party to the crisis nor in alliance with any of the conflicting parties will be perceived as neutral arbiter in defusing tension, dispensation of justice, and restoration of mutualism. Post-conflict societies are characterised with destroyed properties, distorted institutions, fractured economies, dependence, destroyed social bond, and cases of sexual and gender-based violence, mutilations, abductions, and poor civil–military relations. These features make external actors the most qualified to handle reconciliation initiatives in order to hasten healing and forestall recurrence of violence and violations.[25] One of the early steps in

---

[24] UNDP and UN Women, Joint Programme/Project document of the UN Fund for Recovery, Reconstruction and Development in Darfur, Khartoum, February 2016.

[25] Svärd Proscovia, The International Community And Post-War Reconciliation in Africa: A Case Study of the Sierra Leone Truth and Reconciliation Commission; Hayner, 2004.

reconciliation is to answer what is to be reconciled? The answer lies in the factors that prompted the need for reconciliation.[26]

Thus, comprehensive assessment of structural and manifest causes of disaffection and conflict equip reconciliatory efforts with understanding of what to insist on during reconciliation. Conflicts caused by bad governance must be reconciled taking cognisance of accountability, transparency, development, fairness, and involvement of marginalised communities. Conflicts that resulted in amputations, rape and child abuse are particularly difficult because emotions are usually high, tensions raised, and amnesty could be regarded as injustice by the victims. Religious and ethnic conflicts are particularly tricky and difficult to handle because even acceptance of compromise or mediation may be considered a sign of weakness. Hence comprehensive assessment of causes and effects of conflict is veritable in pursuing reconciliation in post-conflict societies.

Similarly, reconciliation should be linked to the policies and programmes of government in order to improve the living conditions of people in post-conflict environment. Economic empowerment, improvement in access to and quality of education and healthcare facilities could facilitate reconciliation efforts and redirect the minds of people towards restoration of peace and pursuit of socioeconomic development.[27] A Rwandan widow was asked to forgive after the genocide and she responded, 'How can I forgive, when my livelihood was destroyed and I cannot even pay for the schooling of my children'.[28] This indicates that there could be possibility of forgiveness if her livelihood will be restored and schooling for her children guaranteed.

It, therefore, underscores the essentiality of poverty alleviation and provision of social facilities in post-conflict societies as instrumental goals towards attaining reconciliation. Implementation of the resolutions reached at the reconciliation table is key to building peace and attaining legitimacy of the whole process. At this stage, the local capacity and involvement of parties come into play. The implementation of recommendations could rebuild political and social infrastructure such as rule of law, democracy, societal reorientation and reorganisation, introduction of courses related to the conflict in the education sector, or empowering research centres to focus on reconciliation and reconstruction to hasten societal regeneration as well as addressing and mitigating causes of conflict.[29] The importance of implementation lies in the fact that silence after reconciliation translates to doing nothing and an indication that the perpetrators of wrongdoings succeeded.

---

[26] Eugenia Zorbas, Reconciliation in Post-Genocide Rwanda, *African Journal of Legal Studies*, Africa Law Institute (2004) ISSN: 1708-7384. 1 AJLS 29–52. http://www.africa lawinstitute.org/ajls/vol1/no1/zorbas.pdf.

[27] Amadu Sesay, DOES ONE SIZE FIT ALL? The Sierra Leone Truth and Reconciliation Commission Revisited. Discussion Paper 36. Stockholm, Elanders Gotab AB, 2007.

[28] Ervin Staub, Genocide and Mass Killing: Origins, Prevention, Healing and Reconciliation, *Political Psychology* (2000), 21 (2), 379.

[29] Svärd, n.d.

On the other hand, confessions, publicising apologies, or sometimes acceptance of blames help in soothing and healing than submitting documents and the outcome of reconciliation efforts.[30] Albeit with high dose of care, cultural and history museums can form part of reconciliation efforts by having monuments of artefacts that tell the awful story to make people unwilling to repeat the same mistakes. However, without careful handiwork, such efforts could raise tensions and flare emotions which could do exactly the opposite of what it was intended to achieve.[31] In Rwanda, a National Day of mourning is observed annually where a scene of genocide is selected and the President leads the effort to exhume bodies and give them national burial aired on national televisions.[32]

SOCIAL COHESION: PROMOTING CONVERGENCE ACROSS GROUPS

Social cohesion is now recognised as a desirable characteristic of a society; thus, it is not an individual trait alone. It is a multidimensional process that comprises of phenomena on the individual attitudes and orientation, features of a society, groups, and societal institutions of governance.[33] Social cohesion entails accepting differences in society while ensuring equity so that differences and disparities do not undermine stability and cause conflict. Despite the lack of common definition of social cohesion, most scholars have agreed on these three dimensions of social cohesion—social relations, sense of belonging, and orientation towards the common good.[34]

A cohesive society has the following characteristics. One, pursuit of shared vision of socioeconomic advancement. Two, members of the societies shared a sense of belonging and possesses similar life opportunities. Three, high degree of trust exists among the people and between people and their local institutions and leaders. This is as a result of strong bond and cordial relationship between people from different backgrounds. Four, members of the society have widespread knowledge of their rights and responsibility as citizens. Five, legitimate and responsive governance institutions and leaders that support inclusive economic development.[35]

Social cohesion helps prevent sociopolitical polarisation by tapping into the local peacebuilding networks of a society which can manage and interrupt conflict-forming dynamics and provide space for new forms of political

---

[30] Zorbas, note 27 above.

[31] As above.

[32] As above.

[33] David Shiefer and Jolanda van de Noll above note 12.

[34] Iffat Idris, *Building Social Cohesion in Post-Conflict Situations* (London: GSDRC, 2016).

[35] Charleen Chiong and Loic Menzies, *Can Schools Make Our Society More Cohesive?* (London: LKMco).

consensus. Social cohesion creates stronger bonds within and across different groups and fosters greater trust in both formal and informal governance process. This is even more important where there is a history or current context of conflict, hostility, or mistrust between different identity groups or the state and its citizens. The nature and extent of socioeconomic divisions within a given society strengthen or weekend social cohesion.

The UN Secretary-General António Guterres has argued that social exclusion, polarisation, corruption, extreme socioeconomic inequalities, disputes over scarce natural resources, and poor governance undermine social cohesion and contribute to conditions which may lead to conflict.[36] When certain segment of a given society is denied access to political power or are excluded from decision-making process, this creates grievances that will lead to violent uprising. The proponents of more peaceful societies emphasise that providing security, good governance, and equitable distribution of scarce resources and opportunities by leaders across all members of a society promote inclusion which strengthen social cohesion. This creates trust between local institutions and the population and it will increase the support of communities for the government. Whereas unequal distribution of resources or opportunities leads to social exclusion.[37]

Furthermore, strengthening social capital in addition to tackling inequalities is crucial to strengthen social cohesion.[38] Social capital is the foundation of collective action, collaboration, and self-organisation and it exists in the relations between and among people, and between people and their leaders. It consists of those things that are required to bring about collective action such as reciprocity, participation, and a culture of trust and tolerance. The importance of social capital is the connectedness it brings between people and groups which has a variety of advantages for building social cohesion and societal resilience.[39] Social cohesion appears to be based on the willingness of people in a given society to cooperate with each other despite their diversity.

This willingness of diverse groups to cooperate means they may form partnerships and have a reasonable chance of realising social justice and socioeconomic progress. In the context of deeply divided societies, participation and inclusion are vital principles. Therefore, understanding the differentiation between forms of engagement is necessary to pinpoint their impact on social cohesion. While participation in collective activities increases the sense of belonging in a particular community by instilling the feeling that an individual or a group is recognised as a member of that society, it possesses

---

[36] SEEDS above note 9.

[37] As above.

[38] Haidar Huma, *Rural Stakeholder Engagement in Social Cohesion, Reconciliation and Peacebuilding Projects* (London: K4D, 2019).

[39] I.M. Machina, Community Resilience to the *Boko Haram* Insurgency in Jigawa State, in Jibrin Ibrahim, Chom Bagu, and Y.Z. Ya'u (eds), *Understanding Community Resilience in the Context of Boko Haram Insurgency in Nigeria* (Kano: CITAD, 2017), pp. 239–285.

risk of reinforcing existing patterns of societal division and exclusion. The extent social interactions in associations, political parties, unions, or non-governmental organisations strengthen shared values, sense of belonging, and trust differs.

For example, engagement in a sports club might strengthen the social ties within a society to a different degree compared to engagement in a charity or cultural organisation. Also, the degree to which participation in a political party promotes cohesion depends on the party's political orientation and agenda. Social networks and civic associations in Africa have been diluted over the years, pushed to the back burner in respect to more intense ethnic, regional, or religious associations. Therefore, programmes should seek to ensure the representation of marginalised and minority groups in forums and strengthen institutions' capacity to resolve conflict, and bring groups together to build trust'.[40]

Identity reconfiguration of societal fault lines that divide societies is necessary through education and sensitisation. There is a need to reconfigure identity and redefine member's identity through reorientation of values in order to change people's perceptions of other groups in the society. Therefore, promoting sound and equitable socioeconomic policies and education will help in strengthening social cohesion as demonstrated by Dan Kuwali in Chapters 12 and 34. Schools are key avenues for promoting social cohesion and it is imperative for policymakers to focus on promoting social cohesion in schools through civic education and training. Schools offer unique safe spaces for students from diverse background to form relationships which might be difficult to take place outside the school environment.

Robust curriculum that introduces students to subjects such as civic education, citizenship, coexistence, and reconciliation will expose students to their rights, obligations as citizens and reduce anti-social behaviour. This will empower students from different background and address the feeling of exclusion and marginalisation.[41] This will develop a shared sense of belonging among students and offer opportunities for mixing students from different ethnic and socioeconomic background and equip them with skills and knowledge to enable them become active citizens.[42] This will create a new identity of mutual respect and understanding of each other.

Community-based participation and development programmes should also be designed to improve the delivery of essential public services that will build trust, social capital, and inclusion by bringing members of the society to work together to achieve these goals. For example, strengthening the capacity of local leaders in rural communities in Zimbabwe played a crucial role in conflict resolution and members of communities are satisfied with their leaders' conflict

---

[40] Andrew McLean, *Community Security and Social Cohesion: Towards a UNDP Approach* (Geneva: UNDP, 2009).

[41] Charleen Chiong and Loic Menzies above note 36.

[42] As above.

resolution efforts. In addition, peace committees established in rural communities in Zimbabwe prove to be effective in addressing communities' basic needs and challenges. Peace communities are small informal local structures designed to allow local communities to participate in peacebuilding efforts and these committees enjoyed legitimacy because they are trusted by the local population.

Thus, policymakers and organisations should involve the members of a given community in the design and decision-making process and consult them in order to identify and strengthen influential actors such as traditional and religious leaders and teachers. They should also involve marginalised groups such as young people, women, and disabled people.[43] In Liberia, women were equipped and trained on alternative dispute resolution that increased the rates of peaceful property resolution in rural communities. Dialogue and conflict resolution is another programme that will promote social cohesion and reconciliation in societies by building the capacity of communities to resolve conflict without resort to violence.

Previous experience showed that when communities work together to achieve development goals, politically motivated, and other forms of violence are significantly reduced. Also, cohesive communities with high levels of trust tend to make better financial decisions that improve people's lives in the long run. With the 2030 Agenda, the world has reaffirmed the mutually reinforcing relationship between peace and sustainable development, noting that the best means of prevention and of sustaining peace is inclusive and sustainable development; and, that sustainable development cannot be achieved in the absence of the conditions for sustainable peace, such as reconciliation, social cohesion, and peaceful coexistence.

Conclusion

This chapter examined three inter-related approaches; coexistence, reconciliation, and social cohesion as strategies to achieve peace and security at various levels of societies in Africa. Drawing from the examination of these three inter-related approaches, the chapter provided evidence-based and concrete recommendations for decision-makers and policymakers that will guide them in building strong and cohesive societies in Africa and pursue sustainable peace and development, more especially in fragile and post-conflict societies. This chapter critique popular assumptions that societal fault lines such as ethnicity, diversity, and religious differences are the causes of conflict in Africa.

Rather, the myriad of conflicts bedevilling the African continent today is caused mainly by failure and challenges of societies to manage these societal fault lines, coupled with socioeconomic factors such as poverty, weak economies and institutions, poor governance, and socioeconomic grievances. Thus, there is a need to strengthen societal capacities to manage diversity

---

[43] Huma above note 39.

and differences in order to pursue peaceful coexistence and sustainable peace and development. This chapter argued that to support societal resilience and strengthen strong state–society relations in societies in Africa, policy and decision-makers and civil society organisations should focus on addressing the underlying conditions that lead to conflict or conflict relapse.

Programmes and approaches that will revive harmonious relationship between individuals or groups of people in African states should be prioritised. This chapter recommend that to enable societies transition from a divided past to a shared future, restoration of social cohesion and amicable settlement of disputes must be diversified to cover all segments of society especially the vulnerable groups including women, youths, minority groups, migrants, and those living with disability and relevant stakeholders such as such religious and cultural leaders. This should also be preceded by renewal of friendly relations and mutual trust among conflicting communities.

CHAPTER 29

Enhancing Conflict Resolution in Africa

Elias O. Opongo

INTRODUCTION

Africa has been registering positive economic growth in the last ten years, with significant reduction in conflicts across the continent. The Sub-Saharan Africa currently has six main active conflicts: Central Africa Republic (CAR), the eastern regions of The Democratic Republic of Congo; Somalia, Mali, Cameroon, and South Sudan. In addition, the continent continues to experience sporadic situations of insecurity due to inter-ethnic or religious conflicts as well as terrorist attacks in countries such as Ethiopia, Nigeria, Mozambique, Niger, Burkina Faso, and Guinea-Conakry. In Chapter 21, Archiles Bwete and his colleagues have illustrated that election-related violence has also been experienced in Kenya, Zimbabwe, Togo, Guinea-Conakry, Uganda and Ivory Coast. Other low-key intercommunal conflicts have taken place in a number of countries mainly due to competition for natural resources such as water and pasture, especially among the pastoralist; land conflicts; and mineral–resource conflicts.

As demonstrated by Dan Kuwali in Chapters 13 and 27, it can be concluded that the African continent faces four categories of conflicts: armed conflicts that are largely between the state and armed groups; sectarian violence (ethnic or religious) led by militia or organized armed groups; political violence advanced by the state against the population, especially through the use of

E. O. Opongo (✉)
Centre for Research, Training and Publications (CRTP), Institute of Peace Studies and International Relations, Hekima University College, Nairobi, Kenya

© The Author(s), under exclusive license to Springer Nature Switzerland AG 2022
D. Kuwali (ed.), *The Palgrave Handbook of Sustainable Peace and Security in Africa*, https://doi.org/10.1007/978-3-030-82020-6_29

505

506   E. O. OPONGO

the security forces; and lastly, low-key communal conflicts. These categories of conflicts in Africa are not mutually exclusive and should be analyzed concomitantly, with a back-and-forth sequencing in order to distinguish the diverse parameters of the specific impacts of the conflicts.

Hence, advancement of conflict resolution in Africa ought to take into account the complexities of the conflicts and the extent to which they have impacted the stability of a state. The discussion in this chapter will begin by making a broad analysis of African conflicts, and the diverse causes and impacts of these conflicts. The next stage will be to analyze three levels of peace engagement in the continent.

First, is the conflict intervention approaches at continental or regional levels. These have been carried out by the African Union (AU) at different levels under the framework of the African Peace and Security Architecture (APSA) as elaborated by Kuwali in Chapter 4. As explained in Part II of this Handbook, the second are the regional bodies that have undertaken peace initiatives to end conflicts in the region. These regional bodies include Intergovernmental Authority on Development (IGAD), the Southern Africa Development Community (SADC), the Economic Community of West African States (ECOWAS), and the Economic Community of *Central African* States (ECCAS). Lastly, civil society organizations (CSOs), non-governmental organizations (NGOs) as well are religious institutions have played an important role in conflict resolution in Africa.

CIVIL CONFLICTS IN AFRICA

In the last 50 years, Africa has had high incidences of civil wars, largely attributed to sectarian conflicts, whether ethnic, religious, or regional; competition for natural resources[1]; violent extremism, whether religiously or politically motivated; economic and political marginalization of particular sections of the population; poor governance; unemployment of the youth who become susceptible to recruitment to armed militia groups; and cross-border instabilities. This means that violent conflicts in Africa cannot be solely identified or linked to one single cause.

As such, it is important to analyze the African conflicts from multiple layers within a much broader framework of actors, causes, trends, and impacts. Other causes of conflict may include poverty[2], climate change impact[3], regional political dynamics, foreign countries that fund proxy armed groups to destabilize a country and render the later vulnerable to natural resource exploitation and

---

[1] De Ree Joppe, and Eleonora Nillesen, "Aiding Violence or Peace? The Impact of Foreign Aid on the Risk of Civil Conflict in Sub-Saharan Africa", *Journal of Development Economics* (2009) 88(2), pp. 301–313.

[2] Østby Gudrun et al., "Regional Inequalities and Civil Conflict in Sub-Saharan Africa", *International Studies Quarterly* (2009) 53(2), pp. 301–324.

[3] Clionadh Raleigh, "Political Marginalization, Climate Change, and Conflict in African Sahel States", *International Studies Review* (2010) 12(1), pp. 69–86.

illegal trade in arms that lead to proliferation of small arms and light weapons (SALW) in agreement with Gilbert Mittawa in Chapter 22. The actors in conflicts are often political agents, either as state representatives or militia groups fighting the government. The actors can also be armed groups from one sectarian grouping (ethnic or religious).

Competition over control of natural resources has been one of the major causes of conflicts on the continent as revealed by Godard Busingye in Chapter 19 and George Chipembere Lwanda in Chapter 30. Natural resources have been used to finance war and sometimes act as the fuel that prolongs it, even as the masses suffer the atrocities, and the country's development remains retarded. States endowed with natural resources stand a higher risk of falling into conflict since the same resources can be hijacked by groups fighting with or against a sitting government.[4] Such conflicts have been witnessed in The Democratic Republic of the Congo (DRC), Sierra Leone, South Sudan, Angola, among others. The DRC, which is the richest country in the world in terms of mineral resources, remains the epitome of resource-based conflicts, with close to 100 armed groups operating in the eastern region of that country.[5] South Sudan has large oil reserves but at the same time has been embroiled in conflict since 2013, just two years after its independence. While the conflict has largely been based on competition for state and territorial control, the lucrative oil resource has been the main source of revenue for the government, which has subsequently used it to prolong the conflict,[6] and derail attempts at peace agreements.

Expansion of democratic space has been evident in the continent since 1990s. However, this space has been shrinking with the adaptation of more controlled system of governance that tends to limit state control to a small clique of individuals. There has been a wave of constitutional changes to retain political stalwarts in power without any term limits. Such has been witnessed in Cameroon, Rwanda, Uganda, Burkina Faso, Mali, Ivory Coast, Burundi, DRC, Togo, among others. In his book, *Africa Unchained*, George Ayittey makes a distinction between African cheetahs and hippos. He refers to *cheetahs* as leaders who are young and innovative, seeking social, political, and economic change in their countries and the continent.

On the one hand, the *hippos* are not willing to accept any change nor leave their political seats to the younger generations or new politicians to take over. The incumbent control has to a great extent created discontent and grievance among opposition groups, and in some cases led to violent conflicts in countries such as DRC, Burundi, Uganda, Mali, and Ivory Coast. Wangari Maathai,

[4] Obi Cyril, "Oil as the 'Curse' of Conflict in Africa: Peering through the Smoke and Mirrors", *Review of African Political Economy* (2010) 37(126), pp. 483–495.

[5] The Guardian, "Militia Raids Kill Dozens as DRC Plunges Deeper into Instability" (2020), < https://www.theguardian.com/world/2020/jan/31/militia-group-raids-villages-in-eastern-drc-after-army-crackdown > (accessed on 17 January 2021).

[6] Hendrix Cullen and Sarah Glaser, "Trends and Triggers: Climate, Climate Change and Civil Conflict in Sub-Saharan Africa", *Political geography* (2007) 26(6), pp. 695–715.

a Nobel laureate, laments that while younger leaders have given Africa hope for change, some of them have already shown signs of staying longer in power, initiated conflicts with their neighbors, and perpetuated political discontent.[7] It is, therefore, important to strengthen institutions of governance as a strategy for stability as Tadziwana Kapeni has rightly argued in Chapter 17.

With political marginalization comes economic marginalization. Africa is one of the richest continents in the world, with a high GDP growth of between 3.4 and 4.1%.[8] The continent has a great potential to become a major economic powerhouse if the Africa free trade agreement is implemented. In 2018, African states agreed to establish the African Continental Free Trade Agreement (AfCFTA) which has a potential of "a joint economic output of more than \$3 billion (€2.6 billion) and more than 1.5 billion consumers."[9] The free trade arrangement is the largest in the world, considering that 54 countries are signatories to the agreement. Despite registering economic growth and the continent's potential for global international trade force, most African countries have huge disparities between the poor and the rich.

Hence, economic growth has been less inclusive, and has focused on national economic growth, based on foreign incomes that rely on export–import dynamics, and less on the population's well-being. In fact, in 2020, only about a third of African countries achieved inclusive economic growth with a capacity to reduce poverty and inequality.[10] Scholars also warn that horizontal economic inequalities are easy triggers for conflicts since often, discontented populations tend to build their grievances against the state, which could boil up into an overt conflict. Economic marginalization has been a trigger to conflicts, among other factors, in countries such as Zimbabwe, Kenya, Ethiopia, South Sudan, Uganda, Cameroon, Ivory Coast, South Africa, to mention but a few.

As explained by Mittawa in Chapter 22, illegal arms trade has led to proliferation of illicit small arms and light weapons which has in turn been a major trigger to conflicts in Africa. While the real statistics of the actual number of illicit arms is not clear, the UN estimates that there are over one billion small arms and light weapons in circulation worldwide.[11] Currently, there are

---

[7] Wangari Maathai, *The Challenge for Africa* (London: Arrow Books, 2011), p. 126.

[8] Africa Development Bank, "Africa Economic Outlook 2020", < https://www.afdb. org/en/knowledge/publications/african-economic-outlook > (accessed on 18 January 2021).

[9] Deutsche Welle (DW), "Africa's Vision for the Future—Much More Than a Free Trade Deal", < https://www.dw.com/en/africas-vision-for-the-future-much-more-than-a-free-trade-deal/a-49486333 > (accessed on 16 January 2021).

[10] As above.

[11] United Nations, "Spread of 1 Billion Small Arms, Light Weapons Remains Major Threat Worldwide, High Representative for Disarmament Affairs Tells Security Council." Security Council 8713th Meeting (am), 5 February 2020, https://www.un.org/press/en/2020/sc14098.doc.htm (accessed on 8 February 2021).

approximately 30 million illicit firearms in circulation across Africa.[12] Porous borders, poor governance of arms control by states, protracted conflicts, international illegal arms trade, interethnic and regional conflicts, poaching through the use of illicit arms has led to lucrative sale of animal products like elephant ivories and rhino horns, among others. The Council of Foreign Relations estimates the annual monetary turnover from illicit arms trade to be US$1 billion, which is about 10–20 percent of the global trade in illicit firearms.[13] The problem of illicit arms trade has been large in the last 7–10 years, and many countries have become unstable due to easy access of illicit arms to militia groups.

The impact of conflicts in Africa has been devastating, leading to millions of deaths, mass displacements, state fragility, and regional instability. For example, according to the United Nations High Commission for Refugees (UNHCR) 79.5 million people were displaced by the end of 2019, South Sudan was among the five countries that account for two-thirds of displaced persons in the world, alongside Syria, Venezuela, Afghanistan, and Myanmar.[14] Africa contributed immensely to total global displacement, particularly given political instabilities in South Sudan, Burkina Faso, Mali, northern Nigeria, Ethiopia, Somalia, DRC, Cameroon, Libya, among others.

A study by Lancet in 2018 found that conflicts in Africa, over a period of 20 years, contributed to 5 million deaths of children under 5 years.[15] The estimates of the number of people who have died in the protracted conflict in the DRC have been controversial since the International Rescue Committees suggested a figure of 5.4 million between the periods of 1998–2001.[16] However, while the exact figures may not be known due to inaccessibility of the conflict zones, there are definitely millions of people who have died since the conflict begun. The South Sudan conflict that has been going on intermittently since 2013, led to deaths of more than 400,000 people by 2018.[17] The Central Africa Republic (CAR) has equally experienced protracted conflict with multiplication of diverse rebel groups. In 2021, an estimated 2.8 million

[12] Deutsche Welle, "Stemming the Flow of Illicit Arms in Africa", < https://www.dw.com/en/stemming-the-flow-of-illicit-arms-in-africa/a-49761552 > (accessed on 16 January 2021).

[13] Council on Foreign Relations, "The Global Regime for Transnational Crime", 25 June 2013. < http://www.cfr.org/transnational-crime/global-regime-transnationalcrime/p28656 > (accessed on 16 January 2021).

[14] UNHCR, "1 Percent of Humanity Displaced: UNHCR Global Trends Report." 2020. < https://www.unhcr.org/news/press/2020/6/5ee9db2e4/1-cent-humanity-displaced-unhcr-global-trends-report.html > (accessed on 16 January 2021).

[15] Zachary Wagner et al., *Armed Conflicts and Child Mortality in Africa: A Geospatial Analysis* (London: Lancet, 2018).

[16] Relief Web, "IRC Study Shows Congo's Neglected Crisis Leaves 5.4 Million Dead", IRC study shows Congo's neglected crisis leaves 5.4 million dead—Democratic Republic of the Congo.

[17] Catholic Relief Services, "South Sudan's Civil War: Nearly 400,000 Estimated Dead", *CRS Insight,* 28 September 2018.

510   E. O. OPONGO

people (57% of the population), were in dire need of humanitarian assistance and protection.[18] Tens of thousands have died in CAR, and the conflict escalated in 2021 with the formation of the Coalition of Patriots for Change (CPC) that brought together the *Seleka and Anti-Balaka* main rebel groups, as well as other militia entities. Former President of CAR, François Bozize is the political leader of the coalition.[19]

Africa has also experienced three coup d'etats in two years: Mali in August 2020; Guinea in September 2021; and Sudan in April 2020 and October 2021.The conflict in Ethiopia, which erupted on November 4, 2020 between Ethiopia government forces and Tigray People's Liberation Front (TPLF), is likely to lead to regional instability, mass displacement, and deaths.

Conflict Resolution in Africa

Conflict resolution in Africa has taken different approaches in the continent, such as mediation and negotiation processes, preventive diplomacy, conflict intervention, human rights' lobbying, and peacekeeping interventions. The civil society and religious organizations have equally played important roles in peacebuilding. Localized mechanisms through cultural and religious interventions have equally borne fruits in resolving conflicts in Africa. Regional intergovernmental interventions by states at both continental and regional level, have also had significant impact. These interventions have been carried out by intergovernmental organizations such as: the United Nations, African Union, Intergovernmental Authority on Development (IGAD), East Africa Community (EAC), the Southern Africa Development Community (SADC), the Economic Community of West African States (ECOWAS), and the Economic Community of *Central African* States (ECCAS), among others.

The strategies applied by these institutions have mainly included mediation and negotiations, economic and political sanctions, military intervention through peacekeeping/peace enforcement forces, and diplomatic initiatives, among others. African Union has over the years developed structures and institutions on conflict intervention, as well as peacebuilding strategies that monitor potential conflicts before they erupt.

---

[18] Relief Web, "Central African Republic: Situation Report, 30 October 2020", 2021. < https://reliefweb.int/report/central-african-republic/central-african-republic-situation-report-30-october-2020 > (accessed on 16 January 2021).

[19] Al Jazeera, "CAR Rebel Groups Announce Ceasefire Ahead of Sunday Vote", 2020. < https://www.aljazeera.com/news/2020/12/24/car-rebel-groups-announce-ceasefire-before-elections > (accessed on 18 January 2021).

The African Union Conflict Resolution Strategy

In order to address conflicts in Africa, the African Union established the African Peace and Security Architecture (APSA).[20] The AU's member states, bureaucrats, and external donor states set up APSA to allow the AU to have a greater role in managing conflicts on the continent.[21] The AU has undergone tremendous changes in its peace operations and conflict resolution initiatives given the shifting dynamics of conflicts in the continent. The creation of the APSA was meant to enable the AU to achieve its goals for a conflict-free continent under the loud theme of *Silencing the Guns: Pre-requisites for Realising a Conflict-free Africa by the Year 2020*. The aim was to make sure that the burden of conflicts is not passed on to the next generation of Africans.[22] However, the continent did not achieve its objective of ending conflicts in *Silencing the Guns* by 2020 and the AU has instead pushed the target to 2030, in light of Agenda 2030 on Sustainable Development Goals (SDGs).

The African Union (AU) also came up with Agenda 2063 that was geared toward ending conflicts in Africa through strategic mediation processes, multilateral conflict resolution, and preventive diplomacy. The Agenda was intended to achieve its vision of a peaceful and economically prosperous Africa in 50 years, beginning 2013–2063. The Agenda 2063 has seven aspirations, and the 4th Aspiration focuses on creating a peaceful and secure Africa. The goals of this aspiration are to ensure the preservation of peace, security, and stability, with a fully functional and operational African Peace and Security Architecture (APSA). The hope is that by 2063, Africa will have the capacity to secure peace and protect its citizens and their interests, through common defense, with clear security policies.

The APSA is inclusive and offers a participatory process that involves different Departments at the African Union Commission (AUC) as well as at the Regional Economic Commissions. The APSA's overall aim is to ensure that it promotes peace, security, and sustainable development that will lead to stability across the continent. It will also ensure that it keeps to the AU's 2000 Constitutive Act in line with the aspirations of the people of Africa.

The APSA consists of structures, objectives, principles, and values aimed at working toward the prevention, management, and resolution of conflicts in the continent. The implementation of the APSA is critical, given it makes a seamless link between peace, security, and development as major components for Africa's agency in international relations and development in the

---

[20] Boulden Jane (ed.), *Responding To Conflict in Africa: The United Nations and Regional Organizations* (Springer, 2013).

[21] As above.

[22] Deng Francis and William Zartman (eds.), *Conflict Resolution in Africa* (Brookings Institution Press, 2011).

twenty-first century.[23] The APSA aims at achieving common defense and security policy; safeguarding sovereignty and territorial integrity of each nation, as well as encouraging democratic principles, human rights, good governance, and sustainable development for all its member states. The administrative and structural support of APSA is anchored on the Peace and Security Council (PSC) Protocol, adopted in 2002, in Durban, and came into force in 2003. The adoption of PSC called on member states to hasten the political and economic integration on the continent, promote peace, security, and stability.[24]

The AU has been implementing the African Peace and Security Architecture (APSA) and has made significant progress in taking initiatives for peace through regional conflict mediation on conflicts in South Sudan, Ethiopia, Gambia, Sudan, Zimbabwe, DRC, Somalia, Burundi, among others. As already stated, the PSC is APSA's main pillar that supports the discharge of the latter's mandate, through different structures. These include: The Continental Early Warning System (CEWS), the African Standby Force (ASF), the Panel of the Wise, and the Peace Fund.[25] The Panel of the Wise (PoW) is made up of members nominated by the AU Commission, and comes from each of the five regions of the continent, and acts as a body to the APSA. It operates under quiet preventive diplomacy, often at the invitation of the PSC or the Chairperson of the Commission.

Since its inauguration in 2007, the POW has been actively involved in intervening against conflicts in countries such as Kenya, Egypt, and Madagascar including Madagascar, Egypt, and Kenya. The POW "works closely with regional structures such as the Council of the Wise of ECOWAS; the Committee of Elders of the Common Market for Eastern and Southern Africa; the ad hoc mediators of SADC; and the AUC's Continental Early Warning System."[26] The African Union, in its 2020 report, acknowledges that the Peace Fund, alongside AU's many other operations is inadequately funded,

---

[23] Sarkin Jeremy, "The Role of The United Nations, The African Union and Africa's Sub-Regional Organizations in Dealing With Africa's Human Rights Problems: Connecting Humanitarian Intervention and the Responsibility to Protect", *Journal of African Law* (2009) 53(1), pp. 1–33.

[24] MacFarlane Neil and Thomas Weiss, "Regional Organizations and Regional Security", *Security Studies* (1992) 2(1), pp. 6–37.

[25] Ofuatey-Kodjoe Wentworth, "Regional organizations and the Resolution of Internal Conflict: The ECOWAS Intervention in Liberia", *International Peacekeeping* (1994) 1(3), pp. 261–302.

[26] Robert, Garenge, "Preventive Diplomacy and the AU Panel of the Wise in Africa's Electoral-related Conflicts." May 2015. Governance and APRM Programme. Policy Briefings 136. < https://www.aprmtoolkit.saiia.org.za/documents/academic-papers/536-preventative-diplomacy-and-the-au-s-panel-of-the-wise-in-africa-s-electoral-related-confli cts/file > (accessed on 8 Feb 2021).

and that the Peace Fund only got 30% of its projected budget in 2019.[27] The main focus of CEWS is to monitor conflicts in the continent and come up with early warning mechanisms that help the Africa Union to take action in good time before the conflict escalates. The African Standby Force (ASF) takes the hard approach to peacebuilding, and is composed of well-trained military and police forces, ready to be deployed in case of any conflict.[28] According to the AU's Africa Peace and Security sector, "initial concept of the ASF was that of a quick reaction capacity that would enable Africans to respond swiftly to a crisis unhampered by any heavy political and instrumental burdens."[29] The standby force has the responsibility of offering peace support to countries in conflict; rapid deployment in situations of escalating conflict with a potential to erupt into a major conflict; peacebuilding and post-conflict disarmament and resettlement of former combats; providing security for humanitarian assistance, among other functions.

The African Union has also taken diverse initiatives for peacekeeping in the region. The peace intervention initiatives operate under the African Union Commission's Peace Support Operations Division (PSOD), equally referred to as the African Standby Force Continental Planning Element. Through the PSOD, the AU has been able to deploy security forces for peace support operations in different countries. In Somalia, the peace operations have been carried out under The African Union Mission in Somalia (AMISOM) established in 2007. In the Central Africa Republic (CAR) peace interventions have been through the Mission for the Consolidation of Peace in the CAR (MICOPAX) deployed in 2008, and was led by the Economic Community of Central African States (ECCAS).

The AU Peace and Security Council gave a go-ahead to the deployment of the African-led International Support Mission in the Central African Republic (MISCA), which now operates through the collaboration of the UN under the United Nations Multidimensional Integrated Stabilization Mission in the Central African Republic (MINUSCA). The Central Africa Republic, as explained above continues to experience protracted conflicts leading to instability in the country. The African Union Mission in Sudan (AMISON) was formed to stabilize the country's western region of Darfur, through control of the advancements of rebel forces and establishment of the rule of law; in South Sudan the Africa Union is in a joint operation under the United Nations Mission in the Republic of South Sudan (UNMISS). In 2016, the IGAD countries increased their forces in South Sudan to end the escalation of violence in the country.

---

[27] African Union, Financing the African Union: Towards the Financial Autonomy of the African Union. June 2020. https://au.int/sites/default/files/documents/38739-doc-rep ort_on_financing_of_the_union_jun_2020_002.pdf (accessed on 8 Feb 2021).

[28] Appiah, Juliana A., "Africa Peace and Security Architecture: Reflections on Over a Decade of Promoting Peace and Security in Africa", *Africa Insight* (2018) 47(4), 29–39.

[29] As above.

514   E. O. OPONGO

In Mali, the African-led International Support Mission to Mali (AFISMA) was put together in 2012 at the request of both the Malian government and the Economic Community of West African States (ECOWAS). The Malian government was faced with fierce military aggression by the Tuaregs in the northern part of the country; the African Union-led Regional Cooperation Initiative for the Elimination of the Lord's Resistance Army (AU-led RCI-LRA), is yet another initiative led by the African Union. The Lord's Resistance Army (LRA) carried a 22-year conflict against the Ugandan government. The conflict took place mainly in northern Uganda. Following the 2006 ceasefire, the failed peace agreement in 2008, and filed charges against the LRA leaders by both the International Criminal Court (ICC) and Ugandan government, the LRA scattered into the DRC, CAR, and South Sudan, carrying out further atrocities against civilians. The RCI-LRA has the responsibility of ensuring total defeat of the LRA in all the border regions of Uganda, Central African Republic, South Sudan, and The Democratic Republic of the Congo (DRC), in order to establish peace, security, and sustainable development in the region.

The APSA also collaborates with the *Regional* Economic Communities/*Regional Mechanisms* (RECs/RMs) for *conflict prevention, management and resolution,* and the promotion of peace, security, and stability in Africa. The PSC Protocol provides for partnerships between the United Nations (UN), the AU, the RECs, and other relevant international stakeholders.[30] There have been other regional initiatives for peace that have complemented the African Union's efforts for stabilizing the continent. However, an obstacle to achieving peace has been the AU's failure to establish a functioning and effective Early Warning System as agreed at various forums. This system would have allowed the various stakeholders to identify signposts/indicators that threaten peace or frustrate peace efforts.

REGIONAL INTERVENTIONS ON CONFLICTS

There are diverse regional initiatives for peace that have been instrumental in de-escalating conflict in Africa. The Great Lakes Region has been one of the most turbulent regions in Africa. To help deal with the conflict challenges, the International Conference of the Great Lakes Region (ICGLR) was formed in 2003. The ICGLR, an intergovernmental body of the Great Lakes countries was meant to implement creative and collective approaches for the prevention, management, and resolution of disputes in the region. For monitoring peace in the region, the IGCLR involves citizens and actors at the grassroots level, through close cooperation with the civil society organizations. In November 2004, the ICGLR signed the Declaration of Dar-es Salaam at the first summit of Heads of State and government in Tanzania.

---

[30] Mazzeo Domenico (ed.), *African Regional Organizations* (Cambridge University Press, 1984).

The heads of state confirmed their political will to resolve conflicts in the Great Lakes Region. This was followed by the Nairobi Pact signed on 15th December 2006, which focused on security, stability, and development in the region. In 2012, the ICGLR put in place mechanisms and instruments to consolidate peace through the cooperation between the ICGLR and civil society organizations (CSOs). This is particularly important given that many civil society organizations work for peace within the Great Lakes Region. Hence, on the CSOs' experience, especially in community peacebuilding, is crucially important. In February 2013, 11 countries signed the Peace, Security, and Cooperation Framework for The Democratic Republic of Congo, given the regional impact of the DRC conflict and its potential to destabilize the region.[31] The countries committed themselves to a collective approach to peace and security.

While there has been considerable progress made from the agreements and protocols above, and other peace initiatives by the ICGLR, the major challenge has been that the member states have not shown adequate commitment to implement the articles in the agreements. However, the ICGLR still has the potential to bring peace in the Great Lakes region, as long as there is extensive collaboration and commitment between the member states, other regional bodies, and the African Union.

The IGAD initiatives for peace in the Eastern and Horn of Africa have contributed to peace in Burundi, Kenya, South Sudan, Ethiopia, and Sudan. One of the most successful cases was the peace mediation process that led to Sudan's Comprehensive Peace Agreement in 2005, and the subsequent secession of the South from North Sudan. Unfortunately, two years after its independence in 2011, South Sudan fell into conflict. The IGAD, in collaboration with the African Union, international community, and other players, made several attempts to bring peace into South Sudan.

The conflict was largely been between President Salva Kiir' and his deputy, Riek Machar, and continued intermittently between 2013 and 2020. The episodic eruption of conflicts and high tensions in different parts of the country had an impact on the southern regions that had been relatively peaceful and considered as the country's breadbasket. These regions experienced attacks from militia, rebel groups, and cattle rustlers.[32] With the multiplication of militia groups and persistent conflicts, the government gradually lost control over coercive power and monopoly of violence, and was

---

[31] ACCORD, "The International Conference on the Great Lakes Region as a Peacebuilding Instrument for Civil Society Organisations", < https://www.accord.org.za/pub lication/international-conference-great-lakes-region-peacebuilding-instrument-civil-society-organisations/ > (accessed on 17 January 2021).

[32] Al-Salem Waleed et al., "A Review of Visceral leishmaniasis During the Conflict in South Sudan and the Consequences for East African Countries", *Parasites & Vectors* (2016) 9(1), p. 460.

subsequently unable to manage justice, provide basic services to the citizens and guarantee their security.[33]

To end the South Sudan conflict, IGAD persistently lobbied South Sudan leaders to come to the negotiation table, and in September 2018, the two factions signed a peace deal known as Revitalized Peace Agreement that called for cessation of violence, a coalition government, and consultative review of the administration boundaries in the country. However, despite the signing of the peace agreement there were reports from the Transitional Security Arrangements Monitoring and Verification Mechanism (CTSAMVM), South Sudan's ceasefire monitoring body, of continued fighting in Yei and Wau areas.[34] South Sudan's National Constitutional Amendment Committee (NCAC) worked on the legal framework for the implementation of revitalized peace agreement and its subsequent incorporation into the constitution.[35] However, in February 2020, the Deputy President Riek Machar agreed to come to Juba and be part of a coalition government meant to lead South Sudan to sustainable peace. IGAD has therefore continued to strengthen its operations for peace in the continent, and through The IGAD Security Sector Program (IGAD SSP), it has been able to support its member states in combating terrorism, maritime piracy, and security threats, address transnational organized crimes and ensure sustainable regional response to conflict.

The African Union, in collaboration with the East Africa Community (EAC) intervened in the Burundi conflict that emerged in May 2015 when the then President Pierre Nkurunziza refused to step down at the end of his term, and added himself another term of five more years in power. This led to demonstrations and deaths of hundreds of civilians. In January 2016, the African Union held its 26th summit in Addis Ababa and took a decision to deploy 5000 peacekeepers to Burundi. The peacekeeping force was named, the African Prevention Mission (MAPROBU), and had the mandate to protect civilians caught up in the political crisis. However, the Burundi government vehemently opposed the decision and stated that no peacekeepers will be allowed into the country without its permission.

In the long run, the troops were not deployed to Burundi on the basis that MAPROBU was premature and not ready for the mission. In the meantime, protests raged in Burundi with more civilian deaths reported from the brutal police force and a youth militia force known as *Imbonerakure* (those

---

[33] Pendle Naomi, "Interrupting the Balance: Reconsidering the Complexities of Conflict in South Sudan", *Disaster* (2014) 38(2), pp. 227–248.

[34] Sudan Tribute, "South Sudan Monitoring Body Urges to Order Commanders to Stop Clashes", 2018, < http://www.sudantribune.com/spip.php?article66570 > (accessed on 8 November 2020).

[35] Sudan Tribute, "South Sudan Constitutional Body Holds Meetings in Juba", 2018, < http://www.sudantribune.com/spip.php?article66568 > (accessed on 8 November 2020).

who see far), formed by the government.[36] With the mounting crisis, the African Union, East African Community, and the international community put pressure on Burundi to get to the dialogue table. In February 2017, the East African Community (EAC) mediated talks between the government and opposition. Eventually, President Nkurunziza agreed to step down at the end of his term, and in May 2020 elections were held and Evariste Ndayishimiye was elected president. Nkurunziza died the next month, June 2020, from health complications.

As shown by Mphatso Boti Phiri in Chapter 9, the Southern African Development Community (SADC) is one of the regional economic commissions in Southern Africa that seeks to promote sustainable economic growth and socioeconomic development through integration, good governance, and durable peace and security. The SADC has intervened a number of times in the DRC. For instance, in 2013, SADC deployed the Force Intervention Brigade (FIB), constituting of battalions from Malawi, South Africa, and Tanzania to neutralize the M23 rebel in Eastern DRC. Equally, the African Union and the International Conference of the Great Lakes Region (ICGLR) have intervened in the DRC crisis. Former President Joseph Kabila extended his term in office for two years, and during this period there was police brutality in the country and human rights abuse.[37]

Following the national elections in December 2018, Felix Tshisekedi was elected president. Upon taking office Tshisekedi committed himself to dismantling dozens of Congolese and foreign armed groups blighting the troubled Eastern part of the country.[38] However, there are still many rebel groups operating in the region. The United Nations Security Council has been working with President Tshisekedi in bid to find better ways of stabilizing the country. The success list of SADC is however limited and it has failed, despite several attempts to bring peace and stability in Zimbabwe.

Rather than challenge Zimbabwe to respect human rights and end corruption, the SADC members, in their summit meeting in Tanzania in 2019, instead called for an end to sanctions against Zimbabwe by the international community, despite the fact that the sanctions mainly targeted to specific individuals in the government. Human Rights Watch noted in 2020 that the SADC leaders, had "failed to publicly address Zimbabwe's failure to respect

---

[36] Human Rights Watch, "World Report 2016: Burundi", < https://www.hrw.org/world-report/2016/country-chapters/burundi > (accessed on 19 December 2020).

[37] Human Rights Watch, "World Report 2019: Democratic Republic of Congo", < https://www.hrw.org/world-report/2019/country-chapters/democratic-republic-congo# > (accessed on 2 January 2021).

[38] International Crisis Group, "De-escalating Tensions in the Great Lakes", 2020, < https://www.crisisgroup.org/africa/central-africa/democratic-republic-congo/de-escalating-tensions-great-lakes > (accessed on 19 December 2020).

518   E. O. OPONGO

human rights, good governance, and the rule of law, key pillars essential for the country's sustainable socio-economic recovery."[39]

The West African developing states established the Economic Community of West African States (ECOWAS) in 1975, aimed at promoting regional integration and establishing an economic union of the region's Anglophone, Francophone, and Lusophone countries. This was part of their plan to encourage economic development and prosperity among the respective countries. Unfortunately, the 1990s and early 2000s, were years of widespread conflicts and instability in the sub-region and most parts of the continent. It dawned on the leaders that economic prosperity would never be realized without peace and security. That was the turning point for the states as they began the process of developing further security protocols that had been set up back in 1978. Today the region has institutionalized elaborate peacekeeping, security, and conflict resolution mechanisms.

Exposure to both internal and external threats drove member states to add a defense protocol to the ECOWAS Treaty. The protocol required the member states to commit to giving mutual aid and assistance for defense against any armed threat or aggression if or when directed at a member state, and if it came to be viewed as "any armed threat or aggression directed against any Member State shall constitute a threat or aggression against the entire Community."[40] The protocol further laid out the conditions under which the stipulated action would be necessary. These would be whenever there were incidences of armed conflict between two or more member states following the failure of peaceful means, or in case of conflict within a state, especially if the conflict is confirmed to be engineered and supported from outside the region. It also set up response mechanisms that would include a sub-regional intervention force, Defense Council, Defense Committee, and a complete Allied Armed Forces of the Community (AAFC). The ECOWAS military arm ECOMOG managed to intervene in conflicts in Liberia, Sierra Leonne, Guinea-Bissau, among other peace initiatives.

Terrorism has been a major menace in the continent. There have been diverse efforts, regionally and internationally, to address violent extremism, religious radicalization and recruitment of youth into terrorist cells. The main terrorist groups include the Al Shabaab, Boko Haram, armed groups affiliated with the Islamic States (ISIS), among others. The Al Shabaab have been active in Eastern Africa, mainly in Somalia, Kenya, and Uganda; Boko Haram has made numerous attacks in Nigeria, Niger, Chad, and Cameron; ISIS-related

---

[39] Human Rights Watch, "Zimbabwe Events 2019." World Report 2020: Zimbabwe | Human Rights Watch < https://www.hrw.org/world-report/2020/country-chapters/zimbabwe > (accessed on 8 February 2021).

[40] ECOWAS, "Protocol Relating to Mutual Assistance on Defence." ECOWAS - Legal Docs A/SP3/5/81 (akomantoso.com), May 29 1981.

terrorist groups have made attacks in the DRC[41] and Mozambique; other terrorist groups carried out attacks in Burkina Faso, Mali, and Ivory Coast.

To address the Boko Haram menace in West Africa, the Peace and Security Council (PSC) of the African Union (AU) in January 2015 launched the mobilization of a Multi-National Joint Task Force (MNJTF), largely composed of troops from Benin, Chad, Nigeria, Cameroon, and Niger to address the menace of the terrorist group, the Boko Haram in northeastern Nigeria and the Lake Chad Basin region. The MNJTF's main tasks sought to "regain control of the areas under Boko Haram threat and occupation, support local agencies in the affected regions to maintain state authority and provide protection to the civilian population."[42] However, the presence of France in the region has in some cases been counter-productive and destabilizing especially in Chad and the Central African Republic (CAR).[43] Kenya and Somalia have mobilized their forces to fight Boko Haram[44] and reduce the latter's spread in the region. The African Union Mission in Somalia (AMISON) has faced the daunting task of stabilizing Somalia, and reducing the spread of Boko Haram.

CIVIL SOCIETY ORGANIZATIONS (CSOS)

In Africa, civil society organizations have played a major role in peacebuilding, human rights advocacy, conflict resolution, and support for the respect of the rule of law. This has been evident in African countries such as Ghana, Kenya, Burundi, Nigeria, Zimbabwe, Lesotho, Sudan, Ethiopia, Uganda, The Democratic Republic of Congo, Mali, and Guinea, among others. West African region has gone through turbulent periods of conflicts and challenges to peace stability. This has been characterized by civil wars in countries like Liberia and Sierra Leone, and political disputes in Guinea, Guinea-Bissau, Cote

---

[41] Draps Paul, "The Evolution of the Terrorist Threat in DR Congo", < http://www.esisc.org/publications/briefings/the-evolution-of-the-terrorist-threat-in-dr-congo > (accessed on 17 January 2021).

[42] Gbenga Adetokubnbo Owojaiye, "Regional Military Integration in West Africa: A Case Study of the Multi-national Joint Task Force in the Fight Against Boko Haram", A thesis presented to the Faculty of the U.S. Army Command and General Staff College (Fort Leavenworth, Kansas, 2003).

[43] Ramani, Samuel, "France and the United States Are Making West Africa's Security Situation Worse." *Foreign Policy*. September 12, 2020. < https://foreignpolicy.com/2020/09/12/france-united-states-sahel-making-west-africa-niger-mali-burkina-faso-sec urity-situation-worse/ > (accessed on 8 February 2021).

[44] P. Williams, "After Westgate: Opportunities and Challenges in the War against Al-Shabaab", *International Affairs 2014 (Royal Institute of International Affairs (1944)* 90(4), pp. 907–923. < http://www.jstor.org/stable/2453820 > (accessed on 12 January 2021).

D'Ivoire, and Mali.[45] In general, a number of countries in West Africa have had protracted conflicts while others have gone through prolonged civil wars.

The West Africa Network for Peacebuilding (WANEP) was established to promote peace, and lobby for human security and development in West Africa, following many years of conflict in the region. WANEP, in collaboration with many civil society organizations have made significant contribution to peace through civic education, human rights advocacy, conflict resolution, support to former combatants, among other initiatives. In South Africa, civil society and religious groups, in collaboration with the state, lobbied for the formation of the Truth and Reconciliation Commission (TRC) which became a major instrument for post-conflict reconstruction in South Africa. Civil society groups have also strongly advocated against corruption in the governments and called for more accountable governance. In Kenya and Zimbabwe, CSOs have been at the forefront in lobbying for fair elections, ending police brutality and human rights abuses, fair distribution of land and natural resources, as well as respect for the rule of law.

Between 1998 and 2002 The Democratic Republic of Congo, experienced violent conflicts which involved national armies of at least eight African countries. During this period, civil society organizations emerged as the voice of reason, not only denouncing war-related crimes, but also calling for a mediation process to end the conflict.[46] In fact, the Inter-Congolese Dialogue, led by the former Botswana President Ketumle Masire, agreed to the participation of the civil society in the peace negotiation held in South Africa between 2002 and 2003. During election periods, Congolese civil society organizations have been active in advocating for electoral justice and respect of human rights, despite the state's constant use of force against civilians.

It was also through the efforts of CSOs in lobbying against the use of rape as a tool of war that the ICC gained grounds in the DRC, and rape charges were brought against rebel leaders.[47] Article 7 of the Rome Statutes recognizes rape as a crime against humanity,[48] and subsequently Congolese rebel leaders, Jean-Pierre Bemba Gombo and Bosco Ntanganda were sentenced by

---

[45] Chukwuemeka B. Eze," The Role of CSOs in Promoting Human Rights Protection, Mass Atrocities Prevention, and Civilian Protection in Armed Conflicts", (2016).

[46] Sadiki Koko, "The Role of Civil Society in Conflict Resolution in the Democratic Republic of the Congo, 1998–2006", < https://www.accord.org.za/ajcr-issues/role-civil-society-conflict-resolution-democratic-republic-congo-1998-2006/ > (accessed on January 2021).

[47] Ibuda I. Patrick, "Applying and 'Misapplying' the Rome Statute in the Democratic Republic of Congo", < https://www.cambridge.org/core/books/contested-justice/applying-and-misapplying-the-rome-statute-in-the-democratic-republic-of-congo/B95ACFA30BFE75EC58AA135639CAB3BE/core-reader > (accessed on 20 December 2020).

[48] Njoroge Fraciah Muringi, "Evolution of Rape as a War Crime and a Crime Against Humanity", 25 July 2016, Available at SSRN: < https://ssrn.com/abstract=2813970 > or < http://dx.doi.org/10.2139/ssrn.2813970 > .

the ICC for 18 years[49] and 30 years, respectively, for crimes against humanity, including rape and sexual abuse of civilians.[50]

However, CSOs have faced numerous challenges in Africa. Most governments control CSOs' activities by introducing restrictive legislations such as anti-terror laws, complex registration processes, limits on access and publication of information, limit to the right to peaceful assembly, and limits on funding sources. Governments also dictate what civil society groups should do and when they do not abide by the demands of the government, they tend to face closure.[51] In some countries, CSOs have been accused of being part of the opposition or a rebel movement. In such situations, governments have prevented CSOs from operating. In a peaceful and democratic environment CSOs are able to strengthen their legitimacy through working in networks and coalitions[52] while lobbying for human rights, rule of law, protection of the environment, and sustainable economic policies and infrastructure.

Religious organizations have been instrumental in promoting peace in the continent. They have worked across faiths through their leadership structures, human rights sectors, humanitarian organizations, and local and international networks. For example, bishops and other religious leaders have issued statements against political violence, human rights abuses, corruption, marginalization of the poor, and violent conflicts in countries such as: Nigeria, South Sudan, Kenya, Zimbabwe, Burundi, Burkina Faso, and South Africa. The Catholic Justice and Peace Commissions all over Africa have been active agents of peace and conflict intervention, have particularly done tremendous job in community peacebuilding.

For example, in Kenya, DRC and Burundi the Catholic Church spoke against electoral malpractices in 2017, 2018, and 2020, respectively. In Nigeria, South Africa and Zimbabwe the church has spoken strongly against corruption, violence, and bad governance. Religious leaders have also come together in Kenya, Tanzania, Mozambique, Nigeria, Ivory Coast, Burkina Faso, Mali, Chad, and Niger to speak against religious extremism and violence. Perhaps, one of the most successful cases of peace intervention by a religious group has been that of Sant'Egidio in Mozambique.

Sant'Egidio was founded in Italy in 1968 and grew to over 50,000 members in about 70 countries. It is a church-based lay association that has been officially recognized by the Catholic Church and allowed sovereign

---

[49] Time, "Congolese Rebel Leader Gets 18 Years in Prison for War Crimes Including Rape", < https://time.com/4377708/congo-bemba-rape-war-crimes-icc/ > (accessed on 7 January 2021).

[50] Al Jazeera, "ICC Sentences Congolese Rebel Chief Ntaganda to 30 years in Jail", < https://www.aljazeera.com/news/2019/11/7/icc-sentences-congolese-rebel-chief-ntaganda-to-30-years-in-jail > (accessed on 7 January 2021).

[51] As above.

[52] Varshney Ashutosh, "Ethnic conflict and Civil Society: India and Beyond", *World politics* (2001), pp. 362–398.

statute.[53] The institution played an important role in mediating against the Mozambique conflict. Mozambique fell into violent conflict two years after gaining its independence in 1975, and the conflict lasted between 1977 to 1992. The conflict led to close to one million deaths and more than 5.7 million persons displaced.[54]

There were several peace attempts to end that conflict, but none of them were successful. It is against this background that Sant'Egidio emerged, through the initiative of the Bishop of Beira, Don Jaime Goncalves, who was conversant with Sant'Egidio's mission of fostering peace.[55] Sant'Egidio's peace mediation begun in 1989 and culminated into a peace agreement in Rome in 1992. The religious peace organization managed to convince protagonists, RENAMO and FRELIMO, to come to the dialogue table.[56] The back-and-forth struggle for peace in the four years of mediation and negotiations, only succeeded because of the neutrality of Sant'Egidio as chief mediator, and support of the different countries that were interested in peaceful transition in Mozambique.

Following the peace agreement, the United Nations took up the responsibility of the implementation of the peace agreement.[57] Mozambique experienced peace for several decades until October 2017 when violent jihadist extremist groups surfaced in northernmost Cabo Delgado province and sustained violent attacks on civilians for several years. The case of Mozambique demonstrates the fragility of most African countries and the extent to which efforts toward peace stability ought to take a multifaceted approach.

Conclusion

The advancement of conflict resolution in Africa is crucial for the political stability and economic sustainability in Africa. While compared to 1980s and 1990s, conflicts have significantly reduced in Africa, there are still a number of countries that face political and economic fragility. The reducing democratic space in the continent and many parts of the world is a matter of concern, and is likely to destabilize a number of countries. The clamor for electoral justice will in future draw some countries into armed conflicts, especially where the incumbent persistently violates the constitution and rigs elections to stay in power. Of greater concern too is the bulging number of youth and high rates

[53] Mullenbach Mark J., "Deciding to Keep Peace: An Analysis of International Influences on the Establishment of Third-Party Peacekeeping Missions", *International Studies Quarterly* (2005) 49(3), pp. 529–555.

[54] Vines Alex, *Still Killing: Landmines in Southern Africa* (New York: Human Rights Watch, 1997), pp. 66–71.

[55] Paris Roland, "Peacebuilding and the Limits of Liberal Internationalism", *International Security* (1997) 22(2), pp. 54–89.

[56] Baranyi Stephen, (ed.), *The Paradoxes of Peacebuilding Post-9/11* (UBC Press, 2009).

[57] Paris Roland, "International Peacebuilding and the 'Mission Civilisatrice'", *Review of International Studies* (2002), pp. 637–656.

of unemployment, coupled with poor economic policies leaned on excessive borrowing that has entrenched some countries into a debt crisis. The youth are vulnerable to recruitment into militia and terrorist groups, as an alternative source of self-affirmation and realization of basic economic needs. Hence, the future of peace sustainability in Africa lies in multidimensional interventions that integrate economic sustainability, respect for the rule of law, advancement of democratic space and human rights values, as well as increasing employment opportunities for the youth.

CHAPTER 30

Preventing Illicit Resources Outflows from Africa

George Chikondi Chipembere Lwanda

INTRODUCTION

In 2015, the Africa Union (AU) adopted the Africa Agenda 2063[1,2] (AA-2063) as the continent's long-term blueprint for transforming African societies into inclusive and sustainably developing societies as projected by Youssef Mahmoud and Chimwemwe Fabiano in Chapter 3.[3] The AA-2063 is articulated as having 7 aspirations, 20 goals, and 5 transformational outcomes. To support this, the AU developed 6 continental frameworks to facilitate the development of key sectors that are critical to the attainment of AA-2063.[4]

[1] African Union Commission (2017), 'Agenda 2063: The Africa We Want', https://au.int/en/agenda2063/overview, accessed 15 August.

[2] As above.

[3] As above.

[4] African Commission (2017), note 1 above.

[5] African Union (2009), 'Africa Mining Vision' (Addis Ababa).

An interactive tool that presents more disaggregated results of the study can be found at https://public.tableau.com/profile/george.lwanda#!/vizhome/PreventingillicitresourceoutflowsfromAfrica-acompaniontool/Countriesquestionscovered?publish=yes.

G. C. C. Lwanda (✉)
United Nations, Resident Coordinator System, Banjul, Gambia

© The Author(s), under exclusive license to Springer Nature Switzerland AG 2022
D. Kuwali (ed.), *The Palgrave Handbook of Sustainable Peace and Security in Africa*, https://doi.org/10.1007/978-3-030-82020-6_30

Among the continental frameworks is the Africa Mining Vision (AMV) which aims at ensuring "transparent, equitable and optimal exploitation of mineral resources to underpin broad-based sustainable growth and socio-economic development."[5]

In addition to the continental frameworks, 15 flagship projects were developed by the AU to accelerate the achievement of the AA-2063 goals.[6] Among these is the "silencing the guns by 2020."[7] The STGIA2020 aims at making peace a reality for all and ridding the continent of wars, violent conflicts, and human rights abuses. Additional to the AA-2063, silencing the guns initiative neatly dovetails with the United Nations (UN) Sustainable Development Goal (SDG) 16.4 which targets the significant reduction in illicit financial and arms flow by 2030. From the above, it follows that the greater the synergy between the AA-2063 flagship projects and the continental frameworks, the greater the likelihood that the continent will be able to achieve the aspirations of the AA-2063.

This chapter attempts to assess the synergies between the AMV and the Silencing the Guns in Africa by leveraging data from the 2017 Resource Governance Index (RGI) to identify gaps between law and practice in the governance of the mining sector in 19 African countries. These 19 countries are highlighted in Fig. 30.1 overleaf. It is the argument of this paper that the gap between law and practice in the governance of the mining sector has a bearing on the sector's susceptibility to illicit financial flows. This gap can be analyzed from various dimensions. However, our focus will primarily dwell on gaps between law and practice in mineral licensing, taxation, licensing, the management of SOE's and national budgeting. Interested readers may also go to the following link for more details on the study's results.[8]

THE NEED TO SILENCE GUNS IN AFRICA

According to data from the Uppsala Conflict Data Program (UCDP) accessed on 1 February 2021, Africa has been one of the most violent regions globally particularly since 1989 (see Fig. 30.1 overleaf). This trend has earned

---

[6] Commission (2017), as above note 1.

[7] Stockholm International Peace Research Institute (2020), 'SIPRI 2020 Yearbook', in SIPRI (ed.) (Stockholm, Sweden).

[8] https://public.tableau.com/profile/george.lwanda#!/vizhome/Preventingillicitreso urceoutflowsfromAfrica-acompaniontool/Countriesquestionscovered?publish=yes.

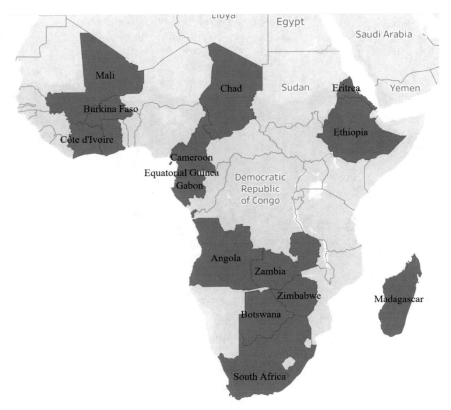

Fig. 30.1 Countries covered

the continent the stigma of a "continent at war with itself."[9] The continent continues to experience various forms of conflict with the majority being interstate in nature and caused by a range of poor development outcome indicators.[10] As illustrated in Fig. 30.2, the number of armed conflicts in Africa has been rising significantly since 2012.[11] This has led to estimated loss of 27,000 lives between 2013 and 2017 alone.[12]

---

[9] David Francis (2006), *Uniting Africa: Building Regional Peace and Security Systems* (London: Ashgate Publishing), 296.

[10] Wafula Okumu, Andrews Atta-Asamoah, and Roba Sharamo (2020), 'Silencing the Guns in Africa by 2020-Achievements, Opportunities and Challenges' (Pretoria, South Africa: Institute of Security Studies).

[11] Okumu et al. as above. See Peace Research Institute (2018), 'Conflict Trends in Africa 1989–2017', in Peace Research Institute (ed.), *Conflict Trends* (06/2018; Oslo, Norway). See also Stockholm International Peace Research Institute note 7 above.

[12] Okumu et al. (2020), note 10 above.

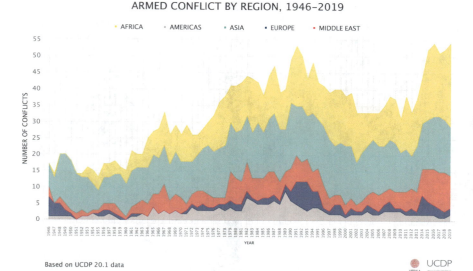

Fig. 30.2 Number of armed conflicts globally (1946–2019)

The actual number of countries afflicted by armed conflict depends on the source consulted. The Stockholm International Peace Research Institute (SIPRI) estimates that at least 15 countries in Sub-Sahara Africa had active armed conflicts in 2019 while the UCDP estimates the number at 25. Key among the factors driving these conflicts has been illicit trade in arms.

Linking Mineral Resources and Armed Conflicts in Africa

A vast body of research suggests that while minerals are never the sole source of conflict, mineral-rich developing countries face a greater risk of violent conflict and poor governance.[13] This is because conflicts need to be financed

---

[13] Ian Bannon and Paul Collier (2003), *Natural Resources and Conflict: What We Can Do* (*Natural Resources and Violent Conflict: Options and Actions*; Washington, DC: World Bank); Ibrahim Elbadawi and Sambanis Nicholas (2002), 'How Much Civil War Will We See? Explaining the Prevalence of Civil War', *Journal of Conflict Resolution*, 46 (June), 307–34; Marcena Hunter (2019), 'Illicit Financial Flows—Artisanal and Small-Scalegold Mining in Ghana and Liberia', in Jorge Moreira da Silva (ed.), *OECD Development Co-Operation Working Paper Series* (Paris, France: OECD); George Lwanda (2003), 'Conflict Diamonds and the African "Resource Curse"', in Vasu Goundem (ed.), *Conflict Trends* (2003/4; Durban, South Africa: African Centre for the Constructive Resolution of Disputes [ACCORD]); Michael Ross (2002), 'Resources and Rebellion in Aceh, Indonesia', in Yale—World Bank Project on the Economics of Political Violence (ed.), Peace Research Institute 2018.

30 PREVENTING ILLICIT RESOURCES OUTFLOWS FROM AFRICA 529

Table 30.1 African conflicts fueled by minerals

Country	Date	Underlying resource
Algeria	1992–2003	Gas, oil
Angola	1975–2002	Diamonds, oil
CAR	2012–date	Diamonds, gold
Chad	1980–1994	Oil, uranium
Congo-Brazzaville	1993–2003	Oil
DRC	1993–date	Diamonds, gold, uranium
Liberia	1989–1996	Diamonds
Libya	2012–date	Oil
Mali		Gold
Mozambique	2017–date	Oil, gas
Sierra Leone	1991–1999	Diamonds
Sudan	1983–2005	Oil
Zimbabwe	2010–date	Diamonds, gold

Source Lwanda (2003) with some additions

and with "organized violence and mayhem" as their only competitive advantage, armed groups often defer to the illicit exploitation of the mining value chain to finance conflict.[14]

There is general consensus that minerals tend to exacerbate and prolong conflicts and elude the attainment of peace.[15] The absence of peace has often compelled governments to incur disproportionately high expenditure on the military services; prolonged conflict increases crime and displacement of people which is accompanied by capital flight and reduced investment into the country.[16] Statistics in Table 30.1 point to how armed conflict has been exacerbated or prolonged by illicit trade along the minerals value chain in 13 African countries.

[14] Bannon and Collier (2003), note 13 above; Nicolas Cook (2012), 'Conflict Minerals in Central Africa: U.S. and International Responses' (Washington, DC: US Congressional Research Service); Michael Ross (2003), *The Natural Resource Curse: How Wealth Can Make You Poor*, in Ian Bannon and Paul Collier (eds.) (*Natural Resources and Violent Conflict: Options and Actions*; Washington, DC: World Bank).

[15] Bannon and Collier (2003), as above; Cook (2012), as above; Elbadawi and Nicholas (2002), note 13 above.

[16] Abiodun Alao, *Natural Resources and Conflict in Africa the Tragedy of Endowment* (Rochester Studies in African History and the Diaspora; Texas, USA: University of Rochester Press), 378; Bannon and Collier (2003), note 13 above; Sylvester Bongani Maphosa (2012), 'Natural Resources and Conflict: Unlocking the Economic Dimension of Peace-Building in Africa', *AISA Policy Brief* (Pretoria, South Africa: Africa Institute of South Africa).

Defining Illicit Financial Flows

There is no globally accepted definition of illicit financial flows (IFF), partly because it covers a broad range of activities and realities.[17] Because of the focus on the mineral value chain, this chapter defines illicit financial flows as money illegally earned, transferred, or used during/in the mineral licensing, taxation, and revenue management processes of a country. This narrow definition is not a proposed new definition of IFF but rather a definition that emphasizes the fact that the chapter is focused on IFF within the mineral value and how the mismatch between law and practice curtails or facilitates it. It is also definition that permits the analysis to concentrate on the domestic aspect of IFF.

Additionally, the chapter's concentration on mineral resource outflow is not to ignore illicit financial inflows. It is the chapter's contention that its focus on silencing guns in Africa necessarily incorporates the inflow of IFF, that is to say, while minerals illicitly flow out of Africa, they flow back into the continent through the processes illustrated in Fig. 30.3.

Figure 30.3 illustrates how IFF and security interact. It proposes that opacity is the single-most factor that gives rise to IFF through four broad practices; (a) money laundering, (b) corruption, (c) tax abuse (which includes tax evasion and avoidance), and (d) market abuse.[18] The result of these practices on economic and human development can be significant and cross-border. Among the most extreme threats, this poses conflict, state illegitimacy and

---

[17] Tiberius Barassa (2018), 'Illicit Financial Flows in Kenya: Mapping of the Literature and Synthesis of the Evidence', in Martin Atela (ed.) (Nairobi, Kenya: Partnership for African Social and Governance Research); Barry Cooper et al. (2018), 'Illicit Financial Flows: A Financial Integrity Perspective' (Tygervalley, South Africa: Centre for Financial Regulation and Inclusion); Maya Forstater (2018), 'Defining and Measuring Illicit Financial Flows' (New York, USA: Council on Foreign Relations); Maria Helena, Meyer Dolve, and Saul Mullard (2019), 'Addressing Illicit Financial Flows for Anti-Corruption at Country Level: A Primer for Development Practitioners' (2019:8; Bergen, Norway: CMR Michelsen Institute); Miles Kahler (2018), 'Countering Illicit Financial Flows: Expanding Agenda, Fragmented Governance' (New York: Council for Foreign Relations); Luckystar Miyandazi and Martin Ronceray (2018), 'Understanding Illicit Financial Flows and Efforts to Combat Them in Europe and Africa', in ECDMP (ed.) (Maastricht); I. Musselli and Bonanomi E. Bürgi (2020), 'Illicit Financial Flows: Concepts and Definition', Irene Ovonji-Odida and Algresia Akwi-Ogojo (2019), 'Illicit Financial Flows: Conceptual and Practical Issues', *Tax Cooperation Policy Brief* (Geneva, Switzerland); Aitor Pérez, and Iliana Olivié (2015), 'Europe Beyond Aid: Illicit Financial Flows Policy Responses in Europe and Implications for Developing Countries' (Washington, DC, USA: Centre for Global Development); Kingshuk Roy and Rohith Jyothish (2015), 'Illicit Financial Flows: Overview of Concepts, Methodologies and Regional Perspectives', in Pooja Rangaprasad and Rohith Jyothish (eds.) (New Delhi, India: Centre for Budget and Governance Accountability); UNCTAD (2020), 'Tackling Illicit Financial Flows for Sustainable Development in Africa', *Economic Development in Africa Report* (Geneva: UNCTAD); UNECA (2014), 'Illicit Financial Flows: Report of the High Level Panel on Illicit Financial Flows from Africa' (Addis Ababa: UNECA).

[18] Barassa (2018) as above; Miyandazi and Ronceray (2018), as above; Ovonji-Odida and Akwi-Ogojo (2019) as above; UNECA (2014), as above.

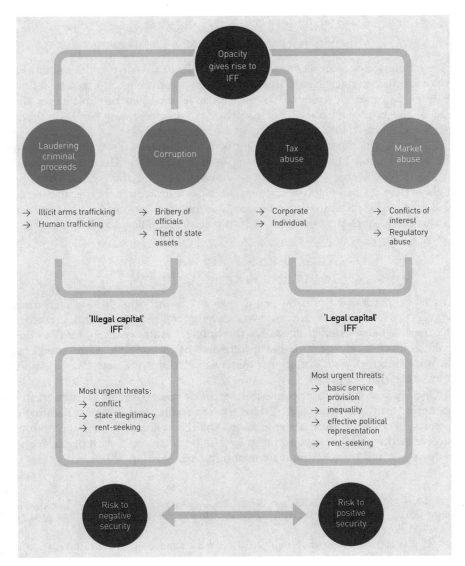

Fig. 30.3 IFF and security interaction (*Source* Tax Justice Network, 2014)

rent-seeking. IFF also curtail, and in certain instances, reverses human development gains by robbing citizens of basic services, exacerbating inequality, and entrenching rent-seeking.

Why the Mining Sector Is Prone to Illicit Financial Flows

The mining sector faces six broad governance challenges that, at the minimum, make it prone to illicit financial flows; (a) the sector is characterized by a flow of huge amounts of money.[19] In Africa, these are often multiple times the size of the economy's GDP.[20] This provides an opportunity for IFF-related activities such as trade misinvoicing, and transfer pricing.[21]

Second, there is a frequent blurring between public and private interests in the sector (Billon 2011; Gillies 2010; Signé et al. 2020). Third, competition in the mining sector is almost always limited. Fourth, the mining sector is highly technical and involves complex financial transactions. Lastly, the sector is almost always, a source of economic and political power.[22] The last three factors often motivate a complex web of collusion in illicit activity.

Good Governance as a Curb to Illicit Financial Flows

The fact that for every mineral-rich developing country that has suffered from armed conflict, there are at least two other mineral-rich developing countries that have avoided conflict illustrates that mineral endowment alone does not make conflict inevitable.[23] Good governance of the mining sector is among the major factors that distinguish mineral-rich countries that avoid conflict from those that do not.[24]

Good governance in the mineral sector is also correlated with greater economic growth. Eisen et al. (2020) use the results of a study by Kaufmann to show how good governance, measured by the ability to curtail corruption, is correlated with higher economic growth in both countries with high mineral endowment and those without mineral resources (see Fig. 30.4).[25]

---

[19] Billon (2011), Buenaventura and Biyani (2020), Centre for Natural Resource Governance (2013), Gillies (2010), Grynberg et al. (2019), Njie (2015), UNCTAD (2020), Williams (2010).

[20] D. Kar and D. Cartwright-Smith (2010), 'Illicit Financial Flows from Africa: Hidden Resource for Development' (Washington, DC, USA); L. Ndikumana and J. Boyce (2011), 'Capital Flight from Sub-Saharan Africa: Linkages with External Borrowing and Policy Options', *International Review of Applied Economics*, 25 (2), 149–70.

[21] Almounsor (2005), H. Mpenya et al. (2016), Signé et al. (2020).

[22] Alao; Billon (2011), H. Mpenya et al. (2016), Kar and Cartwright-Smith (2010), Maphosa (2012), Ross (2002).

[23] Maphosa (2012), Ross (2002, 2003), De Soysa (2002).

[24] Roman Grynberg, Jacob Nyambe, and Fwasa Singogo (2019), 'Illicit Financial Flows, Theft and Gold Smuggling in Africa', *Tanzanian Economic Review*, 9 (1), 35–59; Samaran Malick Njie (2015), 'Illicit Financial Flows and the Extractive Sector in Africa' (University of Ottawa); Oxfam International (2017), 'From Aspiration to Reality: Unpacking the Africa Mining Vision' (London, UK); NRGI (2018).

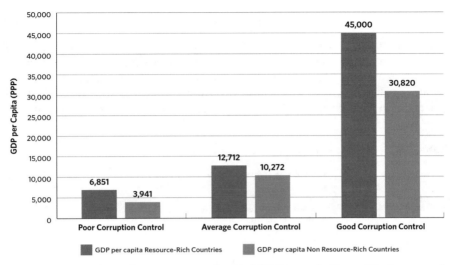

Fig. 30.4 Correlation between corruption and GDP growth (*Source* Kaufmann et al. 2010)

One of the reasons for this is that, by its nature, good governance aims to erode and remove opacity making it critical to curtailing IFF. Within the African mineral sector development context, the prominence of good governance is emphasized by the fact that the Africa Mining Vision (AMV)—one of the Africa 2063 Frameworks—aims to ensure a "sustainable and well-governed" mining sector as one of its main objectives.[26] The AMV founding document contends that, among other factors, governance deficiencies make it impossible to convert mineral endowment into successful and sustainable development.[27]

---

[25] Norman Eisen, et al. (2020), 'The TAP-Plus Approach to Anti-Corruption in the Natural Resource Value Chain' (Washington, DC, USA: Brookings Institute).

[26] African Union (2009, 2017), Commission (2017), Oxfam International (2017), as above.

[27] African Union (2009).

534 G. C. C. LWANDA

METHODOLOGY

The chapter analyzes the results of 38 questions related to a country's mining laws and 66 questions related to actual practice in the NRGI's 2017 Resource Governance Index (RGI). These questions cover 5 areas of mineral governance; (a) licensing, (b) local impact, (c)national budgeting, (d) SOEs, and (e) taxation (see Table 30.2). For each of the five themes, each country's

Table 30.2 Overview of thematic areas assessed

Theme	Examples of vulnerability to IFF	Number of law questions	Number of Practice questions
Licensing	• High risk of corruption if award criteria is not clear and there is no access to information on the selection process • Risk of mining activities in protected areas such as national monument sites and national parks if award criteria is not clear • Risk of an unfair fiscal framework due to opacity on the licenses issued	11	17
Local impact	• High risk of extensive environmental damage with dire consequences on the livelihoods of mining communities if there are no rules requiring for EIA/SIAs • High risk of extensive environmental damage with dire consequences on the livelihoods if there is lack of enforcement of mining laws on EIAs	8	3
National budgeting	• High risk of IFF if fiscal policy is not delinked from resource revenue volatility • High risk of IFF if there is a blurring of public and private interests • High risk of IFF if state institutions are not capacitated with the required technically competent personnel • High risk of IFF if mineral rules are not enforced	2	12

(continued)

30 PREVENTING ILLICIT RESOURCES OUTFLOWS FROM AFRICA 535

Table 30.2 (continued)

Theme	Examples of vulnerability to IFF	Number of law questions	Number of Practice questions
SOE	High risk of corruption, market abuse, and other IFF if there is no compliance with the highest standards of corporate governance	8	22

Taxation	• High risk of bribes, nepotism, and rent-seeking if
	  – Fiscal regime weak
	  – Enforcement of laws weak
	• High risk of fraud when oversight institutions and accountability mechanisms weak
	• High risk of transfer pricing and/or overpricing if there is a lack of enforcement of laws
		9	10

law was compared with the actual practice. Licensing, taxation, local impact, and management of SOEs together measure the sector's ability to realize value (NRGI 2017) while national budgeting is the only measure used in this chapter to assess revenue management (Fig. 30.5).[28]

The key to selection of the five themes was availability of comparable data across all 19 countries. Additionally, the five areas are prone to IFF activity in cases where the mineral governance regime is unable to address key issues such as controversies over ownership, complications arising from the extraction process, problems associated with revenue collection and allocation, unclear corporate governance practices, and free, prior, and informed consent. Table 30.2 lists examples that make each theme prone to IFF.

POLICY IMPLICATIONS

The results suggest that the mineral sector of the 19 countries is vulnerable to rampant IFF. This is largely because of gaps between the law and practice in the governance of minerals. One of the reasons for this could be the large number of African countries that have recently changed their mining

---

[28] In addition to national budgeting, the 2017 RGI includes subnational resource revenue sharing and the management of sovereign wealth funds as measures of revenue management. The chapter only uses national budgeting. Lack of data for all the countries covered was the limiting factor.

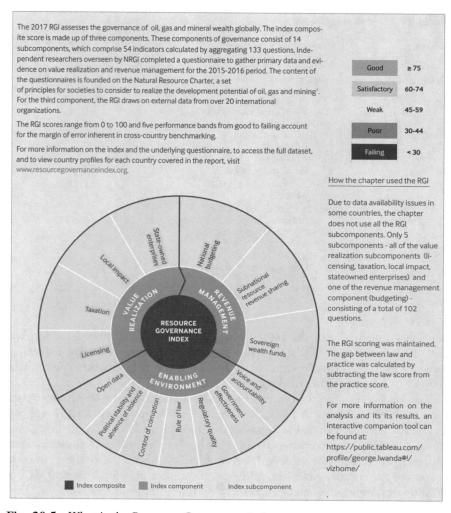

Fig. 30.5 What is the Resource Governance Index

laws.[29] Robust legal framework materializes only when institutions and practices to implement the rules are in place and in the case of these 19 African countries, there generally is a need for urgent institutional capacity building to strengthen the rule of law in the mining sector if they are to avoid IFF becoming endemic.[30]

---

[29] Hany Besada and Philip Martin (2013), 'Mining Codes in Africa Emergence of a "Fourth Generation?"' (North-South Institute).

[30] Natural Resource Governance Index (NRGI) (2018), 'Resource Governance Index: From Legal Reform to Implementation in Sub-Saharan Africa' (London, UK).

30 PREVENTING ILLICIT RESOURCES OUTFLOWS FROM AFRICA   537

Table 30.3   General summary of the likelihood of IFF activity

Theme	Likelihood of IFF	Suggested broad intervention
Local impact	Endemic	Very urgent institutional capacity building interventions (requiring significant amount of resources—human and capital) to entrench Rule of Law and arrest endemic IFF
Licensing	Considerable	Urgent institutional capacity building to strengthen Rule of Law and prevent IFF from becoming endemic
Taxation	Considerable	Urgent institutional capacity building to strengthen Rule of Law and prevent IFF from becoming endemic
National budgeting	Considerable	Urgent institutional capacity building to strengthen Rule of Law and prevent IFF from becoming endemic
SOE	Stoppable	Law and practice dovetail but law is generally not a par with global good practice

Table 30.3 summarizes the proposed likelihood of IFF activity in each of the five areas. Illicit activity is most likely endemic in the management of the environmental and social impacts of mining where the gap between law and practice is biggest. The results suggest that practices in place to curtail IFF activity in the management of the environmental and social impacts of mining are failing. Reflecting the gap between law and practice; laws governing national budgeting of mineral revenues are generally satisfactory in most of the countries, but practice is poor with minimal procedures and practice in place to be able to curtail IFF activity. Activities related with IFF are most likely considerable.

Taxation is a unique area because it is the only one in which the countries generally have satisfactory law that is matched by practice. This reflects growing levels of sophistication in fighting IFF across the continent and suggests that the law and practice in countries are well placed to fight IFF.[31] This however is only true in instances which the law is up to date with global standards and best practices. Simply having practice that is in sync with the law is inefficient when the law is outdated.

While the common trends identified above can be detected, there is great variability among the countries as illustrated in Table 30.4. As illustrated in the table, practice in several countries is ahead of the law in some of the five areas. Botswana (taxation, national budgeting, and SOE management), Angola (SOE management, national budgeting, and licensing), Ghana (national budgeting, licensing, and local impact) and Zambia (SOE management and national budgeting) are leaders. This is commendable as it implies

[31] As above.

538   G. C. C. LWANDA

Table 30.4   General summary of the likelihood of IFF activity

Theme	Countries where practice is ahead of law - better placed to fight IFF	Countries where IFF is most likely endemic — practice significantly lags law
Local impact	Niger, Ivory Coast, Zambia	Angola, Burkina Faso, Ethiopia, Equatorial Guinea, Gabon Madagascar, Mali, Nigeria, Sierra Leone, South Africa, Zimbabwe
Licensing	Angola, Cameroon, Gabon, Mali, Nigeria, Sierra Leone, and Zambia	Equatorial Guinea, Ethiopia
Taxation	Angola, Botswana, Ivory Coast, Madagascar, Niger, and Nigeria	Equatorial Guinea, Eritrea, Gabon
National budgeting	**Angola**, Botswana, Eritrea, *Ethiopia, Ghana, Madagascar, Sierra Leone*, **South Africa**, *Zambia, Zimbabwe*	Burkina Faso, Cameroon, Chad, Equatorial Guinea, Ivory Coast, Gabon, Mali, Niger, Nigeria
SOE	Angola, Botswana, Cameroon, *Chad*, Gabon, Ghana, Nigeria, Zimbabwe	

that the country is well placed to fight IFF in the areas in which practice is ahead of the law. However, it is worth emphasizing the imperative that steps are taken to ensure that mining laws catch up with practice if the country is going to be able to maximize curtailing IFF.

The table also shows the areas (and country) in which IFF is most likely endemic. Countries listed in red are countries where the results show that the gap between law and practice is so large that the law is most likely generally ignored. In this regard, the law seems to be generally ignored in the management of environmental and social impacts in 8 countries (Angola, Equatorial Guinea, Ethiopia, Mali, Nigeria, Sierra Leone, South Africa, and Zimbabwe). Additionally, the law is most likely ignored when it comes to national budgeting in Equatorial Guinea and Chad and mineral taxation in Equatorial Guinea and Eritrea.

The situation in Equatorial Guinea is really concerning. Despite having one of the laws that is coherent with global practice, mining laws are generally ignored in four out of the five areas of analysis (the management of the environmental and social impacts of mining, national budgeting, taxation, and licensing). Consequently, Equatorial Guinea has the widest gap between law and practice. IFF activity is most likely endemic in the mineral sectors of Equatorial Guinea as well as Eritrea and Gabon.

The table also shows that no country is a leader across all five areas. For example, while South Africa leads in national budgeting, law on the management of local impacts of mining is ignored and practice in mineral licensing is weaker than the law. Similarly, Nigeria leads in SOE management, taxation, and licensing but is among the weakest in national budgeting while Cameroon is a leader in mineral licensing but lags significantly in national budgeting.

CONCLUSION: EIGHT PRIORITY FOCUS AREAS TO FIGHT IFF IN MINERAL GOVERNANCE

Table 30.5 summarizes the mining governance practices in the 19 countries that are most suited to fighting IFF. At the licensing stage, progress has been made mostly in the disclosure of mineral licensing qualification criteria as well as the disclosure of license winners. National budgeting practice has been of highest standards in the management of resource revenue coupled with debt and budget management. Practice among SOEs is most coherent with global practice when it comes to disclosing their production figures as well as financial receipts. This has also been accompanied by gains in the timely disclosure of production volumes and the value of exports.

While these practices are necessary for fighting IFF, they are by far not sufficient. Significant practices that ensure that the sector remains shrouded in considerable governance opacity remain. Table 30.6 summarizes proposed

Table 30.5 Areas of significant progress fighting IFF activity

Theme	Issue	Correlation coefficient
Licensing	Qualification criteria disclosure	0.071
	Block allocation disclosure	0.074
	License winner disclosure	0.076
National budgeting	Resource revenue disclosure	0.054
	Fiscal rule monitoring timeframe	0.088
	Government expenditure disclosure	0.102
	Debt currency denomination	0.118
	Debt level disclosure	0.144
	Budget disclosure	0.151
State owned enterprise	Government-SOE receipt disclosure	0.069
	SOE production volume disclosure	0.069
Taxation	Export value disclosure	0.062
	Production volume disclosure	0.094
	Production disclosure timeliness	0.109
	Payment disclosure timeliness	0.112

Table 30.6 Summary of proposed priority focus areas

Theme	Issue	Correlation coefficient
Licensing	Cadaster coverage	−0.890
	Beneficial ownership disclosure	−0.100
	Public official's asset disclosure	−0.096
	License applicant disclosure	−0.091
	Contract disclosure timeliness	−0.088
	Historical contract disclosure	−0.075
	Reserves disclosure machine readability	−0.051
	Cadaster interest holders	−0.046
Local impact	EIA/SIA disclosure practice	−0.077
National budgeting	Online data portal coverage	−0.123
	Online data portal machine readability	−0.123
	Online data portal open license	−0.123
	Online data portal timeliness	−0.123
	Fiscal rule adherence	−0.091
State owned enterprise	SOE subsidiaries cost and revenue disclosure	−0.940
	SOE joint ventures disclosure	−0.088
	SOE code of conduct	−0.078
	SOE production buyer's disclosure	−0.073
	SOE non-commercial activity	−0.055

priority areas requiring urgent change in practice for greater transparency. Transparency, in turn, enables and strengthens the fight against IFF. At least, seven recommendations on how Africa can enhance its fight against the illicit flow of resources arise from the results in Table 30.6.

First, government's need to ensure that senior public officials are required to disclose their financial interests in mining companies. Second, is the need for the disclosure of license applicants. Third, governments need to normalize having publicly available and up to date registries of contracts and licenses including details of the beneficial owners of companies and regardless of when the contract or license was awarded. Without urgently implementing this, IFF activity will remain a core characteristic of the sector's mineral licensing regimes.

Fourth, delinking fiscal expenditure from mineral rents needs urgent implication in Africa. This includes putting in place and adhering to fiscal rules that place quantitative limits on national budget aggregates aimed at curtailing excessive spending during good times and higher taxes. Fifth, African governments need to leverage on the power of digital interventions to support to curtail IFF. In this regard, making data on the management of mineral revenues available online and in machine-readable mode is important.

30 PREVENTING ILLICIT RESOURCES OUTFLOWS FROM AFRICA   541

Sixth, state-owned enterprises must have a publicly available code of conduct which, among other things, requires it to publicly disclose joint ventures, non-commercial activity that it is involved in, the names of companies buying its production and costs and revenues from subsidiaries.

REFERENCES

African Union (2009), 'Africa Mining Vision' (Addis Ababa).

——— (2017), 'Agenda 2063: The Africa We Want', https://au.int/en/agenda 2063/overview, accessed 15 August.

Alao, Abiodun, *Natural Resources and Conflict in Africa The Tragedy Of Endowment* (Rochester Studies in African History and the Diaspora; Texas, USA: University of Rochester Press), 378.

Almounsor, A (ed.), (2005), *A Development Comparative Approach to Capital Flight: The Case of the Middle East and North Africa, 1970–2002*, ed. G Epstein (Capital Flight and Capital Controls in Developing Countries, Cheltenham, UK: Edward Elgar).

Bannon, Ian, and Collier, Paul (2003a), *Natural Resources and Conflict: What We Can Do* (Natural Resources and Violent Conflict: Options and Actions; Washington, DC: World Bank).

——— (2003b), *Natural Resources and Violent Conflict: Options and Actions* (Washington, DC: World Bank).

Barassa, Tiberius (2018), 'Illicit Financial Flows In Kenya: Mapping of the Literature and Synthesis of the Evidence', in Martin Atela (ed.) (Nairobi, Kenya: Partnership for African Social and Governance Research).

Besada, Hany, and Martin, Philip (2013), 'Mining Codes in Africa Emergence of a "Fourth Generation?"' (North-South Institute).

Billon, Philippe Le (2011), 'Extractive Sectors and Illicit Financial Flows: What Role for Revenue Governance Initiatives?', in Anti-Corruption Resource Centre (ed.), (Bergen, Norway: Chr. Michelson Institute).

Buenaventura, Mae, and Biyani, Neeti (2020), 'Combating Illicit Financial Flows in Extractives Sector in Asia: A Toolkit on Illicit Financial Flows' (Financial Transparency Coalition).

Centre for Natural Resource Governance (2013), 'Illicit Financial Flows in Zimbabwe's Artisanal Mining Sector' (Harare, Zimbabwe).

Commission, African Union (2017), 'Flagship Projects of Agenda 2063', https://au.int/en/agenda2063/flagship-projects, accessed 15 August.

Cook, Nicolas (2012), 'Conflict Minerals in Central Africa: U.S. and International Responses' (Washington, DC: US Congressional Research Service).

Cooper, Barry, et al. (2018), 'Illicit Financial Flows: A Financial Intergrity Perspective' (Tygervalley, South Africa: Centre for Financisl Regulation and Inclusion).

De Soysa, I (2002), 'Paradise Is a Bazaar? Greed, Creed, and Governance in Civil War 1989–1999', *Journal of Peace Research*, 39 (4), 395–416.

Eisen, Norman, et al. (2020), 'The TAP-Plus Approach to Anti-Corruption in the Natural Resource Value Chain' (Washington DC, USA: Brookings Institute).

Elbadawi, Ibrahim, and Nicholas, Sambanis (2002), 'How Much Civil War Will We See? Explaining the Prevalence of Civil War', *Journal of Conflict Resolution*, 46 (June), 307–34.

Forstater, Maya (2018), 'Defining and Measuring Illicit Financial Flows' (New York, USA: Council on Foreign Relations).

Francis, David (2006), *Uniting Africa: Building Regional Peace and Security Systems* (London: Ashgate), 296.

Gillies, A (2010), 'Fuelling Transparency and Accountability in the Natural Resources and Energy Markets', Paper presented at *14th International AntiCorruption Conference* (Bangkok, Thailand).

Grynberg, Roman, Nyambe, Jacob, and Singogo, Fwasa (2019), 'Illicit Financial Flows, Theft and Gold Smuggling in Africa', *Tanzanian Economic Review*, 9 (1), 35–59.

Helena, Maria, Dolve, Meyer, and Mullard, Saul (2019), 'Addressing Illicit Financial Flows for Anti-Corruption at Country Level: A Primer for Development Practitioners' (2019:8; Bergen, Norway: CMR Michelsen Institute).

Hunter, Marcena (2019), 'Illicit Financial Flows—Artisanal and Small-Scalegold Mining in Ghana and Liberia', in Jorge Moreira da Silva (ed.), *OECD Development Co-Operation Working Paper Series* (Paris, France: OECD).

Kahler, Miles (2018), 'Countering Illicit Financial Flows: Expanding Agenda, Fragmented Governance' (New York: Council for Foreign Relations).

Kar, D, and Cartwright-Smith, D (2010), 'Illicit Financial Flows from Africa: Hidden Resource for Development' (Washington, DC, USA).

Kaufmann, Daniel, Kraay, Aart, and Mastruzzi, Massimo (2010, September), The Worldwide Governance Indicators: Methodology and Analytical Issues. *World Bank Policy Research Working Paper No. 5430*, Available at SSRN: https://ssrn.com/abstract=1682130.

Lwanda, George (2003), 'Conflict Diamonds and the African "Resource Curse"', in Vasu Goundem (ed.), *Conflict Trends* (2003/4; Durban, South Africa: African Centre for the Constructive Resolution of Disputes [ACCORD]).

Maphosa, Sylvester Bongani (2012), 'Natural Resources and Conflict: Unlocking the Economic Dimension of Peace-Building in Africa', *AISA Policy Brief* (Pretoria, South Africa: Africa Institute of South Africa).

Miyandazi, Luckystar, and Ronceray, Martin (2018), 'Understanding Illicit Financial Flows and Efforts to Combat Them in Europe and Africa', in ECDMP (ed.) (Maastricht).

Mpenya, H, Metseyem, C, and Epo, B (2016), 'Natural Resources and Capital Flight in Cameroon', *African Development Review*, 28 (S1), 88–99.

Musselli, I, and Bürgi, Bonanomi E (2020), 'Illicit Financial Flows: Concepts and Definition', *Revue internationale de politique de développement*.

Ndikumana, L, and Boyce, J (2011), 'Capital Flight from Sub-Saharan Africa: Linkages with External Borrowing and Policy Options', *International Review of Applied Economics*, 25 (2), 149–70.

Njie, Samaran Malick (2015), 'Illicit Financial Flows and the Extractive Sector in Africa' (University of Ottawa).

NRGI (2017), '2017 Resource Governance Index' (London, UK).

——— (2018), 'Resource Governance Index: From Legal Reform to Implementation in Sub-Saharan Africa' (London, UK).

Okumu, Wafula, Atta-Asamoah, Andrews, and Sharamo, Roba (2020), 'Silencing the Guns in Africa by 2020-Achievements, Opportunities and Challenges' (Pretoria, South Africa: Institute of Security Studies).

Ovonji-Odida, Irene, and Akwi-Ogojo, Algresia (2019), 'Illicit Financial Flows: Conceptual and Practical Issues', *Tax Cooperation Policy Brief* (Geneva, Switzerland).

Oxfam International (2017), 'From Aspiration to Reality: Unpacking the Africa Mining Vision' (London, UK).

Peace Research Institute (2018), 'Conflict Trends in Africa 1989–2017', in Peace Reserach Institute (ed.), *Conflict Trends* (06/2018; Oslo, Norway).

Pérez, Aitor, and Olivié, Iliana (2015), 'Europe Beyond Aid: Illicit Finanial Flows Policy Responses in Europe and Implications for Developing Countries' (Washington, DC, USA: Centre for Global Development).

Ross, Michael (2002), 'Resources and Rebellion in Aceh, Indonesia', in Yale–World Bank Project on the Economics of Political Violence (ed.).

———. (2003), *The Natural Resource Curse: How Wealth Can Make You Poor*, eds. Ian Bannon and Paul Collier (Natural Resources and Violent Conflict: Options and Actions; Washington, DC: World Bank).

Roy, Kingshuk, and Jyothish, Rohith (2015), 'Illicit Financial Flows: Overview of Concepts, Methodologies and Regional Perspectives', in Pooja Rangaprasad and Rohith Jyothish (eds.) (New Delhi, India: Centre for Budget and Governance Accountability).

Signé, Landry, Sow, Mariama, and Madden, Payce (2020), 'Illicit Financial Flows in Africa: Drivers, Destinations, and Policy Options' (Brookings Institute).

Stockholm International Peace Research Institute (2020), 'SIPRI 2020 Yearbook', in SIPRI (ed.) (Stockholm, Sweden).

UNCTAD (2020), 'Tackling Illicit Financial Flows for Sustainable Development in Africa', *Economic Development in Africa Report* (Geneva: UNCTAD).

UNECA (2014), 'Illicit Financial Flows: Report of the High Level Panel on Illicit Financial Flows from Africa' (Addis Ababa: UNECA).

Williams, A (2010), 'Shining a Light on the Resource Curse: An Empirical Analysis of the Relationship Between Natural Resources, Transparency, and Economic Growth', *World Development*, 39 (4), 490–505.

CHAPTER 31

Curbing the Migrant Crisis in the Mediterranean Sea

Godard Busingye and Daniel Mayombo

INTRODUCTION

The migrant crisis in the Mediterranean Sea stems not only from the African continent, but includes other regions such as Asia, Latin America, and the Middle East. Armed conflicts, political persecution, poverty, and to some extent unfavourable climatic conditions are some of the push effects that drive persons to leave their homes and venture to cross the Mediterranean Sea, even with the knowledge that the chances of successfully crossing to their desired destinations are minimal. Theoretically, each of the identified causes of this crisis can be addressed from a human rights-based approach, if their root causes can be identified. Once the root causes are addressed, then it becomes easier to curb the crisis in the Mediterranean Sea.

The migrant crisis in the Mediterranean Sea is largely characterised by death of migrants who attempt to cross the Sea in large numbers and on boats operated by gangs of human traffickers/smugglers. They use boats that are unlicensed and not always seaworthy. Some of the migrants drown in the waters when the boats they are travelling in capsize, while others die en route in the boats due to various reasons including starvation, coldness, and disease. Others die on boats when the authorities in Europe deny them

G. Busingye (✉)
Kampala International University, Kampala, Uganda

D. Mayombo
Uganda Peoples' Defence Forces, Kampala, Uganda

© The Author(s), under exclusive license to Springer Nature
Switzerland AG 2022
D. Kuwali (ed.), *The Palgrave Handbook of Sustainable Peace and Security in Africa*, https://doi.org/10.1007/978-3-030-82020-6_31

545

landing access rights, yet they would have been saved if they disembarked the dangerous boats.[1] The various causes of the migrant crisis will require tailor-made solutions curb the migrant crisis in the Mediterranean Sea.

Part of the African initiatives to curb this crisis is encapsulated in the AU Agenda 2063 and Vision 2020, which set the targets for silencing guns on the continent.[2] Silencing the guns on the African continent is part of the global drive to have a peaceful and all-inclusive world where everyone is free to live in a country of his or her choice, and enjoy all rights that are inherent to human beings.[3] These rights are many and each of them is closely related to the migrant crisis in the Mediterranean Sea in one way or the other. The rights include all those provided for under the Universal Declaration of Human Rights,[4] and those under the International Covenant on Civil and Political Rights.[5] Civil and political rights are "[a] class of rights that protect individuals' freedom from infringement by governments, social organizations, and private individuals. They ensure one's entitlement to participate in the civil and political life of the society and State without discrimination or repression".[6]

In line with the discussion by Gloria Phiri and Chikondi Mandala in Chapter 18, both the universal and the civil and political human rights may be violated by State and non-state actors. The motivation to violate human rights is firmly rooted in ideologies that espouse selfishness and the driving force. Political ideologies are prone to the problem of committing atrocities against rivals. Atrocities committed within the ambit of the various political ideologies on the African continent using the gun top the list of all the atrocities that lead

[1] See, for example, Reuters, Hardline Italian Minister Faces Trial Over Blocked Migrants, U.S. news, 24 January 2019, accessed at: Hardline Italian Minister Faces Trial Over Blocked Migrants, on 13 February 2020, where it was reported that A special tribunal has recommended that Interior Minister Matteo Salvini face trial for refusing to let 150 migrants disembark last year from a rescue ship docked in Sicily.

[2] Agenda 2063 is Africa's blueprint and master plan for transforming Africa into the global powerhouse of the future. It is the continent's strategic framework that aims to deliver on its goal for inclusive and sustainable development and is a concrete manifestation of the pan-African drive for unity, self-determination, freedom, progress and collective prosperity pursued under Pan-Africanism and African Renaissance.

[3] Sharon Tshipa, 'Silencing the Guns': Toward a United, Prosperous and Peaceful Africa, DEVEX Global Development Career Forum, accessed at: https://www.devex.com/news/silencing-the-guns-toward-a-united-prosperous-and-peaceful-africa-84979, on 8 February 2020.

[4] See generally the Universal Declaration of Human Rights, 1948, which inter alia provides that human rights accrue tor human beings by virtue of their so being.

[5] International Covenant on Civil and Political Rights, Adopted and opened for signature, ratification and accession by General Assembly resolution 2200A (XXI) of 16 December 1966, entry into force 23 March 1976, in accordance with Article 49.

[6] International Covenant on Civil and Political Rights, Adopted and opened for signature, ratification and accession by General Assembly resolution 2200A (XXI) of 16 December 1966, entry into force 23 March 1976, in accordance with Article 49.

to mass migrations from Africa to Europe, through the Mediterranean Sea.[7] Historically, the gun was introduced on the African continent by the Arab slave traders and the Western colonisers, who the slave traders worked for.

From a historic perspective, the African feudal leaders, chiefs, and clan leaders were unable to prevent the slave traders and colonial aggressors from taking over their land and political power, because the gun wielded by the latter gave them an advantage over the spear, bows, and arrows and other rudimentary instruments of power at their disposal.[8] After the African continent had been depleted of its rich human resource by slave traders, and the subsequent conquest of the continent by foreign powers, largely from the Western world, it became difficult to guarantee security of Africans in their home countries.

Colonial and post-colonial interests have, therefore, and correctly so, been partly blamed for conflicts in countries such as the Democratic Republic of the Congo (DRC), the Central African Republic (CAR), and the Republic of Mali.[9] Political instability linked to the colonial and post-colonial State historical interest in such countries, coupled with commission of mass atrocities in these and other African countries, culminates in mass exodus of nationals to take refuge in perceived safe-havens. During times of political instability, some nationals are witch-hunted by those supposed to protect them and their property. Political instability equally destroys means of livelihoods, which leads to deteriorating standards of living.

The politically witch-hunted and the poor, who are able to escape from their countries, constitute some of the African migrants that risk crossing the Mediterranean Sea to Europe in search of better life alternatives. The crisis in the Mediterranean Sea is further aggravated by the failure of some African governments to ensure that their citizens access and enjoy all such rights as are necessary for their well-being. Such rights include the right to work in a safe and secure environment, right to education, right to health care. The

[7] Ben Quinn, Conflict and Arms, Mass Atrocities Feared in South Sudan as Ethnic Violence Is Stoked by Hunger, *The Guardian*, 2015, https://www.theguardian.com/global-development/2016/dec/18/mass-atrocities-feared-in-south-sudan-as-ethnic-violence-is-stoked-by-hunger, on 8 February 2020.

[8] See for example, South African History Online, Basotho Wars 1858–1868, 2011, accessed at: https://www.sahistory.org.za/article/basotho-wars-1858-1868, on 13 February 2020.

[9] Alfred Burimaso, Political Leadership Crisis in the Post-Colonial African States: The Case of the Democratic Republic of Congo (DRC), MA Dissertation, Department of Political Studies, Faculty of Humanities, University of Witwatersrand, Johannesburg, Republic of South Africa, 2013, accessed at: http://wiredspace.wits.ac.za/bitstream/handle/10539/13693/Corrected%20report.pdf?sequence=2, on 3 February 2020; see also Robert Blanton, T. David Mason, and Brian Athow, Colonial Style and Post-Colonial Ethnic Conflict in Africa, *Journal of Peace Research* (2001) 38(4): 473–491, https://doi.org/10.1177/0022343301038004005.

most violated human rights which rhyme with theme of silencing the guns are those related to the political and economic rights of the victims.[10]

By way of illustration, lack of inclusiveness in sharing the national cake in the political and economic arenas causes dissent on the part of the excluded. Due to poor and immature political ideologies in some African countries, those who ascend to political power practice exclusionary politics based on religion, ethnicity, and regionalism. In the case of Uganda, during the country's period of turmoil, 1962–1986, the country was divided on several sectarian lines.[11] The witch-hunted, and who had means to escape from the country migrated to different parts of the world, including Europe. Social exclusion, largely based on gender, is also another contributing factor to mass exodus of persons from their countries to Europe through the Mediterranean Sea. Cases of female genital mutilation and forced early marriages are still rampant in Africa, and those why defy the cultural practices are witch-hunted, some of them flee their countries to faraway lands, including Europe.[12]

Political dissent breeds instability in countries, where the gun has been the main tool of resolving the feuds between the government forces and the dissidents. The unresolved feuds between governments and the dissident forces constitute a key factor in generating mass movements of migrants from the African continent to Europe through the Mediterranean Sea. It suffices to note that Europe is not the only safe haven for all those persons who flee their countries due to the aforementioned reasons. Some of the affected persons take refuge in other African countries where their security is guaranteed.

In the case of migrants from South Sudan, Somalia, and Eritrea, where there are reported cases of political witch-hunt, female genital mutilation, and forced early marriages, victims have moved to countries like Kenya and Uganda in large numbers.[13] It is, however, possible that if such persons had means of

[10] See Phumla Williams, Silencing the Guns and Firearms Amnesty, *Daily Post*, January 2020, accessed at: https://dailypost.ng/2020/01/20/phumla-williams-silencing-the-guns-and-firearms-amnesty/, on 3 February 2020.

[11] J. J. Carney, *The Politics of Ecumenism in Uganda, 1962–1986*, Cambridge University Press, 30 October 2017, accessed online at: https://www.cambridge.org/core/journals/church-history/article/abs/politics-of-ecumenism-in-uganda-19621986/B1E3170FDC6E BD706916BB28AB0FF01A, on 25 February 2021; see also Andy Lancaster, *The Divisive Nature of Ethnicity in Ugandan Politics, Before and After Independence*, 25 May 2012, available at: https://www.e-ir.info/2012/05/25/the-divisive-nature-of-ethnicity-in-uga ndan-politics-before-and-after-independence/.

[12] Satang Nabaneh and Adamson S. Muula, Female Genital Mutilation/Cutting in Africa: A Complex Legal and Ethical Landscape, *International Journal of Gynaecology & Obstetrics* (2019), available at: https://doi.org/10.1002/ijgo.12792; see also M. J. Maluleke, Culture, Tradition, Custom, Law and Gender Equality, *Potchefstroom Electronic Law Journal/Potchefstroomse Elektroniese Regsblad* (2012) 15(1), available at: http://dx.doi.org/10.4314/pelj.v15i1.1.

[13] Frank Ahimbisibwe, Uganda and the Refugee Problem: Challenges and Opportunities, *African Journal of Political Science and International Relations* (2018) 13(5), https://doi.org/10.5897/AJPSIR2018.1101; Norwegian Refugee Council, More Refugees Flee to Uganda Than Across Mediterranean, Press Release, 25 January 2017; World Health

crossing to Europe, and actually some of them later do so, they would not stay on the African continent. Apart from relative peace in particular African countries, do not provide better living conditions for refugees due to the poverty levels in many of them. Indeed, the African Union roadmap for implementing Agenda 2063 and Vision 2020, acknowledges the nexus between peace and security, governance, and development in sustaining peace.[14]

Many Africans, who flee their countries attempt crossing the Mediterranean Sea in order to access any European country for refuge. Those who manage to cross the dangerous waters of the Mediterranean Sea are sometimes denied landing rights in Europe. Some die while on boats waiting to be granted landing rights in Europe due to starvation, disease, or harsh cold conditions on the waters.[15] Others are held for long periods in detention homes before being screened and either returned to Africa, or granted asylum status in Europe.[16]

Much as many African countries are breeding grounds for the migrant crisis on the Mediterranean Sea, Somalia, Eritrea, Ethiopia, and Egypt are ranked high among African countries from which majority of the migrants to Europe through the Mediterranean Sea originate.[17] The foregoing discussion identifies different causes for the migrant crisis on the Mediterranean Sea. It specifically identifies that there are African continent endogenic factors and also the exogenic factors, which contribute to the migrant crisis in the Mediterranean Sea.

THE AFRO-EURO MIGRANT CRISIS

Ideally, each person should have unfettered right to live in a country of his or her choice, even if it is not their birthplace. This, however, has not been the case for some Africans who are forced to leave their countries of origin

Organization, Female Genital Mutilation—New Knowledge Spurs Optimism, Progress, No. 72 (2006), available at: https://www.who.int/reproductivehealth/topics/fgm/progre ss72_fgm.pdf, accessed on 25 February 2021.

[14] ISS, PSC Report, Silencing the Guns Beyond 2020, 5 August 2019, accessed at: https://issafrica.org/pscreport/psc-insights/silencing-the-guns-beyond-2020, on 3 February 2020.

[15] See Philip Hoare, 'The Sea Does Not Care': The Wretched History of Migrant Voyages, The Guardian, Tuesday, 21 April 2015, accessed at: https://www.theguardian. com/world/2015/apr/21/the-sea-does-not-care-wretched-history-migrant-voyages-med iterranean-tragedy, on 24 January 2020; See also Priyanka Boghani Digital Reporter and Producer, For Those Crossing the Mediterranean, a Higher Risk of Death, FRONTLINE, 27 October 2016, accessed at: https://www.pbs.org/wgbh/frontline/article/for-those-crossing-the-mediterranean-a-higher-risk-of-death/, on 24 January 2020.

[16] Priyali Sur, Why Record Numbers of African Migrants Are Showing Up at the U.S.–Mexican Border, June 2019, accessed at: https://www.alipac.us/f12/why-record-numbers-african-migrants-showing-up-u-s-mexican-border-373866/, on 3 February 2020.

[17] Human Rights Watch, The Mediterranean Migration Crisis: Why People Flee, What the EU Should Do, accessed at: https://www.hrw.org/report/2015/06/19/mediterra nean-migration-crisis/why-people-flee-what-eu-should-do, on 24 January 2020.

only to fail to reach the yearned for European countries, when they die in the Mediterranean Sea. Even for the few who cross the Mediterranean Sea, there is no guarantee that they will be allowed to land or stay in Europe. Some of them are forced back on the dangerous boats and returned to the African continent against their will. Many of them end up in detention camps in Libya or other coastal countries.

In some instances, those in detention are smuggled out and again trafficked over the Mediterranean Sea to Europe. This creates a cyclic problem of the ever-increasing numbers of African migrants that are trafficked over the Mediterranean Sea. The United Nations (UN) and the African continent have mechanisms, policies, and laws to prevent forced migrations from home countries. Europe has policies and laws for accommodating refugees. These mechanisms, policies, and laws, are, however, not strictly adhered to for the case of migrants who attempt to cross the Mediterranean Sea. Curbing the migrant crisis in the Mediterranean Sea, therefore, is an uphill task, because it stems from diverse angles and cannot be handled using a single approach.

The push factors for the migrant crisis on the Mediterranean Sea include, exclusionary governance democracies, violent armed conflicts, poverty, gender discrimination, and climate change on the African continent. Worst of all, not everyone who attempts crossing the Mediterranean Sea on the small boats owned by gangs of human traffickers makes it to the intended destination. Many of these boats are not seaworthy, and coupled with the problem of overloading them, occasionally capsise and their occupants die at sea. Diena et al., consider the Mediterranean as the most dangerous part of the journey for the African migrants crossing to Europe. These authors state that [t]he Central Mediterranean is the most dangerous crossing for irregular migrants in the world. At any given point in time, over half a million potential migrants wait in Libya to travel to Italy with the aid of human smugglers.[18]

Kolade blames this crisis on the Global South and Europe unequal power relations. The unequal power relations between the Global South and Europe is indeed historical stemming largely from the 1884 Berlin Conference which portioned the African continent and divided it amongst European countries in the same way a party cake is sliced and distributed amongst the celebrants. Kolade further asserts "while continued shipwrecks in the Mediterranean Sea, such as the 19 April 2015 incident that claimed an estimated 800 lives, have drawn attention to irregular migration in Europe, it is important to observe that the history of Global South to Europe migration is long and complex. The current crisis in the Mediterranean, which the UN has called, 'a tragedy of

---

[18] Claudio Deiana, Vikram Maheshri, and Giovanni Mastrobuoni, *Irregular Migration and the Unintended Consequences of Search and Rescue Operations in the Central Mediterranean Sea*, 2019, p. 1.

epic proportions' is the culmination of decades of unequal power relationships between the Global South and Europe".[19]

There remains, amidst all these challenges, a problem of either underreporting the migrant crisis in the Mediterranean Sea or even downplaying it as trivial. Unless the problem of the Global North–South is addressed, and the contemporary African leaders address their in-house issues, many more Africans will for now and in the foreseeable future continue to venture crossing the Mediterranean Sea in the aforementioned circumstances. On the part of European countries, the blatant refusal of the already stressed African migrants that cross the Mediterranean Sea, constitutes a violation of human rights.

IDEOLOGICAL CAUSES TO THE MIGRANT CRISIS IN THE MEDITERRANEAN SEA

The UN Charter, which is the guiding instrument in terms of international peace and security, enjoins everyone in the world to practice tolerance and live together in peace with one another as good neighbours, and to unite strength to maintain international peace and security.[20] Tolerance and living together in peace, however, are obstacles to the oppressive ideology of patriarchy, which is intertwined with the capitalist, and colonial and post-colonial African modelled State structures. Patriarchy, often referred to as the rule of fathers, as an ideology is oppressive and intolerant to any dissenting views, especially in the socioeconomic and political arenas.[21] Its contribution to the migrant crisis in the Mediterranean Sea cannot be ignored, especially when it is clear that many Africans flee their homes due to politically related reasons, including persecutions and denial of equitable share in the national cake.

The ideology of patriarchy in regard to its connection with the migrant crisis in the Mediterranean Sea, however, needs to be understood before being blamed. This ideology has been specifically criticised by feminism perspective, suffice to mention that it is so powerful and engrained in the minds of many African leaders to the extent that it overshadows implementation of their intended manifestos as they descend to power.[22] Critiquing the ideology of patriarchy, Becker points out that it is "[a] social structure that is

---

[19] Ifeoluwa Kolade, Swimming Against the Tides: Examining the EU Response to Irregular Migration Through the Mediterranean Sea, Geneva International Centre for Justice, 2015, p. 1.

[20] The Charter of the United Nations, 1945, Preamble.

[21] Mary Becker, Patriarchy and Inequality: Towards a Substantive Feminism, *University of Chicago Legal Forum* 1999(1), Article 3, available at: http://chicagounbound.uchicago.edu/uclf/vol1999/iss1/3.

[22] Lawrence O. Bamikole, Nkrumah and the Triple Heritage Thesis and Development in Africana Societies, *International Journal of Business, Humanities and Technology* 2(2), March 2012, accessed at: http://ijbhtnet.com/journals/Vol_2_No_2_March_2012/9.pdf, on 3 February 2020.

male-centred, male-identified, male-dominated, and which valorizes qualities narrowly defined as masculine".[23]

From the perspective of feminism, State structures, which are constructed by Constitutions crafted with a patriarchal mind, might appear inclusive of everyone in the country by virtue of the wording. On the face of it, those Constitutions are so tailored to suit the normative demands to observe human rights within the ambit of the UN.[24] They, however, silently protect the mighty and the ruling class vested interests, which enable members of those classes to gain uncontrollable political power and also amass wealth that they must protect at the cost of the rest of the citizenry. Moreover, whatever is done in their favour is facilitated by resources contributed by all citizens through the available State structures. The socially, economically, and politically weak, then descend into the dungeons of poverty, from which it is difficult to come from. In the dungeons, they remain excluded from directly benefiting from the State resources and discriminated against even in programmes fallaciously presented as pro-poor. The outcome is creation of socioeconomic and of course political echelons which do not talk to each other on a roundtable.

In this problematic setting, the politically empowered are the only ones who can access, at leisure the national resources. The system then ejects the poor, using the gun to politically persecute them. Those who survive death, and cannot adapt themselves to the harsh political conditions in the country, flee their homes in search of a better life elsewhere.[25] Europe seems to provide the better option for those fleeing their home countries under such circumstances. After fleeing their home countries, the next dangerous obstacle to this category of persons is how to reach their destination. Crossing the Mediterranean Sea, by any means available, however, does not guarantee their safe arrival to the desired destinations. Liss observes that, "migrants relying on the services of people smugglers. Many attempt the cross the Mediterranean Sea in small, crammed boats that are often unsuitable for such journeys".[26] Indeed, many migrants perish in these waters.

In order to reverse the situation and curb the migrant crisis in the Mediterranean Sea, it is necessary to interrogate the root causes of the crisis using a human rights-based approach, espoused within the purview of feminism perspective. A human rights-based approach will then help to inform the home

---

[23] Mary Becker, Patriarchy and Inequality: Towards a Substantive Feminism, *University of Chicago Legal Forum* 1999(1), Article 3, available at: http://chicagounbound.uchicago.edu/uclf/vol1999/iss1/3.

[24] See for example.

[25] See for example, Lauren Ploch Blanchard, *Conflict in South Sudan and the Challenges Ahead, Congressional Research Service*, 22 September 2016, accessed at: https://fas.org/sgp/crs/row/R43344.pdf, on 13 February 2020.

[26] Carolin Liss, *Turning a Blind Eye? The Rescue of Migrants in the Mediterranean*, Peace Research Institute Frankfurt, Germany, 2019, accessed at: https://blog.prif.org/2019/04/09/turning-a-blind-eye-the-rescue-of-migrants-in-the-mediterranean/, on 21 January 2020.

governments and the intended recipients of these people that each one on the planet earth deserves a chance to live. Indeed, over time, the European Parliament has come to appreciate that "with the unprecedented migration and refugee crisis in the Mediterranean, migration quickly became a central priority of European Union (EU) institutions and the need for a more holistic approach became more pressing".[27]

A human rights-based approach will in addition to awareness raising both in the home countries and in Europe, identify why the crisis of African migrants in the Mediterranean Sea continue to be on the radar of international discussions. Questions will be raised as to whether or not the crisis is beyond human comprehension and management or is a neglected problem. The answers obtained will then be used to attack and dismantle the centres of oppression in specific African countries which contribute the largest share to this crisis. It will specifically help to provide a mechanism for addressing the push and pull factors for the African migrants to move Europe in the era of information revolution when everyone knows what lies ahead of his or her actions. Indeed, it must always be foreseen that for the Mediterranean Sea, survival is the exception, not the norm.

According to the EU, "push factors designate the reasons for migrants to leave their country of origin, while pull factors are the reasons encouraging them to come, in this case, to Europe. According to the UN Special Rapporteur on the human rights of migrants, migration to Europe by boats is 'largely driven by conflict, persecution and poverty (push factors) as well as unmet needs with the labour market (pull factors)".[28] Other push and pull factors that greatly contribute to the migrant crisis on the Mediterranean Sea include, "social systems of group-based oppression co-existing with sexism in patriarchal structures. Ethnicity, religion, class, and many other variables structure inequality. How much privilege a person has depending on the social positions he or she occupies and how those positions are valued in his or her society".[29]

On the face of it, Europe appears to have a solution to the migrant crisis in the Mediterranean Sea. The European former colonial powers of the majority of African States which eject many of their citizens to Europe through the Mediterranean Sea, may, however, not provide a lasting solution to the crisis because they are party to the problem. It is not a surprise, for example, that the British Government quietly announced its decision to withdraw support for Mare Nostrum, a search and rescue operation for migrants in the Mediterranean Sea. Britain's position was expressed thus they "do not support planned search and rescue operations in the Mediterranean [...] to avoid an unintended

[27] European Union, Directorate-General for External Policies Policy Department, Migrants in the Mediterranean: Protecting Human Rights, 2015.

[28] European Union, Directorate-General for External Policies Policy Department, Migrants in the Mediterranean: Protecting Human Rights, 2015.

[29] Mary Becker, Patriarchy and Inequality: Towards a Substantive Feminism, *University of Chicago Legal Forum* 1999(1), Article 3, p. 25, available at: http://chicagounbound.uchicago.edu/uclf/vol1999/iss1/3.

'pull factor', encouraging more migrants to attempt the dangerous sea crossing and thereby leading to more tragic and unnecessary deaths".[30]

Whether Britain's message can be interpreted as being moral, ethical, or legal remains a subject of intellectual debate. Considering that Britain has exited the European Union, it is possible that the crisis in the Mediterranean Sea will escalate due to the disharmony in the ideological contestations in Europe about this crisis. It is, however, possible that, with her human rights background, Britain continued with the support for the search and rescue operations on the deadly waters of the Mediterranean Sea. From the foregoing, it is important that the patriarchal African State structures adopt a human rights-based approach in dealing with the issue of political dissent, because this is possible and is done on other continents, so that the agenda for silencing the guns on the African continent can successfully be implemented.

Moreover, the commitment exhibited recently by the African Heads of State and Government at the 39th African Union (AU) Summit in Addis Ababa, Ethiopia, to silence the guns is encouraging. In its recent meeting, the African Union Summit re-echoed the need to silence the guns on the continent, much as realistically, this would not be achieved by the end of 2020. Indeed, a report by the Africa Times reporter noted that the AU has always wanted to silence the guns on the continent, but their wishes have never been fulfilled."[31] Much as it is clear that African leaders are committed to silencing the guns in their countries, there still remains a problem of non-state actors, who are fighting the lawfully established governments. It is clear from the ongoing war on terror in Somalia, Nigeria and other African States, that Governments alone do not have the capacity to silence guns in their countries. They need brotherly and sisterly support from all member States of the United Nations to defeat the terrorists, and then be able to create stable and peaceful environment for each and every citizen to live in. Terrorist groups with Al-Qaeda links, continue to destabilise the continent, and governments cannot simply watch what is going on without responding to the attacks.

The responsibility incumbent on African leaders is to ensure that they address those aspects where they have control first so that their actions do not trigger off mass migrations to Europe. Moreover, if there is stability in a country, fighting terrorism would be a concerted effort of each and every citizen in the country, and there would be no one providing assistance to the terrorists. It, therefore, remains a challenge to the bespoken leaders of the African continent to ensure that they dismantle, and thereafter, reconstruct their ideological leanings to ensure that they accommodate each and everyone in the governance of the continent. Effort by the African leaders can

---

[30] The Lancet, *Migrant Crisis in the Mediterranean* 385(9979), P1698, 2 May 2015, https://doi.org/10.1016/S0140-6736(15)60875-3.

[31] *Africa Times* Reporter, African Union Summit Focuses on 'Silencing the Guns', *Africa Times Magazine*, accessed at: https://africatimes.com/2020/02/10/african-union-summit-focuses-on-silencing-the-guns/, on 11 February 2020.

bear fruits if they are synchronised with those undertaken under the European continental framework for the African migrants who cross to Europe via the Mediterranean Sea.

Attempts by some countries in Europe to address the crisis when migrants are already at Sea cannot provide a solution to the root causes of the crisis emanating from the African continent. Probably a demand that Africa's former colonisers step up their cooperation with the African Union to address the problem from the roots, and on the African continent could provide a seemingly lasting solution to the crisis on the Mediterranean Sea. Heavy investment by the former colonial masters on the African continent is likely to create more job opportunities for the unemployed who, when desperate, turn against their governments as dissidents, and is likely to help to stabilise the debt-burdened African economies, for the benefit of the global community.

The Legal Framework for Taming the Migrant Crisis on the Mediterranean Sea

The push factors for the African migrants who attempt to cross the Mediterranean Sea could be minimised if the legal framework for taming them was strictly implemented, especially within the ambit of the UN framework. For example, under Article 1(3), the UN Charter envisions the global body to be a centre for harmonizing the attainment of, "international cooperation in solving international problems of an economic, social, cultural, or humanitarian character, and in promoting and encouraging respect for human rights and for fundamental freedoms for all without distinction as to race, sex, language, or religion; and (4) for harmonizing the actions of nations in the attainment of these common ends".

The push factors that culminate in the migrant crisis on the Mediterranean Sea have been identified to be in the realm of economic, social, cultural, or humanitarian, which embody the political factors. These fall squarely within the mandate of the UN to address, unless it is argued that the framers of the UN Charter were over-ambitious and provided for what cannot reasonably be handled by the Organisation. In case the UN was unable to address the root causes of the migrant crisis of African migrants in the Mediterranean Sea, still, within the ambit of the UN Charter, the African continent would remain empowered to do so. Article 52(1), the UN Charter empowers regional bodies to deal with matters which, ordinarily would fall within the mandate of the UN. It provides, "nothing in the present Charter precludes the existence of regional arrangements or agencies for dealing with such matters relating to the maintenance of international peace and security as are appropriate for regional action, provided that such arrangements or agencies and their activities are consistent with the Purposes and Principles of the United Nations".

Indeed, the root causes of the migrant crisis in the Mediterranean Sea that stem from the African continent fall within the category for which the UN was formed to address, but whose handling can be done by regional bodies.

The fact that the UN Charter gives mandate to the AU, as a regional body to handle matters within the purview of the Charter signifies a trust on the part of the UN that regional bodies have capacity to handle such. Failure to address any of the root causes of the migrant crisis in the Mediterranean Sea by the leaders of the African continent, then amounts to a betrayal of the whole community of the UN.

It should, however, be noted that some of the causes might be out of the purview of the African leaders, especially if there are foreign interests such as those of the terrorists supported by the Islamic Jihadists. Where the duty to silence guns is out of the purview of the African leaders such as in the case of Islamic-linked Jihad terrorists (Al-Qaeda, Al Shabaab, and Boko Haram), African leaders are supposed to work closely with the UN institutions to address the problem. Moreover, under Article 55, the UN Charter anticipates, "creation of conditions of stability and well-being which are necessary for peaceful and friendly relations among nations based on respect for the principle of equal rights and self-determination of peoples, the United Nations shall promote: a. higher standards of living, full employment, and conditions of economic and social progress and development".

Relying on the wording in the UN Charter and taking them as a must-have been done, however, does not of itself provide a solution to the problem. It is also important to interrogate the reasons why the UN and even the African continental frameworks have not utilised the framework established by the UN Charter to address the problem at hand. The UN and even the African continent are constituted by sovereign States each with a totally different background and at different levels of development with each other. Ideologically, there is no like-mindedness amongst these States. Each has a different historical background that conditions what actions it takes in a global framework. Crises attributable to poverty, may however, not be addressed effectively without concerted effort within the UN framework. Above all, poverty, unlike richness, cannot be shared, but rather it aggravates the already worse situation.

A number of issues associated with the migrant crisis in the Mediterranean Sea may, however, not necessarily have only a legal solution, but rather a combination of legal, social, cultural, economic, and even political solutions. The slogan African solutions to African problems which now is nearing the level of a continental anthem is aimed at addressing, in a holistic manner, all the continental problems, and at the same time. Alas, this is not possible. The UN through its various organs and agencies may provide guidance to the continent and individual States, but this may not be readily adhered to, especially by African political leaders, who are expected to be the driving force for development in the various spheres of the continent.

Some leaders, especially where the gun has remained "loud", adopt dictatorial, and exclusionary leadership styles which alienate some sections of their citizenry, contrary to the letter and spirit of the human rights principles enshrined in the UN Charter. Denial of basic human rights to nationals, which within the United and even continental and national constitutional frameworks is an abomination, characterizes such countries, hence creating fertile grounds for mass exodus of citizens to Europe through the Mediterranean Sea. Many of those who attempt to cross the deadly Sea die before reaching their anticipated destination. Most of their bodies are never recovered from the waters. By way of illustration, about 1900 migrants died in 2019 and 979 in 2020 in the Mediterranean Sea while attempting to cross Europe.[32] It is not possible to use a general broom to sweep all corners of the house at the same time, some dirt and even cobwebs will remain in some corners of the house. Based on this analogy, it becomes necessary that the African continent develops its own mechanisms which suit the continent and the African member States so that their implementation is easy.

On its part, the AU has realised that there is a continental problem of lack of commitment to include all Africans in the decision-making processes that concern the human rights of the continental citizens as proven by Prince Bright Majiga in Chapter 11. In support of this view, Godwin observes that "despite the efforts of this great organisation towards the success of all countries under its umbrella, we still live in an Africa where Xenophobia is on the rise".[33] Godwin notes that most of the problems on the African continent can be resolved if there was commitment by leaders to stamp corruption in their countries. Indeed, corruption leads to other vices such as exclusiveness from centres of political and economic power.

Lack of inclusiveness, especially in political decision-making processes creates dissent and is a fertile ground for rebellion within States, the end result being using the gun to suppress the advocates of an all-inclusive political and socioeconomic environment. In a bid to address the known problem, the AU put in place mechanisms, in line with the UN Charter, which if followed to the letter, no African would dream of leaving his or her country to go and perish in the Mediterranean Sea. In its Preamble, the AU Constitutive Act inter alia provides "inspired by the noble ideals which guided the founding fathers of our Continental Organization and generations of Pan-Africanists in their determination to promote unity, solidarity, cohesion and cooperation among the peoples of Africa and African States".

Deriving from this inspiration, the continent, in AU Constitute Act developed and agreed on an objective to guide its activities. The Objectives of the AU as set out in the Constitutive Act point to the fact that African leaders are committed to addressing the problems which compel Africans to flee their continent for better life. Unfortunately, little has been done to translate these

---

[32] Simona Varrella, Deaths of Migrants in the Mediterranean Sea 2014–2020, *Statista*, 27 November 2020, available at: https://www.statista.com/statistics/1082077/deaths-of-migrants-in-the-mediterranean-sea/, accessed on 25 February 2021.

[33] Gabla Godwin, *African Union; Its Mandate, Failure and What Needs to Be Done*, Ghana Web, 2017, accessed at: https://www.ghanaweb.com/GhanaHomePage/features/African-Union-its-mandate-failure-and-what-needs-to-be-done-541144, on 5 February 2020.

aspirations into action, implying that the problem of Africans fleeing the continent via the Mediterranean Sea is yet to be fully addressed.[34] These objectives are rosy and actually cover a wide range of issues, related to maintenance of peace and security on the continent, if adhered to. When adhered to, there would be nothing more needed to prevent mass movements of Africans from their home countries to Europe, through the riskiest routes on land and eventually the deadly waters of the Mediterranean Sea. The missing good on the African continent, however, is the unity of her peoples, who share a common history, but who are now divided after several years of colonisation that divided them using the ideology of imperialism.

The founders of the Pan-African Movement, many of who are long dead, had a vision, which, to their disappointment could not be realised at least in their lifetime. Persistent violent conflicts, which greatly contribute to the problem of ejecting Africans from their continent, are a common feature on the continent. The AU appears to be frustrated by the high turnover of violent conflicts on the continent, but the frustrations are not about to end because those who sponsor the conflicts and continue fuelling them are not necessarily Africans. Africans, are never given a chance, in the globalised set-up to provide solutions to their problems. Arms proliferation on the African continent, for example, is a lucrative business for the arms manufacturers and dealers from the developed world. In support of this view, Lado, writes, "the thriving of religious terrorist groups such as The Lord's Resistance Army, Boko Haram, Al-Qaeda in the Islamic Maghreb (AQIM), Movement for Unity and Jihad in West Africa (MUJAO), Al-Shabaab [...] which are largely responsible for the spread of religious violence in Sub-Saharan Africa, is boosted by the illicit international arms trade that the international community has failed to take seriously enough in its quest for global security and peace".[35]

Condemnation of violent conflicts and unconstitutional change of governments, respect for democratic principles, human rights, the rule of law, and good governance, are some of the artistic language styles used in the AU Constitutive Act.[36] Sadly, the language used by African leaders in the AU General Assembly does not bring out clear actionable points based on the seemingly authoritative language in the Constitutive Act. The language used is conspicuously in the form of lamentations. In regard to the Road Map for silencing the guns on the continent, the AU General Assembly, laments, "expressing Deep Concern over the persistence of violent conflicts and crisis situations in some parts of the African continent, as well as the scourges related to this persistence, which have resulted in losses of innocent lives, untold

[34] The African Union Constitutive Act, 2000, Article 3.

[35] Ludovic Lado, *Arms Trafficking and the Business of Rebellion in Sub-Saharan Africa, Africa Up Close*, The Wilson Centre, 2014, accessed at: https://africaupclose.wilsoncenter.org/arms-trafficking-and-the-business-of-rebellion-in-sub-saharan-africa/, on 5 February 2020.

[36] See Article 4 of the Constitute Act of the African Union, adopted at 11 July 2000—Lome, Togo.

suffering to the people, internally displaced persons and refugees, destruction of infrastructure and the environment, as well as derailment of national development programmes and projects among others".[37]

After expressing themselves thus, still African leaders do not provide a solution and pockets of instability such as those in the Great Lakes Region of the continent, the Northern part of the continent—Libya, Tunisia, and Egypt have continued to be the most fertile grounds for Africans leaving their continent to Europe via the Mediterranean Sea.

CONCLUSION

From a broad perspective, the migrant crisis in the Mediterranean Sea arises from a number of causes, but these can be narrowed down to one major cause of commission of mass atrocities largely by politicians, in order to be in position to provide a solution to the crisis. The crisis, which is sought to be curbed is multifaceted, but the most prominent component is death at sea. Migrants crossing the Mediterranean Sea to Europe come from different regions of the world, but this chapter narrowed down the scope to the African continent in order to give a detailed account of the root causes of the crisis and also what solutions might be available to address this crisis.

Using a human rights-based approach, the chapter, therefore, discussed and proposed ways to curb the migrant crisis in the Mediterranean Sea which has been pronounced by rising number of migrants from Africa to Europe. The discussion identified that armed conflicts, political persecution, poverty, gender discrimination, and unfavourable climatic conditions force many Africans out of their home countries to trek long distances on land, and eventually risk the journey of crossing the waters of the Mediterranean Sea to Europe. Historical ideological leanings of African States, including colonial and post-colonial ideologies, greatly contribute to the problem of exclusiveness in governance and decision-making processes concerning citizens in their home countries. This culminates in dissent, which is a fertile breeding ground for conflicts.

Unfortunately, African migrants to Europe are smuggled by gangs of human traffickers, sometimes on unseaworthy boats. Many of the migrants die at Sea due to drowning, disease, starvation, coldness, or other causes. Sadly, their intended European Host Nations are not always ready to welcome them into their countries. Some of the migrants die when they are in detention on the boats or after disembarking the boats, but still waiting for clearance to enter Europe.

The African Union is aware of the reasons as to why Africans leave their countries and risk crossing the Mediterranean Sea in the aforementioned circumstances. In order to address the root causes of the problem, which is

---

[37] AU Assembly, Decision on The African Union Master Roadmap of Practical Steps for Silencing the Guns in Africa by the Year 2020 Doc. Assembly/AU/6(XXVIII), p. 1.

largely armed conflicts, the AU adopted Agenda 2063 and Vision 2020 on silencing the guns. Unfortunately, the desire to silence guns on the African continent by 2020 has not been realised, much as African political leaders remain hopeful that at one point in time, this will be achieved.

From the aforegoing narrative, the chapter recommends that Africans should re-consider their political inclinations with a view to unpacking and repackaging them for a better and all-inclusive future governance system where each and everyone's views are accommodatable in the country. European countries, which are the ultimate recipients of African migrants should put in place better mechanisms, policies, and laws to ensure that migrants who successfully cross the Mediterranean Sea are received and handled in Europe just like any other asylum seekers. European countries, especially the former colonial masters of African countries should invest heavily in African countries and create conditions to address the problems that lead Africans to flee their countries. The United Nations should remain seized of its fundamental mandate of ensuring peace and security in the world so that no continent suffers such mass atrocities as the African continent. This will ensure that Africans will in the future, not be subjected to such inhuman conditions that force them to risk their lives by attempting to cross the deadly waters of the Mediterranean Sea in the aforementioned circumstances.

CHAPTER 32

Financing the African Peace and Security Agenda

Cephas Lumina

INTRODUCTION

In recognition of the inextricable link between peace, security, and sustainable development,[1] the African Union (AU) has adopted initiatives to address violent conflicts in Africa, notably the African Peace and Security Architecture (APSA) established in 2002 as the AU's principal framework for the promotion of peace, security and stability in Africa. Dan Kuwali has ably outlined the roles and functions of the APSA in Chapter 4. Suffice to say that at the core of the APSA is the Peace and Security Council (PSC). The PSC which

[1] The establishment of the OAU in 1963 was, to some extent, driven by the realisation by African Heads of State and Government that in order to attain "human progress, conditions and for peace and security must be established and maintained in Africa." *See* OAU Charter, 25 May 1963, preamble; and Wafula Okumu, Andrews Atta-Asamoah and Roba D Sharamo, *Silencing the Guns in Africa by 2020: Achievements, Opportunities and Challenges*, ISS Monograph No. 203 (Pretoria: Institute for Security Studies, 2020), p. 2. In establishing the AU to replace the OAU in 2000, the Assembly of Heads of State and Government were cognisant of the fact that "the scourge of conflicts in Africa constitutes a major impediment to the socio-economic development of the continent and of the need to promote peace, security and stability as a prerequisite for the implementation of our development and integration agenda." *See* Constitutive Act of the African Union, 11 July 2000, OAU Doc. CAB/LEG/23.15 (2001), preamble, para. 8. The nexus between security and

C. Lumina (✉)
University of Lusaka, Lusaka, Zambia

© The Author(s), under exclusive license to Springer Nature
Switzerland AG 2022
D. Kuwali (ed.), *The Palgrave Handbook of Sustainable Peace
and Security in Africa*, https://doi.org/10.1007/978-3-030-82020-6_32

561

was created to, among other things, "promote peace, security and stability in Africa, in order to guarantee the protection and preservation of life and property, the well-being of the African people and their environment, as well as the creation of conditions conducive to sustainable development".[2]

Significantly, in May 2013, the AU Heads of State and Government, acknowledging the adverse impact of conflicts on the continent's socioeconomic development, pledged "not to bequeath the burden of conflict to the next generation of Africans" and undertook "to end all wars in Africa by 2020".[3] This was translated into the AU's "Silencing the Guns by 2020" initiative.[4]

The effective implementation of this ambitious peace and security agenda requires adequate, predictable, and sustainable financing, but the AU's current context of chronic underfunding as a consequence of irregular contributions by AU member states and the AU's excessive dependency on external funding poses a huge challenge in this regard.[5] While the AU has made repeated efforts to enhance the annual contributions by member states and reduce dependency on external funding these have, at least until 2017, largely been unsuccessful.[6] This chapter discusses these challenges as well as the initiatives undertaken by the AU to secure sustainable and predictable financing for peace and security in Africa.

---

socio-economic development is also reflected in numerous decisions, declarations and policies adopted by the OAU/AU. *See, e.g.*, OAU, Declaration on the Establishment within the OAU of a Mechanism for Conflict Prevention, Management and Resolution (Cairo Declaration), adopted by the Twenty-Ninth Ordinary Session of the OAU Assembly of Heads of State and Government, 28–30 June 1993, Cairo, Egypt, para. 9; Protocol Relating to the Establishment of the Peace and Security Council of the African Union (PSC Protocol), 9 July 2002, preamble, para. 10 and principle 4(d); African Union, 50th Anniversary Solemn Declaration, adopted by the Twenty-first Ordinary Session of the Assembly of Heads of State and Government, 26 May 2013, Addis Ababa, Ethiopia; African Union Commission, *Agenda 2063: First Ten-Year Implementation Plan 2014–2023*, September 2015, https://au.int/sites/default/files/documents/33126-doc-ten_year_implementation_book.pdf (accessed on 6 February 2021); and African Union Commission, *Agenda 2063: The Africa We Want*, Popular Version, May 2016, https://au.int/sites/default/files/documents/33126-doc-03_popular_version.pdf (accessed on 6 February 2021).

[2] PSC Protocol, art. 3(a).

[3] African Union, 50th Anniversary Solemn Declaration, part E.

[4] This initiative, which is one of the 14 flagship projects of Agenda 2063, acknowledges that conflict and violence are major threats to development. *See* https://au.int/en/agenda 2063/flagship-projects (accessed on 6 February 2021).

[5] *See* African Union Peace Fund, *Securing Predictable and Sustainable Financing for Peace in Africa*, August 2016, para. 5, https://au.int/sites/default/files/documents/35299-doc-au_peace_fund_background_2016.pdf (accessed on 6 February 2021).

[6] Kesa Pharatlhatlhe and Jan Vanheukelom, *Financing the African Union: On Mindsets and Money*, ECDPM Discussion Paper No. 240, February 2019, https://ecdpm.org/pub lications/financing-the-african-union-on-mindsets-and-money/ (accessed on 6 February 2021).

The AU Financing Context

The AU has two main sources of funding for its operational costs, programmes, and peace support operations.[7] These are member states and development partners. Both sources are problematic, and each has contributed to the AU's chronic underfunding.[8]

Assessed Contributions of Member States

Assessed contributions from its 55 member states constitute the first source of AU funding. These contributions are calculated based on triennial assessments to be paid at the start of each budget year (1 January–31 December). The scale of assessment, which is reviewed every three years, is based on a three-tier system (related to member states' gross domestic product) and the principles of fairness and solidarity.[9] In 2019, the AU Assembly decided that no member state shall pay less than $350,000 or more than $35,000,000 as a contribution to the regular budget and Peace Fund combined.[10]

It is notable, however, that member states often fail to remit their contributions on time or at all. Until 2015, the AU collected on average 67% of assessed contributions, with approximately 30 member states—more than half the AU membership—defaulting either partially or completely annually.[11] The shortfall in member states' contributions creates a significant funding gap between planned budget and actual funding, which undermines the AU's ability to effectively implement its entire agenda, including peace and security.

---

[7] The operations budget mainly finances the costs of running the organisation, its organs, specialised technical agencies, representational offices and agencies around the world. Operational costs amount to an estimated $110 million on average annually over the last few years and are financed exclusively by AU member states. The programme budget covers the execution of programmes approved by the Assembly.

[8] African Union Peace Fund, *Securing Predictable and Sustainable Financing*.

[9] Assembly/AU/Dec.734 (XXXII), Decision on the Scale of Assessment for the Regular Budget and the Peace Fund, adopted by the Thirty-Second Ordinary Session of the Assembly of the African Union, 10–11 February 2019, with reservations by Seychelles (SEY/AU/3/1 Note No. 16/2019, dated 26 March 2019) and Egypt (Note Verbale dated 27 March 2019). For the period 2020–2022, the scale is: Tier 1 (all countries with a GDP of more than 4%)—assessed at 45.151% of the Union's assessed budget; Tier 2 (all countries with a GDP above 1% but less than 4%)—assessed at 32.749% of the AU's assessed budget; and Tier 3 (all countries with a GDP of 1% or less)—assessed at 22.100% of the AU's assessed budget.

[10] Assembly/AU/Dec.734 (XXXII), Decision on the Scale of Assessment for the Regular Budget and the Peace Fund, adopted by the Thirty-Second Ordinary Session of the Assembly of the African Union, 10–11 February 2019, para. 8.

[11] African Union, *Background Paper on Implementing the Kigali Decision on Financing the Union*, September 2016, p. 6, https://au.int/sites/default/files/pages/31955-file-background_paper_on_implementing_the_kigali_decision_on_financing_the_union.pdf (accessed on 23 February 2021).

The management of the AU Commission has attributed the problem of irregular contributions by member states "to the emergent challenges that most member states are experiencing for example insecurity including food insecurity due to prolonged drought, and emergent conflicts which affect the distribution of national resources".[12] It can also be argued that the new sovereign debt crisis facing several AU member states is undermining their capacity to fulfil their financial commitments to the organisation. In 2020, 22 African states were in debt crisis and with government external debt service payments (including principal and interest) ranging from 7.5 to 59.5% of government revenue, many had little fiscal space.[13] Moreover, the economic turmoil caused by the COVID-19 pandemic is pushing many of these countries deeper into crisis, with governments unable to pay their debt or afford basic services such as healthcare and education.[14] The AU has underscored the negative impact of this situation on its member states' contributions as follows:

> The COVID-19 has had devastating effects on African economies resulting in disruption of production and a sharp reduction in demand. The spillovers from a sharp deterioration in global growth and tighter financial conditions as well as severe decline in commodity prices have largely affected the revenue generation capacity of most Member States, and hence their contributions to the AU.[15]

In an attempt to address the perennial problem of member states' non-payment of their assessed contributions, the AU Assembly adopted a new three-tier sanctions regime in November 2018.[16] The sanctions—which are

[12] African Union Commission, *Report of the Board of External Auditors on the Consolidated Financial Statements of the African Union for the Year Ended 31 December 2017*, June 2018, p. 4, https://au.int/sites/default/files/documents/36042-doc-au_audit_rep ort_consolidated_fs_for_the_year_ended_31st_dec._2017.pdf (accessed on 23 February 2021).

[13] *See* https://data.jubileedebt.org.uk (accessed on 24 February 2021).

[14] *See* Jubilee Debt Campaign, *Coronavirus Debt, Summer 2020*, https://jubile edebt.org.uk/wp-content/uploads/2021/01/Drop-it-Summer-2020_WEBz.pdf (accessed on 24 February 2021).

[15] African Union, Bureau of the Chairperson, *Taking Stock, Charting the Future: African Union Commission End of Term Report 2017–2021* (African Union, 2021), p. 39, https://au.int/en/documents/20210203/african-union-commission-end-term-rep ort-2017-2021 (accessed on 22 February 2021).

[16] Ext/Assembly/AU/Dec.3 (XI), Decision on the New African Union Sanctions Regime for the Non-Payment of Contributions, adopted by the Eleventh Extraordinary Session of the Assembly of the African Union, 17–18 November 2018.

in three categories: cautionary,[17] intermediate,[18] and comprehensive[19]—are linked to the length of time a member state fails to pay its assessed contributions, partially or in full: the longer the period, the more rights the member state loses.[20] The sanctions regime has also provided relief to member states that default due to circumstances beyond their control which render them temporarily unable to pay their assessed contributions.

As of October 2020, a third of AU member states were under sanctions for non-payment of their assessed contributions.[21] Nonetheless, the sanctions regime is generally considered to be weak. This is primarily because the AU does not publicise information on member state payments or defaults—a mechanism that could serve to put defaulting states under pressure to settle their arrears. It has been suggested that the absence of such information is most likely due to the fact that several member states perceive such country-specific listing as a "name and shame" practice that offends "the pan-African ethos of solidarity and non-interference".[22]

Funding from Development Partners

The AU is predominantly reliant on development partners to fund its budget (including peace support operations). Between 2017 and 2020, development partners funded the AU budget by an average of 62% annually.[23] Development partners fund the overwhelming portion of the peace support operations budget which is itself the largest component of the organisation's budget. For

---

[17] Cautionary sanctions, which deprive member states of rights to speak at AU meetings, apply to member states who fail to pay at least 50% of their assessed contributions after the second quarter (six months) of each financial year in which the contribution is due.

[18] Intermediate sanctions apply to members who are in arrears for one year. Such member states are subject to cautionary sanctions plus deprivation of voting rights, eligibility for office, the right to host summits and AU institutions and the right to have their nationals participate in electoral and human rights observation missions and for a year. In addition, such states may not be invited to AU meetings or have their nationals recruited into AU positions during the applicable period.

[19] Comprehensive sanctions apply where a member state defaults on its payments for two years. Such states are liable to all the cautionary and intermediate sanctions, as well as suspension of their right to participate in meetings of the AU for two years.

[20] Ext/Assembly/AU/Dec.3 (XI), Decision on the New African Union Sanctions Regime, para. 3.

[21] Frank Mattheis and Ueli Staeger, "How Member States and Partners Impede the African Union's Quest for Financial Autonomy," *The Conversation*, 22 December 2020, https://theconversation.com/how-member-states-and-partners-impede-the-africa-unions-quest-for-financial-autonomy-15111 (accessed on 18 February 2021).

[22] Pharatlhatlhe and Vanheukelom, *Financing the African Union*, p. 4.

[23] African Union, *Taking Stock*, p. 39. *See also* African Union, *2020 Budget Framework Paper for the African Union (Draft)*, September 2018, pp. 6 and 8, https://archives.au.int/bitstream/handle/123456789/6585/EX%20CL%201104%20%28XXXIV%29%20i%20BFW%20_E.pdf?sequence=1&isAllowed=y (accessed on 23 February 2021).

example, the total approved budget for 2019 was \$681.4 million of which \$158.5 million was the operating budget, \$249.7 the programme budget and \$273.3 the peace support operations budget. Of the peace operations budget, 96% (that is, \$262 million) was to be solicited from international partners and the rest (that is, \$11.3 million)—a mere 4% of the budget—was to come from member states' assessed contributions.[24] The total approved budget for 2020 was \$647.3 million of which \$157.2 million was the operating budget, \$216.9 the programme budget and \$273.1 million the peace support operations. With regards to the peace support operations budget, 38% was to come from member states' assessed contributions and 61% solicited from development partners.[25]

While this external financing helps address some of the funding gaps, it is beset with challenges that affect the timing, predictability, and volume of funding from development partners. These challenges relate to, inter alia, development partner procedures and practices related to the array of conditionalities to which funding is tied.[26] Significantly, the multiplicity of external funding channels has occasioned fragmentation and high transaction costs associated with the numerous reporting requirements.[27] There is also a concern as to whether the AU budget truly reflects the organisation's priorities or it masked development partners' preferences.[28]

Clearly, the AU "is currently not financed in a predictable, sustainable, equitable or accountable manner".[29] In particular, the failure of a significant number of member states to fulfil their financial commitments and the AU's excessive dependency on external funding have both contributed to its precarious financial situation.[30] Indeed, "the combination of fragmented, unpredictable, and at times erratic sources of funding" continues to have an adverse effect on the AU's ability to effectively implement its programmes,

[24] African Union, *2020 Budget Framework Paper*, p. 6. *See also* Assembly/AU/Dec.699 (XXXI), Decision on the 2019 African Union Budget and the 2018 Supplementary Budget, adopted by the Thirty-First Ordinary Session of the Assembly of the African Union, 1–2 July 2018.

[25] *See* https://au.int/en/articles/african-union-sustainable-funding-strategy-gains-mom entum (accessed on 23 February 2021).

[26] *See* Pharatlhatlhe and Vanheukelom, *Financing the African Union. See also* Philomena Apiko and Luckystar Miyandazi, *Self-Financing the African Union: One Levy, Multiple Reforms*, ECDPM Discussion Paper No. 258, September 2019, p. 3, https://ecdpm.org/wp-content/uploads/Self-Financing-African-Union-Levy-Reforms-ECDPM-Discussion-Paper-258.pdf (accessed on 6 February 2021); Pharatlhatlhe and Jan Vanheukelom, *Financing the African Union.*

[27] African Union Peace Fund, *Securing Predictable and Sustainable Financing*, p. 2.

[28] Pharatlhatlhe and Vanheukelom, *Financing the African Union*, citing Jan Vanheukelom, *The Political Economy of Regional Integration in Africa: The African Union Report*, ECDPM, https://ecdpm.org/publications/political-economy-regional-int egration-african-union/ (accessed on 6 February 2021).

[29] *See* https://au.int/en/aureforms/financing (accessed on 6 February 2021).

[30] *See* https://au.int/en/aureforms/financing (accessed on 6 February 2021).

including the peace and security agenda.[31] In 2016, for example, the AU failed to pay allowances to AMISOM troops for at least six months.[32] This was attributable to the complex set of arrangements and mechanisms for funding AMISOM.[33]

THE FINANCING MECHANISMS

The financing measures for the African Peace and Security Architecture is outlined below.

The AU Peace Fund

The Peace Fund was established in June 1993 as the main financing instrument for peace and security activities of the Organisation of African Unity (OAU).[34] After the establishment of the AU, the Fund became one of the five components of the APSA.[35] The Fund, which is overseen by a Board of Trustees comprising five African members representing the five AU regions and two

---

[31] See Pharatlhatlhe and Vanheukelom, *Financing the African Union.*

[32] See Catherine Byaruhanga, "African Union Troops in Somalia Not Paid for Six Months," BBC Africa, 27 June 2016, https://www.bbc.com/news/world-africa.366 24520 (accessed on 18 February 2021). *See also* Mattheis and Staeger, "How Member States and Partners Impede the African Union's Quest for Financial Autonomy," *The Conversation*, 22 December 2020, https://theconversation.com/how-member-states-and-partners-impede-the-africa-unions-quest-for-financial-autonomy-15111 (accessed on 18 February 2021).

[33] Paul D Williams, "Paying for AMISOM: Are Politics and Bureaucracy Undermining the AU's Largest Peace Operation?" 11 January 2017, https://theglobalobservatory.org/2017/01/amisom-african-union-peacekeeping-financing/ (accessed on 18 February 2021). There are several sources of funding for AMISOM, including AU member states, the AU Peace Fund, the UN Trust Fund for AMISOM, the UN Trust Fund for Somali Transitional Security Institutions, UN assessed peacekeeping contributions and AU partners, such as the EU. Under the system of financing the AU's peace operations set out in the PSC Protocol, the costs of any AU peace support operation would be borne by the AU member states that contributed troops and police during the first three months. The AU would then reimburse these countries within a maximum period of six months and then finance the operation. Nevertheless, this system has never worked in practice due to the failure of AU member states to provide the required funds. In 2016, the EU, which pays AMISOM troop allowances, took several decisions regarding payment of these allowances, including placing a cap on the applicable amounts and adopting measures to mitigate its financial risks in the event of non-compliance by the AU with the EU's financial standards. These decisions contributed to delays in the payment of allowances for AMISOM peacekeepers.

[34] The OAU Peace Fund, as it was then known, was established as a key component of the OAU Mechanism for Conflict Prevention, Management and Resolution which was mandated to prevent, manage and resolve conflicts in Africa. *See* Cairo Declaration, paras. 13, 15 and 23.

[35] See PSC Protocol, art. 21. The other components of APSA are the Peace and Security Council (the main pillar), the Panel of the Wise, the Continental Early Warning System and the African Standby Force.

international partners (the EU and the UN),[36] was designed to finance activities in three thematic areas: mediation and preventive diplomacy; institutional capacity; and peace support operations.

The Fund is to be replenished through financial appropriations from the regular AU budget, including voluntary contributions from member states and arrears of assessed contributions.[37] Moreover, the Fund may accept contributions from other sources within Africa, including the private sector, civil society, and individuals, and may also be replenished through appropriate fundraising activities.

In August 2009, AU member states agreed to increase contributions to the Peace Fund from 6 to 12% of the AU regular budget. In January 2010, it was agreed that the increase would be implemented over a period of three years, beginning in 2011. In July 2016, the AU Assembly decided to endow the Peace Fund with $400 million in member state contributions to be drawn from the 0.2% levy that had been instituted to finance the overall AU budget.

According to the AU, the percentage contributions from the regular budget have been very low, reaching only 7% in 2016. This situation is attributable to the high levels of arrears and late payment of member states assessed contributions. While some member states have made additional voluntary contributions to the Fund, these are irregular and unpredictable. Consequently, the Fund remains excessively dependent on external partners.

The Fund was launched in November 2018 and was expected to be fully operational in 2020 but this deadline has been extended to 2023 because the Fund has received fewer contributions from member states than projected.[38]

Article 21(4) of the Protocol Relating to the Establishment of the Peace and Security Council also envisaged the creation of a replenishable Revolving Trust Fund as part of the Peace Fund to provide a standing reserve for specific projects in the event of emergencies and unforeseen priorities. The level of funding required for the trust fund was to be determined by the relevant AU policy organs upon recommendation of the Peace and Security Council. It is, however, unclear whether this fund has been created.[39]

---

[36] The other elements of the governance and management structure are: an Independent Evaluation Panel, which will be established to regularly review the effectiveness and impact of the Fund; an Executive Management Committee, will provide strategic management oversight of the Fund; a Fund Manager, who will manage the finances; and a Peace Fund Secretariat that will manage the day to day operations of the Fund.

[37] PSC Protocol, art. 21(2).

[38] *See* Giulia Paravicini, "African Union Delays Plans to Start Using Fund for Security Operations," 11 February 2020, https://www.reuters.com/article/us-africanunion-sum mit/african-union-delays-plan-to-start-using-fund-for-security-operations-idUSKBN20 50D9 (accessed on 1 January 2021).

[39] According to a 2016 AU report, the revolving trust fund "has never been established" but it was "expected that once the Peace Fund (was) optimally operational, this revolving facility (would) become fully functional." *See* African Peace Fund, *Securing Predictable and Sustainable Financing*, p. 6.

As stated earlier, peace support operations constitute the largest part of the AU budget. However, AU member states' contributions to the Peace Fund remain well below the levels expected, leaving the AU heavily dependent on external funding. Moreover, the array of external partners has made funding complicated and unpredictable.[40]

The EU Funding Mechanisms

Since 2004, the European Union (EU) has contributed to AU conflict prevention efforts primarily through its African Peace Facility (APF), a fund established by an ACP-EU Council of Ministers' decision in December 2003 in response to a request by the AU for predictable funds to support peace and security in Africa.[41] The APF, which has its legal basis in the Cotonou Agreement,[42] focuses on supporting the AU and African sub-regional organisations in their efforts to prevent and resolve conflicts.

As of the end of 2019, the EU had provided more than €2.7 billion in financial support to the AU and other African institutions in three key areas: (a) African-led peace support operations[43]; (b) capacity building, which contributes to the operationalisation of the APSA through enhancing the institutional capacities of the AU Commission and African Regional Economic Communities (RECs)/Regional Mechanisms (RMs); and (c) the Early Response Mechanism (ERM), which was established in 2009 and provides funding for African-led rapid reaction conflict prevention activities.[44]

---

[40] *See also* Corinna Jentzsch, "Opportunities and Challenges to Financing African Union Peace Operations," *African Conflict and Peacebuilding Review* (2014) 4(2), p. 89.

[41] Decision No. 3/2003 of the ACP-EU Council of Ministers of 11 December 2003 on the use of resources from the long-term development envelope of the ninth EDF for the creation of a Peace Facility for Africa. The EU also provides funding support for peace and security in Africa from the general budget using instruments such as the Pan-African Programme; the Instrument contributing to Peace and Stability; Common Security and Defence Policy missions; and the "EU Emergency Trust Fund for Africa". *See* European Court of Auditors, *The African Peace and Security Architecture: Need to Refocus EU Support*, Special Report No. 20 (European Union, 2018), p. 9, fn. 20.

[42] The Partnership agreement between the members of the African, Caribbean and Pacific Group of States of the one part, and the European Community and its Member States, of the other part, 23 June 2000 ("the Cotonou Agreement"), art. 11. The Cotonou Agreement is the overarching framework for EU relations with African, Caribbean and Pacific (ACP) countries.

[43] As of the end of 2019, there were seven peace support operations underway in Somalia, the Sahel, the Lake Chad Basin, South Sudan, Guinea Bissau, The Gambia and Burundi. *See* European Union, *African Peace Facility Annual Report 2019*, p. 3, https://africa-eu-partnership.org/sites/default/files/documents/apf_annual_report_2019_en.pdf (accessed on 18 February 2021).

[44] In 2019, the ERM played a role in preventing electoral violence in Sierra Leone, make possible national dialogue in Lesotho, supported the implementation of the peace agreement in the Central African Republic, and financed AU research on conflict prevention in the Sahel. *See* European Union, *African Peace Facility Report 2019*, p. 3.

Ninety-three per cent of the APF (that is, €2.681 billion) has been allocated to peace support operations. Since 2004, the APF has provided financial support to 16 African-led peace support operations with diverse mandates, from preventing conflict in the Gambia to ceasefire monitoring in South Sudan and fighting terrorism in the Sahel and the Lake Chad Basin.[45] During the period 2007–2019, more than €1.94 billion in APF funding was channelled through the AU to support just one operation, the African Union Mission in Somalia (AMISOM). In 2019, the United Kingdom made a voluntary contribution of €7.9 million, leading to an increase in the EU's annual contribution to AMISOM to €207.9 million.[46] The bulk of these funds covered the cost of salaries and allowances for the troops and other personnel involved in the mission.[47]

The capacity building component of the APF received €171.8 million (6%) between 2004 and 2018. Under this component, several support programmes have been implemented to give the AU and the RECs/RMs the necessary instruments to address security challenges through "effective and efficient institutions." The most important of these is the APSA Support Programmes which seek to enhance the capacity of and efficiency of the AU, RECs, and RMs to prevent and/or respond to crises and conflicts in Africa through implementing and operationalising the APSA.

Between its creation in 2009 and 2020, the ERM received approximately €28 million (1%) from the APF. Despite this relatively small allocation, the ERM has supported 40 interventions across the continent and is generally considered as the most successful APF-funded programme.[48] It provides immediately available funds for initiatives aimed at preventing, managing, and resolving violent conflicts, and to use unforeseen opportunities for peacebuilding.[49] Consistent with its character, the ERM funds activities of a temporary nature. It should be noted that the maximum duration of mediation, political negotiation, and preventive diplomacy initiatives is 24 months, while all other initiatives addressing urgent and unforeseen needs in crisis situations can be approved for a maximum of 12 months.

While the APF has made a notable contribution to peace and security in Africa, it is not a sustainable source of financing for several reasons. First, it was designed as a temporary arrangement financed from the European Development Fund (EDF), the main instrument through which the EU finances

---

[45] *See* International Crisis Group, *How to Spend It: New EU Funding for African Peace and Security*, Africa Report No. 297, 14 January 2021, p. 3, https://www.crisisgroup.org/africa/african-union-regional-bodies/297-how-spend-it-new-eu-funding-african-peace-and-security (accessed on 18 February 2021); and European Union, *African Peace Facility Report 2019*, p. 10.

[46] *See* European Union, *African Peace Facility Report 2019*, p. 13.

[47] *See* European Union, *African Peace Facility Report 2019*, p. 13.

[48] International Crisis Group, *How to Spend It*, p. 4.

[49] *See* European Union, *African Peace Facility Report 2019*, p. 22.

most of its development programmes for ACP partner states.[50] Second, it was established within the overall framework of the Cotonou Agreement. Given that this agreement has expired and negotiations on a new agreement ended only on 3 December 2020,[51] the whole range of EU relations with ACP states and related financing instruments is under review. Third, it has been contended that, in its current form, the APF "is unlikely to be able to meet demand in the next few years as pressure for expanding the AU mission in Somalia grows and new missions become necessary".[52]

The APF has since been subsumed under two new EU global funding mechanisms established in March and June 2021, respectively: the European Peace Facility (EPF) and the Neighbourhood, Development and International Cooperation Instrument (NDICI)—'Global Europe,'[53] enabling the EU to provide military support anywhere in the world. The peace support operations element of the APF has been absorbed into the EPF, which has a budget of €5 billion for the period 2021 to 2027. Support for institutional capacity building and the ERM has been incorporated into the NDICI, through which all EU international development assistance will be channelled.

The new EU strategy is evidently driven by two key factors. First, in 2018, a European Court of Arbitrators evaluation found that EU support for the development of the APSA "has had a poor effect and needed refocusing".[54] As a consequence of the shortfall in contributions by AU member states to the AU budget and the Peace Fund, the APSA had become too dependent on external funding and the EU's financial contributions had, for the most

---

[50] This is for legal reasons: the EU Treaties do not allow Community funds to finance military operations. The EDF is not part of the EU budget but is funded directly by EU member states and has its financial rules. *See* Mark Furness, *Sustaining EU Financing for Security and Development: The Difficult Case of the African Peace Security*, German Development Institute Briefing Paper 7/2011, p. 1, https://www.die-gdi.de/en/briefing-paper/article/sustaining-eu-financing-for-security-and-development-the-difficult-case-of-the-african-peace-facility/ (accessed on 6 February 2021).

[51] *See* https://ec.europa.eu/international-partnerships/news/post-cotonou-negotiators-reach-political-deal-new-euafrica-caribbean-pacific-partnership_en (accessed on 5 November 2021).

[52] *See* Furness, *Sustaining EU Financing for Security and Development*, p. 1.

[53] The APF has since been subsumed under two new EU global funding mechanisms established in March and June 2021, respectively: the European Peace Facility (EPF) and the Neighbourhood, Development and International Cooperation Instrument (NDICI) – 'Global Europe,' enabling the EU to provide military support anywhere in the world. The peace support operations element of the APF has been absorbed into the EPF, which has a budget of €5 billion for the period 2021 to 2027. Support for institutional capacity building and the ERM has been incorporated into the NDICI, through which all EU international development assistance will be channelled.

[54] European Court of Auditors, *The African Peace and Security Architecture: Need to Refocus EU Support*, Special Report No. 20/2018, p. 33, https://www.eca.europa.eu/Lists/ECADocuments/SR18_20/SR_APSA_EN.pdf (accessed on 6 February 2021).

part, been used for the AU's basic operational costs—mainly staff-related expenses—rather than for capacity building as intended.

Second, the new funding strategy seeks to "enhance the EU's ability to safeguard European security interests and prevent conflict, build peace and strengthen security around the world".[55] Many EU policymakers consider many of Africa's security challenges as a threat to European stability. The new funding strategy will allow the EU to bypass the AU and directly finance African-led peace support operations even when they are not operating under an AU Peace and Security Council mandate, and to provide bilateral financial support for training and equipment to African militaries.[56] Neither option was available to the EU under the APF since the EU Treaty prohibits the use of the Union's budget to finance expenditure with military and defence implications.[57] But, as an "off-budget" mechanism financed through contributions by EU member states and not subject to EU rules, the EPF will allow the EU to contribute to the funding of EU military operations, to fund partners' military peace support operations, and to support actions with military or defence implications in furtherance of the EU's Common Foreign Security and Policy.[58] The flexibility of the new funding strategy thus allows the EU to better pursue its own strategic interests in Africa and elsewhere in the world.

Nevertheless, numerous concerns have been raised about the new EU funding strategy. In November 2020, for example, 40 civil society organisations robustly opposed plans to finance military training and lethal weapons under the EPF, warning that such support could fuel conflicts and human rights abuses, as well as increase the risk of harm to civilians.[59] It has been argued, persuasively, that the financing of military training and lethal equipment for national militaries can be particularly risky in states where corruption and mismanagement are pervasive in the security forces, rendering it a challenge "to ensure that equipment is used for the intended purpose and does

---

[55] *See* European Parliament, "New Boost for Jobs, Growth and Investment," *Legislative Train 01.2021*, https://www.europarl.europa.eu/legislative-train/theme-new-boost-for-jobs-growth-and-investment/file-mff-european-peace-facility (accessed on 22 February 2021). *See also* Council of the European Union, *Proposal of the High Representative of the Union for Foreign Affairs and Security Policy, with the Support of the Commission, to the Council of 13/06/2018 for a Council Decision Establishing a European Peace Facility*, HR (2018) 94, https://data.consilium.europa.eu/doc/document/ST-9736-2018-INIT/en/pdf (accessed on 5 February 2021).

[56] International Crisis Group, *How to Spend It*, pp. 19–21.

[57] Consolidated Version of the Treaty on European Union, 7 February 1992, *Official Journal of the European Communities*, C 326/15, 26 October 2012, art. 41(2).

[58] Council of the European Union, *Proposal of the High Representative of the Union for Foreign Affairs and Security Policy*, p. 2.

[59] *See* "European 'Peace' Facility: Causing Harm or Bringing Peace?" Joint Civil Society Statement, November 2020, https://www.nhc.nl/assets/uploads/2020/11/Joint-CSO-Statement-on-the-European-Peace-Facility.pdf (accessed on 22 February 2021).

not fall into the wrong hands".[60] And, as the August 2020 military coup in Mali demonstrates, militaries themselves can become a threat to stability.[61] In response, EU member states introduced safeguards to ensure adherence to international standards, notably through risk assessments and traceability measures.[62] In addition, member states that are unwilling to fund lethal military equipment may opt-out.[63] It is, notable however, that some have cast doubt on the EU's ability to conduct risk assessments appropriately.[64]

There is also concern that the new funding strategy could potentially contribute to unpredictability of funding for the AU's peace and security priorities. Given that the EPF, unlike the APF, is a global financing instrument, there is a possibility that African priorities may be "downscaled vis-à-vis possible demands originating from other conflict-affected regions in the world".[65] As the International Crisis Group has aptly observed:

> On one hand, the EPF will have a budget of €5 billion for seven years. This amount is roughly three times as much as the APF's total commitments for the previous seven-year budget cycle (about €1.6 billion for 2014-2020, which include activities such as institutional capacity building that the EPF will not cover). On the other hand, while the EPF's pot of money might appear bigger, the range of potential beneficiaries is also wider, since the EPF will cover common costs of the EU's own military operations (such as the EU training missions in Mali and Somalia), security initiatives outside Africa, and potential contributions to ad hoc coalitions and national militaries in Africa, none of which the APF included. The future of EU funding for the APF's non-military components (parts of the Early Response Mechanism and support to AU institutions), which will be integrated into the EU's new development fund, is equally uncertain after the last generation of APF-funded programs end in 2024.[66]

[60] International Crisis Group, *How to Spend It*, p. ii. *See also* Peter Fabricius, "EU Peace and Security Funds Can Now Bypass the African Union," *ISS Today*, 5 February 2021, https://issafrica.org/iss-today/eu-peace-and-security-funds-can-now-bypass-the-afr>ican-union#:~:text=The%20APF%20will%20now%20give,regional%20and%20national%20military%20initiatives (accessed on 8 February 2021).

[61] International Crisis Group, *How to Spend It*, p. ii.

[62] Pierre Marcos and Donatienne Ruy, "A European Peace Facility to Bolster European Foreign Policy?" 2 February 2021, Centre for Strategic and International Studies, https://www.csis.org/analysis/european-peace-facility-bolster-european-foreign-policy (accessed on 21 February 2021).

[63] Marcos and Ruy, "A European Peace Facility". *See also* International Crisis Group, *How to Spend It*, p. 9.

[64] International Crisis Group, *How to Spend It*, p. 17, fn. 83.

[65] Volker Hauck, *The Latest on the European Peace Facility and What's in It for the African Union*, ECDPM Briefing Note No. 120, September 2020, p. 6, https://ecdpm.org/wp-content/uploads/Latest-European-Peace-Facility-What-Afr>ican-Union-Briefing-Note-120-ECDPM-September-2020.pdf (accessed on 6 February 2021).

[66] International Crisis Group, *How to Spend It*, p. 11.

A further concern is that the EPF could weaken AU's oversight of continental peace and security funding decisions. The AU Commission has expressed concern that with the EU providing funding directly to the RECs, the Commission's coordination role will be significantly diminished.[67] Under the APF, the AU wielded considerable power to direct where and how EU funding for peace and security would be spent. According to the International Crisis Group, the APF "has helped the EU streamline its support and avoid unco-ordinated requests from myriad African institutions" and helped reinforce the AU's central role in continental peace and security.[68]

Several proposals to address some of the foregoing concerns have been made, including that the EU should: (a) refrain from funding lethal equip-ment for militaries in fragile African states; (b) maintain strong support for AU peace and security efforts; (c) preserve an oversight role for the AU; and (d) establish robust monitoring mechanisms to prevent EU funded training and equipment from being used by abusive and unaccountable security and military actors.[69]

Other Sources of Funding

Besides the EU, a broad range of actors provide funding support for peace and security in Africa. These include international organisations, such as the United Nations (UN) and the North Atlantic Treaty Organisation (NATO), and individual countries such as the United States, China, Turkey, and EU member states.[70] It should be noted, however, that an AU proposal for the use of UN assessed contributions as a means of providing predictable and sustainable funding for AU peace support operations based on a 25:75 AU-UN split remains unresolved largely because of misgivings about the AU's ability to pay its share.[71]

While the Peace Fund is able to accept contributions from sources within Africa, including the private sector, civil society, and individuals, and also to raise funds through "appropriate fundraising activities", it is unclear whether or to what extent it has done so to date.

[67] Fabricius, "EU Peace and Security Funds Can Now Bypass the African Union."

[68] International Crisis Group, *How to Spend It*, p. 11.

[69] International Crisis Group, *How to Spend It*, pp. 19–21.

[70] European Union, *African Peace Facility Report 2019*, p. 7.

[71] International Crisis Group, *The Price of Peace: Securing UN Financing for AU Peace Operations*, Africa Report No. 286, 31 January 2020, p. I, https://www.crisisgroup.org/africa/286-price-peace-securing-un-financing-au-peace-operations (accessed on 6 February 2021).

SECURING RELIABLE FINANCING: THE KIGALI FINANCING DECISION

To ensure the availability of reliable and predictable funding, reduce dependency on external funding, and to enhance ownership of its peace and security activities, the AU has launched several initiatives to increase member states' assessed contributions and to explore alternative ways to finance the organisation, including its peace support operations.[72]

In June 2015, the AU Assembly adopted a decision on assessed contributions of member states, based on "the principle of solidarity, equitable payment and capacity to pay", which targeted funding the AU at 100% of the operational budget; 75% of the programme budget; and 25% of the peace support operations budget.[73] In September, the meeting of the Peace and Security Council at the level of Heads of State and Government requested the Chairperson of the AU Commission to appoint a High Representative for the Peace Fund. Furthermore, in December, the AU adopted the APSA Roadmap 2016–2020, whose objectives are, inter alia, "to ensure that the financial ownership of APSA has increased and dependency on donors and international partners decreased substantially".[74]

In January 2016, the former President of the African Development Bank, Donald Kaberuka, was appointed High Representative for the Peace Fund with a mandate that included mobilising additional resources for AU peace and security-related activities.

In July 2016, the AU Assembly decided, on the basis of the progress report submitted by Kaberuka on the subject,[75] to institute and implement a 0.2% levy on all eligible imports into the continent to finance the AU operational, programme, and peace support operations budgets, beginning in 2017.[76] It

---

[72] Philomena Apiko and Faten Aggad, *Can the 0.2% Levy Fund Peace and Security in Africa?* ECDPM Briefing Note No. 103, April 2018, p. 4, https://ecdpm.org/wp-content/uploads/BN-103-Financing-the-African-Union.pdf (accessed on 5 February 2021).

[73] Assembly/AU/Dec. 578 (XXV), Decision on the Scale of Assessment and Alternative Sources of Financing the African Union, adopted by the Twenty-Fifth Ordinary Session of the Assembly of the African Union, 14–15 June 2015, para. 2.

[74] African Union Commission, *APSA Roadmap 2016–2020*, December 2015, p. 59, https://www.peaceau.org/uploads/2015-en-apsa-roadmap-final.pdf (accessed on 20 February 2021).

[75] Kaberuka's progress report proposed a 0.2% levy on all eligible African imports to fund the AU's operating, programme and peace and security budgets. *See* Assembly/AU/Dec.605 (XXVII), Decision on the Outcome of the Retreat of the Assembly of the African Union, para. 5(a)(ii).

[76] Assembly/AU/Dec.605 (XXVII), Decision on the Outcome of the Retreat of the Assembly of the African Union, para. 5(a)(i). The purpose of the decision is to: provide reliable and predictable funding for continental peace and security through the Peace Fund; provide an equitable and predictable source of financing for the AU; reduce dependency on partner funds for implementation of continent development and integration programmes; and relieve the pressure on national treasuries with respect to meeting national obligations for payment of assessed contributions of the AU.

also decided to endow the Peace Fund from the 0.2% levy with $325 million in 2017, rising to a total of $400 million by 2020.[77] This amount was to be raised from equal contributions from each of the five AU regions which would enable the AU to meet its commitment to fund 25% of African-led peace support operations by 2020, a target set in 2015 by the AU Assembly.

The endowment represents a maximum amount to be replenished annually as necessary. Thus, the Fund will only be replenished once it has been drawn down below a pre-determined annual threshold.

How is the levy applied? The taxable base of the import levy is the value of eligible goods originating from a non-AU member state imported into the territory of a member state for consumption in the member state in accordance with the applicable national law.[78] The revenue collected under the import levy is then remitted to the AU in accordance with each member state's approved assessed contribution, including the Peace Fund. Any surplus collected by member states after fulfilment of their obligations under the assessed contribution are, for the time being, to be retained by them while any deficits between the assessed contribution and revenues collected are to be covered by the member state.

The AU import levy applies to the Cost Insurance and Freight (CIF) value at the port of disembarkation for imports arriving by sea and road and the customs value at the airport of disembarkation for goods arriving by air. The revenue would be collected by local authorities and held in central bank accounts, from where it would be paid to the AU. It should be noted, however, that the Kigali Financing Decision has some flexibility built into it, allowing member states to implement the Decision in a manner consistent with their national and international commitments provided they respect the principles of predictability and compliance.

---

[77] Assembly/AU/Dec.605 (XXVII), Decision on the Outcome of the Retreat of the Assembly of the African Union, para. 5(b)(i). The Assembly further requested the AU Commission to conduct "a study on the management of African mineral resources, with particular focus on optimizing revenue through harmonization of royalties and fiscal regimes." See Assembly/AU/Dec.605 (XXVII), Decision on the Outcome of the Retreat of the Assembly of the African Union, Assembly/AU/Dec.605 (XXVII), para. 6.

[78] However, there are some exemptions, including: (a) good originating from outside the territory of a member state for domestic consumption and re-exported to another member state; (b) goods received as aid, gifts and non-repayable grants by a state or by legal entities constituted under public law and destined for charitable works recognised as being for the common good; (c) goods originating from non-member states, imported as part of financing agreements with foreign partners, subject to a clause expressly exempting such goods from any fiscal or para-fiscal levy; (d) goods imported by enterprises before the entry into force of the AU Guidelines; (e) goods on which the AU import levy has been previously applied; and (f) capital goods and raw materials as per national regulations. See African Union, "FAQs (Frequently Asked Questions) About Financing of the Union," https://au.int/sites/default/files/newsevents/workingdocuments/32614-dw-faqs.pdf (accessed on 6 February 2021).

32 FINANCING THE AFRICAN PEACE AND SECURITY AGENDA

Challenges of Implementing the Kigali Financing Decision

Progress in the implementation of the Kigali Financing Decision has been rather slow. As of December 2020, 26 member states (slightly less than half of the total AU membership) were at various stages of implementation of the Kigali Decision through the adoption of relevant national laws and collection of the levy.[79]

There are several reasons for the slow pace of implementation. Firstly, there have been technical, legal, and regulatory challenges. Most AU member states did not have the legal and regulatory frameworks needed to implement the Kigali Financing Decision. Member states have to decide which goods are eligible for the 0.2% levy and which national financial institution or customs authority should be responsible for its collection.[80] In most cases, these decisions entail time-consuming changes to legislation and tariff books (as the levy is a new tariff) as well as the creation of new domestic mechanisms.[81] In response to these concerns, the AU Assembly, in February 2019, mandated the AU Commission to provide technical support to member states in accelerating the implementation of the 0.2% levy.[82] It is unclear if any member states have thus far requested such support.

Secondly, some concerns have been raised—both by some AU member states and non-member states—regarding the 0.2% import levy's compatibility with the World Trade Organisation (WTO) rules, especially the most favoured nation principle (MFN), given that the levy only covers non-African imports.[83] At the meeting of the WTO Council for Trade in Goods in March 2018, for instance, the United States stated that it opposed the use of trade measures to fund the Kigali Decision, arguing that the levy "in all probability" contravened AU member states' WTO obligations.[84] The EU, Canada, Japan, and Norway all emphasised the need for implementation of the Decision to be

---

[79] African Union, *Taking Stock*, p. 38.

[80] Philomena Apiko and Luckystar Miyandazi, *Self-Financing the African Union: One Levy, Multiple Reforms*, ECDPM Discussion Paper No. 258, September 2019, p. 9, https://ecdpm.org/publications/self-financing-african-union-one-levy-multiple-reforms/ (accessed on 6 February 2021).

[81] Apiko and Miyandazi, *Self-Financing the African Union*, pp. 9–10.

[82] Assembly/AU/Dec. 733 (XXXII), Decision on Financing the Union, adopted by the Thirty-Second Ordinary Session of the Assembly of the African Union, 10–11 February 2019, para. 5(i).

[83] The most favoured nation (MFN) principle requires that WTO members apply the same tariffs on a like product imported from other WTO members. *See* Article 1 of the Generalised Agreement on tariffs and Trade, 1994. Forty-four African states are members of the WTO.

[84] World Trade Organisation, Minutes of the Meeting of the Council for Trade in Goods held on 23 and 26 March 2018, 5 October 2018, G/C/M/131, paras. 22.2–22.3. Two years earlier, the United States and Japan had raised concerns regarding the compatibility of the levy with the WTO rules, particularly the MFN principle, before the WTO's General

consistent with WTO obligations.[85] Speaking on behalf of the African Group, South Africa said that it had taken note of the statements by the United States and others and would convey these to the AU.[86]

Nevertheless, the AU maintains that the 0.2% levy "is not in contradiction of other international agreements", pointing out that:

> [T]he levy is not new and indeed variations of such levy are already being used by several regional organisations globally... Such levies are ordinarily applied within the framework of customs unions and Free Trade Areas and do not conflict international norms. With the intended introduction of the Continental Free Trade Area in 2017, which will in essence include an Africa-wide customs union, such a levy therefore becomes possible and fully justifiable.[87]

While it remains to be seen how the WTO will resolve the concerns raised by the US and other WTO member states should it become necessary to do so, a 2018 study by the European Centre for Development Policy Management (ECDPM) lends support to the AU's position.[88] This study proposed several policy options to deal with the WTO-related challenges of the AU import levy, including the MFN principle. These proposals include: (a) the African Continental Free Trade Area[89] as "a possible option to the violation of the MFN principle"; (b) the use, by AU member states, of waivers to WTO obligations including the MFN principle; and (c) the use of the Kenyan model which derives the 0.2% import levy from an already existing charge to avoid excess customs duties and charges.[90]

A subsequent study by the ECDPM presents an additional and somewhat more compelling argument that the AU could invoke the security exception under Article XXI(c) of the General Agreement on Tariffs and Trade (GATT),

Council while the EU underscored the need to ensure that any measures would be WTO-compliant. *See* WTO, Minutes of the Meeting of the General Council held on 7 December 2016, 21 February 2017, WT/GC/M/165, paras. 17.2–17.5, 17.8–17.9.

[85] WTO, Minutes of the Meeting of the Council for Trade in Goods, 23 and 26 March 2018, paras. 22.4–22.7.

[86] WTO, Minutes of the Meeting of the Council for Trade in Goods, 23 and 26 March 2018, para. 22.8.

[87] *See* African Union, "FAQs (Frequently Asked Questions) About Financing of the Union."

[88] Philomena Apiko and Faten Aggad, *Analysis of the Implementation of the African Union's 0.2% Levy: Progress and Challenges*, ECDPM Briefing Note No. 98, February 2018, https://ecdpm.org/wp-content/uploads/BN98-Apiko-Aggad-November-2017.pdf (accessed on 22 February 2021).

[89] The African Continental Free Trade Area Agreement was adopted by the Tenth Extraordinary Session of the Assembly of Heads of State and Government at Kigali, Rwanda, on 21 March 2018 and entered into force on 30 May 2019. Fifty four of the 55 AU member states have signed the agreement while 36 had ratified it as at 5 February 2021. The free trade area was launched on 1 January 2021.

[90] Apiko and Aggad, *Analysis of the Implementation of the African Union's 0.2% Levy.*

which permits any contracting party to take "any action in pursuance of its obligations under the UN Charter for the maintenance of international peace and security", as a possible justification for the use of the 0.2% levy.[91] These proposals require further exploration but it is outside the scope of this chapter to do so.

Thirdly, when the Kigali Financing Decision was adopted, it was anticipated that the 0.2% levy would generate $400 million for the AU Peace Fund by 2020 (this deadline has been extended by 24 months to 2023).[92] Nonetheless, the amount collected thus far falls significantly short of this target.[93] As of November 2020, 51 member states had contributed total of $179.5 million to the Peace Fund[94]—well short of the annual target. Additionally, some member states collecting funds from the levy have not been remitting these funds in full and, to compound matters, there is no enforcement mechanism to ensure that funds collected are remitted.[95]

Finally, several Small Island States have raised concerns that their economies are small and insufficiently diversified, and are greatly reliant on tourism.[96] These states have indicated that an increase in the tariffs on the modest quantity of imports could potentially have a negative impact on their economies.[97] Some member states, such as the Saharawi Arab Democratic Republic, have small market-based economies with no tangible productive industry and their imports (mostly food) are mostly for humanitarian purposes.[98]

CONCLUSION

The AU has developed an ambitious continental peace and security agenda. Nevertheless, its financial commitments have, for the most part, fallen far short of what is required to effectively implement this agenda. Unsustainable

---

[91] *See* Philomena Apiko and Faten Aggad, *Can the 0.2% Levy Fund Peace and Security in Africa? A Stronger AU–UN Partnership in Accordance with WTO Rules*, ECDPM Briefing Note No. 103, April 2018, p. 15, https://ecdpm.org/wp-content/uploads/BN-103-Financing-the-African-Union.pdf (accessed on 22 February 2021).

[92] Assembly/AU/Dec.752 (XXXIII), Decision on the Joint Sitting Report of the Ministerial Committee on Scale of Assessment and Contributions and the Committee of Fifteen Ministers of Finance (F15), para. 6, adopted by the Thirty-Third Ordinary Session of the Assembly of the Union, 9–10 February 2020.

[93] African Union, *Taking Stock*, p. 38.

[94] African Union, *Taking Stock*, p. 38.

[95] African Union, *Financing the Union: Towards the Financial Autonomy of the African Union, Status Report—An Update*, Version Four, 16 June 2020, p. 4, https://au.int/en/documents/20200616/financing-union-towards-financial-autonomy-african-union (accessed on 6 February 2021).

[96] African Union, *Financing the Union*, p. 4.

[97] African Union, *Financing the Union*, p. 4.

[98] African Union, *Financing the Union*, p. 4.

funding arrangements, marked by shortfalls in member states' annual contributions to the AU budget and excessive dependency on external funding, have left the AU perennially underfunded, with negative implications for its peace and security operations. And, notwithstanding repeated efforts at bolstering financial autonomy, the AU remains predominantly reliant on non-member state contributions. In this context, the reduction, by development partners, of their financial contributions to major peace support operations in Africa as well as the potential limitations of the new EU global peace and security funding arrangements, underscore the need for the AU to intensify its efforts to secure sustainable and predictable funding.[99]

Although the Kigali Financing Decision is an important step in the AU's quest for financial self-reliance, it remains to be seen whether it will yield the resources needed for the implementation of the AU peace and security agenda. The slow implementation of the Kigali Decision to date does little to inspire confidence that the AU will finally attain the financial autonomy it needs to effectively implement its ambitious peace and security agenda. To be fair, the AU recognises the need to adopt "complementary measures" to reinforce "the Kigali Decision",[100] but it is unclear precisely what such measures would be.

[99] Apiko and Aggad, *Can the 0.2% Levy Fund Peace and Security in Africa? A Stronger AU–UN Partnership in Accordance with WTO Rules*, ECDPM Briefing Note No. 103, April 2018, p. 2.

[100] *See* https://au.int/aureforms/financing (accessed on 6 February 2021).

CHAPTER 33

Commend and Condemn: Combating Corruption in Africa

Dan Kuwali

INTRODUCTION

Corruption is not only about bribes. Corruption does not only raise the cost of doing business and lead to squandering of public resources, it is also corrosive to the national psyche.[1] People, especially the poor are disadvantaged when resources are wasted. There is no single comprehensive and universally accepted definition of corruption. Generally, corruption is referred to as the abuse of power for private gain.[2] From a public choice theory, corruption can be viewed as attempts by individuals or groups to subvert existing rules and generate extralegal income and wealth for themselves.[3] Corruption is often classified into two categories: grand corruption and petty corruption.

[1] Government of the Republic of Malawi (GoM)/United Nations Development Programme (UNDP), "Malawi Post 2015 Development Agenda: Report on National Consultations on Post MDGs", 8 May 2013, p. 19.

[2] The Corrupt Practices Act (CPA) in Malawi defines corrupt practice as "offering, giving, receiving, obtaining or soliciting of any advantage to influence the action of any public officer or any official or any other person in the discharge of the duties of that public officer, official or other person. See for example section 33.3 of the Corrupt Practices Act, Chapter 7:04 of the Laws of Malawi.

[3] John Mukum Mbaku, *Corruption in Africa: Causes, Consequences and Cleanups*, Lexington Books, 2010, p. 4.

D. Kuwali (✉)
University of Pretoria, Pretoria, South Africa

© The Author(s), under exclusive license to Springer Nature
Switzerland AG 2022
D. Kuwali (ed.), *The Palgrave Handbook of Sustainable Peace
and Security in Africa*, https://doi.org/10.1007/978-3-030-82020-6_33

581

582   D. KUWALI

Grand corruption is further seen through the lens of political corruption and bureaucratic corruption.

Actions and practices which constitute corruption include: bribery, extortion, abuse of discretion, abuse of office, and conflict of interest, state capture, among others. Corruption should be distinguished from fraud which can loosely be seen as wrongful or criminal deception intended to result in financial or personal gain. That is why it is important to understand the different kinds of corruption in order to develop smart and actionable responses.

Africa is the poorest region of the world and also the only one with poor prospects for the future. Corruption is attributed to be one of the most significant contribution of this state of affairs on the continent.[4] Although the African Union (AU) designated 2018 as the year for "winning the fight against corruption" and considering that corruption is a punishable offense in nearly every African State, Africa is still widely considered as the world's most corrupt continent. Of the ten countries considered most corrupt in the world, six are in Sub-Saharan Africa. The continent ranks lowest among global regions in the Corruption Perceptions Index (CPI). Countries in Africa average 32 out of 100 in their CPI scores, and six out of the bottom ten countries are African.

About one billion people (90%) of the continent's 1.2 billion population live under very or extremely corrupt governments, a rate that exceeds most of the rest of the world. Corruption is a recipe to fuel greed and grievance which is attributed to be one of the root causes of conflict.[5] Since the terrorist attacks in the United States of America on 11 September 2001, corruption has also become a major concern for countries fighting transnational terrorism as terrorists have corrupted public officials in some developing countries to use their financial institutions for money laundering to finance terrorist activities elsewhere.[6]

In agreement with Prince Bright Majiga in Chapter 11, Tadziwana Kapeni in Chapter 17 and Godard Busingye in Chapter 19, corruption is an entrenched part of African political culture. It is regarded as a contributing factor to underdevelopment and impoverishment of many African States as it fuels inequalities and undermines access to public service and scares off investors and discourages further development. African countries lose billions of dollars in revenue through corruption, misappropriated funds account for a 25% loss of development resources in Africa while over US$50 billion worth of stolen assets flow out of Africa every year.[7]

---

[4] See Mbaku, note 3 above, p. x.

[5] Paul Collier and Anke Hoeffler, 'Greed and Grievance in Civil War', Policy Research Working Paper; No. 2355. World Bank, Washington, DC. World Bank, 2000. Also available at: <https://openknowledge.worldbank.org/handle/10986/18853 License: CC BY 3.0 IGO>.

[6] Mbaku, note 3 above, p. x.

[7] Organisation for Economic Co-operation and Development, 'Implementing the OECD Principles for Integrity in Public Procurement', available at: <https://www.oecd-ilibrary.org/governance/implementing-the-oecd-principles-for-integrity-in-public-procurement_9789264201385-en> (accessed 1 January 2021).

Therefore, ending corruption is a top priority for peace, security and prosperity on the continent. This explains why the AU has established an Advisory Board on Corruption, which is an organ tasked to advise on, and address the problem of, corruption on the continent. The Board is also mandated to advocate for the ratification and implementation of the African Union Convention on Preventing and Combating Corruption (AUCPCC) by member states. This chapter clarifies the definition of corruption before discussing its causes and effects on the African continent. It then delves into the specifics of preventing corruption in Africa.

THE SPECTRE OF CORRUPTION: MEANING AND CAUSES OF CORRUPTION IN AFRICA

As already seen, owing to its complexity and various perceptions about the vice, corruption cannot be limited to a single meaning. However, common to various attempts at the definition of corruption and its practice is that corruption entails abuse of public resources for private gain. Factors that promote corruption include: absence of ethical code of conduct; lack of effective supervision; outdated policies, procedures and regulations; bureaucratic delays in provision of services and delivery of goods; discretionary powers minus accountability; monopoly in provision of services; living beyond one's means; organizational culture that tolerates corruption; greed and opportunity; and lack of effective punitive sanctions and penalties for offenders.

For example, in the Malawian case of *Republic v Lutepo*, the court lamented at the inadequacy of the maximum sentence reserved for the offense of money laundering, which underscore one of the challenges in fighting corruption in Malawi (see Footnote 5). The recent proliferation of alternative currencies may make it easier to transfer and retain funds anonymously and, therefore, more difficult for anticorruption agencies to trace and seize dirty money. With fast-paced innovations in Internet gaming and software, terrorists, and other organized criminal groups are also finding it easier to launder and transfer funds across jurisdictions without any footprints.[8]

THE NEXUS BETWEEN CORRUPTION, SECURITY AND DEVELOPMENT IN AFRICA

The notion of security has significantly evolved since the end of the Cold War, from a state-centric and military-focused definition to a broader and human-centered approach of human security. The Human Development Report (United Nations Development Programme [UNDP] 1994) coined the term "human security" as security of humanity as a collective where individual

---

[8] Ministry of Defence, 'Strategic Trends Programme: Global Strategic Trends-Out to 2045', Fifth Edition, 2014, p. xxii.

584   D. KUWALI

citizens have freedom from want and freedom from fear. Therefore, contemporary concept of security goes beyond state security and encompasses human security which requires that individuals should enjoy their rights and freedoms, feel secure, and have access to resources and basic day-to-day needs.[9] In this way, security is better achieved by addressing threats to human security through socioeconomic development and not military might alone.[10]

As most of the countries in Africa are not at war, their major threat to peace and security are human security challenges which also have disruptive effects of development of the country.[11] Therefore, to sustain peace, security, and development in Africa, it is necessary that more attention should be put on addressing the human security challenges by creating favorable conditions for social, political, and development than the use of military force.[12] It is easy to notice that the outstanding security problems facing most African countries are non-military, but rather relate to human insecurity and human development and, therefore, require political and economic solutions. This explains why combating corruption should be priority for African countries in order to spur social-economic development on the continent.

THE EFFECTS OF CORRUPTION ON PEACE, SECURITY, AND PROSPERITY IN AFRICA

There is a paucity of research on the relationship between corruption and armed conflict.[13] MacLachlan is one of the few writers who have discussed the connection between corruption, development, peace, and security.[14] MacLachlan notes that "if peace and security are to take hold and create conditions for development, addressing defence and security corruption – especially in fragile and conflict-affected states – must be a priority."[15] Corruption has a

[9] Ayodele Aderinwale, 'The Conference on Security, Stability, Development and Cooperation in Africa-Framework and the Role of Regional Institutions', in Moufids Goucha and Jakkie Cilliers (eds.), *Peace, Human Security and Conflict Prevention in Africa*, ISS/UNESCO, Paris/Pretoria, 2000.

[10] United Nations Development Programme (UNDP), Human Development Report, 7 July 1994.

[11] Aderinwale, 'note 9 above'.

[12] Ernie Regehr and Peter Whelan, 'Reshaping the Security Envelope: Defence Policy in a Human Security Context', Project Ploughshares Working Paper 04-4, 2004, p. 1.

[13] Jens Christopher Andvig, 'Corruption and Armed Conflicts: Some Stirring Around the Governance Soup', NUPI Working Papers, Norwegian Institute of International Affairs (NUPI), Oslo. Also available at: <Corruption and Armed Conflicts: Some Stirring Around in the Governance Soup—GSDRC> (accessed 1 January 2021).

[14] As above.

[15] See also Dr. Karolina MacLachlan, 'Corruption and Conflict: Hand in Glove', available at: <Corruption and Conflict: Hand in Glove (nato.int)> (accessed 29 January 2021).

bearing on peace, security, and prosperity of a country in as much as it damages the economic, social, and institutional fabric of a country.

Corruption does not only destroy social cohesion and trust, it undermines talent and efficiency, rewards the undeserving, lowers standards of performance, is unjust, tarnishes the image of a nation, and has a negative effect on business and investment in a country.[16] The cancerous growth of corruption destroys the economic growth of a country and deprives the general public of resources as it is only the corrupt few who benefit. To this end, corruption, which mainly derives from greed, begets grievance, which begets and later perpetuates conflict.[17]

In Chapter 17, Kapeni agrees that lack of transparency coupled with secrecy and perceived security needs and national prestige leave room for corruption and often makes it difficult to reform defense and security institutions. Yet without reforming them, stability and security cannot take root.[18] MacLachlan has given an example of South Sudan stating that:

> In the early years after independence in South Sudan, for example, the ruling elite diverted oil revenues to fund patronage networks through defence sector expenditures. A bloated military budget was used to pay the salaries of 230,000 soldiers and militia members belonging to various patronage networks. Meanwhile, other departments' budgets were raided and resources redirected to the defence sector: in 2012, when defence and security expenditure constituted 35 per cent of South Sudan's budget, donors funded 75 per cent of South Sudan's health sector.

Corruption in the defense and security sector is often covered by increased defense spending thereby diverting resources from other public services such as health and education. For example, in 2016, 22 African states spent over 5% of their budgets on defense, while seven countries spent over 10%, which called for a robust defense governance. However, in most countries where defense spending is high, there are no effective oversight mechanisms. The drawback in many countries is that defense budgets are mostly opaque and exempt from external scrutiny.[19]

Similarly, a country may see higher gross domestic product, but the benefits of growth may be siphoned into bank accounts of opportunistic politicians, politically connected elites, and other senior bureaucrats. Opportunistic politicians have sought to gain economic benefits through corrupt practices by flouting rules, regulations, and procedures with impunity, especially among the Executive, which is perceived to lack proper checks and balances in several

---

[16] Anver Versi, 'Let's Exorcise Corruption Once and for All', *African Business*, April 2010, p. 11. See also Dan Kuwali, 'Governance or Government Reform?—Transforming Governmentality in Malawi', 5(2) *Malawi Law Journal* (2011), pp. 139–147.

[17] See generally Collier and Hoeffler, note 5 above.

[18] MacLachlan, note 15 above.

[19] As above.

586   D. KUWALI

countries in Africa. Corruption is also an obstacle to effective state-building to bring about more participatory and accountable governance structures hence exacerbating poor governance which is a recipe for conflict. Unless African countries find ways to effectively deal with corruption, corruption will remain a constraint top economic, social, political, peace, security, and development on the continent.

CHALLENGES IN FIGHTING CORRUPTION IN AFRICA

Corruption is so pervasive in Africa and is a direct consequence of poorly developed and inappropriate institutional arrangement. Mbaku has traced the genesis of corruption in Africa to the lack of engagement of the citizenry by most of the immediate independence leaders in state reconstruction through democratic constitution-making[20] According to Mbaku:

> Instead, constitution making was top-down, elite-driven, opportunistic, and reluctant. Hence the outcome was laws and institution that were not locally-focused and did not reflect the values of the people to be governed by them. The institutional arrangement adopted did not promote indigenous entrepreneurship nor did they enhance peaceful coexistence of each country's numerous population groups. Instead, they provided incentives, which encouraged people to invest in rent seeking, corruption and other forms of opportunism. Such distorted incentives stunted wealth creation and significantly damaged economic growth and development.[21]

The mist that surrounds corruption, to an extent, contributes to limited understanding of the vice and subsequently, poor interventions in attempts to curb the problem. Below are some factors that have stalled the fight against corruption in Africa.

Corruption May Be Committed by Persons in Positions of Power

Corruption can be categorized as a white-collar crime. Corruption provides incumbent leaders of people in positions of power with incentives to resist change, especially institutional reforms that could curtail their privileges and deny them access to extralegal income from the economy.[22] The fact that there is a possibility that cases of corruption can be committed by people in positions of influence, it may be difficult to prosecute such cases without external interference. This thinking also lends credence to an earlier study which noted the majority of the people in prisons in Malawi, for example, reveals are mostly

---

[20] Mbaku, note 3 above, p. 4.

[21] As above.

[22] As above.

those who are impecunious and without influence.[23] Attempts at resisting change are also buoyed by realistic fear of persecution upon relinquishment of power. Others have lamented that the fight against corruption only targets the "small fish" and leaves out "the big fish."

The Weak Tone and Tenor of National Anti-Corruption Legislation

To name a piece of legislation, for example, the Nigerian Corrupt Practices and Other Related Offences Act, or the Corrupt Practices Act in Malawi does not say much than indicating that it is a catalogue of acts that constitute corruption. A good example of progressive legislation that condemns corruption is found in South Africa, which has enacted the Prevention and Combating of Corrupt Activities Act, 2004 or the Zambian Anti-Corruption Act, 2012. Kenya also has an impressive array of legislation to combat corruption, which includes Public Officers Ethics Act, 2003, Anti-Corruption and Economic Crimes Act, 2003, Proceeds of Crime and Anti-Money Laundering Act, 2009 and Ethics and Anti-Corruption Commission Act, 2011. Such nomenclature of a piece of legislation unequivocally shows that a country seeks to eradicate corruption. The gold standard in nomenclature is the African Union Convention on Preventing and Combating Corruption. The United Nations (UN) came up with the Convention Against Corruption, which clearly declares the world organization's abhorrence against corruption.

The Nonexistence or Docility of National Systems to Promote Ethics and Integrity

Corruption thrives in societies with weak religious and moral teachings hence the need for mechanisms to promote integrity and ethical values to eradicate decay of moral values. Although most countries have enacted legislation to prevent and combat corruption, the law is not supported by institutions to inculcate a culture of ethics and integrity. For example, in Malawi, the National Integrity System (NIS), which is mandated to facilitate the establishment of Institutional Integrity Committees in all the sectors with a view of promoting transparency and accountability has largely been moribund. While Tanzania promulgated a Code of Ethics and Conduct for Public Service in 2005,[24] Kenya has entrenched guiding principles for leadership and integrity in chapter six of its 2010 Constitution. National ethics and integrity mechanisms are effective tools for preventing and fighting corruption, especially deterring potential offenders from engaging in corrupt practices. If implemented with

---

[23] For more elaborate recommendations, see Fidelis Edge Kanyongolo, *Malawi: Justice Sector and the Rule of Law*, OSISA, 2006.

[24] United Republic of Tanzania, Code of Ethics and Conduct for Public Service, Minister of State, President's Office, Public Service Management. Also available at: <PREAMBLE (policyforum-tz.org)> (accessed 31 January 2021).

commitment, national ethics and integrity mechanisms could empower citizens to demand accountability from public officers and any person in position of authority.

Lack of Vigilance of Sectoral Anti-Corruption Initiatives

By and large, fighting corruption in Africa is seen as the responsibility of the anti-corruption authorities alone, and not the government as a whole and its citizenry. This significantly affects efforts at fighting the vice. In countries where there are sectoral initiatives to combat corruption, the vigilance of these sectoral anti-corruption initiatives has not matched the prevalence of the rising corruption in the country.

Perceived Tolerance of Corruption by Citizens

Although the general public has a crucial role to play in preventing corruption, they may accept wrongdoings out of fear of reprisals, lack of other avenues for redress, or ignorance of their rights. Where arrests are not made or investigations are not carried out following credible information from whistleblowers, citizens may choose to rather keep quiet for their own safety than risking their lives for what they perceive as futile endeavors.[25] Whistleblowers are a key component in the fight against corruption as they can timely raise a red flag to arrest the greed and insatiable appetite for public resources for personal gain by unscrupulous individuals.

ARRESTING CORRUPTION IN AFRICA

Granted, there is no silver bullet for fighting corruption. The AU Convention on Preventing and Combating Corruption was adopted in Maputo, Mozambique on 11 July 2003 and came into force in 2006. To date, the Convention has been ratified by 44 out of the 55 AU Member States.[26] Since adoption of the Convention, African states have showed commitment in arresting corruption including the enactment of domestic laws to fight corruption and establishment of anti-corruption institutions. However, more work is still needed to adopt preventative measures against corruption. The success of corruption prevention measures requires a fundamental shift of culture to a state where the citizens no longer accept corrupt practices as just the way Government works in their country. Mbaku has theorized that:

[25] Dan Kuwali, 'Reckless Business: Afropolitan View on Corporate Accountability for Atrocities', in Jernej Letnar Cernic and Nicolas Carrillo Santarelli (eds.), *The Future of Business and Human Rights*, Intersentia, 2017, pp. 209–227.

[26] African Union, AU Convention on Preventing and Combating Corruption, available at: <https://au.in/sites/default/files/treaties/36382-treats-0028-african-union-convention-on-preventing-and-combating-corruption-e.pdf> (accessed 20 February 2021).

33 COMMEND AND CONDEMN: COMBATING CORRUPTION IN AFRICA 589

According to the theory of public choice, corruption is post-constitution opportunism and as a consequence, cleanups must begin with a negotiated change of the rules in order to affect the incentive structures faced by market participants. Corruption is a market outcome determined by the behaviour of those participants in the market. Thus, to change such an outcome, it is necessary to change the behaviour of market participants. The most effective way to accomplish that (i.e., change the behaviour of market participants) is to change the market incentive structure.[27]

Corruption prevention requires a robust system to detect and eliminate the causes and conditions of corruption through the development and implementation of appropriate measures for deterrence of persons from committing corrupt practices. While there cannot be a one-cap fits all approach to combating corruption, the purpose of corruption prevention should be to minimize, as much as possible, its crippling effect on the economy, democracy, promotion of social welfare, consolidating national security, and improving the quality of provision of public services (see Footnote 18). This discussion outlines ten (10) strategies on how to prevent corruption and mitigate its effects in Africa. The centerpiece of this ten-point strategy is a commend and condemn policy to applaud and reward corruption-free officers and ostracize, name and shame corrupt officials and their accomplices. These strategies can be grouped into five (5) categories that involve: institutional reform, capacity building, mindset change, a reward and punish policy as well as monitoring and evaluation mechanisms as outlined below.[28]

Institutional Reform

Promote Financial Probity
There is a need for reform of the public administration and finance management in order to promote financial probity and professionalism in handing public resources. Reforms focusing on improving financial management and strengthening the role of auditing agencies have greater impact than public sector reforms on curbing corruption. One such reform is the disclosure of budget information, which prevents waste and misappropriation of resources (see Footnote 20). Kenya and Tanzania have good examples of legislative and institutional frameworks in order to promote integrity, transparency, and improve service delivery in all sectors, and to promote public involvement in the fight against corruption at national level.

---

[27] Mbaku, as above note 3, p. x.

[28] For example, Transparency International-Sri Lanka promotes transparent and participatory budgeting by training local communities to comment on the proposed budgets of their local government. The more open and transparent the budgetary process, spending, procurement of goods and services, tax exemption and the way Government manages public resources, the less opportunity it will provide for malfeasance and abuse.

Enhance Transparency and Access to Information

Countries that are successful at curbing corruption have a long tradition of government openness, freedom of the press, transparency, and access to information (see Footnote 21). The rationale is that access to information increases the responsiveness of government bodies, while simultaneously having a positive effect on the levels of public participation in the affairs of a country. Therefore, countries in Africa should promote a culture of transparency, accountability, integrity, and honesty. Governments should support watchdog institutions in preventing and pursuing all corruption cases (see Footnote 23). In this respect, press freedoms and levels of literacy will, likewise, shape in important ways the context for reforms (see Footnote 24). Considering authoritative tendencies that some African states have been subjected to, the importance of transparency cannot be emphasized.

Efficient and Effective Service Delivery

Corruption thrives in institutions where there is no transparency and accountability, and where the public is not empowered to question the conduct of the institution. Hence the need to efficient, effective, and equitable provision of public services. As a matter of policy, all public institutions should develop client service charters with clearly spell out mission, values, work procedures, and obligations of the institution. This will ensure transparency, accountability, and efficiency in public institutions including the rights of clients.[29] Related to service delivery is also the need to cut the unnecessary red-tape which impede doing business. For example, the multitude of regulations governing the registration of a new business, registration of land, engaging in international trade, may not only be burdensome but can also breed corruption as people prefer to cut corners. Given the secrecy attached to military spending and mining deals in Africa, efforts to enhance efficient, responsive systems need to be the rule rather than an exception.

Embracing Smart Technology

There is a need to use the power of technology to build dynamic and continuous exchanges between key stakeholders, namely: government, citizens, business, civil society groups, media, academia, among others. Just as government-induced distortions provide many opportunities for corruption, it is also the case that frequent, direct contact between government officials and citizens can open the way for illicit transactions. One way to address this problem is to use readily available technologies to encourage more of an arms-length relationship between officials and civil society. In this respect, the burgeoning use of online transactions can be an effective mechanism to reduce

---

[29] The client charters will also clearly indicate rights and duties of the public in order to allow the public to demand for an explanation where they feel they have not been treated fairly by public institutions.

corruption in Africa.[30] Chile is one country that has used the latest technologies to create one of the world's most transparent public procurement systems in the world.[31]

Capacity Building

Integrity Checks of Public Officers

Public officers should be individuals who lead by example, possess a character of integrity, and demonstrate professionalism if they are to resist corruption in the conduct of their work. Lithuania is a good example as it has introduced "integrity checks" where information is required for individuals seeking or holding public offices to assess the person's credibility and reduce the probability of the occurrence of corruption in government entities. Therefore, governments in Africa should ensure that public officers in key positions go through integrity checks during the recruitment phase as well as declare their assets before assuming office, and every year thereafter.[32] It is evident that stringent anti-money laundering measures have given rise to a situation where people involved in corrupt activities no longer deposit the proceeds of crime in banks but instead operate on cash basis. This explains the discovery of voluminous stashes of cash in some people's vehicles and villas, following dubious transactions.[33] This is why there should also be lifestyle audits for public servants to curb unlawful and unjustifiable accumulation of wealth by public servants and to deter a culture of living beyond one's means. This process can dovetail with the requirement for asset declaration by public officers and politically exposed persons.

Empower Citizens

Strengthening citizens' demand for anti-corruption and empowering them to hold government accountable is a sustainable approach that helps to build mutual trust between citizens and government. For example, community monitoring initiatives can contribute to the detection of corruption, reduced leakages of funds, and improved quantity and quality of public services. The civil society has the important role of safeguarding democracy by empowering

---

[30] The reason being that the awarding of contracts in public procurement can involve a measure of bureaucratic discretion, kickbacks, and collusion, online transaction can contain procedures that guarantee adequate levels of openness, competition, a level playing field for suppliers, and fairly clear bidding procedures. Narayan Manandhar, 'Anti-Corruption Strategies: Understanding What Works, What doesn't and Why? Lessons Learned from the Asia–Pacific Region', United Nations Development Programme, 2014.

[31] ChileCompra was launched in 2003, and is a public electronic system for purchasing and hiring, based on an Internet platform. See Manandhar, note 24 above.

[32] See the functions of the Civil Service Commission, the Public Appointment Committee of Parliament and such other entities.

[33] See for example, *Republic v Isaac Sithole and Another* (Criminal Case, High Court of Malawi) (Unreported).

people to actively participate in affairs of the state, and advocating for policy reforms or formulation.[34] Citizens must be encouraged to engage in whistle blowing, with assurances of protection and investigation into issues raised. As a success story, to monitor local elections, Transparency International-Slovenia produced an interactive map that the public populated with pictures and reports of potential irregularities in the election. As a result, cases of public funds being misused to support certain candidates were spotted. This is an undertaking that can be replicated in Africa, albeit with adjustments to local realities.

Mindset Change

Inculcate a Culture of Integrity and Honesty

Corruption thrives in a society where there is moral decay. In such a society, people do not mind the consequences of illegal acts on others as they compete for resources. Teachings in morality, especially among the youth, may help to nip corruption in the bud as they promote a culture of ethical conduct. Therefore, all sectors, especially faith-based organizations should promote public campaigns in moral and ethical values, transparency, and accountability. On their part, governments should facilitate a review of the school curriculum to include issues of corruption prevention in the syllabus.[35] On their part, faith-based organizations should check the growing tendency of hailing the so-called "miracle money" as it is a recipe to promote unhealthy competition among followers which may lead to corruption. Given their proximity to the grassroots, traditional leaders should be educating their subjects to desist from engaging in corrupt practices, report suspected corruption, and demand accountability from public officers and other people in positions of authority.

[34] Transparency International-Philippines, which is an affiliate of Transparent International seeks to develop preventive mechanisms and incentives to prevent corruption. It also aims to strengthen integrity systems. See Manandhar, note 24 above.

[35] For example, in the Philippines, there are programs for staff education and training on values and integrity in the performance of duty; inclusion of training on honesty and integrity in public office in early education programs; a system of incentives and rewards to encourage appropriate conduct by public officials and employees; "Citizen First programme; deployment of resident Ombudsmen to graft-prone departments; and organization of a Junior Graftwatch programme to involve the youth in the fight against corruption); public disclosure of detected instances of corruption" other measures of corruption provided for by law. See Manandhar, note 24 above.

Punish and Reward Policy

End Impunity

Effective law enforcement is essential to ensure that perpetrators of corruption are punished and break the cycle of impunity. Successful enforcement approaches are supported by a strong legal framework, law enforcement mechanisms, and an independent and effective judiciary. The anti-corruption legislation should also consider including corporate criminal liability and public interest litigation. Focus should not be limited to criminal prosecutions which has a higher burden of proof but should also consider civil litigation which has a lower burden of proof. Law enforcement should not only end at conviction after prosecution but should proceed to penetrate and recover the tainted assets and funds. Civil society can support the process with initiatives such as Transparency International's "Unmask the Corrupt" campaign. At the same time, there is need to close all loopholes for illegal self-enrichment by public officials and politicians. Without access to the international financial system, corrupt public officials throughout the world would not be able to launder and hide the proceeds of looted state assets. Major financial centers urgently need to put in place ways to stop their banks and cooperating offshore financial centers from absorbing illicit flows of money.

Commend and Condemn

While punishing corruption is a vital component of any effective anti-corruption effort, there is a need to adopt a policy aimed at increasing the benefits of being honest and costs of being corrupt. This shows the need to formulate a policy where good character and professionalism is commended and rewarded through provision of relevant incentives while bad character and corruption is condemned and punished. A sensible combination of reward and punishment should be the driving force for reforms to fight corruption. Likewise, it is also necessary to pay civil servants adequately. There is an inverse relationship between the level of public sector wages and the incidence of corruption.[36] Whether civil servants are appropriately compensated or grossly underpaid will clearly affect motivation and incentives. If the public sector wages are too low, employees may find themselves under pressure to supplement their income in "unofficial" ways.

Monitoring and Evaluation Mechanisms

Monitoring and Evaluation of the Anti-Corruption Strategies

Monitoring and evaluation (M&E) contributes to learning by doing. This explains the importance of monitoring and evaluation in the implementation of anti-corruption strategies.[37] Any good anti-corruption strategy must be

---

[36] Please indicate source of this information.

[37] Manandhar, note 24 above, p. 2.

continually monitored and evaluated to make sure it can be easily adapted as situations on the ground change. The implementation, monitoring and evaluation of anti-corruption strategies should be done by members drawn from all sectors of the economy and not the civil society alone.

CONCLUSION

Corruption is generally understood as the abuse of public resources and authority for private gain. Corruption, which is commonplace in the African political culture, is a direct consequence of poorly developed and inappropriate institutional arrangement that encourages the citizenry to invest in rent-seeking and other forms of opportunism.[38] Corruption is a destabilizing factor, which disproportionately affects the poor, facilitates terrorism, and escalates conflicts. The AU has not be able to achieve its ambition of "winning the fight against corruption" in 2018. Instead, Africa is still widely regarded as the world's most corrupt continent. This vice is regarded as a contributing factor to underdevelopment and impoverishment of many African States as it fuels inequalities and undermines access to public service and scare off investors and discourages further development.

Corruption is deep-rooted in greed, which begets grievance that perpetuates conflict on the continent.[39] The violence fueled by greed and grievance often mutate social and economic development, stall international trade and commerce, unleash massive flows of refugees, create resource shortages, disrupt vital social services, including health care and education on the continent.[40] Ethnic and religious conflicts, border disputes, nationalist struggles, and resource disputes need to be contained and abated.[41] Corruption is also a challenge in the fight against transnational terrorism where terrorists have corrupted public officials to facilitate money laundering to finance terrorist activities.[42] The lack of transparency in defense spending coupled with secrecy in security matters further provide a fertile ground for corruption in the defense and security sector.[43]

The fight against corruption is the responsibility of everyone. Therefore, everyone has a duty in eradicating corruption by actively taking part in the implementation of anti-corruption legislation and strategies and condemning

[38] Mbaku, note 3 above, p. x.

[39] See also Collier and Hoeffler, note 5 above.

[40] James E. Doyle, 'Why Eliminate Nuclear Weapons?', *Survival: Global Politics and Strategy*, February–March 2013, 55(1), 1 February 2013, pp. 7–34, available at: <http://www.iiss.org/en/publications/survival/sections/2013-94b0/survival--global-politics-and-strategy-february-march-2013-3db7/55-1-02-doyle-a88b>.

[41] UNESCO, 'Making the World Safe', available at: <http://www.unesco.org/education/tlsf/mods/theme_a/interact/www.worldgame.org/wwwproject/what17.shtml> (accessed 2 February 2021).

[42] Mbaku, note 3 above, p. x.

[43] MacLachlan, note 15 above.

corrupt practices by demanding justice. However, the results of law enforcement may turn out to be short-term, it is also crucial to engage in proactive prevention strategies that include programs to transform the mindset of the population in Africa by inculcating a culture of integrity, honest, professionalism ethical conduct, and living within one's means, especially for the youth. This transformation may help to spur economic development on the continent, which is the poorest and less peaceful continent in the world.

PART VI

Securing Sustainable Peace and Security in Africa

CHAPTER 34

Conclusion

Dan Kuwali

IN SEARCH FOR SUSTAINABLE PEACE AND SECURITY IN AFRICA

Armed conflicts have occasioned high human cost and suffering in Africa. The concept of peace in Africa is not merely the absence of violence, but also the ability of a society to respond to the needs of its citizens, reduce the number of conflicts, and resolve existing disputes.[1] While security relates to the protection from harm in every imaginable way.[2] Peace in this case will not merely be the absence of violence, but the ability of a society to respond to the needs of its citizens, reduce the number of conflicts, and resolve existing disputes. While security, will be protection from harm in every imaginable way.[3] However, in Chapter 3, Youssef Mahmoud and Chimwemwe Fabiano note that despite the clear normative shift ushered by United Nations (UN) Security Council Resolution 2282 of 2016 on sustaining peace, the policy and

---

[1] Olusola Adeyoose, "Achieving Sustainable Peace and Security in Africa", *The Guardian*, 22 October 2017. Available at: https://guardian.ng/opinion/achieving-sustainable-peace-and-security-in-Africa/ (accessed 23 February 2021).

[2] As above.

[3] As above.

D. Kuwali (✉)
University of Pretoria, Pretoria, South Africa

© The Author(s), under exclusive license to Springer Nature Switzerland AG 2022
D. Kuwali (ed.), *The Palgrave Handbook of Sustainable Peace and Security in Africa*, https://doi.org/10.1007/978-3-030-82020-6_34

600   D. KUWALI

programmatic interpretations remain beholden to the liberal, top-down peace-building agenda largely focused on rebuilding the neocolonial state, politics, and economy. According to the UN Security Council,

> 'sustaining peace' [...] should be broadly understood as a goal and a process to build a common vision of a society, ensuring that the needs of all segments of the population are taken into account, which encompasses activities aimed at preventing the outbreak, escalation, continuation and recurrence of conflict, addressing root causes, assisting parties to conflict to end hostilities, ensuring national reconciliation and moving towards recovery, reconstruction and development.[4]

In practice, sustaining peace continues to be perceived as a package of interventions relevant solely to contexts where conflict is manifest, proximate, or threatens to return. Sustained peace is still linked together with the predominant belief that if the root causes are analyzed and addressed, peace will ensue. Thus, the factors associated with peace are understood to be the inverse of those leading to war and conflict, despite evidence to the contrary.[5] In agreement with Desire Hakorimana and Godard Busingye in Chapter 2, it would seem that the "silencing the guns" vision as articulated under Aspiration 4 of the AU Agenda 2063 has also fallen prey to the same assumption, namely that if guns were removed by 2020, there would be peace on the continent. While violent conflict remains one of the biggest challenges standing in the way of a peaceful and prosperous Africa, conflicts do not start simply because arms are available.[6] There is a concern that as long as Africa's aspirations for peace continue to be depicted negatively, that is as the absence of conflict, sustaining peace will remain an elusive goal.[7]

In Chapter 28, Ibrahim Machina Mohammed and Lawan Cheri also submit that building peace in fragile and post-conflict contexts therefore requires a variety of measures and strategies to strengthen societal capacities to manage diversity and divisions in order to pursue sustainable peace and development and address the underlying conditions that lead to conflict or conflict relapse. According to Mohammed and Cheri, it is necessary to strengthen societal capacities to manage diversity and differences and pursue sustainable peace and development. The two are of the view that the current approaches to building peace in Africa focuses on state-centric approach using hard power military approach while neglecting programs to build harmonious relationship between individuals, groups, and their institutions. That is why these

---

[4] United Nations Security Council 2282 (2016).

[5] Paul F. Diehl, "Exploring Peace: Looking Beyond War and Negative Peace", *International Studies Quarterly* (2016).

[6] Youssef Mahmoud, "What Kind of Leadership Does Sustaining Peace Require?" *Global Observatory* (2019), International Peace Institute.

[7] Youssef Mahmoud, "Freeing Prevention From Conflict: Investing in Sustaining Peace", *Global Observatory*.

peacebuilding efforts have been inadequate and struggle to effectively "silence the guns by 2020." Thus, to effectively prevent conflict and ensure sustainable peace in Africa, reviving harmonious relationships between individuals or groups of people in African states is now considered essential in the promotion of peace and stability.[8]

African scholars and practitioners have documented and conceptualized the rich repertoire of African indigenous and endogenous approaches to peacebuilding, sustaining peace, and conflict management in post-colonial Africa.[9] The examples of community-based peacemaking processes include that practiced by the *Tiv* community in Nigeria, the *Guurti* system in Somaliland, the *Mato Oput* in Northern Uganda and the *Ubuntu* tradition in southern Africa and the traditional *Gacaca* system in post-genocide Rwanda that combines both punitive and restorative justice as a means to fast-track transitional justice and reconciliation processes.[10] These indigenous processes have a value-added in terms of sustaining peace, given that they are inclusive and draw upon local cultural assumptions, norms, and values as well as grass-root notions of justice. Hakorima and Busingye like Mahmoud and Fabiano recommend that some of these practices if strategically leveraged can go a long way toward tempering the top-down, liberal peacebuilding prescriptions, and help build lasting peace.[11] According to Mahmoud and Fabiano, since peace is both an enabler and outcome of AU Agenda 2063 and the UN 2030 Agenda for sustainable development, a deliberate integration of these traditional peacebuilding approaches would make the progress achieved thus far less reversible.

According to Mahmoud and Fabiano, a peace and conflict analysis in the context of the African Agenda for sustaining peace requires to take two simultaneous steps; first, analyze the drivers of conflict with a view to addressing its immediate deleterious consequences; and second, map the resilient capacities of peace that are still working and propose ways for strengthening them. Among these capacities are the indigenous and endogenous infrastructures of peace outlined above. Sustainable peace has greater chance to take root, if peacebuilders build on what people have and what they know.[12]

On the one hand, there seems to be agreement that "top-down one-size-fits-all approaches to policymaking in peace and development are often

---

[8] Haider, H. & Mcloughlin, C. *State-Society Relations and Citizenship in Situations of Conflict and Fragility: Topic Guide Supplement*. Birmingham: GSDRC (2016).

[9] Tim Murithi, "African Indigenous and Endogenous Approaches to Peace and Conflict Resolution", in David J. Francis (ed.), *Peace and Conflict in Africa*.

[10] David J. Francis (ed.), *Peace and Conflict in Africa*.

[11] However, Mahmoud and Fabiano put a caveat concerning the limitations inherent in some of these processes including a predisposition to patriarchy and gender-based violence.

[12] Youssef Mahmoud, et al. "Sustaining Peace in Practice: Building on What Works" (2018).

ineffectual and unsustainable."[13] On the other, there seems to be consensus that community-initiated programs are usually more effective. In the words of Mahmoud and Fabiano, "peace, like a tree, grows from the bottom up. Unlike the rule of law and security, it cannot be enforced from the top. It must be woven into society from within and from below by fostering systemic partnerships and incentives to maintain it." As discussed by Mphatso Jones Boti-Phiri in Chapter 25 as well as Thomasin Gondwe and Laika Nakanga in Chapter 26, community-initiated programs ensure that the needs for all segments of the population to be taken into account and allow for more genuine inclusion of women, the youth, and other marginalized groups who typically have a more grounded and informed insight of the local challenges and sustainable solutions. It is up to local communities in partnership with intermediate and national governance structures to shape the outcome.

The underlying drivers of instability that give rise to armed groups on the continent relate to socioeconomic challenges such as high youth unemployment rate, lack of equal opportunities, urbanization, poverty, inequality, proliferation of small armed and light weapons (SALW), competition over natural resources; bad governance and corruption. According to Godard Busingye in Chapter 21 and George Lwanda in Chapter 30, conflicts and violence on the continent have also been sparked by conflict over scarce land and resources, existential fear between communities that are stoked by lawlessness and competition over access to local positions of authority.

In a continent awash with SALW, natural resources, and a desperate population, there remains a "market for violence."[14] Surveying the current state of the peace and security landscape in Africa is a complex task. Although there has been a reduction in external aggressions and inter-state armed conflicts, there has been an increase in the number of non-international armed conflicts in Africa.[15] There continues to be a deterioration in peace in Africa, particularly in countries such as South Sudan, Somalia, Libya, The Democratic Republic of the Congo (DRC), Central African Republic (CAR), and Sudan.[16] Terrorists networks have taken advantage of the chaos and disorder in countries like DRC, Chad, and Libya to establish themselves on the continent. Southern Africa, especially Mozambique, West Africa, the Sahel, and North Africa are caught between the terrorist presence of Al Shabaab, Al-Qaeda in Islamic Maghreb (AQIM), and the Islamic State of Iraq and Levant (ISIL). Asymmetric warfare, terrorism, and violent extremism, ethnic tensions, violent

---

[13] Peter T. Coleman, et al. *The Science of Sustaining Peace.*

[14] See Shamil Idriss and Mike Jobbins, "Achieving Peace in the Great Lakes Region", *Africa in Focus.* Brookings. 6 February 2015. Available at: www.brookings.edu/blog/africa-in-focus/2015/02/06/achieving-peace-in-the-great-lakes-region/ (accessed 23 February 2021).

[15] Adeyoose, note 1 above.

[16] Global Peace Index, Statistics Times, as of 11 June 2020. Available at: https://statisticstimes.com/ranking/globa-peace-index.php (accessed 23 February 2021).

electoral crises, transnational crimes, resource conflicts, global pandemics, among others, are some of the challenges that have hampered the development of the continent.[17]

While analyzing the root causes of conflict is an important aspect of peacebuilding, the causes of sustainable peace would be better served if the challenges facing countries under stress are framed in terms of the inadequate self-organizing capacity of the society to anticipate, manage, mitigate, and resolve conflicts.[18] To this end, the search for underlying causes becomes the search for why this capacity is inadequate, and how it can be reinforced—rather than merely looking for the causes of today's conflicts. According to Mahmoud and Fabiano, this analytical shift helps identify opportunities for strengthening what is already working even amidst devastation.[19] Focusing on what is still going strong and not only what is wrong, takes people away from the obsessive examination of their conflicts, and provides a welcome opportunity to embrace a different challenge.[20] In protracted conflicts, attempting to understand the causes of the problem often involves looking backward and apportioning blame, which cannot a conducive environment for repairing broken relations, let alone rebuilding trust and laying the foundations for lasting peace.

Eliminating Perennial Problems to State and Human Security in Africa

In Chapter 12, Tadziwana Kapeni contends that poor leadership and governance state in some parts of Africa is a product of the continent's leaders' refusal to defer to the governed. Such poor governance and leadership provoke people's anger, a development that has potential to destabilize states and thereby pose a threat to peace and security on the continent. Kapeni is correct that, as it has been noted in Rwanda, among other countries, with good leadership and good governance skills, a country can develop politically, socially, and economically.

There has been a rise in organized crimes in Africa, which are exacerbated by corruption among law enforcement officials, globalization, advancement in technology, porous borders as well as weak governments and civil wars in some parts of Africa. In order to arrest the problem of organized crimes, Mlowoka Noel Kayira advocates for a holistic approach that will enable the AU and its member states to join efforts to prevent, monitor, investigate, and prosecute perpetrators of these crimes in Chapter 18.

[17] Adeyoose, note 1 above.

[18] Cedric de Coning, "Peace: Can a New Approach Change the UN?".

[19] Phil Vernon, "The Root Causes of What? How Root Causes Analysis Can Get in the Way of Peacebuilding", *Peacebuilding, International Development & Poetry* (2018).

[20] Cormac Russell, "Sustainable Community Development: From What's Wrong to What's Strong", *Tedx Exeter*.

The quest to silence guns In Africa may not be achieved in the absence of democratic management of Africa's natural resources in some States. The greed for political power, and insatiable interest of external actors in Africa's natural resources have fueled armed conflicts on the continent. In Chapter 19, Busingye says that illegal exploitation of Africa's natural resources must be stopped and recommends the adoption of all-inclusive democracy that promotes accountability by political leaders to the citizenry in all African States and African Governments rejecting former colonial interference on which natural resources should be harnessed and destined to which markets.

The trajectory of acts of piracy and attacks against shipping vessels on African coastal lines is still rising both in number and frequency. International initiatives to combat piracy have proven insufficient and ineffective since most of them primarily address the effects of piracy through military means. As such, Prince Bright Majiga in Chapter 20 recommends the adoption of both military and non-military approaches that would go a long way in addressing the problem of piracy on the continent.

Most conflicts in Africa have also emerged from mismanagement of elections. In Chapter 22, Archiles Bwete and his colleagues posit that apart from malpractices relating to electoral outcomes, in some cases, African politicians have appealed to the electorate both overtly and covertly relying on patronage, tribalism, religion, and any other form of sectarianism. As the youth are the common perpetrators of electoral violence, it is imperative that young party cadres are constructively engaged to desist from violence while addressing the socioeconomic challenges they face. Apart their part, Governments should not, and cannot, wage war against their own people because they have the primary responsibility under international human rights law to protect their own citizens. African Governments should also respect and comply with the principles of governing election contained in the AU Declaration on the Principles Governing Democratic Elections in Africa.[21]

Although SALW by themselves do not cause conflicts, they have fueled and exacerbated conflicts on the continent, generating more insecurity, deepening the sense of crisis, and adding to the number of casualties. It is for this reason that Gilbert Mittawa in Chapter 22 recommends adoption of a coherent international and regional strategies for regulation of SALW. This is particularly true considering that without a coordinated regional approach; efforts of any one country to control the presence of arms on its territory could easily be undermined. The possibility of terrorists to acquire weapons of mass destruction increases the threat for the African continent to be unsafe. Hence Christable Tusiime, Sarah Mukashaba, and Godard Busingye in Chapter 23 recommend the adoption of a coordinated continental approach to their non-proliferation onto or within the continent.

---

[21] African Union, "African Union Declaration on the Principles Governing Democratic Elections in Africa", AHG/Decl.1 (XXXVIII) (2002).

COUNTERING CONTEMPORARY THREATS TO PEACE AND SECURITY ON THE CONTINENT

The bulge of unemployed youth has contributed to the rise in popular protests, organized crime, and armed conflict on the continent. As captured by Dan Kuwali in Chapter 13 and supported by Mphatso Boti-Phiri in Chapter 25, engaging unemployed youths is critical to prevent them from being used by terrorists and non-state armed group (NSAGs). This means that job creation to cater for the unemployed population is also important to attain security.[22] Addressing the problem of NSAGs remains an important step, but defeat of the rebel groups will not secure peace.

The rise in the use of the Internet on the continent has come with the rise in digital crimes. According to Tabitha Mwangi, Tracy Asava and Iretioluwa Akerele in Chapter 10, to mitigate cybersecurity risks on the continent, African governments should be at the center of all cybersecurity issues given the national security threat posed by information communication technology (ICT); increase the number of cybersecurity experts; have bilateral and multilateral partnerships for effective intelligence gathering, sharing and analysis; effective implementation of domestic and regional cybersecurity-related legislation such as the AU Convention on Cyber Security and Personal Data Protection; and transition from reactive to proactive cybersecurity policies through multidisciplinary approaches between public and private sector players.

The grievances that have spurred a proliferation of protests on the continent can be attributed to, among others, poor leadership, poor governance, corruption, shabbily run elections. In some cases, such as Egypt and Zimbabwe, these protests have resulted in regime change. As rightly noted by Majiga in Chapter 11, instead of suppressing or ignoring dissenting voices, governments need to address citizens' grievances through meaningful and progressive dialogue. Majiga correctly advises that preemptively, states need to improve their governance systems and also provide socioeconomic development to their citizens in order to reduce areas of discontent.

With regards to the rise in violent extremism on the continent, Kuwali notes in Chapter 12 that this is a result of political instability that has created power vacuum and security lapses, discrimination, religious marginalization, economic crises including social penury, and the proliferation of small arms and light weapons. According to Kuwali, using force alone to curb extremism can exacerbate the problem hence the need for a multipronged approach, which includes methods to win hearts and minds that include economic inclusion, particularly of the youth, and non-discriminatory socioeconomic development. To deter commission of violent crimes, it is important to uphold the rule of law. Adequate funding for acquisition of equipment and regular

---

[22] Adeyoose, note 1 above.

training of law enforcement agencies will help improve their capacity to sustain peace.[23]

In Chapter 13, Kuwali observes that the evolving threats to peace, safety, and security of the population in Africa are not military in nature but concern human security. Most of the threats hinge on the deprivation of social and economic well-being of the citizens including social and political marginalization as well as health care and environmental degradation Therefore, a long-term strategy to overcome threats to peace and security in Africa should involve addressing security, good governance, and socioeconomic development challenges. There is also a need to redesign the Common African Defence and Security Policy and its implementation strategy in order to factor in these contemporary and future security challenges. The APSA should also actively engage States to adopt mediation to resolve disputes and eradicate marginalization, especially of the youth as well as promoting socioeconomic well-being of their citizens indiscriminately.

In Chapter 15, Chikondi Mandala and John Phuka aptly note that health is a prerequisite for the attainment of peace. For example, epidemics and pandemics create social disruption, economic loss, and general hardship. This upheaval affects peace and security in the world by fostering an environment of restrictions on movement, strain on economic activity, overburdened health systems, and a lack of basic social amenities. As it is impossible to be at peace when there is infirmity and the mind is feeble. Making health care affordable via creation and strengthening of insurance schemes will enable even the least privileged of our population access care when the need arises. And this will in effect bring about peace and security.[24]

Peter Makossah and Gilbert Mittawa agree in Chapter 14 that the social media is now a catalyst for change, and an intermediary for peace and security. He argues that social media is a necessary evil that has become an integral part of political uprisings and revolutions all over the world. It has opened up new opportunities for public engagement and interactive dialogue and changed the relationship between the secretive states and their citizens. Largely, social media is a medium of peace and security as it offers an obsequious platform for people to confront each other and conduct rational discussions to form common understandings, even across socioeconomic, religious, and ethnic divisions.

SECURING SUSTAINABLE PEACE AND SECURITY IN AFRICA

As such, securing peace and security in Africa is dependent on good governance, which requires responsible leadership, participatory citizenship, and fair political representation. According to the UN Security Council, a comprehensive approach to sustaining peace requires:

[23] Adeyoose, note 1 above.

[24] As above.

the prevention of conflict and addressing its root causes, strengthening the rule of law at the international and national levels, and promoting sustained and sustainable economic growth, poverty eradication, social development, sustainable development, national reconciliation and unity including through inclusive dialogue and mediation, access to justice and transitional justice, accountability, good governance, democracy, accountable institutions, gender equality and respect for, and protection of, human rights and fundamental freedoms.[25]

It follows, therefore, that to secure sustainable peace and security in Africa; governments should respect human rights obligations that require equitable distribution of resources, bridging the poverty gap and ensuring minority voices are heard. It is also imperative to strengthen democratic institutions, promote representative governance and abhor all forms of discrimination in order to achieve sustainable peace and security on the continent.[26]

The majority of youth in Africa do not have stable economic opportunities. One-third of the nearly 420 million youth aged between 15 and 35 in Africa are unemployed and disgruntled, while another third is employed in vulnerable conditions, and only one in six youths is in wage employment.[27] Therefore, engaging unemployed youths will prevent them from being willing tools in the hands of extremist groups and non-state armed groups.[28] Mahmoud and Fabiano in Chapter 4 have also recommended that Africa also needs to incubate leadership in order to inculcate a culture of sustaining peace on the continent. Leadership for sustaining peace focuses on the processes that create and nurture an empowering environment that unleashes the positive energy and potential of people at all levels of society so they can resolve conflict non-violently and participate in co-charting a path toward every day, positive peace.[29] As such, Mahmoud and Fabiano recommend the integration of such leadership component in the entrepreneurial leadership courses offered by the African Leadership University at its Mauritius campus.

Sexual violence continues to be a common feature of conflicts and state violence, used as a weapon of war on the continent. There is need for more international scrutiny and legislation against such heinous activities including strict compliance with United Nations Security Council Resolutions.

The emergence of COVID-19 has brought health to the front and center on issues of peace and security. Making health care affordable via creation and strengthening of insurance schemes will enable even the least privileged

[25] United Nations, Security Council Resolution 2282 (2016).

[26] As above.

[27] African Development Bank Group, "Jobs for Youths in Africa: Catalyzing Youth Opportunity Across Africa". Available at: https://afdb-org/kr/wp-content/uploads/2018/02/Bottom-3-English.pdf(accessed 2 March 2021).

[28] As above.

[29] Youssef Mahmoud, "What Kind of Leadership Does Sustaining Peace Require?" *Global Observatory* (2019). See also Roger Mac Ginty, "Everyday Peace: Bottom-Up and Local Agency in Conflict-Affected Societies", *Security Dialogue* (2014).

of our population access care when the need arises thereby bringing about peace and security.[30] With a peaceful and secure Africa, we will be able to develop human capital and attain sustainable development.[31] It is reassuring that the AU recognizes that national and regional governance institutions need to be strengthened to counter contemporary challenges to peace and security. The AU's African Governance Architecture (AGA) should be fully engaged and integrated in responses to Africa's peace and security and development challenges.[32] There should also be coordination between the APSA and the New Partnership for Africa's Development (NEPAD), which explicitly recognizes that: "[p]eace, security, democracy, good governance, human rights, and sound economic management are conditions for sustainable development."[33]

Given the nature of the peace and security on the continent, the APSA cannot work in isolation, it has to consistently and coherently coordinate with human rights institutions and organs meant to promote socioeconomic well-being of individuals on the continent. Therefore, coordination of AGA, APSA, NEPAD, and the AU Human and People's Rights legal and judicial frameworks is critical in the implementation of the AU Master Roadmap of Practical Steps to Silence the Guns in Africa by Year 2020 (Lusaka Master Roadmap 2016).[34] States should mobilize the private sector for investment and job creation in order to provide employment to the youths who are at the front and center of escalating the violence on the continent. The AU should also explore options for strengthening collaboration between the African Development Bank and the World Bank in conflict-affected countries. The scale and nature of peace challenges could be met through close strategic and operational partnerships among national Governments, the AU, the UN, and other key stakeholders.[35]

As a component of NEPAD, the African Peer Review Mechanism (APRM) is designed to promote structural conflict prevention through good governance. Importantly, the Conference on Security Stability, Defence, and Cooperation in Africa (CSSDCA) propounds that stability calls for the rule of law and "good governance" and the full protection of human rights, which are key

---

[30] Adeyoose, note 25 above.

[31] As above.

[32] Shamil Idriss and Mike Jobbins, "Achieving Peace in the Great Lakes Region", *Africa in Focus*. Brookings (6 February 2015). Available at: www.brookings.edu/blog/africa-in-focus/2015/02/06/achieving-peace-in-the-great-lakes-region/ (accessed 23 February 2021).

[33] *See also* United Nations, Declaration on the New Partnership for Africa's Development, UN Doc.GA/57/L.2/Rev.1 (16 September 2002).

[34] African Union, the AU Master Roadmap of Practical Steps to Silence the Guns in Africa by Year 2020 (Lusaka Master Roadmap 2016). Available at: https://au.int/sitesdefault/files/documents/37996-doc-au-roadmap-silencing-guns-2020.pdf.en-pdf (accessed 24 February 2021).

[35] United Nations, Security Council Resolution 2282 (2016).

to the prevention of human rights violations, and the root causes of conflicts.[36] Considering that development, security, and human rights are intertwined in a symbiotic relationship, the AU should focus more on improving human security and promoting rule of law, good governance, and economic development in AU States, which are crucial to the prevention of conflicts.[37] Therefore, in light of the AU's current context of chronic underfunding and excessive dependency on external funding, the best way to cut costs for the APSA is to avoid conflicts, promote good governance, and respect for human rights and the rule of law. With a peaceful and secured Africa, the continent we will be able to develop human capital and attain sustainable development.[38]

There is similarly the need to stem all forms of inequality to prevent civil unrest in our communities. We cannot achieve sustainable peace as long as women are discriminated against, and minority groups are sidelined. By allowing equitable distribution of resources, bridging the poverty gap and ensuring minority voices are heard; we will be taken steps in the right direction. We equally need to strengthen our democratic institutions, promote representative governance and shun all forms of discrimination to achieve sustainable peace and security.[39] The picture that is emerging from this discussion is that the key to achieve peace and security in Africa is good governance, which entails responsible leadership, participatory citizenship, free, fair, and just political representation. Good governance has the attendant attributes to improving socioeconomic well-being of the population in terms of quality education, affordable health care, job creation, financial security, food security, and an effective criminal justice system that fights corruption and impunity.[40]

Since armed conflicts place a significant strain on the shoe-string resources for the AU, the best way to save these precious resources is to prevent armed conflicts on the continent. In Chapter 32, Cephas Lumina recommends that the APSA requires predictable and flexible financing in order to be effective. In agreement, Mahmoud and Fabiano in Chapter 3, advocate for the need for sustainable and predictable financing the majority of which should be provided by Africans. According to Mahmoud and Fabiano, one of the proposed components of the African Agenda 2063 that can benefit from a meaningful financial support is the development of a positive peace index to measure peacefulness on the continent with an aim of making a judicious assessment of the multiple factors that account for the prevailing oases of peace which tend to be overshadowed by the few conflict situations on the continent.

---

[36] *See* Department of Foreign Affairs, *The Report on the Implementation of the Conference on Security Stability, Defence and Cooperation in Africa*, Republic of South Africa ['CSSDCA'], p. 2.

[37] J. Busumtwi-Sam, "Architects of Peace: The African Union and NEPAD", 7 *Georgetown Journal of International Affairs* (2006), pp. 71–81, pp. 76–77.

[38] Adeyoose, note 1 above.

[39] As above.

[40] As above.

INDEX

A

abuse, 10, 53, 60, 62, 65, 77, 87, 96, 128, 195, 209, 224, 247–250, 256, 264, 277, 281–285, 287, 288, 379, 386–391, 396, 450, 451, 456, 458, 461, 462, 468–470, 479, 484, 498, 517, 520, 521, 526, 530, 572, 581–583, 594
actionable intelligence, 54
actors, 461, 463, 467, 468, 472, 474, 484
acts of piracy, 344, 353
adequate legislation, 581
adoption, 390, 409, 413, 588
advancement, 303
Africa, 126, 127, 129, 132, 135, 137, 489–491, 493–497, 501–503, 526–528, 530, 532, 533, 539, 540
African coastal lines, 343
African leadership, 300
African luminaries, vii
African Peace and Security Architecture, 7, 21, 47, 83, 98, 240, 339, 442, 506, 511, 512, 561, 567
the African Peer Review Mechanism (APRM), 608
African people, 369, 381
African Union Assembly of Head of States and Government, 51
Africa's peace and security, 608
Afrobarometer, 184, 185
agrometeorology, 148

albinism, 224, 228
all-inclusive economic and political strategies, 11
all-inclusive governance framework for natural resources, 341
Al Shabaab, 48, 283, 287
amorphous enemy, 217, 239
armed conflicts, 461–475, 480–487, 489, 490, 493, 505, 518, 522, 545, 550, 559, 560
armor, 405
arrest, 588
Artificial Intelligence, 221
assets declaration, 591
asymmetric, 162, 217, 239
attacks, 343–345, 347, 349–351, 354, 355, 357, 359, 360
AU Agenda 2063, 4, 10, 39, 43, 77, 92, 304, 600, 601
AU Human and People's Rights, 608
AU Master Roadmap 2016, 5, 13
The AU's African Governance Architecture (AGA), 608
AU's "Silencing the Guns by 2020" initiative, 562
autonomous, 222

B

biological, 398, 400–404, 409, 413
Boko Haram, 110, 114–117, 122, 124
building blocks, 430

© The Editor(s) (if applicable) and The Author(s), under exclusive license to Springer Nature Switzerland AG 2022
D. Kuwali (ed.), *The Palgrave Handbook of Sustainable Peace and Security in Africa*, https://doi.org/10.1007/978-3-030-82020-6

612 INDEX

build peace, 490, 495

C

capacity building, 151, 152
capitalism, 18, 19
carabinieri, 58
categories of conflicts, 505, 506
categorisation, 401
changing and dynamic nature, 463
charismatic leader, 293
child trafficking, 277, 285
choking-off, 207
chronic underfunding, 609
civil wars, 308, 320
civil unrest, 8
coherent and coordinated international
    and regional strategies, 396
cohesion, 126, 137
collaborative leadership, 293
colonial powers, 109
commend and condemn strategy, 589
common causes, 10
common descent, 18
conditionalities, 566
the Conference on Security Stability,
    Defence and Cooperation in Africa
    (CSSDCA), 608
conflict resolution approaches, 127
conflicts in Africa, 4, 5, 10, 11, 48–50,
    54, 57, 68, 126, 161, 230, 246,
    300, 339, 450, 462, 463, 472, 506,
    508–511, 527, 528, 561, 570, 602,
    604
conservative Muslims, 116
containment, 258, 260, 263, 264
contextualise, 139
continent, 159–161, 163, 171,
    174–179, 433–439, 441–443, 461,
    463, 468, 470–472, 483–487,
    489–491, 495, 502
continent's largest economies, 8
contributing factor, 10, 310, 548, 582,
    594
coordinated continental approach, 413
coordination, 608
correlation, 533, 539, 540
corresponding early response
    mechanisms, 8

corruption, 183, 184, 187, 188, 192,
    304, 307, 308, 314, 315, 319, 321,
    581–594
counter, 345, 348, 351, 354, 356, 359,
    363
counter contemporary challenges, 608
countering terrorism, 201, 202
counter-radicalisation, 202, 203, 209,
    210, 213, 216
country, 292, 293, 296–298
coups d'états, 191
Covid-19, 253–258, 260–271
crises, 110–113, 124
crisis management, 9, 226, 267, 450
crystal ball, 218
curbing conflicts, 11
cyber-attack, 244
Cybercrimes, vii
cybercriminals, 159, 162, 169, 176–178
cyber skills, 161
cyber threats, 9
cyclone, 145, 147, 149–152

D

data protection, 50
de-escalation, 39
defensive, 401
democracy, 366, 374–376, 378, 380,
    604, 607, 608
democratic governance, 49, 71
democratic management of natural
    resources, 323
deradicalisation, 211
Destabilisation, vii
destabilise, 205
development, 600, 601, 603, 605, 607,
    609
development challenges, 606, 608
disaster preparedness, 143, 145–151,
    154, 155
discontent, 84, 85, 182, 184, 185, 191
displacements of persons, 545
dissuade migrants, 11
doctrine, 116
downscaled, 573
drive conflicts, 11

E

early warning mechanisms, 55
economically, 10
education, 376, 380
effective and efficient conflict resolution mechanisms, 505
effective implementation, 562
effet utile, 65
electoral violence, 366, 373, 380
elusive, 404, 417
e-mail bombing, 166
emerging, 256, 268
Emerging consensus, vii
emerging powers, 160
ending conflicts, 11, 511
end state, 99
engaged, 13
entrepreneurial leadership, 293
epicentre, 9, 105, 462
epidemics, 253, 257, 258, 260, 265, 270
equitable, 526
eradicate marginalization, 240
ethnicities, 99
ethnicity and economic factors, 10
ethnic or religious, 505, 507
excessive dependency, 609
exclusivist identities, 217
existential, 602
exogenic forces, 34
external actors, 323, 340
external funding, 609
extraordinary traits, 293
extremist groups, 242

F

Facebook, 242–244, 246, 247
Fambul Tok, 42
financial resources, 343
financial self-reliance, 580
financing mechanisms, 567
firm punishment, 581
fiscal policy, 534
flexibility, 9
former colonial interference, 323
formidable preventive mechanisms, 8
Francophone, 120
fuel armed conflicts, 340
future hostilities, 239
future of violence, 218

G

Gacaca, 43
gangs of human traffickers, 545, 550, 559
gendarmerie, 58
gender discrimination, 550, 559
geopolitical complexities, 8
global, 403–405, 407, 408, 410
globalization, 307–309
Global Peace Index, 36
good governance, 603, 606–609
good leadership, 292, 296
governance and leadership, 291, 292, 300
governance deficiencies, 533
governance structure, 276
governance systems, 182
government revenue, 564
governments, 161, 162, 164, 165, 168, 170, 174–178
greed, 582, 583, 585, 588, 594
grievances, 182, 184, 187
guns, 96
Guurti, 43

H

hacktivists, 165, 166
hate speeches, 225
Hellenic, 20
holistic, 318
hostilities, 223, 226, 239
Human Cost of Uncontrolled Arms, 126
human dignity, 218
human rights, 545, 546, 548, 551–559, 604, 607–609
human rights institutions, 608
human rights obligations, 10, 12, 194, 236
human security, 603, 606, 609

I

identity politics, 8
ideological, 217

614 INDEX

illicit proliferation of arms, 8
illicit resource outflows, 525
illicit small arms and light weapons
(SALW), 383–385, 387, 388, 390,
392, 395, 396
immense promise, 417
imperial colonialism, 34
implementation, 446–450, 453–456,
458, 459
inclusion, 449–452, 454, 455
increased Internet penetration, 9
initiatives, 561, 562, 570, 573, 575
innocent civilians, 217, 219, 239
innovations, 9
insatiable appetite, 588
instability, 126, 130, 135
Instagram, 244
institutionalisation, 192, 193
insurgency, 11, 81, 114, 119, 124, 135,
214, 226, 227, 239, 276, 354
insurgent groups, 120
insurgents, 11, 102, 110, 114, 117,
118, 120, 122–124, 222, 226, 227,
255, 315, 465, 470
integral, 241
integrity checks, 591
intelligence, 204, 214
interconnected, 505
intergovernmental, 143, 144, 148, 151,
154
intergroup integration, 41
interlocking nature of crises, 8
intermarriage, 40
international cooperation, 143
interpersonal dialogues, 256
intertwined, 609
investigate, 318
Issos, 117

J
Jihad, 83, 86, 114, 116, 138, 227, 246,
390, 522, 556
judicial, 277, 281

K
key factors, 11, 90, 201, 571
killer robots, 222

L
law enforcement officials, 317
least peaceful continent, 3
legislative frameworks, 9, 207
liberal peacebuilding, 38, 43
liberal peacebuilding project, 8
lifestyle audit, 591
Linas-Marcoussis Agreement, 112
lockdown, 260, 261, 263, 268
low-key communal conflicts, 506
Lusaka Master Roadmap 2016, 608
Lusophone, 120

K
2017 Kigali Financing Decision, 561

M
majority, 505
malaria, 9, 381
manage threats, 146
marginalisation, 201, 213
Mato Oput, 43
mechanisms, 270, 271, 461–463, 466,
467, 473–475, 479, 480, 483, 484,
487
mediation, 230, 240
mediocrity, 294
Mediterranean Sea, 545–560
mercenarism, 117
micro-blogging, 243
Middle East and North Africa (MENA),
86, 89
migrant crisis, 545, 546, 549–553, 555,
556, 559
militias, 85
mitigate, 169
monitor, 321
monitoring and evaluation, 148
Multidimensional peace support
operations, viii
multidisciplinary approaches, 9, 605
Muslim Brotherhood, 82, 87
myriad, 277, 288
MySpace, 243

INDEX 615

N

national and regional governance institutions, 608
National Early Warning Centres, 146, 151
national interest, 143
natural disaster, 148
natural resources, 323–329, 331–338, 340, 341
necessary evil, 9, 606
negative forces, 127, 129–131, 140
Negrosim, 20
neighbourhood, 96, 101, 106
neo-colonial state, 35, 38
nepotistic grounds, 298
New Partnership for Africa's Development (NEPAD), 608
noxious, 402
nuclear, 398, 400–405, 409–413

O

objectivity, 130, 136, 137
offending state, 275
offensive, 401
online election interference, 161–163, 179
openness, 292, 296, 298
operational, 450, 455
operational effectiveness, 445
opportunistic, 585, 586
optimal exploitation, 526
organised crimes, 304, 314
overthrew, 96, 97

P

Pan African, 18, 19, 28, 29, 31, 34
pandemics, 253, 255, 256, 264, 265, 269, 271
pangas, 103
parameters, 9
participation, 447–450, 452–455, 457–459
Partner States, 95–107
Pax Africana, 16, 20
peace, 95–107, 417–419, 429, 431, 432, 599–603, 605–609

peace and security, 127, 129, 131–133, 135–141, 255, 256, 258, 602, 603, 605–609
peace and security architectures, 404, 410
Peace and Security Council, 47, 52
Peace Building Commission (PBC), 37
peacekeeping operations, 446
peace processes, 448–452, 457, 458
people's anger, 603
perennial problems, 3, 10
perpetrators, 306
Persian, 117
personal gain, 582, 588
platforms, 163, 167, 169, 170, 177, 178
political governance regimes, 545
political or ideological agenda, 217
political landscape, 8
politically, 10
political persecution, 545, 559
political structures, 126
political uprisings, 9, 606
political violence, 505, 521
politics and economy, 35, 38
poor governance, 183
poor leadership, 184
poorly run elections, 185
population, 160, 161, 166, 177, 505, 506, 508, 510, 519
porous borders, 8, 10, 99–102, 106, 201, 218, 228, 310, 311, 320, 386, 509, 603
post-Cold War, 109
post-election violence, 11, 103, 223, 366–381
post-electoral violence, 367, 381
poverty, 545, 549, 550, 552, 553, 556, 559
practical steps, 11, 395
precarious expeditions, 545
pre-colonial state, 18
prevalence, 288
prevent, 308
prevent crises, 8
preventing, 525
prevention of human rights violations, 609
proactive cybersecurity policy, 9
professionalization, 417, 419

616 INDEX

prognosis, 9, 22
programmatic, 37, 38, 41, 46
prohibition of weapons of mass
    destruction (WMD), 406
proliferation, 109, 110, 119, 383–393,
    396
proliferation of popular protests, 182
promoting peace, 491, 493, 495
promoting socio-economic development,
    526
promotion, 376, 378, 379
propaganda, 200, 204, 209, 212, 216
proper oversight, 463
prophylactic, 401
prosecute, 318
protection of human rights, 608
protection of human rights in Africa,
    277
provoke, 65
proxy wars, 6, 8
public and private sector players, 9
public despondency, 47
public resources, 581, 583, 588, 589,
    594
pyrotechnic, 402

R
radicalisation, 199, 200, 202, 203, 205,
    206, 210, 211, 215
radicalism, 199, 213
rapprochement, 188
rebuilding, 35, 38, 44
reconciliation, 491, 492, 496–502
regional, 408, 413
regulate, 10, 98, 206, 229, 239, 291,
    294, 295, 397, 400, 405–407, 409,
    411, 412, 472, 487
Repercussion, 172
resilience, 269, 271
resolutions, 445–448, 450, 451, 454,
    455, 458, 459
resolve disputes, 240
responses, 608
responsibilities, 463
rethinking, 545
revolutions, 242–245
right to privacy, 218, 221, 237
risks, 161, 162

robust regional approach, 8
romanticise, 193
root causes of conflicts, 603, 609
rule of law, 376, 378, 379, 418–420,
    422, 432, 602, 605, 607–609

S
safety, 95–100, 102–107
sectarian violence, 505
secure, 562, 580
security, 95–103, 105–107, 417–420,
    432, 599, 602, 605, 606, 608, 609
security and human rights, 609
self-sustaining, 37
sensitization, 10
seriously, 463
sex trafficking, 49
shabbily run elections, 9
shipping vessels, 343
silence the guns, 5, 6, 11, 47, 48, 242,
    250, 293, 339, 394, 396, 554
small arms and light weapons (SALW), 5
socially, 10
social media, 241–251
socioeconomic, 602, 604–606, 608, 609
socio-economic conditions, 124
socioeconomic development, 198, 202,
    215, 388, 395, 396
soul-searching, 281
sound economic management, 608
sources, 563, 566–568, 570, 574, 575
spilling over, 8
state and armed groups, 505
state-building, 39
state-to-state conflict, 8
status quo, 98
strategic, 452, 454, 455
strategies, 490, 491, 502
structural conflict prevention, 608
susceptibility, 526
sustainable and predictable financing,
    562
sustainable development, 601, 607–609
sustainable peace, 6, 7, 12
symbiotic relationship, 609

T
tactical levels, 453, 455

technical and logistical capability, 343
technical capacity, 147
technology, 316
ten C's strategy, 215
terrorism, 81, 84, 86, 87
terrorist groups, 9
thematic areas, 568
threat, 345, 346, 348–350, 356, 359, 362–364
threat to peace and security, 291
thrill seekers, 166
timely decisive action, 8
Tiv, 43
top-down approaches, 92
transaction costs, 144
transnational, 201, 202
transparency, 269, 291, 292, 296, 298
triggered, 182, 186
troubled continent, 3
trust, 419, 429, 430, 432
truth-seeking, 281
Twitter, 242–244, 246, 247
two-legged tripod, 8

U
Ubuntu, 19
uncensured, 227
undefined battlefield, 217, 239
undermine, 384, 392, 396
unemployment, 437, 441

unfavourable climatic conditions, 545, 559
unimaginable loss, 11
unscrupulous, 588
unseaworthy boats, 559
UN Security Council, 445, 446

V
violation, 276, 277, 280–285, 288, 289
violent extremism, 218, 219, 239

W
weak governments, 310, 311
western civilization, 16
Western World, 17, 30
widespread volatility, 258
women, 445–459
worrying surge, 343

X
Xenophobia, vii
xenophobic attacks, 230, 239

Y
yield, 561, 580
youth bulge, 434, 436–438
youth unemployment, 434, 437–442
YouTube, 242, 245, 246

Printed in the United States
by Baker & Taylor Publisher Services